Collaboration with Parents and Families
of Children and Youth with Exceptionalities

Collaboration with Parents and Families of Children and Youth with Exceptionalities

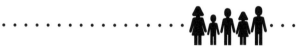

SECOND EDITION

Edited by
Marvin J. Fine
and
Richard L. Simpson

An International Publisher

8700 Shoal Creek Boulevard
Austin, Texas 78757-6897
800/897-3202   Fax 800/397-7633
Order online at http://www.proedinc.com

An International Publisher

© 2000, 1991 by PRO-ED, Inc.
8700 Shoal Creek Boulevard
Austin, Texas 78757-6897
800/897-3202   Fax 800/397-7633
Order online at http://www.proedinc.com

Library of Congress Cataloging-in-Publication Data

Collaboration with parents and families of children and youth with
    exceptionalities / edited by Marvin J. Fine, Richard L. Simpson. —
    2nd ed.
        p.   cm.
    Rev. ed. of: Collaboration with parents of exceptional children,
    c1991.
    Includes bibliographical references and indexes.
    ISBN 0-89079-818-4 (softcover : alk. paper)
    1. Exceptional children.   2. Handicapped children.   3. Parents of
exceptional children.   4. Exceptional children—Family
relationships.   I. Fine, Marvin J.   II. Simpson, Richard L.
    III. Collaboration with parents of exceptional children.
HQ773.5.C59   1999
362.82—dc21   99-25038
                                                                                    CIP

This book is designed in Italia and New Century Schoolbook.

Production Director: Alan Grimes
Production Coordinator: Dolly Fisk Jackson
Managing Editor: Chris Olson
Art Director: Thomas Barkley
Designer: Jason Crosier
Print Buyer: Alicia Woods
Preproduction Coordinator: Chris Anne Worsham
Staff Copyeditor: Martin Wilson
Project Editor: Jenny Stern
Publishing Assistant: Jason Morris

Printed in the United States of America

1   2   3   4   5   6   7   8   9   10   04   03   02   01   00

Contents

Section II: Educational and Intervention Considerations *131*

Section III: Focus on Exceptionality *215*

Contributors

Judy K. C. Bentley
Southwest Texas State University
Department of Curriculum and
  Instruction
San Marcos, TX 78666

Mary Bolger
University of Colorado at Denver
P.O. Box 173364
Denver, CO 80217-3364

Mary Dwyer Brandt
ADD Center
2504 East 7th Street, Suite D
Tulsa, OK 74136

Harriet C. Cobb
James Madison University
Department of Psychology, MSC 7401
Harrisburg, VA 22807

Steven E. Colson
University of Kansas Medical Center
Department of Special Education
3901 Rainbow Boulevard
Kansas City, KS 66160-7335

Vivian I. Correa
University of Florida
Department of Special Education, G-315
  Norman Hall
Gainesville, FL 32611

Francis J. DeMatteo
Indiana University of Pennsylvania
Department of Educational and School
  Psychology
Indiana, PA 15705-1087

Donald D. Deshler
University of Kansas
Center for Research on Learning,
  Dole Human Development Center
Lawrence, KS 66045

Beth Doll
University of Colorado at Denver
P.O. Box 173364
Denver, CO 80217-3364

Carl J. Dunst
Orelena Hawks Puckett Institute
189 East Chestnut Street
Asheville, NC 28801

Amy Farabaugh
Northeastern University
Department of Counseling Psychology,
  Rehabilitation, and Special
  Education
Boston, MA 02115

Craig R. Fiedler
University of Wisconsin–Oshkosh
Department of Special Education
Oshkosh, WI 54901

Marvin J. Fine
University of Kansas
Department of Psychology and Research
  in Education
213 Bailey Hall
Lawrence, KS 66045-2338

Marian C. Fish
Queens College/CUNY
Department of Educational and
  Community Programs
Flushing, NY 11367-1597

Regina M. Foley
Southern Illinois University at
  Carbondale
Department of Education Psychology
  and Special Education
Carbondale, IL 62901-4618

Reva C. Friedman
University of Kansas
Department of Psychology and Research
  in Education
Dole Human Development Center
Lawrence, KS 66045

Rick Gershberg
Northeastern University
Department of Counseling Psychology,
  Rehabilitation, and Special Education
Boston, MA 02115

Thomas P. Guck
Creighton University School of Medicine
Department of Family Practice
601 North 30th Street
Omaha, NE 68131

J. Stephen Hazel
Responsive Health Care
11791 West 112th Street
Overland Park, KS 66210

Hazel Jones
University of Florida
Department of Special Education
G 315 Norman Hall
Gainesville, FL 32611

Mindy Sloan Kohler
California Department of Education
Sacramento, CA

Roberta Krehbiel
University of New Mexico Health
  Sciences Center
Developmental Care Program
Department of Pediatrics/Division of
  Neonatology
Albuquerque, NM 87131

Roger L. Kroth
University of New Mexico
Department of Special Education
  Albuquerque, NM 87106

Lou Ann Kruse
Psychological Services Center
Danville, KY

Steven W. Lee
University of Kansas
Department of Psychology and Research
  in Education
Bailey Hall
Lawrence, KS 66045-2338

Edward M. Levinson
Indiana University of Pennsylvania
Department of Educational and School
  Psychology
Indiana, PA 15705-1087

Emanuel J. Mason
Northeastern University
Department of Counseling Psychology,
  Rehabilitation, and Special
  Education
Boston, MA 02115

Lynne McKee
Indiana University of Pennsylvania
Department of Educational and School
  Psychology
Indiana, PA 15705-1087

Nancy A. Mundschenk
Southern Illinois University
  at Carbondale
Department of Educational Psychology
  and Special Education
Carbondale, IL 62901-4618

Michal S. Nissenbaum
University of Kansas
Department of Psychology and Research
  in Education
213 Bailey Hall
Lawrence, KS 66045-2338

H. Thompson Prout
University of Kentucky
Department of Educational and
  Counseling Psychology
College of Education
Lexington, KY 40508-0017

Susan M. Prout
University of Kentucky
Department of Special Education
  and Rehabilitation Counseling
College of Education
Lexington, KY 40508-0017

Ronald E. Reeve
University of Virginia
Curry Programs in Clinical and School
  Psychology
Curry School of Education, Ruffner Hall
405 Emmet Street
Charlottesville, VA 22903

Jean B. Schumaker
University of Kansas
Center for Research on Learning,
  Dole Human Development Center
Lawrence, KS 66045

Julia S. Shaftel
University of Kansas
Department of Psychology and Research
  in Education
213 Bailey Hall
Lawrence, KS 66045-2338

Richard L. Simpson
University of Kansas
Department of Special Education,
  University of Kansas Medical Center
3901 Rainbow Boulevard
Kansas City, KS 66160-7335

Donna M. Snyder
Orelena Hawks Puckett Institute
189 East Chestnut Street
Asheville, NC 28801

Wayne H. Swanger
University of Wisconsin–Oshkosh
Department of Special Education
Oshkosh, WI 54901

Carol M. Trivette
Orelena Hawks Puckett Institute
189 East Chestnut Street
Asheville, NC 28801

Pauline H. Turner
University of New Mexico
Family Studies
103 Simpson Hall
Albuquerque, NM 87131

Sue Vernon
Edge Enterprises, Inc.
708 West 9th Street, Suite 101
Lawerence, KS 66044

Peggy Jo Wallis
Wallis Associates
21 Green Meadow Drive
Clifton Park, NY 12065

Chriss Walther-Thomas
The College of William and Mary
Department of Special Education
Williamsburg, VA 23187

Jo Webber
Southwest Texas State University
Department of Curriculum and
  Instruction
San Marcos, TX 78666

Joyce K. Zurkowski
University of Kansas Medical Center
Department of Special Education
3901 Rainbow Boulevard
Kansas City, KS 66160-7335

Preface

The last several decades have witnessed dramatic changes in society's perception and treatment of individuals with exceptionalities. The increased sophistication of early diagnosis of problematic conditions, the deinstitutionalization of people with disabilities, the growth of community-based services, and the legislative mandates for public school involvement have all contributed to the care, training, and education of individuals with exceptionalities, with direct implications for parents and families.

Numerous myths have affected not only the community's perception of parents of children with exceptionalities, but also the perceptions and behaviors of professionals. Although it is true that these parents typically undergo an initial process of adjustment—as well as recurring periods of adjustment at various stages of the child's life—many of them are able to develop effective coping skills, maintain a functional integrity within their families, and be proactive and advocacy oriented in efforts on behalf of their children. The perception by professionals that parents are often in need of extensive psychotherapy, unable to accept the realities of their child, or recalcitrant receivers of professional services is rapidly being replaced by a more constructive view. "Exceptional" parents are often eager to learn as much as they can about their child's exceptionality, able to acquire specific skills necessary to facilitate the growth and development of their child, and able to participate in partnership with professionals in the care, treatment, and education of their child.

These optimistic observations are not meant to deny that some parents are in need of ongoing therapeutic assistance as they continue to struggle with the nature of their child's problems and with their relationship with the child. However, there is evidence that even parents who have trouble accepting their child's exceptionality can be empowered to assume a partnership role with professionals. It is around the theme of parents as partners with the professional community in the care, treatment, and education of their child with an exceptionality that this book has been written. Professionals, and particularly those people in training for professional roles that will put them in contact with parents of exceptional children, can benefit from the sympathetic and collaborative orientation of this book.

It has been observed many times that the greatest gift that can be given to people in need is the skill necessary for them to help themselves, so that they become less dependent upon others. This book expresses exactly that theme—the importance of educating and empowering parents and families so that they can become active partners with the professional community in meeting the needs of their own children.

The first section, "The Family and Exceptionality," consists of six chapters that underscore the theme of the book and set the stage for the subsequent sections. The introductory chapter by Fine and Nissenbaum reviews the literature on parental and family response to a child with a disability, presents implications for professionals, and describes a collaborative–empowerment model.

Dunst, Trivette, and Snyder elaborate the concept of family empowerment in Chapter 2. They explore the meaning of the terms *partnership* and *collaboration* from a behavioral science perspective and then place partnerships into the context of empowerment and effective help-giving relationships.

Much of the existing literature on children with disabilities speaks as if intact two-parent families were the norm. This stance ignores what is the reality in many families: variations on the traditional parenting–family structure. Chapter 3 by Fish focuses on the issues and the needs of single-parent, stepparent, foster-parent, adoptive parent, and gay- and lesbian-parent families.

Chapter 4 on siblings, by Mason, Kruse, Farabaugh, Gershberg, and Kohler, brings our attention to the often-forgotten members of the family. These children can be at risk for stress—if not already experiencing it—with regard to their place in the family, and they may be struggling with related personal adjustment issues. Professionals focusing on the obvious parental concern with the child with an exceptionality may miss the less evident needs of the siblings.

Chapter 5, authored by Simpson and Zurkowski, examines the issue of educational reform as it relates to parents and families of children and youth with exceptionalities. Indeed, as pointed out in the chapter, school reform and restructuring, recent legislative and policy enactments, and other societal changes have had significant influence on professional–family interactions and collaboration.

Chapter 6 offers a developmental perspective on families of children with exceptionalities. Turner examines the typical stages of development from infancy to adulthood and how the stages might vary in children with disabilities.

Section II focuses on important educational and intervention considerations. The section begins with Chapter 7 by Correa and Jones on multicultural issues. This important chapter sensitizes the reader to the potential cultural or ethnic variability among families with children with disabilities. Krehbiel and Kroth bring their rich backgrounds of professional contact with parents and families to Chapter 8 on communication. The "how, what, and when" of the professional's communication are inextricably connected to facilitating a collaborative partnership with parents and families.

Chapter 9 on counseling approaches, by Reeve and Cobb, argues for sensitivity and caring by professionals. The authors delineate models of counseling and a range of counseling issues that parents, siblings, and families may experience. The final chapter in this section, by Fine and Shaftel, describes an intervention model for parents who already have or may develop the potential for abusing their child with a disability. These parents need to be understood sympathetically and shown ways to strengthen positive parenting attitudes and skills.

Section III examines the impact of different exceptionalities on the family and discusses specific ways in which parents can be assisted. The emphasis again is on educating, collaborating with, and empowering parents. The exceptionalities discussed include mental retardation (Prout and Prout), developmental disabilities (Doll and Bolger), chronic illness (Lee and Guck), learning disabilities (Vernon, Walther-Thomas, Schumaker, Deshler, and Hazel), and autism (Webber, Simpson, and Bentley). Friedman expands the spectrum of exceptionality by discussing the gifted child. Colson and Brandt discuss children and youth with attention-deficit/hyperactivity disorder, and Mundschenk and Foley address the special concerns related to children and youth with emotional and behavioral disorders.

The last section of the book considers three very important topics for professionals: sexuality, transitions, and advocacy. Chapter 19 by Wallis focuses on the sexuality of people with disabilities. In the past not only parents but often professionals acted as if people with disabilities were not sexual beings or as if their sexuality was somewhat aberrant.

Levinson, McKee, and DeMatteo discuss the child who is in transition from the more sheltered school–family setting into the world of job training and employment, as well as into a more independent style of living. Transition can be a time of stress for parents that invites the support and assistance of professionals.

The last chapter, by Fiedler and Swanger, concerns the important area of professionals advocating for parents. Despite legislation that has created a role for parent involvement, parent participation remains limited in educational programs and life planning for children with disabilities. Fiedler and Swanger's framework for parent advocacy is education oriented and includes procedures for assisting parents to achieve fuller participation in their child's educational life.

We hope that this book will inspire readers to use their own creativity and initiative on behalf of a productive parent–professional partnership. Long after parents and families have finished their work with a given professional, they will continue to be involved in the life of their child with an exceptionality. Each of us needs to view our contribution as part of a continuity of sensitive and caring parent–professional involvement that supports the empowerment of parents and families.

The Family and Exceptionality

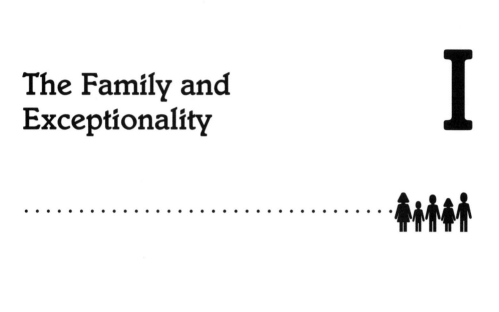

The Child with Disabilities and the Family: Implications for Professionals

1

Marvin J. Fine and Michal S. Nissenbaum

Parent participation in the education and care of children with disabilities or special needs has increased substantially over the last several decades. This change is a result of deinstitutionalization and other trends, as well as the passage of significant legislation affecting the care and treatment of these individuals (Newman, 1983; Peterson & Cooper, 1989; Simpson & Fiedler, 1989). Extensive parent efforts over many years have influenced national policy and community attitudes toward children with disabilities. The passage of the Education for All Handicapped Children Act in 1975 ensured a free and appropriate public education for children with disabilities. Subsequently the Education of the Handicapped Act Amendments (1986) extended services to younger children with an increased emphasis on family needs and involvement (Florian, 1995). The more recent Individuals with Disabilities Education Act (IDEA) Amendments (1997) offered even greater assurance that qualified children would receive appropriate educational services and that their parents would be actively involved.

There is evidence, however, that the dream of effective and comprehensive services for all children with disabilities and the active inclusion of their parents has not yet been realized (Simpson & Fiedler, 1989; Turnbull & Leonard, 1981; Yoshida, Fenton, Kaufman, & Maxwell, 1978). In particular, policy makers' ideas about parent involvement have sometimes missed the realities of parental readiness and preferences with regard to involvement (Turnbull & Turnbull, 1982). It is the recognition of the value of parent involvement on behalf of the child with disabilities, along with the awareness of recurrent problems in parent involvement, that has prompted the preparation of this book.

This chapter will focus on how the presence of a child with disabilities in the family can affect parents, other family members, and professionals. In addition to addressing a number of specific issues that professionals should consider when working with parents, the chapter will include a description of a model of collaborative involvement. The model can serve as a framework for professionals who are convinced that parents should be empowered to work effectively on behalf of their own children.

The attitudes and preconceptions of professionals affect their success in their work with families of children with disabilities. Professionals who do not have an adequate frame of reference may be inclined to "sniff out" pathology in these families. This inclination may be based on several factors, including misconceptions regarding the impact of a child with special needs on the family, the role of parents working on behalf of their child, and the nature of normal family functioning. As a number of authors have pointed out, the existence of stress within a family does not in itself constitute dysfunctionality; rather a family is dysfunctional if it is unable to organize itself over time to cope with stressful events (Hanline, 1991; Lewis, 1986; McCubbin & Figley, 1983; Selye, 1974).

With these observations in mind, the first section of this chapter will discuss families and how they function. This section should offer the reader a background against which to understand the nature of parental response to, and involvement with, a child with disabilities.

What Are Families and How Do They Function?

There are numerous definitions of the family. But from a pragmatic point of view a family could be termed a collection of individuals who are connected to each other by blood ties or strong emotional ties, and who in most circumstances reside together. (A child may go off to college but is still considered a member of that family.) The *nuclear* family refers to the parents and children in the home setting, while the *extended* family includes relatives and others of close emotional ties who are probably outside of the home and may be of different generations. *Blended* or *reconstituted* families are also common, given the frequency of remarriages that include "yours," "mine," and "ours." Estimates indicate that by the year 2000 the majority of families will involve some kind of "reconstruction" (Glick & Lin, 1986).

These observations may have implied the stereotype of the two-parent, middle-class family. Indeed, Foster, Berger, and McLean (1981) have criticized existing conceptual models of parent involvement because they assume the prevalence of two-parent families, mother having a primary childcare role rather than employment role, and father eager to be involved in community activities. But in fact the divorce figures reveal the existence of many single-parent families, while the economic realities speak to the frequent necessity of both parents or the single parent working. Single-parent families are more likely to experience financial hardship than two-parent families.

Also, a growing number of couples prefer to establish careers and an adequate income before having children. The implications of having a child with disabilities for a couple in their late 30s who were planning to have only one child may be quite different from those affecting a family with two typically developing children whose third child has a disability. A child with a disability will have a different impact on a family that can afford private services, support caretakers, and vacations for the parent(s), than on a family with more limited finances.

The Family as a System

It is important for professionals to understand the family as a "system" of members who establish roles and relationships and grow, develop, and change while interacting with each other. Any change in the family, whether it be a teenager starting to drive or the presence of a child with disabilities, will have an impact on the family as a whole. Seldom is it "business as usual" for one portion of a family when another portion is undergoing changes. Families have rules; patterns of communication, affection, and power; and ways of dealing with problems and stress. A child with disabilities is not just a concern for the parents but has an impact throughout the family system, including economics, vacations, social relationships, and family satisfaction. It is encouraging to see the literature on these children assuming more of a family systems perspective (Bailey & Simeonsson, 1988; Foster, 1988; Foster et al., 1981; Seligman & Darling, 1989, 1997; Simpson & Fiedler, 1989; Turnbull, Summers, & Brotherson, 1986; Turnbull & Turnbull, 1997).

Ethnic and Cultural Considerations

A family is rooted in a matrix of influences and traditions, including of course its ethnic or cultural background. Numerous authors have emphasized that ethnicity and culture are important considerations in understanding the dynamics of any family (Harry, 1992; McAdoo, 1993; McGoldrick, Pearce, & Giordano, 1982). They suggest that these factors can have an impact on the family's values, which in turn influence how the family might accept a child with disabilities.

For example, some cultures might consider the birth of an infant with disabilities to mean that the family has been somehow cursed or victimized (see Chapter 7). In other cases cultural values make it easier for a family to accommodate such a child. Winton (1988a) observed that, "The values of some cultures encourage passivity and ascribe events to fate or outside uncontrollable sources. For these families, a simple acceptance of the child with disabilities may be their natural response; reliance on outside help may be minimal" (p. 313).

Along with having particular culturally based perceptions of children with disabilities, some groups may be more self-protective and resistant to outsiders. A strong "we–they" attitude might persist that would affect their seeking and accepting help. This is not to say that the members of such groups will refuse help, but rather that the involved professionals need to be aware of such cultural or ethnic values and proceed in an appropriate way. Professionals who ignore or are insensitive to such cultural or ethnic considerations can impair their relationship with the parents and reinforce negative stereotypes. In the absence of such sensitivity by professionals, the family may become more convinced that "others" do not understand them; then the parents' reluctance to communicate or share may confirm the suspicion by a professional that "those people" reject services.

Kalyanpur and Harry (1997) offer the "Posture of Reciprocity" as a collaborative model for enhancing cultural awareness in professionals. This model emphasizes the importance of identifying one's own cultural values and assumptions, determining if the family shares these same values, respecting differences in values, and making adaptations so that both perspectives are considered. In essence the professional and the family examine their own cultural values as a means of developing mutual goals for the child.

In addition to these steps, special efforts at relationship building and the development of trust may be necessary before the parents willingly ask for help or follow directions. Professional understanding of how the family views the child is a key to achieving parent participation.

Life Cycle Considerations

Professionals interacting with families need to understand that families typically move through a developmental process or life cycle (Carter & McGoldrick, 1980; Foster et al., 1981). At different points in the life cycle the family will need to adapt to changes and transitions. Consider the young family composed of husband and wife in their 20s, attempting to establish an economic base and career direction. Children often are born into this context of parents trying to move forward professionally as well as cope economically with the demands of a young family. As the children grow older, so of course do the parents, and their needs and aspirations become modified by the realities of their lives; all the while the children are learning and developing within the microsystem of the family as well as in contact with outside influences such as school and community.

At some point in time the family may extend over a range of age and developmental stages, including, for example, the preschool and elementary levels. In a matter of years the same family may have a child at the secondary level and a child already moving out of the home into young adulthood. The parents by this time have usually grown into that status referred to as middle age and are dealing with related personal, social, and economic issues.

When a child with disabilities is present, the maturation of the family unit can slow down (Farber, 1959). Turnbull and Turnbull (1997) describe families of children with disabilities as often having "off time" transitions between stages in the life cycle. When other families reach a point of greater individual independence, the family with a child with disabilities may be functioning as if it still had a young dependent child.

The importance of these family life cycle considerations for professionals cannot be overstated. Professionals can only fully appreciate the implications for the family of the child with disabilities by being aware of the family context and how the perceived demands or responsibilities of that child interface with the ongoing development and functioning of the family (Hanline, 1991; Turnbull & Turnbull, 1997).

Boundaries and Hierarchies

In the context of family dynamics, the term *boundary* refers to the delineation of the roles and relationships within a family that are necessary in order to have a functional unit. *Boundary* also implies that there are subsystems within the family that are distinct from each other (Minuchin & Fishman, 1981). For example, the parent subsystem and child subsystem have different places in the family hierarchy. The parent subsystem subsumes certain roles and responsibilities including, of course, leadership and protection for the family. It may perform many tasks, from ensuring the economic survival of the family to imparting values to children. The child subsystem differs in terms of power, authority, and responsibility, although, as children move toward maturity and independence, they assume more prerogatives.

In instances where parents are unsure in their parenting role, one of the children may become a "parental child" and assume more power than might be appropriate. The parent who is constantly stressed and alone may use the sibling for emotional support and advice on decisions regarding the child with special needs. The demands on the family of caring for a child with disabilities might even require that the typically developing siblings assume more responsibilities than would otherwise occur. Such added responsibilities might be accepted well by the siblings and even contribute toward greater family solidarity. But in some instances the siblings may want to expand their responsibilities into other areas of decision making that challenge parental authority ("If I'm old enough to take care of Suzy while you run errands, I'm old enough to decide who my friends are!").

Healthy, functional, or strong families have reasonably clear boundaries and lines of authority. They have some flexibility to accommodate changes and shifts as children grow, but the parents retain their clear executive leadership position. At times of stress the parents are able to work together to support each other and to serve as models for and give support to the rest of the family. Single parenting and other parenting configurations may present some challenges to the development of appropriate boundaries. There may be a real need for greater sibling participation in childcare and other family responsibilities. These considerations are discussed in Chapter 3.

Enmeshment and Disengagement

Families show considerable differences in the degree of emotional closeness among the members (Minuchin & Fishman, 1981; Minuchin, Rosmand, & Baker, 1979). Some families have a very strong "we" nature; everyone is expected to behave, think, and feel in prescribed ways. In these instances the family may exercise a whole range of forces to ensure that this unity prevails. It may be difficult for siblings of the child with disabilities to express their frustrations or resentments in the face of family values or beliefs such as, "We all accept and love Billy despite his disabilities" or "It's God's way of testing us." The sibling may grow in resentment and feel alienated within the family.

Children growing up in enmeshed families may fail to achieve reasonable differentiation from the family; this is exemplified by the kinds of shared and overlapping decision making that occur and the ways in which family or parental approval is constantly sought. Even after the children reach a point at which they would typically have more autonomy, their strong emotional tie to the nuclear family thwarts their attempts to function as adults and to establish their own home and family. Achieving functional adulthood requires young people to differentiate themselves adequately from the family of origin; emotional enmeshment can be understood as interfering with this necessary differentiation.

Some family members may disengage from the family to achieve a greater degree of independence. In instances where the siblings of the child with disabilities might feel overwhelmed by the responsibilities they were forced to assume, they might seek ways of separating emotionally from the family. The distancing by siblings may be seen by other family members as rejection of the child with disabilities. Some families may need to consult a professional to understand and cope with these dynamics. In such cases it is likely that the ostensibly disengaged person is continuing to struggle with feelings of guilt and anger.

Substantial connectedness within families is desirable to encourage children to internalize values and to develop a sense of being a part of the unit. But as children mature and increase their capacity to reason, they should be given opportunities to differentiate themselves appropriately from the family and to gain a greater sense of individuality. This normal process may be more challenging in families with a child whose special needs have pulled family members into committed caretaking roles.

Intimacy and Communication

Although both intimacy and communication have been dealt with as separate entities by writers on family structure and style, there are close parallels between these two factors (Roman & Raley, 1980; Stinnett & DeFrain, 1989). In other words, families that are characterized by a high degree of intimacy in the form of caring and positive feeling for each other also have fairly effective communication patterns. This seems to follow logically. It would be difficult to think of many situations in which family members have a high degree of intimacy without a reasonably high degree of communication.

In some instances parents may have a strong love for their children, yet their style of communication is one of holding back from tangible expressions of that feeling. Families that refrain from expressing feelings, even physically, may also be reluctant to talk about their feelings and concerns; this reticence can lead to a blunting of empathy and sensitivity among family members.

Families in which the parents model and children develop reasonably open and intimate patterns of communication cope more easily with normal crises as they arise. Families that are characterized by limited or inadequate communication do not have the shared background of thoughts and feelings that could help them talk about and understand some event or need such as the care of a child with disabilities. Family members are more likely to feel confused, scared, or alienated if they are unable to deal openly with the new event and support one another.

Some Thoughts for Professionals

These aspects of family functioning are some of the ways in which families differ. It is important for professionals to keep in mind that many families may be equipped, by way of family structure and functioning, including affectional ties, communication, and problem-solving skills, to cope adequately with most crises, including those presented by a child with disabilities. Other families, already in conflict or marginal in adjustment, may act more dysfunctional under stress. Such families may not have developed the kinds of dynamics that can tolerate increased stress. In these vulnerable or marginally functional families, the presence of a child with disabilities is more likely to precipitate personal catastrophic reactions including divorce or separation, alienation of family members, and other severe emotional and behavioral reactions.

Professionals should acknowledge that while the presence of a child with disabilities can precipitate a great deal of stress, no family is exempt from experiencing stress. The Social Readjustment Rating Scale (Holmes & Rahe, 1967) is an index of stress that individuals or families might experience. It seems that almost any kind of change has a stress value to it. The breadwinner being fired is certainly stressful, but achieving a promotion can also be quite stressful. Good adaptation in a family is not the absence of stress but the family's historic ways of mobilizing itself and its resources to cope with stressful events.

The impact on the family of a child with disabilities and the implications for professionals will be discussed subsequently in more detail. But before moving on to the next section, we present a useful exercise for the reader. The following questions provide an opportunity for you to analyze your own family background. This activity can enhance your appreciation of family structure and dynamics as well as the rich variations across families; it can enable you to develop a broader and more personalized perspective on how families function.

Family Analysis Questionnaire

1. Describe your family's cultural or ethnic background. What family values, behaviors, attitudes, and customs have been handed down?

2. What was happening in your family at the time of your birth (e.g., family composition, economic status, housing, employment)?

3. What was the significance of your birth to your family (e.g., were you a long-awaited child, financial burden)?

4. What role(s) did you assume within your family as compared to other members (e.g., the studious child, the bad child)?

5. What subgroups existed in your family and how clear were the boundaries (e.g., parent subsystem–child subsystem, older vs. younger children)?

6. What rules (implicit and explicit) existed in your family?

7. What alliances existed and how did they shift (e.g., mother and son vs. father on discipline, mother and father vs. daughter on school issues)?

8. How and by whom were decisions made (e.g., money, child management, vacations)?

9. How was affection expressed (physically, verbally, by whom, to whom, etc.)?

10. What kinds and patterns of communication existed? (Were there family secrets?)

11. In what ways and in what areas were you and your siblings able or unable to establish independence or interdependence?

12. How did your family connect and interact with the extended family?

13. How did your family connect and interact with the community?

14. How was spirituality or religion treated in the family? (Was there active religious affiliation?)

15. How did family patterns shift as the children got older?

16. Were there characteristic ways that your family responded to crises? (Organize your thoughts around specific crises.)

17. How do you think your family would have reacted to a child with disabilities? You might speculate in terms of which child (oldest or youngest) and the nature and severity of the disability.

The Family's Accommodation of the Child with Disabilities

The foregoing section on families presented a systemic view: that of members reciprocally interacting, affecting others, and being affected by others; of people assuming roles and relationships; and all of this happening against the background of individual and family development, life cycle, and ethnic considerations. The section showed that historical family patterns include ways of responding and coping with stressful events; also, that some families are precariously balanced in terms of their functionality, and a particularly stressful event can unbalance the family. Knowing this range of background information and concepts, professionals can develop a sensitive and sympathetic understanding of the reciprocal relationship between children with disabilities and the rest of the family.

The literature can be extremely useful in depicting "typical" family patterns, but research findings can also lead professionals to expect families to fit the generalizations ("believing is seeing"). Moreover many studies on the effects of a child with disabilities on the family have flaws in their research methodology (Dyson, 1991; Foster, 1988; Foster & Berger, 1985). Examples of such problems include inadequate control groups, a wide range of ages (which increases the difficulty in generalizing results to a single age group or degree of severity), a focus on parental responses rather than family dynamics, and omission of some of the considerations that might mediate the effects that the parents experience.

Awareness of research limitations should support a cautious stance with regard to applying specific findings to all parents. Parents in fact respond differently and uniquely to their situations. There may be enough similarities to give professionals some sense of anticipation and to sharpen their sensitivities, but they need to remain open to the individuality of each situation.

The next section first considers two questions that are often of concern to professionals working with parents and families and then turns to a discussion of intervention implications.

Are there stages parents experience on
learning that their child has a disability?

Blacher (1984), reviewing the literature on parental reactions, found a general pattern of parental adaptability to the child with disabilities, but noted that individual family differences also exist. She was concerned that the methodological problems of studying parental reactions could lead to different conclusions. Of great importance, however, were the mediating considerations. For example, a child with disabilities may have dramatically different implications for a single-parent versus a two-parent family (Schilling, Kirkham, Snow, & Schinke, 1986; see also Chapter 3). Two parents supporting each other emotionally and physically are a more viable picture of functionality than a single parent struggling with the logistics of family life, employment, and what may be the added demands of a child with disabilities. The presence of typically developing children and the solidity of the marital relationship as mentioned earlier also become factors influencing the impact on the parents and in turn the parents' responses to the child with disabilities (Barnett & Boyce, 1995; Trute & Hauch, 1988).

In some instances the etiology of the child's status is clearly established, while in many other instances it is only inferred. The parents may vary in terms of their sense of personal responsibility and accountability for the child's condition depending on what they learn and have been told. For example, a mother who was abusing drugs or alcohol during pregnancy may respond differently to the subsequent birth of a child with disabilities than a parent for whom either the cause was not known or the cause was considered to be outside the parent's control.

Numerous other factors can mediate parental reaction to a child with disabilities, including religiosity (Zuk, 1959), severity of the disability (Fewell & Gelb, 1983; Grossman, 1972), socioeconomic level (Hampson, Hulgus, Beavers, & Beavers, 1988), and even the parents' employment outside of the home (Freedman, Litchfield, & Warfield, 1995). The family's support network is considered to be a major factor (Dunst, Trivette, & Cross, 1986; Kazak, 1986), along with the important ethnic or cultural and life cycle influences discussed earlier. McDowell, Saylor, Taylor, and Boyce (1995) found that stress levels in parents of children with disabilities varied depending on whether the family was white or nonwhite.

With these considerations in mind, to conclude that all parents go through some common sequence such as denial, anger, bargaining, depression, and finally acceptance (Huber, 1979) or shock; denial; sadness, anger, or anxiety; adaptation; and finally reorganization (Drotar, Baskiewicz, Irvin, Kennell, & Klaus, 1975) may miss the uniqueness of a given family. It may be more useful for a professional to anticipate that family members will go through some process in their attempts to come to terms with the events, but that it will likely vary with the individual family. The professional must listen, explore, and interact with the family members in order to appreciate the family's process of adaptation and where individual families are in that process. The professional should avoid concluding that the family or family members are "stuck" at a hypothetical point in the adaptation process; in fact, different family members may be progressing in their own idiosyncratic ways.

Is acceptance the endpoint of the process of family adjustment?

One of the problematic notions of the "stages of adjustment" view of family adaptation is that some idealized acceptance stage is often implicitly if not explicitly promoted as the point that healthy families should reach. The literature, however, suggests that "chronic sorrow" (Olshansky, 1962; Searle, 1978; Wikler, Wasow, & Hatfield, 1981) is not unusual and reflects the family's continued need to adapt to changes in circumstances. Although the parents may move from a shock or grief position to a more proactive and adaptive position, they will witness many life events and transitions that prompt them to reappraise the child's limitations and to come to terms again and again with what is and what may never be.

Consider the hypothetical situation of parents of a preschool child who is experiencing some developmental disabilities. Their initial concerns on behalf of the child relate to determining and then acquiring appropriate educational and developmental experiences for that child. Within several years the child's move from community (infant and toddler services) to school (Part B services) gives rise to a host of new issues surrounding the transition. Because of the mandates under which public schools must operate to serve children with disabilities, the labeling process becomes more explicit and categorical. Parents who may have adapted to notions of "developmental delays" are now facing a whole new set of diagnostic and placement criteria, some of which may appear to be in conflict with their earlier understanding of the child's disability (Peterson & Cooper, 1989). Also, because the child is now going to a different setting, the parents face new issues of transportation and time management.

As the child enters adolescence, questions related to sexuality often arise. What normal leeway should the adolescent be allowed in dating and socializing, and when do the parents need to assume a more controlling, supervisory stance? How does sexual information get communicated to the child (see Chapter 15)? Eventually the child progresses from a public school setting into the community by way of field-based training or sheltered workshop types of facilities. For a number of children with disabilities, the question of whether they will ever be able to function independently in the community looms prominent (see Chapter 20). But many children do eventually move to more independent functioning. At that point the parents may have to face their own relationship issues that they were able to avoid earlier because of the constant focus on the child.

This brief review of some developmental and educational milestones was meant to underscore the number of recurring points at which parents have to confront their child's limitations as well as capabilities and work with the child, school personnel, and community members in all aspects of life planning. On these occasions the parents may find themselves struggling again with feelings of sadness or grief over the realities of the child's situation, as it compares to what the parents had hoped and wished for at different times. This way of viewing the extended periods of adjustment and readjustment argues for a continuum of services over the life span of the individuals with disabilities (Werth & Oseroff, 1987; Wikler et al., 1981), particularly during transition and other critical periods (Hanline, 1991).

Professionals in Their Contacts with Parents

As mentioned earlier, professionals should not assume automatically that parents of children with disabilities are "pathological," overwhelmed, or inadequate, especially in light of the growing body of literature to the contrary (Hampson et al., 1988; Kazak & Marvin, 1984; Longo & Bond, 1984; Palfrey, Walker, Butler, & Singer, 1989; Trute & Hauch, 1988). Longo and Bond (1984) completed their extensive review of the literature with the observation that there is

> sufficient evidence to suggest that more optimistic attitudes and frameworks can be employed when working with families of handicapped children. Overall, many families cope adequately with the added complications of the disabled member; marriages are not necessarily torn apart by the presence of a chronically ill child nor do parents automatically become dysfunctional under these circumstances. (p. 64)

Widerstrom and Dudley-Marling (1986) reviewed the literature on living with a child with disabilities in terms of what they felt were some myths possibly held by professionals. Their findings supported the conclusions of Longo and Bond that these families seem to be managing much better than some of the early literature would have predicted. Their concern is that professionals who bring a negative anticipation to their interaction with families may in different ways interfere with the family's progress. They go on to state that "If, on the other hand, families are generally seen as capable of dealing effectively with the stress of having a handicapped child, it is more likely that the prophecy will self-fulfill and good adjustment will result" (Widerstrom & Dudley-Marling, p. 366).

As mentioned earlier, the presence of a support network is a major mediating factor in how the parents respond to the potential stress of raising the child with disabilities (Dunst et al., 1986; Trute & Hauch, 1988). Some parents may need to seek or develop such a support system. The professional can be a helpful resource in identifying existing support groups, community services, and organizations that the parents can contact.

Rubin and Quinn-Curran (1983) have written on institutional impediments that parents often confront, and many authors have detailed the nature of professionals' biases (Darling, 1983); it seems apparent that the "helping" systems can in some instances become a major source of stress for parents and the family. Parents who "scout out" different options for services may be seen as shopping for more optimistic feedback, rather than attempting to represent the best interests of the child and family. The view by professionals of assertive parents as "aggressive," "disturbed," or "over-emotionally involved" may again discount the legitimate role of a parent.

Professionals unfamiliar with the life cycle aspects of the individual with disabilities and family might not appreciate the sadness that often recurs as parents have to work with the child and the "system" in relation to new developmental or social milestones. They might mistakenly see parents as "stuck" at some point in the hypothesized process of adaptation. Such a perception disregards the often cyclical nature of the adaptation process and the manner in which the family organizes itself regarding the child with disabilities.

The data on siblings also seem to be somewhat problematic (Seligman & Darling, 1997; Skrtic, Summers, Brotherson, & Turnbull, 1984); there is documentation of siblings benefiting or at least not exhibiting notable negative effects due to the presence of a child with disabilities (Crnic & Leconte, 1986; Labato, 1990), as well as research that suggests that siblings experience some difficulties (Harvey & Greenway, 1984; Senel & Akkok, 1995; Tritt & Esses, 1988). Perhaps the best way for professionals to address the issue of siblings is, as Hannah and Midlarsky (1985, 1987) suggest, to consider them as potentially at risk for some problems within the family but not to make the automatic assumption that such problems exist. Certainly in some instances parents can benefit from examining what demands have been placed on siblings, whether the family has become overly focused on the child with disabilities, and how everyone in the family can work together to meet the needs of each member.

It is interesting to note that in families without an individual with special needs, one child might believe that the parents favor another child, that parental expectations of different children in the family are unfair, and so on. Parents deal with these occurrences by talking about them and examining how in fact different children are being treated. For the most part these concerns are readily understandable from a normal, developmental, sibling rivalry point of view without being indicative of family dysfunction. But given the family of a child with disabilities, professionals may be inclined to look at the same kinds of complaints by the siblings in a very different light. These observations again underscore the need for the professionals to have a "normal family" frame of reference so as not to pathologize certain events.

A notable study by Palfrey et al. (1989) involved interviews with parents of 1,726 students in special education. To the authors' surprise the majority of parents did not report any particular stress because of the child with disabilities. The authors, while wondering about parental denial, also considered that many parents might have reached a reasonable point of acceptance and learned how to cope adequately with the child's disability.

This study did analyze parental reports of stress with regard to numerous variables. The fact that the majority of parents did not report any particular stress was not meant as a "whitewash" of the potential stressful effects of raising a child with disabilities. For example, 63% of the parents of children with physical or multiple disabilities reported relatively more stress on the family, whereas only 23% of parents of children with speech or learning difficulties reported family stress. Also, parents with a higher educational background reported more stress than parents of lower educational and socioeconomic backgrounds. The area of marital satisfaction was least affected of all the domains that were considered.

Those parents experiencing stress could benefit from a range of counseling, educational, and support programs. The authors felt that greater involvement by parents in their children's educational program enhanced their sense of empowerment. Professionals may need to develop new strategies to promote greater parental participation and also become more involved with families to reach a better understanding of the specific sources of stress and options for assisting those families.

A sensitive and comprehensive interview with parents can help to identify specific sources of stress as well as family needs (Seligman & Darling, 1989, 1997; Turnbull & Turnbull, 1997; Winton, 1988b). Although checklists and rating scales can be useful, the involved professionals should consider a follow-up interview to explore indicated areas of stress or concern, as well as to encourage discussion of concerns not identified on the instruments. Most important, the professionals should be prepared to identify strengths that can be incorporated into subsequent collaborative intervention efforts. There are also checklists and rating scales available for parents to complete that can reveal areas of concern, stress, and need (Bailey, 1988; Holroyd, 1987; Seligman & Darling, 1989, 1997).

Normal family considerations can assist the involved professionals in maintaining a perspective on the family of a child with disabilities. Concepts of healthy family functioning can also precipitate some directions for professionals to move with specific families. Families who have become excessively enmeshed around the child with disabilities may need help in "loosening up," involving others in the childcare picture, and reaching for social support.

Siblings may have been moved into inappropriate parental roles, and the family might benefit from a clearer demarcation of subsystem boundaries.

Increased communication within the family about the child may be helpful to all family members and can encourage a diminishment of secrets and stigma associated with that child. Open communication can help family members to learn that their various reactions are normal and appropriate.

More community support services are becoming available in the forms of library materials, parent discussion groups, and individual, family, and group counseling. An important role of professionals is assisting parents and families to assess their needs and to seek out appropriate services and resources. It has been noted that families of children with disabilities participate in fewer activities in the community than other families (Barnett & Boyce, 1995; Ehrmann, Aeschleman, & Svanum, 1995).

The availability of support groups and a support network are consistently identified by professionals and parents of children with disabilities as being extremely important (Dunst et al., 1986; Dunst, Trivette, & Deal, 1988; Trute & Hauch, 1988). Support from others often mediates the potential stress of raising a child with special needs and can be informative in terms of other community resources (Smith, Gabard, Dale, & Druker, 1994). The contribution of professionals should include exploring with parents their awareness and use of support groups and their establishing of a support network.

Palfrey et al. (1989) observed that the past decade has witnessed a greater emphasis on individualizing approaches to children with disabilities and their families. These authors believe that individualization, which includes an appreciation of the needs and characteristics of a given family, can lead to a fuller use of human services programs. Such individualization is consistent with the theme of this book, that of productive collaboration by professionals with parents of children with disabilities.

A Collaborative Model of Parent Involvement

The several laws pertaining to education and treatment of children with disabilities stress the importance of collaboration in decision making and program implementation. In particular, parent participation in the child's education has been underscored, with emphasis on collaboration as the preferred method by which the professional and the family can interact (Buysse, Schulte, Pierce, & Terry, 1994). Collaborative consultation assumes that the consultant (the professional) and the consultee (the family) are equal partners in the collaborative process (Fine, 1990; Sheridan, 1992). Sheridan (1992) suggests that while participants are equal in making decisions, the knowledge each brings to the process differs; together, the participants can develop new ideas and solutions. Although the consultant typically is more familiar with the collaborative process and may have a more objective view of the situation, the family can be a rich resource, having observed on a day-to-day basis the child's difficulties as well as strengths.

The partnership that professionals such as mental health workers and educators can form with the parents of children with disabilities has the potential to educate the parents and strengthen their capacity to act on behalf of their children. But professionals' beliefs about the parents' capacity to help themselves can influence perceptions and behaviors and strongly affect the helping relationship for better or worse (Brickman et al., 1982).

The collaborative model being proposed represents a frame of reference that can guide mental health professionals and educators in their contacts with parents of children with disabilities. The model represents a value stance and conveys a positive view of parent involvement including some important perceptions of potential parental competency and effectiveness. A number of writers have influenced the conceptualization of the proposed model, and their works can serve as helpful resources to the reader (Bailey & Simeonsson, 1988; Dunst et al., 1986; Ehly, Conoley, & Rosenthal, 1985; Seligman & Darling, 1989, 1997; Simpson & Fiedler, 1989; Turnbull & Turnbull, 1997).

There are four main objectives to the collaborative model of parent involvement; these can be acted out creatively and with varying emphases by the involved professionals. The four objectives are

1. To include parents in decision making;
2. To educate parents for participation in decision making;
3. To assist parents therapeutically, as needed, so they can cope with specific impediments to their participation; and
4. To enable and empower parents to work actively on behalf of their child.

Functional Aspects of the Model

The model should prove useful and applicable for professionals working in different contexts with parents; however, it is probably most effectively implemented by professionals who view themselves operating out of a flexible consultative orientation. Some functional aspects of the model will be discussed in the remainder of this section.

1. *The model initially represents an existential stance that the helping professional can take toward parents.* Professionals bring to their relationship with parents of children with disabilities a set of attitudes and attributes that represents a kind of worldview. Professionals who respond to parents as potential partners and collaborators have a different set of attitudes, expectations, and behaviors than those who see parents as too emotionally

involved, adversaries, or patients. Different "messages" are likely to be sent and received by the parents and responded to in various ways.

Being on the receiving end of somebody's negative attributions is not a particularly pleasant experience and may precipitate a hostile reaction. Perhaps even worse, parents in this position may become convinced of their inadequacies. The helping professional can be a significant person in the life of parents and, as such, can strongly influence the parents' concept of themselves as active and responsible participants on behalf of their child.

2. *The model is developmental* in the sense that it recognizes that parents may not be prepared for full collaborative participation at a particular point in time but can be assisted toward greater future involvement. The important element here is that parents not be viewed as being in some kind of static and unchangeable posture but as capable of expanding their understanding and skills. This position leads logically to the next aspect of the model.

3. *The model is proactive* in its recognition that certain activities can help the parents move toward greater participatory capabilities in the future. These activities, while often prompted at the time of a problem or crisis, should be made more a part of the ongoing relationship between the helping professional and parents. As a result parents will be better prepared to deal with the range of needs and issues that may subsequently arise. The proactive aspect of the model can focus on three areas: educational, therapeutic, and organizational.

The *educational* dimension relates to the input of needed information, as well as the teaching of specific skills. The skills can focus on many areas from child management to effective communication to parent participation in staffing or IEP (Individualized Education Plan) meetings.

The *therapeutic* dimension occurs as professionals assist parents in processing and understanding their feelings and experiences. The broad goals of the therapeutic dimension are to support the parents in working through whatever personal issues may exist in relation to the child and helping them gain a greater sense of objectivity and awareness in the parenting role.

The *organizational* dimension recognizes the social support needs of parents both for their own emotional well-being and for their efforts on behalf of exceptional children. The notion of networking is extremely important; parents working together are able to construct organizational vehicles that can serve them and their children well. Examples of such organizational vehicles are clearinghouses for information on community resources, directories of individuals who can assist with specific kinds parental problems such as estate planning, and programs for advocacy, planning, or educational purposes.

4. *The model is family–ecologically oriented* in its sensitivity to the family constellation and the day-to-day realities of the parents living with a child with disabilities. For example, the professional who advises parents "to get out and relax" without regard for the difficulties in finding a sitter capable of caring for their child with disabilities has missed an important point in the

parents' reality. Such considerations are especially important when dealing with a single-parent situation.

The model recognizes that the parents may need help in resolving a number of family issues in order for them to be able to take time for themselves. The professional should ask about babysitter problems, financial issues, as well as the attitudes toward childcare that impede or support the parents' ability to take time for themselves. What are the implications of decisions on other family members? For example, how are older siblings used and what is the impact of the babysitting requirements on sibling–family relationships?

Tied in with the notion that parents and child interact within a broad ecology is the awareness that parents benefit from an appreciation of institutional issues. For example, parents should try to be sensitive to teacher needs, such as sufficient time for appropriate planning, inservices, and emotionally renewing experiences.

5. *The model requires multiple roles on the part of the helping professional.* As stated earlier, a consultative stance can represent a useful orientation for the professional in affording the flexibility to pursue a range of activities selectively. As an example, in instances where the parent and school might be experiencing some conflict, the helping professional can assume the role of *mediator* and arrange some sessions that involve the parents and school personnel.

At times the professional may take a more *advocacy-oriented* stance by contributing educational and training information so that parents are better prepared to confront school personnel or participate in planning meetings. From a *therapeutic* stance, the professional may schedule sessions with one or both parents, possibly siblings, or even the whole family, in order to help them deal with different issues. And finally the helping professional may assume the role of *expert* by way of giving specific information, opinions, or recommendations.

These multiple roles have the potential of precipitating role confusion on the part of the helping professional, with concomitant loss of objectivity and neutrality. In a sense professionals always face such dangers when they assume a caring and helping attitude toward a client. When mental health professionals are aware they will be assuming multiple roles, they can be more sensitive to how the roles shift and can even talk about such shifts with the parents. The more open and direct the relationship, the less likely that confusion or misperceptions will arise.

6. *The model promotes a constructive and positive stance* rather than an adversarial one with side-taking that could lead to a polarization of positions. This constructive and positive stance not only improves the helping professional's relationship with parents but also promotes a positive attitude in parents in their dealings with other professionals and agencies.

This focus on the positive requires certain skills on the part of the professional, including the most important skill of being able to reframe events in a positive and constructive light. This kind of stance encourages people to work together, to see each other as contributors, and to engage in networking and group planning.

7. *The model has a problem-solving emphasis.* Professionals and parents should direct their energies to such questions as "What can we do now?" and "Where do we go from here?" Some parents may have a litany of complaints against the systems that they have encountered. Although the parents may need to be heard and to have their feelings and thoughts validated, the helping professional should avoid supporting the parents' obsessing or remaining fixated on their complaints and empower them to take action. They should focus constructively on "what can be" rather than on "what should have been."

Also, the professional's approach to problem solving ought to be more than just an attempt to push people into action. It should involve some step-by-step thinking along the lines of setting goals or objectives, evaluating resources, deciding on appropriate steps in view of the logistical issues, determining who should be involved and in what ways, and, finally, establishing a reasonably concrete timeline for activity. Opportunities for evaluation, feedback, and processing also need to be built into an effective problem-solving approach.

8. *The model views parents as teachers as well as learners.* Collaboration implies that people not only work together in a mutually supportive fashion but that they teach and learn from each other. Many assumptions that professionals hold about what is best for the child or how the parents can accomplish a particular goal need to be checked out with the parents. The parents may have learned how to deal with specific child management or training issues in different and creative ways. The professional community has much to learn from parents who live day to day with a child with disabilities and have had to cope over time with the child in home and school as well as with the "helping" service bureaucracies.

Many professionals who are eager to advise others such as parents of a child with disabilities would do well to listen and observe carefully before recommending new strategies or approaches to a problem situation. What the professional sees as a problem may not be one for the parents; what the parents believe to be a problem is one for the parents. A collaborative partnership requires a valuing of the beliefs and perceptions of parents by professionals, and an appreciation of the parents' insights, ideas, and experiences with the child with disabilities.

Summary

This chapter has approached the child with disabilities in the family from the perspective of the need of involved professionals to (a) understand normal family development, (b) appreciate individual variations among families of children with disabilities, and (c) develop a collaborative orientation to working with parents and families. Research has demonstrated that professionals with negative attitudes and misconceptions can impede the active participation by parents in the care and education of their children with disabilities.

The literature has become progressively more optimistic about parents being able to cope satisfactorily with a child with disabilities. Parent involvement continues to receive legislated support, although individual parents may need assistance in learning how to be effectively involved. The rights of parents to limit formal involvement in certain programs also need to be accepted and appreciated by professionals. After all, not every parent of typically developing children is enthusiastic about attending school functions and parent–teacher conferences, or serving on parent advisory, curriculum, or school policy committees.

We may be approaching a new era of awareness and response to the needs of individuals with disabilities and their families. It is to be hoped that helping professionals such as psychologists, social workers, psychiatrists, counselors, rehabilitation personnel, and educators will assume leadership roles rather than acting out less positive or more adversarial roles.

References

Bailey, D. B. (1988). Assessing family stress and needs. In D. B. Bailey & R. J. Simeonsson (Eds.), *Family assessment in early intervention* (pp. 95–118). Columbus, OH: Merrill.

Bailey, D. B., & Simeonsson, R. J. (1988). *Family assessment in early intervention.* Columbus, OH: Merrill.

Barnett, W. S., & Boyce, G. C. (1995). Effects of children with Down syndrome on parents' activities. *American Journal on Mental Retardation, 100,* 115–127.

Blacher, J. (1984). Sequential stages of parental adjustment to the birth of a child with handicaps: Fact or artifact? *Mental Retardation, 22,* 55–68.

Brickman, P., Rabinowitz, V., Karuza, J., Coates, D., Cohn, E., & Kidder, L. (1982). Models of helping and coping. *American Psychologist, 37,* 368–384.

Buysse, V., Schulte, A. C., Pierce, P. P., & Terry, D. (1994). Models and styles of consultation: Preferences of professionals in early intervention. *Journal of Early Intervention, 18,* 302–310.

Carter, E., & McGoldrick, M. (1980). *The family life cycle: A framework for family therapy.* New York: Gardner Press.

Crnic, K. A., & Leconte, J. M. (1986). Understanding sibling needs and influences. In R. R. Fewell & P. F. Vadasy (Eds.), *Families of handicapped children* (pp. 75–98). Austin, TX: PRO-ED.

Darling, R. B. (1983). Parent–professional interaction: The roots of misunderstanding. In M. Seligman (Ed.), *The family with a handicapped child* (pp. 95–121). Orlando, FL: Grune & Stratton.

Drotar, D., Baskiewicz, A., Irvin, N., Kennell, J., & Klaus, M. (1975). The adaptation of parents to the birth of an infant with congenital malformation: A hypothetical model. *Pediatrics, 56,* 710–717.

Dunst, C. J., Trivette, C. M., & Cross, A. (1986). Mediation influences of social support: Personal, family, and child outcome. *American Journal of Mental Deficiency, 90,* 403–417.

Dunst, C. J., Trivette, C. M., & Deal, A. G. (1988). *Enabling and empowering families*. Cambridge, MA: Brookline Books.

Dyson, L. (1991). Families of young handicapped children: Parental stress and family functioning. *American Journal on Mental Retardation, 95,* 623–629.

Education for All Handicapped Children Act of 1975, 20 U.S.C. § 1400 *et seq.*

Education of the Handicapped Act Amendments of 1986, 20 U.S.C. § 1400 *et seq.*

Ehly, S., Conoley, J., & Rosenthal, D. (1985). *Working with parents of exceptional children*. St. Louis, MO: Mosby.

Ehrmann, L. C., Aeschleman, S. R., & Svanum, S. (1995). Parental reports of community activity patterns: A comparison between young children with disabilities and their non-disabled peers. *Research in Developmental Disabilities, 16,* 331–343.

Farber, B. (1959). Effects of a severely mentally retarded child on family integration. *Monographs of the Society for Research in Child Development, 24* (Whole no. 71).

Fewell, R. R., & Gelb, S. A. (1983). Parenting moderately handicapped persons. In M. Seligman (Ed.), *The family with a handicapped child: Understanding and treatment* (pp. 175–202). Orlando, FL: Grune & Stratton.

Fine, M. J. (1990). Facilitating home–school relationships: A family-oriented approach to collaborative consultation. *Journal of Educational and Psychological Consultation, 1,* 169–187.

Florian, L. (1995). Part H early intervention program: Legislative history and intent of the law. *Topics in Early Childhood Special Education, 15,* 247–262.

Foster, M. (1988). A systems perspective and families of handicapped children. *Journal of Family Psychology, 2,* 54–56.

Foster, M., & Berger, M. (1985). Research with families with handicapped children: A multi-level systemic perspective. In L. L'Abate (Ed.), *The handbook of family psychology and therapy* (Vol. II, pp. 741–780). Homewood, IL: Dorsey.

Foster, M., Berger, M., & McLean, M. (1981). Rethinking a good idea: A reassessment of parent involvement. *Topics in Early Childhood Special Education, 1,* 55–65.

Freedman, R. I., Litchfield, L. C., & Warfield, M. E. (1995). Balancing work and family: Perspectives of parents of children with developmental disabilities. *Families in Society, 76,* 507–514.

Glick, P., & Lin, S. (1986). Recent changes in divorce and remarriage. *Journal of Marriage and the Family, 48,* 737–747.

Grossman, F. K. (1972). *Brothers and sisters of retarded children: An exploratory study*. Syracuse, NY: Syracuse University Press.

Hampson, R., Hulgus, Y., Beavers, W., & Beavers, J. (1988). The assessment of competence in families with a retarded child. *Journal of Family Psychology, 3,* 32–53.

Hanline, M. F. (1991). Transitions and critical events in the family life cycle: Implications for providing support to families of children with disabilities. *Psychology in the Schools, 28,* 53–59.

Hannah, M. E., & Midlarsky, E. (1985). Siblings of the handicapped: A literature review for school psychologist. *School Psychology Review, 14,* 510–520.

Hannah, M. E., & Midlarsky, E. (1987). Siblings of the handicapped: Maladjustment and its prevention. *Techniques, 3,* 188–195.

Harry, B. (1992). *Cultural diversity, families, and the special education system: Communication and empowerment*. New York: Teachers College Press.

Harvey, D. H. P., & Greenway, A. P. (1984). The self concept of physically handicapped children and their non-handicapped siblings: An empirical investigation. *Journal of Child Psychology and Psychiatry, 25,* 273–284.

Holmes, T. H., & Rahe, R. H. (1967). The Social Readjustment Rating Scale. *Journal of Psychosomatic Research, 2,* 213–218.

Holroyd, J. (1987). *Questionnaire on Resources and Stress for families with chronically ill or handicapped members.* Brandon, VT: Clinical Psychology.

Huber, C. H. (1979). Parents of the handicapped child: Facilitating acceptance through group counseling. *Personnel and Guidance Journal, 57,* 267–269.

Individuals with Disabilities Education Act Amendments of 1997, 20 U.S.C. § 1400 *et seq.*

Kalyanpur, M., & Harry, B. (1997). A posture of reciprocity: A practical approach to collaboration between professionals and parents of culturally diverse backgrounds. *Journal of Child and Family Studies, 6,* 485–509.

Kazak, A. E. (1986). Families with physically handicapped children: Social ecology and family systems. *Family Process, 25,* 265–281.

Kazak, A. E., & Marvin, R. S. (1984). Differences, difficulties and adaptation: Stress and social networks in families with a handicapped child. *Family Relations, 33,* 67–76.

Labato, D. L. (1990). *Brothers, sisters, and special needs.* Baltimore, MD: Brookes.

Lewis, J. (1986). Family structure and stress. *Family Process, 25,* 235–247.

Longo, D., & Bond, L. (1984). Families of the handicapped child: Research and practice. *Family Relations, 33,* 57–65.

McAdoo, H. P. (1993). *Family ethnicity: Strength in diversity.* Newbury Park, CA: Sage.

McCubbin, H. I., & Figley, C. (1983). Bridging normative and catastrophic family stress. In H. McCubbin & C. Figley (Eds.), *Stress and the family, Vol. 1: Coping with normative transitions* (pp. 218–228). New York: Brunner/Mazel.

McDowell, A. D., Saylor, C. F., Taylor, M. J., & Boyce, G. C. (1995). Ethnicity and parenting stress change during early intervention. *Early Childhood Development and Care, 111,* 131–140.

McGoldrick, M., Pearce, J., & Giordano, J. (Eds.). (1982). *Ethnicity and family therapy.* New York: Guilford.

Minuchin, S., & Fishman, H. (1981). *Family therapy techniques.* Cambridge, MA: Harvard University Press.

Minuchin, S., Rosmand, B., & Baker, L. (1979). *Psychosomatic families: Anorexia nervosa in context.* Cambridge, MA: Harvard University Press.

Newman, J. (1983). Handicapped persons and their families: Philosophical, historical, and legislative perspectives. In M. Seligman (Ed.), *The family with a handicapped child: Understanding and treatment* (pp. 3–250). Orlando, FL: Grune & Stratton.

Olshansky, S. (1962). Chronic sorrow: A response to having a mentally defective child. *Social Casework, 43,* 190-193.

Palfrey, J., Walker, D., Butler, J., & Singer, J. (1989). Patterns of response in families of chronically disabled children. An assessment in five metropolitan school districts. *American Journal of Orthopsychiatry, 59,* 94-103.

Peterson, N. L., & Cooper, C. (1989). Parent education and involvement in early intervention programs for handicapped children: A different perspective on parent needs and the parent-professional relationship. In M. Fine (Ed.), *The second handbook on parent education: Contemporary perspectives* (pp. 197–234). New York: Academic Press.

Roman, M., & Raley, P. (1980). *The indelible family.* New York: Rawson, Wade.

Rubin, S., & Quinn-Curran, N. (1983). Lost, then found: Parents journey through the community service maze. In M. Seligman (Ed.), *The family with a handicapped child* (pp. 63–94). Orlando, FL: Grune & Stratton.

Schilling, R. F., Kirkham, M. A., Snow, W. H., & Schinke, S. P. (1986). Single mothers with handicapped children: Different from their married counterparts? *Family Relations, 35,* 69–77.

Searle, S. (1978). Stages of parent reaction. *The Exceptional Parent, 8,* 23–27.

Seligman, M., & Darling, R. B. (1989). *Ordinary families, special children: A systems approach to childhood disability.* New York: Guilford Press.

Seligman, M., & Darling, R. B. (1997). *Ordinary families, special children: A systems approach to childhood disability* (2nd ed.). New York: Guilford Press.

Selye, H. (1974). *Stress without distress.* New York: Lippincott.

Senel, H. G., & Akkok, F. (1995). Stress levels and attitudes of normal siblings of children with disabilities. *International Journal for the Advancement of Counseling, 18,* 61–68.

Sheridan, S. M. (1992). What do we mean when we say "collaboration"? *Journal of Educational and Psychological Consultation, 3,* 89–92.

Simpson, R. L., & Fiedler, C. R. (1989). Parent participation in individualized educational program (IEP) conferences: A case for individualization. In M. Fine (Ed.), *The second handbook on parent education: Contemporary perspectives* (pp. 145–170). New York: Academic Press.

Skrtic, T. M., Summers, J. A., Brotherson, M. J., & Turnbull, A. P. (1984). Severely handicapped children and their brothers and sisters. In J. Blacher (Ed.), *Severely handicapped young children and their families.* Orlando: Academic Press.

Smith, K., Gabard, D., Dale, D., & Druker, A. (1994). Parental options about attending parent support groups. *Children's Health Care, 23,* 127–136.

Stinnett, N., & DeFrain, J. (1989). The healthy family: Is it possible: In M. J. Fine (Ed.), *The second handbook on parent education: Contemporary perspectives* (pp. 53–74). New York: Academic Press.

Tritt, S. G., & Esses, L. M. (1988). Psychological adaptation of siblings of children with chronic medical illness. *American Journal of Orthopsychiatry, 58,* 211–220.

Trute, B., & Hauch, C. (1988). Building on family strengths: A study of families with positive adjustment to the birth of a developmentally disabled child. *Journal of Marital & Family Therapy, 14,* 185–194.

Turnbull, A. P., & Leonard, J. (1981). Parent involvement in special education: Emerging advocacy roles. *School Psychology Review, 10,* 32–44.

Turnbull, A. P., Summers, J., & Brotherson, M. (1986). Family life cycle: Theoretical and empirical implications and future directions for families with mentally retarded members. In J. Gallagher & P. Vietze (Eds.), *Families of handicapped persons: Research, programs, and policy issues* (pp. 45–65). Baltimore: Brookes.

Turnbull, A. P., & Turnbull, H. R. (1982). Parent involvement in the education of handicapped children: A critique. *Mental Retardation, 20,* 115–122.

Turnbull, A. P., & Turnbull, H. R. (1997). *Families, professionals, and exceptionality: A special partnership* (3rd ed.). Columbus, OH: Merrill.

Werth, L., & Oseroff, A. (1987). Continued counseling intervention: Lifetime support for the family with a handicapped member. *The American Journal of Family Therapy, 15,* 333–342.

Widerstrom, A., & Dudley-Marling, C. (1986). Living with a handicapped child: Myth and reality. *Childhood Education, 62,* 359, 362, 364–367.

Wikler, L., Wasow, M., & Hatfield, E. (1981). Chronic sorrow revisited: Parent vs. professional depiction of the adjustment of parents of mentally retarded children. *American Journal of Orthopsychiatry, 51,* 63–70.

Winton, P. J. (1988a). Effective communication between parents and professionals. In D. Bailey & R. Simeonsson (Eds.), *Family assessment in early intervention* (pp. 207–228). Columbus, OH: Merrill.

Winton, P. J. (1988b). The family focused interview: An assessment and goal setting mechanism. In D. Bailey & R. Simeonsson (Eds.), *Family assessment in early intervention* (pp. 185–205). Columbus, OH: Merrill.

Yoshida, R., Fenton, K., Kaufman, M., & Maxwell, J. (1978). Parent involvement in the special education pupil planning process: The school's perspective. *Exceptional Children, 44,* 531–534.

Zuk, G. (1959). The religious factor and the role of guild in parental acceptance of the retarded child. *American Journal of Mental Deficiency, 64,* 139–147.

Family–Professional Partnerships: A Behavioral Science Perspective

2

Carl J. Dunst, Carol M. Trivette, and Donna M. Snyder

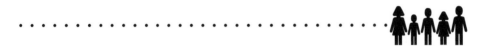

T he terms *partnership* and *collaboration,* which are often used inter-changeably, are now employed widely in the early intervention (Filer & Mahoney, 1996; Stonestreet, Johnston, & Acton, 1991), preschool education (Brand, 1996), elementary and secondary education (Connors & Epstein, 1995; Epstein, 1992), human services (DeChillo, Koren, & Schultze, 1994), maternal and child health care (Bishop, 1993), and other fields (Clark et al., 1996; Galegher, Kraut, & Egido, 1990) to describe working relationships among people, groups, or organizations. However, the terms have now been so widely used in so many different ways that they lack a precise meaning. The published literature, which is replete with references to partnerships and collaboration, does not yield a consistent operational definition of these terms or a set of defining characteristics.

If professionals cannot agree on an operational definition or the defining characteristics of a phenomenon such as a partnership or collaboration, then they cannot reliably know that the phenomenon has occurred. Claims abound in the published literature that partnerships and collaborations are ideal models for relationships among people, groups, and organizations, but the enthusiasts seem to disagree on the important features of these kinds of relationships. Much of the literature on partnerships and collaborations is long on rhetoric and short on specificity; good research is almost nonexistent.

In this chapter we take a behavioral science approach to studying part-nerships and collaborations. Such an approach considers partnerships and collaborations to be behavioral constructs and their conceptualization, oper-ationalization, and measurement (by observation, self-report, paper and pen-cil, etc.) the focus of study and concern. Approaching partnerships and col-laborations from a behavioral science perspective cannot help but promote a better understanding of the phenomena, supply a better method for investi-gating these relationships, and provide guidance for informing practice.

According to Wolman (1973), concepts and constructs that cannot be defined operationally have no place in science. This rigorous standard leads to what we know will be an unpopular assertion: Current discussions of partnerships and collaborations as part of a philosophy of care are not useful from a behavioral science point of view. These accounts may be interesting and helpful for encouraging changes in the relationships among people, groups, and organizations, but accepting them as a truism impedes rather than advances science and the ability to draw empirically based implications for practice.

This chapter focuses on the meaning, characteristics, and consequences of family–professional partnerships. The contents build upon our previous work (Dunst, Johanson, Rounds, Trivette, & Hamby, 1992; Dunst & Paget, 1991; Dunst, Trivette, & Johanson, 1994) as well as that of others (e.g., Bishop, 1993; Christenson, Rounds, & Franklin, 1992; DeChillo et al., 1994; Dinnebeil, Hale, & Rule, 1996; Edmondson, n.d.; Vosler-Hunter, 1988). The chapter is divided into five sections. The first introduces the reader to a behavioral science approach to studying behavioral phenomena. The second section includes a description of a way of viewing partnerships and collaborations as particular kinds of relationships among people, groups, and organizations. In the third section we critically review and analyze the family–professional partnership and collaboration literature, with a focus on whether the theoretical, descriptive, and empirical evidence is consistent with good science. The fourth section places family–professional partnerships in a broader context of empowerment processes and effective helpgiving practices. The chapter concludes with a discussion of the kinds of research needed to advance our understanding of the meaning of family–professional partnerships.

A Behavioral Science Perspective

Behavioral scientists take a particular approach to studying social and behavioral phenomena (intelligence, well-being, wealth, risk taking, etc.). They identify a phenomenon and give it a name (e.g., family-centeredness), develop an operational definition, specify the various indicators of the phenomenon, describe how the phenomenon compares to other related ones, and determine procedures for measuring and investigating the phenomenon. This process links conceptualization to operationalization. According to Babbie (1983), "*conceptualization* is the refinement and specification of abstract concepts, and *operationalization* is the development of specific research procedures [operations] that will result in empirical observations representing those concepts in the real world" (p. 122). (The reader is referred to Babbie for a highly readable description of a behavioral science approach.)

A few examples of how the above works for different kinds of phenomena should help illustrate conceptualization and operationalization. Take, for example, the highly charged phenomenon of child maltreatment. The term most certainly evokes a wide range of images (and emotions). From a scientific perspective, however, it is possible to be fairly precise about its meaning. Zuravin (1991), for example, operationally defined child abuse as acts of commission and harm, and child neglect as acts of omission and endangerment. On the one hand these operational distinctions make clear what child maltreatment is and on the other hand differentiate between conceptually similar but distinct forms of maltreatment. Consequently the definition and distinctions help make the terms more explicit. But Zuravin (1991) did not stop there. For instance, she specified 14 subtypes of neglect that make indicators of the concept even more explicit. These in turn lead to the ability to select relevant measures for assessing the presence or absence of child neglect (Dunst, Trivette, & Gowen, 1993).

We can also consider psychological anxiety and depression as behavioral phenomena. The similarities and differences between both mental states have long been the focus of psychological and psychiatric study (see Kendall & Watson, 1989). Both are negative emotions, but anxiety is a state dominated by arousal and heightened fear, whereas depression is characterized by lethargy and sadness. Conceptualizations of anxiety and depression operationalized in this manner have resulted in fairly detailed sets of indicators for judging the presence or absence of both mental states (e.g., Watson & Tellegen, 1985) and for understanding both the distinctive and overlapping features of these two kinds of emotions (Watson & Kendall, 1989). With these conceptualizations and operationalizations in mind, professionals can select and use appropriate measurement procedures for studying either or both phenomena (see Kendall & Watson, 1989).

Delimiting the Universe of the Construct

This and the next section of the chapter use a behavioral science perspective for reviewing and critically analyzing available evidence with regard to the conceptualization and operationalization of the terms partnership and collaboration. As previously noted, both terms are now widely used to describe the interactional and transactional relationships between people, groups, and organizations. As is the case for any behavioral phenomenon, having operational definitions of partnership and collaboration, together with an agreed upon list of indicators of the constructs, is highly desirable from a behavioral science perspective.

A first step in operationally defining the terms is to differentiate partnerships and collaborations from other kinds of relationships. Within the framework of set theory, all relationships, regardless of their kind, may be considered the universe of interactions and transactions among people, groups, and organizations. Partnerships and collaborations are a particular set of these relationships. Further, the set of relationships that are partnerships and collaborations has many kinds of subsets, including family–professional partnerships, interagency collaboration, and so on. Figure 2.1 shows these interrelationships graphically. U is the universe of all relationships, and A is the set of relationships called partnerships and collaboration. $\overline{A}$, the complement of A, is the set of relationships that by definition would not meet criteria for being either partnerships or collaborations. A_1, a subset of A, may be thought of as a particular kind of partnership or collaborative relationship (e.g., a family–professional partnership). This simple but useful way of thinking about partnerships and collaborations is a good starting point for better conceptualization and operationalization. However, as is described in the next section of the chapter, the distinction between partnerships or collaborations and other kinds of relationships is not at all clear, thus making the exact meaning of the terms elusive at best.

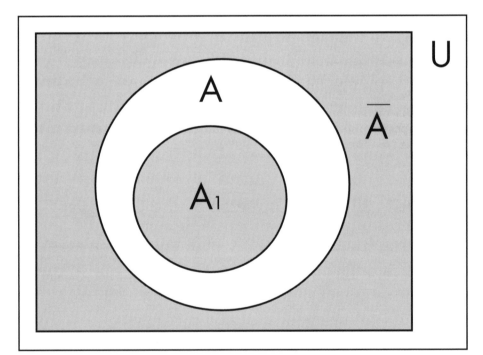

Figure 2.1. A Venn diagram depicting the universe of human, group, and organization relationships (U), the set of partnership and collaborative relationships (A), a subset of those kinds of relationships (A_1), and those relationships that are not partnership and collaborative in nature $(\overline{A})$.

A second step toward a better understanding of the concepts partnership and collaboration involves other differentiations. We suggest that the term partnership be reserved for descriptions of a relationship between people, and that the term collaboration be used to describe a relationship between groups, organizations, and agencies at least with regard to human services, education, and health care programs and practices. This recommendation is based on evidence that the most important characteristics of person–person relationships are different from those of group–group, organization–organization, and agency–agency relationships (compare, e.g., Roberts, Rule, & Innocenti, 1998, and Swan & Morgan, 1993).

We also recommend that professionals using the terms always specify the kind of partnership or collaboration. For example, by using the more descriptive terms *family–professional partnerships, interagency collaboration,* and the like, they cannot help but contribute to a better understanding and appreciation of the phenomena. The more clearly and exactly a concept is described, the more likely the users will have a shared understanding. The term partnership, for example, can and does mean many things to different people, but the term family–professional partnership at least reduces the possibilities by specifying the relationship between a family and one or more professionals.

Babbie (1983) describes a useful way of making the meaning of terms more precise once a phenomenon of interest has been isolated from the universe of conceptually related concepts and ideas. According to Babbie, there are three kinds of definitions—real, nominal, and operational—representing different degrees of precision with regard to operationalization. Real definitions are simply the reification of terms but are so general that they are essentially useless for purposes of advancing an understanding of a concept. Babbie continues:

> A *nominal* definition is one that is *assigned* to a term. In the midst of disagreement and confusion over what a term really means, the scientist specifies a working definition. . . . As a next step, we must specify what we are going to observe, how we will do it, and what interpretations we are going to place on various possible observations. All of these further specifications make up what is called an *operational definition* of the concept. (p. 109)

As the next section shows, professionals have not yet reached the point where they have an operational definition of family–professional partnerships.

Dimensions of Family–Professional Partnerships

During the past decade there has been a flurry of research and practice focusing on various aspects of parent–professional and family–professional partnerships. The number of references that include the term partnership (and collaboration) is mind boggling. We attempt to make sense of this burgeoning body of work by focusing on two dimensions of the construct, definitions and characteristics, and critically examining this work from a behavioral science perspective.

Definition of Partnerships

An extensive review of the partnership and collaboration literature by Dunst and Paget (1991) with an eye toward identification of definitions of parent–professional and family–professional partnerships proved unfruitful. This led Dunst and Paget to borrow a legal definition (Clifford & Warner, 1987; Phillips & Rasberry, 1981; Uniform Partnership Act, 1989, Supp. 1999, Section G [1]) and define a family–professional partnership as "An association between a family and one or more professionals who function collaboratively using agreed-upon roles in pursuit of a joint interest or common goal" (p. 29).

This definition or variations of it have been used by others as the basis for investigating the meaning of family–professional partnerships and for proposing new expanded definitions (Brandt, 1993; DeChillo et al., 1994; Dinnebeil et al., 1996; Dinnebeil & Rule, 1994; Roberts et al., 1998; Rosin, 1996). According to DeChillo et al. (1994), partnerships are "commonly understood as two or more parties working together in pursuit of a common goal. . . . The commonly agreed essence of [family–professional] relationships being reciprocity, with shared power and decision making" (p. 565). Dunst, Johanson, et al. (1992) argued that the particular differentiating feature of family–professional partnerships is that the transactions and interactions between partners are *mutual, complementary, joint,* and *reciprocal.* Traits of these partnerships include, but are not limited to, mutual trust, mutual respect, joint decision making, and joint action. An example of an undated definition incorporating these features of family–professional relationships is as follows:

> **Family–professional partnership**—Parents and other family members working together with professionals in pursuit of a common goal where the relationship between the family and professional is based on shared decision making, shared responsibility, mutual trust, and mutual respect.

Several things can be said about this definition from a behavioral science perspective. First, it is a nominal and not an operational definition (Babbie, 1983). Although the definition is more than just a label, it does not go far enough in terms of specifying the indicators that would operationalize the term. Second, the definition includes numerous terms that demand further definition and explanation (e.g., what do we mean by "working together," "shared responsibility," and "mutual respect"?). Third, there is a need to determine if this is a shared definition (M. Wolery, personal comunication, 1998). Does the reader agree that the definition captures the essence of what constitutes a family–professional partnership? Is this type of partnership, as defined, distinguishable from other kinds of relationships?

If we accept for the moment that this updated definition is a reasonable one, the next step from a behavioral science perspective is to specify the indicators that determine if a relationship is a family–professional partnership. These indicators (dimensions, elements, etc.) are examined next.

Operational Characteristics of Partnerships

Researchers have expended considerable effort to identify the operational features of family–professional partnerships and used both inductive and deductive approaches (see especially Brandt, 1993; Christenson et al., 1992; DeChillo et al., 1994; DeGangi, Royeen, & Wietlisbach, 1992; Dinnebeil et al., 1996; Dinnebeil & Rule, 1994; Dunst, Johanson, et al., 1992; Dunst & Paget, 1991; Dunst, Trivette, Davis, & Cornwell, 1994; Edmondson, n.d.; Minke & Scott, 1995; Paget & Chapman, 1992; Rosin, 1996; Vosler-Hunter, 1988). For an inductive approach they might typically start with some "general" ideas about family–professional partnership characteristics, use different kinds of data collection methods to discover these indicators, and reach tentative conclusions about the defining characteristics of the construct (Christenson et al., 1992; Dinnebeil et al., 1996; Dinnebeil & Rule, 1994; Dunst, Johanson, et al., 1992; Paget & Chapman, 1992). These efforts have entailed both primary data collection (DeGangi et al., 1992; Dinnebeil et al., 1996; Dinnebeil & Rule, 1994; Dunst, Johanson, et al., 1992) and secondary data analysis, summary, and abstraction (Christenson et al., 1992; Paget & Chapman, 1992; Roberts et al., 1998; Rosin, 1996). For a deductive approach they might begin with a "specific" idea about the indicators of family–professional partnerships, use data collection to determine the presence or absence of these characteristics in relationships, and then reach conclusions about whether hypothesized expectations were supported or refuted by the data (DeChillo et al., 1994; Dunst, Trivette, Gordon, & Starnes, 1993).

The majority of efforts identifying the indicators of family–professional partnerships have been inductive rather than deductive. This focus on the inductive approach accounts to a large degree for the lack of consistency in what researchers, practitioners, parents, and other partnership enthusiasts claim are the key features of family–professional partnerships. In using inductive methods, different researchers tend to pay attention to different aspects of family–professional relationships and consequently draw somewhat different conclusions. Nonetheless, these efforts to understand the meaning and defining characteristics of family–professional partnerships have provided a rich source of information about these kinds of relationships (see especially DeChillo et al., 1994; DeGangi et al., 1992; Dinnebeil et al.,

1996; Dinnebeil & Rule, 1994; Dunst, Johanson, et al., 1992). Our review and synthesis of the family–professional partnership literature has led to the following observations and critiques:

There is very little agreement about the number of characteristics that are the indicators of family–professional partnerships. A review of the literature by DeChillo and others (1994) found that the number of proposed characteristics varied from 4 to 26. Our own review similarly found the number of characteristics listed as key features varying from 3 to 26. Having different numbers of indicators is not necessarily problematic from a behavioral science point of view. What is problematic is the fact that there has been little discussion about whether a small or large number of indicators is needed to identify when a family and professional relationship is a partnership. To a large degree, the number of characteristics seems to have more to do with writer preference than it does with any attempt to distill those characteristics that define a partnership.

There is very little agreement about the particular characteristics that are the indicators of family–professional partnerships. Content analysis of the characteristics that different writers identify as the key indicators of family–professional partnerships finds much less consistency than at first glance appears to be the case. For example, close inspection of the three sets of characteristics (DeChillo et al., 1994; Dunst & Paget, 1991; Vosler-Hunter, 1988) listed by Roberts et al. (1998) finds, with few exceptions, that they are more different than similar. Of the 20 characteristics listed in the three sets of indicators, fewer than 50% of them are found in the pairwise lists. Similarly, comparisons of the indicators studied by Dunst, Johanson, et al. (1992) and Paget and Chapman (1992) find some overlap but surprisingly many more differences. These writers list 58 indicators, but only 20% appear in both compilations.

As more and more proposed lists appear in the literature, the sheer number of characteristics identified as the indicators of family–professional partnerships grows almost exponentially. Again, from a behavioral science perspective this is not necessarily a problem (although it becomes unwieldy and overwhelming). The problem is that few if any researchers have tried to determine if the different characteristics are interchangeable indicators of the construct (Babbie, 1983). The interchangeability of indicators means that different characteristics of a concept or construct essentially can be used as identical indicators of the phenomenon of interest. The extent to which this is the case for family–professional partnership indicators is not known because interchangeability analyses have not been done.

Different writers tend to emphasize the importance of different sets of partnership indicators in claiming the identification of defining characteristics. Some writers tend to emphasize the interpersonal aspects of family and professional relationships (Crais, 1993; Wayman, Lynch, & Hanson, 1990), some the nature of communication between partners (Able-Boone, 1996), some the action-oriented aspects of relationships (DeChillo et al., 1994), while others claim that family–professional partnerships are characterized by two or more sets of characteristics (Dunst, Johanson, et al., 1992). It is not at all rare for complex constructs like family–professional partnerships to have multiple dimensions. But few researchers have focused on the extent to which this is the case with regard to family–professional partnerships (see Dinnebeil et al., 1996; Dunst, Johanson, et al., 1992, for exceptions). As a result, there is more confusion than agreement about how many dimensions exist and whether certain dimensions are more important than others or even are hierarchical in nature. For example, is the development of interpersonal relationships a necessary condition for people to work together to achieve a desired goal or outcome?

There is very little agreement about the relative importance of different indicators of family–professional partnerships. Simply put, we do not know the operational features of family–professional partnerships because studies have shown little consensus about the defining characteristics of the construct (Dinnebeil et al., 1996; Dinnebeil & Rule, 1994; Dunst, Johanson, et al., 1992). For instance, Dunst, Johanson, et al. (1992) asked 69 parents and 102 professionals to list the characteristics they believed made a parent–professional relationship into a *partnership*. The researchers elicited a total of 94 separate descriptors, which they reduced to 26 characteristics by combining those that had similar meaning. However, only two characteristics were listed by 50% of the study participants (trust and mutual respect), and only five characteristics (19%) were listed by one third of the participants as important indicators—hardly evidence of agreement concerning the defining characteristics of family–professional partnerships.

A similarly low level of consensus was found by DeGangi et al. (1992) using focus groups to identify the qualities contributing to partnership relationships. A total of 17 characteristics were listed by five focus groups, but there was only 30% to 40% agreement within groups. Even less agreement was found in a study by Dinnebeil and Rule (1994), where only 1 of 12 indicators was identified by more than 50% of the study participants. Most characteristics (83%) were identified by fewer than 20% of the participants as defining features of family–professional partnerships.

Agreement between parents and professionals about the key characteristics of partnerships also is not very strong from a behavioral science perspective (Dinnebeil et al., 1996; Dinnebeil & Rule, 1994). Dinnebeil and Rule (1994), for example, reported no overlap in the characteristics identified by parents and professionals as contributing to productive family–professional partnerships. Lack of consensus has also been found among different groups of professionals. Close inspection of findings by DeGangi et al. (1992) for five focus groups of professionals finds very little consensus with regard to the defining characteristics of effective family–professional partnerships. For the 17 qualities listed, only 4 (23%) of the indicators were listed by 60% or more of the groups.

On the whole there is not sufficient consensus for a claim that the indicators of family–professional partnerships are known. Even if 75% agreement is used as a liberal index of reliability, data in no study even comes close to reaching this level of consensus.

The characteristics said to be the operational indicators of family–professional partnerships are not different from those for other kinds of relationships. The most damaging evidence against the contention that researchers know the indicators of family–professional partnerships is the fact that the characteristics that are said to define the phenomenon are not unique to the phenomenon. This is especially problematic because a good operational definition of a construct includes indicators that differentiate the construct from other related ones. The characteristics that family–professional partnership enthusiasts claim are defining ones in fact overlap considerably with those identified as the key features of caring relationships (Powell-Cope, 1994; Swanson, 1991), codes of ethics (Sokoly & Dokecki, 1992), effective interpersonal communication (Beckman, Frank, & Newcomb, 1996; DeVito, 1986; Forester, 1980), empowering relationships (Riessman, 1990; Swift & Levin, 1987; Whitmore & Kerans, 1988), and effective helpgiving (Brammer, 1993; Brickman et al., 1983; Brickman et al., 1982; Dunst, Trivette, & Hamby, 1996; Karuza, Zevon, Rabinowitz, & Brickman, 1982; Maple, 1977). Consider the following parent description from research by Dinnebeil et al. (1996), which is used to illustrate the meaning of family–professional partnerships: "Our [service coordinator] is friendly, enthusiastic about accomplishments, loving, caring, nonjudgmental, encouraging, honest, a good listener, prompt, committed, a good shoulder to lean on, and very receptive to my child" (p. 337). These characteristics are almost identical to the characteristics of effective helpgivers listed, for example, by Brammer (1993) and Dunst et al. (1996). Again, from a behavioral science perspective, constructs are useful to the extent that they have operationally defined characteristics, and that these characteristics differentiate the phenomenon from other related but conceptually different constructs. Classes of related constructs can have overlapping indicators. But when the indicators of two or more constructs overlap almost entirely, the phenomena may not in fact be distinct.

The almost sole reliance on inductive approaches for studying family–professional partnerships has hampered understanding of the meaning of the construct. Except for research by DeChillo (1993) and DeChillo et al. (1994), and corroborating research by Dunst, Trivette, Gordon, and Starnes (1993) and Dunst, Trivette, Davis, and Cornwell (1994), the majority of studies on family–professional partnerships have been inductive in nature and almost entirely qualitative in focus. Inductive research methodologies can be useful for theory construction (Glaser & Strauss, 1967), but this kind of research on family–professional partnerships has not advanced our understanding of the phenomenon from a behavioral science point of view. Research as a whole has not been well focused which in part is attributable to the lack of deductive approaches to studying the phenomenon. Indeed, the most widely used approaches to studying family–professional partnerships have resulted in less and not more specificity in operationalizing the construct. It is almost as if the family–professional partnership has become a concept that means everything to everybody. A construct that has become so widely (mis)used in so many different ways is not valuable from a behavioral science perspective.

Summary of the Review and Analysis

The findings from our review and critical analysis of the family–professional partnership literature indicate that the operational characteristics of the construct have not been clearly articulated, and available research does not substantiate claims about those elements uniquely defining the phenomenon. From a behavioral science perspective, the research on family–professional partnerships leaves a lot to be desired. (The kinds of research we believe would be helpful will be described in the concluding section of the chapter.) The state of current knowledge of family–professional partnerships has led us to reexamine and rethink our own claims about the theoretical importance of the partnership construct and its contributions to improving practice (e.g., Dunst, 1985; Dunst, Trivette, & Deal, 1988). In contrast to many family–professional partnership enthusiasts who argue for primacy of these kinds of relationships to optimize the benefits of family-oriented interventions, we now contend that the defining features of effective transactions between parents and professionals are a special case of a more general helping process. Family–professional partnerships are not the only or even primary context for helping relationships to have positive consequences. The reasons and rationale for these assertions are described next.

Family–Professional Partnerships, Empowerment, and Effective Helpgiving Practices

In addition to defining and delineating the indicators of a construct operationally, a behavioral science approach also examines the factors producing variations in a behavioral phenomenon and relates the phenomenon of interest to other aspects of behavior and functioning. Our own view of family–professional partnerships has been operationalized in the context of both empowerment theory (Dunst, Trivette, & LaPointe, 1992) and effective helpgiving practices (Dunst & Trivette, 1996; Dunst et al., 1996). This section of the chapter casts a wider net around the family–professional partnership construct, placing it in a broader framework for studying and understanding both its causes and consequences. On the one hand this conceptual–empirical model directly addresses at least some of the concerns raised above, and on the other hand considers family–professional partnerships as one element of an empowering process and as a fundamentally important part of a particular kind of effective helpgiving. The reader is referred to Davies (1985), DeChillo (1993), DeChillo et al. (1994), Elizur (1996), and Stevenson and Srebnik (1996) for descriptions of other work placing partnerships in the context of broader based theoretical models and approaches.

Empowerment and Partnerships

The term *empowerment* is now used widely as a concept for reorienting policy and clinical practice so that interventions of various sorts have competency-enhancing rather than dependency-forming consequences. A review of the empowerment literature by Dunst, Trivette, and LaPointe (1992) found the term used as a conceptual, phenomenological, and behavioral construct in six different but conceptually coherent ways: as *philosophy, paradigm, process, partnership, performance,* and *perception.*

An integration of these six key elements of empowerment suggests the three-component model shown in Figure 2.2. It depicts the relationships between an *empowerment ideology* (philosophy and paradigms), *participatory experiences* (process and partnership), and *empowerment outcomes* (performance and perceptions). The foundation of the model is the adoption of an *empowerment ideology* that delineates the beliefs and attitudes contributing to positive attributions about people's capabilities and the meaningful participation of people in decisions, choices, and actions affecting their welfare. *Participatory experiences* include various kinds of opportunities that strengthen existing capabilities and promote acquisition of new competencies. These experiences, opportunities, and processes bring people together in ways that engender collective action that is reciprocal and mutually beneficial. In our model, partnerships are considered one type of participatory experience. *Empowerment outcomes* include both the behaviors that are strengthened or learned as a result of participatory experiences, and the appraisals people make about their own capabilities and their control over important life events and situations. The substantive importance of control appraisals as an empowerment outcome derives from the fact that "Five decades of research have established it as a robust predictor of people's behavior, emotion, motivation, performance, and success and failure in many domains of life" (Skinner, 1995, p. 3).

The model depicted in Figure 2.2 shows an empowerment ideology having influences on both participatory experiences and empowering outcomes, and

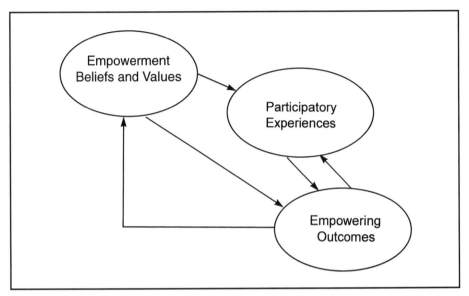

Figure 2.2. Relationship among three major components of empowering processes and consequences.

participatory experiences having influences on empowering outcomes. The feedback loops from the empowering outcome component to both the ideology and participatory experiences components indicate that at least two things are apt to occur as people become more capable. First, they are more likely to seek out other kinds of participatory experiences, and second, their increased competence is likely to strengthen others' perceptions of them as being more capable. Accordingly, the feedback loops reflect the fact that empowerment is a "regenerative process, in which outcomes produced at one stage in the process in turn contribute energy to further participation in the process" (Cochran, 1992, p. 9).

Empowerment and Effective Helpgiving Practices

Our efforts to understand the causes and consequences of empowerment have included a line of research focusing on the characteristics of effective helpgiving practices and how helpgiving functions as an empowering process (Dunst & Trivette, 1988, 1996). This research began with an extensive review of the helpgiving literature with particular emphasis on helpgiving practices found to be competency enhancing and having empowering consequences (Dunst, Trivette, Davis, & Cornwell, 1994). The literature review identified some 20 different kinds of attitudes, behaviors, and practices that met these criteria. These included those helpgiving characteristics typically considered critical and desirable, chief of which are a helpgiver's sincere sense of caring, warmth, honesty, and empathy; active and reflective listening; and maintenance of confidentiality.

In addition a variety of less typical helpgiving approaches were identified, including positive helpgiver assumptions about the capabilities of help receivers; practices that emphasized help-receiver strengths rather than weaknesses; and attention to solutions to rather than causes of people's problems. They also included the active involvement of help receivers in the helpgiving process; a focus of the helpgiving process on needs and concerns identified by the help receiver; the provision of information necessary for help receivers to make informed choices; an emphasis on help-receiver decisions about courses of action to meet needs or achieve desired goals; and the enhancement and promotion of help-receiver knowledge and skills needed to take action in ways that are competency producing. Still further, helpgiving practices associated with empowerment outcomes included helpgiver suggestions and advice that were normative and ecologically relevant to the help receiver; acknowledgement, acceptance, and support of help receivers' decisions; and helpgiver affirmation about the roles help receivers played in achieving positive outcomes. Collectively these characteristics constitute the kinds of helpgiving practices increasing the likelihood that help receivers will experience positive empowering effects (Dunst, Johanson, et al., 1992; Dunst & Paget, 1991; Dunst & Trivette, 1988, Dunst, Trivette, & Thompson, 1990).

To ascertain whether effective helping is unidimensional or multidimensional, the 20 types of helpgiving attitudes, behaviors, and practices identified through the literature review were used to generate an item pool of 40 possible indicators of the various kinds of helpgiving practices. The 40 items became the basis for developing the Helpgiving Practices Scale (Trivette & Dunst, 1994). A psychometric analysis indicated that 25 of the scale items reliably measured helpgiving practices (Dunst et al., 1996). A factor analysis of the 25 items administered to a sample of 220 parents of young children participating in a number of different kinds of human services programs yielded two interpretable solutions. The first factor, labeled *participatory practices,* included a preponderance of helpgiving behaviors that Maple (1977) described as the essential components of *shared decision making* and what Rappaport (1981, 1987) described as the kinds of *enabling experiences* that are likely to have empowering consequences. The items were action-oriented and emphasized the strengthening of help-receiver existing capabilities and the promotion of new competencies. The items termed *participatory practices* are ones that meaningfully involve people in help giver–help receiver exchanges and that are most likely to result in positive control appraisals about one's existing and emerging capabilities (Bandura, 1977, 1997; Brickman et al., 1982; Rappaport, 1981, 1987; Swift & Levin, 1987; Zimmerman, 1990a, 1990b; Zimmerman, Israel, Schulz, & Checkoway, 1992; Zimmerman & Rappaport, 1988).

The second factor, labeled *relational practices,* includes a combination of items focusing on help-receiver attributions about helpgivers, and the help receiver's assessment of the presumed beliefs of the helpgiver toward the help receiver. These include behaviors typically associated with "good" clinical practice (compassion, sense of caring, active listening, etc.), and help-receiver attributions about the helpgiver's beliefs concerning help-receiver capabilities (Brammer, 1993). The items are best described as ones capturing the attitudinal and relational aspects of helpgiver–help receiver exchanges (see especially Dunst & Trivette, 1996).

Effective Helpgiving and Partnerships

Comparisons of the item content of the two clusters of helpgiving practices found by Dunst et al. (1996) with the characteristics thought to be the defining features of family–professional partnerships find considerable overlap, so much so that we have come to think about partnerships as a special case of effective helpgiving practices. The participatory practices factor includes indicators described by family–professional enthusiasts as those involving reciprocity, shared decision making, and joint action between partners, whereas the relational practices factor includes indicators described in the family–professional partnership literature as interpersonal and attitudinal in nature. More specifically, participatory helpgiving practices emphasize helpgivers and help receivers working together to identify desired goals and courses of action to achieve those goals, bidirectional information sharing so that informed choices and decisions can be made, and joint problem solving and actions by both parties to promote a sense of competence and capability. Relational helpgiving practices include positive helpgiver and help-receiver attributions about the existing and potential capabilities of partners, mutual trust and respect, honesty in sharing information that is relevant to the helpgiving relationship or is needed to make informed choices and decisions, active listening and the willingness to take each other's views and opinions into consideration, and an overall sense of camaraderie in working together. Comparisons of these various kinds of helpgiving attitudes, propensities, and behaviors with those found on lists of family–professional partnership characteristics (e.g., Dunst, Johanson, et al., 1992; Paget & Chapman, 1992) are so similar that claims that these features distinguish family–professional partnerships from participatory (Riessman, 1990) and shared decision making (Maple, 1977) helping relationships are unwarranted. Moreover, as is illustrated next, the particular kinds of indicators some family–professional partnership enthusiasts claim are the most important are not, when examined in relationship to other aspects of behavior functioning.

Consequences of Effective Helpgiving

Our research, which established the two domains and clusters of helpgiving practices, is but one way of operationally discerning the indicators of a behavioral construct. A next step in a behavioral science approach to this kind of research is to determine if the different sets of indicators both in combination and independently are related to other phenomena hypothesized to be influenced by helpgiving. The manner in which helpgiving in general and both participatory and relational helpgiving more specifically are related to differences in empowering outcomes (see Figure 2.2) has been the focus of our own research (Dunst, Trivette, Boyd, & Brookfield, 1994; Dunst, Trivette, Gordon, & Starnes, 1993; Dunst et al., 1992, 1996; Trivette, Dunst, Boyd, & Hamby, 1996; Trivette, Dunst, & Hamby, 1996a, 1996b; Trivette, Dunst, Hamby, & LaPointe, 1996) and that of others (Judge, 1997). The measures of helpgiving in these studies have been the Helpgiving Practices Scale (Trivette & Dunst, 1994) and methods for detecting the presence or absence of specific kinds of helpgiving indicators (Dunst, Trivette, Davis, & Cornwell, 1994; Dunst, Trivette, Gordon, & Starnes, 1993). Our research on the relationship between help giving and empowerment has included the use of a number of personal control-apprised measures as the dependent variables. Two consistent patterns of findings have emerged from this line of research. First, helpgiving practices are the principal and most potent determinant of variations in control appraisals, beyond any effects associated with child, parent, and family factors, and practitioner personal characteristics or program characteristics. Second, whereas relational helpgiving has not been found to be at all related to variations in control appraisals, participatory helpgiving practices account for nearly all the variation in how helpgiving is related to these kinds of empowering consequences.

The findings from these studies indicate, contrary to claims by some family–professional partnership enthusiasts, that the participatory and not the relational aspects of family–professional transactions are the most important features of these kinds of relationships in terms of empowering effects. Thus, while good relational skills may be necessary, they are not a sufficient condition for family–professional partnerships to have positive effects with regard to the amount of control or choice reported by families.

Conclusions

We used a behavioral science approach in this chapter to examine and critically analyze the family–professional partnership construct. This approach is specifically concerned with the link between conceptualization and operationalization. Based on our analysis we concluded that the family–professional partnership construct has not been operationally defined; the indicators used to discern the presence or absence of the behavioral aspects of the phenomenon have not been well specified, nor are they unique to the phenomenon. Moreover, the current state of affairs concerning our understanding of family–professional partnerships appears to have been hampered by the almost sole reliance on inductive rather than deductive approaches to studying the construct.

The finding that the indicators identified as the defining characteristics of family–professional partnerships overlap considerably with the operational indicators of other constructs poses the greatest challenge to claims that the phenomenon is real. The single exception to this is the observation that partnerships in general and family–professional partnerships more specifically appear to differ from other kinds of relationships *only* in terms of mutuality and reciprocity between partners. As noted by Dunst, Johanson, et al. (1992), and reiterated here, what appears to differentiate partnerships operationally from other kinds of relationships is the operative *mutual* and its related behavioral features. We suggest a line of research that would operationalize what is meant by mutual trust, mutual respect, mutual agreement, joint decision making and action, reciprocal planning, and so on, and conduct studies to determine if (1) these features are in fact present in relationships between parents and other family members working together with professionals in pursuit of a common goal and (2) these indicators are absent in other kinds of family and professional relationships.

We recommend the use of deductive rather than inductive approaches to conducting the above kind of studies. Inductive approaches have been valuable, but their continued use has blurred rather than clarified the meaning of family–professional partnerships. Further advances will be made only to the extent that we target the operational definition and the identification of the indicators of the construct as has been done with other related concepts, including, but not limited to, effective helpgiving (Brickman et al., 1982, 1983; Dunst & Trivette, 1996; Dunst et al., 1996) and empowerment (Dunst et al., 1992; Zimmerman, 1990a, 1990b; Zimmerman et al., 1992). The reader is referred to DeChillo (1993) and DeChillo et al. (1994) for examples of deductive approaches to studying family–professional partnerships.

In addition to improving conceptualization and operationalization of family–professional partnerships, researchers need to place the construct in wider theoretical contexts to enhance understanding of its causes and consequences. Partnerships are formed because of mutual interests and desires (Clifford & Warner, 1987; Phillips & Rasberry, 1981), and their formation is expected to produce positive effects beyond those attributed to "one person going it alone." Research on how family–professional partnerships come to be, and the benefits associated with these kinds of relationships, cannot help but improve the knowledge base concerning the relative importance of the concept. The reader is referred to DeChillo (1993), DeChillo et al. (1994),

Dunst, Trivette, Boyd, and Brookfield (1994), Dunst et al. (1996), Judge (1997), Thompson et al. (1997), Trivette, Dunst, Boyd, and Hamby (1996), Trivette, Dunst, Hamby, and LaPointe (1996), Trivette et al. (1996a, 1996b), Zimmerman and Rappaport (1988), and Zimmerman et al. (1992) for different ways that this goal can be accomplished.

As part of research investigating family–professional partnerships in the context of broader based theoretical frameworks, it seems especially important that the construct be viewed as multidimensional. Collaborating evidence indicates that, at least in terms of its relationship to certain outcomes, particular dimensions of family–professional partnerships are more important predictors than others in explaining variations in different aspects of behavior and functioning (DeChillo, 1993; DeChillo et al., 1994; Dunst & Trivette, 1996; Trivette, Dunst, Boyd, & Hamby, 1996; Trivette et al., 1996a, 1996b). This kind of research would isolate what it is about family–professional partnerships that make a difference in observed effects. This is especially important for informing practice: We want to be able to place emphasis on the "right" elements of these kinds of relationships so we can draw the practical implications that ought to be a major focus of applied research.

Acknowledgment

Appreciation is extended to Debbie Morgan for typing different versions of this chapter and for preparing the graphic material.

References

Able-Boone, H. (1996). Ethics and early intervention: Toward more relationship-focused interventions. *Infants and Young Children, 9,* 15–21.

Babbie, E. (1983). *The practice of social research* (3rd ed.). Belmont, CA: Wadsworth.

Bandura, A. (1977). Self-efficacy: Toward a unifying theory of behavioral change. *Psychological Review, 84,* 191–215.

Bandura, A. (1997). *Self-efficacy: The exercise of control.* New York: Freeman.

Beckman, P., Frank, N., & Newcomb, S. (1996). Qualities and skills for communicating with families. In P. Beckman (Ed.), *Strategies for working with families of young children with disabilities* (pp. 31–46). Baltimore: Brookes.

Bishop, K. (Ed.). (1993). *Family–professional collaboration for children with special health needs and their families.* (ERIC Document Reproduction No. ED381518).

Brammer, L. (1993). *The helping relationship: Process and skills* (5th ed.). Boston: Allyn & Bacon.

Brand, S. (1996). Making parent involvement a reality: Helping teachers develop partnerships with parents. *Young Children, 51,* 76–81.

Brandt, P. (1993). Negotiation and problem-solving strategies: Collaboration between families and professionals. *Infants and Young Children, 5*, 78–84.

Brickman, P., Kidder, L. H., Coates, D., Rabinowitz, V., Cohn, E., & Karuza, J. (1983). The dilemmas of helping: Making aid fair and effective. In J. Fisher, A. Nadler, & B. DePaulo (Eds.), *New directions in helping: Vol. 1. Recipient reactions to aid* (pp. 18–51). San Diego, CA: Academic Press.

Brickman, P., Rabinowitz, V., Karuza, J., Coates, D., Cohn, E., & Kidder, L. (1982). Models of helping and coping. *American Psychologist, 37*, 368–384.

Christenson, S., Rounds, T., & Franklin, M. J. (1992). Home–school collaboration: Effects, issues and opportunities. In S. Christenson & J. Conoley (Eds.), *Home–school collaboration* (pp. 19–51). Silver Spring, MD: National Association of School Psychologists.

Clark, C., Moss, P. A., Goering, S., Herter, R. J., Lamar, B., Leonard, D., Robbins, S., Russell, M., Templin, M., & Wascha, K. (1996). Collaboration as dialogue: Teachers and researchers engaged in conversation and professional development. *American Educational Research Journal, 33*, 193–231.

Clifford, D., & Warner, R. (1987). *The partnership book* (3rd ed.). Berkeley, CA: Nolo Press.

Cochran, M. (1992). Parent empowerment: Developing a conceptual framework. *Family Science Review, 5/6*, 3–21.

Connors, L., & Epstein, J. (1995). Parent and school partnerships. In M. Bornstein (Ed.), *Handbook of parenting: Vol. 4. Applied and practical parenting* (pp. 437–458). Mahwah, NJ: Erlbaum.

Crais, E. (1993). Families and professionals as collaborators in assessment. *Topics in Language Disorders, 14*, 29–40.

Davies, D. (1995). Collaboration and family empowerment as strategies to achieve comprehensive services. In L. Rigsby, M. Reynolds, & M. Wang (Eds.), *School–community connections: Exploring issues for research and practice* (pp. 267–280). San Francisco: Jossey-Bass.

DeChillo, N. (1993). Collaboration between social workers and families of patients with mental illness. *Families in Society: The Journal of Contemporary Human Services, 74*, 104–115.

DeChillo, N., Koren, P., & Schultze, K. (1994). From paternalism to partnership: Family and professional collaboration in children's mental health. *American Journal of Orthopsychiatry, 64*, 564–576.

DeGangi, G., Royeen, C., & Wietlisbach, S. (1992). How to examine the individualized family service plan process: Preliminary findings and a procedural guide. *Infants and Young Children, 5*, 42–56.

DeVito, J. (1986). *The interpersonal communication book* (5th ed.). New York: Harper & Row.

Dinnebeil, L., Hale, L., & Rule, S. (1996). A qualitative analysis of parents' and service coordinators' descriptions of variables that influence collaborative relationships. *Topics in Early Childhood Special Education, 16*, 322–347.

Dinnebeil, L., & Rule, S. (1994). Variables that influence collaboration between parents and service providers. *Journal of Early Intervention, 18*, 349–361.

Dunst, C. J. (1985). Rethinking early intervention. *Analysis and Intervention in Developmental Disabilities, 5*, 165–201.

Dunst, C. J., Johanson, C., Rounds, T., Trivette, C., & Hamby, D. (1992). Characteristics of parent–professional partnerships. In S. Christenson & J. Conoley (Eds.), *Home–school collaboration* (pp. 157–174). Washington, DC: National Association of School Psychologists.

Dunst, C. J., & Paget K. (1991). Parent–professional partnerships and family empowerment. In M. Fine (Ed.), *Collaboration with parents of exceptional children* (pp. 25–44). Brandon, VT: Clinical Psychology.

Dunst, C. J., & Trivette, C. M. (1988). Helping, helplessness, and harm. In J. Witt, S. Elliott, & F. Gesham (Eds.), *Handbook of behavior therapy in education* (pp. 343–376). New York: Plenum Press.

Dunst, C. J., & Trivette, C. M. (1996). Empowerment, effective helpgiving practices, and family-centered care. *Pediatric Nursing, 22,* 334–337, 343.

Dunst, C. J., Trivette, C. M., Boyd, K., & Brookfield, J. (1994). Helpgiving practices and the self-efficacy appraisals of parents. In C. J. Dunst, C. M. Trivette, & A. G. Deal (Eds.), *Supporting and strengthening families: Methods, strategies, and practices* (pp. 212–220). Cambridge, MA: Brookline Books.

Dunst, C. J., Trivette, C. M., Davis, M., & Cornwell, J. (1994). Characteristics of effective helpgiving practices. In C. J. Dunst, C. M. Trivette, & A. G. Deal (Eds.), *Supporting and strengthening families: Methods, strategies, and practices* (pp. 171–186). Cambridge, MA: Brookline Books.

Dunst, C. J., Trivette, C. M., & Deal, A. G. (1988). *Enabling and empowering families: Principles and guidelines for practice.* Cambridge, MA: Brookline Books.

Dunst, C. J., Trivette, C. M., Gordon, N., & Starnes, L. (1993). Family-centered case manager practices: Characteristics and consequences. In G. S. Singer & L. Powers (Eds.), *Families, disabilities, and empowerment* (pp. 89–118). Baltimore: Brookes.

Dunst, C. J., Trivette, C. M., & Gowen, J. W. (1993, December). *Intrafamily and extrafamily factors associated with child neglect.* Final report, U.S. Department of Health and Human Services, Administration for Children and Families, National Center on Child Abuse and Neglect.

Dunst, C. J., Trivette, C. M., & Hamby, D. (1996). Measuring the helpgiving practices of human services practitioners. *Human Relations, 49,* 815–835.

Dunst, C. J., Trivette, C. M., & Johanson, C. (1994). Parent–professional collaboration and partnerships. In C. J. Dunst, C. M. Trivette, & A. G. Deal (Eds.), *Supporting and strengthening families: Methods, strategies and practices* (pp. 197–211). Cambridge, MA: Brookline Books.

Dunst, C. J., Trivette, C. M., & LaPointe, N. (1992). Toward clarification of the meaning and key elements of empowerment. *Family Science Review, 5/6,* 111–130.

Dunst, C. J., Trivette, C. M., & Thompson, R. (1990). Supporting and strengthening family functioning: Toward a congruence between principles and practice. *Prevention in the Human Services, 9*(1), 19–43.

Edmondson, R. (n.d.). Parent–professional partnerships in early intervention. In P. Pierce (Ed.), *Baby power.* Chapel Hill: Center for Literacy and Disabilities Studies, University of North Carolina at Chapel Hill.

Elizur, Y. (1996). Involvement, collaboration, and empowerment: A model for consultation with human-service agencies and the development of family-oriented care. *Family Process, 35,* 191–210.

Epstein, J. L. (1992). School and family partnerships. In M. Alkin (Ed.), *Encyclopedia of educational research* (6th ed., pp. 1139–1512). New York: Macmillan.

Filer, J. D., & Mahoney, G. J. (1996). Collaboration between families and early intervention service providers. *Infants and Young Children, 9,* 22–30.

Forester, J. (1980). Critical theory and organization analysis. *American Planning Association Journal, 6,* 275–286.

Galegher, J., Kraut, R. E., & Egido, C. (Eds.). (1990). *Intellectual teamwork: Social and technological foundations of cooperative work* (pp. 149–171). Hillsdale, NJ: Erlbaum.

Glaser, B., & Strauss, A. (1967). *The discovery of grounded theory.* Chicago: Aldine.

Judge, S. L. (1997). Parental perceptions of helpgiving practices and control appraisals in early intervention programs. *Topics in Early Childhood Special Education, 17,* 457–476.

Karuza, J., Jr., Zevon, M. A., Rabinowitz, V. C., & Brickman, P. (1982). Attribution of responsibility by helpers and recipients. In T. A. Wills (Ed.), *Basic processes in helping relationships* (pp. 107–129). New York: Academic Press.

Kendall, P., & Watson, D. (Eds.). (1989). *Anxiety and depression: Distinctive and overlapping features.* San Diego, CA: Academic Press.

Maple, F. F. (1977). *Shared decision making.* Beverly Hills, CA: Sage.

Minke, K., & Scott, M. (1995). Parent–professional relationships in early intervention: A qualitative investigation. *Topics in Early Childhood Special Education, 15,* 335–352.

Paget, K., & Chapman, S. (1992). Home–school partnerships and preschool services: From self-assessment to innovation. In S. Christenson & J. Conoley (Eds.), *Home–school collaboration* (pp. 265–288). Silver Spring, MD: National Association of School Psychologists.

Phillips, M., & Rasberry, S. (1981). *Honest business.* New York: Random House.

Powell-Cope, G. (1994). Family caregivers of people with AIDS: Negotiating partnerships with professional health care providers. *Nursing Research, 43,* 324–330.

Rappaport, J. (1981). In praise of paradox: A social policy of empowerment over prevention. *American Journal of Community Psychology, 9,* 1–25.

Rappaport, J. (1987). Terms of empowerment/exemplars of prevention: Toward a theory for community psychology. *American Journal of Community Psychology, 15,* 121–148.

Riessman, F. (1990). Restructuring help: A human services paradigm for the 1990s. *American Journal of Community Psychology, 18,* 221–230.

Roberts, R., Rule, S., & Innocenti, M. (1998). *Strengthening the family–professional partnership in services to young children.* Baltimore: Brookes.

Rosin, P. (1996). Parent and service provider partnerships in early intervention. In P. Rosin, A. Whitehead, L. Tuckman, G. Jesien, A. Begun, & L. Irwin (Eds.), *Partnerships in family-centered care.* Baltimore: Brookes.

Rosin, P., Whitehead, A., Tuckman, L., Jesien, G., Begun, A., & Irwin, L. (1996). *Partnerships in family-centered care.* Baltimore: Brookes.

Skinner, E. (1995). *Perceived control, motivation, and coping.* Thousand Oaks, CA: Sage.

Sokoly, M., & Dokecki, P. (1992). Ethical perspectives on family-centered early intervention. *Infants and Young Children, 4,* 23–32.

Stevenson, J., & Srebnik, D. (1996, February). *Congruence between parent–professional ratings of level of functioning: Relationship to collaboration and satisfaction.* Presentation made at the 9th annual research conference: A system of care for children's mental health, Tampa Bay, FL.

Stonestreet, R., Johnston, R., & Acton, S. (1991). Guidelines for real partnerships with parents. *Infant-Toddler Intervention: The Transdisciplinary Journal, 1,* 37–46.

Swan, W., & Morgan, J. (1993). *Collaborating for comprehensive services for young children and their families.* Baltimore: Brookes.

Swanson, K. (1991). Empirical development of a middle range theory of caring. *Nursing Research, 40,* 161–166.

Swift, C., & Levin, G. (1987). Empowerment: An emerging mental health technology. *Journal of Primary Prevention, 8*(1/2), 71–94.

Thompson, L., Lobb, C., Elling, R., Herman, S., Jurkiewicz, T., & Hulleza, C. (1997). Pathways to family empowerment: Effects of family-centered delivery of early intervention services. *Exceptional Children, 64,* 99–113.

Trivette, C. M., & Dunst, C. J. (1994). *Helpgiving Practices Scale.* Unpublished scale, Orelena Hawks Puckett Institute, Asheville, NC.

Trivette, C. M., Dunst, C. J., Boyd, K., & Hamby, D. W. (1996). Family-oriented program models, helpgiving practices, and parental control appraisals. *Exceptional Children, 62,* 237–248.

Trivette, C. M., Dunst, C. J., & Hamby, D. W. (1996a). Characteristics and consequences of help-giving practices in human services programs. *American Journal of Community Psychology, 24,* 273–293.

Trivette, C. M., Dunst, C. J., & Hamby, D. W. (1996b). Factors associated with perceived control appraisals in a family-centered early intervention program. *Journal of Early Intervention, 20,* 165–178.

Trivette, C. M., Dunst, C. J., Hamby, D. W., & LaPointe, N. (1996). Key elements of empowerment and their implications for early intervention. *Infant-Toddler Intervention: The Transdisciplinary Journal, 6,* 59–73.

Vosler-Hunter, R. (1988). Elements of parent/professional collaboration: *Focal Point, 2*(2), 1–3. (Bulletin of The Research and Training Center, Portland State University, Portland, OR.)

Watson, D., & Kendall, P. (1989). Common and differentiating features in anxiety and depression: Current findings and future directions. In P. Kendall & D. Watson (Eds.), *Anxiety and depression: Distinctive and overlapping features* (pp. 493–508). San Diego, CA: Academic Press.

Watson, D., & Tellegen, A. (1985). Toward a consensual structure of mood. *Psychological Bulletin, 98,* 219–235.

Wayman, K., Lynch, E., & Hanson, M. (1990). Home-based early childhood services: Cultural sensitivity in a family systems approach. *Topics in Early Childhood Special Education, 10,* 56–75.

Whitmore, E., & Kerans, P. (1988). Participation, empowerment, and welfare. *Canadian Review of Social Policy, 22,* 51–60.

Wolman, B. (1973). Concerning psychology and the philosophy of science. In B. Wolman (Ed.), *Handbook of general psychology* (pp. 22–48). Englewood Cliffs, NJ: Prentice Hall.

Zimmerman, M. A. (1990a). Toward a theory of learned hopefulness: A structural model analysis of participation and empowerment. *Journal of Research in Personality, 24,* 71–86.

Zimmerman, M. A. (1990b). Taking aim on empowerment research: On the distinction between individual and psychological concepts. *American Journal of Community Psychology, 18,* 169–177.

Zimmerman, M. A., Israel, B., Schulz, A., & Checkoway, B. (1992). Further explorations in empowerment theory: An empirical analysis of psychological empowerment. *American Journal of Community Psychology, 20,* 707–727.

Zimmerman, M. A., & Rappaport, J. (1988). Citizen participation, perceived control, and psychological empowerment. *American Journal of Community Psychology, 16,* 725–750.

Zuravin, S. (1991). Research definitions of child physical abuse and neglect: Current problems. In R. Starr & D. Wolfe (Eds.), *The effects of child abuse and neglect: Issues and research* (pp. 100–128). New York: Guilford Press.

Children with Special Needs in Nontraditional Families

Marian C. Fish

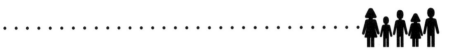

The recent literature, both scholarly and popular, on establishing partnerships between professionals and parents of children with special needs has been primarily directed at two-parent households. Yet the traditional two-parent family is only one of many family forms today and represents a minority of households in the United States (Asprodites, 1996b; Laird, 1993). An increasing percentage of children with special needs are being raised in nontraditional families, such as single-parent, blended, foster, adoptive, and homosexual homes (Asprodites, 1996b; Carlson, 1995; Glick, 1984). Current statistics indicate that half of first marriages end in divorce and over 50% of divorces involve children (Knoff & Bishop, 1997). Moreover, 35% of children are likely to live with a stepparent before age 18 (Visher & Visher, 1993), one out of every six babies is born to unmarried parents (Golden & Capuzzi, 1986), close to half a million children in the United States are under the auspices of the child welfare system (Pasztor & Wynne, 1995), and 6 to 14 million children have gay or lesbian parents (Patterson, 1992). Thus, there is an urgent need for professionals to develop knowledge about these families as they become more commonplace.

In general, nontraditional families and families of children with special needs both experience more stress than other families (Simpson, 1982; Weisz & Tomkins, 1996). Researchers recognize that families of children with special needs benefit from family-focused interventions (Weisz & Tomkins, 1996), and that their relationships with helping professionals are frequently long term (Boyer & Chesteen, 1992). These facts suggest that parents of children with disabilities in nontraditional families have an even greater need for positive relationships with professionals than do other parents.

The basic principles in a collaborative relationship between professionals and parents of children with special needs apply to children across all types of families, yet an understanding by the professional of characteristics and concerns relevant to nontraditional families may enhance the relationship.

Just as family cultural background or ethnicity is an important consideration in working with parents, the different structure of nontraditional family units may raise special issues. Of course, even among these subgroups of families, there is much diversity, and generalizations should be made with care. Nonetheless, there are common needs and experiences shared by parents in each type of nontraditional family.

This chapter examines five nontraditional family types: single-parent, blended or with stepchildren, foster, adoptive, and gay and lesbian families. The chapter (a) identifies characteristics and issues associated with single-parent families and (b) provides guidelines for professionals who work with these parents.

Single Parents: Characteristics and Issues

The single-parent family in the United States today arises from diverse origins, including separation (70%), death (14%), parent never married (10%), and temporary circumstances (6%) (Golden & Capuzzi, 1986). Four critical variables for professionals to consider are (a) sex of parent remaining with the family, (b) reason for only one partner (death, divorce, separation, or parent never married), (c) permanent or temporary absence of noncustodial parent, and (d) total or partial absence of noncustodial parent (Young & Ruth, 1983). Research in this area is muddled and often does not address specific subgroups. Yet the manner in which one becomes a single parent may affect functioning (Golden & Capuzzi, 1986). For example, blame of the spouse may be prevalent in separation cases, whereas the child may be blamed if the mother was never married. Or, when a spouse in an intact marriage dies, the widow(er) often has continued support and functions as a representative of the couple (Golden & Capuzzi, 1986).

Virtually all studies view single parents from a deficit model, looking for evidence that single parenting results in unhappy children while ignoring positive outcomes. Contrary to this commonly held belief, Atlas (1981) found that 75% of single-parent families reported they were doing well and that the children were well adjusted. More recently, however, poorer child outcomes have been reported in single-parent families when compared to those families with two biological parents (Carlson, 1995).

An overwhelming majority 90% of single parents are mothers who work outside the home (Carlson, 1995). Further, a high proportion of single mothers are African American. Fifty-five percent of African American babies live in mother–child families (Bianchi, 1995). Numerous authors have described common characteristics of single-parent families (Carlson, 1985, 1995; Golden & Capuzzi, 1986; Simpson, 1982; Weiss, 1979). Carlson (1985) sees single-parent families as having the same functions as two-parent households, but with more role strain resulting from fewer participants to carry out these functions.

One mother described her experience: "Being a single, divorced parent under the best of circumstances is very demanding and often frustrating and unrewarding" ("Demands on single parents," 1984, p. 48). The custodial parent attempting to fulfill two roles may face financial constraints, family management overload (both child care and household), and emotional overload (Weiss, 1979).

Financial Constraints

One of the major problems faced by single parents is economic survival (Carlson, 1995). A single mother after a divorce and an unwed teenage mother are both vulnerable to financial problems. In fact, 25% of all single-mother households and 50% of African American single mothers who never married are below the poverty line (Carlson, 1995; Golden & Capuzzi, 1986). Parents with youngsters with special needs may have additional expenses, such as laundry, structural modifications to the home, or damage repair (Horne, 1985). Frequently, expenses covered by a spouse such as insurance or health benefits are not available. Moreover, children may hold the mother responsible for the change in lifestyle (Simpson, 1982).

Family Management

When the parent becomes single, the family structure and functioning alter. The parent often assumes responsibilities of the absent partner and may have to learn or relearn tasks (Young & Ruth, 1983). For example, if a father always handled automobile repair and maintenance, the single mother may need to assume this role. Similarly, a single father who never cooked would need to explore the kitchen. These additional household tasks do not excuse the single parent from the major responsibility of childcare. Research shows that boys are especially vulnerable to discipline problems in families headed by women (Carlson, 1995; Simpson, 1982). When the household includes a child with special needs, childcare responsibilities are often greater and may include trips to specialists or direct physical care. Here is how one mother described her life with a daughter with mental retardation:

> It is not a one-time demand. . . . Each day presents . . . the challenge of figuring out how to do everything . . . while managing the handicapped child. . . . That might entail, for instance, grocery shopping with the retarded child in tow. When Beckie was little, such an excursion required only the extra energy needed to carry her on my hip and choose groceries one handed. . . . But, when she hit her teens a completely new ingredient was added to the challenge. (Turnbull & Turnbull, 1985, pp. 143–144)

It is often hard to find babysitters for children with special needs. At times the parent may use other siblings to take over some of the roles of the missing parent. The parent must take care not to exploit these youngsters or assign them inappropriate tasks.

Emotional Overload

Along with financial and household burdens is the emotional overload. One single mother wrote, "I am tired, lonely and isolated" (Barnes, 1986, p. 47). Feelings of being emotionally overwhelmed and angry are commonly reported. When stressed, a single parent may attribute blame to the child for a marital breakup, particularly if that child has special needs. Feelings of social isolation are widely reported. The child with special needs places various restrictions on the social life of two parents, according to researchers. The parents engage in far fewer leisure time activities and social interactions (Horne, 1985). Single mothers have greater difficulty establishing new relationships and developing a social support network. When describing her child with mental retardation, one mother said, "Sometimes I felt very lonely. Weekends were even harder. I was still the caretaker, and it was hard to find sitters, no neighbor offered to take her" ("Demands on single parents," 1984, p. 48). Another mother said, "I felt sorry for myself" (Barnes, 1986). These economic, management, and personal experiences often result in decreased efficiency and a reassessment of priorities by single parents because they are not able to assume the roles of two parents.

Single Parents: Guidelines for Professionals

When working collaboratively with single parents of children with special needs, professionals should begin by recognizing the overwhelming responsibilities that these parents face daily. With time at a premium and care for the child with special needs often difficult to arrange, the parents may require flexible appointment scheduling, including evenings or weekends. Some professionals may be able to schedule home meetings as well; if not, phone calls may be effective. At the least, professionals should not be discouraged by canceled appointments or spotty attendance; these do not indicate a lack of interest or caring, but rather that a more crucial priority has arisen. Understanding on these occasions can enhance, and perhaps save, a relationship with a single parent.

To counter the isolation of the single parent, professionals can help them to find or develop a support network. Parents Without Partners, for example, is a volunteer agency with chapters throughout the country where single parents can meet. A less formal network is one of extended family, old friends, and neighbors. It is important to locate other single parents either to share babysitting or to join the mother and child on a trip or outing. Social and recreational outlets for parents and children provide relief from isolation.

Respite care, the provision of temporary relief services, is a highly valued service, but one that is not available in many states or available only on a limited basis (Blacher, 1984). Also, children with complicated medical needs or severe behavioral problems may not be eligible. A local Association for Retarded Citizens may have a list of respite care providers. However, in helping to identify these resources, professionals must be careful that they do not begin fulfilling some of the functions of the absent parent; single parents must be allowed to accept these responsibilities (Young & Ruth, 1983).

With regard to family management, professionals should work with parents to establish guidelines for their relationship with their children. They can help organize domestic responsibilities so that children are not asked to assume parental roles. The professional and parent can delineate appropriate boundaries between parent and children, define roles, and specify lines of authority. Additionally, the professional can encourage parents to take care of themselves physically and to take time for their personal needs. Just giving them this information may not be enough; where necessary, the professional should teach them skills necessary to accomplish these tasks (e.g., relaxation training, time management, behavior management).

There is considerable evidence that positive parental relationships are a major factor in a child's successful adjustment. Whenever possible, professionals should involve the noncustodial parent in the collaborative planning and facilitate a cooperative relationship between the biological parents.

In general, the professional working with single-parent families with children with special needs should provide information and support that take into consideration the fact that family economic, interpersonal, and cultural resources are less available than in two-parent families (Carlson, 1995).

Stepparents: Characteristics and Issues

A stepfamily is a household containing a child who is biologically related to only one of the adults (Visher & Visher, 1993); usually, either one or both partners have been previously married with at least one of the partners having children from that previous marriage (Katz & Stein, 1983). It is estimated that 1,300 new stepfamilies are being formed each day in the United States and that there are approximately 35 million stepparents (Jarmulowski, 1985). Currently, about 20% of children under age 19 are stepchildren or half-siblings (Visher & Visher, 1993). The nontraditional makeup of stepfamilies (also known as reconstituted, blended, or remarried families) affects many aspects of everyday life, from sending greeting cards to filling out school record forms to planning holidays and special occasions. Although the stepfamily seems similar to the nuclear family, it is more complex because it joins (at least) two households, with children often living in one home and visiting another.

The uniqueness of a stepfamily stems from its formation out of a past that has involved loss (a death or the dissolution of a previous family unit) and the disruption of attachment (Golden & Capuzzi, 1986). All members of a stepfamily bring with them expectations of how families are supposed to function and their memories of their experiences in their prior families. For example, one stepfather described a meal with his stepchildren as follows:

> Sometimes we sit around the dinner table and the children chatter to their mother with great excitement about events before they knew me— the family gatherings, the celebrations, the vacations—the usual family experiences I once shared with my own boys. I want to be part of it, but can't. It is their history. (Giordano, 1985, p. 78)

In stepfamilies the relationship between the biological parent and children predates the new marriage (Visher & Visher, 1979). As a result, a number of common features distinguish the internal functioning of these families from that of other family types (Katz & Stein, 1983). There is, unfortunately, no research on the child with special needs in stepfamilies from which to draw information. It is necessary to extrapolate from the many discussions of other stepfamilies to those with a child with special needs.

Unrealistic expectations of family members is probably the most cited characteristic of stepfamilies. The sprouting of instant love between stepparents and stepchildren resulting in one big, happy family (e.g., "The Brady Bunch") is one myth, while the wicked stepmother of fairy tales is the other common myth. One stepmother illustrated these feelings as follows: "I want his children to love me and be with us all the time. I do not want them at all" (Maglin, 1985, p. 40). Conflicts may result when a stepparent tries to assume the role of the "absent" parent prematurely. This is a particular burden for stepmothers who have the cultural expectation of caregiver and try to live up to it. One mother described her feelings when her husband's son with mental retardation came to live with them: "For one who thought she knew a lot, the last three years have . . . been a humbling experience" (Turnbull & Turnbull, 1985, p. 128). She reported one bad experience shopping: "As the screams became louder and the crowds larger, I felt more and more helpless and inept. My image of being a model mother able to handle difficult situations was beginning to crumble" (Turnbull & Turnbull, 1985, p. 128).

Conflicts may be intensified with a child with special needs in the family if the noncustodial, biological parent is especially concerned about the parenting ability of the stepparent and conveys this message to the child. Competition may arise between parents, resulting in problems over visitation, lifestyle, or discipline.

Parenting skills comprise an area in which issues arise. Because the new marital couple has not developed as a team, they have no shared history of childrearing. A stepparent may not know what is appropriate discipline, and this uncertainty may easily be exacerbated with a child with special needs. The stepparent not only has to understand developmental stages and age-appropriate behavior but also must modify and adjust expectations for a child with special needs. This process can be made more complex by differing guidelines in custodial and noncustodial households.

The lack of clear role definition inherent in stepfamilies underlies all of these characteristics. Though the manpower is available in terms of number of family members, role ambiguity remains, as members assume instant multiple roles. Complicating these situations is the lack of established patterns and rituals to help families with this transition (McGoldrick & Carter, 1980). One stepmother said, "I experience a complex emotional package of jealousy, anger, and fear. I am jealous of his ex-wife. I am jealous of his children, especially his two daughters. I feel inadequate" (Maglin, 1985, p. 40).

There is some preliminary evidence that remarriage is harder on girls than on boys (Kutner, 1988). Younger children usually adapt to stepfamilies more quickly than older children, and, generally, adolescents have the most difficult time.

Stepparents: Guidelines for Professionals

The major emphasis in collaboration with stepparents should be on clarification of roles and boundaries. Subsystems that must be established include the remarried couple, the divorced couple(s), the custodial parent–child, and the stepparent–stepchild (Carlson, 1985). It is important to explore and dispel false expectations stepparents can develop about their role as a parent that lead to feelings of being overburdened, unappreciated, or left out (Golden & Capuzzi, 1986). The professional can point out the special parenting issues unique to this type of family structure. Generally, the biological parent retains the primary parenting role. It can take 4 years or longer for the stepparent to be accepted in an equal parenting role. The professional must be aware of the stages of the parent–child relationship and adjust expectations accordingly. Roles and boundaries need to be clarified, not only within the remarried family, but also with regard to the noncustodial parent or family. This can be especially important when a child with special needs is involved, for example, when educational decisions must be made. The constructive involvement of the noncustodial parent assures the child of the continued support of both parents, regardless of the changed marital status. If this does not occur, a child may "develop" problems to keep the two biological parents in a relationship (Carlson, 1985).

Professionals can help parents negotiate and develop new traditions (Visher & Visher, 1993). For example, discussion may center on how to address family members, what to do on holidays and occasions such as Mother's and Father's Day, and how to fill out school forms. Children may have some pragmatic issues such as how friends will find them if their parents have a different last name. An interesting fact is that a stepparent is not legally related to his or her stepchildren (adoption changes the legal relationship, but it is uncommon); they cannot make medical decisions about them, for example, if the school calls with an emergency, or even educational decisions. Though new alliances are formed, old ones that are still important should be preserved (Visher & Visher, 1982). As was suggested above, noncustodial parents should be included in decision making for the child, for example, in school conferences and meetings. The professional might want to encourage the institutions with which the family interacts to send information to all involved adults.

A key aspect in working with remarried families is to solidify the couple's relationship. A child with special needs who requires much attention from the biological custodial parent can truly stress the marital relationship. Social networks may be restricted and recreational activities limited. Established organizations such as Remarried, Inc. (Santa Ana, California), and the Stepfamily Association of America, Inc., are possible sources of support. Also, a number of books are available that can help parents understand the uniqueness of stepparenting (e.g., Visher & Visher, 1979; Weiss, 1979). Finally, several programs have been developed such as Strengthening Stepfamilies (Albert & Einstein, 1986) to give information and skills to adults in stepfamilies. On the positive side, stepchildren often have a wide circle of interested family members who can be counted on for support.

The child with disabilities in a stepfamily provides a special challenge to the stepparent. As one mother pointed out, "Retardation is chronic; that is one of the fundamental problems for families. I am just beginning to realize the impact of lifelong responsibilities and the need to fortify my coping abilities for the adult years" (Turnbull & Turnbull, 1985, p. 140). The stepparent of a child with special needs is accepting a challenging role.

Foster Parents: Characteristics and Issues

The child welfare system in the United States is responsible for over 462,000 children who live in foster care, kinship care, or some other residential care arrangement (Clay, 1997); projections suggest continued growth of out-of-home care to over a half million children in the 1990s (Pasztor & Wynne, 1995). These increasing numbers have been attributed to the effects of AIDS, alcohol and drug abuse, poverty, and homelessness.

Foster family care is provided when a child's own family is unable to provide adequate care (Lewit, 1993). Reasons may include (a) child abuse and neglect; (b) poor physical or mental health of the parent; (c) arrest or incarceration of the parent; (d) family violence, drug abuse, or alcoholism; and (e) political or economic upheaval (e.g., Vietnamese boat children). Despite the permanency planning movement, which encourages placement in permanent homes rather than multiple temporary placements, foster children change homes on average 2.7 times (Lombana, 1983). Most of the foster youngsters do not return to their biological parents nor are they adopted (Lewis, 1984).

Recently the placement of children with special needs in foster (and adoptive) homes has increased with the realization of the negative effects of institutional living on a child's development. The needs of children requiring out-of-home care have become more complex; behavioral and emotional problems exhibited by a child before foster care placement may be aggravated by the placement itself (Shealy, 1995). Children in foster care may have physical, emotional, or mental handicaps; it is estimated that almost one third have severe emotional problems (Clay, 1997). Pasztor and Wynne recently noted, "Today, most of the infants, children, and youths needing family foster care services have special needs" (1995, p. vii). Research shows a disproportionate number of foster children in special education classes in schools as well (McKellar, 1997).

Foster homes are identified and supervised by authorized social service agencies. Generally a social worker serves as case manager. Despite the increased need for foster family care, fewer families are willing and able to provide foster care services (Pasztor & Wynne, 1995). Reasons include the need for more families to have two wage earners and the low "board rates" paid to foster families for basic childcare (Phillips, 1998). In particular, there are shortages of urban families, families of color, and families willing to care for children with special medical needs (Pasztor & Wynne, 1995). At times the situation of the foster placement is only marginally better than that of the family of origin (Triseliotis, 1980). Those who choose to become foster parents do so for a variety of reasons, and more attention is being paid to recruitment and retention of foster families (Pasztor & Wynne, 1995).

Of primary interest is the role ambiguity that foster parents experience. The status of the foster parents is unclear: They are expected to provide care for a child with special needs in a normal family setting, yet they have limited authority over the child. Ultimate responsibility for the child rests with the child welfare agency and its representative, the caseworker. Thus decisions about the child's education or medical care are always made after conferring with the agency. In fact many decisions are made by the agency alone without consultation with the foster parents who live with the child. This is problematic because the high turnover of casework staff can lead to a lack of continuity in planning. Lombana (1983) points out that foster parents are pulled in many directions; they are supposed to be advocates for the child, collaborators with the welfare agency, and supporters of the natural parents, yet frequently these three roles are in conflict.

A major characteristic of foster families is the temporary, or at least uncertain, duration of the foster child's placement. As a result the family lacks not only a historical perspective on the child's development but also the expectation of participating in the child's future. This sense of temporariness may restrain parents from becoming overly involved with the child; they know the relationship can be terminated at any time. For children with special needs with physical, emotional, or educational problems, the upheaval and future uncertainty may contribute to insecurity and low self-esteem (Lombana, 1983). These children may blame themselves when they are moved around from home to home. Inconsistency of care is a serious problem for children with special needs who need structure and regularity in their daily lives.

Another concern in foster care is keeping siblings together. Between 65% and 85% of children entering the foster care system have siblings, but 75% are placed separately despite advantages of keeping them together (Phillips, 1998).

Foster Parents: Guidelines for Professionals

Clarification of role responsibilities is a major objective for foster parent–professional collaboration. Initially the collaboration may be three-way, that is, foster parent–professional–caseworker. If adoption is unlikely, the professional can try to reframe the foster family as the child's "permanent" family, giving them greater authority and decision-making power (Lewis, 1984). The caseworker then has less involvement, and the foster parents have more control. This shift may be more difficult to implement in the case of a child with special needs. The foster parents frequently need permission from the agency for medical, tutoring, or therapeutic services, which are costly; this means greater reliance on the caseworker. In some cases the natural parents, if available, may be especially involved with a child with special needs. But ideally foster parents should be fully in charge of children with special needs, who require consistency and certainty. Foster parents should be treated with respect by the professional and the caseworker. In particular, if the children have come from institutions, it is important that the permanency of the relationship be acknowledged. When there are disagreements between caseworker and foster parents, professionals should take care not to side with one against the other (Lewis, 1984).

One of the major roles of a professional in a collaboration with foster parents is to facilitate skill acquisition. Many of the foster parents with children with special needs have limited knowledge or training about parenting skills in general, and specifically with regard to these special needs—despite good intentions. These parents can benefit from skill training either within the relationship or through parent education programs. Further, for foster parents not familiar with children with special needs and services available to them, the professional can serve initially as a translator of language, roles, and procedures, particularly with regard to institutions such as schools or hospitals. Parent groups for special youngsters can be held in the school.

Foster parents who gather information about the child will better understand the child's needs. For example, instructional methods in one school were successful for a child with mental retardation, but were not shared with the new school. The foster parents called the original teacher who then provided the information for both the new teacher and the foster parents. In another case one sensitive foster mother did not use the foster child's native language with him, though she was fluent in it. She realized that he felt her use of the language intruded on his relationship with his natural mother, which he wanted to keep separate (Walsh, 1982). Ideally foster parents should have access to developmental profiles, assessment results, and other information from the child's past. They may wish to contact former caretakers and family members. In fact, some researchers have suggested that foster families become a resource in permanency planning for children. Rather than competing with biological families for a child's affection, foster parents can give emotional support and model healthy family relationships and parenting skills for the biological families (Ryan, McFadden, & Warren, 1981). Of course, this approach applies to situations where children will be returning to birth parents.

All foster parents have to deal with the normal fears and fantasies of children removed from their natural parents. But the foster parents of a child with mental retardation may find he has greater difficulty understanding the situation and may blame himself. There is very limited literature on the child with special needs in a foster family despite the prevalence of this type of placement. The books that might be helpful to parents are not specifically aimed at these special children (e.g., Felker, 1977; Sarason, Lindner, & Crnic, 1976).

Foster parents are often treated as pariahs by others in the community who suspect their motives or who simply avoid those who are different. As with other nontraditional parents, social isolation may occur, and the establishment or reestablishment of a support network is a priority. Extended family, neighbors, and friends are helpful resources.

Finally, for those families where siblings are separated, facilitating reunions or get-togethers for the children encourages bonding and a sense of belonging (Phillips, 1998). Two initiatives have helped foster families that accommodate sibling groups and are particularly important for children with special needs. The first provides more phone lines so foster families can contact agency supervisors, and the second establishes a Medicaid hot line to address children's health issues (Phillips, 1998). Encouraging kinship care in which children are placed with relatives is also being used more frequently.

Adoptive Parents: Characteristics and Issues

Adoption is a different way of building a family but is neither better nor worse than other ways (Gilman, 1987). Many of the experiences of adoptive parents are similar to those of other families. But these parents must also cope with the adopted child's experiences of loss (Anderson, Piantanida, & Anderson, 1993).

There are approximately 1.5 million adoptive families in the United States. An estimated 2% to 4% of children are adopted. In 1992, 127,000 children were adopted in the United States, about half by relatives such as stepparents; about 10% of the children were adopted from outside the United States (Lewin, 1997; Wrobel & Grotevant, 1997).

Over the last 25 years a dramatic shift in child welfare adoption practice, influenced by permanency planning, has increased special needs adoptions (Rosenthal, Groze, & Morgan, 1996). The permanency planning philosophy favors a lifelong permanent home for every child and has focused attention on adoption of children other than newborns. Special needs adoptions account for approximately half of public agency adoptions, are broadly defined and include (a) children of older ages without permanent homes (over 6; varies by state); (b) children of ethnicity different from the adoptive parents; (c) children with developmental, behavioral, emotional, or medical problems; (d) children adopted internationally; and (e) children in sibling groups (Rosenthal & Groze, 1994; Wrobel & Grotevant, 1997). Adoptions of children with special needs are at higher risk for disruption (termination either before or after legalization) than other adoptions (Wrobel & Grotevant, 1997). Rosenthal and Groze (1994) identified some predictors of increased risk of disruption: (a) older age of child at adoptive placement; (b) inadequate background information or unrealistic parental expectations; (c) rigidity in family functioning patterns, in particular the father's noninvolvement in parenting tasks; (d) low levels of support from relatives or friends; (e) history of physical and particularly sexual abuse prior to adoption; (f) psychiatric hospitalization prior to adoption; (g) acting-out, externalized behavioral problems including sexual acting out; and (h) adoptive placement with new adoptive parents rather than adoption by foster parents. Better outcomes are associated with families who adopt children with physical disabilities, mental retardation or medical conditions rather than behavioral difficulties (Glidden, 1990; Lightburn & Pine, 1995).

Although the literature suggests that adoptive parents are psychologically diverse, and that the age of child at adoption, current age of child, and sibling situation all influence the adjustment of the adoptive family, these families do share some common characteristics and issues.

Adjustment to parenthood in adoptive families is likely to be more intense than in families with biological children since adoption often comes after a long (childless) period where much energy has been invested in becoming parents. Further, adoptive families can expect an intense and protracted process of family formation, during which family members develop a sense of belonging and identification (Anderson et al., 1993). At the same time that parents are nurturing and encouraging closeness, they must establish their authority and rules for the family. Often there is a tension between these two processes which may be exacerbated with adolescent adoptees, for example, who have different developmental needs (Anderson et al., 1993). Associated with family formation is the establishment of subsystems, both generational and relationship, which is made more difficult when children have experienced abuse or assumed parental roles in prior placements (Anderson et al., 1993). Also, when a child is adopted by a family that has other children, parents must be prepared to deal with rivalries and jealousies that may arise. Parents may be faced with loyalty conflicts.

The issue of "telling," that is, choosing when and how to explain to the child that she was adopted, is faced by all adoptive families (Anderson et al., 1993). Children's comprehension of adoption is developmental, and discussion of this issue will be ongoing in the family as the child matures cognitively (Wrobel & Grotevant, 1997). Similarly, parents will need to satisfy the child's curiosity about the past.

Adoptive parents' unrealistic expectations for the child often lead to feelings of guilt and shame. As one mother described, the difficulties can be overwhelming:

> Before Adam came I had read everything I could get my hands on about cerebral palsy. I was prepared for his not walking and speech difficulties. However, reading about a disability and living with a child on a daily basis who has that disability are two different things . . . I was overwhelmed with it all . . . fear and guilt and tremendous feelings of failure. (Gilman, 1987, p. 211)

Practical concerns abound as well. Parents must be sure that health insurance, wills, and life insurance, for example, apply to an adopted child (Rosenthal & Groze, 1994). They must also be prepared to deal with the reactions of extended family and neighbors.

Adoptive Parents: Guidelines for Professionals

Adoption of a child with special needs is a lifelong process (Groze & Gruenewald, 1991). Parents have described the need for continued subsidies and respite care; some have felt unsupported, isolated, and abandoned by the agency (Berry, 1990). Rosenthal and Groze (1994) have emphasized the need for ongoing postadoptive services.

The collaboration between professionals and the adoptive parents has as its goal the successful functioning of the family. Professionals can assist parents in the process of family formation by facilitating the establishment of clear subsystem boundaries, encouraging the active participation of fathers as well as mothers, and addressing sibling issues. Parents adopting a child with special needs should expect a different life cycle sequence and heightened sensitivity to events that affect family integrity (Anderson et al., 1993). The childless couple who adopts a child with special needs must move from an adult-centered world to one in which the child plays a major role. Clearly, the stage at which the professional sees the parents determines the particular concerns of family integration. Becoming a member of a family is often hardest for a child who has spent long periods in institutional care. The child's adjustment may be precarious, and behaviors may be inappropriate. The professional and parents should discuss facilitating the integration of the child's biological and adoptive heritage into his identity.

Professionals support parents in obtaining accurate information about the child's history (Berry, 1990; Lightburn & Pine, 1996). Older children bring lengthy histories to their adoptive families, and parents must understand their strengths, weaknesses, and "survival behaviors" (Groze, 1996). As with foster children, often the information relevant to current education or medical care has been lost or buried; misdiagnosis may have occurred, as when a child labeled retarded turns out to be hearing impaired.

The professional is a source of information on special needs, abuse, and parenting skills (Berry, 1990). Information related to the child's special needs is useful for parents to develop realistic expectations. Some adoptive parents are uniquely capable of dealing with a specific disability (e.g., a teacher of the deaf might adopt a child who is hearing impaired). Others must be helped to learn about the disability and perhaps how to parent. Locating parent education programs or developing new ones collaboratively can be beneficial.

Children who have been sexually abused are more likely to act out sexually and have other behavior problems. Poorer adoption outcomes are associated with children with special needs who have behavior problems (Lightburn & Pine, 1996). Behavioral training might improve the stability of some adoptive placements (Berry, 1990).

As with other nontraditional families, helping to locate community resources, education and advocacy groups, and social supports are important aims of the collaboration. Parents need to explore future resources for the child who, as an adult, may require a sheltered environment or other life-planning transition services. Helpful agencies and organizations include the Child Welfare League of America (Washington, DC), the North American Council on Adoptable Children (NACAC) (Minneapolis, MN), and Families Adopting Children Everywhere (FACE) (Baltimore, MD). The National Resource Center for Special Needs Adoption (P.O. Box 377, Chelsea, MI 48118) has children with special needs as its focus. Finally, the emotional and physical exhaustion common to all parents with children with special needs can be addressed by identifying or developing respite care.

Gay and Lesbian Parents:
Characteristics and Issues

Until recently there has been only limited acknowledgement of gay and lesbian families and scant attention to this type of family in the literature (Laird, 1993; Victor & Fish, 1995). In this alternative family arrangement, same-sex couples, male (gay) or female (lesbian), or single parents self-identified as gay, lesbian, or bisexual are heads of families (Asprodites, 1996b). It is estimated that there are 1 to 5 million lesbian mothers and 1 to 3 million gay fathers in the United States (Patterson, 1992).

Most children in these families were born in the context of heterosexual relationships that later ended, though in recent years lesbians have begun to have biological children more frequently. Because adoption in many cases is made difficult for gay and lesbian couples, they are often willing to adopt children who are hard to place, for example, children who are transracial or have special needs (Okun, 1996). While the literature on gay and lesbian families with children is itself limited, virtually none exists on gay and lesbian families with children with special needs.

Gay and lesbian families vary in functioning as do heterosexual families and encounter many of the same issues in forming a family. These include negotiating rules and roles and defining boundaries. Often gay and lesbian parents have had to overcome enormous obstacles to become primary parents and therefore may be especially committed and energetic as parents (Okun, 1996). In addition, however, they must deal with those issues that are specific to their sexual orientation in a society that is often not accepting of their alternative family definition and commitment to parenting (Okun, 1996). Pervasive societal homophobia takes its toll on gay and lesbian families and is a major stressor (Laird, 1993). Gay and lesbian families are probably the most vulnerable to prejudice and discrimination and are actively stigmatized and marginalized in American society. They are denied legal and social recognition that is given to heterosexual married partners. Thus, they struggle with the tension between wanting to live life openly and fearing the repercussions for disclosure (Asprodites, 1996b). Some fear that because of their sexual orientation they could lose custody of children or have to relinquish visitation rights (Okun, 1996). Their secrecy and fear of exposure may have an impact on a child's willingness to socialize. Children of gay and lesbian parents are likely to face social discrimination, perhaps ridicule and teasing from peers, and are often harassed during adolescence (Asprodites, 1996b); they may be rejected by peers or embarrassed to bring friends home. This may exacerbate feelings of isolation and loneliness already more prevalent in families with children with special needs. Moreover, gay and lesbian families may not have the support of their families of origin or other friends and relatives who usually provide parents with both physical and psychological assistance.

A common theme in the research is that gay and lesbian families lack clear traditions and guidelines and have no real role models (e.g., Okun, 1996), although these findings are questioned by Laird (1993). At the very least they have no socially approved language to describe coparents; no established religious, legal, or family rituals; and more loosely defined career and home responsibilities (Laird, 1993; Okun, 1996; Victor & Fish, 1995).

Parenting issues specific to gay and lesbian families include providing opposite gender role models for children and helping children from a prior marriage adjust to the new coparenting relationship. If both parents bring children to a family, sibling issues arise, just as with heterosexual stepfamilies. Once again, these issues can be magnified when one sibling has special needs.

Gay and lesbian families must deal with a number of common misconceptions: that their children's emotional health, interpersonal relationships, sexual orientation, and gender development are in some way compromised and inferior to children of heterosexuals (Asprodites, 1996b; Victor & Fish, 1995). None of these has been substantiated in the literature (Asprodites, 1996b). Not surprisingly, gay men face skepticism, and sometimes bias, as males who are primary parents. Frequently, questions are raised about parenting skills of both gay and lesbian households. No significant differences in parenting skills have been found for lesbian and heterosexual mothers (Victor & Fish, 1995).

Finally, financial issues such as sharing benefits with partners and children present major problems for gay and lesbian parents. This is particularly salient with regard to children with special needs who require additional, often costly services.

Gay and Lesbian Parents: Guidelines for Professionals

Professionals collaborating with gay and lesbian families should initially examine themselves for homophobic feelings and negative stereotypes (Clay, 1990; Okun, 1996; Victor & Fish, 1995). They should be willing to acknowledge discomfort due to ignorance, inexperience, religious training, or personal values and to make an informed decision about proceeding with the collaboration (Victor & Fish, 1995).

Once they have established the collaboration, the professional and parents should address the issues that arise from forming a family in a homophobic and heterosexist society. Concerns about inclusion and safety are prevalent (Okun, 1996). Children should be safe from harassment and discrimination, and the professional may want to help families and children develop coping skills to respond to threats (Asprodites, 1996b). Preventing isolation and loneliness through support groups and community programs is especially relevant for youngsters with special needs. Also, children may need assistance "disclosing" to their friends; role-playing has been found to be effective for this, but most important is the support of parents.

The general family issues are similar to those of heterosexual couples, especially stepparents, and are described in the stepparent section. Roles and tasks need to be defined. If children are from previous partners, for example, facilitating discussion between the biological parent and partner to decide on the partner's role is necessary. When a child with special needs is involved, these relationships become more complex.

Unrealistic expectations of gays and lesbians as parents may be addressed through parenting groups or counseling with limit setting and discipline issues taking center stage (Laird, 1993). Children with special needs can stress the family system, so establishing a strong parental subsystem is essential.

Professionals serve as a resource for needed information. A number of books and videos about gay and lesbian families are described by Asprodites (1996a) and Victor and Fish (1995). Organizations that have developed training programs and curricula include the National Education Association (Washington, DC), Equity Institute (Emeryville, CA), Lesbian and Gay Parents Association (San Francisco, CA), Gay and Lesbian Alliance Against Defamation (GLAAD, Hollywood, CA), and Project of the Study of Gay and Lesbian Issues in Schools (Dr. Arthur Lipkin, Harvard Graduate School of Education, Cambridge, MA) (Asprodites, 1996a).

Summary

Successful professional–parent collaboration involves joint decision making, mutual respect, recognizing and acknowledging strengths, skill acquisition, and empowering parents to work actively on behalf of their children with special needs. This chapter focused on working with nontraditional families, where professionals may need to modify their approach in some way to recognize the special characteristics and needs of these families.

References

Albert, L., & Einstein, E. (1986). *Strengthening stepfamilies.* Circle Pines, MN: American Guidance Service.

Anderson, S., Piantanida, M., & Anderson, C. (1993). Normal processes in adoptive families. In F. Walsh (Ed.). *Normal family processes* (2nd ed., pp. 254–281). New York: Guilford.

Asprodites, C. (1996a, December). Resources for gay/lesbian parents and their children. *NASP Communique.*

Asprodites, C. (1996b, December). Responding to the needs of children in gay families. *NASP Communique*, pp. 12–14.

Atlas, S. L. (1981). *Single parenting: A practical resource guide.* Englewood Cliffs, NJ: Prentice Hall.

Barnes, K. (1986). Surviving as a single parent. *The Exceptional Parent, 16,* 47–49.

Berry, M. (1990). Preparing and supporting special needs adoptive families: A review of the literature. *Child and Adolescent Social Work, 7,* 403–418.

Bianchi, S. M. (1995). The changing demographic and socioeconomic characteristics of single parent families. *Marriage and Family Review, 20,* 71–97.

Blacher, J. (Ed.). (1984). *Severely handicapped young children and their families.* Orlando, FL: Academic Press.

Boyer, P., & Chesteen, H. (1992). Professional helpfulness? The experiences of parents of handicapped children with counselors and social workers. *Journal of Child and Youth Care, 7,* 37–48.

Carlson, C. (1985). Best practices in working with single-parent and stepfamilies. In A. Thomas & J. Grimes (Eds.), *Best practices in school psychology* (pp. 43–60). Kent, OH: National Association of School Psychologists.

Carlson, C. (1995). Single parenting and stepparenting. In G. G. Bear, K. M. Minke, & A. Thomas (Eds.), *Children's needs II: Development, problems and alternatives* (pp. 615–631). Bethesda, MD: National Association of School Psychologists.

Clay, J. (1990). Working with lesbian and gay parents and their children. *Young Children, 45,* 31–35.

Clay, R. A. (1997). Today's foster-care system is facing new challenges. *American Psychological Association Monitor,* p. 14.

Demands on single parents. (1984). *The Exceptional Parent, 14,* 43–49.

Felker, E. H. (1977). *Foster parenting young children: Guidelines from a foster parent.* New York: Child Welfare League of America.

Gilman, L. (1987). *The adoption resource book.* New York: Harper & Row.

Giordano, J. (1985, February). A stepfather tries to find his role. *Ms,* pp. 50, 78.

Glick, P. (1984). Marriage, divorce and living arrangements: Prospective changes. *Journal of Family Issues, 5,* 7–26.

Glidden, L. M. (1990). The wanted ones: Families adopting children with mental retardation. *Journal of Children in Contemporary Society, 21,* 363–378.

Golden, L. B., & Capuzzi, D. (1986). *Helping families help children.* Springfield, IL: Thomas.

Groze, V. (1996). A 1 and 2 year follow-up study of adoptive families and special needs children. *Children and Youth Services Review, 18,* 57–82.

Groze, V., & Gruenewald, A. (1991). PARTNERS: A model program for special-needs adoptive families in stress. *Child Welfare, LXX,* 581–589.

Horne, M. D. (1985). *Professional, peer and parent reactions.* Hillsdale, NJ: Erlbaum.

Jarmulowski, V. (1985, February). The blended family: Who are they? *Ms,* pp. 33–34.

Katz, L., & Stein, S. (1983). Treating stepfamilies. In B. B. Wolman & G. Stricker (Eds.), *Handbook of family therapy* (pp. 387–420). New York: Plenum Press.

Knoff, H. M., & Bishop, M. D. (1997). Divorce. In G. G. Bear, K. M. Minke, & A. Thomas (Eds), *Children's needs II: Development, problems and alternatives* (pp. 593–604). Bethesda, MD: National Association of School Psychologists.

Kutner, L. (1988, June). Parent and child. *New York Times,* p. C10.

Laird, J. (1993). Lesbian and gay families. In F. Walsh (Ed.), *Normal family processes* (2nd ed., pp. 282–328). New York: Guilford.

Lewin, T. (1997, November 9). U.S. is divided on adoption, survey of attitudes asserts. *New York Times.*

Lewis, H. C. (1984). Child welfare agencies. In M. Berger & G. J. Jurkovic (Eds.), *Practicing family therapy in diverse settings* (pp. 180–210). San Francisco, CA: Jossey-Bass.

Lewit, E. M. (1993). Children in foster care. *The Future of Children, 3,* 192–200.

Lightburn, A., & Pine, B. A. (1995). Supporting and enhancing the adoption of children with developmental disabilities. *Children and Youth Services Review, 18,* 139–162.

Lombana, J. H. (1983). *Home–school partnerships.* New York: Grune & Stratton.

Maglin, N. B. (1985, February). It could not be more complicated. *Ms,* pp. 40–45.

McGoldrick, M., & Carter, E. A. (1980). Forming a remarried family. In E. A. Carter & M. McGoldrick (Eds.), *The family life cycle* (pp. 265–294). New York: Gardner.

McKellar, N. (1997). Foster homes. In G. G. Bear, K. M. Minke, & A. Thomas (Eds.), *Children's needs II: Development, problems and alternatives* (pp. 697–706). Bethesda, MD: National Association of School Psychologists.

Okun, B. F. (1996). *Understanding diverse families: What practitioners need to know.* New York: Guilford.

Pasztor, E. M., & Wynne, S. F. (1995). *Foster parent retention and recruitment.* Washington, DC: Child Welfare League of America.

Patterson, C. (1992). Children of gay and lesbian parents. *Child Development, 63,* 1025–1042.

Phillips, C. (1998, January). Foster care system struggles to keep siblings living together. *American Psychological Association Monitor,* pp. 26–27.

Rosenthal, J. A., & Groze, V. K. (1994). A longitudinal study of special-needs adoptive families. *Child Welfare, 73,* 689–706.

Rosenthal, J. A., Groze, V., & Morgan, J. (1996). Services for families adopting children via public child welfare agencies: Use, helpfulness, and need. *Children and Youth Services Review, 18,* 163–182.

Ryan, P., McFadden, E. J., & Warren, B. (1981). Foster families: A resource for helping parents. In A. N. Maluccio & P. Sinanoglu (Eds.), *The challenge of partnership: Working with parents of children in foster care* (pp. 189–199). New York: Child Welfare League of America.

Sarason, I. G., Lindner, K. C., & Crnic, K. (1976). *A guide for foster parents.* New York: Human Science Press.

Shealy, C. N. (1995). From *Boys Town* to *Oliver Twist:* Separating fact from fiction in welfare reform and out-of-home placement of children and youth. *American Psychologist, 50,* 565–580.

Simpson, R. L. (1982). *Conferencing parents of exceptional children.* Rockville, MD: Aspen.

Triseliotis, J. (1980). *New developments in foster care and adoption.* London: Routledge & Kegan Paul.

Turnbull, H. R., & Turnbull, A. P. (Eds.). (1985). *Parents speak out.* Columbus, OH: Merrill.

Victor, S. B., & Fish, M. C. (1995). Lesbian mothers and their children: A review for school psychologists. *School Psychology Review, 24,* 456–479.

Visher, E. B., & Visher, J. S. (1979). *Stepfamilies: A guide to working with stepparents and stepchildren.* New York: Brunner/Mazel.

Visher, E. B., & Visher, J. S. (1982). Stepfamilies and stepparenting. In F. Walsh (Ed.), *Normal family processes* (pp. 331–353). New York: Guilford.

Visher, E. B., & Visher, J. S. (1993). Remarriage families and stepparenting. In F. Walsh (Ed.), *Normal family processes* (2nd ed., pp. 235–253). New York: Guilford.

Walsh, F. (Ed.). (1982). *Normal family processes.* New York: Guilford.

Weiss, R. (1979). *Going it alone.* New York: Basic Books.

Weisz, V., & Tomkins, A. (1996). The right to a family environment for children with disabilities. *American Psychologist, 51,* 1239–1245.

Wrobel, G. M., & Grotevant, H. D. (1997). Adoption. In G. G. Bear, K. M. Minke, & A. Thomas (Eds.), *Children's needs II: Development, problems and alternatives* (pp. 641–652). Bethesda, MD: National Association of School Psychologists.

Young, H. H., & Ruth, B. M. (1983). Special treatment problems with the one-parent family. In B. B. Wolman & G. Stricker (Eds.), *Handbook of family and marital therapy* (pp. 377–386). New York: Plenum Press.

Children with Exceptionalities and Their Siblings: Opportunities for Collaboration Between Family and School

Emanuel J. Mason, Lou Ann Kruse, Amy Farabaugh, Rick Gershberg, and Mindy Sloan Kohler

E very child is a member of at least two overlapping systems, the home and the school, and these have a profound influence on the developing child. The effects of these two systems are particularly evident in the siblings of children with disabilities. The siblings may experience stress in the home setting that affects their performance at school, while their school performance may reinforce dysfunctional patterns at home. By viewing the home and school as overlapping systems, a school professional can identify the shared responsibilities and potential for collaboration with regard to reducing the stress on these siblings and their families.

In this chapter we will first consider the structure of a family and how a child with a disability might affect other family members. We will look at such factors as birth order, age, and gender of the children; socioeconomic status; family size; nature of the child's disability; and the resulting family dynamics. We will also view the school as a complex system that creates pressures and dynamics affecting the members of the school population. To illustrate the interaction of the home and school systems, we will present three hypothetical profiles of children with disabilities in disengaged families. Finally we will discuss the goals and establishment of a home–school partnership and show how it might benefit the children in the three illustrations.

The Family as a System

A family is a social system that is structured by rules, patterns of communication, and positions of relative power. Roles of individual family members are influenced by culture, tradition, social patterns, and family structure. The structure permits the family to function as a unit and defines each member's role (Goldenberg & Goldenberg, 1996). Within the family structure, subsystems may form based on gender, interests, environmental contexts, or

69

function, and every family member plays unique roles in these subgroupings. Some members are more heavily involved in some subgroupings than others. For example, in a family subgroup that is devoted to hiking and other outdoor activities, one parent may choose not to participate regularly or may be involved only to pack lunches or drive to the site of the outings. Further, these roles may be flexible so that one parent may participate on an irregular basis.

In the well-balanced family these roles are mutually supportive and permit growth, satisfaction, expression, and development of a sense of self-efficacy, competence, and personal worth in all family members. Roles are typically flexible in such a family and are maintained in response to ongoing communication between family members and the various contexts and functions of the family. Figure 4.1 shows that each member's position in the family is influenced by the other family members.

Channels of effective communication can break down. When this happens, the balanced structure of the family is affected. Research suggests that reduction in the supportiveness in the environment can produce unfavorable

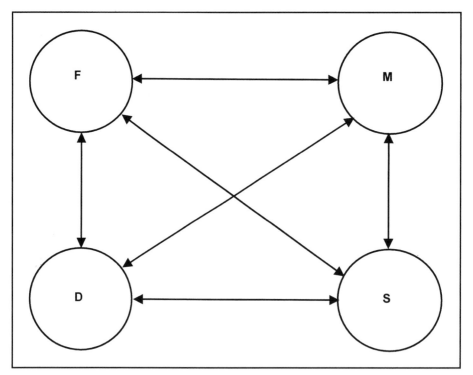

Figure 4.1. The well-functioning family with a child with a disability has balance and reciprocity among all family members (M = mother, F = father, D = child with a disability, S = sibling of child with disability).

effects on self-concept in the siblings of children with disabilities (Ferrari, 1984; Harvey & Greenway, 1984). On the other hand, the presence of a brother or sister with a disability may afford opportunities for the nondisabled child to develop a sense of responsibility and to expand the sibling role to include helping, teaching, and caregiving. These actions could lead to an increased sense of competence, independence, and feelings of self-worth.

The literature presents a complicated picture regarding whether the nondisabled sibling is at risk for learning or adjustment difficulties. For example, it has been reported that siblings of children with Down syndrome were similar to children with nondisabled siblings in terms of marital satisfaction of parents, levels of parental depression, family cohesion, and warmth of relationships between siblings (Fisman et al., 1996). But other studies conflict with these findings (e.g., Beckman, 1991; Cahill & Glidden, 1996). Further, Dyson (1996) noted in her research that parents of children with learning disabilities exhibited higher levels of stress than parents of nondisabled children. Brody and Stoneman (1986) found that increased stress and fatigue experienced by the parents could reduce the quantity and quality of their interactions with the children with no disability. Such stress can create a risk for problems among family members.

Birth Order, Age, and Gender

Although the effects of birth order alone seem mixed with regard to the siblings of children with disabilities (Gath, 1974; Stoneman, Brody, Davis, Crapps, & Malone, 1991; Tew & Laurence, 1975), when considered in the context of age and gender, some interesting consistencies appear in the literature. Generally, older sisters of children with disabilities had more caregiving responsibilities than other siblings (Cleveland & Miller, 1977; Gath, 1972, 1974; Grossman, 1972; Stoneman, Brody, & MacKinnon, 1986; Stoneman et al., 1991). These older sisters may feel stress and resentment for loss of their childhood and freedom. Teachers have reported these older sisters to be less social at school than their peers, but to be better adjusted when the sibling with the disability did not live at home. In contrast, younger sisters of children with disabilities exhibit no more adjustment problems than younger brothers (Breslau, 1982; Breslau, Weitzman, & Messenger, 1981), even though these younger sisters tend to assume more teaching and helping roles in the family than their counterparts who do not have siblings with disabilities (Brody, Stoneman, Davis, & Crapps, 1991).

Brothers seem to be affected differently than sisters. For example, younger sisters tend to assume more of a care-taking role than their male counter parts for the child with a disability (Brody et al., 1991; Lavigne & Ryan, 1979). Breslau (1982), on the other hand, found that younger males exhibited more symptoms of poor mental health, particularly when the sibling with the disability was male and close in age to the younger brother, and the disability was severe (Trevino, 1979). Older brothers may be the least involved and consequently the most isolated of the siblings.

The effects of birth order, age, and gender can be compounded by the nature of the disability. For example, brothers seem to become less involved than sisters when retardation is the disability and the male is the older sibling (Cleveland & Miller, 1977; Grossman, 1972). Researchers have found that older siblings with retardation can become more involved with and closer to their younger siblings than would be the case if the disability were not present (Brody et al., 1991). Further, as children in a family grow older, a child with retardation may be passed in abilities and knowledge by younger siblings. The resulting role reversal can lead to resentment and rejection directed toward the older sibling with the disability (Simeonsson & McHale, 1981). When the disabling condition is cystic fibrosis, the impact on family structure may be most severe when the affected child is the first born (Johnson, Muyskens, Bryce, Palmer, & Rodnan, 1985).

Socioeconomic Status of the Family

Families with less financial security may experience greater difficulty meeting the needs of children with disabilities because fewer resources are available to pay for assistance and services (Featherstone, 1980; Grossman, 1972; Seligman, 1983; Simeonsson & McHale, 1981). Faced with financial strain, family members, particularly siblings, might unconsciously or directly blame the child with the disability for the family's financial condition. Families of lower socioeconomic status tend to be heavily invested in basic economic survival and may not be in a position, psychologically, physically, or financially, to deal with the added responsibilities of a child with a disability (McHale, Simeonsson, & Sloan, 1984).

On the other hand, affluent families who take advantage of their financial resources to secure assistance in the care of the child with a disability (e.g., residential programs, summer camps, and professional services) often feel guilty about leaving responsibility for the care of their child to others (Grossman, 1972). These parents may also feel they are neglecting other children in the family and attempt to compensate by indulging the other children with material goods as a surrogate for attention and emotional support. Middle-class families' problems often appear linked to disappointed aspirations and worries about the ability of the child with the disability to be independent at maturity.

Family Size

In larger families, the hopes and aspirations of the parents can be spread over several children, thus dispersing the pressures on any one child to compensate for the member with a disability. Further, the more children present, the more the responsibilities for the child with the disability are dispersed in the family constellation (Trevino, 1979). For these reasons, siblings without disabilities from larger families usually appear better adjusted than those from smaller families (Gath, 1973; Grossman, 1972; Trevino, 1979).

Disability Type and Severity

The type of disability may not significantly affect the adjustment of the siblings who have no disability (Breslau et al., 1981). For example, Lobato (1983) summarized a number of studies of siblings of children with Down syndrome, hearing impairment, autism, cerebral palsy, and childhood cancers and noted that the type of disability alone did not appear to contribute significantly to the siblings' adjustment. Individual traits such as temperament and behavior of the child can override the influence of a particular disability (McHale et al., 1984).

When severity is defined as the amount of help needed in such basic activities of daily life as toileting, eating, and dressing, siblings of children with disabilities show the most negative effects when the degree of disability is either mild or severe; a child with moderate disability has less an effect on siblings than those with no disabilities (Farber, 1960; Grossman, 1972; Hewitt, Newsom, & Newsom, 1970; Tew & Laurence, 1975). The reasons for the better situation posed by moderately handicapping conditions are not clear. Possibly the nondisabled sibling may feel resentment and jealousy toward the child with the mild disability due to what appears to be parental favoritism toward a child who does not seem very incapacitated. But the presence of a severe disability places more responsibility on the nondisabled sibling, leading to complex feelings and pressures.

Family Dynamics

It is clear from what has been reviewed so far that a child with a disability can have an impact on family relationships. A family that functions well will presumably make better adjustment to the child with the disability. Further, family problems may not be as prevalent among families with a child with a disability as once thought (Cahill & Glidden, 1996).

Disengagement is a common form of adaptation among families that are faced with problems of any kind. A disengaged family is one in which members are isolated, autonomous, independent, and striving for mastery of its difficulties. Disengagement tends to limit warmth, affection, nurturance, and social support within the family. For example, the parents may rest all their hopes and aspirations on their children without disability. However, these siblings may not be psychologically, intellectually, or emotionally suited to attain these lofty expectations. When they fail to meet the expected standards, these children frequently react with anger, irritation, aggression, and disobedience (Barragan, 1976; Dyson, 1996). On the other hand, when they succeed, they often feel ignored and unappreciated. Anger resulting from the parental push to excel may be compounded by resentment toward the parents and sibling with a disability regarding money spent for caregiving and other services that could have been used for family activities, comforts, education, or other needs.

How the parents perceive, feel about, and react to their child with a disability is extremely important (Grossman, 1972). Parents with a child who has a minor disability often display more disengaged reactions and stronger neglect reactions (Perosa & Perosa, 1981). For example, a parent may indulge in material ways a child who has a learning disability, while at the same time rejecting the child emotionally (Faerstein, 1981). Parents who overindulge, overprotect, and become otherwise overinvolved with their children with disabilities, without dealing with their own feelings (e.g., shame, rejection, anxiety) can establish a pattern of confusion for the family. Their contradictory messages toward the child who has the disability leave other siblings with little support for resolving their own confused feelings about the situation. Another common pattern is for the child who does not have the disability to feel left out of discussions or deliberations on family matters and to resent being omitted. The feelings of parents and children alike are complex and conflicting. Without proper opportunity for communication between family members, these confused feelings remain troubling and unresolved.

Communication among family members is crucial to the preservation of effective functioning. The potential negative consequences of having a child with a disability in the family is reduced when family members understand the nature of the disability and can communicate about it within the family. This communication is most effective when conversation concerning the child with the disability involves all family members.

The School as a System

In school the child is in a system similar to the family. The child must meet obligations and perform according to standards established by others, participate with peers, and respond to pressures to fill a role as both student and member of a social group. The actions of students, teachers, and administrators are all interrelated. For instance, because of the number of students in a class, the teacher is not able to respond effectively and appropriately to all the needs of each child. This occasional lack of attention can cause some children to increase behavior that pressures the teacher to respond and also affects others in the classroom. At the same time, teachers look to the children for recognition and approval of their efforts and investment in the class-room. Further, teachers and administrators are engaged in a mutually dependent relationship in which each one's perceived success relies to some extent on the reactions of the others. In this way the dynamics of the school are formed and stabilized. This view of the school as a system permits consideration of ways to destabilize and realign destructive interactive patterns that might form.

In situations in which the school system is functioning effectively, channels of communication are open between the child, her peers, and the teacher. (See Figure 4.2.) A child who brings problems from home into the classroom may seek ways to express pent-up anger, frustration, or needs for recognition. Teachers may not recognize the child's activity as expressing frustrations from the home setting, and they may unwittingly respond in such a way as to reinforce the withdrawal, aggression, or other undesirable behavior patterns.

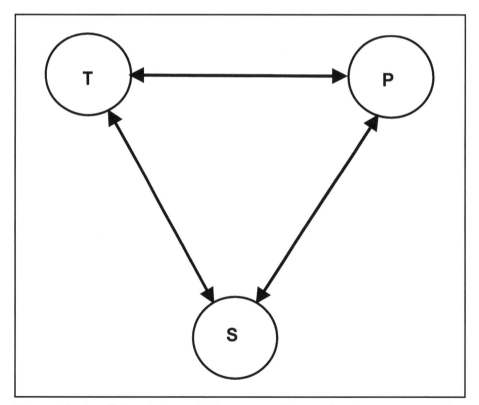

Figure 4.2. A well-functioning school structure (T = teacher, P = peer group, S = sibling of child with disability).

Home and School: Collaborative Overlapping Systems

That the child is part of overlapping systems including the home and school is well recognized (Gutkin & Curtis, 1992). Events that occur in one of these arenas may have direct consequences for the other. Minuchin, Rosman, and Baker (1979) used the term "psychofamilial" to describe the connection between family functioning and disorders that may show themselves at school; the school becomes the location of the child's transferred and displaced family struggles (Ehrlich, 1983; Fine & Holt, 1983). Further, focusing on school-related problems can serve as a diversion from stress factors for family members. Because the child is a member of two systems, his behavior must be viewed within the contexts of these systems. Collaboration between home and school (a) provides for a more complete perspective and understanding of the child's difficulty, (b) promotes direct parent–teacher involvement in the solution, and (c) encourages development of a comprehensive intervention plan that will have a positive impact beyond the school setting.

Plas (1986), as well as several contributors to the present book, suggested methods for implementing the systemic approach in schools and for overcoming the inertia of the traditional approaches to children's problems in school settings. Power and Bartholomew (1985) illustrated how a collaborative approach may be implemented through a systems perspective, which brings together the school and home spheres of control. Erwin and Rainforth (1996) discussed the fostering of a family-centered approach for home–school collaboration that involves the sharing of resources of the families, the teachers, and other school and counseling professionals.

Three Hypothetical Illustrations

Figure 4.3 diagrams the structural dynamics in three different disengaged families and one balanced family. Each of these illustrations is a composite based on cases described in the literature or familiar to the authors. The illustrations focus on the siblings of children with disabilities: Nathan, a child who is frozen out of the lines of communication of the family and left to fend for himself; Jennifer, a very responsible teenager who cares for her brother who has a disability after school while her parents both work to meet their medical bills and other expenses; and Tommy, a high-achieving "super kid" whose performance level is determined by pressure from his family to compensate for his brother who has a severe disability. As you read the brief descriptions, it might help to compare the structural diagrams in Figure 4.3, which represent how each family is communicating and relating, to the well-functioning family and school situations depicted in Figures 4.1 and 4.2.

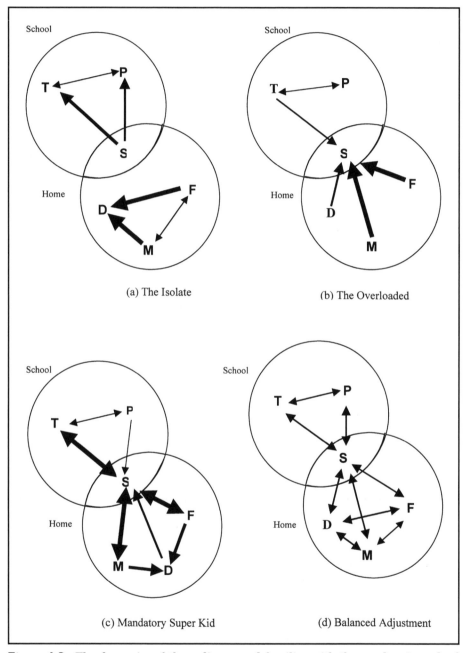

(a) The Isolate

(b) The Overloaded

(c) Mandatory Super Kid

(d) Balanced Adjustment

Figure 4.3. The dynamics of three disengaged families with the overlapping school situation (darker lines represent increased intensity of relationship). (T = teacher, P = peer group, S = sibling of child with disability, D = child with a disability, F = father, M = mother.)

In addition to the family structure, the diagrams depict the overlapping school setting and the adjustment the child has made to the family disengagement. The darker the line, the more overloaded the relationship. These illustrations can aid school-based professionals to understand what must be accomplished to mount a collaborative effort between family and school.

Professionals working with these families should remember that there are rarely any villains. No one is deliberately and individually responsible for causing the family's difficulties. Rather, everyone is mired in a system that is not working. The members of the family system often do not recognize the dysfunction. Parents may deny problems or rationalize their children's roles. Furthermore, awareness that the family is struggling can increase the parents' defensiveness, which can impede cooperative involvement with the school. For positive changes to occur in the system, several things need to happen. The children need help breaking out of the roles they find themselves filling. The parents need help changing what they are doing or not doing. Teachers, and perhaps others in the school who work with the child, need help changing their responses to the child's behavior. The intention of a school professional is to improve the adjustment and learning of the child and support, but not replace, any family therapy or other direct intervention taking place outside of the school setting. The examples and recommendations in the next section may be helpful to school professionals in that role.

The Isolate (Figure 4.3a)

Nathan is 11 years old. His sister is 9 and has had a severe disability from birth. Since the beginning of the school year, Nathan has been experiencing difficulties in the classroom and several times has been kept after school for disciplinary reasons. Teachers complain that Nathan is aggressive, disrespectful, and stubborn. He frequently draws attention to himself in class by calling out. In addition, Nathan is often tardy or skips classes. He seems to have no close friends. Nathan's teachers report that he shows limited social skills on the playground. In conferences with teachers, Nathan's parents indicate a very different perception of their son. They report that he is independent and confident, and they display little concern about his emotional adjustment or ability in social situations. Their expectations for Nathan's achievement seem vague. Family activities are almost nonexistent. Usually one parent or the other is engaged with their daughter with the disability while Nathan is left to amuse himself. The family rarely does anything as a unit. The parents are reluctant to discuss the future with teachers and have not considered who will assume responsibility for caring for their daughter when they become too old to be her primary caregivers. The parents seem very busy with their daughter and admit that they have not discussed her disability with Nathan ("He is only a kid!"). They acknowledge that they do not talk very much to him (or each other).

The Overloaded Child (Figure 4.3b)

Jennifer is 14 years old and has a 12-year-old brother who has a disability. Jennifer's parents both work to support the family. Therefore Jennifer is responsible for her brother's care after school. Her brother attends a special school and is brought home by the school bus at 3:45. Jennifer meets the bus each day, does physical therapy with her brother, cleans the house, and prepares dinner before her parents arrive home from work. She has few friends, does not participate in extracurricular activities after school, and has a limited social life. Her teachers report that Jennifer is a pleasant student but seems withdrawn and distracted when compared to the other children. Some teachers said that they felt she was depressed. The teachers also report that Jennifer's grades are average and that she follows directions and does everything asked of her. Jennifer says that she enjoys taking care of her brother but sometimes resents being the only one who is available to care for him.

The Mandatory Super Kid (Figure 4.3c)

Ten-year-old Tommy, who is 7 years younger than his brother who has a severe disability, has an A average in academic subjects and excels in all the major seasonal sports at school. His teachers and coaches report that although Tommy seems to do well at whatever he tries, he does not seem to be enjoying himself. One of his teachers says, "Tommy is grimly devoted to excellence." In other words Tommy seems to feel he has no choice but to do well in everything. His homework assignments are often turned in late but are perfectly done. He seldom completes classwork within the time allotted, but the work that is done is always perfect. Group cognitive assessments suggest that Tommy's current academic abilities exceed the level at which he should be expected to perform. Although Tommy plays team sports and is always desired as a teammate because of his athletic ability, he seems to have few friends off the athletic field. Both Tommy and his parents have high, and somewhat unrealistic, expectations and aspirations for him. His mother expects him to be "a famous physician," while his father expects him to "at least be a state governor." Although Tommy has few friends among his peers, his parents happily report that he mixes well in adult company.

Establishing Collaborative Relationships Between School and Home

The three illustrations show how family dysfunction centering around a child with a disability can affect the school performance of a sibling who is not disabled. Changing these established patterns requires cooperation between school and home; power conflicts only hinder the process. It is difficult for parents to discuss responsibility for events that occur at school, and for the school professionals to share responsibility for events that happen in the school. Parents and professionals might consider five goals for home–school collaboration:

1. Break the dysfunctional behavior patterns in the family and at school.

2. Establish and reinforce new patterns of behavior for members of both the home and school systems.

3. Open channels of communication between teachers and parents.

4. Open channels of communication between the family members.

5. Involve parents actively and constructively in the planning and decision making regarding their child's school experiences.

An overall strategy for establishing such a collaborative relationship might include the following elements:

1. *Power equalization.* School professionals are viewed by parents as being in a position of relative power within the schools (Orford, 1992). Teachers and other school staff must overcome this perception by development of communication channels and relationships that convey the reality of partnership of interest in the child's education. Effective collaboration occurs when school professionals succeed in making parents into capable partners in the planning and decision making for the child.

2. *Education of all concerned.* Parents may need help to understand the dynamics of family interaction and the role each member plays in the family constellation. They should be made aware of the pressures to perform or assume responsibility that are placed upon siblings who are not disabled, and the frustration, deprivation, jealousy, guilt, and isolation these pressures can induce. In addition, school personnel should be prepared to understand the role that the nondisabled sibling plays in the family, and how this role may

explain the student's learning or adjustment problems at school. Further, both parents and teachers should be prepared to avoid natural and territorial barriers as they pursue a collaborative effort to support cooperative goals.

3. *Inclusion of parents as partners in the decision making and planning for the child that does not have a disability.* Professionals must assume that parents know something about their children and are concerned for their well-being. Parents should recognize that school personnel are likewise concerned about these children, see them for a significant part of the day, and are willing to work cooperatively. By planning interventions together, school personnel and parents can integrate their efforts on behalf of the child.

4. *Family consultation or counseling.* Parents may require therapeutic consultation to recognize the character of the problem in their own family and be able to take action to change destructive patterns, particularly in terms of issues extending beyond school.

Implementation of a collaborative effort between the school and the parents is usually done by a school-based helping professional such as a school psychologist or guidance counselor. However, anyone able to function with the confidence of both the school staff and the parents on behalf of the child (such as a physician, pastor, or community mental health worker) can probably play an active role in the implementation. This professional can act initially as consultant and information resource between parents and school and in this manner bring the two together to establish the collaboration. This may require a slightly different stance than other forms of consultative services. The initial goal of the consultant is to bring the two groups (not always congruently oriented) into a productive collaborative relationship, rather than to provide information directly to help them work out the problems on their own.

The helping professional may provide several services to parents during the course of the collaborative relationship. For example, initially the professional might act as a mediator between the school and home, then serve more of an information resource function, and still later take an advocacy position for the child with or without the disability. Other roles might be more based in therapeutic intervention.

Strategies for the School-Based Professional To Establish Collaboration Between Parents and School

The following strategies would be helpful in establishing a collaborative relationship between the school and the family. These are general strategies for use in a variety of situations. More specific strategies to address the Isolate, Overloaded Child, or Super Kid follow. The suggested strategies are not in any particular order. Implementation should be determined by the settings, people involved, and the collaborative process.

- A complex assortment of tradition, personal feelings and investment, social expectation, and well-established rules underline the actions of both parents and school workers in relationship to the sibling of the child with a disability. Therefore, both should prepare themselves for the collaborative relationship before the first joint meeting is held. Parents and teachers should recognize that neither intends to usurp the power of, or undermine, the other within their respective domain (home or school), and that both are interested in helping the child. They should acknowledge explicitly from the outset that each party has something to gain from cooperating with the other.

- Parents can be prepared to address what they would like the school to do and what they themselves might be able to do if the school would permit them. Similar planning with the teachers and relevant school personnel could facilitate progress at the first meeting between parents and school.

- The professional should help both parents and school personnel understand the home–school dynamics of the child.

- The professional should arrange for regular follow-up contacts between parents and teachers to update the collaborative relationship and to change strategies and activities at home and in school as the child's behavior changes, with the goal of furthering the child's adjustment and learning.

- The professional might try to maintain a neutral role, collaborative to both parents and school staff, monitoring progress at home and in school, and promoting communication and coordination between the two settings.

Strategies for The Isolate (Nathan)

General Goals: At home the goals are to increase Nathan's involvement in the family, strengthen family interaction and communication, improve quality and quantity of Nathan's interactions with his peers, reduce the amount of family energy focused on the sibling with the disability, and set clearer objectives and expectations for Nathan at home. The goals for the school are to identify responsibilities for Nathan and reward successful performance, increase constructive participation in class and social interaction with classmates, and raise the level of verbal communication.

Specific Strategies:

1. Parents and teachers agree to hold regular meetings to discuss Nathan and his activities at home and school.

2. Parents and teachers agree to provide honest answers to Nathan's questions about his sister and what is expected of him and to tell him when they do not know the answer to a particular question.

3. Parents agree to spend time with Nathan in family activities (e.g., hobbies, homework, outings) and include him in family discussions.

4. Parents agree to strengthen Nathan's sense of his own importance by giving him opportunities to participate in family planning and decision making.

5. Teachers agree to design small group activities for the classroom in which any child, including Nathan, would find it difficult to avoid participation, such as group learning activities in which each member of the group is responsible for some part of a lesson.

6. Teachers agree to appoint Nathan to classroom committees and responsibilities that would involve him with his peers (e.g., a committee planning a class Christmas party, or one planning a class production of a play).

7. Teachers agree to encourage Nathan to speak or write about his feelings, home, and sister's disability, without involving the whole class in ways that might embarrass him.

8. Teachers agree to contact the parents when something out of the usual occurs and to involve both parents actively in these discussions.

9. Teachers recognize that they should not reveal information to the parents that Nathan provides in confidence without discussing the situation first with Nathan (unless withholding the information might put him in danger).

10. Parents agree to help Nathan understand his sister's condition and the long-term implications of it. They begin the dialogue by asking the first questions.

11. Parents agree to provide material about their daughter's disabilities for Nathan to read and then discuss these materials with him. They may obtain this material from the library or their physician's office.

12. Parents agree to talk about the future together and to include Nathan in these discussions. Topics might include such things as who will care for their daughter when she is an adult. What will her life be like, and what will Nathan's responsibilities for her be.

13. Parents agree that when they cannot answer a question, they will tell Nathan and seek help with these answers from school professionals (e.g., school psychologist, social worker, teacher, guidance counselor), the family physician, or other families with children who have disabilities.

14. Both parents agree to plan together how to bring Nathan into family discussions and activities and recognize him for his efforts in school and at home. In addition, parents agree to schedule regular family discussions in which Nathan takes part. At these discussions, parents should ask for Nathan's opinions about family plans and decisions.

15. Parents agree to show interest in Nathan's school activities by asking him what his day was like and about his activities. They will also show him that they are concerned about his activities outside of school by talking with him about his friends, preferences, and interests.

16. Parents agree to encourage Nathan's participation in social and recreational groups outside of school such as teams or scouts.

17. Parents agree to attend regular meetings with the teacher to learn about Nathan's performance in school, on the playground, and with peers and to relate to the teacher any significant changes in behavior or performance at home.

Strategies for The Overloaded Child (Jennifer)

General Goals: At home the goals are to decentralize the focus from the overloaded child, to establish more communication between all the family members, and to create more balance in the distribution of responsibilities within the family. Parents will provide opportunity for experiences more typical of adolescence by reducing some of Jennifer's caregiving and family responsibilities and to increase the time the family spends together. Goals for the school are to increase Jennifer's participation in class and extracurricular activities.

Specific Strategies:

1. Parents and teachers agree to encourage Jennifer to participate in extracurricular activities that they feel she would enjoy.

2. Teachers agree to regular meetings with parents regarding Jennifer's participation in school settings.

3. Teachers agree to help parents meet with the school social worker who can suggest community resources for caregiving and other services for children with disabilities.

4. Parents agree to help Jennifer identify interests (e.g., reading, hobbies) that she can enjoy while at home with her brother with a disability.

5. Teachers agree to encourage Jennifer to work with other students on class projects and to organize small group activities in class in which Jennifer will have to participate.

6. Parents agree to prepare a list of responsibilities and chores with Jennifer and assign them on a rotational basis.

7. Parents agree to initiate a "day off" for the overloaded child so that she can participate in activities with her peers outside of the home.

8. Members of the family agree to schedule weekly meetings to discuss problems, feelings, and successes of each member because the family seems to have opportunity to meet informally and spontaneously to discuss these matters. Activities involving the whole family may be planned at these meetings.

9. Parents agree to contact teachers to discuss Jennifer's progress and performance. They will ask for teachers' assistance in identifying things that should be built into Jennifer's schedule of responsibilities.

10. Parents agree to encourage Jennifer to express to them her feelings and frustrations and provide a model for this by discussing their own feelings with her.

Strategies with the Super Kid (Tommy)

General Goals: Goals for home and school are to help Tommy develop social skills and foster relationships that are more reciprocal with his sibling with a disability, parents, and peers and to redirect the intense pressure for achievement and excellence that Tommy perceives. Also, parents will make their expectations for Tommy more realistic.

Specific Strategies:

1. Teachers agree to maintain a realistic perspective on Tommy's capabilities. They will remember that Tommy's parents are probably at least as invested as the boy in having him overcompensate for his brother's handicap.

2. Teachers agree to communicate to parents information about test scores, grades, work performance, and peer interaction. At the same time they will sound favorably disposed toward the child and recognize frankly how hard he works to achieve his level of performance. The teachers will avoid sounding too accusatory toward the parents in order not to arouse unnecessary defenses.

3. Teachers will suggest that parents ask the school psychologist or counselor to explain in greater depth the meaning of test scores and other information if this seems necessary.

4. Teachers agree to arrange for Tommy's feelings and interests to be explored by the counselor or school psychologist and then enlist their aid in explaining these interests to the parents and Tommy.

5. Teachers agree to be warm and supportive of Tommy, even when he is late with homework or assignments or on the rare occasion that his work is not outstanding, and to encourage the parents to recognize his efforts regardless of the outcome. Tommy is hard enough on himself without additional pressure from teachers and parents.

6. The school psychologist agrees to discuss with the parents the implications of Tommy's need to excel in terms of its effects on his future growth and emotional development, self-concept, self-esteem, and social relationships.

7. Parents agree to suggest ways that their son involve himself more with his peers in his various activities.

8. Parents agree to explore with Tommy any interests beyond school work and sports that would not put him in competition with his peers (e.g., building model airplanes, studying birds or insects, or learning to play a musical instrument). These should be activities that would provide

opportunity for enjoyment and making friends with children his own age who have similar interests.

9. Parents agree to schedule times for family activities such as picnics and other outings, in which all members participate and which provide times to discuss feelings, goals, and aspirations and other matters of importance to individual family members.

Summary

The nondisabled sibling of a child with a disability is more likely to experience intense pressures, unresolved expectations, and conflicting feelings than a peer who does not have a brother or sister with a disability. Increased pressure from financial needs, caregiving responsibilities, and lack of opportunity for communication and self-expression within the family can become major sources of frustration for the nondisabled sibling and may lead to disengagement and dysfunction in the family system. Often the child's behavior at school reflects this disruption of family functioning at home. School-based professionals can provide mental health and psychological services for the child and, through collaboration with parents, can coordinate the family and school systems to address the child's problems and frustrations.

References

Barragan, M. (1976). The child centered family. In P. J. Guerin (Ed.), *Family therapy: Theory and practice* (pp. 232–248). New York: Gardner.

Beckman, P. (1991). Comparison of mothers' and fathers' perceptions of the effect of young children with and without disabilities. *American Journal on Mental Retardation, 95,* 585–595.

Breslau, N. (1982). Siblings of disabled children: Birth order and age spacing effects. *Journal of Abnormal Child Psychology, 10,* 85–96.

Breslau, N., Weitzman, M., & Messenger, K. (1981). Psychological functioning of siblings of disabled children. *Pediatrics, 61,* 344–353.

Brody, G. H., & Stoneman, Z. (1986). Contextual issues in the study of sibling socialization. In J. J. Gallagher & P. M. Vietze (Eds.), *Families of handicapped persons: Research, programs and policy issues* (pp. 197–217). Baltimore: Brookes.

Brody, G. H., Stoneman, Z., Davis, C. H., & Crapps, J. M. (1991). Observations of the role relations between older children with mental retardation and their younger siblings. *American Journal on Mental Retardation, 95,* 527–536.

Cahill, B. M., & Glidden, L. (1996). Influence of child diagnosis on family and parental functioning: Down syndrome versus other disabilities. *American Journal on Mental Retardation, 101*(2), 149–160.

Cleveland, D. W., & Miller, N. (1977). Attitude and life commitments of older siblings of mentally retarded adults. *Mental Retardation, 15,* 38–41.

Dyson, L. (1996). The experiences of families of children with learning disabilities: Parental stress, family functioning and sibling self-concept. *Journal of Learning Disabilities, 29,* 280–286.

Ehrlich, M. I. (1983). Psychofamilial correlates of school disorders. *Journal of School Psychology, 21,* 191–199.

Erwin, E. J., & Rainforth, B. (1996). Partnerships for collaboration: Building bridges in early care and education. In E. J. Erwin (Ed.), *Putting children first: Visions for a brighter future for young children and their families* (pp. 227–251). Baltimore: Brookes.

Faerstein, L. W. (1981). Stress and coping in families of learning disabled children: A literature review. *Journal of Learning Disabilities, 14,* 420–423.

Farber, B. (1960). Family organization and crises: Maintenance of integration in families with a severely mentally retarded child. *Monographs of the Society for Research in Child Development, 25* (Serial No. 75), 1–95.

Featherstone, H. (1980). *A difference in the family: Life with a disabled child.* New York: Basic Books.

Ferrari, M. (1984). Chronic illness: Psychosocial effects on siblings. 1. Chronically ill boys. *Journal of Child Psychology and Psychiatry, 25,* 459–476.

Fine, M. J., & Holt, P. (1983). Intervening with school problems: A family systems perspective. *Psychology in the Schools, 20,* 59–66.

Fisman, S., Wolf, L., Ellison, D., Gillis, B., Freeman, T., & Szatmari, P. (1996). Risk and protective factors affecting the adjustment of siblings of children with chronic disabilities. *Journal of the American Academy of Child and Adolescent Psychiatry, 35,* 1532–1541.

Gath, A. (1972). The mental health of congenitally abnormal children. *Journal of Child Psychology and Psychiatry, 13,* 211–218.

Gath, A. (1973). The school-age siblings of mongol children. *British Journal of Psychiatry, 123,* 161–167.

Gath, A. (1974). Siblings' reactions to mental handicap: A comparison of brothers and sisters of mongol children. *Journal of Child Psychology and Psychiatry, 15,* 187–198.

Goldenberg, I., & Goldenberg, H. (1996). *Family therapy: An overview* (4th ed.). Monterey, CA: Brooks/Cole.

Grossman, F. K. (1972). *Brothers and sisters of retarded children: An exploratory study.* Syracuse, NY: Syracuse University Press.

Gutkin, T. B., & Curtis, M. (1992). School-based consultation: Theory, techniques, and research. In T. B. Gutkin & C. R. Reynolds (Eds.), *Handbook of school psychology* (2nd ed., pp. 603–604). New York: Wiley.

Harvey, D. H. P., & Greenway, A. P. (1984). The self-concept of physically handicapped children and their nonhandicapped siblings: An empirical investigation. *Journal of Child Psychology and Psychiatry, 25,* 273–274.

Hewitt, S., Newsom, J., & Newsom, E. (1970). *The family and the handicapped child.* London: George Allen & Unwin.

Johnson, M. C., Muyskens, M., Bryce, M., Palmer, J., & Rodnan, J. (1985). A comparison of family adaptations to having a child with cystic fibrosis. *Journal of Marital and Family Therapy, 11,* 305–312.

Lavigne, J., & Ryan, M. (1979). Psychological adjustment of siblings with chronic illness. *Pediatrics, 63,* 616–627.

Lobato, D. (1983). Siblings of handicapped children: A review. *Journal of Autism and Developmental Disorders, 13,* 347–364.

McHale, S. M., Simeonsson, R. J., & Sloan, J. L. (1984). Children with handicapped brothers and sisters. In E. Schopler & G. Mesibov (Eds.), *The effects of autism on the family.* New York: Plenum.

Minuchin, S., Rosman, B. L., & Baker, L. (1979). *Psychosomatic families: Anorexia nervosa in context.* Cambridge, MA: Harvard University Press.

Orford, J. (1992). *Community psychology: Theory and practice.* New York: Wiley.

Perosa, L. M., & Perosa, S. L. (1981). The school counselor's use of structural family therapy with learning disabled students. *The School Counselor, 29,* 152–155.

Plas, J. M. (1986). *Systems psychology in the schools.* New York: Pergamon Press.

Power, T. J., & Bartholomew, K. L. (1985). Getting uncaught in the middle: A case study in family–school system consultation. *School Psychology Review, 14,* 222–229.

Seligman, M. (1983). *Family with a handicapped child: Understanding and treatment.* New York: Grune & Stratton.

Simeonsson, R. J., & McHale, S. W. (1981). Review: Research on handicapped children: Sibling relationships. *Child Care, Health, and Development, 7,* 153–171.

Stoneman, Z., Brody, G. H., Davis, C. H., Crapps, J. M., & Malone, D. M. (1991). Ascribed role relations between children with mental retardation and their siblings. *American Journal on Mental Retardation, 95,* 537–550.

Stoneman, Z., Brody, G. H., & MacKinnon, C. E. (1986). Same-sex and cross-sex siblings: Activity choices, roles, behavior, and gender stereotypes. *Sex Roles, 15,* 495–511.

Summers, C. R., White, K. R., & Summer, M. (1994). Siblings of children with a disability: A review and analysis of the empirical literature. *Journal of Social Behavior and Personality, 9*(5), 169–184.

Tew, B., & Laurence, K. (1975). Mothers, brothers, and sisters of patients with spina bifida. *Developmental Medicine and Child Neurology, 15,* 69–76.

Trevino, F. (1979). Siblings of handicapped children: Identifying those at risk. *Social Casework, 60,* 488–493.

Parent and Professional Collaborative Relationships in an Era of Change

5

Richard L. Simpson and Joyce K. Zurkowski

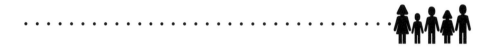

The world of the rapidly approaching 21st century will differ significantly from what it is today (Coontz, 1995; Elkind, 1995), and every facet of life and every institution, including schools, must prepare to meet the changes that lie ahead. Amidst the many changes in this country, the involvement of parents and families in their children's education is likely to remain an important aim of both parents and professionals (Sailor & Skrtic, 1996). By forming and maintaining collaborative relationships, parents, families, and professionals can respond to and prepare for the ongoing changes that will significantly alter family life and education in the future (Clark & Berkowitz, 1995). This chapter will focus on societal changes that will affect specifically the relationships between parents and families of children with disabilities and educational professionals. We will examine families of the 21st century, disability-related legislative enactments and legal rulings, school reform, and service delivery restructuring.

Families of the 21st Century

In order for professionals to collaborate effectively with families of the future, they must recognize that these families will be different from those of previous generations. Families in the United States in the 21st century will be more diverse than at any previous point in our society in terms of racial, cultural, structural, and economic considerations.

Indeed, today's families represent a variety of racial and cultural groups, each with their own distinct value system (Hardin & Littlejohn, 1995). Asian American, Hispanic, and African American populations have grown from 2 to 17 times more rapidly than their Caucasian counterparts over the last 20 years. In fact, it has been estimated that in the year 2000, 1 in 3 classroom students will be African American, Hispanic, or Native American (Individuals with Disabilities Education Act [IDEA] Amendments, 1997). This country will be composed of a populace about which few generalities can be applied.

In addition to coming from a variety of cultural and racial backgrounds, our students will also come from families of differing compositions. Today, in spite of stabilized divorce and separation rates, significant numbers of children continue to live in one-parent or reconstituted families (Dawson, 1991). It is estimated that half of all children born today will be living with only one parent at some point in their lives (U.S. President, 1995). As reported by Fields and Smith (1998), these children have lower academic achievement scores and an increased likelihood of dropping out of school. The effects of being raised by a single parent can be emotional as well, exhibited through increased levels of anxiety, depression, and aggression among these students.

Families will also continue to be affected by socioeconomic conditions. Tragically, poverty has increased during the past decades, most notably for children. In fact, over recent years, U.S. children have become the poorest of any other age group. In 1996, although children were only 27% of the total population, they were 40% of the poor. Since the early 1980s, 20% or more of U.S. children have lived in families with incomes that have fallen below the poverty line (Weinberg, 1997). Poverty conditions have had a particularly negative effect on minority families (Correa & Weismentel, 1991; Hanson & Lynch, 1992; Kozol, 1991; Scherer, 1993). As recently as 1994, 30% of young black children lived in families with incomes below 50% of the federal poverty threshold compared to 6% of young white children (National Center for Children in Poverty, 1996).

As reported by the National Center for Children in Poverty (1996), the children of families in poverty are exposed to many risk factors which can affect their development and their parents' ability to engage in collaborative relationships. Inadequate nutrition can cause delayed or stunted physical growth and motor skill development, as well as decreased social interaction (Brown & Pollit, 1996). Maternal substance abuse can lead to poor fetal brain development, which can affect all developmental areas. Children of mothers who are depressed frequently experience a nonstimulating environment. Their emotional needs tend to be ignored, leading to inactivity, withdrawal, and shortened attention spans (Belle, 1990). Environmental toxins can cause brain damage as well as resulting motor and neurological difficulties. Trauma and abuse, two of the most devastating side effects of poverty, have physical, emotional, and social consequences. Overall, children living in poverty suffer from a decreased quality of daily care (Burchinal, Lee, & Ramey, 1989).

As can be seen, professionals of the 21st century will need to form effective collaborative relationships with families whose ethnic, cultural, structural, and socioeconomic conditions, beliefs, and values may be very different from their own (Mundschenk & Foley, 1995). As part of the process of forming such partnerships, professionals will first need to develop an understanding of their own value systems, and come to recognize how values influence individuals' actions and responses (Raths, Harmin, & Simon, 1966; Rutherford & Edgar, 1979). Just as importantly, they will need to understand, respect, and accept the values of the varied individuals and families with whom they interact. They must be willing to look beyond common stereotypes of differing racial, cultural, and economic backgrounds. Without such acceptance and understanding, the trust needed to form and nurture collaborative relationships will be missing (Friend & Cook, 1992; Salend & Taylor, 1993).

Forming and maintaining effective collaborative relationships between professionals and the families of the 21st century will require additional planning, coordination, and sensitivity. For example, the many single parents will have economic and time constraints beyond those of other families (Karpowitz, 1980; Schulz, 1987). Parents and children in single-parent and blended families often experience increased stress (Hetherington, Arnett, & Hollier, 1985; Lambie & Daniels-Mohring, 1993; Martin, 1975). Moreover, some parents undergoing changes related to divorce, separation, and remarriage may appear to be uninterested in forming and participating in collaborative partnerships with professionals to deal with their child's school-related problems. Nevertheless, professionals must attempt to maintain open lines of communication with these parents and families and to involve them in their child's education. Indeed, many parents and families undergoing transitions associated with divorce, separation, and remarriage will both benefit from and contribute to effective parent–professional partnerships.

Economic concerns may also make families initially appear to be less motivated to form partnerships with professionals. There are no simple answers for responding to the needs of poor families. The multiple needs of families living in poverty require a coordinated effort by a variety of social agencies and professionals.

Thus, to reach children and families with such varied needs, educators must be willing to abandon the narrow perception that the only role of education is developing students' academic skills and knowledge. Parent–professional collaboration in the 21st century must reflect culturally sensitive, family supportive, and economically responsive attitudes.

Legal Decisions and Legislative Changes Related to Individuals with Disabilities

The history of special education clearly confirms that most advances made on behalf of exceptional children and youth and their families have been achieved through court rulings and legislative enactments (Hehir & Latus, 1992; Turnbull, 1993). Increased parent–professional collaboration has resulted in part from a heightened awareness of the benefits of such cooperative involvement. Legal, legislative, advocacy, and political efforts, however, have been the primary basis by which parents and families have established their position as collaborators. Historically, parents and families of exceptional children were forced to resort to legal and legislative strategies largely because of limited opportunities to participate with professionals as partners in educational decision making.

Court Rulings

Court decisions such as *Pennsylvania Association of Retarded Citizens v. the Commonwealth of Pennsylvania* (1971) and *Mills v. the Board of Education, District of Columbia* (1972) set the stage for parent advocacy. In the Pennsylvania case, an advocacy group filed suit against the state for allegedly failing to provide a public education for all children with mental retardation. Results of the suit included an order that the state's children with retardation were entitled to educational services, and that as much as possible these children were to be educated in programs that were like those of children without retardation. Similarly *Mills v. the Board of Education* involved parents filing a class action suit against the school system for failing to provide a public education for all children. As in the Pennsylvania case ruling, the court decreed that all students, including those with disabilities, must be afforded appropriate educational opportunities.

Parents and schools have continued to rely on direction from the courts with regard to determining appropriate services for students with special needs. In the *Board of Education of the Hendrick Hudson School District v. Rowley* (1982), the Supreme Court interpreted the free appropriate education provision (FAPE) of the Education for All Handicapped Children Act (1975). The court posited a two-part test to determine whether a school has provided FAPE. The first part dealt with state compliance with the provisions set forth in the act, and the second examined whether or not the Individualized Education Program (IEP) was designed to enable the child to receive educational benefit. *Irving Independent School District v. Tatro* (1984) dealt with related service issues under the same act. Specifically, the Supreme Court delineated which medical services a school is under obligation to provide.

Honig v. Doe (1988) discussed discipline options for students with disabilities. The Supreme Court ruled that schools could remove students from their current educational placement if maintaining those students in such placements was substantially likely to result in injury either to themselves or others.

In *Daniel R.R. v. State Board of Education* (1989), the concept of least restrictive environment provision of the Education for All Handicapped Children Act (1975) was further discussed by the Fifth Circuit Court. The decision established a multipronged test to determine school district compliance with this law: (1) Has the state taken steps to accommodate the student with disabilities in general education? (2) Will the student receive educational benefit from general education, including the availability of language models? (3) What impact will the presence of the student with disabilities have on the other students? and (4) If the general education environment is determined not to be satisfactory, has the student been mainstreamed to the maximum extent appropriate?

Legislative Changes

Legislative efforts on behalf of children with disabilities culminated with the 1975 passage of P.L. 94-142, the Education for All Handicapped Children Act. This monumental enactment provided for a free and appropriate public education for all children with disabilities. Further, the Education of the Handicapped Act Amendments, P.L. 99-457 (Part H), passed in 1986, mandated comprehensive multidisciplinary services for infants and toddlers and their families. In 1990, the Individuals with Disabilities Education Act (IDEA) (P.L. 101-476), an amendment to the Education for All Handicapped Children's Act, required school personnel to provide transition services to students with disabilities.

IDEA was reauthorized in 1997 with a number of significant changes. Modifications included (a) provisions that required states to establish performance goals and indicators for students with disabilities that were compatible and consistent with other state performance goals, and to include students with disabilities in statewide and districtwide assessments; (b) attempts to link more closely the evaluation procedures for students with disabilities with instructional programming, including the general education curriculum; and (c) procedures to streamline steps used to develop and modify students' IEPs.

Perhaps most significantly, Congress' belief that the education of students with disabilities can be improved by "strengthening the role of parents and ensuring that families of such children have meaningful opportunities to participate in the education of their children at school and at home" [20 USC §1400(c)(5)(B)] is reflected throughout these aforementioned laws. Informed consent by parents is required for evaluation, reevaluation, and initial placement. The law also mandates that parents be provided with the opportunity to participate actively throughout the special education process, starting with being part of the team that determines whether their child is a student with a disability. As participants in the evaluation process, parents contribute valuable information and have a voice in determining what types of information and data are required to make such a determination. Parents are also encouraged to be part of both the IEP and placement teams. The IEP is required to reflect the concerns of the parents regarding their children's education. As part of the placement team, parents participate in determining an appropriate setting for the education of their child.

Further changes directly related to parents include streamlined parent procedural safeguard notices and mediation programs to resolve parent and school district conflicts. Finally, and perhaps most controversially, the reauthorized IDEA (1997) enactment includes changes related to disciplinary measures for students with disabilities. Stricter procedures have been established for disciplining and dismissing from school students with disabilities who violate school rules. Parents, as part of the IEP team, again have an active role to play in this disciplinary process, determining whether the behavior was a manifestation of the child's disability and selecting an appropriate interim alternative educational setting when such a placement must be made.

These legal changes will potentially have a significant impact on students with disabilities, their parents and families, as well as parent–professional collaborative relationships. The changes will create new opportunities for parents and professionals to work together, along with an even greater need for these partnerships (Dunst & Paget, 1991; Simpson & Fiedler, 1989). Indeed, successful implementation of these proposed changes may well be contingent upon formation of successful parent–professional collaborative links. Meyen's comment in 1978 regarding the impact of laws passed at that time continues to be applicable to those laws recently passed: "The consequences of these changes are so far-reaching that they affect not only the education of exceptional children but the future education of all children" (p. 3).

Parent involvement has undergone significant changes over the past three decades, largely as a result of these legal rulings and legislative enactments. Parent participation and collaboration have crystallized and will likely continue to be significant elements of exceptional education programs. Professionals must continue to familiarize themselves with educational legislation, legal rulings, and local, state, and national policies related to individuals with exceptionalities, especially since these are virtually guaranteed to change over the coming years. History has clearly affirmed that when parents are denied opportunities for collaboration and involvement with professionals who work with their children, they will seek other avenues. The most common of these options, legal and legislative alternatives, rarely if ever results in outcomes that are better than those based on collaboration (Cronin, Slade, Bechtel, & Anderson, 1992; Fiedler, 1986; McAfee & Vergason, 1979).

In recognition of the importance of legitimate parent involvement, parent empowerment must be encouraged as an important component of parent–professional collaboration, and nurtured as a mutually beneficial process. Rappaport (1984) observed that "Empowerment is easy to define in its absence; powerlessness, real or imagined; learned helplessness; alienation; loss of a sense of control over one's life. It is more difficult to define positively only because it takes on a different form in different people and contexts" (p. 3). When parents and families are empowered to engage in meaningful collaboration, problem solving, and decision making with professionals, positive outcomes are likely to result (Dixon, 1992; Mundschenk & Foley, 1995). Thus, a process based on parent–professional collaborative relationships, as opposed to reliance on uniform interpretations or formal rulings related to legal and legislative matters, offers an important direction for future parent–professional affiliations.

School Reform

Beginning with publication of *A Nation at Risk: The Imperative for Educational Reform* (National Commission on Excellence in Education, 1983) and continuing through the 1990s, *school reform* rhetoric and related activities have been commonplace. In this context, school reform refers to the variety of attempts to improve education, including curriculum reform, assessment standards, and discipline. Ironically, this school reform has had considerable impact on parents and families of children with disabilities even though relatively little reform attention initially focused on these students (Shaw et al., 1990; U.S. Department of Education, 1993). Primarily designed to raise educational standards, modify curricula to enhance development of higher order thinking skills, and increase flexible use of educational resources, the initial school reform gave relatively little consideration to the unique needs of children and youth with disabilities. The genesis of this oversight is easy to understand: Improved math and science performance was a major element of school reform effort, based on the assumption that the condition of the American economy was fundamentally tied to the quality of the schools.

Early reformers either failed to recognize or considered as unimportant the fact that primarily basing school improvement on such an assumption bodes poorly for students with disabilities. Indeed, one of the most commonly referenced school reform documents, *America 2000: An Education Strategy* (U.S. Department of Education, 1991), virtually ignored children and youth with special needs. In response to this oversight, Ysseldyke, Algozzine, and Thurlow (1992) observed that "in a summary of the 'education reform decade' (ETS Policy Information Center, 1990), there was not a single mention of students with disabilities or even special education" (p. 140). School reform initiatives have generally failed to consider the needs of students with disabilities and their parents (National Council on Disability, 1989; Roach & Caruso, 1997).

Fortunately, recent school reform efforts have begun to include issues germane to the needs of students with disabilities. Some have interpreted this shift as recognition that excellence can flourish only in an environment of equity (Doktor & Poertner, 1996; Villa, Thousand, Stainback, & Stainback, 1992). Others have been less charitable and optimistic in their assessment, noting that the highly significant and ever-changing trends associated with school reform still fail to consider adequately the needs of students with disabilities and their families (Zigmond et al., 1995).

Despite this lack of direct and deliberate attention to students with disabilities within the school reform movement, their parents and families have been affected in a number of ways. School reform initiatives such as specifying educational goals and outcomes, raising academic requirements (e.g., high school students required to enroll in more science and math courses; all students given more homework assignments), establishing more stringent behavioral conduct codes, evaluating the performance of all students using normative measures, tying the availability of school resources to performance, and increasing the quantity and quality of what is taught have had spillover impact on students with disabilities. Parents and families have responded strongly to these changes, many of which appear to run counter to their children's needs (e.g., requiring longer school days, supplanting direct service programs with consultation models, requiring all students to complete core curricula, and increasing parent responsibility for student learning and behavior).

These parent concerns have led to increased recognition that school reform will not succeed without the support of all parents and families, including those of children and youth with disabilities. Former Secretary of Education Terrel Bell (1993), for instance, made the following observations about the need for increased parent involvement in his musings about school reform:

> In school reform initiatives of the future, we must pay more attention to that other educational institution: the home. We must learn more about how to motivate parents, workers in child-care centers, and others to make after-school hours and weekends more educationally productive. We will soon have a greater number of formal programs of parent involvement. We need to begin a tradition of parents and schools working together to establish individualized education plans for every student, as is now required by federal law only for handicapped children. (pp. 596–597)

Obviously much remains to be done relative to making parents and families of children and youth with exceptionalities more involved in efforts to reform schools. While not a universal panacea, collaboration between professionals and parents is a key to this process. Effectively responding to the needs of all students in a climate of school reform will involve addressing a variety of difficult issues, and acceptable solutions will require the collective effort of both professionals and families (Lambie & Daniels-Mohring, 1993; Paul & Simeonsson, 1993; Simpson, 1996).

Service Delivery Restructuring

Not only has there been an attempt to change *what* we teach through school reform, much effort has been put into changing the very *structure* of the schools themselves. Many of these attempted changes greatly affect students with disabilities and their families. Two such movements have been school-linked services and inclusive education.

School-Linked Services

Professionals agree that parents and families of children and adolescents with disabilities often need a significant number of services and resources (Knapp, 1995). Professionals generally favor programs and services that address the needs of entire families, rather than exclusively focusing on children independent of their families (Simpson, 1996). Yet, in spite of such widespread agreement, many needs of children with disabilities and their families are going unmet. Of the estimated 12% of children in the United States who need mental health services, only about 20% receive appropriate treatment (Day & Roberts, 1991). Knitzer, Steinberg, and Fleisch (1990) noted similarly that over 50% of the school districts they surveyed did not offer counseling services, and when counseling was offered, it was provided only on a short-term basis and often paid for by parents. They further reported that community mental health programs, psychotherapy, and related counseling support resources were generally lacking, and that there was little continuity and limited communication among educational, legal, and mental health programs. The issue of lack of services available through the schools and in the community is compounded by the lack of accessibility of private services due to the estimated 41 million people in the United States, including over 10 million children, without health insurance (Weinberg, 1997).

There is no question that these conditions significantly limit and put a strain on collaborative efforts among parents and professionals. Whereas collaboration allows parents and professionals to identify and use cooperatively their various resources, when the resources are insufficient or nonexistent, a foundational element of the collaborative process is unavailable. Such a significant problem affects children with disabilities, as well as the formation and maintenance of effective parent–professional partnerships.

A long-term solution to this challenge will likely come in the form of sufficient community social and family support resources in combination with increased competence among professionals in building partnerships with community programs and families. School-linked services provide one avenue to meet this challenge; they bring together education, social welfare, and health care into one collaborative effort, allowing families to access integrated service provision (Sailor & Skrtic, 1996). This model increases the likelihood of not only improved parent–professional partnerships, but also school, home, and community communication. This collaboration should facilitate improved services and outcomes for students.

Inclusive Education

IDEA currently specifies that the placement decision process for a student with a disability must begin with a consideration of the appropriateness of assigning the student to a general education setting. The law further states that placement in an alternative setting should be considered only if general education placement is determined to be unacceptable. This mandate, combined with the ethical and moral arguments raised by parents in the 1980s regarding their children's rights to participate with typically achieving peers, has led to another form of school restructuring known as inclusive education. Interpretation of the least restrictive environment (LRE) provision of IDEA has led to much debate regarding when and under what circumstances inclusion becomes best practice. Commenting on this issue, Lieberman (1992) noted,

> There seem to be two different camps of full integration advocates. One group does not attempt to justify its position in logical, pragmatic, or curricular terms. When asked what has to be done in order to make full integration work successfully, they generally reply that nothing has to be done. Just do it. Just doing it will make it happen. (p. 22)

Unfortunately, many school districts adopted this "just do it" model without adequate planning or preparation. In 1993 Kauffman observed that "empirical evidence does not indicate that we currently have effective and reliable strategies for improving and sustaining outcomes for all students in regular classrooms" (p. 8). Although schools have developed many effective strategies that allow children with disabilities to participate meaningfully with their nondisabled peers since Kauffman made his statement, they are still far from able to serve all students all the time in what is traditionally considered general education. In order to expand further the vision of delivering an appropriate education in the least restrictive environment, ongoing dialogue must continue, and it must include both professionals and families. The "all or nothing" approach of the 1980s must give way to a realistic restructuring of schools to meet the needs of all students more effectively. Finding a balance between the "free appropriate public education" and "least restrictive environment" provisions of IDEA, needs to be a joint effort between all involved parties (Idstein, Gizzi, Ferrero, & Miller, 1994; Kauffman & Hallahan, 1995). Only through joint planning and open lines of communication can creative and effective solutions to these challenges of school restructuring be developed (O'Shea & O'Shea, 1997). Better services for all students should be the result of these efforts.

Summary

Twenty years ago, Isakson (1979) suggested that professionals hoping to interact effectively with parents must "recognize the strengths in families and capitalize on those so that they can get on with the business they were trained for" (p. 78). This sage advice stands strong as we examine the role of parent–professional collaboration in the 21st century. Professionals must recognize the significant role they play in the lives of families with children with disabilities. They must equally acknowledge that parents and families must be allowed to share the responsibility for educating their children. Collaborative parent–professional relationships will only come about as a result of meaningful dialogue between parents and professionals, with its focus on the needs of children with disabilities. Parents, schools, and communities working together on behalf of all children and youth, including those with disabilities, will need to meet the increasing challenges. The potential positive outcomes associated with families and professionals effectively working together can significantly contribute to children's education and development in the 21st century.

References

Bell, T. (1993). Reflections one decade after *A Nation at Risk*. *Phi Delta Kappan, 74,* 592–604.

Belle, D. (1990). Poverty and women's mental health. *American Psychologist, 45*(3), 385–389.

Board of Education of the Hendrick Hudson School District v. Rowley, 458 U.S. 176 (1982).

Brown, L., & Pollit, E. (1996). Malnutrition, poverty and intellectual development. *Scientific American, 274*(2), 38–43.

Burchinal, M., Lee, M., & Ramey, C. (1989). Type of daycare and preschool intellectual development in disadvantaged children. *Child Development, 60*(1), 128–137.

Clark, R. L., & Berkowitz, R. E. (1995). *Federal expenditures on children, 1960–1995.* Washington, DC: The Urban Institute.

Coontz, S. (1995). The American family and the nostalgia trap. *Phi Delta Kappan, 76,* K1–K20.

Correa, V., & Weismentel, J. (1991). Multicultural issues related to families with an exceptional child. In M. J. Fine (Ed.), *Collaboration with parents of exceptional children* (pp. 83–102). Brandon, VT: Clinical Psychology.

Cronin, M., Slade, D. L., Bechtel, C., & Anderson, P. (1992). Home–school partnerships: A cooperative approach to intervention. *Intervention in School and Clinic, 27,* 286–292.

Daniel R.R. v. State Board of Education, 874 F.2d 1036 (5th cir. 1989).

Dawson, D. A. (1991). Family structure and children's health and well-being: Data from the 1988 national health interview survey on child health. *Journal of Marriage and the Family, 53,* 573–584.

Day, C., & Roberts, M. C. (1991). Activities of the child and adolescent service system program for improving mental health services for children and families. *Journal of Clinical Child Psychology, 20,* 340–350.

Dixon, A. P. (1992). Parents: Full partners in the decision-making process. *NASSP Bulletin, 76*(543), 15–18.

Doktor, J. E., & Poertner, J. (1996). Kentucky's family resource centers. *Remedial and Special Education, 17*(5), 293–302.

Dunst, C. J., & Paget, K. D. (1991). Parent–professional partnerships and family empowerment. In M. J. Fine (Ed.), *Collaboration with parents of exceptional children.* Brandon, VT: Clinical Psychology.

Education for All Handicapped Children Act of 1975, 20 U.S.C. § 1400 *et seq.*

Education of the Handicapped Act Amendments of 1986, 20 U.S.C. § 1400 *et seq.*

Elkind, D. (1995). School and family in the postmodern world. *Phi Delta Kappan, 76,* 8–14.

ETS Policy Information Center. (1990). *The education reform decade.* Princeton, NJ: Educational Testing Service.

Fiedler, C. R. (1986). Enhancing parent–school personnel partnerships. *Focus on Autistic Behavior, 1*(4), 1–8

Fields, J. M., & Smith, K. E. (1998, April). *Poverty, family structure, and child well-being: Indicators from the SIPP.* Paper presented at the annual meeting of the Population Association of America, Chicago.

Friend, M., & Cook, L. (1992). *Interactions: Collaboration skills for school professionals.* New York: Longman.

Hanson, M. J., & Lynch, E. W. (1992). Family diversity: Implications for policy and practice. *Topics in Early Childhood Special Education, 12*(3), 283–306.

Hardin, D. M., & Littlejohn, W. (1995). Family–school collaboration: Elements of effectiveness and program models. *Preventing School Failure, 39*(1), 4–8.

Hehir, T., & Latus, T. (1992). *Special education at the century's end.* Cambridge, MA: Harvard Educational Review.

Hetherington, E. M., Arnett, J., & Hollier, A. (1985). The effects of remarriage on children and families. In P. Karoly & S. Wolchik (Eds.), *Family transition* (pp. 71–97). New York: Garland Press.

Honig v. Doe, 479 U.S. 1084 (1988).

Idstein, P., Gizzi, P., Ferrero, K., & Miller, S. (1994). There are others in the mainstream. *Phi Delta Kappan, 75*(9), 718–720.

Individuals with Disabilities Education Act of 1990, 20 U.S.C. § 1400 *et seq.*

Individuals with Disabilities Education Act Amendments of 1997, 20 U.S.C. § 1400 *et seq.*

Irving Independent School District v. Tatro, 468 U.S. 883 (1984).

Isakson, R. L. (1979, September). Whatever happened to the Waltons? *Instructor,* pp. 77–79.

Karpowitz, D. H. (1980). A conceptualization of the American family. In M. J. Fine (Ed.), *Handbook on parent education* (pp. 27–50). New York: Academic Press.

Kauffman, J. M. (1993). How we might achieve the radical reform of special education. *Exceptional Children, 60*(1), 6–16.

Kauffman, J. M., & Hallahan, D. P. (1995). *The illusion of full inclusion.* Austin, TX: PRO-ED.

Knapp, M. S. (1995). How shall we study comprehensive, collaborative services for children and families? *Educational Researcher, 24*(4), 5–16.

Knitzer, J., Steinberg, Z., & Fleisch, B. (1990). *At the schoolhouse door: An examination of programs and policies for children with behavior and emotional problems.* New York: Bank Street College of Education.

Kozol, J. (1991). *Savage inequalities: Children in America's schools.* New York: Crown.

Lambie, R., & Daniels-Mohring, D. (1993). *Family systems within educational contexts.* Denver: Love.

Lieberman, L. M. (1992). Preserving special education . . . For those who need it. In W. Stainback & S. Stainback (Eds.), *Controversial issues confronting special education* (pp. 13–25). Boston: Allyn & Bacon.

Martin, B. (1975). Parent–child relations. In F. D. Horowitz (Ed.), *Review of child development research* (Vol. 4, pp. 121–142). Chicago: University of Chicago Press.

McAfee, J. K., & Vergason, G. A. (1979). Parent involvement in the process of special education: Establishing the new partnership. *Focus on Exceptional Children, 11*(2), 1–15.

Meyen, E. L. (1978). *Exceptional children and youth: An introduction.* Denver: Love.

Mills v. Board of Education, 348 F. Supp. 866 (D.D.C. 1972).

Mundschenk, N., & Foley, R. (1995). Collaborative relationships between school and home: Implications for service delivery. *Preventing School Failure, 39*(1), 16–20.

National Center for Children in Poverty. (1996). *One in four: America's youngest poor.* New York: Author.

National Commission on Excellence in Education. (1983). *A nation at risk: The imperative for educational reform.* Washington, DC: U.S. Government Printing Office.

National Council on Disability. (1989). *The education of students with disabilities: Where do we stand?* Washington, DC: Author.

O'Shea, D. J., & O'Shea, L. J. (1997). Collaboration and school reform: A twenty-first-century perspective. *Journal of Learning Disabilities, 30*(4), 449–462.

Paul, J. L., & Simeonsson, R. J. (1993). *Children with special needs.* Fort Worth, TX: Harcourt Brace Jovanovich.

Pennsylvania Association of Retarded Citizens v. Commonwealth of Pennsylvania, 343 F. Supp. 279 (E.D. Pa. 1972).

Rappaport, J. (1984). Studies in empowerment: Introduction to the issues. In J. Rappaport, C. Swift, & R. Hess (Eds.), *Studies in empowerment: Steps towards understanding and action* (pp. 1–7). New York: Haworth Press.

Raths, L., Harmin, M., & Simon, S. (1966). *Values and teaching.* Columbus, OH: Merrill.

Roach, V. E., & Caruso, M. G. (1997). Policy and practice: Observations and recommendations to promote inclusive practices. *Education and Treatment of Children, 20*(1), 105–121.

Rutherford, R. B., & Edgar, E. (1979). *Teachers and parents: A guide to interaction and cooperation.* Boston: Allyn & Bacon.

Sailor, W., & Skrtic, T. M. (1996). School/community partnerships and educational reform. *Remedial and Special Education, 17*(5), 267–270.

Salend, S., & Taylor, L. (1993). Working with families: A cross cultural perspective. *Remedial and Special Education, 14,* 25–32.

Scherer, M. (1993). On savage inequalities: A conversation with Jonathan Kozol. *Educational Leadership, 50*(4), 4–9.

Schulz, J. B. (1987). *Parents and professionals in special education.* Boston: Allyn & Bacon.

Shaw, S., Biklen, D., Conlon, S., Dunn, J., Kramer, J., & DeRoma Wagner, V. (1990). Special education and school reform. In L. M. Bullock & R. L. Simpson (Eds.), *Critical issues in special education: Implications for personnel preparation.* Denton: University of North Texas.

Simpson, R. L. (1996). *Working with parents and families of exceptional children and youth.* Austin, TX: PRO-ED.

Simpson, R. L., & Fiedler, C. R. (1989). Parent participation in individualized education program conferences: A case for individualization. In M. Fine (Ed.), *The second handbook on parent education* (pp. 145–171). New York: Academic Press.

Turnbull, H. R. (1993). *Free appropriate public education: The law and children with disabilities.* Denver: Love.

U.S. Department of Education. (1991). *America 2000: An education strategy.* Washington, DC: Author.

U.S. Department of Education. (1993). *Reinventing Chapter 1: The current Chapter 1 program and new directions.* Washington, DC: Author.

U.S. President. (1995). *The economic report of the President transmitted to the Congress* (pp. 178–179).

Villa, R. A., Thousand, J. S., Stainback, W., & Stainback, S. (1992). *Restructuring for caring and effective education: An administrative guide to creating heterogeneous schools.* Baltimore: Brookes.

Weinberg, D. H. (1997). *Income and poverty.* Press briefing, Washington, DC.

Ysseldyke, J. E., Algozzine, B., & Thurlow, M. L. (1992). *Critical issues in special education.* Boston: Houghton Mifflin.

Zigmond, N., Jenkins, J., Fuchs, L. S., Deno, S., Fuchs, D., Baker, J. N., Jenkins, L., & Couthino, M. (1995). Special education in restructured schools. *Phi Delta Kappan, 76*(7), 531–540.

The Developmental Nature of Parent–Child Relationships: The Impact of Disabilities

6

Pauline H. Turner

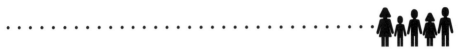

eing a parent is one of the most important adult roles in American society, yet it is one for which most adults are poorly prepared. Effective parenting is difficult, especially in times of economic stress, social change, and growing concern about the well-being of future generations. Most parents are concerned about their children's futures in the face of increasing violence and crime, widespread use of drugs and alcohol, growing poverty, and dissatisfaction with the educational system. At the same time, parents are working harder, access to extended family support systems is shrinking, and families are becoming more isolated.

The transition to parenthood with the birth of the first child is widely recognized to be a time of major changes in the family system, often bringing stress to the marital relationship or to the single parent. As each child is born into a family, a new family system (and multiple subsystems) emerge, with each part of the system affecting every other part. Most families' expectations about their future lives with children do not match the reality (Kalmuss, Davidson, & Cushman, 1992). Research has found that following the birth of a baby, especially the first one, feelings of love for the spouse decline, ambivalence about marriage increases, communication decreases, marital satisfaction decreases, and conflicts increase (Belsky & Rovine, 1990; Belsky, Youngblade, Rovine, & Volling, 1991; MacDermid, Huston, & McHale, 1990; Wallace & Gotlib, 1990). However, while the first stage of parenting probably produces the most intense negative effects, it also produces the most intense positive effects, with parents expressing the greatest degree of satisfaction in the earliest stages of parenting and the least satisfaction when children are adolescents (Goetting, 1986).

Adjustment to the birth of a child with disabilities is considerably more difficult. Most parents plan for and expect healthy happy babies. When an impairment is immediately obvious, the acknowledgment of it is traumatic. The initial reaction may be one of disbelief, and the degree of disbelief appears to be related to the degree of the visibility of the handicap. Most parents experience a grieving process as they try to separate from a significant lost dream and reevaluate their attitudes and expectations. The states of grieving may include denial, anxiety, guilt, depression, and anger, and these feelings may overlap or occur simultaneously. Many parents conceptualize the worst before they deal with reality, and confrontation of reality is facilitated by acceptance of both the child's and the parents' limitations (Moses, 1983).

Thus, transition to parenthood and the subsequent addition of other children into the family are stressful times for many parents and perhaps traumatic for some, especially for those families whose children have obvious disabilities. Nevertheless, most families do, in fact, make healthy adjustments. The adjustment process is affected by socioeconomic status, the availability and use of support systems, marital stability, family constellation, and psychological health of parents. For parents of children with disabilities, adjustment also is affected by cultural beliefs, religious beliefs, the nature and visibility of the disability, and coping strategies of family members (Hamner & Turner, 1996).

Most parents grow and develop with their children. Erikson (1963) described eight stages in the development of individuals from birth to death, with individuals in the seventh stage (the childbearing and childrearing years) striving for a sense of generativity—the interest in establishing and guiding the next generation or caring for others. As children grow and develop, parents adapt their parenting practices, attempting to mesh their own developmental needs with those of their children. This chapter describes that normal developmental process and how it may be affected by children with disabilities.

Parenting and Young Children

Infants

Parents begin their journey with their children in the primary role of caregivers. Both mothers and fathers demonstrate nurturant caregiving behaviors toward their infants, who are helpless and dependent on adults for all of their needs. Parents protect and provide life support to their babies, including the physical necessities and the psychological warmth that they need in order to develop optimally. At least three factors appear to have a major influence on the quality of these early relationships: (1) the quality of the parents' own early experiences (the care each received as children); (2) the conditions of the present situation (family stability, marital discord, job security, health, degree of stress in daily life, etc.); and (3) the characteristics of the infant herself. Parental attitudes and accuracy of perceptions about the baby's characteristics and needs are additional influences. Some studies have shown that the infant's behavior is related to the mother's and father's expectations, for example, what they believe the infant can do.

Responding to Infant Characteristics

Ventura (1987) found that infants' fussy behavior in relation to feeding or soothing techniques was the major source of stress reported by 35% of the mothers and 20% of the fathers in her sample. Mothers reported feeling guilty, helpless, or angry when caring for their fussy infants. Wilkie and Ames (1986) found fathers experienced more stress than mothers when they had a crying baby. Other studies have found that the more difficult the child is temperamentally, the less responsive the mother is likely to be. Difficult babies cry a lot and have irregular schedules. They are hard to soothe and do not adapt easily to new people and situations. These babies do not fare well with impatient unresponsive mothers, but they may, in fact, contribute to their mothers' impatience and unresponsiveness. "Goodness of fit" does not occur in such cases between mother and infant (Thomas & Chess, 1977). Babies also contribute to the parent–child interaction by their state of awareness (asleep, awake, drowsy, alert); by the types of signaling they demonstrate through vocalizing, touching, or looking; by the amount of attention they seek; and by the extent of responsiveness they demonstrate (Hamner & Turner, 1996).

Imagine what might happen to the early relationships between parents and their infants when infants have obvious physical or mental disabilities. In addition to the basic needs that all babies have, these children have their own special needs, often not understood by parents at first. They may be significantly more fussy and more difficult to soothe; they may require infinitely more strenuous caregiving; they may be unresponsive; their activity level, adaptability, and biological rhythmicity may be quite different from typical babies; and parents may have inappropriate expectations for their behavior. In many cases these babies remain in the hospital, diminishing the parents' ability to bond with them and to develop individualized reciprocal relationships with them. Babies at risk for mental retardation due to neurological sequelae may require prolonged feedings with immature suckings, failing to provide adequate reward to the mother. The child who lacks muscle tone, is floppy, and is difficult to handle is usually picked up less often. This reduced contact may inhibit opportunities to learn and thus increase the cognitive disability (Gath, 1993). Blind infants who are unable to establish eye contact with their parents lack an important means for sustaining reciprocal interactions that contribute to positive social and emotional behaviors. Further, they do not display the clearly differentiated facial expressions of sighted babies and smile less often. In these instances, parents must work harder to get the relationship off to a good start, while still grieving over the loss of a normal child.

Establishing Basic Trust

In Erikson's psychosocial framework (Erikson, 1963), the first year of an infant's life is crucial for establishing basic trust, which forms the foundation for lifelong healthy development. The degree to which the child comes to trust the world, other people, and himself depends to a considerable extent on the quality of care he receives. The infant whose needs are met when they arise; whose discomforts are quickly removed; and who is cuddled, fondled, played with, and talked to develops a sense of the world as a safe place to be and of people as helpful and dependable. When, however, the care is inconsistent, inadequate, and rejecting, it fosters a basic mistrust, an attitude of fear and suspicion on the part of the infant, toward the world in general and toward people in particular, that will carry through to later stages of development. If basic needs are not met, the child feels somehow empty, cheated, at a loss, and ill at ease with others and with himself.

In the beginning, much of the infant's world is bound to her physiological needs. If she is fed when she is hungry, changed when she is wet, helped to sleep or rest when she is tired, and cared for by the same few people whom she eventually comes to recognize as significant, then her day-to-day environment becomes orderly, predictable, and consistent. She comes to know that certain things happen at particular times and that familiar people come when she needs them. She learns to recognize, too, the particular patterns of responses of her special caregivers—their tones of voice, their odors, and the way their bodies feel when she is held close. All of these consistent predictable subtleties help her to learn who she is and that she can depend on others for her safety.

Trust also is built from the child's own behavior; that is, he begins to view himself as competent by his ability to act on his environment and his success in eliciting certain responses from his caregivers. If, however, the infant is cared for by a number of different people; if there is no predictability in his feeding, sleeping, or being played with; if he is unable to act on his environment and successfully elicit responses from his caregivers; and especially if he is abused or neglected, then his sense of basic trust in others as dependable and himself as competent is impeded. Parents of infants with disabilities may be inconsistent in their caregiving, partly because they may not clearly understand the needs of their children and partly because their children may be unable to elicit responsive care from them. Further, competent substitute caregiving may be more difficult to find. Helping these infants establish basic healthy trust can be a challenge.

Fostering Attachment

Profoundly related to a sense of trust during the first year is the security of attachment the infant develops for her mother and other primary caregivers.

Attachment refers to the special bond that the infant forms with significant adults in her life. A sense of trust is crucial for the formation of this special bond. Both biological and environmental factors work interdependently to facilitate the infant's attachment to significant others. Maternal sensitivity is the central feature that fosters secure attachment. Specifically, mothers who foster security are more responsive to their infants' cries, are more affectionate and tender, are more positive in affect, and interfere less often in their infants' ongoing behavior (Isabella & Belsky, 1991). Mothers who are overinvolved with their infants and who intrude too much into their infants' activities lead their infants to develop defenses whereby they shut down from within, demonstrating insecure–avoidant behavior that is a self-protecting strategy. On the other hand, mothers who are underinvolved— unresponsive, inconsistent, detached from the child—may cause insecure– resistant behavior, which includes ambivalence, anger, and frustration over the inability to connect with the mother.

Somewhere between 3 and 6 months of age, infants begin to show preference for significant others by directing more of their signaling behaviors toward them, such as eye contact, smiling, cooing and babbling, and so forth. By about 8 months, babies begin to show visible separation and stranger anxiety when separated from the primary attachment figure(s) and when in the presence of strangers. At the same time, babies seek proximity to attachment figures by crawling toward them, much as ducklings follow their mothers. These behaviors, though sometimes misunderstood by parents and other caregivers, are healthy manifestations of attachment to significant others. Most experts believe that secure attachments during infancy are essential for later social and emotional development, and that secure attachments of infants to parents are based upon prior secure bonding of parents to their infants, a process that is begun in the first minutes after birth: This original parent–infant tie is the major source for all the infant's subsequent attachments and is the formative relationship in the course of which the child develops a sense of himself. Throughout his lifetime the strength and character of this attachment will influence the quality of all future bonds to other individuals (Klaus & Kennell, 1982).

Klaus and Kennell (1982) noted that mothers under stress have more difficulty bonding to their infants, as do parents whose infants have obvious malformations. Delayed or diminished bonding by parents may delay or diminish the security of the infant's attachment to parents. Further, parents of infants with disabilities may be more at risk for either overinvolvement or underinvolvement with their infants, threatening the security of attachment. Infants with disabilities such as blindness or deafness or who have difficulty responding positively to caregivers' behavior (e.g., very premature infants or those prenatally exposed to drugs) may be in some jeopardy during this stage. For example, a hyperirritable infant may cry or turn away when his mother brings her face close or talks to him. He may give her a fleeting look and avert his gaze when she smiles. These infants may have difficulty developing a preference for the human world—an important outcome of attachment (Cook, Tessier, & Klein, 1996). According to Greenspan (1988), parents may need special assistance in learning how to "woo" their infants to ensure the attachment process. In addition, the extent to which health care professionals and others emphasize the normal aspects of a baby will have an impact on parents' expectations and subsequent behaviors.

Providing Infant Stimulation

Infants exhibit curiosity and active participation in learning experiences. They develop significant motor, social, and cognitive skills that have strong implications for healthy development throughout their lives. The kind of stimulation that parents provide during this period appears to be crucial for healthy development. Parents provide stimulation in two ways: by structuring the environment to facilitate sensorimotor activities and by interacting directly with their infants. It is primarily through the senses that infants take in information, and their subsequent actions on this information constitute the major vehicle for learning.

Infants prefer visual stimulation consisting of bright colors, light and dark contrasts (stripes, bull's-eye patterns, geometric shapes), objects that move, and contoured surfaces. By about 5 or 6 months of age, infants seem to prefer moderately discrepant or complex stimuli. The human face is a favorite object for attention because it moves, it talks, and it is contoured. Close face-to-face gazing and vocalizing provide an opportunity for significant visual, auditory, and even tactile stimulation. Frequent changes in position (from back to stomach, from crib to pallet, and from infant seat to swing) provide infants with different visual vantage points. Parents of blind babies must provide many experiences to stimulate their children's other senses. To develop communicative competence, parents can learn to respond to all of the child's attempts to communicate by using alternative signals such as verbal responses, soft touch, imitation of vocalizations, and talking about a variety of content outside the here and now, and by encouraging the child to use a variety of strategies to initiate social interactions (Erwin, 1994).

For auditory stimulation, vocalizing (imitating coos and babbles, talking, singing) is of utmost importance. The amount and type of language used in the home during the period of infancy has been shown to be a critical factor in the child's intellectual development. Exposure to all types of music, daily sounds indoors and outdoors, and reading to the baby all help to provide auditory stimulation. Hearing mothers may become discouraged and frustrated in their attempts to stimulate and interact with their deaf babies and subsequently diminish their efforts. Alternative communication systems and sensory experiences must be developed if the child's cognitive and social development are to proceed normally.

Of all types of sensory stimulation, tactile stimulation seems to be the most important for healthy development. Holding, cuddling, stroking, rocking, and movement have been shown to be essential. Other forms include massaging and bathing. Caregivers can provide these kinds of stimulation during feeding, changing, and other routine activities. Babies of all ages should be held when given a bottle. Toys with varied textures (soft, slick, flexible, rigid, fluffy) provide diverse tactile experiences. Mothers of infants with disabilities may at first be uncomfortable with some of these activities, fearful of harming their fragile children. Reassurance and support may be necessary in the beginning.

The period of infancy—one short year—is crucial for laying the foundation for healthy development. Parents must adapt to the transition to parenthood, establish a strong bond to their infants, provide nurturing caregiving, facilitate a sense of basic trust, contribute to a secure infant–parent attachment, and provide appropriate stimulation—a tall order for any parent. Parents of infants with disabilities also must adjust to having a child who is different from their dreams, and they must meet the special needs these children have. Many of these babies will be delayed in reaching major milestones, such as babbling, sitting alone, rolling over, walking, and saying words, and they may demonstrate infantlike behaviors for years to come. Some few may never demonstrate these behaviors. These parents have special challenges that require the support of family members, friends, health professionals, and early interventionists. A major role of support people is to help parents focus more on the normal aspects of development and behavior and focus less on the child's disabilities.

Toddlers

As children become mobile, the protector role of parents becomes more important. The once "helpless" baby is transformed into an active, tireless, and curious toddler. Tabletops, toilet bowls, faucets, magazines, pet food, electrical outlets, and a host of other things become fascinating. First-time parents (and grandparents who have forgotten) are astonished at the ingenuity toddlers employ to satisfy their curiosity. As protectors, parents must childproof the house and outdoor areas to provide the safest possible environment for toddlers exercising their growing autonomy and increased capacity for learning. Toddlers with disabilities may be especially vulnerable to safety hazards. However, despite parents' best attempts, the precocious toddler will find that one button under the carpet that she can swallow or climb up on the kitchen cabinet to obtain the aspirin bottle on the top shelf. This means that toddlers require the continual watchful eye of adults.

For many parents the transition from caregiver to protector is a difficult one. They are not prepared for the safety measures they must take, and many learn through unfortunate experiences. Accidental poisoning is one of the leading causes of death during the first 2 years of life. Further, caring for toddlers can be physically exhausting, leaving little energy for anything else. Finally, toddlers and older siblings may be in frequent conflict over territory. However, most of toddlers' behavior is a manifestation of their growing autonomy, a healthy stage of development.

Coping with Growing Autonomy

As Brazelton (1974) has said, the years from about 1 to 3 constitute a declaration of independence, and, according to Erikson (1963), they are the stage for developing healthy autonomy or unhealthy shame and doubt. The toddler takes pride in his new accomplishments of walking and climbing, opening and closing, dropping, pushing and pulling, and holding on and letting go. He wants to do everything for himself even though his desires exceed his skills. "Me do it" is a common phrase, and parents must have endless patience with toddlers' attempts to feed themselves, dress themselves, and take control of their toileting. Patient parents help children develop growing autonomy, and impatient inconsistent parents may breed shame and doubt. This stage may be particularly difficult for parents of a toddler with disabilities, especially since the child's delay in reaching major milestones makes the parents painfully aware of the differences between their child and other children of the same age. Further, unusual caregiving demands can be a significant source of stress for parents.

Toddlers' growing sense of autonomy often is coupled with open negativism. Saying "no" helps them to establish themselves as separate from their parents. Brazelton (1974) noted that negativism quickly becomes a first line of defense in order to stall for time—time for inner decision and evaluation. Most parents recognize that negativism is not a personal affront to their authority, and they learn that giving toddlers legitimate choices (the kind of juice to drink or the shirt to wear) helps them to feel independent. They also make it clear when the child does and does not have a choice by the kind of words they use (e.g., "It's bedtime now"). Finally, they avoid overusing the word "no" themselves, saving it for times it is necessary to protect the child.

Parents begin to set limits when their children become mobile, and limits must be clear and enforced consistently in a positive and loving manner. Too many or too few limits can interfere with healthy development. The most important limits relate to the child's own safety and well-being—she does not go into the street, she does not eat the pet food, she does not climb on objects that are not sturdy, and she does not touch hot objects. External control at this stage helps the child know how and when to control herself. Erikson (1963) believed that a lasting sense of good will and pride derives from a sense of self-control without loss of self-esteem. Contests of wills between parents and children can be minimized by making expectations simple, clear, and consistent. When children test these expectations, parents can assist cooperation by reinforcing verbal requests by physical contact (taking the child by the hand and leading him in the desired direction), modeling the expected behavior, and offering legitimate choices. Parents of toddlers with disabilities may be unsure about the balance between appropriate limits and encouraging independent behavior.

Toddlers everywhere have temper tantrums. The differences lie in the intensity and duration. Parents often unknowingly reinforce temper tantrums by paying attention to the child or giving in to her wishes. Neither approach is effective in reducing tantrum behavior. The most effective response is to ignore the behavior, but be sure the child does not hurt herself, others, or property. Children who continue tantrum behavior into the preschool period and beyond usually are those who have been given undue attention in response to the behavior or who have won the contest of wills with their parents by getting what they want.

Facilitating Self-Help Skills

Typically developing toddlers learn to do an amazing number of things for themselves. After they have begun to walk, they learn to feed themselves, drink from a cup instead of a breast or bottle, dress themselves, toilet themselves at appropriate times and places, and carry on conversations with adults and other children. Learning these skills takes time and parental patience. At first, parents and toddlers can share these routines, even if the job is done imperfectly. Providing finger food, toddler drinking cups, clothing that is easy to manipulate, and easy access to the toilet can save parents some frustration. Helping children with disabilities learn self-help skills can be a much more complex process, but mastery of these skills reduces the caregiving burden for parents. Using behavior modification techniques to facilitate learning of self-help skills has been shown to be effective for many children.

Toilet learning seems to be especially frustrating for parents and can serve as an area of significant conflict between parent and child. This conflict can be reduced if parents take their cues from the child, for example, by noting regularity in bowel movements and later in frequency of urination, helping the child understand that he has caused the wet or dirty diaper, and encouraging sufficient language skills to indicate a need to use the toilet. If parents are alert to the cues and provide encouragement rather than punishment, the process will progress smoothly. A positive, reinforcing, and patient attitude on the part of the parent will help the child to gain a sense of autonomy, whereas a critical, harsh, and impatient attitude will promote a sense of doubt and shame and a loss of self-esteem.

Fostering Social and Intellectual Learning

Besides self-help skills, there are four other areas of learning that are crucial for this stage of development: acquiring social skills, understanding language, developing curiosity, and forming the roots of intelligence. Exposure to peers for brief periods on a regular basis can help the toddler learn rudimentary social skills such as waiting one's turn, sharing toys, delaying gratification, and getting along in groups. Toddlers frequently treat their peers as objects rather than as people, especially in the beginning. "Me do it" and "No, mine" indicate the egocentric nature and social immaturity of toddlers. Therefore, demands to share and "be nice" usually are not helpful. Adults can use distraction, offer alternatives, and most importantly, model appropriate social behavior for the child.

Between 18 months and 3 years of age, the child learns nearly 900 words, and she understands more than she uses. The adult role in facilitating this rapid language development includes labeling familiar objects and events; expanding on the child's telegraphic speech; reinforcing language attempts; and modeling appropriate language. These techniques are particularly important for toddlers whose language is delayed. A child's language development is closely correlated with the quantity and quality of language used in the home. Even before the toddler has the language to ask questions, she demonstrates her curiosity by using her senses. Independent locomotion provides important cues about her expanded world and assists her in the formation of rudimentary concepts (Hamner & Turner, 1996).

Ample space for the child to explore, developmentally appropriate toys and materials, excursions to interesting places, and a variety of books stimulate the child's growing curiosity and intellectual development. Discovery learning is important at this stage, and the parent can provide the experiences and the environment to facilitate discovery, combined with physical and verbal interactions with children about their discoveries.

The toddler stage of development can be both frustrating and rewarding for parents. The growing drive toward autonomy challenges parents to find the delicate balance between encouragement, protection, and setting appropriate limits. This task can be particularly challenging for parents of toddlers with disabilities, especially if the child is severely delayed in reaching major milestones or if he places unusual caregiving demands on his parents.

Preschool Children

The chief role that parents assume when their children are preschoolers is that of nurturer. To nurture children is to provide affectionate care and attention, to educate, and to further their development. *Nurturance,* as a psychological process, refers to the satisfaction of emotional needs through words, actions, and physical touch (Bigner, 1989). While the preschool child's environment must remain safe and protective, he does not need the constant watchful eye of parents so necessary for a toddler. To discover the optimal amount of supervision without interference, assistance without indulgence, and warmth and love without suffocation is the challenge that parents face (Hamner & Turner, 1996).

Young children are loud, intrusive, and demanding of their parents' time, attention, and energy. Preschool children seem to alternate between behavioral extremes; that is, phases of cooperative compliant behavior alternate with phases of resistant negative behavior, coupled with emotional extremes of shyness and aggressiveness. These inconsistent behaviors puzzle many parents and often cause them to question their methods of discipline, which vacillate between freedom and control. If parents have not already agreed upon the goals and values they have for their children and their childrearing philosophies, it is crucial that they do so now. A major consideration is how to establish limits and achieve responsible behavior without threatening children's sense of initiative.

Developing Initiative

After the child has attained proficiency in walking and feeding himself, usually during the last part of the third year for typically developing children, he moves into the third stage of psychosocial development, initiative versus guilt (Erikson, 1963). Since most preschoolers no longer need to direct their attention to developing and controlling their bodies, they now focus on increasing participation in the social environment, which consists largely of the basic family unit but also includes other adults and peers to some extent. The child can initiate a variety of motor activities and play on his own and no longer merely responds to or imitates the actions of others. Using language and engaging in fantasy activities are paramount. Children who are given freedom, opportunity, and encouragement to experiment with motor play, to ask questions, and to engage in fantasy play activities will have their sense of initiative reinforced. At this age children are beginning to understand the difference between right and wrong and pleasing and displeasing their parents. If they think that their motor activities are dangerous, that their questions are a nuisance, and that their play is silly and a waste of time, they may develop a sense of guilt about self-initiated activities that can persist through later life stages.

Erikson (1963) noted the following about the stage of initiative:

> Where the child, now so ready to over-manipulate himself, can gradually develop a sense of moral responsibility, where he can gain some insight into the institutions, functions, and roles which will permit his responsible participation, he will find pleasurable accomplishment in wielding tools and weapons, in manipulating meaningful toys . . . and in caring for young children. (p. 256)

Children who are encouraged to explore their environment tend to become eager and carefree about initiating such exploration, whereas children who are overprotected from or punished for such exploration tend to become inhibited. If parents consistently are harsh, young children may develop strong guilt feelings and inhibitions, becoming very dependent and unable to take new initiatives without experiencing anxiety. An environment that encourages exploration has ample space, appropriate toys and equipment, props for fantasy play, and adults who respond to questions and extend children's play and learning. Children who resolve the conflict between initiative and guilt successfully will learn to control their behavior and respect social conventions and moral responsibilities.

Preschool children whose development is delayed or who have moderate to severe disabilities will not demonstrate the same signs of initiative as typically developing preschoolers. Erikson emphasized that children must develop basic trust before autonomy, and they must develop autonomy before initiative. While these stages of psychosocial development are invariant, the rate of psychosocial development varies considerably. Therefore, development is sequentially predictable, but each child develops at his own rate and in his own way.

Facilitating Play and Learning

Play is the major vehicle for learning during the early childhood years, and through play, young children learn in a way that no one can teach them. They learn about their physical world by touching, examining, testing, exploring, evaluating, and imagining. Raw materials (sand, water, dirt, clay) allow sensory experiences that are vital for the formation of basic concepts about their world that facilitate later academic learning. Toys for preschool children should be appropriate to the child's developmental level (challenging but not frustrating), versatile (suitable for a variety of creative uses such as blocks, Legos, etc.), durable (they outlast the child's desire to play with them), safe, aesthetically pleasing, and encouraging of active participation rather than passive observation. Common household items such as pots and pans, measuring spoons and cups, coffee cans filled with odds and ends, nesting cans, plastic bottles with screw-on caps, and blocks made from milk cartons or cigar boxes can offer stimulation and challenge equally as well as expensive educational toys. While toys and raw materials are important for play, the most important ingredient is one or more loving caring adults who are available to answer the child's questions, engage her in imagination and fantasy, introduce her to new words and ideas, and pick up on her cues of curiosity.

Some types of disabilities can inhibit certain types of play, but all preschoolers need the time, opportunity, and an appropriate environment in which to initiate play within their capabilities. Clearly, intervention activities such as speech therapy, physical therapy, and occupational therapy may be necessary to help children function at their maximum potential, but these activities can be presented in the context of play and should be balanced with child-initiated play, preferably in an inclusive context so that typically and atypically developing children can play with and learn from one another.

Developing a Healthy Self-Concept

Three assumptions can be made about self-concept. First, self-concept is learned; second, it is learned early within the socialization process of the family; and third, it is a powerful determinant of behavior. A sense of belonging and a feeling of worth are two aspects of self-concept that traditionally have been emphasized; a more recent framework includes a sense of competence as well, that is, the child's perceived behavioral competencies or his ability to interact successfully with his environment.

The groundwork for self-concept is laid during the period of infancy, and it takes the form of self-awareness that is both affective and cognitive; infants have experiences that help them learn that they are separate and distinct from their environment. The infant becomes increasingly successful in effecting changes in the environment and in the behavior of others. The preschool period seems to be a critical time for the validation of these early impressions that the child has with regard to herself.

Early researchers on self-concept (e.g., Coopersmith, 1967; Sears, 1970) determined that parental warmth, acceptance, and respect for the child, supported by a limit-setting democratic parenting style, resulted in children with high self-esteem, whereas a lack of affection, regard, and the use of severe punishment resulted in lower self-esteem. Parents of children with high self-esteem are attentive to their children, they structure the world of their children along the lines they believe to be appropriate, and they permit relatively great freedom within the structure they have established.

A more recent study (Menaghan & Parcel, 1991) found that mothers who have high self-esteem themselves seem to impart feelings of competence and self-worth to their children, partly by providing a strong home environment. Mothers who perceive that they control their own life chances (have an internal locus of control) consciously create stronger home environments than mothers who see life events, likely extending into household circumstances, as less within their control (have an external locus of control).

Abundant evidence supports the relationship between self-concept and behavior. Correlations between self-concept and achievement have been found as early as kindergarten, though this relationship becomes more prominent during the school-age years. In fact, an individual's chances for success increase as his self-esteem increases (Lefrancois, 1989). Preschool children with poor self-concepts may be overly cautious in attempting new tasks, fearing failure. They often appear anxious, defensive, and withdrawn. Their lack of confidence may result in unpopularity with their peers. During the preschool period, the child begins to judge his self-worth and competence partly on the basis of his competence with adults, but also with his peers.

Children with obvious differences from other children are particularly at risk for poor self-concepts, especially when their world broadens from the family into the larger community. Young children, and even adults, can respond to children who are different in ways that often seem cruel. Some parents are reluctant to take children with disabilities to public places for fear of stares or unkind comments. Further, when preschool children with disabilities begin to interact with their typically developing peers, their awareness of the differences is heightened. It is especially important, then, for parents to have realistic expectations about what their children can do and to help their children develop their sense of worth, belonging, and competence within that framework. All children need successful experiences to feel worthy and competent, and parents must identify and promote the child's strengths rather than overemphasizing his limitations.

Providing Guidance and Discipline

Every family with preschool children struggles with appropriate and effective guidance and discipline techniques. To many adults, discipline and punishment are synonymous. In reality a system of discipline implies a broad positive system of guidance, with particular methods of punishment being only a minor aspect of that system. Research has shown that punishment has limited value in consistently influencing rule-related behavior of children, and nonpunitive techniques have a greater impact on children who have mastered language (Toner, 1986).

Parents seem to be concerned primarily about the degree and type of external control they should have over their children. Thirty years ago Diana Baumrind (1966) described three parental prototypes of control, still applicable today: permissive, authoritative, and authoritarian. Permissive parents avoid exercising any control over their children, are nonpunitive, do not value obedience, use reason rather than power or manipulation, and exert few demands on children. Authoritarian parents, on the other hand, use absolute standards of conduct, value obedience, restrict autonomy and the child's self-will, and use punitive forceful measures to control the child. Baumrind's research, and that of others since, has found that authoritarian parents produce children who are aggressive and hostile, and permissive parents produce children who have no framework for developing self-discipline and few guidelines for making decisions.

Authoritative discipline falls somewhere in between these two extremes, balancing warmth and control. These parents are nurturant; they use reason and explanations for required behavior; they set and maintain reasonable limits with appropriate levels of control; they provide a balance between the values of autonomy and conformity; and they often use inductive techniques— that is, they focus on encouraging children to take into account the potential effects of their behavior on other people and on themselves, stressing the "how" rather than the "what" of behavior. Children of authoritative parents have been found to have more positive interactions with peers and siblings (socioemotional competence) and to demonstrate positive outcomes in almost every area of behavior and development.

Authoritative parents seek alternatives to punishment, often in the form of natural or logical consequences. Natural consequences are those that occur naturally from the behavior; for example, a child who refuses to eat at mealtime does not get food until the next snack or meal. Logical consequences are those that are assigned by the parent to express the reality of the social order, not of the person; for example, a child who is disturbing the rest of the family at mealtime is given the choice to settle down or to leave the table and eat alone. This approach holds children, not their parents, responsible for children's behavior; it allows children to make their own decisions about what courses of action are appropriate; and it permits children to learn from the (impersonal) natural or social order of events rather than forcing them to comply with the wishes of others (Dinkmeyer & McKay, 1989).

Authoritative discipline fosters the development of all children—those developing typically and those developing atypically. All children need reasonable limits, with considerable freedom within those limits to grow and develop. The developmental level of the child should be taken into account when limits are established. For example, children must have sufficient cognitive ability to understand the use of natural and logical consequences. Further, children with some types of disabilities may need a different combination of limits than their typically developing peers. While the strategies remain the same, then, the particulars are unique to each child.

The preschool period represents a time of growing initiative, a time of continual play and exploration, a time when the foundation for a healthy self-concept is built, and a time when childrearing patterns and techniques are established. It also represents a time when most children broaden their experiences into the larger community. For most parents, it represents a time when they can decrease their caregiving, protection, and supervision activities. For parents of most atypical children, it also represents a time when they are obtaining special educational services for their children and establishing working relationships with a variety of health and education professionals.

Parents and Older Children

School-Age Children

The transition of a child from total physical and psychological dependency to self-sufficiency and independence occurs gradually. Starting school, however, is an early major step in the process. Patterns of parent–child interaction established during the early years continue to influence children as they progress in school. The general pattern of stabilization that occurs during the school years makes this period critical. From observations of typically developing children during middle childhood, one can predict with moderate accuracy what the young adult will be like. Personality develops during the school-age years in important ways, and personality attributes stabilize into something similar to their adult form somewhere between the ages of 6 and 10. A wide range of competencies develops rapidly. Middle childhood, then, is a period of active development involving expansion and integration of social, emotional, and cognitive phenomena (Bryant, 1985).

While school-age children continue to need nurturance from their parents, the role of encourager becomes paramount. Continual exposure to adults and children outside the family offers children alternative sources of rewards and evaluations—while simultaneously adding pressure that may increase anxiety due to the evaluative relationship that develops among children, teachers, and peers (Santrock, 1989). Most children must develop, then, a system for coping with occasional incompetencies, failures, and rejection by friends. Encouragement by parents is crucial in helping children cope with these situations successfully, and encouragement appears to be the most corrective influence on behavior during this period. Children whose physical or cognitive skills are limited, or who have difficulty learning are especially in need of encouragement from parents and teachers. As conformity to peers increases, antisocial behavior of children also increases, especially between the third and ninth grades, and parents face new challenges in relating positively to their children.

Developing a Sense of Industry

Erikson (1963) described the school-age years as crucial for developing a sense of industry rather than inferiority. Most school-age children show unceasing energy toward investing all possible efforts in producing, but fears of inferiority emerge when they try to overcome by diligently engaging in opportunities to learn by doing. A new concern with how things are made, how they work, and what they do predominates. It is the age of collections, long-term projects, and "making a mess." Children feel a strong need for a sense of accomplishment, and acceptance by peers is critical for ego development. The sense of competence is the sense of being capable and able to do meaningful tasks. When children's efforts meet with success, when they receive support and approval from parents and teachers, then they develop a sense of industry; but repeated experiences of failure and disapproval evoke a sense of inferiority.

Erikson believed that many of the attitudes toward work and work habits that are exhibited later in life are formed during this period. Therefore, adults need to provide many opportunities for success in a variety of work experiences. Both home and school should teach positive work habits: doing one's best, setting appropriate standards for work attempted, and so on.

Elkind (1970) noted that children developing typically at this stage become capable of deductive reasoning and of playing and learning by rules. They begin to compare their own homes with those of their peers. The assumption that parents are not very bright may emerge at this time, especially when children are able to catch adults in errors of reasoning or fact.

Developing Self-Concept

By the school-age years, most children have clearer perceptions of parental attitudes and behavior. The child's view of the quality of the parent–child relationship, especially with the parent of the same sex, seems to be associated with high self-esteem. However, the child's perception of parental attitudes and behaviors is more influential in determining self-esteem than actual parental attitudes and beliefs. The school-age child's sense of self is very much a reflection of the success of his interactions with others, especially his parents. Other factors relating to self-concept are body image (perceived physical appearance), anxiety level, competence (especially academic), peer acceptance, and family constellation.

Significant research evidence supports the fact that positive self-concept is related to high academic achievement during the school-age years (e.g., Chapman, Lambourne, & Silva, 1990; Mufson, 1989). Low self-concept and low academic achievement interact and feed back negatively on each other. Self-concept seems to drop as children enter school because of the increased sources of evaluation by teachers and peers, but by fifth grade the trend is again upward. It is important to note that the child herself plays a role in others' views of her. Children behave in ways consistent with the ways they see themselves. If a child feels she is worthless, she will expect others to treat her as worthless. In general, as children get older they are increasingly capable of more objective self-evaluation, and a larger percentage of rewards become self-rewards. Parents must help children to identify their strengths and to reward themselves for those while minimizing negative evaluations of weaknesses.

School-age children with disabilities are especially vulnerable to experiences that threaten their self-concepts. The degree of vulnerability depends on their view of themselves when they enter school, the type and degree of disability, and, of course, the responses of the people around them. Children with learning disabilities, for example—the largest group of children receiving special education services—appear to be perfectly normal and often are perceived by their parents and teachers as lazy, stubborn, or unmotivated. Parents may attempt to push these children beyond their capabilities. Unfortunately, many children with learning disabilities develop emotional or behavioral disorders, partly because their learning problems have led to repeated experiences of failure, coupled with rejection by parents, teachers, and peers. Regardless of the type and degree of disability, children with special needs profit from parents who have realistic expectations of them, who provide opportunities for many successful experiences, who are warm and support-ive, who focus on the child's total development, and who are not intrusive and overprotective.

Providing Guidance and Discipline

Authoritative discipline and inductive techniques continue to produce the best results during the school-age period. The use of reasoning to help chil-dren to take the perspective of others is associated with gains in children's empathy and prosocial behaviors such as comforting, sharing, and helping. On the other hand, parental demands for children to control their own feel-ings and emotional displays are likely to lead to anxiety and hidden feelings (Eisenberg et al., 1992). Authoritative discipline tends to foster in children what has been called instrumental competence, including the attributes of social responsibility, independence, achievement orientation, vigor, objectivity, and self-control. Social approval and disapproval, as well as inductive disci-pline methods, facilitate role taking and the child's ability to make inferences about how others feel.

Years ago, Haim Ginott (1969) described discipline techniques that are self-defeating for parents, and these still apply today. They include threats (invitations to repeat a forbidden act only challenge the child's autonomy), bribes (they seldom inspire the child toward continual efforts), promises (may build up unrealistic expectations, as they do not account for situational factors), sarcasm (invites counterattacks), and provoking lies (the child feels he is not allowed to tell the truth for fear of punishment). Ginott fur-ther emphasized that limits should tell the child clearly what constitutes acceptable conduct and what substitute will be accepted. Limits imposed without violence or excessive anger preserve the self-respect of both the par-ent and the child.

Providing Activities for Learning

School-age children learn in the structured environment of the school, in the home, and through out-of-home activities. Play continues to be important during these years because it provides children with situations in which they can test themselves, work out feelings, experiment with roles, learn rules and expectations, and develop and practice skills that will be important for adult life in society. Many of these goals are achieved by play involving peers or by team efforts. Peers provide children with effective models of how to behave among other children, and they reinforce one another. Through group modeling and reinforcement, group norms are established. Children with disabilities need to be involved with peers who are developing both typically and atypically. However, activities that are overly competitive should be avoided.

Both planned and spontaneous family activities provide valuable learning experiences for school-age children, for example, picnics, camping, vacations, cultural events, sports events, parks, and even shopping. Organized activities must be planned with the interests of each family member in mind. Other spontaneous activities are equally important, for example, games, hobbies, family projects, reading together, and family conversations. These often yield the fondest memories for children. There is "math" in the bathroom and "science" in the sink, and parents who take advantage of these opportunities stimulate home learning for their children.

It is essential that parents and teachers establish a partnership relationship if children are to receive maximum benefit from school. This partnership is especially crucial for children with disabilities so that parents can be full participants in planning an appropriate educational environment for their children. Parents are the first and most important teachers of their children, and the information they hold about their children cannot be duplicated by teachers or other professionals. By working together as partners, realistic expectations can be determined and an individualized plan of action initiated (Hamner & Turner, 1996).

Even though less is written about school-age children than about very young children and adolescents, and growth and development slow down during the school-age years, many important events occur, and parents continue to play a crucial role with their children. Having a child go to school for the first time can be a difficult event for all parents, but especially for parents of children with disabilities as they worry about whether the child will receive the kind of services she needs and will make new friends. Helping children achieve a sense of industry and pride in their accomplishments is another challenge for parents, especially those with children of limited abilities. Fostering a healthy self-concept, using effective guidance and discipline techniques, and providing appropriate learning experiences are other important tasks for parents of school-age children.

Adolescents

It is impossible within the scope of this chapter to address adequately the relationships between parents and their teenagers. Therefore, only a few general issues will be included. Many parents in Western society dread their children's approaching adolescence; at best they experience some degree of confusion about parenting an individual who is neither a child nor an adult. Because of the biological, cognitive, and psychosocial changes that occur in adolescence and because of the rapid social changes occurring in our society, the concept of a generation gap between parents and teenagers is widespread. However, research over the past decade has challenged the view of adolescence as a time of storm and stress (Gecas & Seff, 1991). In fact, many adolescents feel respect and fondness for their parents, talk openly with them about concerns and problems, have similar values as their parents, and seek guidance from them on important life decisions (Richardson, Abramowitz, Asp, & Petersen, 1986; Sebald, 1986).

Physical and hormonal changes that occur at puberty often affect adolescent behavior, and significant changes in cognitive development can lead to behavior that is misunderstood by parents. Because of these multiple changes, parents must shift their interactional styles and assume the primary role of counselor to their children. An already established positive communication system between parent and child is perhaps the single most important ingredient in this relationship. By the time children reach adolescence, the communication system in the family already can be described as open or closed, determining how comfortable the teenager will feel in discussing her concerns and problems with her parents. Teenagers generally are more sensitive to parental criticism, less communicative, and more reserved and reclusive than younger children (Small & Eastman, 1991).

Developing a Sense of Identity

The fifth and most important stage in Erikson's (1963) theory of psychosocial development is identity versus role confusion during the period of adolescence. Erikson noted that adolescents experience new feelings, sensations, and desires as they mature physiologically and develop a multitude of ways of looking at and thinking about the world as they mature mentally. In their crucial search for identity formation, adolescents can be described as impatient idealists who believe that there is little difficulty in realizing an imagined ideal. They become capable of constructing theories and philosophies designed to bring the varied and conflicting aspects of society into a harmonious whole.

In seeking ego identity, the adolescent's mind has a certain recognizable quality or character all its own but in a certain measure can be shared thoroughly with others. Adolescence can be seen as a time when all the crises of the previous stages are relived, and those of future stages are rehearsed. In Erikson's view, adolescence is a socially authorized delay of adulthood in which the individual has time to integrate himself into that future role. Identity strivings may result in experiments with nonconforming roles, membership in "cliques," diverse ideologies, or faddish signs and styles that mark one as an "in-grouper." Sexual identity is rehearsed and tested during periods of courtship. The final task for the adolescent is to bring together all the things he has learned about himself and to integrate all the images into a coherent whole that links his past with the future. Identity, then, includes focus on work, sex-role identity and sexuality, and ideology. Failure to achieve a sense of personal identity results in role confusion, which has been associated with severe emotional upheavals and delinquency.

A broad body of research supports the notion that positive family relations (e.g., those high in parental support, communication, involvement, and inductive control) facilitate the development of ego identity in adolescence (Gecas & Seff, 1991), producing independent and self-directed individuals. However, when rapid social and technological changes occur that affect traditional values, adolescents may have difficulty finding continuity between what they have learned and experienced as children and what they are experiencing as adolescents. The search for causes may result in activism, cultism, or even gang affiliation (Hamner & Turner, 1996).

Establishing healthy ego identity may be more complex for teenagers with disabilities. At the secondary level, these adolescents, like all others, must be prepared for adult responsibilities, independence, and employment or continued education. However, studies of what happens to students with disabilities during and after their high school years suggest that a higher percentage of them, compared to students without disabilities, drop out of school, experience great difficulty in finding and holding a job, do not find work suited to their capabilities, do not receive further training or education, or become dependent on their families or public assistance. Teachers of students with mild disabilities are continually faced with the decision of how much to stress academics (e.g., college preparatory courses) versus vocational training. Some experts believe that many adolescents with learning disabilities are written off as academic failures who can never achieve at the postsecondary level and therefore are offered a curriculum that makes few academic demands on them (Hallahan & Kauffman, 1994).

These conditions, coupled with chronic academic failure, can have a profound impact on how the teenager views himself and what he is able to do. McLoughlin, Clark, Mauck, and Petrosko (1987) found that parents perceived greater adverse effects of learning disability in all academic and cognitive areas than adolescents with learning disabilities themselves perceived. Adolescents rated their academic, social, and vocational or career skills as similar to those of most people, but parents rated their performance as lower, especially in reading, writing, school content areas, and socialization. This discrepancy in perception, too, could affect ego identity.

Assessing Parent and Peer Influence

Because of the adolescent's desire to establish a sense of identity and increasing degrees of independence, peers exert considerable influence. Research has found that teenagers want to be attuned to the standards of their peers in the specifics of their social lives, for example, dress, dating, social events, extracurricular activities, and drinking. However, in matters of finances, education, and career plans, they seek advice and counsel from their parents. In areas of sexuality, substance use, and gang activity, peers are extremely influential. Parental support is very important at this stage of development, relating positively to cognitive development, conformity to adult standards, moral behavior, internal locus of control, self-esteem, instrumental competence, and academic achievement. Lack of parental support is related to negative socialization outcomes for teenagers, such as low self-esteem, delinquency, drug abuse, and other problem behaviors.

Equally important as support is control, but different types of control have different outcomes. Authoritarian or coercive control (threats, force, physical punishment) has negative consequences, whereas authoritative or inductive control has positive outcomes. Failure to distinguish between these two types of control has caused parents to be confused and inconsistent. Much of the conflict and stress of parent–adolescent interactions revolves around the issue of control. Parents have more influence over adolescents when they express a high level of support and exercise inductive control (Gecas & Seff, 1991). It appears, then, that both peers and parents are important for adolescent identity and socialization, though they play vastly different roles. It is interesting to note that McLoughlin et al. (1987) found that adolescents with learning disabilities in their study reported having many friends, but their parents reported that they had few friends. Once again, there is a discrepancy between parents' and children's perceptions. Peers play such a crucial role in adolescent development that parents may need to make extra effort to encourage positive peer interaction between their children with disabilities and other teenagers.

Four major functions of families with adolescents were identified by Small and Eastman (1991). They are as follows:

1. *Meeting basic needs.* Providing a secure place to live, adequate food and nutrition, clothing, and access to health and mental health services and education.

2. *Protecting adolescents.* Monitoring and teaching self-protection skills as teens take on new responsibilities and as they become exposed to a wider range of influences and potential dangers.

3. *Guiding and supporting development.* Facilitating development in the following areas: social, emotional, cognitive, physical, moral, spiritual, sexual, cultural, and educational, through an appropriate balance of support and control, positive communication, reinforcement and appropriate sanctions, and healthy resolutions to conflict.

4. *Advocacy.* Collaborating with other individuals, groups, and institutions that help socialize teenagers.

Anticipating Parent–Adolescent Conflict

The degree of conflict between parents and their teenagers varies from culture to culture and from family to family. Culturally, conflict is greater in periods of rapid social change; similarly, conflict is greater when there is a high degree of parental power and authority. Other factors that contribute to conflict include expression of sexuality or the postponement of sexual expression, experimentation with alcohol and drugs, confusion about the adolescent's economic role, increasing independence from the family and yielding to peer pressure, the failure of schools to meet the adolescent's needs, pressure to choose a life occupation, and discord between parents or dysfunctional parental behavior (Hamner & Turner, 1996).

Parental interest and involvement in the adolescent's activities, but not intrusion, seem crucial in preventing and resolving conflict. Some parental attitudes and behaviors that demonstrate interest and involvement are knowing the names of the teen's friends; being interested in where they go and what they do; welcoming friends into the home; participating appropriately in school and athletic events; and showing tolerance for contemporary styles of dress, music, and harmless teen activities. Parents can reduce conflict by being warm, accepting, nurturant, supportive, and autonomy-granting. Attempts to exert more power when conflict occurs are usually counterproductive. Joint decision making and showing respect for the opinions of teenagers is more beneficial.

Resolving Parent–Teen Issues

Most parents of teens today are concerned with a variety of issues, which include but are not limited to expression of sexuality, substance use, gangs, violence, school failure and dropout, and delinquency. Many agree that it is harder to raise teenagers today than in the past because of increasing negative societal influences. These influences, coupled with less time available for most parents to monitor and supervise their teenagers' activities, leads to a sense of dread for this stage in the family life cycle. Many variables affect the teen's participation in activities that are unacceptable to their parents: peer pressure, academic performance, parental communication and support, risk-taking attitudes, self-esteem, societal attitudes, and personality characteristics of the teen herself. Most often these variables interact in complex ways to affect adolescent behavior.

Teenagers with disabilities are not immune to the influences described above, and some may be uniquely vulnerable. For example, a teenager with mental retardation will experience the same sexual urgings at puberty but lack the full understanding of their meaning and acceptable ways to express them. A teenager with learning disabilities whose self-esteem is fragile may bow to peer influence related to experimentation with drugs in order to be accepted as a member of the group. Teenagers with mental retardation or learning disabilities may be especially likely to drop out of school and become involved in delinquent activities if they can find nothing productive to do. Therefore, while parents of all adolescents can profit from some form of attending education and support, parents of teenagers with disabilities are in critical need of these experiences, whether in the form of attending support groups, developing skills in behavior management, or focusing on positive communication.

Another major issue for parents of adolescents with disabilities and the schools is planning for the transition for their children from secondary school to employment. In the Individuals with Disabilities Education Act of 1990, the federal government mandated transition services for all students with disabilities. The services include a coordinated set of activities that promotes movement from school to postschool activities (e.g., postsecondary education, vocational training, integrated employment, continuing adult education, adult services, independent living, or community participation). Beginning no later than age 16, each student's Individualized Education Program (IEP) must contain a statement of needed transition services and a statement of the linkages or responsibilities of each participating agency before the student leaves the school setting. Nevertheless, transition to adult life is difficult for all adolescents, and especially so for adolescents with disabilities. Implementation of the federal law has met with some obstacles, such as continuing debate over the importance of academics versus vocational preparation. The challenge is to provide the special assistance needed by adolescents and young adults with disabilities that will help them achieve the most rewarding, productive, independent, and integrated adult life as possible (Hallahan & Kauffman, 1994). Partnerships between parents, youth, the schools, and community agencies are essential for meeting this challenge.

Developmental Needs of Parents

Erikson (1963) described the seventh stage in his theory of psychosocial development as generativity versus self-absorption. Generativity is defined as the interest in establishing and guiding the next generation, or a sense of caring for others or becoming involved with creative production. Erikson believed that adults are "triggered" by physical, psychological, and social stimuli to develop this sense, and the parenting role is one of the major vehicles for expressing it. When children are born, they have a need to be loved and protected, and most parents have a reciprocal need to be needed. As the child grows and matures, his needs change, and those of his parents change, too. If we accept Erikson's framework, individuals continue to develop throughout their lives, and at each stage of development, they have needs.

Most parents try to mesh their needs with those of their children, and they are more or less successful at this attempt. However, some parents ignore their own needs continually in order to meet those of their children. For example, when children are young, they are loud and intrusive, and parents need time alone in order to invest in the spousal relationship. Ignoring these needs may damage the marital relationship and, in turn, negatively affect the parent–child relationship. Further, many parents face the challenge of balancing their personal needs, their family's needs, and their career or occupational needs. Continuous priority given to any one of these has a negative impact, but at one time or another, each one takes priority—the balance is delicate. Finally, when children are adolescents, most parents are at the midpoint in their lives, a time that may be as crucial as adolescence itself, quite apart from the fact that they are parents of teenagers. This stage has been referred to as "middlescence," the "deadline decade," or the midlife crisis. It often is, then, a time in which both men and women take a serious look at what they are and what they want to be—the gap between the real and ideal self. In fact, parents may experience a kind of identity crisis themselves at nearly the same time their teenagers are searching for a sense of identity (Hamner & Turner, 1996).

For parents of children with disabilities, these normal developmental needs are compounded by the long-term care of children. This responsibility results in increased financial costs, caregiving burdens, and restrictions on family lifestyle and career opportunities, conditions that often lead to increased stress and poor psychological functioning. It is especially crucial, then, that these families have special support and resources, as well as opportunities for respite care, if they are to balance their own and their children's developmental needs. For too long, experts have focused on the unidirectional nature of parenting: that is, parents providing for the developmental needs of their children. If parents do not find appropriate ways to meet their own needs, the quality of their parenting deteriorates.

Summary

Parenting is a reciprocal developmental process. The parent begins in the role caregiver, and changes to a new role at each stage of the child's development: protector during toddlerhood, nurturer during the preschool period, encourager during the school-age years, and counselor during adolescence. The parents adapt their roles to fit the developmental needs of children. However, some important aspects of parenting should remain the same throughout the child's life, and these have a profound positive influence on developmental outcomes. They include warmth and support, reasoning and explanation, reasonable limits and inductive control, and a balance between autonomy and conformity. The converse of these behaviors has a profound negative influence on developmental outcomes: power-assertive and coercive techniques, punitive control, restrictions on autonomy and self will, and absolute standards of conduct. The child himself also influences parental behavior and developmental outcomes. The goodness of fit between children's and parents' temperament, personality characteristics, and responsivity can enhance or impede parent–child relationships.

Children with disabilities experience developmental needs similar to those of children who are developing typically, though the timing of these needs varies. In addition, they have special needs that relate to the specific type of disability. Their parents, too, experience developmental needs similar to those of other parents, but they are especially vulnerable to increased levels of stress related to family resources, family life events, family cohesion, family support, severity of the child's disability, and family constellation (Innocenti, Huh, & Boyce, 1992). However, there is no evidence that suggests that these families are dysfunctional or pathological. Rather, it is safe to assume that all parents experience certain levels of stress, and providing services and supports to mediate stress is crucial.

References

Baumrind, D. (1966). Effects of authoritative parental control on child behavior. *Child Development, 37*(4), 887–907.

Belsky, J., & Rovine, M. (1990). Patterns of marital change across the transition to parenthood: Pregnancy to three years postpartum. *Journal of Marriage and the Family, 52*(1), 5–19.

Belsky, J., Youngblade, L., Rovine, M., & Volling, B, (1991). Patterns of marital change and parent–child interaction. *Journal of Marriage and the Family, 53*(2), 487–498.

Bigner, J. (1989). *Parent–child relations* (3rd ed.). New York: Macmillan.

Brazelton, T. B. (1974). *Toddlers and parents: A declaration of independence.* New York: Dell.

Bryant, B. (1985). The neighborhood walk: Sources of support in middle childhood. *Monographs of the Society for Research in Child Development, 50*(3), 1–122.

Chapman, J., Lambourne, R., & Silva, P. (1990). Some antecedents of academic self-concept: A longitudinal study. *British Journal of Educational Psychology, 60,* 142–152.

Cook, R., Tessier, A., & Klein, M. D. (1996). *Adapting early childhood curricula for children in inclusive settings.* Englewood Cliffs, NJ: Prentice Hall.

Coopersmith, S. (1967). *The antecedents of self esteem.* San Francisco: Freeman.

Dinkmeyer, D., & McKay, G. (1989). *The parents' handbook* (A part of the complete STEP program). Circle Pines, MN: American Guidance.

Eisenberg, N., Fabes, R., Carlo, G., Troyer, D., Speer, A., Karbon, M., & Switzer, G. (1992). The relations of maternal practices and characteristics to children's vicarious emotional responsiveness. *Child Development, 63*(3), 583–602.

Elkind, D. (1970, April 5). Erikson's eight ages of man. *New York Times Magazine,* pp. 25–28.

Erikson, E. (1963). *Childhood and society.* New York: Norton.

Erwin, E. (1994). Social competence in young children with visual impairments. *Infants and Young Children, 6*(3), 26–33.

Gath, A. (1993). Changes that occur in families as children with intellectual disability grow up. *International Journal of Disability, Development and Education, 40*(3), 167–174.

Gecas, V., & Seff, M. (1991). Families and adolescents: A review of the 1980s. In A. Booth (Ed.), *Contemporary families: Looking forward, looking back* (pp. 208–225). Minneapolis: National Council on Family Relationships.

Ginott, H. (1969). *Between parent and teenager.* New York: Macmillan.

Goetting, A. (1986). Parental satisfaction. *Journal of Family Issues, 7*(1), 83–109.

Greenspan, S. (1988, September). Fostering emotional and social development in infants with disabilities. *Zero to Three, 9*(1), 8–18.

Hallahan, D., & Kauffman, J. (1994). *Exceptional children: Introduction to special education* (6th ed.). Needham Heights, MA: Simon & Schuster.

Hamner, T., & Turner, P. (1996). *Parenting in contemporary society* (3rd ed.). Needham Heights, MA: Allyn & Bacon.

Individuals with Disabilities Education Act of 1990, 20 U.S.C. § 1400 *et seq.*

Innocenti, M., Huh, K., & Boyce, G. (1992). Families of children with disabilities: Normative data and other considerations on parenting stress. *TECSE, 12*(3), 403–427.

Isabella, R., & Belsky, J. (1991). International synchrony and the origins of infant–mother attachment: A replication study. *Child Development, 62*(2), 373–384.

Kalmuss, D., Davidson, A., & Cushman, L. (1992). Parenting expectations, experiences, and adjustment to parenthood: A test of the violated expectations framework. *Journal of Marriage and the Family, 54*(3), 515–526.

Klaus, M., & Kennell, J. (1982). *Parent–infant bonding.* St. Louis: Mosby.

Lefrancois, G. (1989). *Of children: An introduction to child development.* Belmont, CA: Wadsworth.

MacDermid, S., Huston, T., & McHale, S. (1990). Changes in marriage associated with the transition to parenthood: Individual differences as a function of sex-role attitudes and changes in the division of household labor. *Journal of Marriage and the Family, 52*(2), 475–486.

McLoughlin, J., Clark, F., Mauck, A., & Petrosko, J. (1987). A comparison of parent–child perceptions of student learning disabilities. *Journal of Learning Disabilities, 20*(6), 357–360.

Menaghan, E., & Parcel, T. (1991). Determining children's home environment: The impact of maternal characteristics and current occupational and family conditions. *Journal of Marriage and the Family, 53*(2), 417–431.

Moses, K. (1983). The impact of initial diagnosis: Mobilizing family resources. In J. Mulick & S. Pueschel (Eds.), *Parent–professional partnerships in developmental disabilities services* (pp. 11–34). Cambridge, MA: Academic Guild.

Mufson, L. (1989). Factors associated with under-achievement in seventh-grade children. *Journal of Educational Research, 83*(1), 5–10.

Richardson, R., Abramowitz, R., Asp, C., & Petersen, A. (1986). Parent–child relationships in early adolescence: Effects of family structure. *Journal of Marriage and the Family, 48*(4), 805–812.

Santrock, J. (1989). *Lifespan development* (3rd ed.). Dubuque, IA: Brown.

Sears, R. (1970). Relation of early socialization experiences to self-concepts and gender role in middle childhood. *Child Development, 41,* 267–289.

Sebald, H. (1986). Adolescents' shifting orientation toward parents and peers. *Journal of Marriage and the Family, 48*(1), 5–13.

Small, S., & Eastman, G. (1991). Rearing adolescents in contemporary society: A conceptual framework for understanding the responsibilities and needs of parents. *Family Relations, 40,* 455–462.

Thomas, A., & Chess, S. (1977). *Temperament and development.* New York: Brunner/Mazel.

Toner, I. (1986). Punitive and non-punitive discipline and subsequent rule-following in young children. *Child Care Quarterly, 15*(1), 27–37.

Ventura, J. (1987). The stresses of parenthood reexamined. *Family Relations 36*(1), 26–29.

Wallace, P., & Gotlib, I. (1990). Marital adjustment during the transition to parenthood: Stability and predictors of change. *Journal of Marriage and the Family, 52*(1), 21–29.

Wilkie, C., & Ames, E. (1986). The relationship of infant crying to parental stress in the transition to parenthood. *Journal of Marriage and the Family, 48*(3), 545–550.

Educational
and Intervention
Considerations

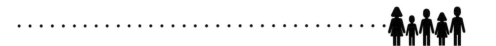

Multicultural Issues Related to Families of Children with Disabilities

7

Vivian I. Correa and Hazel Jones

Involving families in the education of their children has become a major goal for professionals working with students who have disabilities. The reauthorization of the Individuals with Disabilities Education Act (IDEA) in 1997 supported a greater role for families in all facets of their children's education including participation in assessment and Individualized Education Plan (IEP) development, parent training, community parent resource centers, and membership on state improvement planning committees. Furthermore, Part C of IDEA (was Part H), the infants and toddlers programs for children birth to age 3 with disabilities, required a family-centered approach to the development of the Individual Family Service Plan (IFSP). The benefits associated with involving families in planning and implementing interventions have been documented by many researchers (Kroth, 1997; Turnbull & Turnbull, 1997). But with the greater numbers of culturally and linguistically diverse students entering mainstream school programs in the United States and the growing numbers of children of low socioeconomic status (SES), professionals need to reassess their responsibilities and update their skills in order to involve families successfully. The families' cultural and ethnic backgrounds contribute significantly to how they conceptualize, understand, and react to having a child with a disability. Professionals must come to understand the family's (a) needs and social supports necessary for coping with the child with disabilities, (b) willingness to acknowledge the disability and seek appropriate treatment, and (c) perception of and response to agencies and mental health professionals.

The purpose of this chapter is to present a model for developing culturally sensitive home–school partnerships among culturally diverse families of children with disabilities and mental health and special education personnel. The first part of the chapter will examine the cultural characteristics of families. It will cover (a) modern changes in demographics, (b) importance of cultural sensitivity in special education, (c) labels and stereotypes, (d) cultural attributes sometimes associated with various ethnic groups, and (e) the changing role of school professionals in meeting the needs of culturally diverse children and encouraging family involvement in school. The second part of the chapter will provide a step-by-step model that can guide professionals in developing effective special education partnerships with culturally diverse families.

Cultural Characteristics of Families

Changes in U.S. Demographics

There is a growing need for professionals who can work effectively with families from culturally and linguistically diverse backgrounds, as the number of these families continues to increase. Recently published studies of U.S. demographics project that populations of minorities will continue to grow from 1995 to 2005, while the white population will decrease by 3%. The largest increase will be in Hispanic and Asian or Pacific Islander populations (30% and 39%, respectively) (Annie E. Casey Foundation, 1997). Immigrants seeking economic betterment continue to cross the Rio Grande. Many native-born Mexican American families as well as families from some other Hispanic backgrounds are poorer than and have birth rates higher than the U.S. average. The percentage of teenage mothers is also higher among some Hispanic groups, and infants born to these mothers are often at risk for medical and educational problems. Asian populations also continue to immigrate to the United States. Some Asian groups such as the Hmongs from Cambodia bring with them two difficulties: stresses due to war experiences and educational problems due to being from a nonliterate background.

Hodgkinson (1992) projected that by the year 2010, approximately one third of the country's youth will live in four states (New York, Florida, Texas, and California), and more than half of these young people will be "minorities," as we currently define the term. However, the true minority in these states will be non-Hispanic white youth. He further estimated that the majority of high school graduates in North Carolina, South Carolina, Georgia, Florida, Alabama, Mississippi, Louisiana, Texas, New Mexico, Arizona, and California will likewise be the traditionally defined minority students. Unquestionably, professionals who can work effectively with culturally diverse students and their families will be greatly needed. Already, within the public schools the need for personnel who can work with students who have disabilities and are from culturally and linguistically varied backgrounds is becoming monumental.

Importance of Cultural Sensitivity in Special Education

Culture is defined as factors that shape one's sense of group identity: race, ethnicity, religion, geographical locations, income status, gender, and occupations (Turnbull, Turnbull, Shank, & Leal, 1995, p. 8). Culture has an impact on all aspects of family life, including child development, childrearing practices, religiosity, and beliefs about education and disabilities.

Special education professionals provide intervention programs that are responsive to the needs and concerns expressed by families. However, if parents and professionals come from diverse cultural backgrounds and SES, they may differ in their views about educational services and interventions (DeGangi, Wietlisbach, Poisson, & Stein, 1994). For example, mental health professionals who work with children and youth with serious emotional disturbances have expressed concern about meeting the needs of the increasing number of culturally diverse children referred for consultation. In a workshop of the Child and Adolescent Service System Program of the National Institute for Mental Health, professionals delineated stresses that have an impact on the mental health of culturally diverse youth in school systems:

- social environment in which the natural, familiar helping and support systems of cultural groups are not used by professionals;

- poverty, including lack of employment opportunities and poor urban housing and neighborhoods;

- intergroup conflict;

- intergenerational conflicts, as young students adopt values and choose lifestyles of the new culture faster than do older members of families;

- emphasis on extended family in some minority cultures rather than the nuclear family of the majority culture;

- alcohol and substance abuse;

- negative perceptions held by minority groups about mental health care and other types of medical care; and

- lack of sensitivity of professionals to factors such as the extent to which members of minority cultures have adopted the majority culture, the degree of proficiency in English, and the fact that families may have multiple concerns.

Although some of the stresses contributing to the families' and individual family member's inability to function were similar across culturally and linguistically diverse groups, the researchers also noted some differences among the groups and their reactions to life in the United States.

Labels and Stereotypes

It is critical that special education and mental health professionals become acquainted with each family's individual cultural lifestyle, including values, beliefs, and practices associated with having a child with a disability. Unfortunately, many professionals have typically gained this knowledge through exposure to multicultural materials that offer a smattering of stereotypical elements of cultures. Glenn (1989) warns that "[W]e must never speak of culture as an occasion for reinforcing stereotypes—negative or positive—about ethnic groups" (p. 779). Culture is dynamic; professionals must understand the "lived culture" of the family, not the fiestas and folklore that had meaning for the grandfamilies but may not be part of the lives of all immigrants in the United States (Glenn, 1989).

Furthermore, the general labels "Hispanic" and "Asian American," for example, can conceal the differences that exist among national groups. Cuban Americans, Mexican Americans, and Puerto Ricans are the largest groups among Hispanics. Cuban Americans are a refugee population, who came under duress to the United States and cannot return to Cuba. Many Mexican Americans and Puerto Ricans migrated to find better opportunities. Many immigrants enter illegally, and have had minimal experience in school and in urban life. Puerto Ricans, however, are U.S. citizens, who frequently move between the island and the mainland United States. Asian Americans are often pictured as models by the media who report their educational achievements. But the term "Asian" includes some national groups from Southeast Asia who are refugees unaccustomed to urban life. These groups often experience grave problems in U.S. public schools. Although people living in the United States who are of Chinese, Japanese, Korean, Vietnamese, or Filipino descent have all been labeled Asian American, mental health workers and educators should expect many important cultural and familial differences among these groups.

An added difficulty with labels is stereotyping. For example, labeling Asians as models of success obscures the very real problems many Asian students from all the national groups experience, especially in trying to master English (Yao & Houng, 1987). Stereotyping obscures recognition of personal traits. In fact, rigidly assigning specific traits to a cultural group may be just as detrimental as completely ignoring differences among the groups altogether. Some Hispanics are quiet independent people, and some Asians are outgoing and relaxed. Smith (1981) reminds us that "each individual is like all other people, like some people, and like no other person" (p. 180).

Providing professionals with cultural profiles of ethnic groups is effective *only* if the professional can affirm that the cultural pattern does indeed exist within the individual family and may be affecting the family's adjustment to a child with disabilities. For example, parents and immediate family members should be the first source of information about their child's behavior or cause of a disability. A second source of information is other people whose opinions are valued by the parents, such as compadres (godparents) in the Hispanic family and elders in the Asian family. Involving the parents, relatives, and informal support persons in decision making assists professionals in determining culturally responsive educational or medical intervention. For example, professionals who understand the child's home culture may better determine if the child's behaviors in school indicate problems or are a function of the family's cultural beliefs.

A third source of information is community leaders and other members who share the ethnic culture of the family and student. Asking clergy or community leaders to be cultural brokers can greatly assist professionals in better understanding the families and students they work with. Observing members of the cultural group within the community and attending local meetings and religious activities further empowers the professional to become culturally responsive.

Once a cultural belief is validated within the family, mental health and special education personnel can work to modify educational or therapeutic interventions and involve parents and members of the informal family network in a partnership with professionals (Dunst, Trivette, & Deal, 1994; Katz-Levy, Laurie, & Kaufman, 1987). Using cultural information wisely and carefully in working with culturally and linguistically different families empowers professionals to provide more effective services. Valuable information on minority group children and their families can be found through books (e.g., Grant, 1995; McGoldrick, Pearce, & Giordano, 1982; Powell, 1983; Lynch & Hanson, 1992) and journals (e.g., *Equity and Choice, Multicultural Education, Teaching Tolerance*).

Examples of Cultural Attributes

Specific cultural characteristics that may provide mental health and special education personnel with insights into the family of a child with disabilities vary among and within ethnic groups. For example, many Hispanics report that for them the U.S. mental health system seems irrelevant and oppressive. They see the family as the source of problem solving, and of value setting. Frequently, they perceive the U.S. system as being in conflict with traditional Hispanic family values, including their religious and spiritual beliefs. In some Hispanic cultures, for example, the belief that prayer and faith in God is the most powerful intervention for their child with disabilities can influence their attitudes toward special education services. The family may believe it is more important to go to church or pray for assistance from God than to provide the recommended therapeutic services (Correa, Bailey, & Skinner, in preparation).

Asian American families may place great value on conformity to authority and tranquility. Acting in harmony, being humble about one's abilities, and showing deference to authority figures are appropriate behaviors. In working with Asian American students with emotional problems, counselors and mental health caregivers are learning to consider the degree to which mental and emotional stresses have physical manifestations. Students do not wish to display emotions but may experience deeply felt shame and guilt when they fail to achieve at a high level. Asian American students may feel that they have brought shame on their families; the students' painful headaches may be symptoms of inner stress. Furthermore, Chinese parents have been reported as having high educational aspirations for their children, and severe learning disabilities in a child may affect a family's acceptance of the child (Seligman & Darling, 1989). If the family appears to ignore or deny the child's special educational needs, school personnel can at least understand the family's reactions and ask them to speak with other Chinese families who have adjusted to the special needs of their children.

Table 7.1 provides selected examples of cultural beliefs that may assist school personnel and mental health personnel in working with culturally diverse families of children with disabilities. The list is by no means representative of all aspects of cultural beliefs within the ethnic groups. It serves only as a way to demonstrate areas that may need to be considered when providing culturally responsive intervention programs for families and their children with disabilities. Again, professionals are warned not to stereotype families on the basis of ethnicity (Seligman & Darling, 1989).

Meeting the needs of culturally diverse groups is a challenge for many types of professionals. For example, a report of the Task Force on Library and Information Services to Cultural Minorities stated that librarians should reach out to members of diverse groups who may fear what they perceive to be institutions that are government operated (Allen, 1988). Some minority groups may not understand that library service is free, without obligation to the user. In Fresno County, California, an area with a large population of Hispanic farm workers who lacked transporation to the city library, librarians called the bookmobile a "barriomobile." Complete with mural painted on the sides of the vehicle and providing appropriate materials in English and in Spanish, the Biblioteca Ambulante provided library services to Hispanic families (Allen, 1988).

These reports by mental health practitioners, special educators, and librarians indicate that working effectively with families from different language and cultural backgrounds requires that professionals have a positive accepting attitude toward diversity. A willingness to adapt practices to meet the needs of changing populations is essential. Being informed about the background and characteristics of a particular group enables professionals to make a better assessment of the needs of the group and the individual members. The task is challenging and complex. As professionals accumulate knowledge through experience, they can better evaluate and refine their ways of working with families.

Table 7.1

Examples of Cultural Values or Beliefs Affecting Intervention
with Culturally Diverse Families of Children with Disabilities

Ethnic Group	Cultural Values or Beliefs	Implication for Services
Mexican American	• *machismo*	• respect the role of the father in family governance • understand that the father is the "provider" and may be uncomfortable with the child-care role • provide "male-oriented" activities for family involvement • use male professionals when possible • respect the mother's need to postpone decision making until she speaks with her husband
Puerto Rican	• *confianza* (trust)	• understand that families may not openly accept service providers into their lives • anticipate that it might take some time for families to develop trust in a service provider • acknowledge that bilingual and bicultural service providers may develop *confianza* earlier than non-Spanish speaking professionals • demonstrate genuine concern, care, and advocacy for the child with disabilities in order to advance the development of trust • develop respect from the family by learning simple Spanish phrases and appreciating their cultural traditions
	• *compadres*	• include extended family members such as godparents, close friends, and neighbors in school activities • respect the involvement of non–family members in the decision-making process with regard to the child's services • use extrafamilial subsystem to provide support for parents
Japanese	• avoid confrontation	• understand that parents are not likely to challenge professionals in a meeting, even if they are unhappy with the recommendations
Native American	• acceptance of fate	• recognize the families' acceptance of the child's disabilities and focus on child's strengths

The Changing Role of School Professionals

As far back as the 1950s educators commented on the need to construct a bridge between home and school (Hymes, 1953/1974). The bridge was seen in the 1950s as a link allowing families and teachers, through proven techniques, to create a unified environment for children. The goal was to define areas of common understanding between families and teachers. The first area concerned what *children* are—the roles they play, how they grow and develop, and how to help them learn. The second area concerned what good *education* is—what to look for in schools, and how to obtain the desired educational programs within communities. If families and educators could agree on these common areas, then they could form a team, reinforce each other, and work to assist the student.

For example, home and school often shared an outlook in suburbia in the 1950s. Mothers were home and were often school volunteers, PTAs flourished, dads came home in the evening, families ate dinner at the table together, and the children did homework. Few families had the small black-and-white televisions of the era. The schools saw such families as providing the background needed for the education of youth. Suburban mothers, with their station wagons for field trips and their cakes for school parties, were defined as supportive of school efforts. Parents saw the local public schools as the important elements of a democratic society, often with bright new buildings and enthusiastic teachers and coaches, who guided the students toward social and economic success. The support system arising from these common understandings shared by school personnel and parents was successful—at least for white middle-class students with no special needs.

In the 1950s, however, cracks appeared in the areas of common understanding. Following *Brown v. the Board of Education,* a series of challenges to the nation's education system arose. Where were the common areas when African American parents entered previously all-white schools, or when white parents found that their children had an African American teacher? Again, where were the common areas in the 1960s and 1970s, when parents of children with disabilities in regular classrooms came to confer with the teacher? In the 1970s and 1980s, the question arose again, when teachers found that increasing numbers of limited English proficient (LEP) people from a variety of backgrounds were the real-life parents in the school community. As we approach the 21st century, where are the new areas of common understanding between families and teachers, as the populations of disenfranchised groups such as the homeless, poor, and people with HIV continue to grow?

Traditionally in the United States, which is a nation of immigrants, the public schools have had major responsibility for assisting students and their families through the transition from their native culture to that of their adopted country. Such a change may be particularly difficult for families of children with disabilities. Families from some cultures may not understand the nature of the child's disability, the appropriate educational services available to the child, or the expectations of the professionals working with the child (Heron & Harris, 1987). The following scenario serves to illustrate this point:

> Fredrick is a 6-year-old student who has just arrived in the United States from Bosnia. His first-grade teacher, Ms. Johnson, has noticed that Fredrick is withdrawn and has episodes of crying during the school day. Ms. Johnson contacts the school psychologist, Mr. Ramirez, refer-ring Fredrick to receive special education services. Mr. Ramirez asks Ms. Johnson to try some strategies to help Fredrick feel more comfort-able in her classroom, for example, by pairing Fredrick with another first-grader from Bosnia, in a buddy system. Ms. Johnson is opposed. She thinks Fredrick has emotional disabilities and should be removed from her class.
>
> Ms. Johnson also makes a home visit to talk with Fredrick's mother. The mother speaks very little English. Ms. Johnson tries to explain that she is concerned about Fredrick and believes he should be referred for testing and special education services. The mother only understands parts of the conversation. Ms. Johnson does manage to get her to sign the school consent forms for evaluation. She leaves the home shortly after arriving.
>
> Ms. Johnson speaks with Mr. Ramirez about proceeding with the referral into special education. Mr. Ramirez reminds Ms. Johnson of the prereferral process and suggests that she read articles on student behav-iors associated with assimilation to a new culture and second language acquisition. He asks Ms. Johnson to be patient and try some positive strategies for helping Fredrick adjust to the new situation.

School-based professionals like Mr. Ramirez who take on the role of advocates serve as culture brokers between the majority and minority cultures (Correa, 1989). Culture brokers serve as mediators for dealing with the mainstream culture for a family of another culture. Knowledge of both minority and majority cultures and language, as well as the ability to interpret from one group to the other, are essential characteristics of effective culture brokers. Culture brokers assist school personnel in empowering culturally diverse families to adapt to the U.S. school system, which may be very different from the educational systems they have experienced in their former countries.

Building Blocks to Home–School Partnerships

Research continues to show that when families are involved in education, stu-dents of all backgrounds and capabilities benefit (Reynolds, 1992). Teachers want family involvement and report that lack of parental support is their number one problem (Stern & Chandler, 1987). Furthermore, school personnel are under legal mandate to involve parents. For example, any schools receiving Title VII funds to provide special language services (those provided by the federal government under the Bilingual Education Act) are required to inform families of their child's educational program and progress in that program (Cubillos, 1988). Under the 1997 IDEA amendments, parents must be invited to participate actively in conferences where decisions are made about students in special education. If parents do not understand English, federal law requires that schools provide translated materials and an interpreter. Even with provision of materials and interpreters, finding common areas that allow teachers and parents to become partners in the educational process is difficult when school personnel are linguistically and culturally different from the families of the students.

A problem in defining common areas is that school personnel may not have approached the issue from a perspective of knowing about the family's point of view (Hymes, 1953/1974). Some school personnel may not have developed a way of incorporating parents into the educational system as partners, particularly parents who may themselves have had difficulties in school or not attended school. Often school personnel obtain information about families from only a few sources:

- *memory:* what their parents or friends' parents were like;

- *personal experience:* what they themselves and their friends are like as parents, or what they perceive parents to be like;

- *media:* television, newspapers, magazines; and

- *general information:* information in the professional's background that may tend to be general in nature.

Memory, personal experience, the media, and general information may combine to give an idealized mental picture of what a family is or perhaps should be. School personnel who have an image of middle-class parents as school volunteers during the day and supervisors of homework at night expect to involve families in school by planning an Open House as discussed in many teacher preparation courses. This image of families may be far from the reality of non-English–speaking families of a child with disabilities. When the immigrant parents fail to respond to the traditional written school material, the school personnel may perceive them as being nonsupportive and uninterested.

On the other hand, parents from another culture may have images of education drawn from their own memories, experiences, and media. There may be little match between their image of school and the reality in U.S. classrooms. For families from another culture, the freedom, openness, even the wealth and beauty of a U.S. classroom, may not fit with their conception of what an ideal educational situation is. To families from a more authoritarian society, the informality of the U.S. teacher may indicate a lack of professional ability. A school's expectations that the parent participate in the education process may be completely outside the experience of some families. Images on television of teenagers' behavior in schools may frighten families who value obedience and believe in their right to make decisions for their children. For families from diverse language and cultural backgrounds, the trip to school is at best difficult due to lack of comprehension of both the language and the ways of doing things. At worst, the trip may evoke painful memories of their own failure in school or indicate the seeming failure of their children. Finding common areas is a difficult task when school personnel and parents are very different.

Yet there is a base on which to begin to build common areas: the desire of parents and school personnel to have students experience success. Families make a great investment in their children. For many immigrants the major reason for leaving their countries was the opportunity for educating their children in the United States. Immigrant families value education, and wish to be involved with their children's school (National Coalition of Advocates for Students [NCAS], 1988). By being knowledgeable about the United States, the culture and language of students' families, and the school system, school personnel can lead the effort to build partnerships with culturally diverse families based on the common ground of desiring student success. The schools should take the initiative in involving families (Met, 1987); research results indicate that it is the differences in teachers, not parents, that determine the level of parent involvement in school.

Unfortunately, school personnel are not generally succeeding in involving multicultural immigrant families in the educational process. Schools not only fail to reach out to these families, but in many cases, the school personnel are indifferent to attempts at involvement by families whose language and values are unlike their own. Some school personnel are even hostile, perceiving attempts by culturally different groups to express their beliefs about education as threats to the educational professionals' established methodology (NCAS, 1988).

Fortunately, the lack of success of school personnel in reaching out to parents of diverse backgrounds is not universal. Some educational leaders are able to involve parents as supporters of school efforts and as volunteers, regardless of parents' educational and cultural background. They are able to involve both single and married parents and to appreciate the contributions of all parents equally. In fact, these leaders organize and get good results from the involvement of all parents (Becker & Epstein, 1982). Believing that building a mutually beneficial partnership with multicultural families is possible and desirable is the first step in reaching out to any family. Figure 7.1 shows the six building blocks of family involvement needed to bridge the gap of school and home to meet the common goal of educating children.

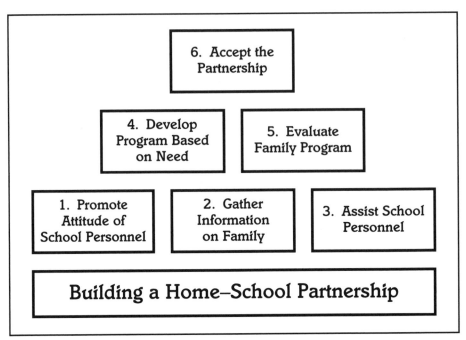

Figure 7.1. Six building blocks needed to form a home–school partnership.

1. Promote Attitude of School Personnel

The first building block for developing a family program that meets the needs of diverse families is promoting a positive attitude in school personnel. Personnel must recognize that families of all backgrounds do want to support the education of their children and have high hopes for their children. For example, Hispanic families often encourage their children to study and apply themselves to school. To many of these minority families, an education means a way to improve their way of life (Florida Department of Education, 1983). The following vignette depicts an inaccurate perception of a Hispanic family by a professional.

Rosa, a 12-year-old Cuban student, was not performing well in her social studies class at her middle school. Her teacher, Ms. Smith, had sent a note home asking the mother to come meet with her regarding the school problem. Ms. Smith had not received a reply to the note. One afternoon in the teacher's lounge, Ms. Smith commented to the school psychologist that Rosa's mom had not responded to the note and that it was obvious this mother didn't care about her child's education. "You know those Hispanic people; they have little education themselves and don't see any value in giving their children a good education," commented Ms. Smith. She further stated that many Hispanic families feel as though education will never get them out of their barrios (local housing projects).

The school psychologist, who was knowledgeable about the Cuban community, interrupted Ms. Smith and stated that he had found the opposite attitude among the Cuban families he had worked with. In fact, he found that Cuban families were very eager to see their children succeed in education and encouraged good performance in school. The school psychologist asked Ms. Smith if she had sent the note home in Spanish, and if she knew that Rosa's mom worked full time in a local grocery store.

Attitudes of school personnel that reflect faulty thinking or inaccurate stereotyping toward families of diverse cultures must change if a collaborative relationship is to work. It is hoped that Ms. Smith learned from this experience and contacted Rosa's mom via a Spanish-speaking interpreter to schedule a conference during the mother's lunch hour or after work.

School personnel should first understand their own images of parenting, and their own values and beliefs, as a frame of reference for the views of others. Culture brokers assist in helping school personnel understand how their values and beliefs might be perceived by people of other cultures and what modifications at the school might help these families to feel part of the school community. When professionals realize that these modifications are minor, not radical, changes, then they are more willing to make the attempt in order to meet the needs of minority culture and language students and their families. Helping school personnel to become both sensitive to cultural groups and willing to enter into partnership is only the first step in building a solid relationship with families and students.

2. Gather Family Information

The second building block for school personnel is learning about the family. One way to begin gathering information is to develop a parent profile that consists of questions regarding socioeconomic characteristics, cultural and linguistic characteristics, and reactions to having a child with a disability. Many authors provide excellent surveys for use with parents (Sandhu, 1988; Thomas, Correa, & Morsink, 1995). Professionals should be cautious when using surveys, however, to ensure that the family's cultural beliefs and values are considered. The following questions might be among those asked in an interview:

- Why have members of the cultural group left their homeland?
- Why have members of the cultural group settled in the local community?
- To what extent do members of the cultural group experience poverty?
- What is the typical family size?
- What roles are assigned to individual family members?
- What customs, values, and beliefs in the culture have relevance in understanding the children's behavior?
- How do members of the cultural group view education?
- How do members of the cultural group view [individuals with disabilities]? (Mattes & Omark, 1984, pp. 43–45)

The information for a family profile can be acquired in a number of ways, for example by providing professional inservices, talking with people knowledgeable about the community, and talking with people who understand the needs of children with disabilities from diverse cultures. Often local clergy or community leaders can provide school personnel with insight into family customs and beliefs. Local public libraries may have resources describing cultural patterns of particular minority groups. School personnel are encouraged to spend time in the community, including making home visits, attending local art or musical events, dining in local restaurants, and listening to local radio or television broadcasts (Correa, 1989).

The literature suggests several tools useful for interviewing families. Turnbull and Turnbull (1997) offer a conversation guide for talking with families that embraces a systems view of the family. The guide includes questions about family characteristics, family interactions, family functions, and family life cycle. Winton and Bailey (1988) suggest that a family interview is a useful tool for uncovering information about family characteristics, strengths, and perceptions in order to help parents take an active role in setting goals for their child. They offer a structure and format for a family-focused interview that includes five phases (the preliminary phase; the introductory phase; the inventory phase; the summary, priority, and goal-setting phase and closure). The ecological map or "eco-map" (Hartman, 1978) is a method for visually mapping the major systems that are part of a family's life. The eco-map provides a picture of the family in their particular situation and considers the important sustaining or discordant connections between the family and their community. These three techniques permit the school professional to gather information not traditionally obtained, allowing new insights on which to build positive family–professional relationships.

Gathering information about the particular cultures represented within a school community can be a complex task. Developing inservice components, bringing in speakers, planning excursions to ethnic restaurants, and sharing the materials and information obtained from reading and travel can be collegial experiences for school personnel. Learning about other cultures, the foods, music, and beliefs, is an enlarging experience for individuals. The following vignette helps illustrate this point.

Carmen, a Salvadoran mother of a 3-year-old child with blindness due to prematurity will be receiving services for her daughter from the local public school system within a few months. The school social worker and early childhood–special education teacher make a home visit for the purpose of orienting the mother to the special services provided by the school program. In talking with the mother, the social worker asks for a description of her daughter's medical diagnosis. Carmen describes what the physicians have told her about retinopathy of prematurity, but she adds that she believes evil spirits had caused the problem. She further states that she is glad the schools were going to teach her daughter, but she would continue to take her daughter for spiritual (*espiritualistas*) treatments. After the home visit, the social worker volunteers to gather information on the spiritual and religious beliefs of Salvadorans. She contacts a local Catholic clergyman and asks him to share information that would be relevant to understanding Carmen's case.

School administrators provide leadership by initiating and participating in the information gathering and sharing. By including English-speaking community leaders, and parents of children with and without disabilities, they extend the learning opportunity and demonstrate that the school as a community wishes to incorporate all families into the education process.

3. Assist School Personnel

The third building block is to assist school personnel with communication skills so they are better able to work with families from culturally diverse groups. The parent profile developed at the school level provides general information about various families' cultures and their perceptions of children with disabilities. Conversations, interviews, and eco-maps provide additional information about particular families and their situations. As mentioned earlier, school personnel must also enhance their own cultural competence. Becoming more aware of one's own culture and its influence on day-to-day life as well as that of the families in the school community is beneficial to developing a partnership with families (Turnbull & Turnbull, 1997).

It is also important for school personnel to understand the potential barriers to getting families involved in school programs. Barriers may include the fact that

- the burden of family care is on elderly family members who are in poor physical condition to travel to school;
- the problem of poverty prohibits transportation and requires long hours of work;
- lack of babysitting support prevents school visits;
- inability to speak or read English prevents understanding school policies and procedures;
- lack of literacy skills in native language hinders the use of materials written in native language; and
- lack of legal documents for citizenship deters entry into school for fear of expulsion.

School professionals need to establish if any of the above barriers are an explanation for lack of school involvement by the culturally diverse families of the students with disabilities. Once the barriers are identified, they can be overcome by various means including transportation, day-care for siblings at school, native language interpreters, or meetings outside of the school facilities.

Once families have agreed to participate in school activities and interact with school personnel, the next step is to assist school personnel in communicating effectively with families from diverse cultures. Professionals should understand that people from different cultures may have different nonverbal communication skills. For example, some researchers have reported that Hispanic people may stand closer to and touch others more often than white people (Sandhu, 1988; Torres, 1983). Additionally, some Asian groups avoid eye contact as a form of respect toward authority figures such as school personnel (Kumabe, Nishida, & Hepworth, 1985). Active listening and other positive communication skills that are sensitive to families from diverse cultures may be helpful for some teachers. As mentioned previously, providing inservice training on multicultural issues and acquiring information about cultural groups through community contacts are excellent ways in which to enhance school professionals' knowledge and thus encourage family involvement in school-related activities.

Furthermore, many professionals often mistakenly perceive the family who speaks very little or no English as inferior or as lacking awareness of conceptual knowledge (Kumabe et al., 1985). The fact that a family is unfamiliar with the complex jargon related to special education is no reason to omit them from conferences and informal meetings. By providing the family with information in their native language and using interpreters during meetings, school personnel can begin to bridge the linguistic and communication gap between families and schools. Remembering that culturally diverse families come to school with many apprehensions, and are often shy about asking questions is critical to understanding the home–school interaction. Sandhu (1988) suggests the following ways for school personnel to work effectively with families of minority culture groups:

- Make a positive first impression by having staff welcome and accommodate parents when enrolling their children.

- Maintain positive communication directly with parents by calling or providing informal meetings instead of sending written notes home with children.

- Familiarize parents with school buildings and school policies by inviting them to a scheduled Parent Teacher Association (PTA) meeting or School Open House for parents. It will be important to invite extended family members or close friends and provide interpreters for families needing English translations.

- Provide frequent and flexible opportunities for conferences by inviting parents to attend school meetings before or after work, or special events at school that coincide with holidays of cultural importance.

Additionally, school personnel must be knowledgeable about the child's learning styles and behaviors. For example, a school psychologist must provide assessment instruments that are culturally nonbiased, and adapt administration of those instruments for the child who does not speak English. Teachers must provide classroom environments and activities that match the learning styles of the minority students (Gilbert & Gay, 1985; Westby & Rouse, 1985). Many limited English proficient students are referred to special education primarily because of behavior which reflects first their adjustment to a new culture and second their learning of a second language (Hoover & Collier, 1985).

4. Develop a Program Based on Need

The fourth building block is planning a family involvement program based on the needs of the particular student and family. There are numerous ways in which school personnel can develop positive partnerships with families. The following are some examples:

- If a sizable number of poor families are headed by women, then having an inexpensive supper to which the mothers can bring all their children may be a way to begin family involvement.

- If the particular cultural group in the school has a national holiday or hero, school personnel can provide a program on or near the day and invite families to assist.

- Materials can be added to the school library about the particular group.

- Families can be invited to serve as bilingual aides; community volunteers who speak the language or are acquainted with the cultural group can be enlisted to assist at school.

- Schools can offer English classes or citizenship classes on a regular basis.

- Schools can provide a community bulletin board notifying families of special services (babysitting, transportation, employment openings, church activities, etc.).

- Families of children with disabilities can meet with other culturally and linguistically diverse families and assist them in understanding special education policy and procedures.

- Families can be given information on basic child development and disciplining techniques, as well as information on disabilities.

- Families can be trained in simple special education instructional strategies and methodologies that can be adapted for the home (e.g., behavior management programs, behavioral contracts, direct instruction).

- Families can be trained in advocacy and leadership skills and serve on advisory councils for bilingual and special education programs.

Developing a program to meet the needs of the families within the school can be the responsibility of a committee of faculty, parents, and community members. Once the school ascertains the needs of families, then it can provide programs that meet these needs. Moreover, community agencies as well as those who provide informal support services to cultural groups can assist in providing programs, transportation, and other services.

5. Evaluate the Parent Program

Professionals working with parents from culturally diverse populations increase the effectiveness of their efforts through continual evaluation of their parent involvement activities. Parents' needs may change throughout the school year; parents from a different cultural group may become involved; parents of students with a certain type of disability may request assistance. School personnel then add to the existing parent involvement program or change emphasis. Monitoring of the parent involvement program can be informal. School personnel can maintain records of conversations with parents about the program. Formal monitoring by means of telephone and written questionnaires can also be beneficial. Asking parents either personally or through a newsletter to recommend new ideas for planning programs encourages their participation. Educators should monitor three areas of parent involvement: (a) whether the planned activities meet parents' needs, (b) whether the level of parent involvement has increased, and (c) whether parents are better informed about the educational program (Sandhu, 1988). If the school has identified culture brokers and an informal support network, then asking these resource people to review the program would assist school personnel in evaluation.

6. Accept the Partnership

The final block in developing a collaborative relationship with multicultural families of students with disabilities is that of acceptance of the partnership. There are obstacles to both parents and teachers in this effort. The word partnership implies equality. As such, it may be difficult for some families to put themselves in a partnership with school personnel. Certain cultural groups may hold professionals up on a pedestal, thinking them to be experts and therefore not questioning decisions or expressing their own desires for their child's education (Correa & Heward, 1996). Teachers, on the other hand, may feel limited by the time constraints of teaching and lack of training to work with families.

The previous blocks provide the school professional with skills to construct and to enhance the home–school relationship. Parents are provided with opportunities to become knowledgeable about and to participate in the education of their children. This final phase requires cooperative efforts of both school professionals and parents in reaching consensus about what educational success is for each student and what is the appropriate instructional plan for that student. Consensus in each situation depends on school and parents having developed areas across cultures for understanding children and education. By absorbing some of the values and traditions about children held by members of a minority cultural group, the school opens the door to cooperation in the education of diverse students and their families. This process of absorbing values applies equally to culturally diverse students and their families. It is their responsibility to come to understand the school system and to participate in working toward the fundamental goals of education in a democracy. School personnel as professionals have the right and responsibility to insist on the policies that are effective in the instruction of students. They have the obligation to see that students acquire the knowledge and understanding of the rights and duties of citizens of this nation. A paradigm of two-way involvement is necessary if common ground is to be found between home and school.

Summary

Developing a cross-cultural partnership of home and school is a challenging task. The shared desire to have students enjoy educational success provides the basis on which to construct such a partnership. School personnel engaged in this task collaborate with each other in the sharing of knowledge and experiences. They can work together on case studies, visit ethnic neighborhoods of the families, attend workshops to develop active listening and communication skills, and set aside time to reflect and evaluate their efforts. Administrators can offer encouragement by personally welcoming culturally diverse parents and supporting the efforts of faculty and other personnel to establish effective school–family programs. The task, as described in this chapter, is approached in steps like erecting a structure of building blocks. In the end the successful completion of the task depends on school professionals' patience, commitment, and belief that incorporating parents of diverse backgrounds into the educational process is a part of modern school life.

School personnel need to be told that theirs is a most important role in determining the future of the nation. A multicultural humanistic environment in which students and families of diverse backgrounds work and live together can flourish with school leadership. Welcoming families of students who differ from the mainstream into the school community, encouraging them to participate, giving them a voice in decisions about the education of their children, and providing them with programs that meet their instructional needs are actions that public schools can take. Learning how to participate in schools can enable multicultural families to participate as citizens in the broader community of city, state, and nation. Schools can thus continue to fulfill their traditional role of educating and empowering families of all backgrounds. In this era of continued high levels of immigration of people of diverse backgrounds into the United States, the public schools that find areas of understanding common to all families set an example for other democratic institutions.

References

Allen, A. (1988). Library services for Hispanic young adults. *Library Trends, 37*(1), 80–105.

The Annie E. Casey Foundation. (1997). *Kids count data book: State profiles of child well-being.* Baltimore: Author.

Becker, H. J., & Epstein, J. L. (1982). Family involvement: A study in teacher practices. *The Elementary School Journal, 83,* 85–102.

Comer, J. P. (1980). *School power: Implications of an intervention project.* New York: Free Press.

Correa, V. I. (1989). Involving culturally diverse families in the educational process. In S. Fradd & M. J. Weismantel (Eds.), *Meeting the needs of culturally and linguistically different students: A handbook for educators* (pp. 130–144). San Diego: College-Hill Press.

Correa, V. I., & Heward, W. L. (1996). Special education in a culturally and linguistically diverse society. In W. L Heward, *Exceptional children: An introduction to special education* (5th ed.). Englewood Cliffs, NJ: Prentice Hall.

Cubillos, E. (1988). *The Bilingual Education Act: 1988 legislation.* Wheaton, MD: National Clearinghouse for Bilingual Education.

DeGangi, G., Wietlisbach, S., Poisson, & Stein, E. (1994). The impact of culture and socioeconomic status on family–professional collaboration: Challenges and solutions. *Topics in Early Childhood Special Education, 14,* 503–520.

Dunst, C. J., Trivette, C. M., & Deal, A. (1994). *Supporting and strengthening families: Vol. I. Methods, strategies, and practices.* Cambridge, MA: Brookline Books.

Florida Department of Education (1983, March). *A resource manual for the development of evaluation of special programs for exceptional children: Vol. III-B. Evaluating the non-English speaking disabilities* (pp. 45–62). Tallahassee, FL: Bureau of Exceptional Education Services.

Gilbert, S. E., & Gay, G. (1985). Improving the success in school of poor black children. *Phi Delta Kappan, 67,* 133–137.

Glenn, C. L. (1989). Just schools for minority children. *Phi Delta Kappan, 10*(70), 777–779.

Grant, C. A. (1995). *Educating for diversity: An anthology of multicultural voices.* Needham Heights, MA: Allyn & Bacon.

Hartman, A. (1978). Diagrammatic assessment of family relationships. *Social Casework, 59,* 465–476.

Heron, T. E., & Harris, K. C. (1987). *The educational consultant: Helping professionals, parents, and mainstreamed students* (3rd ed.). Austin, TX: PRO-ED.

Hodgkinson, H. L. (1992). *A demographic look at tomorrow.* Washington, DC: Center for Demographic Policy, Institute for Educational Leadership. (ERIC Document Reproduction Service No. ED 359 087)

Hoover, J. J., & Collier, C. (1985). Referring culturally different children: Sociocultural considerations. *Academic Therapy, 20,* 503–509.

Hymes, J. I. (1974). *Effective home–school relations.* Sierra Madre, CA: Southern California Association for the Education of Young Children. (Original work published 1953)

Individuals with Disabilities Education Act Amendments of 1997, 20 U.S.C. § 1400 *et seq.*

Katz-Levy, J., Laurie, I. E., & Kaufman, R. (1987). Meeting the mental health needs of disturbed minority children and adolescents: A national perspective. *Children Today, 16,* 10–15.

Kroth, R. L., & Edge, D. (1997). *Strategies for communicating with parents and families of exceptional children* (3rd ed.). Denver: Love.

Kumabe, K. T., Nishida, C., & Hepworth, D. H. (1985). *Bridging ethnocultural diversity in social work and health.* Honolulu: University of Hawaii.

Lynch, E. W., & Hanson, M. J. (1992). *Developing a cross-cultural competence: A guide for working with young children and their families.* Baltimore: Brookes.

Mattes, L. J., & Omark, D. R. (1984). *Speech and language assessment for the bilingual handicapped* (pp. 43–45). San Diego: College-Hill.

McGoldrick, J., Pearce, J., & Giordano, J. (1982). *Ethnicity and family therapy.* New York: Guilford Press.

Met, M. (1987). Family involvement in foreign language learning. *ERIC/CLL News Bulletin, 11*(1), 2–3, 7–8.

National Coalition of Advocates for Students. (1988). *New voices: Immigrant students in U.S. public schools.* Boston: Author.

Powell, G. (1983). *The psychosocial development of minority group children.* New York: Brunner/Mazel.

Reynolds, A. J. (1992). Comparing measures of parental involvement and their effects on academic achievement. *Research Quarterly, 7,* 441–462.

Sandhu, H. K. (1988, Fall). *Family involvement: A resource for the education of limited English proficient students.* Silver Springs, MD: National Clearinghouse for Bilingual Education.

Seligman, M., & Darling, R. (1989). *Ordinary families, special children: A systems approach to childhood disability.* New York: Guilford Press.

Smith, E. (1981). Cultural and historical perspectives in counseling blacks. In D. W. Sue, *Counseling the culturally different: Theory and practices.* New York: Wiley.

Stern, J., & Chandler, M. (1987). *The condition of education.* Washington, DC: U.S. Department of Education.

Thomas, C. C., Correa, V. I., & Morsink, C. V. (1995). *Interactive teaming: Consultation and collaboration in special programs* (2nd ed.). Englewood Cliffs, NJ: Prentice-Hall.

Torres, I. (1983). *Hidden messages: Awareness of nonverbal communication of Hispanics.* Gainesville: University of Florida.

Turnbull, A. P., & Turnbull, H. R. (1997). *Families, professionals, and exceptionality: A special partnership* (3rd ed.). Upper Saddle River, NJ: Prentice Hall.

Turnbull, A., Turnbull, H., Shank, M., & Leal, D. (1995). *Exceptional lives: Special education in today's schools.* Englewood Cliffs, NJ: Prentice Hall.

Westby, C. E., & Rouse, G. R. (1985). Culture in education and the instruction of language learning-disabled students. *Topics in Language Disorders, 5*(4), 15–28.

Winton, P. J., & Bailey, D. B. (1988). The family-focused interview: A collaborative mechanism for family assessment and goal-setting. *Journal of Early Intervention, 12,* 195–207.

Yao, E., & Houng, C. (1987). Teaching English to Asian immigrant children. *Educational Horizons, 66,* 43–45.

Communicating with Families of Children with Disabilities or Chronic Illness

8

Roberta Krehbiel and Roger L. Kroth

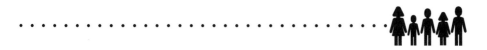

T he term *communication,* as we will use it in this chapter, refers to the interactions that take place between the parents of children with disabilities or chronic illness and the professionals who support them. We will provide an overview of the skills needed for professionals who want to build and nurture a positive and proactive relationship with these parents. The goal of the professional's involvement is to help maximize family potential so the family can independently meet its own needs and prevent the occurrence of secondary problems.

We make several assumptions about the families of children with special needs and the professionals who work with them: First, we recognize that the crisis of diagnosis typically uproots a family's traditional dreams and expectations and creates high levels of stress. Skilled and sensitive professional support can help parents to "reclaim" and readjust. Next, we assume that the mental health professional (psychiatrist, psychologist, counselor, social worker) views the family as unique and strives to respect each family's perspective throughout the relationship. A professional's recognition of the influence of her own personal values, beliefs, biases, and viewpoints can help her to meet the family on neutral ground. Finally, we trust that professionals who work to support families of children with special needs are constantly seeking to expand, refine, and improve their ability to communicate. These interpersonal communication skills are the focus of this chapter. They include *listening, specialized listening, interviewing, responding, problem solving,* and *anticipatory guidance.* The professional's use of these skills can help parents identify ways of coping and adapting to their own worldview. Listening, the most fundamental communication skill, is more than just hearing; it is becoming aware of parental beliefs, values, lifestyles, and preferences in childrearing practices. By careful listening, professionals learn to be empathic, that is, to "take a walk in someone else's shoes."

Listening

Professionals all have definite and diverse ideas about what makes a good listener and so do parents. It is up to the professional to determine what type of listener the parent needs or wants at any given time. Kroth (1985; Kroth & Edge, 1997) conceptualized four types of general listening behavior: passive nonlistening, active nonlistening, passive listening, and active listening. Two of these, passive nonlistening and active nonlistening, are counterproductive to the parent–professional relationship. The passive nonlistener tends to "hear" but not to listen. If asked, the passive nonlistener can repeat back what is said but does not engage in any verbal or nonverbal feedback that shows interest. The active nonlistener, by talking excessively and not following the thoughts of the speaker, never lets the other person get to the point.

In contrast, both passive and active listening support the parent–professional relationship. Kroth suggested that the passive listener is valuable when a parent needs to discharge frustration, anxiety, worries, and aspirations or even to hear their own solutions. A passive listener uses nonverbal messages of acceptance and few words to encourage this discharge. The following excerpt from "Ginny," in Bombeck's *Motherhood, The Second Oldest Profession* (1983), illustrates the need for a passive listener:

> This is the only house on the block that will never have a swing set or a path across the yard. I'm a mother whose kid will never play in the toilet. Never tug at my leg when I'm on the phone. Never tear up my favorite magazine. Never run away from home stark naked. He'll never play patty-cake. Never pull my hair. He'll never even know my name. (p. 75)

The active listener uses reflective verbal comments to help the parent clarify, understand, and solve problems within the context of the family's beliefs and values. Examples of active listening occur throughout this chapter. The professional should shift between active and passive listening behavior, following the lead of the parent.

In their enthusiasm to share their advice and knowledge, professionals often forget to listen. They may become distracted from the content because they are busy formulating a response. Satir (1988) contended that "To the degree that you are involved with internal dialogue, you stop listening" (p. 70). When tempted to fall into certain response patterns due to the feeling of having heard it all before, professionals should remember that parents of children with special needs are not a homogeneous group (Kroth, 1985, 1997), nor are they extremely different from families raising children with no lifelong involvement. A valuable schematic for the professional is the three-link chain of listening–thinking–responding. Benjamin (1974/1981) offers professionals a self-check on their listening skills:

If during the interview you can state in your own words what the interviewee has said and also convey to him in your own words the feelings he has expressed and he then accepts all this as emanating from him, there is an excellent chance that you have listened and understood him. (p. 47)

Specialized Listening

Professionals who have not spent time working with parents of children with special needs can easily fall prey to old myths and potentially destructive stereotypes such as the tendency to see pathology where none exists. This section includes some areas where specialized listening on the part of the professional will help the family's progress. The professional specifically listens for *family resiliency and strengths, feelings of powerlessness and victimization,* and dynamics surrounding *life cycle stages and transitions,* such as normalization, high-risk periods, stigmatization by society, and stress from the burden of care.

Family Resiliency and Strengths

How well a family adapts to a child with special needs depends on the members' resilience: "Resilience is bouncing back after an adversity, being able to recover your previous shape after you have been stretched psychologically. Problems don't predict how people will do" (Wolin & Wolin, 1996, p. 250). Werner and Smith (1992) wrote in *Overcoming the Odds* that resilient people love well, work well, play well, and expect well. We find these descriptions to apply to the majority of families who have children with special needs, and we encourage professionals to keep the thoughts of resiliency foremost in their minds as they work with families in crisis. Stinnett and Defrain (1985) found that all families share six major strengths that the professional, functioning as a specialized listener, can recognize and reinforce: commitment, time, communication, appreciation, coping ability, and spiritual wellness. According to these authors, *commitment* is present if family members are "dedicated to promoting each others' welfare and happiness" (p. 14). Commitment is evident in the following discourse by a parent: "My wife works days and I work the night shift. That's what's best for Kelly and our son, and our family. We have to do this while Kelly is in so much danger and her life is at stake." Stinnett and Defrain reported that strong families also spend planned quality *time* with each other. Part of quality time is devoted to *communication* among family members; and part of the communication is devoted to showing appreciation for individuals in the family. *Coping* with various issues related to raising a family member with a disability and maintaining a sense of *spiritual wellness* are also important strengths for families.

Dunst, Trivette, and Deal (1988) summarized other qualities of strong families termed family functional style: purpose, congruence, problem solving, flexibility and adaptability, positiveness, and a clear set of rules, values, and beliefs. According to these authors, the combination of qualities is important and not all strong families are characterized by the presence of all qualities.

We believe it is necessary for the professional to listen selectively for the positive attributes, resources, and solutions that families generate. Families come for help when they are stuck in situations that require change and see no solutions available (Minuchin, 1974). Professionals must recognize and help families use their strengths in order to expand their repertoire of behaviors. As parents of children with special needs acquire new skills and competence, they will mobilize these strengths in unique and culturally appropriate ways.

Feelings of Powerlessness and Victimization

Specialized listening requires professionals to hear parental concerns about feelings of powerlessness and victimization. When expectations of a typical birth or healthy child are abruptly shattered, the psychological response may be a strong sense of vulnerability, loss of control, and threatened self-esteem. These feelings may lead to disorganization, a slowing of family development, and periodic inability to cope. For some parents this sense of powerlessness can be vicious. Unable to pace their lives, the parents experience more failure as the stress accumulates and previous coping strategies are not successful. The professional listens for the painful statements of powerlessness and helps the parent to reshape or reframe the meaning of the event, restoring a sense of purpose:

MOM: He can't talk. He will never tell me he loves me, or even that he hates me! I am his mother, but I might as well be nothing.

PROFESSIONAL: You need feedback of some kind, and it seems like Raymond will never give it to you.

MOM: Never. Ever. As long as I live. He is trapped in that body with that brain.

PROFESSIONAL: What is he doing instead of talking?

MOM: Something I guess. I know when he hurts and when he is tired and when he needs to eat.

PROFESSIONAL: How do you know this?

MOM: I guess it's in his eyes, his face, his movements.

PROFESSIONAL: So you are becoming a very astute observer, an expert on Raymond.

MOM: Yes. Maybe I should look for some other signs. Maybe some signs of love.

Life Cycle Stages and Transitions

According to most theorists the stages of the family life cycle include the unattached young adult, the couple, the family with children, the family with adolescents, the children leaving home and moving on, and the family in later life (Carter & McGoldrick, 1980). Each stage involves change and requires new learning and mastery of new roles. The transitions from stage to stage are accompanied by varying amounts of stress. Minuchin (1974) believes that professionals must recognize the stress of adapting to change as families make transitions: "With this orientation many more families who enter therapy would be seen and treated as average families in transitional situations, suffering the pains of accommodating to new circumstances" (p. 60).

No better words could be spoken on behalf of families with children who have disabilities or chronic illness. These families must adapt to expected life events, while simultaneously coping with unexpected events, transitions, and stress that accompany a catastrophe. The added stressors that occur because of crisis require that parents cope in ways that may appear dysfunctional to others. We will briefly discuss some potential lifelong stressors: the quest for normalization, high-risk periods, stigmatized social values and personal value changes, and prolonged burden of care.

Quest for Normalization

For families living with children with disabilities or chronic illness, the need to feel normal is powerful:

> We deal with cardiac specialists, pulmonary specialists, nutritionists, several surgeons, public health nurses, neurologists, occupational therapists, physical therapists, speech therapists, an early intervention program, counselor, case manager from children's medical services and the state legislature. This is not normal but we try to make our family as normal as possible. (a parent)

Professionals can help families express feelings of normality by using exploratory questions such as, "How do you find time to be a regular family?" The constant struggle for normality should be viewed as healthy and reinforced, not viewed as denial. For example, for short periods of time some parents might not use what some professionals would consider essential therapy.

These families may be coping by prioritizing therapeutic and educational intervention and limiting the time the child spends with outsiders. They are respecting their child's right to be a child and family member first, a member of society second, and a consumer of social and developmental services last.

High-Risk Periods

Wikler, Wassow, and Hatfield (1981) identified 10 high-risk periods when a child's deviance from normality may rekindle parental grief and stress. These periods are diagnosis, time for walking, time for talking, siblings surpassing the child's growth, alternative placement, entry into school, management crisis, the onset of puberty, 21st birthday, and guardianship. An example of stress related to school entry was described by a parent to the authors:

> I think I am doing so well. Sophia is in preschool with good teachers and therapists. I believe all is going just fine. But I am nervous and anxious about . . . what? I don't know. Maybe I am trying to make something there that isn't.

A parent within earshot of this mother later introduced herself and said she too felt the same, but had identified her worry: In 8 months the children would be going to public school and would have to be "labeled" in order to get services.

Other high-risk periods include repeated hospitalizations and required learning of life-saving equipment, repeated assessment and evaluation of developmental levels, decisions about inclusion in regular education classrooms, and development of a circle of support and acquaintances where the common link is solely disability or chronic illness. In addition parents are forced to interact with specialized physicians, educators, therapists, and childcare people who must be carefully cultivated so that they fully understand the needs of the child. In each of these periods parents may expose personal values and lifestyle preferences that may be criticized by others or found wanting by the professional community.

The professional who listens carefully realizes that each high-risk period involves varying levels of stress. Families must make quantum leaps in their knowledge and readjust emotionally in short amounts of time. With each new situation professionals can assist to reactivate coping mechanisms by asking such questions as "What did you do in the past when . . . ?" In addition the professional and family must sort through these coping mechanisms to be sure they are not in need of revision based on the current stage of family and child development. The following example illustrates this point:

> PARENT: I don't know what is happening. Before, we could tell him what to do and he would do it right away. Now nothing we do works.

PROFESSIONAL: Has the change been sudden?

PARENT: Yes, even drastic. Almost overnight.

PROFESSIONAL: Let's go back and retrace. As you remember, tell me what you did that worked along the way.

The professional can also identify behaviors that interfere with adaptation such as overwhelming emotional reactions or habitual family problem solvers whose inflexibility can bring new learning to a halt.

Stigmatization by Society

A third area for specialized listening is stigmatized social values. Researchers suggest that being a victim is neither socially nor psychologically neutral and that parents can feel blamed, stigmatized for having a child with needs (Affleck et al., 1991)—a recurring nightmare for those families with children who are different in appearance and behavior. The following story was related to the first author by the mother of a child with a syndrome that left her arms and part of her face very deformed:

> We were in line at the grocery store when a woman two baskets back yelled, "Why in the world is that child that way?" I said, "We had her done that way. What do you think of it?" The woman was speechless. The people in the grocery store applauded. . . .

After this incident, the professional had the opportunity to explore this mother's feelings and the recurrence of grief reactions. When the mother's coping strategies of humor and assertiveness were brought to her attention, she was able to share her feelings of guilt at being flippant and not taking the time to educate the bigoted public about children with special needs. This incident reminds us of the serious harm that is done to families when disabilities are perceived as an indication of personal worth. The professional realizes that stigma may alter a family's range of activity and explores that possibility in this interchange:

PROFESSIONAL: That incident was particularly hard for you. Have there been others?

PARENT: Yes. No. Well, not really. We don't take her with us very much. I guess just for that reason.

PROFESSIONAL: It's easier not to deal with the comments.

PARENT: Yes. Right now it is.

PROFESSIONAL: You say "right now." What have you thought of to help you deal with these situations in the future?

There will be times when parents discuss their own past views of disabilities and illness. In most cases, children with special needs were born or diagnosed when the parents were young and their personal experience and exposure to positive aspects of differences were limited. In this regard, parents may need to talk through feelings of discomfort or guilt about how they used to perceive children with special needs relative to more current perspectives.

Stress from Burden of Care

As professionals come into contact with families of children with disabilities and chronic illness, they become more specialized in listening for evidence of stress due to the prolonged burden of care. Stein and Jessop (1982) developed an index that measures five dimensions of this burden. We have supplied a comment to illustrate evidence of each dimension:

- the added dependency of a child who cannot perform age-appropriate activities of daily living independently. (Parent: I finally realized that everything we take for granted is going to take much more time than we ever expected.)

- the psychological burden entailed in the child's prognosis. (Parent: The most difficult part is never knowing what tomorrow is going to bring.)

- a disruption in family routines. (Parent: For the rest of our lives we will never be sure that planned events will work out.)

- the fixed deficits in the child requiring compensatory parental behavior. (Parent: I found myself doing things most fathers don't even think about when their child turns 3.)

- medical or nursing tasks that parents need to perform. (Parent: The fear is always there that you'll do something wrong with all the technical apparatus.)

With such children the burden of care is continuous, and parents are often too exhausted and anxious to seek respite. These families have good reason to shelter their children longer than other parents for no one can make definite statements about the future. Sensitive professionals can encourage the family to explore rest and respite sources both informally through the family and formally through agencies that provide trained caregivers.

Effective listening provides the professional with information on the disability or the illness; the effects of the crisis on the family; the lifestyles, beliefs, and values of the family; the coping styles; and so forth. Effective listening also builds parent confidence in the professional as a trusted ally. Specialized listening, as described in this section, alerts the professional to the underlying family strengths and stressors, which can then be addressed.

Interviewing

In the course of their work with families, professionals gather large amounts of information. They must collect data in ways that are not influenced by biases from personal experience and training, before generating hypotheses about a family's functioning. This section explores techniques of interviewing in which the major goal of the process is to provide parents with the opportunity to volunteer information spontaneously. The professional mentally notes strong and consistent patterns and themes in order to return later for the purposes of clarifying goals and building solutions. We will begin this section by briefly discussing rapport building and the importance of making the parent an informer.

Rapport Building

The professional's responsibility is to begin the relationship with the family through rapport building. Spradley (1979) conceptualized rapport as a continuum because it develops in a patterned manner. Awareness of this continuum of rapport helps the professional exercise patience in the relationship. During early contacts between families and professionals, both sides may feel a sense of apprehension and uncertainty. This is followed by a brief period of exploration and mutual assessment. Both parties may be asking, "What does he want me to say?" "Can she be trusted?" (Spradley, 1979, p. 80). The third stage of rapport is cooperation between the professional and parent who have learned what to expect of each other. During the final stage, termed participation, parents bring new information to the attention of the professional in ways that are reflective of their analysis of the situation. To build rapport the interviewer should continually explain reasons for gathering information and probing into family life: "I want to ask you some general questions about life with your son Tommy so that I can get to know and understand your situation better."

As professionals build rapport they assist the parent in adopting the role of informer. Parents may be unaware that the information they possess about their own lives and beliefs can be used productively. In addition, many parents may not have been asked to share or to give their opinion during past encounters with professionals and therefore do not recognize the potential value of their contribution. One goal during the early stages of the interview is to get the parents to speak unself-consciously in their own language—the language of parents who have very specialized knowledge.

One roadblock in this process is that a parent may be unable to form any sentences to describe the situation. The following exchange illustrates this type of roadblock:

PROFESSIONAL: Would you like to tell me some of the reasons you came to see me today?

PARENT: Yeah, I am having trouble with my husband. He doesn't seem to like Jerry [the child with special needs].

PROFESSIONAL: Can you tell me more about how you know?

PARENT: Not really. I just know.

PROFESSIONAL: How has your husband acted that makes you think he doesn't like Jerry?

PARENT: Nothing. I just know.

The professional must now interact in ways that support the parent in learning how to become an informer. In this way the professional can develop a profile of the family's beliefs, values, and lifestyle preferences.

Ethnographic Interviewing

Professionals can help families of children with disabilities or chronic illness by providing a framework within which they can express their own understandings in their own terms. We will briefly describe ethnographic interviewing (Spradley, 1979) as a technique for gathering the stories of families in an open-ended manner. Spradley's particular approach to ethnographic interviewing is easily remembered and is useful to inexperienced interviewers who are not concerned with research or ethnography per se, but are interested in nonbiased gathering of information.

The actual ethnographic interviewing questions are grouped by Spradley (1979) and labeled as grand tour, mini tour, example, experience, native language, and hypothetical. The grand tour question asks for a description of how things usually exist. The mini tour question is used to investigate some smaller aspect of the description that was given during the grand tour response. Example questions ask parents to clarify some description by giving an example. Experience questions ask parents for any experiences they have had in some particular setting. Native-language questions ask the parents, "How would you refer to it?" Hypothetical questions create a hypothetical situation and ask for the parent's response. We have added an opinion question to Spradley's list.

The following examples, preceded by a rationale for obtaining the information, illustrate the various types of ethnographic interviewing questions. Spradley (1979) reminds us that " expanding the length of the question tends to expand the length of the response" (p. 85). The questions follow the same rules of most interviewing; that is, all should be clear, singular, and neutral or nonjudgmental; and most should be open-ended (Patton, 1980).

▶ Interview Example 1

It is often important to ascertain levels of support in order to get a total profile of the family:

GRAND TOUR: Tell me about your family members who come to mind.

A response to this simple question may yield names and ages of family members over three generations in addition to facts about marriage, divorce, remarriage, illness, death, geographical location, and personal contact.

▶ Interview Example 2

Patterson and McCubbin (1983) discuss a Double ABCX model of adaptation to stress in families who are subjected to catastrophic situations. This model looks at family efforts over time to adapt to multiple stressors. In the model, a is the stressor event that interacts with b, the family's resources. These interact with c, which is the definition the family makes of the event, to produce x, which may be a crisis or disorganization or imbalance in the family. The next example explores the c factor in this model which is the definition the family makes of the event: their appraisal of its impact on the family as a whole as well as on individual members. Consider the following types of ethnographic questions that may provide information about parental perceptions:

GRAND TOUR: Tell me the diagnosis as you understand it.

MINI TOUR: Earlier you said you did not know what this was going to do to your son's grandparents. Would you talk about that some more?

EXAMPLE: You mentioned that you have all kinds of expectations for Arlene. Please share some examples with me.

NATIVE-LANGUAGE: I noticed you used the term "learning disabilities." I think that everyone has their own ideas of what that is. Would you take a minute to tell me what this means in your family?

▶ Interview Example 3

The b factor in the Patterson and McCubbin model (1983) suggests that stress is mediated by the resources (both internal and external) available to the family. We need to know the family's view of their own social support:

GRAND TOUR: Who are the people you consider most helpful to you at this time?

EXAMPLE: Would you tell me some of the specific ways these people contribute their help?

EXAMPLE: Often people would like to help out but just don't know what parents need. What are some of the ways you have "educated" your friends and family?

▶ Interview Example 4

This example involves interviewing a family to gain their perspectives on health and healing.

First, it is necessary to determine the degree of concurrence between expert opinions regarding diagnosis or assessment results and the family's perceptions and concepts of the problem:

GRAND TOUR: Tell me what you or your family think is going on here with Chan.

With this type of question you may get the family's perceptions of health in a medical sense or in a holistic sense. The professional then establishes the family's degree of concern about the child's special needs (the family's major concerns are usually voiced first and more than once as they are sharing information).

HYPOTHETICAL: If you had all of these worries written on cards and you had to put them in order, which would you put at the top of the pile?

The professional may ask questions to arrive at the family's feelings about the interventions and treatments for the child or about the future:

OPINION: In what way is the [school, treatment, inclusion] helpful for your child? What are you doing now that is most helpful for your child?

Assume that at some point during the parent's discussion the mother expresses fear at being required to do a certain type of intervention with her child at home:

HYPOTHETICAL: Imagine yourself doing therapy with Isabel in the tub. What do you see happening?

Please note, if a professional is speaking to a family whose dominant language is not English, and the professional is not fluent in that language, it is wise to ask a knowledgeable colleague whether such phrases as "picture this" or "imagine yourself" are used in that language.

With some families it is necessary to inquire about others helping the child and whether the professional should coordinate with them:

OPINION: You have a lot of people in your family and outside your family who really seem to care about Joseph. Should we talk to any of them before we get going?

During a later interview, the professional determines more exactly the family's expectations about growth or change:

OPINION: As you said, getting Flora to sleep through the night will really help her. How long do you think it will take before she sleeps for at least 3 hours straight?

▶ Interview Example 5

Just when families should increase natural social supports, some supports actually shrink. The professional explores this phenomenon with parents in the following example:

EXPERIENCE: What are you experiencing with your friends now that Carla's behavior is getting so out of hand?

In this approach the interviewer's professional or personal agenda is not involved. If after several visits the professional sees the child completely differently than the family sees him, that agenda remains in the background until trust is built and the professional can comfortably suggest some other views. We assume that listening and interviewing go hand-in-hand and that the professional weaves the two together as necessary and appropriate.

Responding

From a counseling perspective the purpose of responding, which is inherent in active listening, is to work with parents to understand their frame of reference and to assist them in building solutions. Theory and research are translated into practical skills and models in the literature. Although each author may offer a slightly different slant to the communication relationship, all are concerned with the "bridge or barrier" responses available to the professional. Due to the vastness of the topic, we will not discuss the various characteristics or types of responding skills but instead refer to the literature on applied psychology.

There is ample evidence to suggest that some parents of children with developmental disabilities or chronic illness manifest grief reactions at diagnosis (Fortier & Wanlass, 1984; Kubler-Ross, 1969; Olshansky, 1963; Solnit & Stark, 1961), and periodically throughout the life of the child (Menolascino, 1977, Wikler et al., 1981). Moses (1983) writes that parents cannot grieve alone and need support through states of shock, denial, anxiety, anger, guilt, and depression:

PARENT: It might be better if Janey just dies.

PROFESSIONAL: When your pain for Janey is so severe, what pulls you up and keeps you going?

PARENT: I feel like now everyone is rejecting me and our family.

PROFESSIONAL: Just when you need support, people are not coming through for you. What did you do differently in the past to garner support?

PARENT: Right now, I hate everyone connected with "special children."

PROFESSIONAL: Let me ask you a strange question, and you think about it a while. Suppose tonight you went to sleep and a miracle happened, and when you woke up in the morning all of your problems had disappeared, what would be different? (Berg, 1994)

PARENT: Well, my baby wouldn't have Down syndrome.

PROFESSIONAL: Yes, and what would be different?

PARENT: I wouldn't have to wake up and cry.

PROFESSIONAL: What would you be doing instead?

PARENT: I would be, I don't know, singing a song and planning a happy day.

PROFESSIONAL: Tell me about this day.

Affleck et al. (1991) found that many parents restore their sense of meaning and mastery during crises by constructing causal theories. For example, mothers, who are more likely to blame themselves, often increase their confidence by building solutions for the future. These authors also found that a mother's feeling of guilt was mitigated by obtaining "absolution" from friends and family and by focusing on the child's progress.

PARENT: I know it's my fault. I am the one who gave birth to this child.

PROFESSIONAL: It's so painful when you believe you caused your child to be disabled. But you appear to carry on. That's very difficult. How do you do that?

Affleck and his colleagues discovered some negative consequences when mothers blamed others for a crisis. The consequences included greater mood disturbances and caretaking problems, less optimal interactions with the child, and an undercutting of sense of control. If professionals are to influence a family's well-being they must take time to explore the tendency to blame others.

The professional also prepares to explore questions that reflect the feeling of prolonged burden of care, which seems to be universal for parents of children with special needs:

PARENT: Am I doing the right thing for my child?

PROFESSIONAL: Let's begin a list of what you have done that has been helpful so far.

PARENT: Am I the only person going insane trying to deal with this?

PROFESSIONAL: No, you are not alone, but it feels that way because right now you have so many decisions to make—it makes you crazy. What problem is top of the list?

PARENT: Why me? Why my child?

PROFESSIONAL: What answers have you found?

Although we offered a few examples of responses in the above sample questions, we recommend that discussions with parents who have "been through it all" are invaluable to the professional who wishes to gain a deeper insight into families with children who have developmental disabilities.

There are many ways to strengthen or reinforce the parents' efforts to raise a child with special needs through professional responses. Positive, non-patronizing comments made at the appropriate moment serve this purpose:

"You've come a long way in learning medical terminology."

"You've discovered the roots of Paul's refusal to maintain his diet. Tell me how you did that."

"So things are still frustrating and difficult. What did it take to get the routine under control?"

"There are some new parents who would like to talk with a veteran parent. What would you think about talking with them?"

Parents also benefit from verbalizing the positive and articulating their own strengths. Two questions used by Affleck, Tennen, and Gershmann (1985) allow parents to redefine or reframe the crisis as beneficial:

As difficult as this situation has been for you and your family, have there been any benefits, gains, or advantages that come from having a child [with special needs]? Many parents asked themselves the question "Why me?" Do you have an answer to this? (p. 654)

Affleck et al. (1985) also caution against taking the parent too far with positive evaluations and purposeful interpretations: "Such communications, however well-intentioned, may be received hostilely by people who have not drawn such conclusions on their own" (p. 656).

Problem Solving

Ivey and Authier (1978) suggest that parents should leave a professional–parent relationship with competencies that allow them to view old problems from new perspectives and cope with new complications that may arise. Before entering into problem-solving activity with the parent, the professional becomes aware of preferences parents have regarding childrearing. A story from Turnbull, Turnbull, Bronicki, Summers, and Roeder-Gordon (1988) illustrates this point: A young man, whose mother hated doing laundry and had it sent out, was being taught to do laundry in school. The teacher considered this task a part of being able to live independently. To the young man, being independent meant earning enough money to pay someone else to do his laundry. He resisted the task and the teacher's attempts to get him to do it. In that case the conflict escalated because the teacher lacked appropriate knowledge about the lifestyles of the individual family. Professionals need to problem solve with parents, *not* to solve problems for parents.

In order for families to build effective solutions and gain mastery over their situation, they will also need great amounts of information on everything from the etiology of the disabling problem, to taxes and insurance, to specialized toothbrushes. Endless roadblocks, including time limitations and bureaucracy, may prevent parents from obtaining needed information. For problem solving to be successful, the professional must become aware of such roadblocks.

Most problem-solving approaches include problem definition, goal selection, strategy selection and implementation, and evaluation. In the beginning the professional models a problem-solving strategy (perhaps by verbalizing its steps) and uses direct questions such as "What have you tried in order to solve this problem?" and "What would you like to try next?" All stages or steps eventually become the responsibility of the parent with the professional providing guidance, sequencing, and reflection.

Several reasons why some parents have difficulty in problem solving were suggested by Dixon and Glover (1984). First, the parents may never have learned the responses necessary for certain problems. This is especially true for most of the problems facing families of children with special needs and is the reason they turn to professionals for advice on the particular disability or illness. In addition, parents may not recognize that they possess effective problem-solving responses that can be generalized to new situations. Finally, effective problem-solving responses may be blocked by excessive anxiety and other emotional states.

As professionals gain experience in working with families of children with special needs, they become more attuned to the potential stressors that may arise. The final section describes the concept of anticipatory guidance and when it might be used in a way that benefits parents.

Anticipatory Guidance

From a medical perspective, the premise of anticipatory guidance suggests that the optimal time for the introduction of information relating to common problems arising during childrearing is just prior to the age at which such problems are likely to appear. Effective professionals are familiar with the affective, cognitive, and physical development of children and share these developmental patterns with families before they happen. The information helps remove fear, uncertainty, and anxiety and allows parents to make informed decisions.

Anticipatory guidance about development must be given with extreme care to parents of children who have special needs. Even though the children may follow some typical developmental patterns, they may also develop differently in many skill areas. Professionals must neither dwell on the child's future because of the potential for free-floating anxiety nor ignore anticipatory guidance about development. Most parents have built-in clocks and become anxious when milestones are not being reached. They may know intuitively that early disabilities and illness can cause problems in emotional and social development as the child grows older. Only the parents themselves know how much information about the future they need in order to make decisions, and only they know how much information they can handle at any period of time.

The professional can choose among several approaches to anticipatory guidance. He can periodically inquire about the parents' needs by such statements as:

> "Some parents are comfortable knowing about what is supposed to come next and some wish to let the professionals keep up with everything. What is best for your family?"

Through careful listening the professional can recognize a parent's readiness to receive information:

> "For the last two visits you have made comments about whether Sarah will walk. Can your occupational therapist tell you what signs he

is looking for to let him know about Sarah's progression toward walking?"

"I sense your worry about Michael's lying. Let me tell you what I know about lying with children who are his age. . . ."

The anticipation of a crisis can be an ameliorating factor. The professional may choose to prepare the family for certain events that may cause excess stress such as younger sibling advancement, developmental progress reviews, behavior management as the child grows older, and the child's 21st birthday. In this way the family can ready themselves for decision making and better understand their emotional reactions. As the following example illustrates, there also will be times when the professional realizes the family has not allowed certain thoughts about future events to surface and must bring that to their attention:

"Now that Linda is entering puberty, I know you are wondering what should be done to educate her about sex. First, let's talk about how you feel about the appropriate behavior for a teenager. Then let's try to remember her 6-year-old mind as we consider what to do."

Consider the following suggestions regarding anticipatory guidance:

- "Learn" your families. Become skilled in observation. Determine a family's flexibility, adaptability, and readiness levels. Be aware that each family will handle the information you give them in a unique manner.

- Be discreet and couch comments about the future in generic terms. For example a professional might say, "Some families have told me they begin to feel anxious very early even though their child will not change programs until the fall. . . ."

- Share anticipatory guidance information only at "teachable moments." For example, when the parent makes comments about the energy it takes to care for Samuel, the interventionist might observe, "You must have to keep healthy yourself to continue to care for all the family."

- Anticipate that it is natural for families to dwell on normative developmental milestones and give them other information such as Vygotsky's "zone of proximal development." Teach parents to attend to and concentrate on behavior other than typical developmental milestones, such as independence, imitation, initiation, and self-regulation. Use goal attainment scaling to help parents fine-tune their expectations and lessen the discrepancy between expectation and reality.

In conclusion, the purpose of delivering anticipatory guidance is to educate parents about what the future may hold for their child. Such guidance is given with deliberate care and consideration so as not to alarm the family or cause an excess of anxiety. As with delivery of sensitive information, the professional must consider the readiness of the parents, the type of material to be delivered, the environment, timing, and the imprecision of language.

Summary

We have explored several interpersonal communication skills from the perspective of families with children who are disabled or chronically ill: passive and active listening, specialized listening, interviewing, responding, problem solving, and anticipatory guidance. We believe we present a perspective that will enhance the well-being of these families and promote the competence needed to raise children with special needs. These skills represent a minute portion of professional demands. The challenge is to learn from the family, to understand the complexity of families and their ecologic reference, to avoid overgeneralization, and to enjoy working with each family in terms of their uniqueness and diversity.

✎ Exercise 1

Ask a colleague or local parent support group to role-play using the situations below. Practice responding in ways that will enable the parent to feel more in control and not as powerless.

PARENT: The cardiologist thinks an operation will be useless, that the baby will die soon anyway of heart failure. The surgeon disagrees. To her, cardiac surgery will remedy the situation and prolong life.

PARENT: They called me to come to what they call an Education, Appraisal and Review at school. All the paperwork was done when I arrived. They had classified my child as behavior disordered and assigned him to a "W-level" classroom. I was stunned. They even had goals and objectives written out. It was as though I wasn't even there. Wasn't even the father of my child.

PARENT: I know occupational therapy will help Kaye. But they say she's performing motorically according to her age level and therefore she can't qualify. We can't afford outside therapy now with all the bills piling up from her last operation.

PARENT: I take Zakia to clinic on Tuesday and again on Thursday. I have to get off work to do this. If I want to see the doctor who ordered all this I have to go on Friday. I am a pinball.

PARENT: It's the insurance. They will cover Omar at Children's Medical Services if the doctor diagnoses him as multiply handicapped. But the doctor says his hearing loss is not that bad, so he's just (just!) physically handicapped. But we can't afford the specialized hearing aids. . . .

PARENT: I knew something was wrong. I knew it was his shunt. But the doctors said, "No, he just had a revision. It can't be that." But I know my son. I know when he is different.

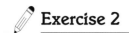 Exercise 2

Assume a parent begins to discuss the meaning of social stigma and asks about the interviewer's personal feelings. Readers should think about their own values and how they would respond to the parent.

 Exercise 3

The following quote illustrates the reality of dealing with social stigma. What response would be made to a parent who relates this information:

So many people said, "I'm so sorry." We were still excited about Stephanie's birth and people were sending condolences. We even received sympathy cards from people instead of cards of congratulations. (Brower 1987, p. 17)

Supplementary Reading

Anderson, P. P., & Fenichel, E. S. (1989). *Serving culturally diverse families of infants and toddlers with disabilities.* National Center for Clinical Infant Programs.

Berry, J. O., & Hardman, M. L. (in press). *Lifespan perspectives on the family and disability.* Needham Heights, MA: Allyn & Bacon.

Bronfenbrenner, U. (1979). *The ecology of human development: Experiments by nature and design.* Cambridge, MA: Harvard University Press.

Davern, L. (1996). Listening to parents of children with disabilities. *Educational Leadership, 53*(7), 61–63.

Fernandez-Villarreal, S., McKinney, L., & Quackenbush, M. (1992). *Handle with care: Helping children prenatally exposed to drugs and alcohol.* Santa Cruz, CA: ETR Associates.

Fuller, M. L., & Olsen, G. (1998). *Home–school relations: Working success with parents and families.* Needham Heights, MA: Allyn & Bacon.

Garbarino, J., & Sherman, D. (1980). High-risk neighborhoods and high-risk families: The human ecology of child maltreatment. *Child Development, 51,* 188–198.

Goldfarb, L. A., Brotherson, M. J., Summers, J. A., & Turnbull, A. P. (1986). *Meeting the challenge of disability or chronic illness: A family guide.* Baltimore: Brookes.

Hobbs, N., Dokeckil, P. R., Hoover-Dempsey, K. V., Moroney, R. M., Shayne, M. W., & Weeks, K. H. (1984). *Strengthening families.* San Francisco: Jossey-Bass.

Kroth, R. L., Olsen, J., & Kroth, J. (1986). Delivering sensitive information: Or, please don't kill the messenger! *Counseling and Human Development, 18*(9), 1–11.

Newbrough, J. R., Simpkins, C. G., & Maurer, H. (1985). A family development approach to studying factors in the management and control of childhood diabetes. *Diabetes Care, 8*(1), 83–92.

Simeonsson, R. J., Bailey, D. B., Huntington, G. S., & Comfort, M. (1986). Testing the concept of goodness of fit in early intervention. *Infant Mental Health Journal, 7*(1), 81–94.

Turnbull, A. P., Brotherson, M. J., & Summers, J. A. (1987). The impact of deinstitutionalization on families. In R. H. Bruininks & K. C. Lakin (Eds.), *Living and learning in the least restrictive environment.* Baltimore: Brookes.

Useful Websites

http://www.dssw.com/DevCare/

http://www.resiliency.com/links.html

http://www.unm.edu/~rkroth

References

Affleck, G., Tennen, H., & Gershman, K. (1985). Cognitive adaptations to high-risk infants: The search for mastery, meaning, and protection from future harm. *American Journal of Mental Deficiency, 89*(6), 653–656.

Affleck, G., Tennen, H., & Rowe, J. (1991). *Infants in crises: How parents cope with newborn intensive care and its aftermath.* New York: Springer-Verlag.

Benjamin, A. (1981). *The helping interview* (3rd ed.). Boston: Houghton Mifflin. (Original work published 1974)

Berg, I. K. (1994). *Family based services: A solution-focused approach.* New York: Norton.

Bombeck, E. (1983). *Motherhood, the second oldest profession.* New York: Dell.

Brower, D. (1987, July/August). The rubberband syndrome. *The Exceptional Parent Magazine,* pp. 17–20.

Carter, E. A., & McGoldrick, M. (1980). *The family life cycle: A framework for family therapy.* New York: Gardner Press.

Dixon, N., & Glover, J. A. (1984). *Counseling: A problem-solving approach.* New York: Wiley.

Dunst, C. J., Trivette, C. M., & Deal, A. G. (1988). *Enabling and empowering families: Principles and guidelines for practice.* Cambridge, MA: Brookline.

Fortier, L. M., & Wanlass, R. L. (1984). Family crisis following the diagnosis of a handicapped child. *Family Relations, 33,* 13–24.

Ivey, A., & Authier, J. (1978). *Microcounseling.* Springfield, IL: Thomas.

Kroth, R. L. (1985). *Communicating with parents of exceptional children.* Denver: Love.

Kroth, R. L., & Edge, D. (1997). *Strategies for communicating with parents and families of exceptional children* (3rd ed.). Denver: Love.

Kubler-Ross, E. (1969). *On death and dying.* New York: Macmillan.

Menolascino, F. J. (1977). *Challenges in mental retardation: Progressive ideology and services.* New York: Human Sciences Press.

Minuchin, S. (1974). *Families and family therapy.* Cambridge, MA: Harvard University Press.

Moses, K. L. (1983). The impact of initial diagnosis: Mobilizing family resources. In J. A. Mulick & S. M. Pueschel (Eds.), *Parent professional partnerships in developmental disabilities services* (pp. 11–34). Cambridge, MA: Academic Guild.

Olshansky, S. (1963). Chronic sorrow: A response to having a mentally defective child. *Social Casework, 43,* 190–193.

Patterson, J. M., & McCubbin, H. I. (1983). Chronic illness: Family stress and coping. In H. I. McCubbin & C. F. Figley (Eds.), *Stress and the family: Coping with normative transitions* (pp. 5–25). New York: Brunner/Mazel.

Patton, M. Q. (1980). *Qualitative evaluation methods.* Beverly Hills: Sage.

Satir, V. (1988). *The newpeoplemaking.* Mountain View, CA: Science and Behavior Books.

Solnit, A. J., & Stark, M. H. (1961). Mourning and the birth of a defective child. *Psychoanalytic Study of the Child, 16,* 523–537.

Spradley, J. P. (1979). *The ethnographic interview.* New York: Holt, Rinehart, & Winston.

Stein, R. E., & Jessop, D. J. (1982). A noncategorical approach to chronic childhood illness. *Public Health Report, 97,* 354–362.

Stinnett, N., & Defrain, J. (1985). *Secrets of strong families.* Boston: Little, Brown.

Turnbull, H. R., Turnbull, A. P., Bronicki, G. J. B., Summers, J. A., & Roeder-Gordon, C. (1988). *Disability and the family: A guide to decisions for adulthood.* Baltimore: Brookes.

Werner, E. E., & Smith, R. S. (1992). Vulnerable but not invincible: A longitudinal study of resilient children and youth. New York: Adams, Bannisterm, Cox.

Wikler, L., Wasow, M., & Hatfield, E. (1981). Chronic sorrow revisited: Parent vs. professional depiction of the adjustment of parents of mentally retarded children. *American Journal of Orthopsychiatry, 51,* 63–70.

Wolin, S., & Wolin, S. J. (1996). The challenge model: Working with strengths in children of substance abusing parents. *Children and Adolescent Psychiatric Clinics of North America, 5*(1), 243–256.

Counseling Approaches with Parents and Families

9

Ronald E. Reeve and Harriet C. Cobb

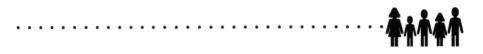

C ounseling is an extremely important service that mental health professionals offer to parents and families of children with disabilities. Physicians, educators, social service personnel, and other professionals also provide essential services, some of which share common characteristics with counseling. However, counseling is a unique type of service. It involves a special kind of relationship between a person who requests help (the client) and a person trained to provide that help (the counselor or therapist) (Patterson, 1986). Although the term *counselor* sometimes is used to refer only to individuals trained in a graduate program in "counseling," we will use the term in a more generic sense to mean a professional trained to do counseling or therapy regardless of professional title. Included are counselors, psychologists, clinical social workers, psychiatrists, and probably half a dozen other professionals.

Counseling approaches may vary widely depending upon (1) the nature and severity of the presenting problem, (2) the theoretical model of the counselor, (3) the developmental level of the child, (4) the point the family has reached in their understanding and acceptance of the disability, (5) the time available, and (6) the economic resources available (if the family is to pay for the service). For example, if the child is mildly disabled the counseling issues may revolve primarily around the educational and peer relations needs of the child. The counselor would encourage the parents to communicate closely with the school and recommend ways in which the child could become involved in appropriate peer-related activities. A supportive consultation role on the part of the therapist would be appropriate. If, however, the child is severely disabled and difficult to manage at home and school, an intensive multidimensional approach may be necessary that could include direct parent counseling, consultation with the school, and family therapy. Regardless of the particular counseling issue, professionals must realize that children with disabilities function within the context of a family system.

Counselors who work primarily from one theoretical model may focus on those aspects of the presenting problem that lend themselves most appropriately to their perspective. For example, the behaviorally oriented counselor may concentrate on teaching parents behavior modification skills and may refer the parents to a family counselor for dealing with emotional issues. A primarily "person-centered" therapist may devote the sessions to assisting the parents in clarifying their feelings about the child with disabilities, then refer them to a school psychologist for consultation regarding educational matters.

Parents with a 5-year-old child with mental retardation, who is about to enter school, face very different issues from those confronting parents of a 22-year-old who is about to enter the world of work. The mental health professional, of course, also must deal quite differently with parents who are just learning the extent of their child's disability, as compared to those who have been to their fourth IEP meeting at the school and are frustrated about the progress their child is making.

Both the time available and economic resources play a role in whether the counseling will be short term and focused on coping with crises or long term and providing a resource to which families can return at various points in their lives.

The counseling process may be thought of as primarily *educative, facilitative,* or *remedial.* The *educative* component refers to the provision of basic information with regard to such things as the nature of the disability, resources available to the family, and specific behavior management techniques. Bibliotherapy can be a useful adjunct to the counseling process, as the use of books can often reinforce the concepts presented to the parents and enable them to absorb information at their own pace. Some parents simply may not be ready to absorb a barrage of information regarding their child's disabling condition until a later stage; the written information is available when they are ready.

In order to fulfill an educative role with parents of a child with a disability, the therapist must be knowledgeable about all issues related to the disability. Counselors who do not possess the information needed should either refer the parents elsewhere or quickly educate themselves, ideally making use of peer supervision in the process. They must know relevant laws regarding rights of people with disabilities for financial assistance, education, access to facilities, vocational training, and so forth. Counselors also must be aware of community resources such as parent support groups, advocacy organizations, and respite care providers. To the extent possible, counselors of families of children with disabilities should become part of the "network" of individuals and organizations concerned with helping people with disabilities in their community, such as the ARC, special education groups, or independence resource centers. A major goal of educative counseling is assisting parents to become as knowledgeable about the disability as possible.

Facilitative counseling involves a balance of providing support and information for the parent (the educative function of counseling) while at the same time reinforcing their effort at independent problem solving. The facilitative component involves assisting the family in identifying its strengths and developing new ways of coping with the inevitable stresses of having a member with a disability. The *remedial* function of counseling refers to the therapeutic task of targeting dysfunctional patterns and developing strategies for helping parents to correct a problem. This is often the most challenging task for a therapist and involves assessing the interactions among family members and perhaps teaching entirely new patterns of relating to each other. In any counseling relationship, and sometimes within a single counseling session, one or all of the functions of counseling (educative, facilitative, and remedial) may be appropriate. Consider the following example.

Case Example: Use of Educative, Facilitative, and Remedial Counseling

The Joneses brought their 8-year-old son, Carl, to a counselor for evaluation. Carl was of average intelligence but had a severe attention-deficit/hyperactivity disorder (ADHD) that was interfering with both schoolwork and his behavior at home. Mrs. Jones expressed concern that Carl was going to be "just like his dad." (Carl's biological father reportedly was a moody restless man who was difficult to live with. He died of cancer when Carl was 2.) Placement in special education and a prescription of Ritalin played a role in improved classroom performance for Carl. However, he continued to be difficult to manage; and his mother remained in counseling for emotional support and guidance in coping with his behavior. Mr. Jones, Carl's stepfather, attended family sessions only sporadically but did attempt to follow through with suggestions for parenting, according to Mrs. Jones. Carl's two siblings attended sessions periodically in an effort to work on Carl's place in the family. Carl had an extremely low self-concept and was prone to compare himself negatively with his brother and sister. Mr. and Mrs. Jones came to realize the dynamics of "scapegoating" and responded by not blaming all family woes on Carl. It was clear, however, that parenting Carl was more challenging than parenting the other two children. Thus, the approach of the counselor was to empathize with the Jones's situation and provide them with coping skills. The therapy was educative, facilitative, and remedial in nature, with bibliotherapy used as a means of providing information about ADHD from an external source. It is interesting to note that the Joneses' response to information about ADHD varied, depending on the developmental stage of the family in relationship to Carl. Initially, Mrs. Jones was convinced that Carl's misbehavior was deliberate.

An insight-oriented focus in the parent counseling seemed to help her acknowledge her "unfinished business" with her first husband. Later, the Joneses tended to perceive Carl's problem as the fault of the school. At the present stage of counseling, they both have a better understanding of the disorder and an appreciation for their role in contributing to effective family functioning.

Theoretical Orientations

A variety of theoretical approaches are potentially appropriate for working with parents and families, including *humanistic, behavioral, cognitive, psychodynamic,* and *systems* orientations (including family systems).

Originally identified as "client-centered" and now referred to as "person-centered," Carl Rogers's theory of counseling is the best known of the *humanistic* approaches (Rogers, 1961). It is based on the premise that people are basically good and generally capable of solving their own problems. Individuals have a natural, internal motivation to move toward "self-actualization," a stage of interpersonal adjustment, and autonomy. The best way for the counselor to understand the client's problem is to take the perspective of his internal frame of reference or perception of reality. This empathic focus on the client's reality is one of the essential conditions for success of therapy, according to Rogers. The other conditions are as follows:

1. two people are in psychological contact;
2. the client is in a state of incongruence and is experiencing anxiety;
3. the therapist is integrated in the relationship and is a "congruent" individual;
4. the therapist feels unconditional positive regard for the client; and
5. the communication of the therapist's unconditional regard and empathy to the client is achieved.

Clearly, establishing an empathic relationship with parents of a child with a disability is a critical element in effective counseling. These parents often experience emotional distance from the many professionals they encounter during the course of initial diagnosis, recurring evaluations, and educational or vocational interventions. For example, one parent of a child with Down syndrome expressed the pain she felt when everyone around her seemed to be emphasizing how "well" she was coping with her child; no one seemed to be in touch with her deep depression related to her awareness of the chronicity of the situation. In her case an important step toward healing was the therapist's empathy with the pain first, without an expectation for the parent to come to terms with the handicap and accept it after some prescribed period of time.

The *behavioral* approaches, based on theories of learning, focus on observable behavioral changes that occur as a result of the counseling. Specifically, the behavioral orientation refers to the systematic application of a variety of techniques, including reinforcements and methods to reduce the frequency of behaviors (e.g., time-out and response cost), to modify target behaviors. (See Kazdin, 1984, for a clear presentation of these techniques.)

As an example, the parents of Alice, a 10-year-old with moderate mental retardation, wanted help changing their daughter's table manners. They reported that, with no apparent provocation, Alice would spit out her food or throw it across the table. Her parents believed that they had established rules for appropriate behavior with their other children, but Alice just ignored them, and punishing her was ineffective. The counselor suggested that the parents administer a token (a sticker on a chart) along with social praise for every 2 minutes of appropriate eating behavior. The frequency of food throwing and spitting decreased dramatically with the use of stickers and praise, so that the parents soon were able to give Alice only one sticker per meal to maintain good table manners. Furthermore, the success of this behavioral program provided a much needed boost for the parents to use positive reinforcements in other situations as well, such as brushing teeth at bedtime, getting dressed in the morning, and so on.

Cognitive approaches are based on the belief that thoughts and emotions are closely intertwined, and that faulty thoughts are at the root of most psychological problems. Cognitive therapists try to help clients identify distortions in their thinking and in their appraisals of situations and then help them to substitute more correct, or more psychological, functional appraisals and interpretations. Albert Ellis's rational emotive therapy (RET) (Ellis, 1979) is an example of a cognitive model that emphasizes changing thoughts so that feelings and behavioral changes can follow.

In recent years most behavioral therapists have come to acknowledge the importance of cognitive variables, and most cognitive therapists now recognize the power of behavioral techniques. This has resulted in a blending of cognitive and behavioral approaches, usually referred to as *cognitive–behavioral,* probably best exemplified by the work of Donald Meichenbaum (1977). He focused on client's self-statements about stress and especially about their perception of their ability to cope with stressors. Meichenbaum assumed that thought influences behavior. Before entering therapy, a client's internal dialogue may consist of negative self-statements and images. In therapy, the counselor attempts to modify the client's conclusions about a specific problem. A "translation" process occurs, in which the therapist offers alternative explanations and interpretations of the client's thoughts and "self-talk." This process enables the client to believe that improvement is truly possible. New coping behaviors are provided for the client to try outside of therapy, and these are discussed in subsequent sessions. Through rehearsal and feedback the client moves toward a more successful mode of coping. For example:

Case Example: Use of Rehearsal and Feedback

A parent of one child with a disability entered therapy with depression and chronic anxiety. He could not shake the belief that he and his wife were being punished for something. Through the cognitive–behavioral interventions provided by his counselor he was able to reframe his belief by accepting the concept that *most* families are faced with obstacles to overcome, and this was theirs. His feeling of being singled out and his guilt were no longer present. The change clearly was a cognitive one. The realistic difficulties associated with having a child with a disability remained; yet the father was able to let go of the sense of doom that was preventing him from moving forward.

The *psychodynamic* approach to counseling is based on Freud's principles of personality development, although in practice Freud's original set of assumptions has been extended considerably. This approach emphasizes the importance of the developmental stage of the client and past parental pressures as contributors to personality dynamics. The individual attempts to cope with anxiety-producing unconscious conflicts by using defense mechanisms. It is the task of the therapist to assist the client in recognizing and overcoming the use of these defenses.

This approach is insight oriented as it attempts to provide the client with a "corrective emotional experience." The aspects of emotional abreaction, intellectual insight, and dealing with repressed memories are all interrelated in the therapy process. A necessary part of therapy includes direction of repressed attitudes toward the therapist, which is known as "transference." The working through of the transference to real-life situations is a goal of the therapy. The concept of "countertransference" refers to the therapist's emotional reactions to the client that may impede the process of counseling. For example, if a counselor believes that dealing with a child with disabilities truly is an insurmountable difficulty, this clearly will interfere with counseling.

Most modern psychodynamic therapies are seen as being of relatively short duration. Although not as readily related to the issues surrounding a child with a disability as some other perspectives, the psychoanalytic approach's principles of transference, countertransference, defense mechanisms, and so on, are useful in understanding the counseling process generally. Any method of assisting the client to grasp the reality of a situation and cope with it is applicable to a variety of psychological issues, certainly including those confronted by parents and families of children with disabilities.

Regardless of the theoretical orientation a counselor may have toward understanding and altering the behavior of individuals, a *systems* perspective is important when approaching parents and families with a child with a disability. A systems viewpoint is multidimensional; it considers the family to be a complex entity with access to a broad range of options to aid in adapting to the stressors of raising a child with a disability. Systems principles include (a) "nonsummerativity," the sum is more than the sum of its parts, and thus it is inappropriate to view an individual member of the family without understanding the broader context in which that person (father, mother, sibling, etc.) is functioning; (b) "homeostasis," the need of a system (such as a family) to maintain a state of equilibrium despite external influences, which leads to conceptualizing the stressor of raising a child with special needs as a perturbation exerted on the family system which necessitates that the entire system respond, realign existing structures, and reorganize itself to deal with change and to allow for coping (Yogman & Brazelton, 1986); and (3) "equifinality," the assumption that the system (e.g., family) is organized to achieve some goal, and a variety of solutions or strategies are available. More than one solution may be adaptive.

The systems perspective is a reminder that families also are part of a larger social context, or "social ecology" (e.g., Bronfenbrenner, 1979). A family interacts with and is influenced by other social systems, including school, daycare, and employment settings, and such social support networks as grandparents, other relatives, and friends. Further, cultural and subcultural beliefs, attitudes, and values must be recognized as potentially important influences on the family. Counselors have an obligation to become knowledgeable about the cultural backgrounds of their clients and to be sensitive to the issues which families of diverse ethnicity or culture may bring (Seligman & Darling, 1989). For example, cultural groups tend to vary regarding who is the most important decision maker in the family; it may be the mother, the father, or a grandparent depending on the family's cultural background. Even the best efforts of a counselor will be rendered ineffective without awareness of the impact of cultural differences.

Family therapy is an established mode of intervention for working with parents of a child with a disability. Family therapy is a broad term that encompasses a diversity of philosophical orientations that have in common the approach of working with the child in the context of all or part of her family. Most family therapists operate from a systems perspective. The parent of an exceptional child often enters counseling as part of a couple or family unit. Although the child may not be the focus of counseling, dealing with the implications of the disability usually is one of the major life issues the client brings.

A fundamental premise of family therapy or counseling is that families are interactive systems that are organized such that a change in one part of the system is likely to result in changes in other parts. A well-functioning family has a hierarchy or clear rules with regard to how decisions are made and which family members have authority to make them. The nature of communication and the balance of power are often indicators of how a family is adapting to a member with a disability.

Boundaries exist within a healthy family, helping to define individual and subsystem roles. For example, in a healthy system the parents have the authority over the children, and the husband and wife participate in a cooperative subsystem. In the "enmeshed" family, boundaries between subsystems do not exist, thus preventing individual members from developing their own identities. On the other hand, boundaries are so rigid in "disengaged" families that it is difficult for cooperation to develop across boundaries. In these families there is little closeness, which precludes, for example, pulling together during crises such as the birth of a child with a disability. A lack of positive affect among family members is associated with family dysfunction.

Case Example: Use of Family Therapy

One of the authors saw a family with five children, one of whom had profound mental retardation. The mother, a single parent, expressed her concern that she doubted that she and her four nondisabled children could cope much longer with the continued needs of the 15-year-old with retardation, although she would not consider residential placement. This mother perceived her family as disconnected and "burned out," with few enjoyable times. The four nondisabled children were 9, 12, 17, and 19 years old. Each shared in responsibilities for the care of their sibling, with little differentiation of roles among themselves, or between the mother and the children.

Counseling focused on establishing and clarifying boundaries for the individual members. The mother and the two older siblings were reinforced in their roles as the "parents." The younger children were then freed of the enormous responsibility they felt, for example, for feeding a brother who might choke to death if they made a mistake. Then, with clearer boundaries established, the counselor helped with practical issues such as providing respite time for each of the three "adults" so that they could engage without guilt in activities away from home. The two younger siblings were freed to be children. Over time, the family was able to focus less on the child with retardation as their ever-present "burden." This appeared to allow them to have fun in family outings and to accept their sibling with retardation more positively, rather than just as their confining consuming responsibility.

Issues Commonly Encountered in Counseling

All families progress through developmental life cycles: becoming a couple, childbearing, entering school, adolescence, postparental years, and aging

(Olson et al., 1984). However, the family with a child with a disability may experience these cycles punctuated by events that affect the family system in unique ways. According to Fewell (1986), certain periods may be especially difficult for families with a child with a disability: encountering the disability, early childhood, initial schooling, adolescence, and beginning adult life. As families progress through these different stages with their child with a disability, certain issues tend to arise during counseling. The rest of the chapter will discuss those issues.

Reactions to the Initial Diagnosis

Regardless of whether their child is found to be disabled at birth or much later, the news precipitates an emotional crisis with which parents must cope. Recent research indicates that the degree of resolution to the diagnosis of disability that parents reach may be more important for long-term outcomes for the child and family than the actual nature and severity of the disabling condition (Marvin & Pianta, 1996). A model commonly cited to help in understanding parents' reactions to the initial diagnosis of their child as having a disability is borrowed from the grief literature (Solnit & Stark, 1961). From this perspective the parents are viewed as having "lost" the idealized, healthy, normal child for whom they had longed and come to expect. With the realization that their child has a disability, parents experience the "death" of their idealized child. The reactions often are intense, perhaps approximating those associated with the actual loss of a loved one. Stages involved in the grieving process have been identified, including shock, denial, guilt, anger and blaming, and eventual achievement of equilibrium as movement is made toward acceptance. However, greatly complicating the grieving process is the fact that the disability remains, placing constant demands on the parents and serving as an ever-present reminder of their loss. Olshansky (1962) used the term "chronic sorrow" to characterize the ongoing feelings parents experience because they cannot completely work through their grief.

Not all professionals who work with parents of children with disabilities accept the grief model as a useful conceptual framework for understanding parents' attempts to cope with the crisis of the initial diagnosis. Although the emotional reactions to the realization that their child has a disability are undoubtedly intense, it may be just as useful to think of this as the equivalent of trying to cope with any other major family crises (e.g., loss of a job, divorce, a sudden move). For one thing, not all parents "work through" the steps delineated in the grieving process; any of the stages may be reexperienced at any time, or a parent may never move beyond the anger and blaming stage. Also, it is important to realize that the two parents do not necessarily move through the stages at the same time. Thus each situation should be evaluated, and each reaction should be considered unique. As Seligman and Darling (1989) point out, several factors may influence the type of reaction a family will have, including socioeconomic status, actual physical appearance of the child, prior information, religiosity, and social support.

The most common mistake professionals make at this point is to be overly optimistic about the severity of the child's problems. A natural human tendency is to want to make the parents feel better. However, making the parents happier by minimizing the child's condition is counterproductive in the long run. At the other extreme, some professionals seem to err by presenting the "worst case scenario." They apparently believe that preparing parents for the worst outcomes will make anything short of that situation easy to accept. Neither extreme is helpful.

Of course, for many parents, this will be their first close encounter with this particular disability. Counselors often can help by steering parents toward clear, accurate, comprehensive information about the child's condition. Factual knowledge is greatly preferable to what the parents may be imagining.

The goals of counseling at this point should include helping the parents to see that their reactions, including their powerful emotions, are normal, automatic, perfectly understandable ways of responding. They need to accept that their feelings are part of a coping, healing process, which will take time and energy but which they almost certainly will survive.

As soon as practically possible, parents can benefit greatly from being put in touch with others who have gone through similar experiences. This contact can help the parents feel less alone and "singled out" for the difficult task of raising a child with a disability. The group experience can provide significant credibility to the notion of eventual acceptance of the situation. *Universality* and *installation of hope* are two of the most important curative factors that group counseling has to offer parents. Counselors should become personally acquainted with support and advocacy groups to which they can confidently send parents, knowing these groups will help normalize the experience for parents encountering this crisis. In addition, such groups often are involved in actively advocating for appropriate social services and education programs for individuals with disabilities. Families that become involved with such support or advocacy groups frequently report finding their feelings of hopelessness being gradually replaced with efficacy or increasing sense of self-empowerment (Singer & Powers, 1993).

However, the counselor must be sensitive to the readiness of the parents to participate in such a group. It is not unusual for parents, particularly those in the early stages of the grief process, to resist the reality of associating with other parents who have children with disabilities. One couple reported that attendance at a picnic sponsored by a support group was a depressing experience. Both parents and children were present, which enabled this couple to see how their then 2-year-old child probably would look as he grew older. The stark reality of a malformed physical appearance was disturbing to them, and they terminated their involvement with the group. The couple would have benefitted from more extensive preparation before entering the group. At a later time this couple found support and comfort from these same families.

Shopping Behavior

Professionals often encounter parents who bring their child in for assessment in order to get another "second opinion" about the nature and severity of the disability despite the fact that the child has already been evaluated numerous times. Related to this, in a counseling situation parents may lodge complaints about the perceived incompetence of the other professionals who have been involved with their child. This may occur because parents are still at the anger and blaming stage of adjusting to having a disabled child. Usually, however, it can best be understood as a normal reaction of people who are confused and frustrated by what seem to them to be contradictory messages from professionals. Indeed some professionals are willing to make firm statements without valid basis for doing so, and others are unwilling to give parents any clear diagnosis or prognosis. Part of the problem, though, is the nature of the disciplines involved. Parents are drawn from the ranks of the normal population, so most do not have backgrounds in medicine, psychology, and education. They tend to think of each of these as much more exact sciences than they actually are.

Counselors can best respond by acknowledging the legitimacy of the parents' frustrations. They then can assess the level of knowledge and understanding the parents have of child development and the disciplines with which their child is involved. Rather than perform an unnecessary expensive evaluation (which also may be traumatizing to the child), the counselor may better spend the time educating the parents and interpreting the professional jargon into understandable language so the parents can know exactly what the professionals were trying to say.

Effects on the Marital Relationship

Having a child can alter the nature of any marital relationship. There may be markedly less time and energy to devote to the spouse, and this can place stress on the relationship. Most parents cope with these changes, in part because of the joy and pride the child also brings to them, and perhaps in part because they know the child will only be with them during this time-limited stage of their lives.

The severity of the strain brought on by having a child with a disability can be influenced by a number of factors. The child is typically not what the parents wanted or expected, requires even more time and energy than other children, and may appear in need of permanent parental care. The financial burden often is great, putting further pressure on the parents. A feeling of embarrassment about having produced a "defective" child may lower the self-esteem of one or both parents, making them less able to function in the relationship with their spouse. One parent might blame the other, citing as evidence some relative with a disability or some real or imagined action such as a fall or medication taken during pregnancy.

If the couple involved had a problematic relationship prior to the child's arrival, the additional stress may be the "final straw." Research regarding marital integration generally presents a mixed picture. Early studies indicated that the number of desertions and divorces was higher in families with a child with a disability compared to control families (Telford & Sawrey, 1981); the rate of suicide and alcoholism was also higher (Block, 1978). More recent research has frequently found no differences in overall rates of marital satisfaction between families with and without a child with special needs (Kazak, Segal-Andrews, & Johnson, 1995; Sabbeth & Leventhal, 1984). Most such parents do manage to cope, and in fact some couples report that the pressure of the child with a disability brought them closer together. In some cases, this appears to be a negative bonding, with parents saying, in effect, "We must stay together at all costs." Clearly, maintaining (or achieving) a satisfactory marital relationship is important if the family is to adapt, and outside professional help can be a key factor in that process.

Fathers tend to be less involved in the day-to-day care of a child with a disability. This can be interpreted as rejection on the father's part, or as an indication of family disengagement. Although these may be accurate perceptions in some cases, counselors will err if they jump to that conclusion. Because of the necessity for *someone* to be home, and given the economic reality that men frequently make more money than women, couples may agree that the husband should be the primary earner and the wife provide the primary care for the child. When that is a shared decision, it actually may indicate a more functional adaptation than equally sharing care but having to survive with fewer economic resources. This is another example of the importance of considering each family as unique and of getting to know their special circumstances prior to acting on assumptions.

Sibling Concerns

While having a child with a disability in the family may greatly affect the parents and their interactions, it also alters the entire family system. Brothers and sisters often report that the presence of a sibling with a disability was the single most important element in their own development. Some of the negative reactions to be expected are the following (Chinn, Winn, & Walters, 1978; Wentworth, 1974): (a) *resentment and jealousy,* because of the parents' extra attention to the child with a disability, the amount of money that goes to treatment, limitations on their own participation in trips and other experiences, requirements that they babysit, and so on; (b) *hostility,* because they may see the sibling with the disability as the source of all their problems, as evidenced in verbal or physical abuse directed toward the sibling, or in disobedience and other acting out behaviors directed toward the parents; (c) *guilt* over having negative feelings toward their sibling, or because of their own good fortune for having been born "normal"; (d) *fear* of acquiring the disability themselves, or that their own offspring might have disabilities, or that they may one day be left to care for the sibling on their own; (e) *shame and embarrassment* about the presence of the child with a disability in the family, including concerns about how to explain his condition to peers and visitors to the home and embarrassment about being seen in public with him; (f) *rejection,* which may manifest itself in denying the reality of the impairment or, more commonly, in withholding affection or pretending the child with the disability does not exist; and (g) *pressure* from unrealistically high expectations placed on them by some parents who seem to want the nondisabled siblings to make up for the other child's limitations by overachieving.

But there are also numerous reports of siblings responding positively, experiencing an increased family closeness and a positive sense of responsibility. Professionals should not automatically conclude that the sibling is being negatively affected.

The impact of the presence of a sibling with a disability varies greatly in form and intensity depending on the relative ages of the children, the presence of other nondisabled siblings, the gender of the siblings, the severity of the disability, the economic status of the family, and a host of other variables. Girls are generally expected to help with the day-to-day care of a sibling with a disability more than boys, so they often will experience the effects more intensely. If the nondisabled sibling is older than the child with a disability, greater expectations for help are likely to be placed on the nondisabled child. Siblings whose families easily can afford to pay for outside help, respite care, special equipment, and so on, can be spared many of the unfortunate side effects felt by children in poorer families.

Nondisabled siblings obviously can benefit from the counseling process. Counselors should consider several factors when working with these siblings. They should check to see what factual knowledge base the siblings have about the disabling condition involved; although the parents may have educated themselves at the time of the initial diagnosis, they may have neglected to provide information continually to their nondisabled children at a level they could understand. If needed, counseling should begin with a major educative component. Contact with other children who have siblings with disabilities in a group counseling format can be extremely valuable in normalizing the experience. Children have models for typical behavior and emotions as they go through most other developmental tasks, but they commonly never encounter another child with a sibling with a disability, who can share how they feel and how they act.

An important goal in counseling siblings is to let them know that it is all right for them to feel hostility or jealousy toward the sibling with the disability. All siblings experience these negative emotions toward each other; this is *normal*. On the other hand, it is also important to help the siblings gain perspective on the extent to which their brother or sister with the disability actually is the big problem in their lives; it is too easy to blame all one's problems on a scapegoat. Another important counseling goal is to help the nondisabled children develop appropriate "scripts" that they can use to explain their sibling's disabilities to people they encounter. Having something specific in mind to say is greatly preferable to the discomfort children feel if they do not know how they might respond in given circumstances. Role playing is a good way to provide practice with these scripts.

Deciding Whether To Have More Children

Especially in families in which the first child has a disability, the issue of having additional children will arise in counseling. Parents may hesitate to do so for fear subsequent children also will have the disability, or out of concerns about their ability to provide well for other children given the cost of caring for the one child, or because of concerns that that child will harm a younger sibling. Counselors must help parents clarify the factors so that they can achieve an appropriate focus. If a genetic component was involved in their child's disability, or if prenatal maternal complications contributed, specialized medical information is essential, and the counselor should either help the parents acquire that information or refer them to people who can provide it. The other issues involved are much more subjective. The counselor can aid by helping the parents to communicate fears, life goals, and other views to each other. Such decisions can be made more objectively in the context of counseling.

Peer Relations

Most children with disabilities have restricted opportunities for interaction with children their own age. Social skills deficits accompany many disabling conditions, and physical impairments limit the activities in which many children with disabilities can engage. Community-sponsored sports and musical activities often are outside the ability levels of these children, and it is in these settings that much informal interaction occurs for nondisabled children. Parents often find that they cannot simply drop the child off to play with friends. The child may experience social rejection; other children frequently are cruel to children who are different. A counselor should encourage the parents not to shield their child from interaction with the outside world because this will prove detrimental to the child's long-term development. Instead, parents can be encouraged to manufacture friendship opportunities by choosing likely candidates and arranging times and places where the interactions can most likely succeed. Supervision can be provided if needed. In addition, counselors can work directly with the child with a disability, or through the parents, to teach social skills to the child. These might include such topics as looking at people when talking to them, dealing with anger, or sharing toys. Guided practice will be necessary, including role playing and controlled experience with peers. A number of social skills training programs, complete with visual aids and other prompts, are commercially available. Children also should be taught "scripts" for how to deal with questions about the nature of their disability, because these are sure to come from other children.

Dealing with Sexual Behavior

Delivering sex education is difficult for many parents, even without the complications of a child with a disability. For children who are mentally retarded or have other disabilities, sex is an especially complicated concern. Some parents think that youth with mental retardation should not be sexually active and avoid providing sexual information in the naive hope that the child will not show an interest in sex. It is difficult to know how much to teach about sexual topics when the likelihood of experiencing a sexual relationship is low, as in the case of some children with severe disabilities. Nonetheless, all humans have sexual feelings that they need to understand at some level. Counselors can help parents get in touch with their own concerns about the sexuality of their child with a disability, then enable them to make informed decisions about how and how much to teach. In circumstances where the parents' discomfort is so high that they cannot deal with the topic alone, the counselor may provide the information for the child either in an individual session or, preferably, in the presence of the parents.

Planning for the Child's Future

Entry into adulthood is an important transition stage both for parents and their child with a disability. The issues of the separation process can be difficult for families in that the normal trend toward increasing independence from the family is complicated by the disability. Parents may need assistance in recognizing their child's normal need for individuation from the family psychologically, while simultaneously requiring more emotional and financial support than a child without disabilities. The family must make many decisions with regard to living arrangements, such as will the "adult" child remain at home or are there other acceptable alternatives such as group homes or supervised apartments? The extent to which the child can earn money independently plays a significant role in the necessity for continued parental responsibility. Extended vocational training or assistance in job placement are factors to be considered in assisting the parents and child in decision making.

The nature of the counseling continues to include educative and facilitative components at this point. Parents may need to be directed toward social service agencies and job training or rehabilitation centers for such things as information about social security benefits related to the disability.

The counselor must be sensitive to the parents' emotional experiences that may have evolved through several stages by this time. Old "crises" may reemerge, such as feelings of deep disappointment about the unfulfilled dreams of having a "perfect" child to launch into the adult world.

Conclusion

Counselors who work with parents and families will be most effective if they view these clients as normal people with a full range of strengths, weaknesses, and life circumstances who, in addition, are attempting to cope with the special challenges involved in having a child with a disability in the family. Thus, although some specialized knowledge base and unique perspectives are important assets for counselors, the most basic requirement for effectiveness in this role is that the professional be a perceptive, sensitive, caring human being who can listen empathetically, evaluate the special circumstances of these clients, and then apply good counseling skills.

References

Block, J. (1978). Impaired children. *Children Today, 7,* 2–6.

Bronfenbrenner, U. (1979). *The ecology of human development.* Cambridge, MA: Harvard University Press.

Chinn, P., Winn, J., & Walters, R. (1978). *Two-way talking with parents of special children.* St. Louis: Mosby.

Ellis, A. (1979). Rational-emotive therapy. In R. J. Corsini (Ed.), *Current psychotherapies* (2nd ed., pp. 185–229). Itasca, IL: Peacock.

Fewell, R. (1986). A disabled child in the family. In R. R. Fewell & P. F. Vadasy (Eds.), *Families of handicapped children* (pp. 3–34). Austin, TX: PRO-ED.

Kazak, A. E., Segal-Andrews, A. M., & Johnson, K. (1995). Pediatric psychology research and practice: A family systems approach. In M. C. Roberts (Ed.), *Psychology handbook of pediatric psychology* (pp. 84–104). New York: Guilford.

Kazdin, A. E. (1994). *Behavior modification in applied settings* (5th ed.). Pacific Grove, CA: Brooks/Cole.

Marvin, R. S., & Pianta, R. C. (1996). Mother's reactions to their child's diagnosis: Relations with security of attachment. *Journal of Clinical Child Psychology, 25*(4), 436–445.

Meichenbaum, D. (1977). *Cognitive behavior modification: An integrative approach.* New York: Plenum Press.

Olshanksy, S. S. (1962). Chronic sorrow: A response to having a mentally defective child. *Social Casework, 43,* 190–193.

Olson, D. H., McCubbin, H. I., Barnes, H., Larsen, A., Muxen, M., & Wilson, M. (1984). *One thousand families: A national survey.* Beverly Hills: Sage.

Patterson, C. H. (1986). *Theories of counseling and psychotherapy* (4th ed.). New York: Harper & Row.

Rogers, C. (1961). *On becoming a person: A therapist's view of psychotherapy.* Boston: Houghton Mifflin.

Sabbeth, B. F., & Leventhal, J. M. (1984). Marital adjustment to chronic childhood illness: A critique of the literature. *Pediatrics, 73,* 762–768.

Seligman, M., & Darling, R. B. (1989). *Ordinary families, special children: A systems approach to childhood disability.* New York: Guilford Press.

Singer, G. H. S., & Powers, L. E. (Eds.). (1993). *Families, disability, and empowerment.* Baltimore: Brookes.

Solnit, A., & Stark, M. (1961). Mourning and the birth of a defective child. *Psychoanalytic Study of the Child, 16,* 523–527.

Telford, C., & Sawrey, J. (1981). *The exceptional individual* (4th ed.). Englewood Cliffs, NJ: Prentice Hall.

Wentworth, E. (1974). *Listen to your heart.* Boston: Houghton Mifflin.

Yogman, M. W., & Brazelton, T. B. (Eds.). (1986). *In support of families.* Cambridge, MA: Harvard University Press.

Intervening with Abusing Parents of Children with Disabilities

10

Marvin J. Fine and Julia S. Shaftel

Since national attention was focused on child abuse over 35 years ago (Kempe, Silverman, Steele, Droegemueller, & Silver, 1962), our awareness of the scope of the problem has grown enormously. Child abuse reports have increased 45% from 1987 to 1996 (Wang & Daro, 1997). According to the 1996 Fifty State Survey conducted by the National Committee to Prevent Child Abuse, over 3 million children were reported to have been victims of abuse or neglect in 1996, and almost 1 million of these cases were substantiated (Wang & Daro, 1997). While the reported incidence rose slightly over 1995, the rate of substantiated abuse represented a 3% decrease from 1995. Greater changes have occurred with respect to substantiated reports of sexual abuse, which decreased 7% from 1995 to 1996 (Wang & Daro, 1997). The authors point out that reporting and substantiation rates are variable across states and over time, and that they reflect social and political conditions, child welfare classification systems, and the willingness of professionals and individuals to report various types of abuse.

The historical bases for the identification of child abuse have been actual physical abuse and neglect. Concerns about other forms of abuse, such as emotional maltreatment and sexual abuse, expanded the numbers of reported and identified abused children in the 1980s (Garbarino, Guttman, & Seeley, 1986; Hart & Brassard, 1987; Wang & Daro, 1997). Children who have been belittled, threatened, or emotionally manipulated can be psychologically damaged in ways that affect their interactions with peers, schooling, and society. Children caught up in parental conflict can easily become psychological casualties, despite both parents' insistence that they love their children and would not knowingly hurt them. And certainly children who have been sexually molested or exploited can develop deep psychological impairments.

Children who have been the victims of abuse are at high risk for a range of lasting personal and social difficulties. Ammerman, Cassisi, Hersen, and Van Hasselt (1986) reviewed the outcome literature in relation to (a) medical and neurological effects, (b) intellectual and cognitive functioning, (c) academic achievement, (d) behavioral disorders and psychopathology, and (e) social development. All of these areas were found to be negatively affected by abuse, with many children showing impairment across all areas. The development of aggressive patterns, learning difficulties, and lower intellectual functioning suggests the potential for long-term and pervasive repercussions of abuse.

Abuse and the Child with Disabilities

Considering the vulnerability of children with disabilities and the stresses that these children might place on their families, it might seem that a greater incidence and possibly more severe kinds of child abuse would occur within such families. In 1993 the National Center on Child Abuse and Neglect concluded that children with disabilities were maltreated at 1.7 times the rate of children without disabilities (Crosse, Kaye, & Ratnofsky, 1993). Furthermore, caseworkers reported that disabilities directly led to or may have contributed to abuse for 47% of the maltreated children with disabilities (Crosse et al., 1993). However, one review of the literature concluded that "the evidence reviewed in this paper does not demonstrate the clear causal link between prior handicaps and abuse. Indeed, more recent prospective research suggests that handicapping conditions are unrelated to abuse" (Starr, Dietrich, Fischoff, Ceresnie, & Zweier, 1984, p. 62). These seemingly contradictory results raise an interesting question: Does the existence of the disability itself cause children with disabilities to become victims of abuse more frequently than children without disabilities?

In another literature review, Ammerman, Van Hasselt, and Hersen (1988) suggested that an increased likelihood of abuse exists among families that include a child with a disability due to factors that are considered high risk in nondisabled populations, such as early separation of parent and child, disruption of attachment, difficult-to-manage crying and other problem behaviors, and increased parental stress due to the requirements of care. Zirpoli (1990) and Waldron (1996) stressed that the interaction of a number of variables, rather than simply the presence of a disabling condition, may increase or even decrease the likelihood of abuse. The interaction of child and parent characteristics with family and environmental factors tends to have a compounding effect, particularly when a life crisis or other precipitating event occurs. In his review of the literature, Zirpoli (1990) examined these variables by category. Caregiver characteristics included having been a victim of abuse or a witness to abusive family interactions, being an immature parent lacking parenting skills, or being a member of a dysfunctional family system. Environmental factors referred to unemployment, poverty, substance abuse, and lack of support systems. Sociocultural variables included cultural acceptance of violence and physical punishment. Finally, child attributes potentially included prematurity, difficult temperament such as irritability and frequent crying, and intense care needs.

Several recent studies have examined the relationship between disability and abuse. A study of 150 psychiatrically hospitalized children with multiple disabilities (Ammerman, Hersen, Van Hasselt, McGonigle, & Lubetsky, 1989) found that 39% of the sample exhibited evidence of abuse or neglect, a much higher proportion than in the overall population. The maltreated children were more likely to live in situations other than with their natural parents and to have more siblings than the nonmaltreated group. The authors found that the physically abused youngsters were less likely to have been diagnosed with organic brain syndrome or mental retardation, conditions that might prompt sympathy on the part of parents and others and help to protect the child against parental anger and abuse.

Benedict, White, Wulff, and Hall (1990) conducted a cohort study in which they found that children with milder impairments were more likely to have been reported as victims of abuse than children with more severe disabilities. These researchers theorized that the disparity between their expectations and the child's actual functioning resulted in significant frustration for these parents, whereas parents of children with severe disabilities did not anticipate considerable improvement. Furthermore, parents of more severely impaired children might have access to greater levels of community support than parents of marginally functioning children who might appear to have age-appropriate characteristics.

A later study examining the relationship between characteristics of disability and child abuse (Ammerman, Hersen, Van Hasselt, Lubetsky, & Sieck, 1994) found that milder levels of the child's functional impairment and higher maternal levels of social isolation and anger were related to greater levels of physical discipline. The significant correlation between certain mother and child characteristics and harsh physical discipline supports the view of the abuse process as systemic. Professionals need to look beyond the mere fact of a disability to the level of impairment and parental response to the stress of caring for the child.

Ammerman and Patz (1996) sought to determine whether child attributes were indicative of increased abuse potential and how they interacted with parental attributes, as well as whether the existence of a disability per se increased the risk for abuse. They found that problematic child characteristics such as hyperactivity and difficulty in adapting to environmental changes were significantly correlated with abuse potential, as were lower levels of social resources and greater parental stress. However, the mere existence of a disability did not help to predict abuse potential above and beyond the existence of salient child characteristics. Children who display difficult behaviors may or may not be impaired, though the existence of these behaviors may be more common among children with disabilities. Challenging behaviors, along with diminished social resources and poorer maternal functioning, are predictive of higher risk for abuse whether the child has a disability or not.

Burrell, Thompson, and Sexton (1994) studied mothers of young children without identified disabilities and with mild to moderate or severe to profound disabilities to examine correlations between abusive behavior and child, family, and environmental characteristics. They found that stress, family resources, and social support were interrelated with child abuse potential, and that mothers of children with disabilities were at risk for elevated levels of child abuse potential. Overall, stress was the most significant correlate of child abuse potential. The authors theorized that the existence of the disability by itself did not create a higher risk for child abuse, but that maternal response to the stress of caring for a child with a disability did.

These studies indicate that the interdependence of parent, child, and environmental characteristics, rather than simply the existence of a disability, is a critical pattern in potential and actual abuse. This is not meant as a disclaimer, however; there is ample evidence that children with disabilities are being abused and that families with a member with a disability can be stressed (Ammerman et al., 1994; Ammerman et al., 1989; Beckman, 1983; Farber, 1959; Gallagher, Beckman, & Cross, 1983). The error of generalization is the automatic assumption that family stress leads to pathologies such as abuse; in fact, many families have been able to develop useful coping and adaptation strategies prompted by the presence and care of the individual with the disability (Crnic, Friedrich, & Greenberg, 1983; Kazak & Marvin, 1984; Longo & Bond, 1984). Longo and Bond (1984) echoed the findings of other researchers about the fallacy of depicting a family as pathologically stressed and experiencing a range of marital and family problems solely because of the presence of an individual with a disability. Tavormina, Boll, Dunn, Luscomb, and Taylor (1981) pointed out that researchers and clinicians operating from such a preconception often stereotype these families as dysfunctional and in doing so perpetuate those beliefs within the professional community.

Moreover, some writers who have discussed the effects of a child with a disability on the family dynamics have ignored the full range of potential stresses placed on any family by children. Barsch (1968) discussed a number of common parental issues that could be misinterpreted in relation to families with a child with a disability instead of being viewed as problems that any parent might experience. If one family with a child with an impairment develops appropriate coping and adaptation strategies and another family with a child with a similar disability is unable to respond in an adaptive way, the issue is not the disability per se but other family, interpersonal, or ecological considerations.

The intent of this chapter is to consider a broad systems and family ecology orientation toward understanding and intervening with abusive families. Although the examples and discussion relate mainly to families with a member with a disability, the analysis and observations have a more heuristic application. The viewpoint being presented is not original but brings together an awareness of family dynamics (Jung & Cook, 1985; Minuchin & Fishman, 1981) with an appreciation of cultural background and the subsystems within which people exist (Bronfenbrenner, 1979). Justice and Justice (1976) presented a psychosocial systems model of individual family members interlocking within a family system which in turn is nested within a broader societal or cultural matrix. This view complements the ideas presented by Belsky (1980) on child maltreatment from an ecological viewpoint, and Jung and Cook's (1985) description of a family systems approach to child assault.

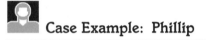 Case Example: Phillip

The case of Phillip illustrates a number of important considerations relevant to understanding the dynamics of abusive families with a child with a disability and to intervening helpfully with such families. Mrs. K. had been a teacher prior to her marriage and had a background of experience with early elementary school children who varied in ability levels and personality characteristics. She came from a family in which people tended to discuss problems, and verbal interchanges were commonplace. Mr. K. came from a family in which obedience on the part of children was an important value. Although corporal punishment was not used extensively or severely, his father had exercised a dominant role in terms of being the disciplinarian, and his word was seldom challenged by the children. Mr. K. did well in mathematics and the sciences and subsequently became an engineer. As he advanced in his company, the nature of his work took him away from home for periods of time, sometimes for weeks. The marriage was described as reasonably happy by both spouses, with Mrs. K. being the more social and verbal partner while her husband was less communicative and intensely involved with his work. There were no conflicts over money or decision making, and in general the couple seemed to be in tacit agreement over their respective marital roles.

The birth of their first child, Phillip, was a happy event following positive anticipation on both their parts. The little boy was a full-term baby without birth complications, but his subsequent development proceeded quite slowly. The father was less aware of the slowness with which the child reached various developmental milestones because of his time away from home. The mother, however, did express a growing concern. The physicians who periodically saw the child generally reassured the mother that Phillip was just a slow developer; they pointed out that the boy had no notable medical or physical problems and would eventually catch up to other children his age. The mother's response was to become progressively more concerned and protective. The father's response was to become gradually more impatient and to begin to believe that the child was stubborn and somehow holding back from displaying more appropriate behavior. Also of note were the reactions of the extended family. Mrs. K.'s parents were sympathetic and supportive of Phillip's difficulties and of the stress on his parents. Mr. K.'s parents were fairly communicative but conveyed a sense of discomfort with the situation and actually commented in passing that no one on their side of the family had ever had those kinds of problems.

The parents finally did receive a descriptive diagnosis from a pediatric clinic that suggested that Phillip was displaying a pattern of irregular development with specific moderate delays. The etiology was unknown and the prognosis was guarded in that Phillip's future progress was considered unpredictable. The recommendation was for Phillip to attend a developmental preschool program that would emphasize motor and language skills. The mother assumed responsibility for the logistics of Phillip's attendance while the father remained skeptical of the medical opinion and the need for a special preschool program.

When Phillip was 3 years old, the couple had a second child whose development proceeded quite normally and whose apparent precocity further set off Phillip as different. The father began to use physical punishment with Phillip and developed a habit of holding Phillip tightly by his shoulders, shaking him, and insisting that he shape up and do what he was supposed to do. Spankings became more frequent and severe. Phillip began to act shy and fearful in group situations, preferred to spend time alone, and became even more reluctant to attempt new experiences. The father's belief that Phillip was willfully choosing to be different and negative was reinforced by Phillip's behavior. The marital relationship began to suffer, the mother became even more protective of Phillip, and the father's interactions with Phillip became more physically and psychologically abusive as he attempted to correct and modify the child's behavior. During this time the father began spending more time in play with the younger child, who was beginning to present discipline problems for the mother.

Much of the writing on child abuse has tended to look at abusive situations in a linear, cause-and-effect fashion. For example, one line of research examined the relationship between abusive parents and their own experiences as abused children (Main & Goldwin, 1984). Some studies have focused on the socioeconomic correlates to abusive situations (Pelton, 1981) and on the extent to which the abused child might even be provoking abuse (Johnson & Morse, 1968). It has become increasingly clear, though, that the study of unitary variables has not been highly productive for a comprehensive understanding of the problem and in planning an intervention program. Evaluating the abusing family as a system seems to be a more useful approach to understanding and ameliorating abusive situations. An examination of the family context is vital because that is where all the variables play themselves out in a systemic manner (Berger, 1980; Fine & Holt, 1983; Garbarino & Gilliam, 1980; Jung & Cook, 1985).

The family as a microsystem includes the nuclear family of parents and children along with whoever else resides in the home. The structure of the family reveals patterns of communication, affection, and authority. Subsystems and boundaries within the nuclear family are often expressed as the parent and child subsystems. The nuclear family is nested within and interconnects to broader systems, including extended family and cultural, educational, and socioeconomic systems. Individuals influence and are influenced reciprocally by these different systems. Family values, historic parenting patterns, and members defining their roles in relation to other family members all influence current functioning. Some families are relatively open to change and evidence a good capacity for adapting successfully to new events. Members close ranks and work together supportively. Other families resist change and are threatened by new events that challenge rigidly adhered-to patterns and beliefs.

Although no one case can reflect all that we know about abusive families and the presence of a child with a disability, Phillip's case exhibited some features common to some other abusive situations. First, the abuse of Phillip appears fairly mild when considered against the backdrop of dramatic accounts of almost sadistic behavior by parents. Yet the majority of actual cases of abuse are likely to be approximations of Phillip's situation rather than the highly dramatic variety. Second, the psychologically damaging impact of the father's behavior must be given considerable weight aside from the physical abuse. We can only speculate as to the effects on Phillip's self-esteem and the anxiety he might experience in new learning situations. Historically, emotional abuse has existed in the shadows of more obvious physical abuse and continues to be reported at a much lower rate—only 3% of the total abuse reported in 1996 (Wang & Daro, 1997).

Phillip's case reflects repeated research conclusions that children with mild disabilities are more likely to become victims of abuse (Ammerman et al., 1994; Benedict et al., 1990; Martin, 1982). Because he was mildly impaired but appeared normal, his father attributed his behavior to willfulness rather than to an aspect of his disability. Parents may find it easier to explain child difficulties as the result of a disabling condition if the impairment is more severe, while unrealistic expectations of the child with a mild disability result in attribution of the challenging behavior to the child (Benedict et al., 1990; Waldron, 1996).

The ambiguity of this type of diagnosis and prognosis is frustrating to parents who want clear answers. They may fall into patterns of wishful thinking or project their misconceptions onto others. Mr. K.'s view of Phillip as choosing to act in a manner different from his younger sibling led to his belief that his wife was being manipulated by the child and that it was up to him to intervene. The father's beliefs about parental responsibilities were learned from his experiences with his own father and required him to be in charge of his family and its well-being. The child's developmental problems struck at the core of the father's sense of adequacy as a parent. These feelings were exacerbated by his own parents' discomfort with Phillip and their defensiveness about possible genetic influences.

Mrs. K.'s background within her own family and in terms of her professional training as a teacher prompted her to seek help and advice from appropriate professionals. Her work with children in the public schools helped her to realize that problem situations often involve ambiguity and that a parent may need to work over time with a child experiencing a problem. The father's more black-and-white view of the world and his sense of certitude about his son led him into a dismissive posture toward the various professionals from whom they attempted to obtain help.

Mr. K. progressively became less willing to discuss the child's difficulties with his wife, and both parents felt increasingly alienated within the family. The parent conflict, anger and blaming, and, in particular, the father's denial, tended to block either parent from seeking community assistance such as a parent support group, thereby exacerbating their respective feelings of isolation. The father was even reluctant to discuss the situation with friends while the mother was more able to use friends for emotional support. A significant contributing factor to incidents of child abuse in families with and without a member with a disability is a sense of aloneness and alienation on the part of family members (Polansky, Chalmers, Buttenweiser, & Williams, 1979).

Mr. K. was apparently more comfortable clinging tenaciously to the belief that Phillip was willfully disobedient than admitting that his child was somehow "defective." Helping the father to understand and accept some of the realities and ambiguities of Phillip's subtle disabilities would be an important although challenging task for the professional worker. Such an acceptance would require him to relinquish the need for a normally functioning child and would probably initiate a related grieving process for the loss of the child that never was.

There is evidence that the sorrow parents may experience about the child with a disability is likely to return at different points during the child's development. As the child fails to meet certain developmental milestones, the realities of the child's condition are again revealed and can trigger a recurrence of the mourning process. This pattern argues for a continuum of services over the life of the person with the disability (Wikler, Wasow, & Hatfield, 1981). We can only speculate as to how the father's closeness to the younger child and the accompanying alienation from his wife and Phillip have influenced the mother's management problems with the younger child. This side-taking and triangulation of relationships reflects the growing dysfunctionality of the family.

The case of Phillip illustrates how having an individual with a disability as a member can have a great many repercussions within the family, depending on what the family members bring to the situation in terms of stability, communication and coping skills, availability of support systems, and even religious belief (Kazak & Marvin, 1984). What other kinds of stress is the family under and what other transitions are occurring in the family? How does the focus of the parental conflict around Phillip reflect some unresolved issues between the parents and serve to detract the parents from facing each other over those issues?

Intervention

Intervention in cases of abuse can mean different things. The removal of the child from an abusive situation always needs to be considered if the child may be in imminent danger. However, this appears to be an infrequently selected option, used in 18% of reported cases of abuse in 1996 (Wang & Daro, 1997). Even in such cases the eventual return of the child to the family is often the ultimate goal, necessitating preparatory work with the parents to ensure the viability of the child's reentry into the family. Alternatively, maintaining the child within the family is the course of action in the majority of substantiated incidents of abuse (Wang & Daro, 1997).

Therapeutic Options

For families with an abuse problem, there are a range of options that may be available or could be developed within any community. Individual or group counseling, family therapy, parent education and training, parent support groups, and some form of direct home supervision are possibilities. Although some parents will voluntarily seek assistance through therapy or parent training, many are directed into treatment by some agency, usually the court or welfare system. There is seldom a comprehensive plan; available services in a community are often used even if only marginally appropriate.

One common intervention is to require the parents to attend parenting sessions such as STEP (Dinkmeyer & McKay, 1977), PET (Gordon, 1970), or Active Parenting (Popkin, 1983). These programs as offered in a community are usually open to any interested persons and might therefore include already competent parents as well as parents with minimal skill, destructive attitudes, and a history of abusive behavior. Parent education programs tend to be informational, oriented toward skill building, and can be helpful to parents. However, personal accountability is low, and the programs are time limited, usually running several sessions.

The first author had the experience of offering general parenting programs and at termination having some parents request written documentation that they had attended. The author was unaware that they had been required to attend because of reported child abuse, found them to be passive participants, and had no real sense of what they had gained or how they might be able to be more effective parents. However, they did satisfy the court's directive. This author is also aware of cases in which parents were required to participate in therapy until the therapist recommended termination. This can create the potentially bizarre scenario of parents having to continue indefinitely with a therapist unwilling to release them because some potential for abuse still exists (as if it did not exist in all of us).

Another alternative is home visit programs operated through social welfare services. These may be particularly beneficial where the parents feel overwhelmed by the day-to-day demands of home management and child care. A visitor, often a paraprofessional with evidence of successful home and child management skills, can prove helpful by being on site to demonstrate, coach, and teach parents more effective skills.

Perhaps more than with a nondisabled child, educational intervention is of major importance. The goal is to help parents to understand the nature of the child's condition, the course of development, and, in an educational manner, to make them aware of the kinds of frustrations and problems that will emerge along the way. It is not uncommon to find abusive parents holding unrealistic developmental expectations for their children.

The alienation factor, as previously indicated, has been identified as a contributor to abuse. Parents of children with disabilities may not be aware of community resources, parent networks, and other kinds of support systems that are available in their community. Respite care is an example of a support option. In cases where the child's disabling condition requires fairly constant attention, the stress on parents can become enormous as they become almost captives of the child's condition. For single parents or couples with a child with severe disabilities and needs, the trapped feeling can be overwhelming and can nurture the potential for growing resentment toward the child. Many communities provide forms of respite care, which is an important avenue for reducing parental pressures.

Another valuable intervention is a series of group meetings with parents of young children with disabilities facilitated by a trained professional who can process their experiences and problems, their successes and failures. This can serve as a reality feedback procedure and one that can help parents to understand that what they are experiencing is normal for parents of children with disabilities. The opportunity to feel less singled out and to share information and experiences can be very supportive. The group is also a more efficient structure for reaching a greater number of persons under conditions of limited professional resources. There are a growing number of support groups that can help parents learn about specific disabilities, how family members can work together, and, most important, that others have had and survived similar experiences.

Attitudinal Considerations

Regardless of the kind of program being implemented, the required participation of the parents can create an impression of the program being punitive. One of the first tasks of the involved professional, regardless of program format, is to encourage a positive perception of the experience in terms of its potential helpfulness and to identify the parents as concerned and loving but probably frustrated in their roles as caregivers for their child with exceptional needs. Because the parents might believe that others (e.g., social welfare agencies or the courts) have not understood them and have been punitive toward them, the parents may be understandably defensive.

Unquestionably, the abusive behavior on the part of parents must terminate. But in many instances the most helpful intervention by professionals will come from a sympathetic view of the plight of the family and its members as opposed to a belief that the abuser is a deranged individual. The pattern of abusive behavior is frequently symptomatic of systemic problems in the family and the frustration and unhappiness of a number of family members (Brassard & Apellaniz, 1992; Fine & Holt, 1983).

Any involved professional should maintain a sympathetic view of the parents as struggling to adapt and cope with the effects of the child on the family. A professional should have the insight and compassion to see through the abusive behavior to the kinds of deep-seated parental concerns and fears that often characterize the abusing parent. Such a posture can be quite difficult to maintain given the professional's aversive reaction to parents who have harmed a child with a disability. Minuchin and Fishman (1981) described this issue in a family therapy situation:

> The therapist is forcing himself to act against his own inclinations. It would give the therapist great pleasure at this point to tell the mother exactly what he thinks of people who mistreat children. But if this child is not to be removed from his parents—which is always a chancy solution—then family change is his best hope. In order to achieve that change, the therapist must keep the family in therapy. This can be done only by creating a therapeutic system in which the parents feel supported and understood before there is any challenge. (p. 41)

A Multidimensional View of Intervention

There is a homeostatic dynamic in families that encourages the maintenance of the status quo: relationship patterns once established have ways of reinforcing themselves. Some changes that occur in dysfunctional families are mainly cosmetic with fundamental patterns of behavior and beliefs remaining intact. The data on the effects of intervention with abusing families are not highly encouraging, with predicted success rates of only 40% to 50% (Starr, 1979).

The reported difficulties in precipitating change in abusing families may be related to relatively superficial levels of intervention. A several-pronged approach based on the interrelationship between (a) education and information, (b) belief and insight, (c) skill acquisition, and (d) problem solving may have greater potential for successful behavior change. As shown in Figure 10.1, those four areas of emphasis overlap and can synergistically reinforce each other. Although formats may differ from program to program, as between a time-limited versus open-ended therapy group, all four areas seem to be critical and distinct elements of a comprehensive program. Any one of the emphases alone, such as information acquisition or insight, is unlikely to move the person into different and lasting attitudinal and behavior patterns.

Programs may be offered through community agencies, schools, or even within the context of a private psychotherapy practice. Usually one location is identified as the primary source of intervention, such as a community mental health clinic. Ideally, there would exist within that one agency sev-

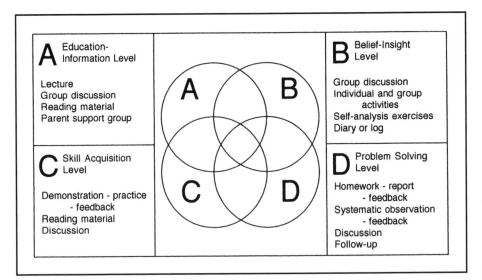

Figure 10.1. The interrelationship among the four areas of family intervention.

eral tracks that parents and families could move through. For example, the parents could be counseled as a couple and also participate in a discussion group with other parents; subsequently they might join a time-limited parent education group. The abused child could receive individual counseling as needed and might in time join the parents for a family therapy experience. Specific educational and community resource components might be built into the overall program. The involved professionals would be able to conceptualize a broad systemic and ecological framework that would allow for connecting the parents selectively to other programs and resources within the community.

In the case of Phillip's parents, couple's therapy would seem indicated to help them work out the anger and hurt that is now pushing them apart. Some family-of-origin focus would assist them in seeing what they brought to the relationship and the way that current extended family relationships are influencing how they are dealing with Phillip.

Their involvement in a parent support group that included educational components would also be helpful. Mr. K. would benefit from specific information on developmental delays in children and hearing from other parents who, like him, are struggling with feelings of frustration and anger over the ambiguities of their child's behavior. To hear others share how they may have tried to force more appropriate behavior from the child, lost control, were hurtful with the child, then remorseful, then angry, then withdrawing, would assist the father in realizing that he was not alone in his reactions and experiences, nor was he a terrible person.

Ideally, through either the couple's therapy group or some other program vehicle, the father could be taught some anger control techniques. Both parents could learn how to be more supportive of each other and come to recognize that Phillip will need their support, understanding, and guidance for the years ahead. Both parents, working together, could gradually help Phillip to feel better about himself, to believe that he can please his parents, and to approach new learning situations with less anxiety. These last happy scenarios may be some time in coming but are achievable to a reasonable degree.

The following discussion elaborates each of the four areas of focus, although professionals are encouraged to develop a comprehensive framework appropriate for their professional contexts. The specifics of program and community resources will vary from community to community, requiring initiative and creativity on the part of professionals.

The Education–Information Level

Books, pamphlets, lectures, and films are ready vehicles for conveying important factual information regarding the disabling condition, its course of development, and how families can productively respond. Information on typical development and appropriate expectations should also be included. Some parents have unrealistic expectations for their child, project a negative intent onto the child when he does not perform, and then feel justified in punishing the child. It is important for parents to appreciate the normal variances of child development and to learn to see each child as an individual. Especially in the case of disabling conditions with ambiguous prognoses, parents can benefit from developmental information to help them sort out the overall picture. Information on families in general, descriptions of problem-solving styles, and discussion of the impact of the child with a disability on all family members, including siblings, can also be helpful. The education–information level is also where information on organizations dealing with specific disabilities and community support services such as a respite care program can be shared.

Typical educational formats may be less threatening than other formats because a minimal level of personal involvement by the participants is acceptable. Even when discussion and personal sharing follows a film, many parents often sit passively listening to the few who become actively engaged in discussion. Each parent involved in a treatment program is going to respond differently. Some will need time to acclimate and to learn how to respond and think through family situations. The parent who sits passively at first, if emotionally supported, may subsequently open up and become a more active participant. If parents are pushed too hard at first to participate, their defensiveness may increase along with progressively less cooperative involvement.

The Belief–Insight Level

The belief–insight level can also involve a combination of educational inputs but should represent calculated occasions for the parents to personalize their experiences. Parent or whole family counseling sessions can more easily bring the feelings of different family members to the surface and reveal dysfunctional patterns that maintain tension and abusive behavior. Parent education programs that utilize some family therapy techniques encouraging exploration of family patterns and family history can also be a valuable input at this level (Fine & Jennings, 1985).

The goals at the belief–insight level are to increase family members' awareness of destructive family patterns, to clarify their own feelings and needs in both the contemporary scene and from a family-of-origin perspective, and to help them achieve a healthier view of themselves and other family members. A cognitive behavioral framework can be helpful in encouraging parents to examine their thoughts and how feelings and behavior can follow. Cognitive strategies can assist parents in overriding an emotional reaction with appropriate behavior. A simple example is a parent who learned that he could still think and choose appropriate interventions with the child, even though he was becoming angry. In another case, the parent became aware of a sequence of thinking that she went through that encouraged angry reactions, then learned a series of positive self-statements she could make that supported a positive response to the child.

Helping parents gain access to social support systems of either a community or extended family nature may require supporting them to change their beliefs about the child and their own needs. An examination of their resistance to reaching out and accepting community support will probably reveal specific thoughts and feelings about the child with the disability, personal responsibility, and the anticipated reactions of others. Professionals should explore these areas with the family because of the positive mediating influences of social support (Dunst, Trivette, & Cross, 1986). Researchers hypothesize that without changes at the belief–insight level, generalizability and permanence of behavior changes by the parents will be limited.

Skill Acquisition and Problem-Solving Levels

The skill acquisition and problem-solving levels can be conceptualized separately but in operation should occur simultaneously. Within a clinic or training group setting, the professional can advise parents on techniques of child-care, discipline, anger management, and mutual support. Specific relaxation and stress reduction techniques can also be demonstrated and practiced. Modeling, role playing, and behavioral rehearsal are other potentially effective, action-oriented ways of training parents.

The professional who is able to observe the parents and child interact in a playroom or through home visits can offer coaching and immediate feedback to the parents. The feedback is extremely important not only for positively reinforcing gains, but also for heading off parent frustration. For example, parents can learn that even if they start to react angrily they can still shift to a more positive response. For some parents, once they show the wrong reaction they feel frustrated and then continue the angry abusive response as if they had no control. This situation is similar to that of people on a diet who take a cookie and then think that if they took one, they may as well have 10 and feel unable to stop.

The cognitive analyses mentioned earlier can be taught as a set of skills to be implemented by the parents at stressful times. The importance of the cognitive components is that they can support parents in developing a self-view of being in control and able to think clearly. These views counteract the historical self-view of some parents as becoming out of control or "losing it" as soon as they experience anger or find themselves in trigger situations.

Once certain skill areas have been identified and demonstrated with opportunities for practice within the session, then the parents will be expected to try out the new skills at home. Some record of specific incidents, data collection, or vignettes can be brought back to regular sessions for processing and, most important, for feedback. Positive reinforcement is crucial at this point. The parents need to see themselves changing and succeeding. The important changes are not only in terms of specific parent–child behaviors but also in parent–parent behaviors of a collaborative, mutually supportive nature, and in overall healthier family interaction patterns.

The Family Emphasis

The professional worker needs to be cognizant at all times that the family is the focus of treatment even through the steps of intervention may seem at times to focus more narrowly on information or specific skills. For example, in a processing discussion about some new behavior the parents have attempted, the inquiry should include who else was involved, how others in the family are responding, whether the grandparents (or whoever else is an important extended member) are aware of what is happening, and what they are saying or doing.

The feedback given to the parents should reinforce what seem to be changes in their thinking and attitudes and in family behavior patterns. As stated, the parents need to begin seeing themselves as more competent in parenting and as more supportive of each other. In essence a positive, family adaptation process has been initiated that should lead to successful outcomes that, in a cyclical fashion, reinforce the new behavior patterns. If this phenomenon occurs, the likelihood of successful, enduring, and generalizable changes in family functioning should increase with the most important consequence of eliminating the child abuse.

Summary

Abuse of any child, with or without a disability, can be conceptualized as an expression of dysfunctionality in the family. Intervention therefore should have a broad family orientation. Although a child with a disability can represent a stressful event to a family, many families do adapt and cope adequately.

The efficacy literature on intervention with families showing child abuse has not been encouraging. The multilevel intervention model proposed here may increase the likelihood of the family undergoing and maintaining positive changes. Each of the focuses—information, belief, skill, and problem solving—interfaces with the others. This framework can serve as a blueprint for professionals developing intervention programs for parents who have been abusive.

The example presented of a child with a mild disability and of fairly mild abuse, although not very dramatic, does illustrate some typical considerations. The professional needs to assume a sympathetic posture with the family struggling to cope, albeit not very effectively, rather than viewing the parent who abused the child as a horrible person. Strengthening the family's positive adaptation and coping skills and eliminating negative reciprocal behavior patterns between parents and the abused child are reasonable goals of intervention. Teaching the parents to be seekers and accepters of professional and peer support is also important.

References

Ammerman, R. T., Cassisi, J. E., Hersen, M., & Van Hasselt, V. B. (1986). Consequences of physical abuse and neglect in children. *Clinical Psychology Review, 6,* 291–310.

Ammerman, R. T., Hersen, M., Van Hasselt, V. B., Lubetsky, M. J., & Sieck, W. R. (1994). Maltreatment in psychiatrically hospitalized children and adolescents with developmental disabilities: Prevalence and correlates. *Journal of the American Academy of Child and Adolescent Psychiatry, 33,* 567–576.

Ammerman, R. T., Hersen, M., Van Hasselt, V. B., McGonigle, J. J., & Lubetsky, M. J. (1989). Abuse and neglect in psychiatrically hospitalized multihandicapped children. *Child Abuse & Neglect, 13,* 335–343.

Ammerman, R. T., & Patz, R. J. (1996). Determinants of child abuse potential: Contribution of parent and child factors. *Journal of Clinical Child Psychology, 25,* 300–307.

Ammerman, R. T., Van Hasselt, V. B., & Hersen, M. (1988). Maltreatment of handicapped children: A critical review. *Journal of Family Violence, 3,* 53–72.

Barsch, R. H. (1968). *The parent of the handicapped child: A study of childrearing practices.* Springfield, IL: Thomas.

Beckman, P. (1983). Influences of selected child characteristics on stress in families of handicapped infants. *American Journal of Mental Deficiency, 80,* 150–156.

Belsky, J. (1980). Child maltreatment: An ecological integration. *American Psychologist, 35,* 320–335.

Benedict, M. I., White, R. B., Wulff, L. M., & Hall, B. J. (1990). Reported maltreatment in children with multiple disabilities. *Child Abuse & Neglect, 14,* 207–217.

Berger, A. M. (1980). The child abusing family: Part I. Methodological issues and parent-related characteristics of abusing families. *The American Journal of Family Therapy, 8,* 52–68.

Brassard, M. R., & Apellaniz, I. M. (1992). The abusive family: Theory and intervention. In M. J. Fine & C. Carlson (Eds.), *The handbook of family–school intervention: A systems perspective* (pp. 215–230). Boston: Allyn & Bacon.

Bronfenbrenner, U. (1979). *The ecology of human development.* Cambridge, MA: Harvard University Press.

Burrell, B., Thompson, B., & Sexton, D. (1994). Predicting child abuse potential across family types. *Child Abuse & Neglect, 18,* 1039–1049.

Crnic, K. A., Friedrich, W. N., & Greenberg, M. T. (1983). Adaptation of families with mentally retarded children: A model of stress, coping, and family ecology. *American Journal of Mental Deficiency, 88,* 125–138.

Crosse, S. B., Kaye, E., & Ratnofsky, A. C. (1993). *A report on the maltreatment of children with disabilities* (Rep. No. 20-10030). Washington, DC: National Center on Child Abuse and Neglect, U.S. Department of Health and Human Services.

Dinkmeyer, D., & McKay, G. (1977). *Systematic training for effective parenting.* Circle Pines, MN: American Guidance Service.

Dunst, C. J., Trivette, C., & Cross, A. H. (1986). Mediating influences of social support: Personal, family, and child outcomes. *American Journal of Mental Deficiency, 90,* 403–417.

Farber, B. (1959). Effects of a severely mentally retarded child on family integration. *Monographs of the Society for Research in Child Development, 24*(71).

Fine, M. J., & Holt, P. (1983). Corporal punishment in the family: A systems perspective. *Psychology in the Schools, 20,* 85–92.

Fine, M. J., & Jennings, J. (1985). What parent education can learn from family therapy. *Social Work in Education, 8,* 14–31.

Gallagher, J. J., Beckman, P., & Cross, A. H. (1983). Families of handicapped children: Sources of stress and its amelioration. *Exceptional Children, 50,* 10–19.

Garbarino, J., & Gilliam, G. (1980). *Understanding abusive families.* Lexington, MA: Lexington Books.

Garbarino, J., Guttman, E., & Seeley, J. (1986). *The psychologically battered child: Strategies for identification, assessment, and intervention.* San Francisco: Jossey-Bass.

Gordon, T. (1970). *Parent effectiveness training.* New York: David McKay.

Hart, S. N., & Brassard, M. R. (1987). A major threat to children's mental health: Psychological maltreatment. *American Psychologist, 42,* 160–165.

Johnson, B., & Morse, H. A. (1968). Injured children and their parents. *Children, 15,* 147–152.

Jung, M., & Cook, P. (1985). A family systems approach to child assault. In J. Meier (Ed.), *Assault against children: Why it happens and how to stop it.* San Diego, CA: College Hill Press.

Justice, B., & Justice, R. (1976). *The abusing family.* New York: Human Sciences Press.

Kazak, A. E., & Marvin, R. S. (1984). Differences, difficulties, and adaptation: Stress and social networks in families with a handicapped child. *Family Relations, 33,* 67–76.

Kempe, C. H., Silverman, F. N., Steele, B. F., Droegemueller, W., & Silver, H. K. (1962). The battered child syndrome. *Journal of the American Medical Association, 181,* 17–24.

Longo, D. C., & Bond, L. (1984). Families of the handicapped child: Research and practice. *Family Relations, 33,* 57–65.

Main, M., & Goldwin, R. (1984). Predicting rejection of her infant from mother's representation of her own experience: Implications for the abused–abusing intergenerational cycle. *Child Abuse & Neglect, 8,* 203–217.

Martin, H. P. (1982). The clinical relevance of prediction and prevention. In R. H. Starr, Jr. (Ed.), *Child abuse prediction: Policy implications.* Cambridge, MA: Ballinger.

Minuchin, S., & Fishman, H. C. (1981). *Family therapy techniques.* Cambridge, MA: Harvard University Press.

Pelton, L. H. (Ed). (1981). *The social context of child abuse and neglect.* New York: Human Services Press.

Polansky, N., Chalmers, M., Buttenweiser, R., & Williams, P. (1979). Isolation of the neglectful family. *American Journal of Orthopsychiatry, 49,* 149–152.

Popkin, M. H. (1983). *Active parenting.* Atlanta: Active Parenting.

Starr, R. H. (1979). Child abuse. *American Psychologist, 34,* 872–878.

Starr, R. H., Dietrich, K. N., Fischoff, J., Ceresnie, S., & Zweier, D. (1984). The contribution of handicapping conditions to child abuse. *Topics in Early Childhood Special Education, 4,* 55–69.

Tavormina, J. B., Boll, T. J., Dunn, N. J., Luscomb, R. L., & Taylor, J. R. (1981). Psychosocial effects on parents of raising a physically handicapped child. *Journal of Abnormal Child Psychology, 9,* 121–131.

Waldron, N. L. (1996). Child abuse and disability: The school's role in prevention and intervention. *Preventing School Failure, 40*(4), 164–168.

Wang, C. T., & Daro, D. (1997). *Current trends in child abuse reporting and fatalities: NCPCA's 1996 annual fifty state survey* [on-line]. Chicago: The National Committee to Prevent Child Abuse. Available: http://www.childabuse.org/5096sum.html

Wikler, L., Wasow, M., & Hatfield, E. (1981). Chronic sorrow revisited: Parents vs. professional depiction of the adjustment of parents of mentally retarded children. *American Journal of Orthopsychiatry, 51,* 63–70.

Zirpoli, T. J. (1990). Physical abuse: Are children with disabilities at greater risk? A look at the facts. *Intervention in School and Clinic, 26,* 6–11.

Focus on Exceptionality

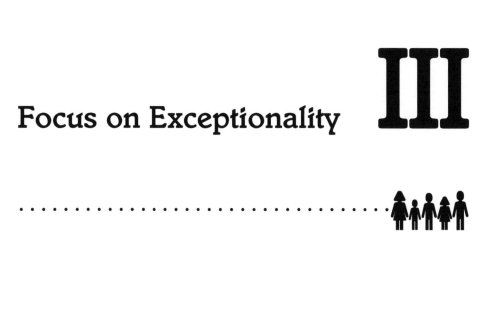

The Family with a Child with Mental Retardation

11

H. Thompson Prout and Susan M. Prout

The identification of intellectual handicaps such as mental retardation has been an issue in the human service, medical, and education professions for many years. Most of the research and concern have focused on the diagnosed individuals themselves and their characteristics, care, education, and adaptation. While the impact on the families of people with mental retardation has long been recognized by practitioners, only within the last decade has the family been emphasized at a research and policy level (e.g., see Gallagher & Vietze, 1986). Professionals now recognize that the presence of a person with mental retardation within a family system has significant impact on that system and its members.

This chapter will review relevant research on individuals with mental retardation and their families and discuss collaborations between professionals and parents. Discussion will focus on potential collaborative roles of professionals, the impact on families, and social–emotional problems of persons with mental retardation. The chapter will conclude with a historical case study focusing on a child with mental retardation at different ages and developmental levels with the concomitant effects on the parents and family.

Collaborative Roles with Parents

The collaborations and interventions with parents of children with mental retardation can take many forms. The professional must assume that parents will be consulting with an assortment of professionals throughout the child's life, and thus the collaboration roles should be viewed within a developmental framework that considers family life cycle issues. Tymchuk (1983) has delineated several models of interventions with parents of persons with mental retardation. The *dynamic* model emphasizes a counseling or therapeutic approach and assumes parental behavior relates directly to how the parents respond psychologically to their child's disability. This model places more importance on the attitudes and feelings of the parents than on actual management strategies for dealing with the child. Laborde and Seligman (1983) call a similar approach "facilitative counseling" that deals largely with parental adjustment. The marital relationship of the parents may also receive some attention in this model. Difficulty in dealing with the child and the disability is viewed as a psychological barrier in the parents. In order to facilitate the parents' adjustment, the professional helps them to explore, examine, and overcome the barrier. The resolution allows the parents to be more effective in their role.

The aim of the *behavioral* model, in contrast, is to help parents improve their parenting skills and their responses to behaviors presented by their children with mental retardation. The emphasis is on teaching parents how to conduct operantly based behavior modification programs in the home, for instance, appropriately reinforcing specified or desired behaviors. This model focuses on training more than counseling or therapeutic approaches.

The *family therapy* model assumes that the family structure or system is affected by the presence of a member with mental retardation. The professional, recognizing that the family is an interacting system, may meet with all the family members in a group. This model goes beyond the others by including siblings of the child with mental retardation. A more functional family system facilitates the adjustment of the child with mental retardation as well as other family members.

The *early intervention* approach or *educational* approach focuses on the parents' role in collaborating with educational or developmental programming for their child. Similar to the behavioral model, it focuses on training parents to work with their child to maximize cognitive, adaptive, and educational development.

We would add three somewhat related models to Tymchuk's (1983) discussion—the role of *collaborative assessment,* the *resource* role of providing information for parents, and the role of fostering family *empowerment.* The *assessment* role is an important collaborative function on a number of levels. Accurate and thorough assessment is a vital part of planning for the child, helping parents accept the disability, and understanding the extent of the child's problems and limitations. Assessment conducted in a *collaborative* style—showing parents the nature of the assessment; perhaps allowing some observation; collecting parental information through structured interviews, checklists, and rating scales; and so forth—facilitates the parents' willingness to collaborate and cooperate with the professionals involved with their child. In addition to focusing on cognitive, adaptive, and educational areas, professionals in this assessment role should thoroughly evaluate the social–emotional functioning of the child. This area, often overlooked, is vital to the child's adjustment and is discussed later in this chapter.

A professional in the resource role provides accurate information about the child's disability and programs to assist the child. The role's main purpose is educational. It may involve providing parents with reading materials, directing them to various community resources, and generally linking them to case management services at various transition points for the child. Explaining appropriate developmental expectations, without setting expectations too low, is a key part of this role.

The *empowerment* role, perhaps, pervades all other roles. The professional encourages the family to gain greater control over decisions made about their children and stresses less dependency and greater self-sufficiency. Birenbaum (1996) notes that empowerment may become even more important with dwindling resources for human service programs.

The Impact of a Child with Mental Retardation on the Family

The Initial Diagnosis and Recognition

Although many parents may suspect that something is "wrong" or "different" with their child, the first official confirmation of developmental delay is traumatic. Depending on the degree and nature of the mental retardation, this official diagnosis may occur at different times for different children. With advances in genetics and medical screening technology, the diagnosis can occur prenatally. Severe or obvious mental retardation is often diagnosed at or shortly after birth, or at least within the first 6 months to 1 year of life. Children with mild mental retardation may not be identified until they enter school. Thus, different families may deal emotionally with the diagnosis at different points in the family development.

Drew, Logan, and Hunter (1988) have described a range of parental reactions and adaptations to the diagnosis of a child's mental retardation. These reactions are influenced by the degree of retardation (discussed below), general family dynamics, specific characteristics of family unit (e.g., single parent, blended family), presence or absence and adjustment of other children, marital dynamics, socioeconomic levels and resources, intelligence of parents, and emotional adjustment coping skills of the parents. Across these parental reactions runs a general theme of the child with mental retardation as a threat to the parents' self-esteem and self-acceptance. These reactions and adaptations to the diagnosis include the following.

Denial. This is a common reaction, particularly after the initial identification of the retardation. Parents may deny that any problem exists or minimize the extent of the problem. At later stages of development, they may attribute the child's limitations to other factors such as poor motivation, laziness, or lack of effort.

Projection of Blame. Projecting blame helps protect the parents' self-esteem with regard to possible causative factors underlying the retardation. If developmental problems are apparent at birth, parents may initially blame the medical professionals involved in the prenatal or early care of their child. They may fabricate or exaggerate what they perceive as improper care for their child and show overt hostility toward the health care professionals. As children with mental retardation grow older and are involved in educational and rehabilitative programs, the parents may blame the professionals in these settings for their child's lack of development and even the failure to overcome the handicap. The blame may manifest itself in overzealous parental advocacy and constant challenging of programming.

Fear. What is not known about mental retardation in general and their child's condition, specifically, may be very scary to the parents. Often, the term "mental retardation" brings to mind the stereotype of the institutionalized, helpless, and inappropriately behaving individual. The parents may have little notion of what to expect behaviorally and developmentally from their child. They may have fears about causative factors and the potential for other children being similarly disabled. The parents may have many questions or fears about care for their child, schooling, the future, available resources, and so on. Further, they may be fearful about reactions from friends, relatives, and the community in general.

Guilt. Guilt is similar to projection of blame except that the blame is directed toward oneself. Parents, and mothers in particular, may search for their causative role in their child's disability. They may obsess on some event or behavior that they feel may have contributed to the disability by exaggerating the significance of these events or behaviors, or blaming themselves for known causative factors (i.e., an infection) over which they had no control.

Mourning or Grief. Some have compared the realization that a child has mental retardation to mourning or grieving for someone who has died. In anticipation of the birth and during early development, parents have dreams about what their child will be like in the future. For example, this anticipation might take the form of parents buying infant sweatshirts for "XYZ University." Upon the diagnosis of mental retardation, these dreams and hopes for the future are negated and drastically altered. It is as if the child they had dreamed of had died. The process of acceptance and adjustment may resemble a grieving pattern for some parents. Unlike the dead child, however, the child with mental retardation who remains in the family may be a constant reminder of the "child that never was."

Withdrawal. After their initial emotional reaction to the diagnosis, the parents may become withdrawn. While in some cases, this response may initially help them to "sort out" issues related to their child's retardation, prolonged withdrawal is maladaptive. The parents may avoid contact with friends, relatives, co-workers, and others, as well as social and community outings and public places.

Rejection. Other emotional reactions may lead to rejecting behaviors toward the child. These may be direct overt behaviors, or may have more subtle psychological manifestations. The rejecting parent may devalue the child by ignoring or minimizing positive attributes, setting unrealistic goals, or simply escaping from the family situation.

Acceptance. The final adjustment, acceptance, may take a long time to achieve. Parents learn to accept and value the child with the disability—and accept themselves. Their obsession with finding causes, blaming others, and other negative emotional reactions decreases significantly. These parents find joy in their child, look forward to the future realistically and positively, and engage in behaviors to normalize their family life.

This acceptance may not be complete throughout the life of the child even after the parents have seemingly adjusted to the disability. Wikler, Wasow, and Hatfield (1981) discussed "chronic sorrow" in parents of children with disabilities. As the child develops and grows older, each new stage or point of "normal" developmental transitions may serve as a reminder of the child's limitations and deficits. Thus parents may experience varying degrees of "acceptance" throughout the child's and family's development. What initially seemed to be a positive and accepting parental attitude about the child's disability may be somewhat less positive as the child grows older.

Degree of Retardation

Many people unfamiliar with mental retardation view these individuals as homogeneous and similarly functioning. This is a common assumption made by parents when first hearing the term in reference to their child. In many cases, parents may assume a worst case scenario: that their child will be severely disabled. The degree of retardation and the associated behaviors vary tremendously as does the child's role in the family. The levels of retardation—mild, moderate, severe, and profound according to the fourth edition of the *Diagnostic and Statistical Manual of Mental Disorders* (DSM–IV, 1994) of the American Psychiatric Association (the American Association on Mental Retardation no long uses these levels), or educable mental retardation/mild mental disability or trainable mental retardation/functional mental disability for schooling purposes—describe very different types of individuals. Inherent in these differences are different impacts and types of stressors within the family (Seligman & Darling, 1989).

Consider the contrasting cases of two "well-behaved" adolescent boys, one with mild mental retardation and one with severe or profound mental retardation. The adolescent with mild mental retardation has a mental or developmental age of approximately 10 years. While somewhat behind his age-mates, he has acquired most of the basic developmental skills, albeit at later times in his development. He has most of his self-care skills (feeding, bathing, dressing, etc.), has some basic academic skills, can go about the community fairly independently, does chores at home, participates in some school and community activities, is partially mainstreamed at school, is taking vocational training for a postschool job, and is responsible enough that his parents can go out at night and leave him alone in the house. He has begun to become quite interested in dating and sexual matters.

The adolescent with severe or profound mental retardation has a mental age of approximately 3 to 4 years. He still lacks most of his basic self-care skills. He can messily feed himself, only recently became completely toilet trained, and needs assistance with dressing and bathing. He needs to be monitored at home and in the community and often gets stared at when his parents take him out in the community. His academic skills are limited to color recognition and partial number and letter naming. His communication is limited to brief descriptive sentences and one- to two-word labeling responses, and he understands only very simple instructions and directions. He attends a self-contained special class and is generally isolated from the rest of his age-mates at school. He can never be left alone at home, and the parents have had a very difficult time finding babysitters. While neither may present significant behavioral concerns for their parents, these two young men present very different current problems for their families. One is relatively independent, nearer the "norm" for his age, and requires less direct time and effort from his parents, although they must deal with prolonged adolescent identity issues. The other is very dependent, very different from his age-mates, and still requires a great deal of direct care from his parents. Further, there are fewer developmental changes for the boy with severe or profound mental retardation, and the parental role has remained constant and demanding. Obviously, the experiences of these parents and families are quite different. Professionals should remember that different degrees of mental retardation in children result in different types of concerns and stressors for the families; the functioning level of the child should be considered an important variable in assessing the family dynamics and adaptation.

Several exploratory studies (Mink, 1986; Mink, Blacher, & Nihira, 1988; Mink, Meyers, & Nihira, 1984; Mink, Nihira, & Meyers, 1983) have examined the differences in families with children of different levels of mental retardation. Across these studies, Mink and her colleagues studied family typologies in families of children in the slow learning, trainable, and severely retarded ranges of mental retardation. Using a clustering procedure, these investigators found that many similar typology patterns existed across these families. However, they also discovered a few distinctive patterns among the families of children with severe mental retardation within family types. The details of these typologies are beyond the scope of this chapter and are detailed in Mink (1986). Cullen, MacLeod, Williams, and Williams (1991) compared families with a member with mental retardation in single- and two-parent households. They found, not surprisingly, more stressors and dissatisfaction in the single-parent households. These studies, taken together, suggest that the presence of a child with mental retardation in a family tends to interact with family dynamics to yield typologies that are relatively similar across levels of retardation. The professional therefore may need to pay considerable attention to the general family typology and not overly focus on the level of retardation. It should be noted that much of the research by Mink's group was done with younger children with mental retardation and their families, and Mink et al. (1988) emphasize the empirical or research nature of their classification system. The clinical significance of the typologies across the family life cycle remains to be demonstrated.

Developmental Impact on Parents and Families

The family life cycle theoretical viewpoint recognizes that the development of both the family and its individual members is interactive; individual development affects the stages of family development and vice versa (see Turnbull, Summers, & Brotherson, 1986, for a discussion of family life cycle theory and its implications for families with members with mental retardation). Wikler (1986) found that developmental transitions such as adolescence and young adulthood were particularly stressful for families. We feel that four points in the development of the person with mental retardation are often critical as stressor, transition, or adjustment periods for the parents and family. The professional might use any of the collaborative roles delineated previously at any of these points, but some may be more effective at certain points. The four points are described next.

Identification and Early Childhood. The parental reactions detailed earlier in this chapter are particularly relevant here. The reaction to the diagnosis of mental retardation is often dominated by affective and emotional responses. As noted above, the point at which the diagnosis is made and the conclusiveness of the diagnosis may vary with the obviousness or the degree of the retardation. Parents of a child with severe mental retardation or a child with a clearly identifiable syndrome may become aware of the disability very early in the child's development. Further, the obviousness of the disability may make it more difficult to deny. The child with mild mental retardation may not be identified until after school entrance. Parents of children with mild mental retardation are likely to have developed a different type of emotional attachment to what they may have presumed to be a "normal" child. Because their child did not seem strikingly different from other children, they may have more difficulty accepting the diagnosis; that is, they may exhibit more denial. Regardless of when the diagnosis is made, the parents are likely to have individual emotional reactions requiring support.

The professional at this identification point needs to assess the child carefully and be able to explain the implications of the assessment to the parents. This explanation should be probabilistic, yet realistic. It should offer the parents prognostic information that neither paints an overly "gloomy" picture of the child's future and thus limits expectations, nor prevents the parents from dealing with the reality of the child's condition. The professional, indeed, walks a fine line in communicating the diagnostic information to the parents. The assessment information should also orient the parents for the appropriate developmental expectations for their child. Because of the emotional response of the parents, the dynamic or therapeutic role may be useful for helping the parents "work through" or adjust to their child's handicap. Assisting the parents with both home-based and school or agency early intervention programming is important, as is serving as a resource in providing information for the parents.

School Entrance. Assuming that the child has been identified prior to reaching school age, most parents will be at some level of adjustment to their child's mental retardation. However, their child's "differentness" starts to become more obvious at school age. The parents begin to deal with special education and its concomitant assessment, placement, and educational planning meetings; different class arrangements; and so forth. Because of the nature of public education, the developmental delays of their child thus become "public." Further, parents see other children the same age as their child progressing, while their child obviously lags behind. The fact that their child has mental retardation and is different may be painfully reinforced by the early school experience.

The professional may continue in the dynamic role by providing support for the parents whose child's retardation has been made more apparent by school entrance. Some of the emotional reactions often observed at the initial diagnosis may reoccur in somewhat different form. The professional in the resource role can help parents understand the various processes, procedures, and parental rights related to involvement with special education. Further, involvement with collaborative planning of the child's education will continue.

Adolescence. As many parents will attest, the adolescent period is a difficult one from a social–emotional standpoint. The "normal" adolescent experiences physical and hormonal changes that also produce social–emotional reactions. For the most part, adolescents with mental retardation are subject to the same physical changes and sexual development, yet they remain cognitively delayed. The child may not as easily understand these changes, and the parents may not be prepared to view their child as a sexual being. Both the parents and the child may need assistance in dealing with human sexuality issues. Further, the appearance of social–emotional problems may be more prominent at this stage of development. Studies (discussed later in this chapter) support a higher incidence of problems in adolescents with mental retardation when compared to nonretarded adolescents. Adolescents with mild mental retardation, in particular, also become more aware of their "differentness" from their age-mates and their limitations at a critical point in identity development.

At this stage the professional can help parents deal with the social–emotional development of their child. The dynamic, family therapy, and behavioral roles may be useful in facilitating emotional and social skill development. The resource function may lead parents to materials about both normal and atypical adolescent development with particular reference to human sexuality issues.

Community and Vocational Transition. This stage involves helping the parents prepare for their child to leave home. Again, the parents are reminded of their child's limitations. Rather than an independent or competitive job or further education, their child may be moving to a supported form of work, supervised job, sheltered workshop, or day treatment program. Instead of moving out on her own, their child may be moving to a supervised setting with other persons with mental retardation. The young adult with mental retardation may have relatively few residential and vocational options, and the parents may find some of them less than desirable. The process of "letting go" and fostering the independence of their child may be difficult for some parents. Thorin, Yovanoff, and Irvin (1996) surveyed parents at this stage and found that they faced groups of "dilemmas." These included providing independence for the young adult while ensuring that health and safety needs were met, wanting a life separate from the young adult while ensuring a good life for her, encouraging a separate social life for the young adult while lessening the degree of parental involvement, and desiring to maximize the young adult's development and growth while still accepting who she is.

Smith, Majeski, and McClenny (1996) studied the needs of aging parents who have offspring with developmental disabilities. They reported positive evaluations of psychoeducational support groups for these parents which focused on longer term planning and interventions for their adult children.

In addition to the supportive role, two roles may be helpful to parents at this stage. The professional in the assessment role evaluates adaptive, community living, social, and vocational skills. The issue of diagnosis has long been resolved, but more criteria-based assessments to determine basic daily living and survival skills help to facilitate a successful and developmentally appropriate transition. The resource role becomes important again at this stage just as it was for helping parents understand special education at school entrance. The parents are again entering a situation where they encounter a wide variety of agencies providing services for adults with disabilities. Parents may be confounded by the options: vocational rehabilitation, day programs, social security, health programs, group homes, supervised apartments, and so on. The professional should help the parents to select the most normalizing and least restrictive vocational and residential situations for their child.

Mental Retardation and Social–Emotional Functioning

In recent years, there has been increased interest in the emotional problems of people with mental retardation. Previously, many of the problematic behaviors and symptoms displayed by these individuals were thought simply to be characteristics of mental retardation and not representative of genuine and separate psychopathology. In fact, social–emotional functioning among mentally retarded persons received little attention from both researchers and practitioners. Perhaps indicative of more contemporary thinking, the DSM–IV (American Psychiatric Association, 1994) notes that "individuals with Mental Retardation have a prevalence of comorbid mental disorders that is estimated to be three to four times greater than the general population" (p. 42).

The prevalence of these problems in children with mental retardation is shown in a study by Cullinan, Epstein, Matson, and Rosemier (1984). Adolescents, ages 13 to 18, in the educable mental retardation range were rated by their teachers on the Behavior Problem Checklist. A similar group of age peers without mental retardation were also rated by their teachers. The adolescents with mild mental retardation showed significantly higher scores on the Conduct Disorder dimension, which assesses aggressive and disruptive behavior patterns, and on the Personality Problem dimension, which assesses difficulties with anxiety and withdrawal. The Conduct and Personality dimensions are the two major factors on the Behavior Problem Checklist and account for the majority of the variance in behavioral deviance. In a similar study, Epstein, Cullinan, and Polloway (1986) used the checklist to compare elementary *and* secondary students with educable levels of mental retardation to those without retardation. Factor analysis on the combined sample yielded factors they labeled aggression, attention disorder, anxiety–inferiority, and social incompetence. For three of the factors—aggression, attention disorder, and anxiety–inferiority—the students with educable levels of mental retardation showed significantly more problems than their peers without mental retardation at all age levels and for both sexes. The researchers also found some differences in the social competence factor but not as consistently as with the other factors. They noted that this factor did not overlap to a great degree with the notion of adaptive behavior. Sevin and Matson (1993), in their review of psychopathology in people with mental retardation, note that studies have consistently found higher rates of psychopathology and emotional disturbance among children and adolescents with mental retardation. In general, many mentally retarded children appear to have significant behavior problems in a variety of areas. Obviously, this higher prevalence would present problems for their families.

Prout, Marcal, and Marcal (1989) used a meta-analysis procedure to analyze self-reported patterns of social–emotional adjustment among people with mental retardation. They looked at studies in which people with mental retardation (predominantly children and adolescents) had completed self-report inventories of major personality variables. The bulk of the measures assessed depression, self-esteem or self-concept, and anxiety. Across these studies, they consistently found that people with mental retardation reported concerns that were more pathological or problematic than those of individuals without mental retardation. That is, they tended to self-report relatively more depression, higher anxiety, lower self-esteem, and so forth.

These studies, among others, highlight the social–emotional problems of children and adolescents with mental retardation. There appears to be a higher prevalence of problems both in the observable behavioral areas as well as in more affective and emotional areas. It is now well accepted that persons with mental retardation are susceptible to psychopathology and emotional problems or disorders. A few generalizations can be made in this regard:

- Persons with mental retardation are susceptible to the full range of emotional and psychological problems as are the "normal" or general population.

- Lowered intelligence places an individual "at risk" for the development of emotional problems and may be seen as a related predisposing factor.

- The incidence and prevalence rates for emotional disorders among persons with mental retardation appear to be significantly above those in the general population.

- Many problems in adjustment and adaptation of persons with mental retardation that are thought to be related to retardation may be more related to problems in social–emotional functioning. For example, the failure of a person with mental retardation in a job placement may be more related to a social–emotional problem than a lack of job skills related to lowered intelligence. In addition to vocational situations, this may be seen in family and residential settings and other life transition situations.

Three other issues are important to consider in this context. First is the concept of *dual diagnosis*. In general, the term refers to the coexistence of two (or more) significant, identifiable, and "separate" disorders, problems, or conditions. It is different from the *multiple diagnosis* concept in that the disorders represent major diagnostic classifications or systems. With respect to mental retardation, dual diagnosis refers to the coexistence of mental retardation and emotional or psychiatric disorders. There has been much debate about causative issues and the necessity to establish primary and secondary diagnosis. Many of these distinctions (i.e., primary vs. secondary), we feel are semantic. Both cognitive and social–emotional functioning are important areas to be addressed.

The second issue relates to the problems in diagnosing emotional disorders in the population with mental retardation. Many of the instruments and assessment techniques used with the general population are either inappropriate for or not normed on individuals with lower cognitive functioning. Some of the adaptive behavior scales include measures of maladaptive behavior, but many of the areas assessed seem to focus on problems more often seen in individuals functioning at or below the moderate mental retardation range. Until recently there have been few measures appropriate for persons with mental retardation. Several measures are now available including the *Emotional Problems Scales* (Prout & Strohmer, 1991), which is designed for adolescents and adults with mild mental retardation and borderline intelligence and includes self-report, behavior rating, problem checklist, and incomplete sentence components; the Nisonger *Child Behavior Rating Form* (Aman, Tassé, Rojahn, & Hammer, 1995) for children and adolescents with developmental disabilities; and the *Reiss Screen for Children's Dual Diagnosis* (Reiss & Valenti-Hein, 1990). Together, these instruments offer a variety of modalities for assessing the presence of psychiatric and emotional problems in children and adolescents with mental retardation.

The third issue involves the concept of *diagnostic overshadowing* (Levitan & Reiss, 1983; Reiss, Levitan, & Syszko, 1982; Reiss & Syszko, 1983; Spengler, Strohmer, & Prout, 1990), the tendency for clinicians and professionals to downplay or ignore mental health problems when they are aware that the person functions in the mentally retarded range. In a series of analogue studies, professionals were presented with case histories that were identical except that in one case the individual was described as having an IQ in the mentally retarded range, and in the other, the person's functioning was described in the average range. When the subject of the case study was described as having mental retardation, the clinicians were less likely to diagnose an emotional disorder and recommend appropriate therapeutic interventions. This tendency may translate to actual underdiagnosing of emotional problems in people with lower cognitive functioning and difficulty in obtaining mental health services for these individuals. The diagnostic overshadowing concept is relevant to both dual diagnosis and the lack of appropriate assessment instrumentation.

Collaborative Issues. Because of the greater incidence of emotional and behavioral problems among people with mental retardation, professional collaboration might include providing mental health services. Assessment should not just focus on the developmental delays of the individual; social–emotional assessment should be included at all levels of development. Collaborative assessment includes the collection of informant data from the parents. If a mental health problem is identified, a variety of mental health services might be provided that have elements of the dynamic, family therapy, or behavioral approaches. In fact, Tymchuk (1983) supports a combined model of intervention when working with parents.

Case Study: Stressor Points

The following is a chronology of events encountered by Robert and Martha as they raised their daughter Katie. These events occurred around the stressor points of identification and early childhood, school entrance, adolescence, and transition. As will be seen, these stressor points also involved collaboration with a variety of professionals throughout Katie's development. This case demonstrates both positive and moderately conflictual collaborations that occur.

Identification and Early Childhood

Katie was born at 30 weeks of gestation with a birth weight of 4 pounds, 1 ounce, and Apgar Score of 4 at 1 minute and a subsequent score of 6. Oxygen was administered immediately following birth due to anoxia. She was delivered vaginally following a labor of 8 hours during which no medication was administered to the mother. However, Martha received medication to delay labor following premature contractions 36 hours prior to the birth. The pregnancy, which occurred when Martha was 33 years old, was uncomplicated, as were her three previous pregnancies. There was no history of any genetic or medical problems among family members and no cause for the premature birth was identified.

Following the delivery, Katie was moved to a neonatal intensive care unit where her condition stabilized after 24 hours. Postnatal testing revealed no identifiable complications or problems. Katie was breast fed during her month of hospital stay until she was discharged at 5 weeks of age with a weight of 5 pounds, 8 ounces.

Robert and Martha were informed by the neonatologist and pediatrician that Katie had approximately a 10% chance of later developmental problems. However, her developmental milestones appeared within normal limits in all areas and no significant medical problems occurred except ear infections, which began at 6 months of age and continued periodically until age 3½. Following a routine pediatric examination at age 2, Katie was referred for a speech and language evaluation at a local clinic due to possible delays in both receptive and expressive language. The concerns about possible delays were based on the parents' observations and reports to their pediatrician. While this referral was stressful for the parents, they hoped that the language delays were related to the frequent ear infections. They also rationalized that since Katie was the youngest of four children, she really had no reason to speak more than a few words in their busy household.

The results of the speech and language evaluation indicated that articulation skills were within normal limits with only developmental errors noted. Oral mechanism was adequate for speech production. However, the language evaluation indicated a receptive delay of approximately 9 months and an expressive delay of 1 year. Katie and her parents were referred to a preschool program for children with language impairments. No reasons for the delays were given but the parents were reassured that early intervention was critical and could help remediate the language deficits. The parents remained hopeful that the delays were limited to the language area.

In addition to accepting the fact that their young daughter had language delays and required special services so early, the parents had difficulty explaining the situation to other family members and friends. Some of these people gave unsolicited advice such as "She's fine–she's just spoiled being the little one." Martha also felt responsible for the problem, feeling that she must have done something "wrong" during the pregnancy to have "caused" the prematurity. She was afraid that Robert blamed her, even though he professed to have no concerns about Katie's development and expressed confidence that she would be fine.

Katie's progress in the language program was minimal. While she acquired new skills and vocabulary, her rate of progress continued to be at roughly 6 months per year. At the end of 18 months in the program (Katie's chronological age now 3 years, 6 months), she was again referred for comprehensive developmental, psychological, and medical evaluation to help identify more clearly her developmental status and educational needs. Her parents, although overtly cooperating with the referral, responded defensively and questioned the necessity of further evaluation. The evaluation indicated generally normal physical development but with delays of approximately 8 months in fine motor skills. Receptive language and cognitive skills were at the 2½-year level, and expressive language at the 2-year level. Additional reports from the parents indicated delays in adaptive skills, particularly in self-help, communication, and socialization areas. A diagnosis of mild mental retardation was explained to the parents.

The parents' response was initially one of confusion about the diagnosis and developmental information that they had been given and how it translated to their view of their daughter. A person with mental retardation, from their perspective, was someone with obvious physical and cognitive problems—this was not their Katie. They felt a great deal of anger and hostility toward the psychologist, physician, and speech–language clinician who conducted the evaluation, as well as toward the preschool program staff for failing to provide an adequate program for Katie.

The process of understanding Katie's developmental delays was prolonged for both parents. Both reported an adjustment period that included increased moodiness and irritability, periodic depression, and questioning of the causes of the problem and the validity of the diagnosis. They often felt frustrated with Katie when she was unable to perform certain tasks, yet they tended to overestimate her progress when she acquired a new skill. Observation of other children Katie's age facilitated their awareness of her delays, but their acceptance of the diagnosis was not complete.

School Entrance

Upon Katie's entrance into kindergarten, her parents began their role as child advocates by rejecting the public school district's recommendation that Katie be placed in a self-contained class for children with developmental delays. In order to obtain full-day educational programming, the parents agreed to a half-day special class placement in a program for children with language impairments and the other half day in a regular kindergarten class. This placement was generally successful for Katie, although socially and academically her skills were well below her regular classmates.

Her subsequent elementary school program involved regular class placements with support services of special education and language therapy. Katie had progressively more difficulty understanding the material in the regular classes and used the special education services to facilitate her understanding of class material as well as to foster basic skill acquisition. Social problems began to arise in the third grade when she refused to do class work and became resistant to attending school. Peer relationships also became more problematic as her interests and social maturity became increasingly different from her classmates, often resulting in Katie being teased or ignored by other students. Her parents responded to her behavioral changes with frustration and anger, which was directed primarily at the school. They did not accept the educational staff's repeated recommendation for a self-contained class placement but did agree to a second-opinion evaluation by professionals outside of the school district. In addition to the educational concerns, the parents were trying to balance

Katie's needs with those of her siblings, who were, at various times, confused about Katie, resentful of attention she received from the parents, and embarrassed by her behavior. Katie's elementary school years were marked by considerable family conflict, as well as ongoing disagreements with school personnel. Gradually the parents became more aware of her educational and developmental deficits in comparison to her age-mates. This gradual awareness seemed to decrease their tendency to blame and disagree with school personnel and led to a degree of resolve within the family.

Adolescence

Following a second-opinion evaluation, which confirmed the findings of previous evaluations by the school personnel and other clinicians, the parents had fewer doubts about the diagnosis and began to focus more on its implications for themselves and Katie. A special class placement was agreed upon that included individual and group social skills training as a support service. Peer interaction difficulties became a dominant concern, particularly as Katie became more interested in boys. Since she was attractive and friendly, her parents and school personnel were concerned about her ability to make appropriate social judgments, especially with respect to sexual relationships.

Katie began to question her parents more persistently about "What's wrong with me?" She began to ask this question during middle school, but as she got older, the questioning became more emotional and frequent. She began resisting her parents' requests with angry outbursts and periods of crying. The stress level in the family continued to increase as Katie progressed in high school where she was not involved in the social activities to which she aspired. She wanted to be involved in sports and cheerleading but did not make the teams at tryouts. She also hoped to go to school dances and the proms.

A positive aspect of the school experience was Katie's success in a child-care vocational training program. Despite this, the parents began to acknowledge their disappointment in their plans for Katie—particularly when their friends' children, many of whom were Katie's age, were formulating college plans and involved in extracurricular activities. The family began private counseling during Katie's high school years as a means of dealing with her depression, low self-esteem, and socialization problems. However, the counseling also provided a mechanism for the family to express their concerns, disappointments, and feelings of guilt. While these feelings were not as intense or as frequent as in the earlier years for the parents, they still continued to appear intermittently.

The family also developed a plan for guardianship upon Katie's reaching age 18. The issue of sibling responsibility in the event of parental death or disability was particularly difficult for the family to consider and resolve.

Transition

As many of the members of Katie's graduating class embarked on college or vocational careers, Katie enrolled in a job training program in childcare sponsored by the Office of Vocational Rehabilitation and conducted at a local rehabilitation center. Following a year of on-site training at the center, for which Katie was paid a small subminimum wage, she was able to gain employment in a day-care setting as an aide.

At the same time, Katie moved into a supervised living apartment with two other young women with mild mental retardation. Initially, both Katie and her parents had difficulty adjusting to their lifestyle changes. These changes, particularly in the areas of control and independence, forced Katie to become more independent and to make her own decisions, responsibilities with which she had little experience. Her parents also had to allow her more freedom to make her own decisions. For the parents, this highlighted their dependence on Katie and the impact that she had on their lives. For them, the absence of Katie from their home and their daily supervision required a major readjustment. They had not realized how much of their lives revolved around caring for her.

Through the residential agency Katie continued to receive counseling related to dating, sexuality, possible marriage, discrimination and normalization issues, self-advocacy, and employment. At times the parents had difficulty accepting the agency's push for Katie's extensive community involvement and independence. They remained involved with some decision making and input with regard to Katie's employment and living arrangements. However, each progression to more independent levels was viewed by the parents with both happiness and cautious concern. These changes invariably were stressful for the parents.

Summary

The presence of a person with mental retardation in a family has significant impact on the parents and the dynamics of the family. The parents' needs range from emotional support to informational. A variety of professional roles are required to deal with the many issues that face individuals with mental retardation and their families. The acceptance of the disability by the parents, the level of the disability, and the social–emotional adjustments of the person with mental retardation are key factors in collaborative work. Further, the professional must view the collaboration across the life span of the person with mental retardation and the concomitant family life cycle.

References

Aman, M. G., Tassé, M. J., Rojahn, J., & Hammer, D. (1995). *Nisonger Child Behavior Rating Form.* Columbus: Ohio State University.

American Psychiatric Association. (1994). *Diagnostic and statistical manual of mental disorders* (4th ed.). Washington, DC: Author.

Birenbaum, A. (1996). Can family empowerment survive a smaller government? *Mental Retardation, 34,* 320–322.

Cullen, J. C., MacLeod, J. A., Williams, P. D., & Williams, A. R. (1991). Coping, satisfaction, and the life cycle of families with mentally retarded persons. *Issues in Comprehensive Pediatric Nursing, 14,* 193–207.

Cullinan, D., Epstein, M. H., Matson, J. L., & Rosemier, R. A. (1984). Behavior problems of mentally retarded and non retarded adolescent pupils. *School Psychology Review, 13,* 381–384.

Drew, L. J., Logan, P. R., & Hunter, M. L. (1988). *Mental retardation: A life cycle approach* (3rd ed.). Columbus, OH: Merrill.

Epstein, M. H., Cullinan, D., & Polloway, E. A. (1986). Patterns of maladjustment among mentally retarded children and youth. *American Journal of Mental Deficiency, 91,* 127–134.

Gallagher, J. J., & Vietze, P. M. (Eds.). (1986). *Families of handicapped persons: Research, programs, and policy issues.* Baltimore: Brookes.

Laborde, P. R., & Seligman, M. (1983). Individual counseling with parents of handicapped children: Rationale and strategies. In M. Seligman (Ed.), *The family with a handicapped child: Understanding and treatment.* Orlando, FL: Grune & Stratton.

Levitan, G. W., & Reiss, S. (1983). Generality of diagnostic overshadowing across disciplines. *Applied Research in Mental Retardation, 4,* 59–64.

Mink, I. T. (1986). Classification of families with mentally retarded children. In J. J. Gallagher & P. M. Vietze (Eds.), *Families of handicapped persons: Research, programs, and policy issues.* Baltimore: Brookes.

Mink, I. T., Blacher, J., & Nihira, K. (1988). Taxonomy of family life styles: III. Replication with families with severely mentally retarded children. *American Journal on Mental Retardation, 93,* 250–264.

Mink, I. T., Meyers, C. E., & Nihira, K. (1984). Taxonomy of family life styles: II. Homes with slow learning children. *American Journal of Mental Deficiency, 89,* 111–123.

Mink, I. T., Nihira, K., & Meyers, C. E. (1983). Taxonomy of family life styles: I. Homes with TMR children. *American Journal of Mental Deficiency, 87,* 484–497.

Prout, H. T., Marcal, S., & Marcal, D. (1989). *A meta-analysis of self-reported personality characteristics of developmentally and learning disabled persons.* Unpublished manuscript.

Prout, H. T., & Strohmer, D. C. (1991). *Emotional Problems Scales.* Odessa, FL: Psychological Assessment Resources.

Reiss, S., Levitan, G. W., & Syszko, J. (1982). Emotional disturbance and mental retardation: Diagnostic overshadowing. *American Journal of Mental Deficiency, 86,* 567–574.

Reiss, S., & Syszko, J. (1983). Diagnostic overshadowing and professional experience with mentally retarded persons. *American Journal of Mental Deficiency, 87,* 396–402.

Reiss, S., & Valenti-Hein, D. (1990). *Reiss Screen for Children's Dual Diagnosis.* Worthington Park, OH: International Diagnostics Systems.

Seligman, M., & Darling, R. B. (1989). *Ordinary families, special children: A systems approach to childhood disability.* New York: Guilford Press.

Sevin, J. A., & Matson, J. L. (1993). An overview of psychopathology. In D. C. Strohmer & H. T. Prout (Eds.), *Counseling & psychotherapy with persons with mental retardation and borderline intelligence.* Brandon, VT: Clinical Psychology Publishing.

Smith, G. C., Majeski, R. J., & McClenny, B. (1996). Psychoeducational support groups for aging parents: Development and preliminary outcomes. *Mental Retardation, 34,* 172–181.

Spengler, P. M., Strohmer, D. C., & Prout, H. T. (1990). Testing the robustness of the diagnostic overshadowing bias. *American Journal on Mental Retardation, 95,* 204–214.

Thorin, E., Yovanoff, P., & Irvin, L. (1996). Dilemmas faced by families during their young adults' transitions to adulthood: A brief report. *Mental Retardation, 34,* 117–120.

Turnbull, A. P., Summers, J. A., & Brotherson, M. J. (1986). Family life cycle: Theoretical and empirical implications and future directions for families with mentally retarded members. In J. J. Gallagher & P. M. Vietze (Eds.), *Families of handicapped persons: Research, programs, and policy issues.* Baltimore: Brookes.

Tymchuk, A. J. (1983). Interventions with parents of the mentally retarded. In J. L. Matson & J. A. Mulick (Eds.), *Handbook of mental retardation.* New York: Pergamon.

Wikler, L. M. (1986). Family stress theory and research on families of children with mental retardation. In J. J. Gallagher & P. M. Vietze (Eds.), *Families of handicapped persons: Research, programs, and policy issues.* Baltimore: Brookes.

Wikler, L. M., Wasow, M., & Hatfield, E. (1981). Chronic sorrow revisited: Attitudes of parents and professionals about adjustment to mental retardation. *American Journal of Orthopsychiatry, 51,* 63–70.

The Family with a Young Child with Disabilities

12

Beth Doll and Mary Bolger

· ·

O ver the past decade, becoming partners with parents in the education of children with disabilities has become the most respected approach for intervention services. Now, a heightened sensitivity toward parents is reflected by recent federal legislation and education initiatives (Education of the Handicapped Act Amendments of 1986 and Individuals with Disabilities Education Act [IDEA] Amendments of 1991 and 1997), which require parent involvement in Individualized Family Service Plans and Individualized Education Plans for children with disabilities. This attention to family conveys a deep respect for the parent–child relationship and serves to protect and strengthen this essential source of support for children. By valuing the competence of parents as much as that of professionals, collaborative services reaffirm parents' skills, knowledge, and the importance of their interaction with their children. Collaboration can provide parents with the confidence and experience to become powerful advocates throughout their children's lives.

Collaborative interventions are especially appropriate to serve the needs of very young children with disabilities, whose dependence on parental care is more marked and whose interaction with parents is more intense and more frequent than that of older children (Peterson, 1987). Gains demonstrated by children in early intervention programs have been shown to be strongly influenced by home environment, the social support available to the family, and family characteristics (Dunst & Leet, 1987). Moreover, emerging evidence suggests that the impact of intervention is more pronounced and more enduring the younger the child is when entering programs of intervention (Strain & Smith, 1996; Strayhorn & Strain, 1986).

Although parent involvement is now mandated by federal statute, translating policy into exemplary practice is not easily achieved. Professionals can ease this translation by using a family-centered approach as a foundation for engaging parents in a collaborative relationship (Friesen & Koroloff, 1990). Family-centered models of service remain responsive to the needs of the entire family including the child with disabilities, thus recognizing the family's role as the child's most important lifelong resource. Parents and professionals work in unison to meet the developmental needs of the child, which are seen to emerge within the reciprocal influence of child–family interactions. The challenge for professionals is to craft their relationship with this family–child system such that it truly enhances rather than disrupts the system's efficacy.

Essential to meeting this challenge is the professionals' recognition that the locus of control over the child's growth must remain within the family. This recognition creates equity within the parent–professional partnership. Parents are included in the decision making and brainstorming that plan a child's program, and their goals and parent-directed activities are integral to their child's services. Professionals working from a family-focused approach are careful to provide parents with comprehensive information about their child's needs, progress, and services so that they can make informed decisions for their child (Lubetsky, Mueller, Madden, Walker, & Len, 1995). Family-centered professionals educate parents on issues related to early intervention so that they can become effective advocates for their child. Family-centered services reinforce learning that occurs at home in the same way that parents reinforce what occurs at school and adjust their teaching and service in ways that parents advise (Peterson, 1987). Because family-centered services evaluate the needs of the child within the family and community network, a lifespan perspective is taken in the selection of goals for the child. This requires that programs be flexible in the services that are offered in order to meet the unique needs of diverse families and their children.

Family-centered services are effective because they realistically accept the choices and knowledge of parents. If the demands that services impose on parents are incompatible with their needs and capacities, intervention efforts can become an extra burden that overwhelms the family and becomes a failure experience. If family participation in intervention is unnecessarily constrained, the experience can underwhelm the family and serve as one more example of professionals patronizing the family. Family-centered services remain sensitive to the needs and experience of the family, allowing professionals to support parents in maintaining their family values and making family decisions while still serving the child with disabilities.

This chapter will review the special characteristics of families of young children with disabilities and the implications these hold for implementing family-centered models of service. In particular, attention will be paid to those professional practices that vest parents with decision making and make it possible for parents to discover and exercise their own expertise in parenting their child with disabilities. Family-centered interventions must, by definition, be individualized to meet the needs of different families, so the chapter will conclude by discussing ways to assess and adjust to these familial differences.

Characteristics of Families of Young Children with Disabilities

Parents of young children with developmental disabilities are often relatively new to the role of raising a child with disabilities and may still be unsure of how to assume it. Until recently, they were part of the uninformed masses that rarely interact with disabled persons, and they may still hold some stereotypic views of their child's disability and its implications. In many cases the nature and implications of their child's developmental condition are as yet uncertain, and the parents are frequently required to tolerate a fair amount of ambiguity about their child's needs or future development. Moreover, their grief over the child's disabling condition is likely to be fresh, and consequently more intense, and may exert a stronger influence over their ability to interact effectively with the nondisabled world. The family of a young child with developmental disabilities is more likely to be a young family, facing the financial and social adjustments that all young families face but that are exacerbated by the special challenges presented by their child with disabilities. The experience of each family will be unique, and the realities of these parental resources must be carefully balanced if collaborative efforts are to be successful. It is unfortunate, then, that characterizations of these families are all too frequently cliché-ridden and shallow. Families require a thorough and honest acknowledgment of their resources, values, and dreams for their child if their needs are to be assessed accurately and served with sensitivity.

Familial Stress

Stress and coping paradigms have been useful for understanding families having a child with disabilities. Professional, financial, social, and marital pressures are frequently more intense for young families while parents work to establish their careers, acquire resources, and adjust to their marriage. Professionals who work with families of infants and preschoolers with disabilities are keenly aware that all of these adjustment difficulties can be intensified by the presence of a child with disabilities. Career responsibilities may intrude into the time needed to care for a child with disabilities, and the medical needs of the child may place a strain on family finances. Indeed, studies that compare families with and without children with disabilities do show that stress is understandably higher among parents raising children with disabilities (Beckman-Bell, 1981; McKinney & Peterson, 1987; Schilling, Gilchrist, & Schinke, 1984). Historically, survey research has suggested that families of persons with disabilities have experienced divorce rates double that of the general population (Tew, Payne, & Lawrence, 1974), higher rates of parental anxiety and depression (Breslau & Davis, 1986), and increases in marital tension (Gath, 1978), suicide (Love, 1973), and desertion (Reed & Reed, 1965).

Those studies that examine the particular sources of this stress demonstrate that it is directly and pragmatically tied to the increased demands of parenting the child (Kazak & Marvin, 1984). With the birth of their child with disabilities, parents report that their family's financial resources become strained (Herman & Thompson, 1995), their activities as a family become restricted (Blackard & Barsh, 1982), and time becomes a treasured rarity (Herman & Thompson, 1995). Stress levels are generally found to be higher in families of children with physical disabilities whose disability, in reality, places more caregiving demands upon the family (McKinney & Peterson, 1987). For example, mothers of children with spina bifida ascribe their stress to their children being less adaptable to change and more demanding of day-to-day care (Kazak & Marvin, 1984). Some of the stresses that these parents face are likely to be chronic as their child with disabilities will acquire self-care skills slowly and with great effort. As an example, one mother living in a rural community described 3 years of driving her son with developmental delays son to daily classes at an early childhood center 25 miles away. Some caregiving may extend indefinitely into the future, as new events produce another cycle of demands. In the face of such demands, family resources can become strained or even exhausted.

Providing care for the child with disabilities will be even more difficult in situations where both parents have employment outside of the home. Families of children with disabilities report that obtaining high-quality flexible child care is a priority (Bailey, Blasco, & Simeonsson, 1992), but that often it has been nearly impossible to find daycare providers willing and trained to assume the demanding task of caring for a child with disabilities (Gallagher, Beckman, & Cross, 1983; Quine & Pahl, 1985). The most prominent barriers to center-based care appear to be limited staff training for work with children with disabilities and limited ability to assume the extensive physical care required by the children (Crowley, 1990). Instead, parents of young children with disabilities report that their child care has most often been provided by relatives rather than daycare centers (Warfield & Hauser-Cram, 1996). Moreover, the type of disability affects parents' ability to find child care. Parents of children with severe developmental disabilities and behavior problems describe the greatest difficulty in locating center-based child care (Warfield & Hauser-Cram, 1996). In many cases, one parent (usually the mother) must give up a career to stay home with the child.

The relationship between having a child with a disability, stress, and adjustment is not direct. Rather, variables related to the child and family interact in complex ways to determine family adaptation. How a family adjusts and their quality of life is influenced by child and family resources. Resources that have been found to contribute to positive coping and adjustment include social support, parental beliefs about developmental disabilities, general beliefs about self-efficacy, family cohesiveness, and family income level (Bristol & Schopler, 1984; Friedrich, Wilturner, & Cohen, 1985). In some cases, the accommodations that families make can strengthen the child–family system. A less flexible but functional division of duties among parents frequently develops with the birth of the child, with mothers assuming a rather heavy caregiving role and fathers taking responsibility for additional financial burdens (Kazak & Marvin, 1984). While both parents may feel constrained by this division, they also become important and inseparable partners in parenting. Parents also report that maternal fatigue and concerns about having another child with disabilities interfere with comfortable sexual intimacy (Kazak & Marvin, 1984). However, general marital satisfaction remains as high as in other families (Dunlap & Hollingsworth, 1977) and may in fact improve due to an increased respect, affection, and consensus shared between parents (Kazak & Marvin, 1984).

Collaborative intervention with these families was inconceivable under the traditional assumption that the birth of a child with developmental disabilities was a traumatic event that created pathological response in the family system (Cummings, 1976). When families were thought to be traumatized, they were not seen as capable of making important contributions to the child's developmental program. Effective collaborators use a coping model in which families of children with disabilities are understood according to the resources they apply toward the demands of childrearing (Turnbull, 1997). Families that are characterized as coping are seen as functional and capable partners in the child's intervention. When parents are viewed as victims of trauma, professionals feel bound to lighten their burden by assuming some of the responsibility for the care of the child with disabilities. When parents' responses to having a child with disabilities are seen as adaptable and coping, professionals are more likely to recognize the commonalities they share with the parents and are obliged to supplement rather than supplant the parental care of the child. Professionals who search for and recognize the families' strengths and effectiveness are more likely to vest essential responsibility for the child with the parents and family.

While acknowledging that early intervention efforts should be collaborative, many professionals continue to find it difficult to devise roles for parents that truly share with them responsibility for the child's program. Too often, involving parents as partners has not acknowledged the breadth of parental competence and potential for parental contribution. Instead, these efforts focus narrowly on training parents to be teachers of their child with disabilities. This is a cost-effective approach because parents typically spend more time with their child than a professional. However, it may have an unintended effect upon family functioning if needs of the individual family members are not recognized. Involving the parent as a teacher may disrupt other family roles and create unintended additional burdens on family members. The role of teacher may decrease the enjoyment the parent derives from interacting with the child. Effective collaboration demands that parental suggestions for goals and activities be accepted as well as parental participation in their implementation. With parent input, it is more likely that parental services to the child will enhance the parent–child system, and that the goals selected will make it possible for the child to contribute to the family's quality of life. As examples, some parent-identified goals for young children with disabilities have included being able to eat at McDonald's without standing out as different, being able to play independently for 15 minutes with a toy, or being able to ask for a drink when thirsty or a snack when hungry.

Professionals should ensure that families are not so stressed by the increased demands of collaboration that the family system becomes dysfunctional. Effective collaboration must respect the reality of the family's caregiving burden and the value of their time. Services that infringe upon the time of the family should be carefully evaluated to see that they are truly necessary. For example, repeated diagnostic evaluations may not improve the child's services measurably and could occupy entire days out of the family's summer. Services should be offered at times that are not in conflict with the caretaking duties of the family and in ways that allow parents to retain control over the family schedule. Early evening can be a difficult time for parents to meet if a child's range of movement exercises must be completed after the meeting adjourns. It is especially important that each professional working with the family be fully aware of the time demands imposed by other professionals, so that the totality of family responsibility is realistic.

Even parents who stridently and effectively advocate for the needs of their child may be less vocal in protecting their personal needs. In some cases parents may feel a need to become super parents, juggling the needs of their children with and without disabilities and meeting all of the expectations that are imposed upon them. They may depend on professionals to suggest moderating the child's program in a way that is knowledgeable about and sensitive to the family needs. If the family is to remain the most desirable and optimal environment for the child, then the family's needs as well as the child's needs must be appropriately addressed in early intervention programs.

Emotional Status of the Family

The intense and unpredictable emotions that punctuate the parenting of a child with developmental disabilities also contribute to familial distress. The sense of loss that accompanies the birth of a child with disabilities has been compared repeatedly to the grief that accompanies death and dying (Lamb, 1983). Parents of children with developmental delays experience cycles of anger, denial, guilt, sadness, and acceptance as they attempt to reconcile the child they have been given with the child they were expecting to raise. Parents of a young child with disabilities have only recently lost the "expected child," and so their grief is likely to be more pronounced. Moreover, the contrasts between the child with disabilities and the expected child are more stark when they observe the frequent and striking milestones that many children are achieving in the preschool years; other children born at the same time are acquiring the independence of talking, walking, exploring, and achieving more rapidly and convincingly than their own child.

Parents often draw strength from the intense emotional bond that they develop with their child. Peterson (1987) provides an excellent discussion of how this bonding can be disrupted when a child is disabled. Emotional attachment is a reciprocal process, affected by the child's responses to the parent as these elicit the parent's responses to the child. A child's disability may prevent her from seeking out the contact and interaction of the parents in the same ways that other children do. A child with a hearing impairment may be unresponsive to his mother's cooing. A child with a visual impairment may not face her father as he enters the room. Children who are austic may resist cuddling during feeding. Thus, parents may not receive the emotional support from their children with disabilities that facilitates bonding and attachment.

Even so, parents of children with disabilities are not trapped into perpetual cycles of grief and anger. Feelings of loss wax and wane and are interspersed with frequent periods of joy while parents discover and take pleasure in their child with disabilities. Professionals should empathize with the rewards of parenting the child with disabilities, as parents frequently complain of being stereotyped as tragic characters and patronized by pity. They notice, with disappointment, that others rarely acknowledge their family's joy. As a father explained, "I know Chris can't talk, but I want people to know how much fun he is to be with."

Parents' emotional adjustment to having a child with disabilities will have an impact upon their involvement as partners in the collaborative process. Being part of special training programs and involved with special educators and therapists is a constant reminder that their child is different. Feelings of anger and resentment over having a child with disabilities may be directed at the professionals working with the parents. The parents may also feel incompetent in responding to their child's needs, particularly if typical childrearing skills are ineffective in securing a response from the child. Loss of self-esteem and feelings of insecurity as a parent may result. Parents' emotional reactions may be difficult for professionals to understand or anticipate if they are viewed independently of the full system of the family. One kindergarten teacher was growing increasingly impatient with a family who refused to discuss their newly enrolled son's social isolation and mechanical language. Then she learned that the boy's 3-year-old brother was identified with a serious hearing loss that same week. The family had inadvertently been buffeted with simultaneous reports of problems in both of their sons. To be sensitive to these emotional responses, professionals need to make themselves familiar with the full spectrum of the family's experience. At a time when parents are less prepared to assume the role of advocate, less expert in their child's needs, and less comfortable in their social role, life events have propelled them into the time-intensive and emotionally challenging role of parenting their young child with disabilities.

If an effective collaborative relationship is to develop between parents of the preschooler with disabilities and the professionals that serve their child, each must value the competence and expertise of the other. This collaboration can be undermined when professionals, overwhelmed by the tragedy and stress they witness, begin to protect and shelter the family. A professional's sympathy can diminish the perceived competence of the family she intends to serve. As an example, parents are sometimes "allowed" to be uninvolved in a program for children with disabilities because the constant reminders of the disability are thought to be so difficult. In one family where this continued for several years, the child's mother finally explained that she felt unnecessary and uninvited when program planning meetings were scheduled with little effort to secure her assistance. Instead of sympathizing and protecting, professionals should express their concern by respecting the integrity and capability of the family system.

Most professionals successfully accommodate the somewhat unpredictable parental feelings of ambivalence, anger, and sadness without feeling personally responsible or blamed for the family's distress. All too often, however, the grieving process is considered to be maladaptive or even pathological. It is useful instead to regard the cycles of grieving as a normal process for a family living through the birth of a child with disabilities. Successful grieving allows the family to work simultaneously to meet the child's immediate needs without giving up hope for the beneficial future of the child or confidence in themselves as persons. Professionals who work closely with the child experience a similar albeit less intense grief and can become similarly unrealistic in their vision of the child and his gifts. Sensitivity to one's own feelings of sadness and enjoyment can enhance recognition of the parents' experience.

Social Support in the Community

The social support provided by neighbors, friends, and relatives is critical to the resilience of children with disabilities and their families. Parents frequently mention this need to blend child, family, and community as the primary goal of early childhood intervention—one that may be overlooked by professional members of the collaborative team. Unfortunately, an unintended but painful consequence of having a child with disabilities can be the narrowing of a family's community to those persons and professionals able to deal with disability issues. Although not socially isolated, families of persons with disabilities report having slightly fewer friends and describe a family and friendship network that is highly interconnected (Kazak & Marvin, 1984). Creating community can be a difficult task if the loved ones who provide the family's social support are awkward in the face of the birth and unskilled at greeting the family with the same ease and familiarity as before. At the same time as they cope with their own grief, parents may be faced with the disappointment of the extended family and community. In an effort to deal with the grief, parents may assume the weighty role of "comforter" for each other and for people outside the family. Still, a hidden "possible" community may exist for some families if both the family and the silent allies wait for the other to make the first move. A touching example of a "hidden community" is articulated by Turnbull (1997), who described her surprise upon discovering that her son with disabilities was being monitored each morning by a neighborhood teacher whose classroom looked out on the bus stop. The unsuspected assistance only became known when the teacher called, concerned because the boy had accepted a ride from an unfamiliar man.

Parent organizations have been stressed as an important means to address social dissonance experienced by some families of children with disabilities. One researcher was even led to suggest that, because of this, early intervention programs would be more effective when conducted in groups (McKinney & Peterson, 1987). Parents agree and frequently describe the group interaction as one of the most appreciated factors in early intervention programs (McKinney & Peterson, 1987), arguing that parent groups address their needs more directly than those organized by professionals. As an example, a group of parents at a local early childhood program established very different goals for their group than the professional staff had anticipated: Rather than talk about behavior management, they wanted to develop ways to deal with their children's anger and sadness and to find ways to interact more normally with parents of children without disabilities.

On the other hand, parent organizations may be less accessible to parents of young children with disabilities because of the serious time constraints, the demands of other young children, and the perceptions parents may have that their child is not like the other children with disabilities in the group. Moreover, parents will be seeking a social niche for themselves within their community that incorporates children both with and without disabilities; parent organizations can prevent them from resuming participation in networks of social support that existed before the birth of their child with disabilities. As an alternative, some parents may require a less organized form of interaction with other parents of children with disabilities. A personal contact with one other parent may substitute for attendance at group meetings or conferences.

Parents of young children with disabilities are also very aware and appropriately concerned that their children are at risk for failure to develop effective social behaviors (Turnbull & Turnbull, 1993). Their children are more likely to be engaged in solitary play, to ignore attempts other children make to initiate play, and to spend more time watching and less time talking than preschoolers without disabilities, as shown by Strain (1983, 1985). Indeed, Strain's research suggests that the successful inclusion of children with disabilities into mixed play groups is an important normalizing experience that mediates some effects of the disability (Strain & Smith, 1996). As one father of a 4-year-old son with Down syndrome poignantly explained, he depends on the altruism of children without disabilities to pull his son into normal play interactions. As a result, families in this group were constantly seeking ways to explain the disability to siblings and neighborhood children without disabilities, as well as ways to blend their children with disabilities into the community of childhood.

The parents' community is the child's community. As the child's earliest and most enduring social partners, families are the logical agents to foster the inclusion of their child into the world of everyday events (Fox & Savelle, 1987). However, young parents are frequently new to the world of childhood and need assistance learning how to communicate in child-compatible words, to view the disability from the child's eye, and to adapt to the brief and unpredictable conversations that children offer. Parents in one support group frequently used opportunities to meet with other parents to talk about this concern. During these group discussions parents shared their expertise, anticipated the questions that children might ask about their child with disabilities, and planned effective answers together. Discussions among families allowed them to clarify in their own minds what they wanted other children to know about their child with disabilities and how to handle the conversation with sensitivity when their child was present. Parents frequently used these opportunities to describe confusing or surprising conversations they had already had with other children and helped each other understand what was meant.

Parents frequently request instruction in explaining disabilities to young children through their natural communication systems: through stories and in play. Reading a well-written story about a disability can make a child more available to conversation by raising his interest, giving him the opportunity to pose innumerable questions for parents to react to, and allowing him to enter more fully the world of the child with disabilities. Professionals can support parents in these attempts by locating books that include models with disabilities. Together, parents and professionals can evaluate whether the book presents disabilities with sensitivity. A detailed explanation of how to locate books about children's disabilities, and a comprehensive model for selecting and presenting books for young children are presented in Doll and Doll (1997).

Dolls with disabilities are another effective strategy for introducing the preschooler without disabilities to the experience of peers with disabilities (Chapel Hill Training Outreach Project, 1983). Cloth dolls can be made by parents or church or community groups and, with props, can be given disabilities similar to those of a child in a play group or preschool. Children can be introduced to the role of disabilities through adult-directed play, and the dolls can then be left in neighborhood play areas to be available for free play. By assuming in play the role of a doll with disabilities, preschoolers can be prompted to experience the disability in a limited way, to discuss it in familiar words, and to explain some of their feelings about disabilities to an available adult.

Spousal Support

The adequacy of a family's community support network does not appear to be the most critical variable in determining whether the family is under excessive strain. Instead, the best predictor of parental stress is the extent to which one spouse perceives the other to be sharing in the parenting burden (Kazak & Marvin, 1984; McKinney & Peterson, 1987). Thus, it is critically important for professionals to respect the spousal relationship when collaborating with parents of preschoolers and infants with disabilities. In many cases professionals must be satisfied to meet with one parent, while the other one cares for the child. The lack of suitable child care or an intractable home care routine can make it impossible for both parents to leave the home simultaneously. Providing child care at meeting sites does not always resolve the conflict if the child is hypersensitive to changes in daily routine or requires special care during that time. Programs that provide training to one parent can make that training available to the other parent via tape recordings or extra copies of handouts. The division of responsibility that parents choose to assume within their marriage must be acknowledged by the professionals who work with them.

Siblings of a Preschooler with Disabilities

The introduction of a child with disabilities into a family system will inevitably alter the experience of that child's nondisabled siblings. Siblings of children with disabilities are frequently given less parental time and share fewer family activities than other children (Dunlap & Hollingsworth, 1977). Parents may need assistance developing family activities that are enjoyable to their children without disabilities as well as to the child with disabilities. These are difficult roles to juggle successfully. In one family a second grader complained that he was given a swimming pool for his birthday because then his younger brother with a disability would play in it too.

Few resources address this need as well as the Let's Play To Grow program sponsored by the John P. Kennedy, Jr. Foundation (1977). Let's Play To Grow materials describe adaptations of such familiar recreational activities as volleyball, soccer, kite flying, dance, and jumping rope that allow children with disabilities to participate and enjoy. The foundation facilitates the integration of the child with disabilities into play activities with friends and relatives without disabilities (both children and adults) by sponsoring the formation of Let's Play To Grow groups in communities and neighborhoods. It endorses the collaborative model by establishing parents as directors of the community play groups and providing technical assistance with mainstreaming and administration of programs through staff in Washington, DC.

Siblings also play an essential role as social agents of a child with disabilities, fostering the inclusion of that child in ongoing interactions with young friends and neighborhood children without disabilities (Fox, Niemeyer, & Savelle, 1992). Key evidence suggests that the play of children with disabilities with their peers is more sophisticated and more interactive than play with children outside the family (Lieber & Beckman, 1990). This leads Beckman and Lieber (1992) to suggest that sibling interactions be used as models for interventions that enhance the social competence of children with disabilities with their peers.

If put to the task, siblings of a child with disabilities can devise their own ways to accommodate disabilities into their daily interactions. Turnbull (1997) includes siblings as members of Action Groups, allowing them to share responsibility for expanding the expectations held for a child with disabilities. Within the group, the siblings have an opportunity to describe their vision for the child's future, to identify barriers that might restrict the child's possible futures, to brainstorm solutions to the problems that are identified, and to suggest ways in which they might contribute to the child's quality of life.

The Family and the Professional World

Because early intervention programs involve multiple professional disciplines, parents of a young child with disabilities are typically involved with educators, nurses, physicians, social workers, nutritionists, psychologists, and other parents. Interacting with multiple professionals from various disciplines can, in and of itself, be an overwhelming task for parents who are already struggling to understand their child's disability. Many parents sit at multidisciplinary meetings in silence and confusion. An inability to decode complicated professional jargon or to negotiate the protocol that governs professional meetings may convince parents that they are indeed ignorant of their child's needs.

In fact, professional protocol should be the least important detail in planning a child's program. Professionals can help parents by collaborating effectively and efficiently with each other: developing treatment programs that coordinate services of the different professionals rather than fragmenting these into discrete services; asking for clarification when it is needed and adding examples to illustrate important points that are made; drawing attention to parent comments by reiterating them or focusing discussion on them; informing the parent about available community resources; and assuming responsibility for effectively working with one another. Most important, professionals need to seek out opportunities for informal interactions with parents if they are to be truly accessible to families of children with disabilities (Peterson, 1987). It is the responsibility of the professional members of collaborative teams to break down any artificial barriers that professional jargon or etiquette may present to parental participation.

To become full participants in planning their child's program, parents need accurate information about their child and the disability. Many parents eventually become expert consumers of the technical literature describing the nature and treatment of their child's condition. However, parents of the young child with disabilities are not yet expert in their child's condition. They frequently have not read widely about the child's disability, are unfamiliar with the vocabulary the professionals use to describe the child, and may be unsure of what changes to expect from the child in the future. Thus, parents need easy access to reference material and repeated conversations with expert parents or other professionals in order to develop an understanding of what is known and what is not known about their child's condition.

In some cases parents themselves, seeking diagnoses and advice, take a child to a multitude of professionals. This is sometimes dismissed as "doctor shopping." In fact, seeking second or even third opinions is the parents' prerogative and can be a reasonable solution to their need for more information and more definitive descriptions of the child's condition and treatment. Parents may seek "permission" and even assistance to obtain second opinions from other professionals and encouragement to keep each person informed of the other's work so that steps are not repeated unnecessarily or overlooked.

One reason that information has been withheld from parents is that it lacks certainty. Assessment procedures are not as reliable when children are young as they will be once the child reaches the age of 10 or 12 (Ulrey & Schnell, 1982). Diagnoses are frequently ambiguous because of this lack of reliability and because there is limited information about how the child will change over time. Powerful risk factors associated with early childhood disabilities have been identified, but clearly these factors do not adequately predict how well the child will be able to adapt to or cope with a disability (Werner, 1986). For example, although it is clear that children are more likely to be disabled if they experience birth complications, the impact of these health traumas on eventual child disability varies tremendously. Much of the variability in child progress is explainable by family variables such as the quality of the parent–child interaction, parents' attitudes toward their child's learning, and the amount of social support given the family (Peterson, 1987; Werner & Smith, 1982).

As a result of the uncertainty, professionals are likely to make ambiguous and difficult to understand statements about the child's abilities or prognosis; so much remains unknown while the child is still young. Different, noncategorical diagnoses are applied to young children with disabilities; children who are autistic, aphasic, or severely retarded may all be called "developmentally delayed." The use of such generic descriptions may be appropriate when a more precise description of the child's condition is truly unavailable. Still, professionals may be knowledgeable of situations in which generic descriptions of a child could limit the family's access to needed services. They may need to assist parents in negotiating the politics of categorical services as these apply to their child. Moreover, in some situations noncategorical labels may mask information about the child that professionals know but are uncomfortable sharing with the parents. For example, one mother had not been told 2 years after her child's automobile accident that the injury had caused permanent paralysis and profound retardation. She had been carefully saving the child's first bicycle, bought a few days before the accident. Withholding critical information from parents can only make the family's adjustment to the child more difficult.

Uncertainty can be emotionally draining as well as difficult to understand. While the extent of a child's disability remains uncertain, both parents and professionals can hope that the disability will be minimal. Professionals sometimes seek to protect the child with disabilities and his parents from a disturbing diagnosis by withholding information about the possibilities until a certain diagnosis was available. This may be done with the best of intentions: parents can draw more hope from the description that their child is developmentally delayed than from the diagnosis of moderate mental retardation. Still, that hope is almost always accompanied by an underlying and pervasive worry that the delay will continue or worsen.

Adjustment to a child's disability takes time. Parents need an opportunity to learn about the diagnosis given their child, to observe the child to see if the diagnosis fits, and to decide whether they can accept that label for their child's condition. When diagnosis is deferred because of the child's young age or uncertain condition, this process of acceptance is also delayed. If alternative diagnoses are not discussed by the time the child enters kindergarten, then definitive categorical labels used in special education programs can be unexpected and alarming for parents. Their dismay is understandable: they have not been given the time they need to evaluate the diagnoses and determine whether these match their own experience of the child.

Parents are most successful in adapting to their child's disability if given a very complete description of all information available about the child and the alternative explanations that can be made based on that information. In some cases, this forthrightness may require discussion of some disturbing diagnostic possibilities such as retardation or pervasive developmental disabilities. Parents, by becoming partners in the diagnostic process, may be able to resolve some of the diagnostic dilemmas by providing informed observations of the nuances of their child's behavior and skills. Thus collaborative approaches to diagnostic decisions are in the best interest of the child as well as the parent.

Individual Plans for Family Services

Just as individuals differ from one another in their values, goals, desires, and needs, so do families. Creating a match between families and services is key to serving families of young children with disabilities effectively. Interventions that match the family's capacities and goals are most likely to enhance the family–child system as well as increase family involvement in the intervention (Peterson, 1987). A family struggling to provide adequate medical care for their medically fragile child may view educational programming as lower on a list of priorities that need to be met. Or parents' feelings of anger over having a child with disabilities may interfere with their participation in an intervention program. One parent, although pleased with a large-motor exercise program developed for her child, confessed that she valued most the fact that the program's equipment attracted other children to play with her son. If parents are to select goals and strategies that are truly compatible with their family, they will have to be provided with a range of options that is as diverse as the families that a program serves.

The hopes and dreams that parents hold for their children with and without disabilities is the fuel that keeps families going despite the challenges they face. Professionals can inspire parents by understanding their dreams and offering guidance in matching their goals to the child's developmental needs and the needs of the family system. In some cases, though, professionals can inadvertently encourage families to oversacrifice by suggesting additional strategies or emphasizing additional needs without regard to the family's resources and goals. Effective program planning seeks a plan of service that realizes the family's vision for the child with disabilities, while also protecting the needs and dreams of other members of the family. Such planning requires the support of a comprehensive analysis of the family's resources, goals, values, vulnerabilities, coping styles, parent–child interactive styles, and needs so that parents can clarify the nature of services and service goals that can encourage and sustain the family. The resulting programs focus on providing resources to all members of the family as necessary to foster more parental involvement, less stress, and more successful interactions with their children (Griest, Forehand, Rogers, Breiner, & Williams, 1982; Wahler & Dumas, 1984).

Family assessments are not easily accomplished. Families change over time, and information about family needs must be updated constantly. Most educators have not received training in conducting family assessment and identifying family-centered goals, and many feel unqualified or uncomfortable about performing the task. Moreover, there are a limited number of clinically sound and educationally relevant assessment tools to evaluate family systems in this manner (Bailey & Simeonsson, 1984; Walsh & Wood, 1983). Two instruments, the Parenting Stress Index (Abidin, 1986) and the Family Resource Scale (Dunst & Leet, 1987), have been used extensively with young children with disabilities and their families and could be used to support a family systems assessment. More recently, two assessment and planning procedures have been articulated that infuse family information and family decision making into intervention programs: Family Centered Consultation (Leviton, Mueller, & Kauffman, 1992) and Group Action Planning (Turnbull, 1997).

The Parenting Stress Index or PSI (Abidin, 1986) provides a useful evaluation of the emotional resources that parents draw upon in their daily interactions with their young child with disabilities. The PSI is a 120-item parent-report checklist that assesses the degree of stress parents are experiencing in their childcare role. The scale yields a total parenting stress score and separate domain scores that represent the portion of parental stress attributable to the child characteristics, the portion attributable to parent characteristics, and the portion attributable to situational life events. The scale is helpful in allowing parents to clarify the degree to which the parent–child interactions have been affected by difficult child characteristics, as well as the emotional resources they can draw on to support that interaction.

Research on the adequacy of family resources for raising a child with disabilities highlights the need to assess not only family resources but also the family's perception of the adequacy of their resources (Herman & Thompson, 1995). By understanding the actual family resources available and the family's perception of how adequate these are, services can be matched to the family's perception of need. The Family Resource Scale (Dunst & Leet, 1987) is an instrument that can be used to assess resource adequacy from the family's perspective. The 30-item rating scale assesses components of interpersonal and intrapersonal support within the family. The components evaluated include financial resources, child care, health care, shelter, and social supports. Moreover, additional probing of family responses can elaborate on whether they believe these resources are adequate to meet their needs and those of their child. Used in this manner, the scale can aid parents in identifying the gaps between their family's daily living needs and the resources available to fill these. Subsequently, the individualized plan for family services can be designed to fill these gaps.

An assessment of family needs only becomes useful once results are integrated into a plan for family services. A family plan is now required under the Education of the Handicapped Act Amendments of 1986. Family plans are most useful if they are co-constructed with the parents and include goals for the child, for the family, and for their interaction that reflect the concerns and expertise of family members and professionals. A family-centered consultation model at the Kennedy-Kreiger Institute has been described by Leviton, Mueller, and Kauffman (1992) as exemplary. Three stages of intervention are followed which include (1) establishing the relationship between the parents and the professionals and setting goals; (2) specifying strategies to achieve the goals; and (3) deciding who will provide the services to achieve the goals. Strategies for periodic review and revision of the plan provide opportunities for family and professional to continue to collaborate in their efforts to serve the child.

Group Action Planning (Turnbull, 1997) is a process that merges family assessment with program planning. Action groups are assemblies of family, friends, professionals, and relatives of a child with a disability who coalesce around the shared purpose of making an enviable life for the child. During Action Group meetings, the participants seek to visualize a future for the child that could be celebrated as rich, joyful, and engaging. Members of the group merge their individual insights to identify interests and strengths of the child with disabilities in addition to needs. Shared problem solving and brainstorming are used to anticipate problems and generate possible solutions. All members of the group have the option of contributing to the child's program of service, adding their unique capacities to the pool of resources that a family might draw upon. An exciting feature of Group Action Planning is its potential for identifying solutions and seeking futures that are unexpected and unbound by tradition. Moreover, the process itself creates a community for a child in ways that traditional multidisciplinary service plans do not. Finally, the resources identified through Group Action Planning may be much more extensive than even the family anticipated.

Summary

Having a child with disabilities is an event that creates change in the family system. In many ways these families respond like many other families faced with a crisis or sudden change. However, there are some factors that are unique responses to having a child with disabilities. These, then, are essential criteria for effective collaboration with families of young children: The professional should be sensitive to the unique challenges facing families of children with disabilities and the coping mechanisms that families use; the professional should also continue to acknowledge the commonalities these families hold with all other families of young children, with and without disabilities; this sensitivity should continue to be reflected in the daily practices of professionals who serve young children with disabilities; the professional should remain sensitive to changes in the unique combination of strengths and needs that each family brings to its childrearing task and directly assess the resources and requirements of each individual family; flexibility and choice should be inherent in the design of service programs so as to accommodate the unique goals of the child and family; and the family should be permitted to exercise its resources and judgment by sharing responsibility for planning and implementing their child's intervention. The collaborative approach to early childhood intervention is more difficult to plan, implement, and evaluate than traditional professional-dominated early intervention models. The challenge is made worthwhile by its sensitivity to children as family members. The family is the most valuable resource for the child with a disability; the family systems approach allows professionals to nurture and protect this resource for the child.

References

Abidin, R. R. (1986). *Parenting Stress Index* (2nd ed.). Charlottesville, VA: Pediatric Psychology Press.

Bailey, D. B., Blasco, P. M., & Simeonsson, R. J. (1992). Needs expressed by mothers and fathers of young children with disabilities. *American Journal on Mental Retardation, 97,* 1–10.

Bailey, D. B., & Simeonsson, R. J. (1984). Critical issues underlying research and intervention with families of young handicapped children. *Journal of the Division of Early Childhood, 9,* 38–48.

Beckman, P. J., & Lieber, J. (1992). Parent–child social relationships and peer social competence of preschool children with disabilities. In S. L. Odom, S. R. McConnell, & M. A. McEvoy (Eds.), *Social competence of young children with disabilities: Issues and strategies for intervention* (pp. 65–92). Baltimore: Brookes.

Beckman-Bell, P. (1981). Child-related stress in families of handicapped children. *Topics in Early Childhood Special Education, 1,* 45–53.

Blackard, M. K., & Barsh, E. T. (1982). Parents' and professionals' perceptions of the handicapped child's impact on the family. *The Journal of the Association for the Severely Handicapped, 7,* 62–70.

Breslau, N., & Davis, G. C. (1986). Chronic stress and major depression. *Archives of General Psychiatry, 43,* 309–314.

Bristol, M. M., & Schopler, F. (1984). A developmental perspective on stress and coping in families of autistic children. In J. Bacher (Ed.), *Severely handicapped young children and their families* (pp. 91–112). Orlando, FL: Academic Press.

Chapel Hill Training Outreach Project. (1983). *New friends: Mainstreaming activities to help young children understand and accept individual differences.* Chapel Hill, NC: Author.

Crowley, A. A. (1990). Integrating handicapped and chronically ill children into day care centers. *Pediatric Nursing, 16,* 39–44.

Cummings, S. T. (1976). The impact of the child's deficiency on the father: A study of fathers of mentally retarded and or chronically ill children. *American Journal of Orthopsychiatry, 6,* 246–255.

Doll, B., & Doll, C. (1997). *Bibliotherapy with young people: Librarians and mental health professionals working together.* Englewood, CO: Libraries Unlimited.

Dunlap, W. R., & Hollingsworth, S. J. (1977). How does a handicapped child affect the family: Implications for practitioners. *Family Coordinator, 26,* 3–17.

Dunst, C., & Leet, H. (1987). Measuring the adequacy of resources in households with young children. *Child Care, Health and Development, 13,* 111–125.

Education of the Handicapped Act Amendments of 1986, 20 U.S.C. § 1400 *et seq.*

Erickson, M. W., & Hauser-Cram, P. (1996). Child care needs, arrangements, and satisfaction of mothers of children with developmental disabilities. *Mental Retardation, 34,* 294–302.

Fox, J. J., Niemeyer, J., & Savelle, S. (1992). Contributions of siblings to the development of social competence interventions for young children with disabilities. In S. L. Odom, S. R. McConnell, & M. A. McEvoy (Eds.), *Social competence of young children with disabilities: Issues and strategies for intervention* (pp. 215–244). Baltimore: Brookes.

Fox, J., & Savelle, S. (1987). Social interaction research and families of behaviorally disordered children: A critical review and forward look. *Behavioral Disorders, 12,* 276–291.

Friedrich, W. N., Wilturner, L. T., & Cohen, D. S. (1985). Coping resources and parenting mentally retarded children. *American Journal of Mental Deficiency, 90,* 130–139.

Friesen, B. J., & Koroloff, N. K. (1990). Family-centered services: Implications for mental health administration and research. *Journal of Mental Health Administration, 17,* 13–25.

Gallagher, J., Beckman, P., & Cross, A. (1983). Families of handicapped children: Sources of stress and its amelioration. *Exceptional Children, 10,* 10–19.

Gath, A. (1978). *Down's syndrome and the family: The early years.* London: Academic Press.

Greist, D. L., Forehand, R., Rogers, T., Breiner, J., & Williams, C. (1982). Effects of parent enhancement therapy on the treatment outcome and generalization of a parent training program. *Behavior Research and Therapy, 20,* 429–436.

Herman, S., & Thompson, L. (1995). Families' perceptions of their resources for caring for children with developmental disabilities. *Mental Retardation, 33,* 73–83.

Individuals with Disabilities Education Act Amendments of 1991, 20 U.S.C. § 1400 *et seq.*

John P. Kennedy, Jr. Foundation. (1977). *Let's play to grow: For families, for schools, for communities.* Washington, DC: Author.

Kazak, A. E., & Marvin, R. S. (1984). Differences, difficulties, and adaptation: Stress and social networks in families with a handicapped child. *Family Relations, 33,* 67–77.

Lamb, M. E. (1983). Fathers of exceptional children. In H. Seligman (Ed.), *The family with a handicapped child* (pp. 125–146). New York: Grune & Stratton.

Leviton, A., Mueller, M., & Kauffman, C. (1992). The family-centered consultation model: Practical applications for professionals. *Infants and Young Children, 4,* 1–8.

Lieber, J., & Beckman, P. J. (1990, April). *The effect of social context on social interaction in toddlers with handicaps.* A paper presented at the annual convention of the American Educational Research Association, Boston.

Love, H. (1973). *The mentally retarded child and his family.* Springfield, IL: Thomas.

Lubetsky, M., Mueller, L., Madden, K., Walker, R., & Len, D. (1995). Family-centered/interdisciplinary team approach to working with families of children who have mental retardation. *Mental Retardation, 33,* 251–255.

McKinney, B., & Peterson, R. A. (1987). Predictors of stress in parents of developmentally delayed children. *Journal of Pediatric Psychology, 12,* 133–150.

Odom, S. L., McConnell, S. R., & McEvoy, M. A. (1992). *Social competence of young children with disabilities: Issues and strategies for intervention.* Baltimore: Brookes.

Peterson, N. L. (1987). *Early intervention for handicapped and at-risk children: An introduction to early childhood special education.* Denver, CO: Love.

Quine, L., & Pahl, J. (1985). Examining the causes of stress in families with severely mentally handicapped children. *British Journal of Social Work, 15,* 501–517.

Reed, E. W., & Reed, S. C. (1965). *Mental retardation: A family study.* Philadelphia: Saunders.

Schilling, R. F., Gilchrist, L. D., & Schinke, S. P. (1984). Coping and social support in families of developmentally disabled children. *Family Relations, 33,* 47–54.

Strain, P. S. (1983). Identification of social skill curriculum targets for severely handicapped children in mainstream preschools. *Applied Research in Mental Retardation, 4,* 369–382.

Strain, P. S. (1985). Programmic research on peers as intervention agents for socially isolated classmates. *The Pointer, 29,* 22–29.

Strain, P. S., & Smith, B. J. (1996). Developing social skills in young children with special needs. *Preventing School Failure, 41,* 24–27.

Strayhorn, J., & Strain, P. S. (1986). Social and language skills for preventive mental health: What, how, who, and when. In P. S. Strain, M. J. Guralnick, & H. M. Walker (Eds.), *Children's social behavior* (pp. 287–330). New York: Academic Press.

Tew, B., Payne, H., & Lawrence, K. (1974). Must a family with a handicapped child be a handicapped family? *Developmental Medicine and Child Neurology, 16,* 95–104.

Turnbull, A. (1997). *Families, professionals and exceptionality: A special partnership.* Columbus, OH: Merrill.

Turnbull, A. P., & Turnbull, R. (1993). Participating research on cognitive coping. In A. P. Turnbull, J. M. Patterson, S. K. Behr, D. L. Murphy, J. G. Marquis, & M. J. Blue-Banning (Eds.), *Cognitive coping, families and disabilities.* Baltimore: Brookes.

Ulrey, G., & Schnell, R. R. (1982). Introduction to assessing young children. In G. Ulrey & S. J. Rogers (Eds.), *Psychological assessment of handicapped infants and young children* (pp. 1–11). New York: Thieme-Stratton.

Wahler, R., & Dumas, J. (1984). Changing the observational coding styles of insular and noninsular mothers: A step towards maintenance of parent training effects. In R. Dangel & R. Polster (Eds.), *Parent training: Foundations of research and practice* (pp. 379–416). New York: Guilford Press.

Walsh, W. M., & Wood, J. I. (1983). Family assessment: Bridging the gap between theory, research and practice. *American Mental Health Counselors Association Journal, 23,* 111–120.

Warfield, M., & Hauser-Cram, P. (1996). Child care needs, arrangements, and satisfaction of mothers of children with developmental disabilities. *Mental Retardation, 5,* 294–302.

Werner, E. E. (1986). A longitudinal study of perinatal risk. In D. C. Farran & J. D. McKinney (Eds.), *Risk in intellectual and psychosocial development* (pp. 3–27). New York: Academic Press.

Werner, E. E., & Smith, R. S. (1982). *Vulnerable but invincible: A longitudinal study of resilient children and youth.* New York: Adams, Bannister, Cox.

The Family with a Chronically Ill Child

13

Steven W. Lee and Thomas P. Guck

• •

T he primary purpose of this chapter is to present the collaborative–consultative model and its application to the family with a chronically ill child. Professionals applying the model can maximize treatment effectiveness if they understand the context in which the model has been developed, particularly (a) the prevalence and impact of chronic illness on children and families; (b) models of care; and (c) the role of schools in working with families with chronically ill children. The first part of this chapter discusses these key factors and provides a backdrop for the second part, which presents the collaborative–consultative model and its use with families with chronically ill children.

Background Issues for the Collaborative–Consultative Model

Prevalence and Impact of Chronic Illness on Children and Families

There appears to be a paradox in the research findings related to the incidence of childhood illness. On the one hand, many thousands of lives have been saved due to the control of infectious diseases through improvements in sanitation, housing, and medical care. Mortality rates in this country fell from 870 per 100,000 children aged 1 to 14 years in 1900 to 33 in 100,000 children in 1987 (National Center for Health Statistics, 1990). Technological and medical advances have produced a dramatic reduction of some of the worst childhood chronic conditions such as polio and rheumatic fever. On the other hand, these same life-saving advances have resulted in many children living with chronic illnesses. For example, children suffering from cystic fibrosis, spina bifida, leukemia, and congenital heart disease now live significantly longer, some even to adulthood (Gortmaker, 1985; Gortmaker & Sappenfield, 1984).

Using data from the 1988 National Health Interview Survey, Newacheck and Taylor (1992) estimated that 31% of a sample of 17,100 children were affected by chronic conditions. The most prevalent conditions included respiratory allergies (9.7%), repeated ear infections (8.3%), and asthma (4.3%). Five percent of those with chronic conditions accounted for 19% of physician contacts and 33% of hospital days. While these statistics are instructive, they do not tell the whole story. Beneath these general observations is the variability in prevalence rates dependent on type of condition, age, developmental maturation, gender, ethnicity, socioeconomic status, and educational background and opportunity (Kazak, 1997).

The impact of chronic conditions on any given child or family can be determined in part by the number, type, and severity of the conditions. Children and their families can be affected by external factors, such as psychosocial support, access to medical and other services, effectiveness of treatment and rehabilitative interventions, and acceptance by the community of children with chronic conditions (Newacheck & Taylor, 1992).

Kerns (1995) has suggested four domains to consider when examining the impact of chronic illness on children and their families. The first is the illness process itself. Chronic illnesses vary according to the biological system involved, their evolving versus resolving natures, their speeds of progression, and so forth. The professional's knowledge about the course of specific illnesses is essential when working with parents. As an example, educating parents about the disease of diabetes and principle of glucose metabolism can establish a collaborative effort that brings about effective regulation of the disease (Hauser et al., 1986; Johnson, 1985). The cyclical nature of some chronic illnesses features acute phases and remission. While in acute phases the children or their parents may reexperience the same grief reaction as with the initial diagnosis (Friederich, 1977). Sheeran, Marvin, and Pianta (1997) suggested a relationship between parents' resolution of the child's diagnosis and the quality of parenting. They further suggested that in grieving the loss of the perfect child, parents may benefit from cognitive strategies that entail changing their mental models of self and child. They learn to modify their image of the perfect healthy child originally anticipated.

The second domain relates to the clinical and symptomatic expression of the disease. The family's response to symptoms can play a crucial role in determining the frequency and severity of symptoms. For example, the longer a child endures a chronic or recurrent pain episode that is unpredictable, and the more the parents search for environmental causes, the greater the risk that the child will develop learned or conditioned pain triggers (McGrath & Hillier, 1996). Modeling and reinforcement of the sick role in childhood by family members has been shown to predict adult illness behavior (Kerns, 1995).

Closely related to symptom presentation is the third domain, which is behavior associated with impairment and disability. Characteristics of the illness can cause varying degree of impairment. The effects on behavior can range from simple symptom management in conditions such as hypertension to more profound impairment associated with disorders of the central nervous system (Kerns, 1995). Family members may contribute to functional disability in the child through reinforcement of inactivity or the processes of enmeshment, overprotectiveness, and rigidity (Drotar, 1997; Sargent, 1983).

Enmeshment refers to a high involvement or overresponsiveness among family members. Furthermore, members of an enmeshed family are highly sensitive to one another and respond to minor upsets with closeness. Individuals within the family lack their own distinct identities; they have difficulty differentiating themselves from the family unit. Overprotectiveness (Sargent, 1983) refers to a tendency to shelter other family members from psychological or physical harm. When this extends to the major areas of family life, "individual competence and autonomy are retarded, and personal control and problem solving are inhibited" (Sargent, 1983, p. 53). Rigidity refers to a tendency to maintain stability within the family unit. Sargent (1983) argues that this tendency may remain even when traditional methods of family interactions become dysfunctional. The inability to communicate then further compounds the family's problems. Sargent (1983) contends that these families have a low tolerance for conflict; the family views small conflicts as disproportionately threatening and intolerable.

The fourth domain is the affective response of the child to his chronic condition. Family variables such as sibling relations (Hanson et al., 1992) and family or parental functioning (Drotar, 1997) can affect psychological adjustment of children with chronic conditions. Lawler, Nakielny, and Wright (1966) noted a much higher degree of psychopathology and marital discord in parents of dying children. Emotional problems such as anxiety, depression, denial, hostility, and an inability to care for the sick child were noted in studies by McCollum and Gibson (1970) and Meyerwitz and Kaplan (1967). Depression in the sick child and the parents (Tropauer, Franz, & Dilgard, 1970), as well as communication difficulties among immediate family members and between the family and relatives, has been noted by Turk (1964). Problems of this sort serve to isolate the family with the ill child and reduce the effect of familial support systems. McCubbin et al. (1983) observed that parents of chronically ill children have an inadequate amount of leisure time either with their families or by themselves; consequently, depression can develop because naturally occurring reinforcement is not obtained from enjoyable activities.

Hannah and Midlarsky (1985) examined specific issues related to the siblings of chronically ill children including the increased responsibilities of caretaking for the sick child and doing additional chores around the home. Parents often devote more time to the sick child, resulting in feelings of neglect and isolation in the siblings. Parents may increase their educational or athletic expectations for the non-ill siblings in compensation for the lost expectations of the sick child. Finally, the researchers point out that family size seems to have a bearing on problems with the siblings as in a larger family, members can share caretaking responsibilities, the sick child is less conspicuous, and therefore "an atmosphere of normality prevails" (p. 514). Smaller families seem more likely to experience dysfunction (Trevino, 1979).

Frequently families and their chronically ill children do adjust to change without an increased need for professional consultation. Family factors can keep children from developing affective disorders by encouraging resilience in the face of their chronic illness (Lavigne & Faier-Routman, 1992, 1993; Wallander & Thompson, 1995). There is some evidence that at least 75% of parents with chronically ill children are not dysfunctional or suffering symptoms of maladjustment (Holmbeck et al., 1997). However, these parents rarely come to the attention of helping professionals.

Models of Health Care

For the past two centuries, health care has been dominated by the medical model. More recently, because of this model's shortcomings, professionals in health care settings began giving greater attention to a new model, the biopsychosocial model. The new model assumes that any health or illness outcome is a consequence of the interplay of biological, psychological, and social factors (Engel, 1977; Schwartz, 1982). Diagnosis and treatment should always consider the interacting role of all three factors. By definition, chronic illness extends over time. The biopsychosocial model views the chronic conditions longitudinally as ongoing multifactorial processes in which there is a dynamic and reciprocal interplay among biological, psychological, and social factors as a more appropriate model of care (Turk, 1996). This model makes explicit the significance of the relationship among child, family, and health care providers. Communication among all parties is reciprocal.

The biopsychosocial model is the cornerstone for the new and emerging fields of health psychology and behavioral medicine (Matarazzo, 1980). However the medical model in many ways continues to govern public policy, health care financing, and treatment approaches. It maintains that all illness can be explained on the basis of aberrant biochemical and neurophysiological processes. It is a reductionistic model focusing on isolating a single cause for a disease. To its credit the medical model has led to technological, surgical, and pharmacological advances that have helped eliminate many childhood diseases. More recently several factors, such as the increasing cost of health care; the nature of chronic illnesses, which requires ongoing management rather than a cure; the recognition of behavioral and lifestyle choices as contributors to health and illness; and a greater desire on the part of patients and families to share in health care decisions, have led to dissatisfaction with the purely medical model (Taylor, 1995).

Perhaps the greatest shortcoming of the medical model is its inability to help health care professionals work collaboratively with families of chronically ill children. Within the medical service delivery model, the focus is on the ill child only and other aspects of the child's life are often ignored. Under the medical model the professional's relationship with parents is often prescriptive; the physician tells the parents and family what the medical people will do and what the parents will do for the ill child. Because the treatment emphasis in the medical model is on the ill child and not on daily family interactions, the model disregards the relationship between the parent and child, which undoubtedly plays a large part in treatment effectiveness (Kazak, 1997). Because the focus is on the ill child only, little or no change occurs elsewhere. The medical model features one-way communication, with little or no interaction or collaboration. The professional's language is often replete with medical terminology and jargon that are unfamiliar to the family. The incomprehensible explanations breed anxiety due to fear of the unknown.

Historically, parents who tried to act as collaborators with medical and other human service providers in the care of children were often met with contempt and lack of cooperation. In fact, parents were often barred in their attempts to be close to their hospitalized child, because hospital personnel believed that the parents' presence would constitute spoiling the child, overprotectiveness, or a neurotic symbiosis (Azarnoff & Hardgrove, 1981). They often felt that better care was afforded by nursing staff during a child's stay in the hospital. Azarnoff and Hardgrove (1981) note that

> parents took great care not to offend the staff by questioning these policies, by appearing to be too close to their child, or by knowing too much. They feared that if they displeased the staff in whose hands their child's well-being rested, revenge on the child might result or care might be withheld. (p. 5)

Rather than collaborating with parents, physicians in the past assumed a superior role. The 1847 American Medical Association Code of Ethics which specifies that the physician's role is to "unite tenderness with firmness and condescension with authority, so as to inspire the minds of their patients with gratitude, respect and confidence" (Gallessich, 1982, p. 20).

Parents have also been criticized by professionals in other fields as being the cause of the behavior problems in their children (Kozloff, 1979). The professionals felt that therapeutic treatment for the parents was every bit as necessary as that for the child if the child was to function adequately.

The view of parents as second-rate caregivers who should be treated with condescension and are likely the primary cause of their child's problems would clearly prohibit true and co-equal collaboration between the professional and the parent. However, research over the last 40 years on the benefits of parental intervention with children, the negative effects of parent–child separations, and the importance of the parent–child bond on the emotional well-being of family members has done much to change the medical and educational communities' views on the value of parental involvement. In addition the federal government, recognizing the need to provide parents' rights in the educational arena, passed the Elementary and Secondary Education Amendments (1974), the Education for All Handicapped Children Act (1975), and the Individuals with Disabilities Education Act Amendments (1997). These laws provided a number of procedural safeguards against the misuse of information about children, as well as the preparation of formal assessments without parental permission and involvement in the process. However, the archaic views mentioned above still linger; they have been ingrained in the medical community over time and are resistant to change. The need for this book is evidence that professional collaboration with parents is still a relatively new and evolving mindset.

The negative views of parents held by professionals reduces the probability of effective treatment for the child from both medical and educational standpoints. Collaboration is of a limited nature because disproportionate power relationships tend to restrict the communication flow between the professionals and parents (Alpert, 1977; Kramer & Nagle, 1980; Kurpius, 1978; Pryzwansky, 1974). The view that parents are not equals in the consultative process and the restricted communication that results does not allow the professional to work as an ally with parents. In contrast, when parents are involved in the medical care, the children seem to recuperate faster, parents express greater satisfaction with the hospital, and children seem to be more cooperative with medical procedures (Wolfer & Visitainer, 1975). Collaborative involvement with parents in some medical settings serves to normalize the environment and thereby reduce stress, provide security for the child, and continue the growth and development of the child within the family (Hardgrove, 1980). The professional who fails to view the parent as a co-equal agent in the care and treatment of the child may jeopardize the quality of care to the child and diminish the probability of an optimal treatment outcome.

The Role of the School in Working with Families of Chronically Ill Children

School is often of great importance in the lives of chronically ill children, as it is their link with the mainstream of the child and adolescent culture. School adjustment in chronically ill children has not been well studied (Drotar, 1981). Researchers do know that chronically ill children often have excessive and intermittent absences. They may be limited in their ability to participate fully in school and they may require special tutoring or homebound instruction. Richman and Harper (1978) found that mildly handicapped children with cleft lip and palate and cerebral palsy significantly underachieved academically when compared with their normal peers. The underachievement was attributed to "the general characteristic of personality inhibition" (Richman & Harper, 1978, p. 16), as chronically ill children may be reluctant to draw attention to themselves. This inhibition may limit competitiveness and drive, which are often necessary for academic achievement.

Chronically ill children often have special needs that the educational system is not equipped to handle. As a result, schools may vary greatly in how they place these children and how they identify educational handicaps. Within the educational system, children with other exceptionalities have somewhat clearer identification criteria and somewhat more uniform educational deficits, which result in more homogeneous educational placements.

The above-mentioned issues serve to distinguish some of the qualitative differences between the problems of chronically ill children and their families and those of families of children with other disabilities. Professionals working with the families of chronically ill children should be aware of these differences and not assume that experience in serving parents and children with other disabilities is sufficient for understanding and consulting with these families.

Despite these concerns, school adjustment of chronically ill children can be quite good (Drotar et al., 1981), but this depends in part on the type of condition. For example, Harper, Richman, and Snider (1980) found that children with a cleft lip and palate showed a higher degree of impulse inhibition in school than a matched sample of children with cerebral palsy. Limitations on sample size in this study as well as other considerations make these results difficult to generalize.

Little research is available on the effects of school interventions for chronically ill children. School psychologists have a variety of intervention modes to choose from, such as the following:

1. *School System Consultation.* Intervention at this level may include advocacy programs or parent support groups. System level programs highlight this level of intervention.

2. *Principal or Teacher Consultation.* The psychologist intervenes in a specific case by consulting with the teacher or principal. There is no direct intervention from the psychologist (consultant) to the ill child.

3. *Counseling the Ill Child.* This familiar approach involves individual psychotherapy with the ill child. Services of this sort may also include counseling with a group of chronically ill children.

4. *Counseling with the Siblings of the Ill Child.* This approach features traditional individual or group counseling with siblings of the ill child.

This unique strategy promotes family stability through the brothers and sisters of the ill child.

5. *Parent Consultation.* The psychologist helps the child indirectly by working with the parents. This technique is the focus of the second section of this chapter.

The Collaborative–Consultative Model and Its Usefulness

A number of factors point to consultation as an important and needed human service intervention. The psychologist working within a consultative framework may serve more children in a shorter time by imparting psychological techniques to parents who can work with their child. From a preventive standpoint, parents may gain skills that will also help them in the future.

Two Types of Consultative Relationships

When a child is diagnosed as chronically ill the family's involvement with medical and educational personnel increases. As a result parents may experience consultative relationships with both medical and educational personnel. The contrast between these two models may leave the parents confused about their role, and perhaps without the ability to participate fully and collaboratively in the consultative process. The following is a critical look at the medical service delivery model presented above in comparison with the collaborative consultation model.

Medical Service Delivery Model. Figure 13.1 shows the medical service delivery model. This traditional approach is characterized by the focus on the ill child only. As noted in the figure, daily interaction takes place between the parents and the ill child as well as the neighbors, relatives, and siblings. The referral (arrow 1) comes from the parent to the physician who examines and assesses the ill child (arrow 2). The physician then reports the findings to the parents and outlines the treatment plan which the physician and others (i.e., nurses, physician's assistant) will carry out (arrow 3). The treatment emanates from the physician (arrow 4) and is directed toward the ill child.

Collaborative–Consultative Service Delivery Model. Figure 13.2 shows the collaborative–consultative service delivery model. This model focuses primarily on the parents and their daily interaction with the child and other important people in the child's life. Secondarily, the model may focus on the ill child as the target of assessment and treatment. In the collaborative–consultative service delivery model, the referral may come from the parent to

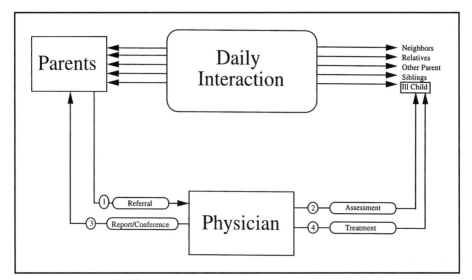

Figure 13.1. Medical service delivery model. From T. B. Gutkin (personal communication, October 1982). Adapted with permission.

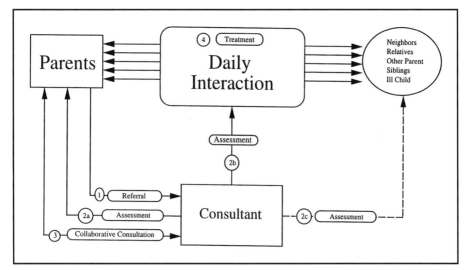

Figure 13.2. Collaborative–consultative service delivery model. From T. B. Gutkin (personal communication, October 1982). Adapted with permission.

the psychologist or consultant (or other education professionals) as shown in Figure 13.2 (arrow 1). The consultant's assessment in this model includes an interview with the parents (arrow 2a) and an evaluation of the daily interaction between the parents and the ill child (arrow 2b). This evaluation may include direct observation of the parent–child interaction or information collected through parent- or child-completed behavior rating scales. Occasionally, the consultant may evaluate the ill child directly (dashed arrow 2c) but this is rarely necessary. After the assessment phase is completed, collaborative consultation is initiated between the parent and the consultant (arrow 3) using a problem-solving format as well as a variety of other consultation techniques. Finally, treatment is initiated by the parent within the daily interaction with the child (arrow #4). In the collaborative–consultative model the parent is responsible for carrying out the treatment.

Model Comparisons

While both of the above-mentioned models have utility within their respective systems, professionals should be fully aware of the sharp contrast between the models. Within the medical service delivery model, the focus is only on the ill child; other aspects of the child's life are often ignored. The medical model approach features little collaborative problem solving with parents and is often prescriptive; the physician tells the parents what the medical people will do and what the parent will do for the ill child. This prescriptive approach decreases the parents' sense of ownership for the treatment plan. Because the treatment focuses exclusively on the ill child, it neglects the relationship between the parents and child, which undoubtedly plays a large part in treatment effectiveness. Serious collaboration with parents requires a positive view of parents as co-equal in terms of influence on the treatment plan. The prescriptive dimension of the medical model reduces the chances that other (nonmedical) approaches advanced by the parents are considered.

Medical model treatments largely ignore the family and how they may be coping with chronic illness. Since the focus is only on the ill child, little or no change in the child's condition results in little reduction in the stress on the family. The medical model for service delivery features one-way communications (note arrows in Figure 13.1), and very little serious collaboration. Lastly, as mentioned the medical orientation uses terminology that is unfamiliar to the parent and breeds anxiety due to fear of the unknown.

In the collaborative–consultative service delivery model, the focus is on the daily interaction of the parents with the ill child and with significant others in the child's life. The process features mutually agreed-upon goals and interventions; parents' sense of ownership for the goals and interventions increases the likelihood that they will be carried out. The collaborative process includes the family, relatives, and neighbors by examining their role in enhancing the environment for the ill child, parents, and siblings. The open and ongoing communication between the consultant and the parents allows for evolving views of the problems of the child and family, and these may be incorporated into the consultation process. The collaborative–consultative process uses a problem-solving orientation in which both the parents and the consultant, working together, examine the problems of the child and family and devise intervention plans. Unlike the medical service delivery model, the collaborative–consultative approach assumes the parent to be competent. Finally, because the problems as depicted by the parent are the focus of the consultative effort, the collaborative–consultative model generally relies on terminology familiar to the parents.

Consultants should be aware that parents of chronically ill children may be getting a vastly different view of working with professionals from the medical community. Parents may have difficulty understanding or adjusting to the collaborative or more participative role. A description of collaboration (i.e., mutual working together, joint responsibility) during the initial consultative session might be quite helpful to the parents and prepare them for full participation.

Collaborative Consultation with Parents of Chronically Ill Children

As previously noted, in collaborative consultation, both the parents and the consultant contribute to problem solving. The consultant should have both process and content expertise. Process expertise refers to skills of engaging and interacting with the parents. Process expertise includes problem-solving methods and communication skills. Process skills can be used with any type of consultee with any type of problem. Content expertise refers to the body of knowledge and skills specific to the issue at hand, in this case chronically ill children and their families. A consultant with content expertise is familiar with the relevant research in the content area and the effectiveness of various intervention approaches.

Collaborative consultation has been the focus of both outcome and process research (Gresham & Kendell, 1987). Outcome research examines the effects of interventions that resulted from collaborative consultation. Gresham and Kendell (1987) summarized the outcomes of consultation with teachers to include "(a) changes in consultees' classroom behavior, (b) changes in consultees' knowledge, perceptions, and or attitudes, (c) changes in clients' classroom behavior, and (d) changes in the frequency of consultation utilization" (p. 310). Other effects have included improved scholastic achievement of children in the intermediate grades (4, 5, and 6) whose parents received consultative services. More recently collaborative consultation approaches have shown positive results in increasing social initiations in withdrawn students (Sheridan, 1997).

Process research refers to studies of the collaborative–consultative process itself (i.e., techniques, communication skills). Gresham and Kendell (1987) concluded that behavioral consultation seemed to result in higher expectations from the teachers for solving problems. Less prescriptive approaches were found to be more effective with teachers: "The odds are 14 times greater that a teacher will identify resources and a way to carry out a consultation plan if the consultant asks rather than tells the teacher" (Gresham & Kendell, 1987, p. 310).

Knoff, Hines, and Kromrey (1995) investigated factors that differentiated effective from noneffective consultants. They explored factors within the context of the development of the Consultant Effectiveness Scale (CES) and found that more effective consultants possessed better (a) interpersonal and problem-solving abilities, (b) consultation process skills, and (c) ethical and professional practice expertise. Competencies like these in working with parents have produced increased active involvement in the problem-solving process (Sheridan, 1997). Further, numerous authors have endorsed the collaborative– consultative approach for working with parents of children with serious medical conditions such as failure to thrive (Black, 1995), seizure disorders (Sachs & Barrett, 1995), and pediatric HIV (Landau, Pryor, & Haefli, 1995).

General approaches to process consultation have been outlined elsewhere (Conoley & Conoley, 1982; Gutkin & Curtis, 1982); therefore this discussion will focus predominantly on the issue of content expertise. But first we will briefly discuss process expertise with reference to important process issues in consulting with the parents of chronically ill children.

Process Expertise

As previously noted, process expertise involves the methods or techniques used in working with parents or other consultees. In this vein, a problem-solving approach using a sequence similar to that shown in Table 13.1, may not only help the parents to solve current problems, but also function preventively. Its ability to prevent future problems depends upon the degree to which the consultant passes along the problem-solving skills to the parent (Gutkin & Curtis, 1982).

The professional who is pursuing the problem-solving sequence in a collaborative way with parents of chronically ill children, can call upon a variety of technical and communication skills that will likely enhance the relationship and make the consultation more fruitful. For example, the professional can communicate to the parents that the relationship is co-equal in terms of power; it is not a supervisory relationship. The parent brings a vast body of

Table 13.1

Problem-Solving Sequence

---

1. Establish a calm and rational atmosphere.
2. Define and clarify the problem(s).
   a. Identify and prioritize all the problems and determine which will be worked with first.
   b. State the problem in concrete behavioral terms. Be specific.
   c. When appropriate, divide the problem into its component parts and determine which component or combination of components should be dealt with first.
   d. Identify the terminal goals.
3. Analyze the forces impinging on the problem.
   a. Identify forces that impede the solution of the problem.
   b. Identify forces that contribute to the solution of the problem.
   c. Identify any neutral forces that must be taken into account in solving the problem.
4. Brainstorm multiple alternative solutions to the problem.
5. Evaluate and choose among alternatives.
6. Specify consultant and consultee responsibilities.
7. Implement the solution(s).
8. Evaluate the effectiveness of the action and recycle if necessary.

---

knowledge about the child and the consultant brings knowledge of education or psychology to the relationship.

Each side has responsibilities. The consultant is responsible for regulating the problem-solving process and contributing some content expertise. The consultant should also be available mentally and physically, model effective problem solving, and be patient. The responsibilities of parents include contributing content expertise (knowledge of the child), being involved in the problem-solving process, and taking action on the plan that results from consultation. Lastly, parents are responsible for initiating, maintaining, and terminating the consultative relationship. The responsibility for success or failure lies jointly with the consultant and the parents.

The relationship between the professional and parents should be viewed as voluntary, and parents should have the freedom to reject any solutions generated. These aspects of the relationship empower the parents to have control over the relationship and ownership for interventions for their child generated from the consultative endeavor.

An array of effective communication skills helps the professional gain and maintain rapport, as well as achieve clarity of communication with the parent. Skills such as paraphrasing, providing accurate empathy, using time purposefully, and developing appropriate styles of opening and closing interviews are all critical to effective consultation. The reader is directed toward Beier (1966), Benjamin (1969), Gutkin and Curtis (1982), and Rogers (1951) for a full discussion of relevant communication techniques.

Content Expertise

Content expertise in working with parents of chronically ill children involves knowledge of intervention strategies that are helpful to parents, siblings, and the ill child. The following is a literature review of relevant findings and some effective techniques.

McCubbin et al. (1983) studied 100 families who had one or more children with cystic fibrosis. A questionnaire administered to the parents identified their coping behaviors. The study found three substantive factors or behavior sets. These were (1) maintaining family integration, cooperation, and an optimistic view of the situation; (2) maintaining social support, self-esteem, and psychological stability; and (3) understanding the medical situation. Factor 1 included parent behaviors such as a belief things will work out, confidence in the medical care, belief in God, and actions that strengthen relationships with family members. Factor 2 included behaviors such as continued involvement with friends, eating, sleeping, getting away, working, and having hobbies. Factor 3 included talking with other parents in the same situation, talking with the medical staff, and reading about how others handled these problems. McCubbin et al. (1983) also noted that positive changes in the child's health were associated with coping Factor 2 with regard to both fathers and mothers.

Hall and Richmond (1984) discussed guidelines for consulting with parents of children with handicaps, some of which are applicable to the parents of chronically ill children. These authors noted that parents need time on their own and time together to relieve the stress and strain of the situation. Groups of parents with similar problems seem to offer support and help parents to feel that they are not alone. The financial burden of a long-standing illness can cause significant stress for the family. The consultant should be knowledgeable about financial help. The consultant should also help parents learn the trust their decisions with reference to their ill child; the parents may seek advice but they are the ones who must ultimately live with the decisions.

Sargent (1983) summarized some guidelines designed for psychotherapists, which may be applicable for consultants working with parents of chronically ill children: Parents should be in charge of managing the illness. The less involved parent should be drawn into the process as much as possible. Parents should agree in planning for their children and should cooperate in responsibility for the sick child.

Friedrich (1977) outlined the value of support groups for parents, which may allow them to "publicly mourn" for their child as well as gain strength from the other group members. Friedrich also noted that a strictly medical approach toward the ill child is anxiety provoking and confusing. Therefore, parents and other human service professionals should also attend to the psychosocial needs of the child.

Cobb and Medway (1978) summarized the literature on general parent consultation and concluded that these consultations are more effective with groups with higher income and education. In addition, they asserted that the modeling of techniques with parents and the intensity of the training are related to successful outcomes.

Potter (1988) stated that parents should help children to be responsible for as much of their own care as possible, providing them with a feeling of control rather than dependence. Parents should be encouraged to ask questions about their child's care from medical personnel.

Potter (1988) also suggested that parents should help the well siblings to develop their own identity and to understand distinctions between themselves and the ill child. Furthermore, siblings should be informed about the nature and progression of the illness. McKeever (1983) likewise asserted that siblings may feel responsible for the ill child's condition and therefore need a clear and rational explanation of the cause of the illness. The effects of an ill child are often far reaching; when consulting with parents of a chronically ill child, the professional should collect information on the academic achievement, sleeping, eating, and mood of the siblings.

If the ill child's school progress is hindered by the illness, then the child may be eligible for special services such as homebound instruction, special counseling, physical or occupational therapy, or in-school special help (Potter, 1988). The parent should maintain contact with a person within the school who can coordinate homework, lessons, and classmate contact for the ill child.

Thompson and Gustafson (1996) reviewed several studies related to intervention strategies for chronically ill children. This review pointed to the effectiveness of school reintegration programs for improving school adjustment and reducing depressive behaviors in chronically ill children. In addition, the development of social competencies in chronically ill children may result in increased social support at school as well as fewer parent-reported behavior problems (Thompson & Gustafson, 1996).

Guidelines for Working with Parents of Chronically Ill Children

The following is a summary of guidelines extracted from the previous review that should be considered by consultants.

1. Use a collaborative approach in working with parents.

2. Help parents to develop an optimistic but realistic view of their child's illness. Optimism seems to help parents to cope.

3. Encourage religious beliefs; these also seem to assist parents in coping.

4. Encourage parents to maintain involvement with relatives and neighbors as well as immediate family.

5. Discuss the importance of supporting the spouse and allowing oneself to be supported.

6. Help parents to encourage independence in the ill child. This may include making the child responsible for her own medication.

7. Encourage parents to get time alone.

8. Help parents to maintain adequate eating and sleeping behavior.

9. Encourage parents to continue working or maintaining hobbies; these activities seem to help with coping.

10. Discuss the value of keeping in shape physically and being well groomed.

11. Help parents to explore support groups.

12. Know the financial services that are available to parents of chronically ill children.

13. Encourage parents to get input from others but ultimately make their own decisions regarding their child.

14. Encourage parents to be in charge of illness management; in particular, encourage the less involved parent.

15. Help parents to ask questions of and continue communication with the medical staff treating their child.

16. Know a list of helpful materials that parents may read relative to their child's illness and other parents' reaction to it.

17. Encourage parents to inform the well siblings about the nature and progression of the child's illness.

18. Help the parent to understand the special services for which their child may be eligible at school and specify a school contact person to coordinate homework, lessons, and classmate contact with their ill child.

19. Encourage efforts for planned school reintegration with attention to social, developmental, medical, and academic considerations. A carefully crafted plan for school reintegration should include school and medical personnel, parents and family, and the ill child.

20. Assess and strengthen the social skills of the ill child with an eye toward how enhancement might result in a better social life for the child.

Summary

This chapter presented the adverse impact of chronic illness on a child and family. We explained how the medical model may hinder meaningful collaboration with parents while the collaborative–consultative model can be a more effective alternative. We discussed aspects of these two models within the context of the specific problems that affect the families of chronically ill children. We also gleaned from the literature some aspects of process and content expertise that can assist the collaborative consultant. This information was provided as a summary of guidelines that may aid the consultant in reducing the stress associated with childhood chronic illness.

References

Alpert, J. L. (1977). Some guidelines for school consultants. *Journal of School Psychology, 15,* 308–317.

Azarnoff, P., & Hardgrove, C. (1981). *The family in the child health care.* New York: Wiley.

Beier, E. (1966). *The silent language of psychotherapy.* Chicago: Aldine.

Benjamin, A. (1969). *The helping interview.* Boston: Houghton Mifflin.

Black, M. M. (1995). Failure to thrive: Strategies for evaluation and intervention. *School Psychology Review, 24,* 171–185.

Cobb, D. E., & Medway, F. J. (1978). Determinants of effectiveness in parent consultation. *Journal of Community Psychology, 6,* 229–240.

Conoley, J. C., & Conoley, C. W. (1982). *School consultation: A guide to practice and training.* New York: Pergamon Press.

Drotar, D. (1981). Psychological perspectives in chronic childhood illness. *Journal of Pediatric Psychology, 6,* 211–228.

Drotar, D. (1997). Relating parent and family functioning to the psychological adjustment of children with chronic health conditions: What have we learned? What do we need to know? *Journal of Pediatric Psychology, 22,* 149–165.

Drotar, D., Doershuk, C. F., Boat, T. F., Stern, R. C., Matthews, L., & Boyer, W. (1981). Psychosocial functioning of children with cystic fibrosis. *Pediatrics, 67,* 338–343.

Education for All Handicapped Children Act of 1975, 20 U.S.C. § 1400 *et seq.*

Elementary and Secondary Education Amendments. (1974). Public Law 93-380.

Engel, G. L. (1977). The need for a new medical model: A challenge for biomedical science. *Science, 196,* 129–136.

Friedrich, W. N. (1977). Ameliorating the psychological impact of chronic disease on the child and family. *Journal of Pediatric Psychology, 2,* 26–31.

Gallessich, J. (1982). *The profession and practice of consultation.* San Francisco: Jossey-Bass.

Gortmaker, S. L. (1985). Demography of chronic childhood diseases. In N. Hobbs & J. M. Perrin (Eds.), *Issues in the care of children with chronic illness.* San Francisco: Jossey-Bass.

Gortmaker, S. L., & Sappenfield, W. (1984). Chronic childhood disorders: Prevalence and impact. *Pediatric Clinic of North America, 31,* 3–18.

Gresham, F. M., & Kendell, G. K. (1987). School consultation research: Methodological critique and future research directions. *School Psychology Review, 16,* 306–316.

Gutkin, T. B., & Curtis, M. J. (1982). School-based consultation: Theory and techniques. In C. R. Reynolds & T. B. Gutkin (Eds.), *The handbook of school psychology* (pp. 796–828). New York: Wiley.

Hall, C. W., & Richmond, B. O. (1984). Consultation with parents of handicapped children. *The Exceptional Child, 31,* 185–191.

Hannah, M. E., & Midlarsky, E. (1985). Siblings of the handicapped: A literature review for school psychologists. *School Psychology Review, 14,* 510–520.

Hanson, C. L., Henggeler, S. W., Harris, M. A., Cigrang, J. A., Schinkel, A. M., Rodrigue, J. R., & Klesges, R. C. (1992). Contributions of sibling relations to the adaptation of youth with insulin-dependent diabetes mellitus. *Journal of Consulting and Clinical Psychology, 60,* 104–112.

Hardgrove, C. (1980). Helping parents on the pediatric ward. A report on a survey of hospitals with 'Living-In' programs. *Paediatrician, 9,* 220–223.

Harper, D. C., Richman, L. C., & Snider, B. C. (1980). School adjustment and degree of physical impairment. *Journal of Pediatric Psychology, 5,* 377–383.

Hauser, S. T., Jacobson, A. M., Wertlieb, D., Weiss-Perry, B., Follansbee, D., Wolfsdorf, J. I., Herskowitz, R. D., Houlihan, J., & Rajapark, D. C. (1986). Children with recently diagnosed diabetes: Interactions with their families. *Health Psychology, 5,* 273–296.

Holmbeck, G. N., Gorey-Ferguson, L., Hudson, T., Seefeldt, T., Shapera, W., Turner, T., & Uhler, J. (1997). Maternal, paternal, and marital functioning in families of preadolescents with spina bifida. *Journal of Pediatric Psychology, 22,* 167–181.

Individuals with Disabilities Education Act Amendments of 1997, 20 U.S.C. § 1400 *et seq.*

Johnson, S. B. (1985). The family and the child with chronic illness. In D. C. Turk & R. D. Kerns (Eds.), *Health, illness, and families: A life-span perspective* (pp. 220–254). New York: Wiley.

Kazak, A. E. (1997). A contextual family/systems approach to pediatric psychology: Introduction to the special issue. *Journal of Pediatric Psychology, 22,* 141–148.

Kerns, R. D. (1995). Family assessment and intervention. In P. M. Nicassio & T. W. Smith (Eds.), *Managing chronic illness: A biopsychosocial perspective* (pp. 207–244). Washington DC: American Psychological Association.

Knoff, H. M., Hines, C. V., & Kromrey, J. D. (1995). Finalizing the Consultant Effectiveness Scale: An analysis and validation of the characteristics of effective consultants. *School Psychology Review, 24,* 480–496.

Kozloff, M. A. (1979). *A program for families of children with learning and behavior problems.* New York: Wiley.

Kramer, J. J., & Nagle, R. J. (1980). Suggestions for the delivery of psychological services in secondary schools. *Psychology in the Schools, 17,* 53–59.

Kurpius, D. J. (1978). Defining and implementing a consultation program in the schools. *School Psychology Digest, 7,* 4–17.

Landau, S., Pryor, J. B., & Haefli, K. (1995). Pediatric HIV: School-based sequelae and curricular interventions for infection prevention and social acceptance. *School Psychology Review, 24,* 213–229.

Lavigne, J. V., & Faier-Routman, J. (1992). Psychological adjustment to pediatric physical disorders: A meta-analytic review. *Journal of Pediatric Psychology, 17,* 133–157.

Lavigne, J. V., & Faier-Routman, J. (1993). Correlates of psychological adjustment to pediatric physical disorders: A meta-analytic review and comparison of existing models. *Journal of Developmental and Behavioral Pediatrics, 14,* 117–123.

Lawler, R. H., Nakielny, W., & Wright, N. A. (1966). Psychological implications of crystic fibrosis. *Canadian Medical Association Journal, 94,* 1043–1046.

Matarazzo, J. D. (1980). Behavioral health and behavioral medicine: Frontiers for a new health psychology. *American Psychologist, 35,* 807–817.

McCollum, A. T., & Gibson, L. E. (1970). Family adaptation to the child with cystic fibrosis. *Journal of Pediatrics, 77,* 571–578.

McCubbin, M. I., McCubbin, M. A., Patterson, J. A., Cauble, A. E., Wilson, L. R., & Warwick, W. (1983, May). CHIP–Coping Healing Inventory for Parents: An assessment of parental coping patterns in the care of the chronically ill child. *Journal of Marriage and the Family,* pp. 359–370.

McGrath, P. A., & Hillier, L. M. (1996). Controlling children's pain. In R. J. Gatchel & D. C. Turk (Eds.), *Psychological approaches to pain management: A practitioner's handbook* (pp. 331–370). New York: Guilford Press.

McKeever, P. (1983). Siblings of chronically ill children: A literature review with implications for research and practice. *American Journal of Orthopsychiatry, 53,* 209–217.

Meyerwitz, J., & Kaplan, H. (1967). Familial responses to stress: The case of cystic fibrosis. *Social Science and Medicine, 1,* 249–266.

National Center for Health Statistics. (1990). *Prevention profile: Health, United States, 1989.* Hyattsville, MD: Public Health Service.

Newacheck, P. W., & Taylor, W. R. (1992). Childhood chronic illness: Prevalence, severity, and impact. *American Journal of Public Health, 82,* 364–371.

Potter, M. L. (1988, March). Children and chronic illness. *Communique,* p. 26.

Pryzwansky, W. A. (1974). A reconsideration of the consultation model for delivery of school-based psychological services. *American Journal of Orthopsychiatry, 44,* 579–583.

Richman, L. C., & Harper, D. C. (1978). School adjustment of children with observable difficulties. *Journal of Abnormal Child Psychology, 6,* 11–18.

Rogers, C. R. (1951). Client-centered therapy: Its current practice, implications and theory. Boston: Houghton Mifflin.

Sachs, H., & Barrett, R. P. (1995). Seizure disorders: A review for school psychologists. *School Psychology Review, 24,* 131–145.

Sargent, J. (1983). The sick child: Family complications. *Developmental and Behavioral Pediatrics, 4,* 50–56.

Schwartz, G. E. (1982). Testing the biopsychosocial model: The ultimate challenge facing behavioral medicine? *Journal of Consulting and Clinical Psychology, 50,* 1040–1053.

Sheeran, T., Marvin, R. S., & Pianta, R. C. (1997). Mother's resolution of their child's diagnosis and self-reported measures of parenting stress, marital relations, and social support. *Journal of Pediatric Psychology, 22,* 197–212.

Sheridan, S. (1997). Conceptual and empirical bases of conjoint behavioral consultation. *School Psychology Quarterly, 12,* 119–133.

Taylor, S. E. (1995). *Health psychology.* New York: McGraw-Hill.

Thompson, R. J., & Gustafson, K. E. (1996). *Adaptation to chronic childhood illness.* Washington, DC: American Psychological Association.

Trevino, F. (1979). Siblings of handicapped children: Identifying those at risk. *Social Casework, 60,* 488–493.

Tropauer, A., Franz, M. N., & Dilgard, V. W. (1970). Psychological aspects of the care of children with cystic fibrosis. *American Journal of Diseases of Children, 199,* 424–432.

Turk, D. C. (1996). Biopsychosocial perspective on chronic pain. In R. J. Gatchel & D. C. Turk (Eds.), *Psychological approaches to pain management: A practitioner's handbook* (pp. 3–32). New York: Guilford.

Turk, J. (1964). Impact of cystic fibrosis on family functioning. *Pediatrics, 34,* 67–71.

Wallander, J. L., & Thompson, R. J. (1995). Psychosocial adjustment of children with chronic physical conditions. In M. C. Roberts (Ed.), *Handbook of pediatric psychology* (pp. 124–141). New York: Guilford.

Wolfer, J., & Visitainer, M. (1975). Pediatric surgical patients and parents. Stress responses and adjustment. *Nursing Research, 24,* 244–255.

A Program for Families of Children and Youth with Learning Disabilities

Sue Vernon, Chriss Walther-Thomas, Jean B. Schumaker, Donald D. Deshler, and J. Stephen Hazel

14

T he challenges of raising a family in today's world are great. Economic pressures, the changing roles of mothers and fathers within the family constellation, and the demands of helping children and adolescents cope with pressure from their peers (e.g., to take drugs and skip school) all contribute to stress on the family unit. This stress can be significantly magnified when a family has a child with learning disabilities (LD). Some of this stress can result from the elusive nature of learning disabilities, which have often been referred to as the "hidden handicap" (Anderson, 1970). That is, to the casual observer, the youth with LD appears to be perfectly normal.

Children with Learning Disabilities and Their Families

Because of the hidden nature of a learning disability, initial acknowledgment of its existence may be difficult for families (Turnbull, Turnbull, Shank, & Leal, 1995). Often a full diagnosis of the disability does not occur until the child has been in school for an extended period of time. Such late diagnosis of a disability can lead to further problems. On the one hand, parents, siblings, and extended family members may be frustrated and confused by the discovery of a disability in a child who seems capable in many ways. On the other hand, some families may be relieved finally to learn there are reasons for the problems they have observed; however, these families may experience guilt that the disability was not identified earlier.

Also because of the hidden nature of learning disabilities, families of children with mild to moderate disabilities may take longer to accept the presence of a permanent disability than parents of children with more clearly defined conditions (Dyson, 1996; Faerstein, 1986). Generally, children with severe disabilities demonstrate consistently delayed patterns of development that are readily observed. Consequently, families of these children are forced to acknowledge discrepancies that exist between these children and their peers who do not have disabilities at an early age (Rappaport, 1965). The problems of children with mild to moderate disabilities are not as easily defined. They often experience wide variations in terms of meeting developmental milestones. They meet many milestones at the "expected time," some milestones earlier than their peers perhaps, and other important milestones much later than their peers, sometimes only after intensive instruction has been devoted to the targeted skills. These inconsistencies in performance make understanding and acceptance of their problems more difficult (Gerber & Reiff, 1992; McLoed, 1993; Willner & Crane, 1979).

Although the signs of LD may not be obvious compared to the signs readily observed in individuals with physical disabilities or severe developmental disabilities, the effects of LD are very real and can touch every aspect of a growing child's life. Because school plays such a prominent role in the lives of most students, success or failure in school determines to a large extent how students define themselves as competent or incompetent individuals (McLoed, 1993). Academic performance also affects how others in the school environment such as peers, teachers, and administrators regard the student. Consequently, poor school performance affects a student's social status as well as academic status. Over time, academic failure, frustration, self-doubt, and negative feedback from others may undermine confidence and self-esteem (Hazel & Schumaker, 1988; Lopez-Reyna & Olufs, 1996; McLoed, 1993).

Not surprisingly, parents of children and youth with LD continually face issues related to school. For example, they often have to decide what academic outcomes are realistic and appropriate (Berk, 1997). If parents push, they worry that the pressure is too great. Often, performance problems of a child in school can become more complicated if the expectations are not reasonable, given the child's condition (e.g., Giannotti & Doyle, 1982; Haager & Vaughn, 1995).

Despite lower expectations for student performance, school failure often leads to family conflicts. Indeed, problems in school are a primary source of conflict between parents and children with disabilities (Giannotti & Doyle, 1982; Powers, Hauser, & Kilner, 1989). The parents who may not clearly understand the nature of the disability may conclude that the child's failure reflects a general lack of ability or effort (Haywood & Switzky, 1986). Primary caregivers who are frustrated and confused about their child's performance may also develop maladaptive parenting behaviors such as inappropriate expectations, overprotection, indulgence, or denial (Odom, McConnell, & McEvoy, 1992).

Given the increased national emphasis on higher academic standards for all students, the academic pressures most students with LD and their families experience are not likely to decrease in the foreseeable future (McDonnell, McLaughlin, & Morison, 1997; U.S. Department of Education, 1997). If more students with LD are going to be successful at school and as adults, professionals need to get the families involved in mentoring and supporting the students academically and socially. Parents and other significant adults often play important roles in teaching, supporting, and encouraging the efforts of youth with disabilities (Carlson, 1997; U.S. Department of Education, 1997; Wagner, 1995).

The same cognitive deficits that often lead to school failure can lead to failure in other areas. As Silver (1983) noted more than 15 years ago, LD is "not just a school disability; it is a total life disability" (p. 58). Indeed, the subtle and complex difficulties associated with a learning disability can involve virtually all aspects of a child's and a family's life (Pfeiffer, Gerber, & Reiff, 1985; Smith, 1998). These children and youth are much like their typical peers; however, their persistent and unexpected underachievement problems may produce devastating effects at home and school (Bender, 1993; Hazel & Schumaker, 1988).

Day-to-day performance problems can have a lasting impact on a child's position within the family. In fact, these problems often affect how children and youth are judged by their parents, siblings, and other extended family members. Because children and youth with LD look "normal," their brothers, sisters, other relatives, and neighbors may misunderstand the source of their omissions and blunders. They may view the child as a burden or source of embarrassment (Osman, 1982). Siblings may believe the child with LD is "failing on purpose" to gain preferential treatment from parents (Amerikaner & Omizo, 1984). The parents' attempts to address the child's unique learning problems may affect other family members. For example, parents may feel that they need to allocate inordinate amounts of family resources to help the child with LD (Cone, Delawyer, & Wolfe, 1985). Margalit (1982) has suggested that pressures due to the costs of special services, fatigue from the daily management of difficult child behaviors and needs, and the self-doubt that many parents experience regarding the appropriateness of their parenting practices can disrupt family equilibrium. Kozloff (1979) suggested that families of children with LD experience an energy drain due to the amount of time needed to cope with factors related to the disability while trying to maintain normal family routines. If this is the case, negative feelings such as resentment, jealousy, and guilt may emerge (Turnbull & Turnbull, 1996).

The child's adolescence may put additional stress on the family equilibrium. Adolescence is often a time of conflict, pressure, and new challenges for greater personal independence (Coburn & Treeger, 1997). During this stage, children are evolving physically, psychologically, intellectually, and socially into young adults. Typically, they explore a wide range of new academic, social, and vocational experiences as they become more competent and independent (Benson, Williams, & Johnson, 1987; Zirpoli & Melloy, 1993). Roles change as teens become more self-reliant and more independent decision makers and as family members redefine their relationships with one another.

Parents often assume that their roles and opinions are less important to their child as a teenager than as a youngster. Emerging research suggests that the opposite is true. Adolescence is a very important time in a child's life for effective parenting (Benson, Williams, & Johnson, 1987). Despite the verbalized opinions of teens, the power of peers, and other external factors, families remain significant influences on many teenagers' academic and social decisions (Dryfoos, 1990; Resnick et al., 1997; Snodgrass, 1991; Zirpoli & Melloy, 1993). Consequently, the actions and expectations of supportive and caring parents can produce positive effects on important choices related to academic goals, school performance, friendships, drug and alcohol use, and sexual activity (Benson et al., 1987; Carnegie Council on Adolescent Development, 1992; Snodgrass, 1991).

Adolescents with LD often need more support from their parents than typical teens as they prepare for independent adulthood (Carlson, 1997; Goldfarb, Brotherson, Summers, & Turnbull, 1986; Hazel & Schumaker, 1988; Hazel, Schumaker, Sherman, & Sheldon-Wildgen, 1982; Turnbull & Turnbull, 1996; Wagner, 1995). After they leave public schools, very few are prepared to participate in postsecondary programs (Murray, Goldstein, & Edgar, 1997). Also, many young adults with disabilities have poorly developed networks of support and often experience poor employment opportunities (Carlson, 1997; Wagner, 1995). Tasks that many typical adolescents and young adults take for granted such as organizing their time, completing assigned homework and special projects, storing and retrieving new information, interpreting social cues, and even reading road signs on the freeway present problems for many individuals with LD (Gerber, Reiff, & Ginsberg, 1996).

Clearly, the ability of family members to understand and cope effectively with the demands associated with the condition affects the happiness of the family and the successful development of the child (Bryan & Bryan, 1981). Unfortunately, even well-intentioned families often lack the knowledge and skills needed to help their children cope with the unique demands of LD. Few school and community resources are available. Many families of students with disabilities have fewer emotional, educational, social, or financial resources than do typical students' families (Dryfoos, 1990; Dunst, Trivette, Starnes, Hamby, & Gordon, 1993; McDonnell et al., 1997; McLoyd, 1998; Wirt & Kirst, 1997). Various authors (e.g., Kroth & Otteni, 1983; Roth & Weller, 1985) have proposed models to guide professionals interested in helping these families; a variety of treatment models have been developed (Nichols, 1996). Many of these have targeted youth with behavioral or legal difficulties. For example, Robin and Foster (1989) proposed a treatment approach for families that uniquely combines family system orientation and techniques with a social-learning approach. Another prototypical intensive family intervention program, Homebuilders, was started in 1974 to provide an alternative to foster care and institutional placement of children (Kinney, Haapala, Booth, & Leavitt, 1990; Nelson, 1994). The program is structured to provide immediate access to intensive services (8 to 10 hours per week) over a brief period of time to two to four families. Multisystemic Therapy (Henggeler & Bourdin, 1990) is another family treatment approach to service delivery. This approach has been shown to be effective in reducing the recidivism for both sexual offenses, nonsexual crimes, and drug-related crimes among juvenile offenders (Bourdin, Henggeler, Blaske, & Stein, 1990; Henggeler et al., 1991). While a few specific skill development programs do exist (e.g., Burke & Herron, 1996; Dinkmeyer & McKay 1976; Patterson & Forgatch, 1987), comprehensive programs that have been empirically validated are not available for parents of children with LD.

Recognizing the need that exists for many families of children and adolescents with LD, the staff of the University of Kansas Center for Research in Learning (KU-CRL) (formerly known as the University of Kansas Institute for Research in Learning Disabilities) has developed and evaluated a family education model. In this chapter the four phases of model development will be described and the results from each phase will be presented. Following this information, conclusions and recommendations for future family education and family involvement efforts will be presented.

Model Development

Survey Phase

The first goal set by the KU-CRL Families Project was to gather information from families of children and youth with LD about the kinds of skills they wanted to learn, the kinds of skills they wanted to teach their children, and the format of the skill development process that they would prefer. As an initial step to reach this goal, 10 couples whose children had LD were interviewed for 2 hours. They were asked questions regarding their concerns and needs with regard to their child with learning disabilities.

Based on the results of these interviews and a literature review, the researchers developed a survey instrument. The survey had six major sections within which parents could respond. In the first section, parents were asked to rate the importance of learning each of 26 skills, identified from the interview and literature review, using a 7-point Likert-type scale (with 1 representing *Not important to learn* and 7 representing *Very important to learn*). For example, parents were asked to rate (within separate items) the importance of learning a skill for "solving family problems" and a skill for "communicating effectively with our youth with learning disabilities." The

26 items focused on six domains of family life: (1) development of interpersonal relationships within the family, (2) preparation of children for independent living and careers, (3) teaching skills, (4) development of self-confidence, (5) teaching of coping strategies (e.g., organizing time, stress management), and (6) the development of a home academic support system.

In the second section of the survey, parents were asked to rank each of these six areas in relation to its importance for families with a child with LD. In the third section, parents were asked to rank the top three sources of support for their child. The options provided in this section included parents, teachers, employers, extended family members, friends, therapists/counselors, and other significant adults in the community such as coaches, clergy, and youth-group leaders. These sources of support were identified from the initial interviews. In the fourth section, parents were asked to identify and rank the three best ways for them to learn new skills. They could choose among options such as weeknight classes, weekend workshops, and Saturday morning classes. In the fifth section, parents were asked to provide information regarding family earnings, number of children, and age at which their child was diagnosed as having a learning disability. In the last section, parents were asked, in an open-ended format, to identify the skill that they would most like to teach their child with LD.

The survey was distributed through the Learning Disabilities Association (LDA) to parent members across the country (LDA was formerly known as the Association for Children and Youth with Learning Disabilities). Of 185 surveys, 107 were returned. Twenty additional surveys were received from one LDA chapter where members copied the survey and distributed it to the other members. Ninety-four percent of the respondents were mothers. Seventy-two percent of the respondents were middle-income families or above. The average number of children per family was 2.8.

Parents indicated by their responses to items in the first section of the survey that all of the 26 listed skills were "important" or "very important" for families of children and youth with LD to learn. The lowest mean rating of a skill was 5.6, and the highest was 6.7 on the 7-point scale. The five most highly rated skills were communicating effectively with children and youth ($M = 6.6$); teaching children and youth how to make important decisions ($M = 6.5$); teaching children and youth how to make friends ($M = 6.5$); developing confidence in children and youth ($M = 6.5$); and building positive family relationships ($M = 6.3$). When respondents ranked the six domains by importance, they ranked them in the following order: (1) fostering self-confidence, (2) developing social skills, (3) teaching coping skills, (4) building family relationships, (5) developing independent living and career planning skills, and (6) providing home academic support.

Overwhelmingly, parents viewed themselves as the greatest source of support for their children. When asked to describe the skill they would most like to teach their children, the majority provided one or more responses. Of

156 responses in this section, 51 (33%) were related to social skills (e.g., starting a conversation, getting along with others, making friends, maintaining friendships, asking for and accepting help), 35 (22%) were related to teaching their children to have confidence in themselves, and 29 (19%) were related to academic skills such as reading, writing, notetaking, studying for tests, and taking tests. Parents also listed such skill areas as independent living, organization, goal setting and self-motivation, coping skills, and problem solving as being important.

Program Development Phase

The survey results indicated that parents were interested in learning a variety of skills for helping their children with LD. Most showed a strong interest in learning skills that would help improve their family's interpersonal relationships. Parents also indicated an interest in teaching social skills, academic skills, and decision-making skills and fostering self-confidence.

Based on these findings, a parent education program called "The Families Program" was developed by the KU-CRL staff to focus on teaching parents the skills that they desired to learn and that would help them cope with the demands they face as parents of children with learning disabilities. The first step in the Development Phase was to specify the philosophical foundation for the program. Five major assumptions were identified. First was the belief that a disability is not necessarily a "problem." As noted by Goldfarb and colleagues (1986), "Disabilities are not problems; they are conditions. Conditions are not problems in themselves, but they may bring problems, or they may make other problems more difficult to solve" (p. 3). Thus, within the Families Program learning disabilities were acknowledged as conditions that could create problems that needed to be addressed. Thus the Families Program was designed to focus primarily on the academic or social learning associated with LD and not on the disabilities themselves.

The second philosophical premise was based on earlier work by KU-CRL researchers (Seabaugh & Schumaker, 1981) who had found that children with LD must have a real stake in their lives and their futures to be motivated to learn new skills. If youth are to become more successful, they must take responsibility for their lives and feel a measure of personal control in decision making. The Families Program therefore emphasized that youth and their parents must form a partnership and relate openly and effectively with each other while working toward successful outcomes together. Parents must be willing to give over some of their basic control to foster the development of their children's personal self-control. Additionally, parents must recognize their role as "coaches" in helping children develop the skills to become competent decision makers and independent successful members of society. Attitudes that suggest "I am your parent, so you will do what I say" were to be replaced by messages that encourage skill development, confidence building, and family support. For example, a parent who adheres to this philosophy might say to a child, "I can tell this is an important issue for you. I would like to work with you to come up with a plan that we can both accept. Are you willing to work with me on it?"

The third assumption associated with the program, that all family members must be involved in the program in some way, was based on the dynamic nature of families and the notion that any family intervention planned to help a child or youth with LD must also consider the possible effects on other family members (Amerikaner & Omizo, 1984). The program organizers had decided early to develop skill practice activities that would involve family members in a collaborative process to improve the situation of the family as a whole.

Fourth, underlying the program was the basic assumption that each family has unique needs (Finn, 1998). Families differ from one another in terms of the types of learning disabilities manifested by their children, family sizes and forms, cultural backgrounds, individual and group commitments to other activities, current skills, socioeconomic factors, and other unique characteristics (e.g., the parents' educational experiences, coping styles, intellectual capacity). Thus, the researchers sought to design a program that was responsive and flexible enough to address the individual needs of each family (Finn, 1998; Turnbull & Turnbull, 1996).

Finally, the program was founded on the concept that a program for families must be skill-based. Beyond just providing parents with useful information, an effective parent education program should also ensure that parents have the opportunities to master skills that will enable them to accomplish their desired teaching and relationship-building goals.

Based on these premises, the literature review, the national survey results, and the collective experiences of KU-CRL staff members, four basic skill-teaching routines were designed during the Program Development Phase. The first, the Relationship-Building Skill, was designed to help parents to develop better relationships with their children by listening more attentively and objectively. The parents were taught to (a) use attentive listening skills, (b) avoid negative judgmental statements, and (c) express empathy, concern, and love verbally during interactions with their child. Relationship Building was selected as the first skill to be taught because it could serve as the foundation upon which parents could base further interactions with their children. Parents, using effective listening and information-gathering skills, could learn more about their children's interests, concerns, ideas, and goals. This information would help them identify appropriate targets for teaching–learning partnerships with their children. Clearly, if a parent was going to draw a child into an ongoing partnership, the focus of this effort must be related to the child's concerns.

The second skill, the Teaching Skill, was designed for use with a variety of instructional content such as social, academic, independent living, time management, and personal organization skills. The fundamental design for this skill was based on instructional methodology developed by Deshler, Alley, Warner, and Schumaker (1981), which was founded on empirically sound learning principles. This methodology had previously been shown to be effective in teaching new skills to students with LD (Hazel et al., 1982; Schumaker, Deshler, et al., 1982).

The third skill, the Problem-Solving Skill, was developed because many parents had indicated that they wanted to help their children acquire more effective decision-making skills. Previous research also indicated that children with LD frequently have difficulty learning to solve problems (Hazel et al., 1982; Schumaker, Hazel, Sherman, & Sheldon, 1982). Thus, the Problem-Solving Skill was designed to facilitate family problem-solving and decision-making processes. Parents using this skill can help the child define a problem, identify potential solutions, evaluate proposed solutions, select the best option, and develop an appropriate action plan for carrying out the solution. The child's role in selecting a solution is important because he is more likely to carry out solutions of his own choosing rather than those that have been chosen for him by others.

The fourth skill was developed in response to the parents' interest in enhancing the self-esteem and confidence of their children. Because self-esteem and confidence grow out of past achievement, the Goal-Achievement Skill was designed to help children and youth set and achieve personal goals. This skill involves helping the child target an area within which she wants to work or improve her performance, set a realistic goal, identify tasks to reach the goal, monitor progress, and determine appropriate personal rewards when the goal is achieved. Emphasized within the Goal-Achievement Skill is the child or youth's role with regard to accepting personal responsibility for completing particular tasks and working collaboratively with a parent to accomplish tasks where additional help may be needed.

The four skills were designed to be generic and applicable in a variety of teaching–learning situations, facilitate widespread use, and allow greater family individualization. Participants could apply the skills to fit their own family situations. For example, using the basic Relationship-Building Skill, parents could explore a wide range of topics such as a child's computer interests, school concerns, or preferences about possible family weekend plans.

Each of the four skills was carefully defined, and the components were specified during the Program Development Phase of the project. For example, the steps of the Teaching Skill are shown in Figure 14.1. These steps were used by parents during the teaching session. The teaching was also enhanced if the parents used the Relationship-Building Skill.

As the first step of the Teaching Skill, the parent names and defines a particular skill for the child. For example, a parent might name and describe a skill called "Asking for Help" by saying something like, "I'd like to teach you

Step 1: **Describe the skill to be taught**

- Name the skill
- Provide an explicit definition of the skill

Step 2: **Provide rationales for using this skill**

- Discuss why this skill is important to your child
- Be specific about the benefits
- Talk about the short-term advantages of the skill
- Personalize the reasons to your child's situation
- Make sure your rationales are believable

Step 3: **Help your child think of situations where the skill can be used**

- Discuss general characteristics of situations in which use of the skill is appropriate
- Help the child think of situations in different settings

Step 4: **Discuss the steps of the skill**

- Discuss each step with your child and why it is important

Step 5: **Provide a model for the skill**

- Demonstrate the skill for the child by using all the steps

Step 6: **Verbally rehearse the steps in the skill**

- Involve your child in verbal rehearsal of steps

Step 7: **Practice the skill in role-play situations**

- Ask your child to practice the skill in a role-play situation
- Provide feedback after each role-play attempt that is positive, corrective, personal, and specific
- Require a criterion level of performance

Step 8: **Plan practices in which your child can use the skill**

- Determine situations when the skill can be used
- Plan a time to check on skill use

Step 9: **Thank your child for cooperation and effort**

- Make a personal, encouraging statement of thanks, or compliment, praise, or show affection

Step 10: **Discuss the benefits of learning the skill**

- Discuss specific benefits of using the skill

Figure 14.1. Component Steps of the Teaching Skill.

a new skill that will let you ask for help when you need it. Let's call it the 'Asking for Help' skill. Asking for Help is an important skill to use to get teachers and other adults to explain something to you or to help you get something done."

In the second step the parent focuses on the advantages of using the specified skill and disadvantages of not using it. Initially the parent asks the child to think about the skill and consider why the skill is important. Following the child's explanation, the parent may provide additional information as appropriate. For example, the parent might ask, "What are some of the good things that might happen if you ask for help and get the help you need?" or "What are bad things that might happen if you don't know how to do something, and you don't ask for help?" If the child is unable to answer, the parent might say, "I think that you'll like the Asking for Help skill because if you use it, you will get the help you need, so you can do your work at school and here at home correctly. If you remember to use this skill, you can avoid having to do work over again and maybe even save yourself time. For example, if you don't know how to ask Ms. Sanchez for help in math, you may have to do those problems over again—and that is frustrating for you! If you have to redo your work, you have less time for activities that you like a lot better— like playing soccer or using the computer. Right? Would you like to learn this skill?"

The third step in the Teaching Skill is to discuss example situations in which the skill can be used. During this step, the parent and child should discuss the characteristics of various situations in which the skill could be used (e.g., "Whenever you're not sure what to do or how to do it"). They also discuss examples of such situations (e.g., "When the teacher has given you an assignment and you don't know how to start").

During the fourth Teaching step the parent describes and explains specific behaviors involved in performing the new skill. This process involves breaking the skill into its component parts and discussing each part in detail. The parts of the Asking for Help skill, when used in a classroom situation, might include raising one's hand for permission to talk, waiting to talk until called upon, explaining the problem, asking for help, listening to the response, asking for clarification as needed, and thanking the person for assistance. As each component is discussed, examples and reasons are elicited from the child or are provided by the parent as needed.

The fifth Teaching step provides a demonstration of the skill in a role-play situation. To present this demonstration, the parent plays the role of the child, and the child assumes the role of the person who is being asked for help. This process enables the child to see how each part of the skill is translated into words and actions within a flowing dialogue.

The sixth step, verbal rehearsal, is critical and may require considerable practice. It involves helping the child learn the names of all the parts of the skill. Here, parents must facilitate and encourage verbal practice of the steps until the child can repeat all of them from memory. It is important that the child remember all of the steps so he can instruct himself as the skill is performed.

The seventh step involves practicing the skill in role-play situations. The parent prompts the child to identify appropriate situations at home, school, and work where the skill can be used. Once situations have been identified, the parent can use them as the context for skill practice in role-play activities. The child performs her own role using the new skill, and the parent plays the other person's part (e.g., music teacher, coach, supervisor). Following each role-play practice, the parent provides praise, constructive feedback, and additional practice as needed. The child is also asked to evaluate her own performance (i.e., "So how did you think you did?"). Practice continues until the child can meet a criterion level of performance in a role-play situation that ensures mastery of the skill.

In the eighth step, planning when the skill will be used, the parent arranges a time for the child to check back and report on the success of his efforts. The ninth and tenth teaching steps involve thanking the child for his efforts and cooperation and discussing the potential benefits of learning and using the skill. These last steps are important because they serve to reinforce the child's efforts and motivate him to use the skill.

In addition to the four basic skills designed for parent use, "family meeting" procedures were also designed to enhance organization and family participation in the child's skill acquisition. Previous studies of families with LD had suggested that many are poorly organized, have few routines to follow, and rarely plan activities together. Consequently, the family meeting "agenda" was developed to enable families to address a variety of family events, concerns, and issues such as family rules, weekend work schedules, individual and family goals, and upcoming vacations. Each agenda included a fun family activity such as playing a card game, making ice cream sundaes, or riding bikes together. This session was designed to enable all family members to spend time together collaborating on individual or family concerns and developing appropriate family goals.

After all of the skills were developed and a family meeting agenda had been designed, the program materials (i.e., session presentation outlines, handouts, role-playing materials, overhead transparencies, homework activities, and record-keeping forms) were developed for use in the Families Program training sessions.

Pilot Test Phase

Four families with children with LD volunteered to participate in the initial pilot test study of the Families Program. For all four families, both parents participated in the program. The ages of the children with LD ranged from

12 to 15 years, and parent ages ranged from 35 to 41 years. Family size ranged from four to six members.

The four basic program skills and the family meeting procedures were taught to the parents within a series of eight weekly training sessions. The first session, a half-day Saturday workshop, covered information about learning disabilities and their potential effects on children. Specifically, the parents learned the definition of learning disabilities; the ramifications of this condition for learning at home, in school, in extracurricular activities, and within social interactions; and the role of parents with regard to helping a child learn. They also discussed the program goals and philosophy and learned the Relationship-Building Skill. In subsequent evening sessions, the participants learned the remaining skills and family meeting procedures. The final two sessions each focused on a skill that participants wanted to teach their children. One session related to social skills teaching. The other related to teaching children how to prepare for tests.

Instruction provided during each session followed a standard format: overview of the parenting skill that included a definition, rationales, example situations, and steps in the skill; a model of the skill followed by small-group practice; feedback to the parents regarding their individual performance of the skill, with additional practice conducted when needed and as time allowed; and a homework assignment that required the parents to use the new skill with their child and to audiotape the interaction. During each subsequent session, the group reviewed the homework assignment and previously learned skills and reported and discussed their problems and successes.

Two types of instruments were used to assess the effectiveness of the program. Role-play assessment instruments evaluated the parents' performance of the basic program skills and social validity questionnaires measured participants' satisfaction with the program. A multiple-baseline across-skills design was used to assess parents' entry-level and acquisition of the four skills. Parents participated in individual role-play sessions at the beginning and end of each workshop session. Some, but not all, skills were tested in each role-playing session. KU-CRL staff members read aloud a description of a parent–child scenario, played the role of the child, and then scored the parent's performance on a checklist that contained the components of a given skill. Each role-play session was audiotaped for later reliability checks by other staff members. Interscorer agreement on individual role-play situations ranged from 65% to 100% with a mean of 85%.

The results of the first field test were encouraging. The mean scores for the parents' pre- and posttest performance of each of the four skills are shown in Table 14.1, and the results of the multiple-baseline probes are shown in Figure 14.2. Across all skills, mean baseline performance was stable. During baseline, participants performed an average of 38% of the skill steps in the Relationship-Building Skill. Following instruction and practice, they performed an average of 69% of the steps. For Problem Solving, parents per-

Table 14.1

Mean Percentage of Skill Steps Performed Correctly (Pilot Test Phase)

	Pretest	Posttest
Relationship-Building Skill	38%	69%
Problem-Solving Skill	15%	81%
Goal-Achievement Skill	9%	59%
Teaching Skill	6%	59%

formed an average of 15% of the skill steps during baseline and 81% of the steps after instruction and practice. For the Goal-Achievement Skill, participants performed an average of 9% of the skill components during baseline. Their performance of this skill increased to an average of 59% of the steps after instruction and practice. Parents performed an average of 6% of the Teaching Skill components during baseline and an average of 59% of the steps after instruction and practice.

Overall, the participants made substantial gains with regard to their performance of the skills. Improvements in skill level only occurred after instruction was provided. Some of the participants performed all of the skills at or above the 75% level (an arbitrarily chosen criterion for mastery). The majority of the group, however, did not achieve mastery. For example, only two of the participants attained mastery on the Relationship-Building Skill and the Goal-Achievement Skill. Only three mastered the Teaching Skill. Performance scores on the Problem-Solving Skill were higher; six of the parents met mastery on this skill.

Although the number of parents mastering each skill was small, significant changes in the parents' behavior as a group were noted. For example, in role-play situations before instruction, most parents in the group conversed with the "child" (a staff member) by asking a series of "yes or no" questions. Parents also tended to dominate the conversation with advice or lectures, sometimes used a harsh voice tone, and on several occasions called the child a derogatory name. Frequently they tried to guess at the cause of the child's problems rather than ask the child to explain the situation. They typically chose solutions for problems with little input from the child, and often they expounded on how well they had addressed a similar problem when they were young.

After instruction and practice, the researchers noted qualitative improvements in the parents' performance in the role-play activities. Parents greeted their child by name or with an affectionate nickname, asked more open-ended questions, and listened more attentively. In addition, they responded to their child in a nonjudgmental manner; made more statements of empa-

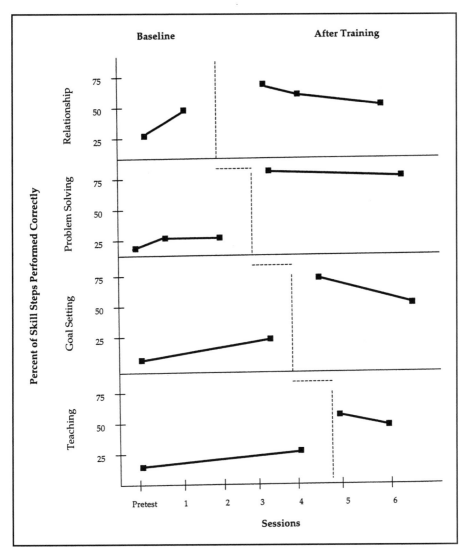

Figure 14.2. Mean scores for the parents' pre- and posttraining performance of each of four skills.

thy, praise, caring, and encouragement; and frequently ended conversations on a more positive note. Additionally, parents were more likely to facilitate their child's identification of problems and solutions in role-plays, encourage the child to take the lead on choosing goals, and help the child develop steps for reaching these goals. The parents also offered appropriate assistance, took time to teach skills, and set up specific times to discuss outcomes of previous conversations. Parents also made statements showing that they cared.

On the questionnaires participants completed, all parents reported that the use of the Families Program skills had enabled them to help their children. For example, one couple reported the successful use of the Teaching Skill with their 13-year-old son, Jeff. The family had moved recently from Chicago, and Jeff was having difficulty adjusting to seventh grade in a new community. He had told his parents that he had trouble talking to peers in his classes. He had heard some girls call him "stuck-up." Jeff's parents used the Teaching Skill to help him learn how to initiate and maintain more positive conversations with peers. They helped him to understand the importance of using the skill, and they provided models of the skill use. Following this, they practiced the skill in repeated role-play situations. They gave Jeff encouragement and feedback on his practice efforts, and he made a commitment to try the skill at school at least once a day for a month. Each day, he selected possible situations at school where he could use the skill and attempted to initiate and maintain a conversation. Together, Jeff and his parents monitored his progress. Every night after dinner, he discussed his conversation attempts with one or both of his parents. His parents reported that he quickly became very skillful at critiquing his own performance. By the end of the first month, he reported that he was talking to more students every day and feeling happier about the new school.

The children also completed consumer-satisfaction questionnaires in which they reported changes in their parents' behavior at the end of their parents' education program. The children were asked about changes they had noticed in routines around their homes. Sixty percent reported positive changes in the ways in which their parents helped them with homework. One youth mentioned that his father had changed because "now he makes me study harder." With regard to changes that the adolescents liked best, their comments included: "[I liked] learning how to set goals," "They [parents] are not as strict, and they are more trusting," "Dad controls his temper," "Mom does goal setting, step-by-step, and talks more," and "Mom doesn't rush through homework. I do it by myself but she sits and makes sure I do it right." Only one youth commented that he did not like the changes in his family. His comment was, "They don't give me answers to my homework anymore." When asked whether or not the Families Program had been useful for their family, 100% of the youth reported that it was useful. They made comments such as, "It [the program] helps with communication," "They [parents] trust me more," "We get along better and get more help from our parents," "Dad talks more," and "My grades have risen."

The results of the parents' consumer satisfaction questionnaires were also positive. Overall, parents reported that the program had been beneficial to them and their families. On a 7-point Likert-type scale (with 7 being *completely satisfied* and 1 being *completely dissatisfied*), parents were very satisfied with the usefulness of the program ($M = 6.6$), instructional methods ($M = 6.4$), clarity of information presented ($M = 6.4$), professionalism of staff ($M = 6.9$), opportunities to ask questions ($M = 6.3$), opportunities to get questions answered completely (M = 6.6), the instructional environment (M = 7.0), and the instructional materials (M = 7.0). The only areas that were rated in the "slightly satisfied" range were the organization of the workshop (M = 5.7) and the amount of time spent for instruction (M = 5.7). For both of these areas, parents indicated that they wanted a longer training program. General positive comments made by parents regarding the program included: "The best thing about the training was coming to a better understanding of my kids and what they're going through with this disability," "The training really helped me as a person to relate to others better, not just my child," "The problem solving and skill teaching have helped more than anything, but the relationship building was also very valuable," and "The most valuable thing about the training was learning how to help my child learn different skills academically and socially." Negative comments focused on the short nature of the training and the role-play activities. The negative comments were: "Not enough time," "Would have liked more sessions," "Role plays were not my thing," and "More feedback needed during role plays."

Revision Phase

The data gathered during the pilot test were useful in identifying areas in which the Families Program was effective and where refinement was needed. The content and the skill development methods of the workshop sessions seemed to be appropriate for and accepted by parents. Parents had attended the sessions regularly with few absences. They indicated that they wanted more skill development sessions, probably because they felt they had not mastered the skills and because they wanted additional support. The skills that were taught, although described as useful by the parents, contained many steps and appeared to be difficult to learn. To facilitate learning, the skill steps were simplified, and the complexity of the skills was substantially reduced. For example, the steps for the Teaching Skill shown in Figure 14.1 were revised to create the steps show in Figure 14.3. Additionally, a mnemonic device (e.g., "TEACHING") was developed to help the parents remember the steps of each skill.

Since participants also seemed to be overwhelmed with the quantity of workshop handouts, parent booklets were developed to correspond to the instructional program. Instructional information, examples, and space to take notes were provided in the booklets. One booklet was developed for each skill.

Field Test Phase

To evaluate the effects of these changes, a field test was conducted in which 10 parents participated. All participants attended the full 9-week skill development program. The program was implemented in the same manner as in

Step 1: Target a skill
- Select a skill to teach
- Describe the skill

Step 2: Explain the rationales for using this skill
- Discuss why the skill is important

Step 3: Analyze the skill
- Break the skill into easy steps
- Discuss each step

Step 4: Conduct a demonstration of the skill
- Model the skill using all of the steps

Step 5: Help your child think of situations to use the skill

Step 6: Involve your child in learning the skill
- Conduct role-play practices
- Give constructive feedback

Step 7: Note your child's commitment to use the skill
- Determine when the skill will be used
- Set up a time to discuss the outcome of using the skill

Step 8: Give support to show you CARE
- Compliment, praise, or show affection
- Acknowledge your child's contribution to the conversation
- Restate the value or the content of the conversation
- Express your positive expectations

Figure 14.3. The TEACHING Skill.

the pilot test using the simplified skills and booklets. One session was devoted to each skill. As in the first study, a multiple-baseline across-skills design was employed. Data were collected during skill development sessions and in each family's home following the end of the parent education program. Summary data on pre- and postintervention skill levels for all parents in the second study are presented in Table 14.2.

The results of the field test showed similar increases in skill performance for participants as in the pilot test. Again, participants made substantial gains with regard to performing the skills, and the multiple-baseline across-skills design demonstrated that skill improvement occurred as a result of the skill instruction and practice provided.

The results of the participant satisfaction survey were positive. Overall, parents felt the skill development program was beneficial to them and their families. On a 7-point scale, they were very satisfied with the usefulness of

Table 14.2

Mean Percentage of Skill Steps Performed Correctly (Field Test)

	Pretest	Posttest
Relationship Skill	50%	76%
Problem-Solving Skill	27%	72%
Goal-Setting Skill	19%	72%
Teaching Skill	21%	59%

the program (M = 6.3), knowledge and preparation of instructors (M = 6.8), the instructors' receptivity to questions and ability to answer questions (M = 6.3), large group activities (M = 6.3), role-play practice (M = 6.3), feedback from staff (M = 6.5), and organization of the workshop sessions (M = 6.3). The only areas that were rated in the "slightly satisfied" range were the workshop materials (M = 5.9), the amount of time spent each session for skill development (M = 5.5), and the homework assignments (M = 5.8). Despite positive ratings, most of the participants indicated that they wanted a longer skill development program. They also noted that the format of the booklets was sometimes hard to follow.

Revision Phase 2

Based on these results and informal feedback from parents during the course of the program, further efforts were made to simplify the content and instructional materials. Shorter mnemonic devices were also developed to facilitate skill acquisition and mastery. For example, the changes to the Teaching Skill, shown earlier in Figures 14.1 and 14.3, are illustrated in Figure 14.4.

Similarly, the Relationship Building Skill was refined to include six steps corresponding to the acronym, "RELATE." The Problem-Solving Skill was modified to include five steps corresponding to the acronym "SOLVE." Finally, the Goal-Setting Skill was changed to a five-step skill called "Make PLANS."

Additionally, a fundamental change was made in the way the program was delivered to parents. In the two earlier versions of the program, staff members were actively involved as instructors, and they played key parts in most role-play activities. In fact, the instructor–participant ratio was approximately 4:10 and each pair of parents had an instructor assigned to work with them during each role-play activity. Recognizing that this ratio would not be practical for most parent educators using the Families Program, a unit on "parent coaching" was added to the program. Parent coaching was developed to facilitate parent role playing during role-play sessions, thereby

Step 1: **Tell the 3 "W's"**
- What: Describe the skill
- Why: Discuss why the skill is important
- When: Give examples of when this skill can be used

Step 2: **Explain the steps in the skill**
- Break the skill into easy steps

Step 3: **Act out the skill for your child**
- Demonstrate the skill using all of the steps

Step 4: **Coach and practice to mastery**
- Verbally rehearse the skills steps
- Practice the skill in role-play situations
- Give performance feedback

Step 5: **Help your child develop a plan to use the skill**
- Determine when and where the skill will be used

Figure 14.4. The TEACH Skill.

reducing the number of staff instructors needed to run the program effectively.

In the parent coaching unit, parents were divided into groups of three and were assigned a role as a "parent," "child," or "coach." Three vignettes were developed for each practice session and participants rotated roles. During the course of a practice session, all three participants had the opportunity to play the part of parent, child, and coach. During a practice vignette, the coach in each group checked off steps on a skill checklist as they were used by the parent. If the parent had difficulty performing a step, the coach reminded the person of the step and encouraged the role players to continue. After the role-play activity was concluded, the coach used the checklist to provide feedback on the skill steps and asked for questions or comments from the role-play participants. Coaches were also asked to make at least one positive comment about the parent's role in the interaction. Basic rules were established for all coaching: (a) keep participants on task, (b) keep the activity moving, (c) help participants be successful, (d) be positive, (e) be specific, (f) be thorough, and (g) have fun!

Booklets containing the revised information were created. Laminated bookmark-type cards were also developed for each skill. Each card listed the skill steps, and parents were encouraged to use the cards as prompts at home. Finally, additional time was allotted in the program for new skill instruction and practice. Two instructional sessions were devoted to the acquisition and mastery of each parenting skill.

Final Field Test

Nine parents participated in the final field-test study. Seven parents participated in the full 9-week skill development program. Two parents dropped out after the second session because of unanticipated family responsibilities and limited time. Role-play data were collected during skill development sessions. Again, a multiple-baseline across-skills design was used. Summary data on pre- and postintervention skill levels for all participants in the final field test of the program are represented in Table 14.3.

Participants in the final field test earned the highest performance scores among the three groups of parents. The multiple-baseline design demonstrated that skill improvement and performance gains occurred as a result of the program.

The results of the participant satisfaction survey were very positive. Overall, parents felt the skill development was beneficial to them and their families. On a 7-point scale, they were very satisfied with the usefulness of the program ($M = 6.4$), material review and discussion ($M = 6.3$), instructional methods ($M = 6.4$), clarity of information presented ($M = 6.4$), professionalism of instructors ($M = 6.9$), opportunities to ask questions and have questions answered completely ($M = 6.6$), large-group activities in the workshop ($M = 6.1$), amount of time for practice ($M = 6.3$), feedback from staff ($M = 6.1$), amount of time for the workshop ($M = 6.3$), overall organization ($M = 6.6$), the skill development environment ($M = 6.6$), the quality of the instructional materials ($M = 6.6$), homework assignment ($M = 6.1$), knowledge of newly acquired skills ($M = 6.0$), usefulness of the new skills ($M = 6.2$), and the helpfulness of the parent coaching component ($M = 6.3$).

Conclusion and Future Recommendations

The results of these three tests of the program indicate that the described approach to parent education can be effective. Parents can learn skills to

Table 14.3

Mean Percentage of Skill Steps Performed Correctly (Final Field Test)

	Pretest	Posttest
Relationship-Building Skill	51%	81%
Problem-Solving Skill	27%	84%
Goal-Setting Skill	17%	73%
Teaching Skill	10%	87%

interact more effectively with their children with LD. The basic four skills developed in this program (i.e., Relationship Building, Problem Solving, Goal Achievement, Teaching) and the family meeting format appear to be applicable to a number of potential parenting concerns. Participants were satisfied with the effects of the program and indicated that they had implemented the techniques in their interactions at home with their children. Following instruction and practice, parents learned and used the skills quickly. Parent coaching procedures appeared to strengthen the instructional program and facilitate participant learning. Additionally, they enabled the program to be presented by only one instructor.

Additional research is needed to determine the efficacy of this model over time. A broad array of questions remain, including: Do participants maintain their use of the Families Program skills over time? If so, which skill(s) do participants use most frequently and why? What are the short-term and long-term effects of parent skill use on the behavior and attitudes of children at home and at school? and What happens to the behaviors and attitudes of other family members?

Replication at other training sites is also needed. In all three studies, KU-CRL program developers were present to ensure the quality of the instruction, troubleshoot problems, and offer ongoing assistance. Without such support, the effectiveness of the model may be different. Additional research studies also need to determine the appropriateness of this model with families representing a broad array of cultural, social, ethnic, and economic backgrounds. Most participants in this project were married couples, Caucasian, average or above-average income earners, and had some post–high school education. Future research should consider possible modifications that would make this program more appropriate and more accessible to single parents, grandparents, other guardians, or participants who may lack many of the educational, economic, or social–emotional resources that most of the participants in this project possessed. Finally, given recent developments in technology and the growing use of home computers, researchers should consider the possible use of electronic methods to enhance parent-learning opportunities. Electronic communication may be viable as systems for initial instruction, simulated practice, ongoing group communication, technical support, long-term performance monitoring, and low-cost, noninvasive home data collection.

The provision of programmatic services such as those described in this development effort is seen as one part of a multicomponent treatment approach to helping families with children and adolescents with learning disabilities. That is, the current program addressed needed skills in both home and school situations; however, many additional intervention efforts are needed to provide support and to ensure success for children with LD. An important example is the use of interventions within the school setting to provide instruction in learning strategies to help children with LD succeed academically (Schumaker & Deshler, 1992). Additionally, interventions may be needed in the area of social skills development to facilitate their successful integration within inclusive general education classrooms (Vernon, Schumaker, & Deshler, 1996). Mentoring programs may also be an important component of a comprehensive intervention approach (Moccia, Schumaker, Hazel, Vernon, & Deshler, 1989).

In conclusion, this program was designed to help families with children and adolescents with learning disabilities who face many academic and social learning challenges. Built on a foundation of information gathered from families of children with LD and existing research literature, the Families Program taught interested parents some skills for strengthening relationships with their children and for teaching their children new skills, effective problem solving, and techniques for setting and attaining personal goals. All of the Families Program skills were taught within the context of an ongoing teaching–learning partnership between parents and their children. The goal of the program was to enhance family functioning through strengthening and empowering the family unit. The means included addressing unique needs of each individual and engaging all members of the family in the intervention. As a method of intervention, the core of the program was skill-building within the family for both parents and children. The importance of the child's personal involvement and commitment to the success of this partnership was recognized as critical. The knowledge and understanding that families had about themselves were used to develop skills and instructional procedures that fostered growth in families. The pilot and field tests indicated that such a program could be effective in improving parent–child interactions in significant areas while producing participant satisfaction. By working collaboratively with families in the development, implementation, and evaluation of such parent-education programs, professionals can develop effective strategies to improve the quality of family interactions over time.

References

Amerikaner, M. J., & Omizo, M. M. (1984). Family interaction and learning disabilities. *Journal of Learning Disabilities, 7,* 540–543.

Anderson, L. E. (1970). *Helping the adolescent with the hidden handicap.* Belmont, CA: Fearon/ Laer Siegler.

Bender, W. N. (1993). *Learning disabilities: Best practices for professionals.* Boston: Andover Medical.

Benson, P., Williams, D., & Johnson, A. (1987). *The quicksilver years, the hopes and fears of early adolescence.* San Francisco: Harper & Row.

Berk, L. E. (1997). *Child development* (4th ed.). Needham Heights, MA: Allyn & Bacon.

Bourdin, C. M., Henggeler, S. W., Blaske, D. M., & Stein, R. (1990). Multisystemic treatment of adolescent sexual offenders. *International Journal of Offender Therapy and Comparative Criminology, 34,* 105–113.

Bryan, T. H., & Bryan, J. H. (1981). Some personal and social experiences of learning disabled children. In B. K. Koegh (Ed.), *Advances in special education*. Greenwich, CT: JAI Press.

Burke, R., & Herron, R. (1996). *Common sense parenting class*. Omaha, NE: Boys Town Press.

Carnegie Council on Adolescent Development. (1992). *A matter of time: Risk and opportunity in the nonschool hours*. New York: Author.

Carlson, E. (1997). *Outcomes for students declassified from special education*. Unpublished dissertation. Williamsburg, VA: College of William & Mary.

Coburn, K. L., & Treeger, M. L. (1997). *Letting go: A parents' guide to understanding the college years*. New York: Harper Perennial.

Cone, J. D., Delawyer, D. D., & Wolfe, V. V. (1985). Assessing parent participation: The parent/family index. *Exceptional Children, 51*, 417–424.

Deshler, D. D., Alley, G. R., Warner, M. M., & Schumaker, J. B. (1981). Instructional practices for promoting skill acquisition and generalization in severely learning disabled adolescents. *Learning Disabilities Quarterly, 4*(4), 415–421.

Dinkmeyer, D., & McKay, G. D. (1976). *Systematic training for effective parenting (STEP)*. Circle Pines, MN: American Guidance Service.

Dryfoos, J. G. (1990). *Adolescents at risk: Prevalence and prevention*. New York: Oxford University Press.

Dunst, C. J., Trivette, C. M., Starnes, A. L., Hamby, D. W., & Gordon, N. J. (1993). *Building and evaluating family support initiatives: A national study of programs for persons with developmental disabilities*. Baltimore: Brookes.

Dyson, L. L. (1996). The experiences of families of children with learning disabilities: Parental stress, family functioning, and sibling self-concept. *Journal of Learning Disabilities, 29*, 280–286.

Faerstein, L. M. (1986). Coping and defense mechanisms of mothers of learning disabled children. *Journal of Learning Disabilities, 9*, 8–11.

Finn, J. D. (1998). Parental encouragement that makes a difference. *Educational Leadership, 55*(8), 20–24.

Gerber, P. J., & Reiff, H. B. (1992). *Speaking for themselves: Ethnographic interviews with adults with learning disabilities*. Ann Arbor: University of Michigan Press.

Gerber, P. J., Reiff, H. B., & Ginsberg, R. (1996). Reframing the learning disabilities experience. *Journal of Learning Disabilities, 29*(1), 98–107.

Giannotti, T. J., & Doyle, R. R. (1982). The effectiveness of parental training on learning disabled children and their parents. *Elementary School Guidance and Counseling, 17*, 131–134.

Goldfarb, L. A., Brotherson, M. J., Summers, J. A., & Turnbull, A. P. (1986). *Meeting the challenge of disability or chronic illness: A family guide*. Hillsdale, NJ: Erlbaum.

Haager, D., & Vaughn, S. (1995). Parent, teacher, peer, and self-reports of the social competence of students with learning disabilities. *Journal of Learning Disabilities, 28*, 205–215, 231.

Haywood, H. C., & Switzky, H. N. (1986). The malleability of intelligence: Cognitive processes as a function of polygenic-experiential interaction. *School Psychology Review, 15*, 245–255.

Hazel, J. S., & Schumaker, J. B. (1988). Social skills and learning disabilities: Current issues and recommendations for future research. In J. F. Kavanagh & T. J. Truss, Jr. (Eds.), *Learning disabilities: Proceedings for the national conference* (pp. 293–344). Parkton, MD: York Press.

Hazel, J. S., Schumaker, J. B., Sherman, J. A., & Sheldon-Wildgen, J. (1982). Application of a group training program in social skills and problem-solving to learning disabled and non-learning disabled adolescents. *Learning Disability Quarterly, 5*, 398–408.

Henggeler, S. W., & Bourdin, C. M. (1990). *Family therapy and beyond: A multisystemic approach to treating the behavior problems of children and adolescents.* Pacific Grove, CA: Brooks/ Cole.

Henggeler, S. W., Bourdin, C. M., Melton, G. B., Mann, B. J., Smith, L. A., Hall, J. A., Cone, L., & Fucci, B. R. (1991). Effects of multisystemic therapy on drug use and abuse in serious juvenile offenders: A progress report from two outcome studies. *Family Dynamics of Addiction Quarterly, 1,* 40–51.

Kinney, J., Haapala, D., Booth, C., & Leavitt, S. (1990). The homebuilders model. In J. K. Kinney, E. M. Tracy, & C. Booth (Eds.), *Reaching high-risk families: Intensive family preservation in human services* (pp. 31–64). New York: Aldine.

Kozloff, M. A. (1979). *A program for families of children with learning and behavior problems.* New York: Wiley.

Kroth, R., & Otteni, H. (1983). Parent education programs that work: A model. *Focus on Exceptional Children, 15*(8), 1–16.

Lopez-Reyna, N., & Olufs, D. (1996, April). *Developing resilience: How families and teachers can help individuals with learning disabilities.* Paper presented at Conference of the International Council for Exceptional Children, Orlando, FL.

Margalit, M. (1982). Learning disabled children and their families: Strategies of extension and adaptation of family therapy. *Journal of Learning Disabilities, 15,* 594–595.

McDonnell, L. M., McLaughlin, M. J., & Morison, P. (Eds.). (1997). *Educating one & all: Students with disabilities and standards-based reform.* Washington, DC: National Academy Press.

McLoed, T. M. (1993). Social/behavioral characteristics. In W. N. Bender (Ed.), *Learning disabilities: Best practices for professionals.* Boston: Andover Medical.

McLoyd, V. C. (1998). Socioeconomic disadvantaged and child development. *American Psychologist, 53*(2), 185–204.

Moccia, R. E., Schumaker, J. S., Hazel, J. S., Vernon, S., & Deshler, D. D. (1989). A mentor program for facilitating the life transitions of individuals with handicapping conditions. *Journal of Reading, Writing, and Learning Disabilities, 5*(2), 177–195.

Murray, C., Goldstein, D. E., & Edgar, E. (1997). The employment and engagement status of high school graduates with LD through the first decade after graduation. *Learning Disabilities Research & Practice, 12*(3), 151–160.

Nelson, K. E. (1994). Innovative delivery models in social services. *Journal of Clinical Child Psychology, 23,* 26–31.

Nichols, W. C. (1996). *Treating people in families.* New York: Guilford.

Odom, S. L., McConnell, S. R., & McEvoy, M. A. (1992). *Social competence of young children with disabilities: Issues and strategies for intervention.* Baltimore: Brookes.

Osman, B. (1982). *No one to play with: The social side of learning disabilities.* New York: Random House.

Patterson, G., & Forgatch, M. (1987). *Parents and adolescents living together.* Eugene, OR: Castalia.

Pfeiffer, S. I., Gerber, P. J., & Reiff, H. B. (1985). Family-oriented intervention with the learning disabled child. *Journal of Reading, Writing, and Learning Disabilities International, 1*(4), 63–69.

Powers, S. I., Hauser, S. T., & Kilner, L. A. (1989). Adolescent mental health. *American Psychologist, 44,* 220–228.

Rappaport, L. (1965). The state of crisis: Theoretical considerations. In H. Parad (Ed.), *Crisis intervention: Selected readings* (pp. 22–31). New York: Family Service Association of America.

Resnick, M. D., Bearman, P. S., Blum, R. W., Bauman, K. E., Harris, K. M., Jones, J., Tabor, J., Beuhring, T., Sieving, R. E., Shew, M., Ireland, M., Bearinger, L. H., & Udry, J. R. (1997). Protecting adolescents from harm: Findings from the national longitudinal study on adolescent health. *Journal of the American Medical Association, 278*(10), 823–832.

Robin, A. L., & Foster, S. L. (1989). *Negotiating parent–adolescent conflict.* New York: Guilford Press.

Roth, L., & Weller, C. (1985). Education/counseling models for parents of learning disabled children. *Academic Therapy, 20*(4), 487–495.

Schumaker, J. B., & Deshler, D. D. (1992). Validation of learning strategy interventions for students with LD: Results of a programmatic research effort. In B. Y. L. Wong (Ed.), *Contemporary intervention research in learning disabilities: An international perspective.* New York: Springer-Verlag.

Schumaker, J. B., Deshler, D. D., Alley, G. R., Warner, M. M., Clark, F. L., & Nolan, S. (1982). Error monitoring: A learning strategy for improving adolescents' academic performance. In W. M. Cruickshank & J. W. Lerner (Eds.), *Best of ACLD* (Vol. 3, pp. 170–183). New York: Syracuse University Press.

Schumaker, J. B., Hazel, J. S., Sherman, J. A., & Sheldon, J. (1982). Social skills performances of learning disabled, non-learning disabled, and delinquent adolescents. *Learning Disability Quarterly, 5,* 388–397.

Seabaugh, G. O., & Schumaker, J. B. (1981). *The effect of self-regulation training on the academic productivity of LD and NLD adolescents* (Research Report No. 37). Lawrence, KS: University of Kansas Institute for Research in Learning Disabilities.

Silver, L. (1983). Therapeutic interventions with learning disabled students and their families. *Topics in Learning and Learning Disabilities, 3*(2), 48–58.

Snodgrass, D. M. (1991). The parent connection. *Adolescence, 26,* 83–87.

Smith, C. R. (1998). *Learning disabilities: The interaction of learner, task, and setting.* Needham Heights, MA: Allyn & Bacon.

Turnbull, A. P., & Turnbull, H. R. (1996). *Families, professionals, and exceptionality: A special partnership* (3rd ed.). Columbus, OH: Prentice Hall.

Turnbull, A. P., Turnbull, H. R., Shank, M., & Leal, D. (1995). *Exceptional lives: Special education in today's schools.* Englewood Cliffs, NJ: Prentice Hall.

U.S. Department of Education. (1997). *The nineteenth annual report to Congress on the implementation of the Individuals with Disabilities Education Act.* Washington, DC: Author.

Vernon, D. S., Schumaker, J. B., & Deshler, D. D. (1996). *The SCORE skills: Social skills for cooperative groups.* Lawrence, KS: Edge Enterprises.

Wagner, M. (Ed.). (1995). *The national longitudinal transition study of special education students: A summary of findings.* Menlo Park, CA: SRI International.

Willner, S., & Crane, R. (1979). A parental dilemma: The child with a marginal handicap. *Social Casework: The Journal of Contemporary Social Work, 1,* 30–35.

Wirt, F. M., & Kirst, M. W. (1997). *The political dynamics of American education.* Berkeley, CA: McCutchan.

Zirpoli, T. J., & Melloy, K. J. (1993). *Behavior management: Application for teachers and parents.* Upper Saddle River, NJ: Merrill/Prentice-Hall.

Jo Webber, Richard L. Simpson,
and Judy K. C. Bentley

Parents and Families of Children with Autism

15

· ·

A utism is a lifelong neurological disorder. Symptoms appear before age 3. Although children with autism may demonstrate characteristics found in other children with disabilities, the combination and severity of their behavioral and communication deficits often prevent any semblance of a typical parent–child relationship.

The characteristics of autism were first described by Leo Kanner in 1943. Others have reworked the definition of autism (American Psychiatric Association [APA], 1994; Creak, 1961; Ritvo & Freeman, 1981; Wing, 1972). However, Kanner's original case study is still regarded as descriptive. Thus, it is generally accepted that autistic children show some combination of the following:

1. *Inability to relate to other people,* including an absence of social smiling, indifference to affection or physical contact, an apparent preference for interaction with objects rather than people, and failure to show distress when a parent leaves the room. As infants these children may fail to make eye contact, smile, or respond to their parents' voices, often prompting an initial fear that their child with autism is deaf.

2. *Language deficits,* including mutism, echolalia, noncommunicative speech, pronoun reversals, abnormal voice tone and inflection, and immature grammar. About half the children with autism never acquire speech. Of those who do, over 75% show abnormal speech, and only about 30% are able to develop functional language (APA, 1994; Miranda-Linné & Melin, 1997). Even the most verbally capable children with autism have delayed speech development and show marked impairment in the ability to initiate or sustain a conversation (APA, 1994; Rappaport, 1996). If a child with autism has not acquired speech by the time she is 7 years old, the likelihood of significant oral language capability is very remote (Bondy & Frost, 1994).

3. *Sensory impairment* characterized by over- or underresponding to sensory input, such as a high threshold for pain, oversensitivity to sound or touch, exaggerated and atypical reactions to light or odors, and fascination with specific stimuli.

4. *Abnormal behaviors* that might include extreme fear, tantrums, uncontrolled giggling and crying, hyperactivity, short attention span, impulsivity, aggressiveness, or a marked absence of emotion.

5. *Self-stimulation and self-injury* such as spinning self and objects, repetitive hand movements, rocking, humming, biting oneself, and head banging.

6. *Inappropriate* play characterized by little interest in developing age-appropriate peer relationships, and lack of spontaneous make-believe play and social imitative play.

7. *Extreme resistance to environmental changes* such as furniture arrangements, everyday schedule, and familiar routes (Koegel, Rincover, & Egel, 1982).

8. *Abnormal eating and sleeping habits* including limiting the diet to certain types of foods, or Pica (the life-threatening and compulsive consumption of inedible materials such as glass, plastic, and metal), and brief intermittent sleep patterns (APA, 1994).

The majority of children with autism show these abnormalities from an early age. However, in a few cases, normal development is observed for the first 2 years of life, followed by sudden regression. Autistic symptoms are often accompanied by mental retardation and, in some cases, seizure disorders. Although there are fewer females with autism, there are more females with autism who also have mental retardation. Regardless of the general level of intelligence, the profile of cognitive skills in individuals with autism is uneven. Older individuals may have excellent rote memory for isolated facts (APA, 1994), but so-called "savant" feats of memory, intelligence, and artistic ability are extremely rare (Happé, 1994).

Despite the fact that Kanner (1985) proposed that these children came into the world *biologically* unable to form "affective contact" (p. 50), his work was most defined by his observation that within this "autistic" group, "there were very few really warmhearted fathers and mothers" (p. 50). These observations set the stage for speculation that the condition was actually caused by cold unresponsive parents. Others have supported this notion of parent responsibility, including Bettelheim (1950), who went so far as to advocate "parentectomy," that is, institutionalizing children with autism so that parents could be replaced with institutional staff and professionals considered more caring and competent. Although a preponderance of current research has refuted the assumption that parents cause autism, pointing instead toward organic causes such as genetic predisposition, abnormal brain structure, and abnormal brain chemistry (e.g., Harvard Medical School, 1997), many parents are still trying to overcome the guilt and the professional bullying associated with that initial blame.

Effects of Autism on Parents and Families

Due to the nature of the disorder and the historical assumptions regarding etiology, parents of children with autism often experience ongoing emotional responses such as grief, guilt, thwarted expectations, disappointment, depression, continuous concern and helplessness, and desperation (Siegel, 1996; Wing, 1974). Retardation and aberrant patterns of cognitive development may cause a child with autism to have a prolonged infancy and toddlerhood, necessitating lifelong care. Most parents therefore will not have the luxury of taking time to deal with their own intense feelings. Because few educational and respite care services have historically been available for children with autism, parents may also encounter great financial burden in acquiring appropriate services. Furthermore, they are not only faced with intense feelings, more work, and greater financial responsibility, but they may receive few rewards from the child himself. Children with autism communicate and relate to others in unique ways. Their lack of typical verbal communication and social reciprocity, coupled with bizarre behaviors, makes autism a disability that does not provide what parents and others expect from loving, or merely satisfactory, relationships.

For families of children with disabilities, the divorce rate is 20% higher than the divorce rate for other families (Siegel, 1996). A single parent of a child with autism, usually the mother, may experience the greatest lack of financial and personal resources. Additionally, siblings may be forced to take on adult responsibilities, consciously or unconsciously, due to the demands on parents. It should come as no surprise, then, that the presence of a child with autism often poses significant challenges for parents and families (Breslau, Staruch, & Mortimer, 1982; Maurice, Green, & Luce, 1996; Simpson & Myles, 1998; Wright, Matlock, & Matlock, 1985). As an illustration of some of these challenges, Handleman and Harris (1986) pointed to several major transitional issues parents and families of children with disabilities, including those with autism, experience across a life span. These issues, from the time of the parents' marriage until their offspring's adulthood, are shown in Table 15.1.

The presence of a child with autism may tend to exacerbate any other problems the family may encounter. For example, from a family systems perspective (Fiedler, 1986; Turnbull, Summers, & Brotherson, 1984), an autistic child affects and in turn is affected by the family's structure, interactions, functions, and life cycles. An understanding of these variables will assist professionals in assessing the impact of a child with autism on a

Table 15.1

Families of Children with Developmental
Disabilities: Transitional Challenges

Phase	Normative	Added or Different
Marriage	Adaptation to spouse's routines, values, etc. Development of negotiation skills. Separation from family of origin. Pursuit of vocational goals.	None
Birth and infancy	Adjustment of routine to include child. Adaptation to changes in marital relationship. Negotiation on philosophy of child care with spouse. Negotiation on extended family involvement with child	Acceptance of diagnosis. Meeting medical needs. Resolving issues of blame, anger. Dealing with sorrow.
Kindergarten	Child's increased independence. Separation between parent and child. Increased influence of other people.	Continued dependence. Acceptance of special school placement. Use of special child management methods.
School years	Growing independence. Personal development of parents. Development of sibling relationships.	Continued dependence. Constraints on parents' growth. Extra burdens on siblings. Growing gap with peers.
Adolescence	Intensive separation. Individuation struggle. Increased marital stress. Need of aging grandparents for attention from parents.	Confirmed dependence. Must encourage separation. Increase in emotional and physical fatigue.
Adulthood	Child's transition to own nuclear family. Renewal of marital relationship. Acceptance of life achievements. Death of spouse.	Continued dependence. Renewal of marriage more difficult. Risk of burnout. Need to plan for child's care after parents' death.

Note. From *Educating the Developmentally Disabled: Meeting the Needs of Children and Families* (pp. 154, 159, 161) by J. S. Handleman and S. L. Harris, 1986, San Diego: College-Hill Press. Copyright 1986 by College-Hill Press. Reprinted with permission.

family, and subsequently in identifying and implementing appropriate support and strategies.

Family structure refers to various familial elements, including socioeconomic status (e.g., the family may be required to spend limited resources for medical and therapeutic services for their autistic child), cultural background, composition (e.g., single-parent families can be easily overwhelmed by the demands of an autistic child), human and nonhuman resources (e.g., respite services and peer support are often unavailable to parents of autistic children), attitudes, and values. Children with autism may have a significant impact on (as well as be impacted by) their family structure in instances where they consume an inequitable share of resources, and when a family's structure fails to match the needs of an autistic child. Additionally, coping strategies and styles may influence the degree to which families are able to accommodate children with autism as well as influence their behavior and development.

Family interactions refer to family members' relationships, including marital, sibling, parental, and extrafamilial. According to Olson, Russell, and Sprenkle (1980), interactions within these subsystems depend on family cohesion (i.e., family members may be overly involved or more or less disengaged from an autistic family member); adaptability (i.e., a family's ability to respond to circumstances associated with accommodating a child with autism); and communication (i.e., family members' ability to send and receive clear messages, provide feedback, reveal their needs and feelings). A child with autism poses significant demands and thereby places great stress on the family's capacity to survive (Lovaas, 1996; Maurice et al., 1996; Siegel, 1996; Zionts & Simpson, 1988). However, family members' ability to engage in positive and effective interactions bodes well for their ability to accommodate a child with autism.

Family functions are the various unique need areas families must consider: economic, educational, vocational, physical, restful or recuperative, affection, socialization, self-definition, and guidance. Each of these functions is significant, and only by responding to each can families operate optimally. Thus, overemphasis on any individual function (e.g., excessive emphasis on home training for a child with autism) may decrease the family's capacity to respond to other equally important needs. Not surprisingly, the autistic child's unique and demanding nature frequently strains the family's ability to maintain a balance of functions.

The *family life cycle* refers to the sequence of developmental and nondevelopmental changes all families experience. Goldenberg and Goldenberg (1980) described the cycle as "successive patterns within the continuity of family living over the years of its existence with members aging and passing through a succession of family roles" (p. 14). Families of children with autism can be expected to experience disruptions in this typical cycle (Fewell, 1986; Siegel, 1996) as is illustrated in Table 15.1. For example, autistic family members will rarely achieve the social and economic independence of those without disabilities and may increase family stress by failing to progress in a manner typical of others. Attempts to compensate for family cycle delay and disruption, including institutionalization, and factors associated with the ability of the family to care for members with autism throughout their lives (e.g., death, infirmity of parents) may also increase stress and erode a family's functioning capacity.

Although children with autism will inevitably have a significant effect on their families (Green, 1996a; Kozloff, 1975; Siegel, 1996; Simpson & Regan, 1986), professionals can help to moderate the nature and extent of this influence through awareness and sensitivity to family issues. Accordingly, collaborative involvement between professionals and families, as well as mutual support, is essential. The underpinnings of effective collaboration include trust, understanding, confidence, and a willingness to allow the other party to participate as a meaningful partner.

Meeting the Needs of Parents and Families of Children with Autism

Awareness of the impact of autism on parents and families is essential for providing adequate support. According to Buscaglia (1975), "a disability is not a desirable thing and there is no reason to believe otherwise. It will, in most cases, cause pain, discomfort, embarrassment, tears, confusion and the expenditure of a great deal of time and money" (p. 11). Thus, almost without exception, parents of children with disabilities have reported difficulties directly associated with their children's condition (Fewell, 1986; Lovaas, 1996; Siegel, 1996; Turnbull & Turnbull, 1978). Gorham (1975) identified a variety of problems and obstacles she and her family experienced when adjusting to and attempting to accommodate her child. Thus it was only after "accumulating some scars which clearly mark us as parents and as members of the 'lost generation'" (p. 522) that they were able to survive the ordeal.

One of the most basic needs of parents and families of children with autism is to secure appropriate direct services. The significance of other parent and family needs cannot be underestimated; however, in most instances these are secondary to finding suitable educational, residential, and treatment programs. Thus a number of parents have observed that until they identified an appropriate school or program for their child with autism, they were unable to consider other needs (Simpson, 1996). The need for and importance of direct service resources for children with autism are often overlooked when considering parent and family needs; however, this basic need will typically override all other parent and family considerations.

Levels of Parent and Family Participation

With the exception of identifying appropriate direct services, needs of parents and families of children with autism are heterogeneous. Thus, several authors have presented strong arguments for individualized parent and family service and support programs (Fiedler, 1986; Kroth, 1985; Siegel, 1996; Simpson & Fiedler, 1989). In accordance with the emphasis on individualization, professionals must permit parents and families to choose the degree and type of involvement that is commensurate with their personal needs and preferences. Involvement may take place at one of five levels: awareness, open communication, advocacy and participation, problem solving and procedural application, and partnership. At any given time, parents and families may be at more than one level of involvement (e.g., parents may demonstrate a desire for open communication as well as advocacy and participation). Additionally, involvement levels may vary across time (e.g., a family may move from awareness to partnership).

Among the five levels of parental involvement, *awareness* is a baseline condition. Parents and families choosing this level of involvement should receive information about autism including its characteristics and patterns, school-related procedures and strategies employed with students with autism, and resources (e.g., counseling, respite care) available to the child and family. Awareness implies a low level of parent and family involvement; however, it nonetheless requires that professionals apprise parents and families of basic facts pertaining to children with autism and parent and family services and programs.

Open communication refers to a level of involvement characterized by effective information sharing and communication between parents, family members, and professionals. This stage should be the desired participation level for all parents and families (i.e., in spite of other involvement, all parents and families should engage in ongoing communication with professionals).

Advocacy and participation characterizes parents and family members who desire to be involved actively in promoting services and programs for their children. Examples of such participation include membership on autism advocacy boards and agencies, volunteer service to organizations serving children and youth with autism, and participation in training programs for parents and families who wish to be involved actively in making educational and treatment decisions (e.g., selecting goals and objectives for Individualized Education Plans).

Problem solving and procedural application is an option for parents and families who are able and motivated to implement programs and procedures for autistic individuals in natural environments. Examples of this level of engagement include application of management programs in home settings, home-based tutoring programs, and training program implementation (e.g., toileting and eating programs).

Partnership refers to participation of parents and families on an equal basis with professionals in identifying, implementing, and evaluating programs for children and youth with autism. At this level of involvement, parents may independently identify goals for their child, develop training procedures for achieving each goal, and evaluate generalization of the skill in other settings.

In many instances, increased parent and family involvement and participation does not necessarily mean "better involvement." For example, parents who choose to participate at an open communication level may function more effectively and thus better satisfy family needs than parents who participate at a partnership level. Accordingly, professionals must accommodate various levels of involvement. To this end, individualizing parent and family participation is the first step to satisfying parent and family needs.

Parent and Family Programs

Not only must professionals individualize their expectations about family participation, but they must also be aware of each family's varied and inconstant needs once their child with autism begins receiving direct services. Typically families need three basic sources of support: (1) information, (2) knowledge and skills to deal with their child, and (3) support from outside the family to assist with coping and problem solving. Programs and services that address these needs usually contain one or more of the following: (a) information sharing; (b) partnership and consumer-advocacy training; (c) natural environment training programs; (d) counseling, therapy and support services; and (e) school and community participation programs. Professionals would do well to assist parents in accessing those components most likely to satisfy their specific needs and preferred level of involvement.

Information sharing is an essential underlying component of effective professional services. Nearly all parents and families of children with autism want and need information about autism, such as definitions (e.g., autism, autistic-like, pervasive developmental disorder, Asperger's syndrome), prevalence, characteristics, etiology, and prognosis. Additionally, many want to discuss why professionals have such difficulty in agreeing on the precise nature and course of treatment for autism and related disorders.

In fact, because little is known about the specific cause(s) of autism and no cure has been found, most parents are very anxious to do something, anything, to help their child. This makes the parents vulnerable to wasting time and money on so-called "therapies" that may be widely used but have no reputable proof of efficacy. Historically, professionals have convinced parents of such "cures" as psychotherapy whereby children have been allowed to play with their feces in order to work through their conflicts (Bettelheim, 1950); swimming with dolphins whereby children with autism are placed in tanks with dolphins so that the dolphins can detect neurological damage in the child and provide therapeutic contact (e.g., Bourne, 1998; Mosley, 1998); and facilitated communication whereby a child's intelligence is released through prompted typing (e.g., Biklen, 1990, 1992). None of these treatments have resulted in meaningful benefits (e.g., Green, 1996a), and they may have actually been detrimental to the children and their families (e.g., Connelly, 1998; Green, 1994; Webber, 1991). In order to prevent the waste of time and money and the ultimate disappointment and mistrust that follow ineffective treatments, professionals must take the responsibility of providing parents with valid information based on sound research. Parents (and professionals) should be wary of claims based on nothing more than testimonials and avoid new treatments which have not yet been tested (Green, 1996b).

Professionals must also disseminate and discuss with parents and family members any findings and recommendations that relate to specific children, including diagnostic information (e.g., cognitive abilities, speech and language skills and deficits, behavioral and social strengths and weaknesses, educational and vocational abilities, neurological deficits). Parents and family members typically wish to discuss and possibly observe educational, vocational, and other treatment programs recommended or being considered for their children. Specifically, educational programs should be discussed (and demonstrated) in terms of their philosophy, opportunities for integration with children without disabilities, management procedures, curricula, ancillary services and support programs (e.g., occupational therapy, speech), and evaluation methods. Special attention must be directed to the unique nature of programs for children with autism, even with parents who may be knowledgeable of educational and treatment methods for children with other types of disabilities.

Specific information needs vary from family to family. For instance, some parents may be concerned about guardianship and legal issues affecting their autistic child. Thus, professionals must be able to provide assistance in these areas, relying, for example, on information such as that provided by Apolloni (1984) and Frolik (1983). Similarly, parents may require information on how to obtain medical and dental services for children with autism, because some practitioners are either unprepared or unwilling to accept children with autism as patients.

Beyond such specific information, ongoing and informational exchange forms a basic foundation for a collaborative relationship between parents and professionals. This collaboration can keep parents involved with their child's development and provide a source of comfort to families. Thus, professionals must regularly discuss with parents and family members any progress and program changes. Moreover, the collaborative partnership is two-sided; parents also share appropriate information with professionals. Such information should include family history, parent expectations, school history, and regular updates on significant developments that occur outside school.

Partnership and consumer-advocacy training refers to training parents and family members to advocate more effectively for their autistic children and to be more efficient participants and consumers of educational and professional services. The Individuals with Disabilities Education Act (IDEA, 1990) (e.g., Hardman, Drew, Egan, & Wolf, 1993) and its most recent reauthorization in 1997 (e.g., Yell & Shriner, 1997) ensure parental involvement in educational programming to include extended educational programs, daily scheduling, behavioral objectives, prevocational and vocational needs and in-home training (Martin, 1997). Unfortunately, parents typically do not receive training to enable them to perform these functions. The small percentage of parents that may actually request advocacy and participation training does not necessarily mean an absence of interest or need. Rather, parents may be unaware that such training is appropriate or available. Hence it is the professional's responsibility to remind them of their rights and be prepared to offer the necessary services.

If training is provided within the partnership and consumer advocacy domain, it should include (a) information about school and community resources (e.g., mental health services, medical care programs, parent organizations); (b) workshops and other training programs regarding parents' rights and responsibilities, particularly as related to IDEA; (c) training programs and information that address participation in Individualized Education Program (IEP) conferences; and (d) techniques of information sharing and professional–parent conferencing. Not every parent and family member will require or want training in this area; however, a collaborative partnership between families and professionals is facilitated when such training opportunities are made available.

Natural environment training programs include opportunities for parents and other family members to acquire behavior management, tutoring, and program implementation skills appropriate for use with children with autism in home and community settings. The extensive needs of children with autism and the proven effectiveness of parents and family members as change agents in natural environments (e.g., Atkeson & Forehand, 1978; Birnbrauer & Leach, 1993; Lovaas, 1987; Simpson & Swenson, 1980) make training in this domain logical for parents and families wishing involvement at the problem-solving and procedural application level.

For example, very impressive results have emerged from programs that train parents in behavioral intervention techniques when their child with autism is very young (e.g., Bondy & Frost, 1994; Brown & Prelock, 1995; Green, 1996a; Lovaas, 1977, 1996; McEachin, Smith, & Lovaas, 1993). Methods employing behavioral interventions for young children with autism have reported (a) acceleration of developmental rates, resulting in IQ gains; (b) language gains; (c) improved social behavior; and (d) decreased symptoms of autism (Rogers, 1996). A landmark longitudinal study by McEachin et al.

(1993) indicated that these gains may be long-lasting if intensive early intervention is employed. The intensive one-to-one training usually recommended may range from 15 to 40 hours per week. This means that parents trained to provide behavioral intervention may facilitate success (e.g., Bondy & Frost, 1994; Lovaas, 1977, 1996; Rogers, 1996).

Most behaviorally based parent training programs proceed from the assumption that autistic children's school progress is enhanced when parents provide some of the intervention. Behavioral treatment has clearly been found to be effective with children with autism (Green, 1996a; Lovaas, 1977, 1996; Lovaas & Newsome, 1976; Risley, 1968; Romanczyk, 1996; Schreibman & Koegel, 1981), and research has shown that parents are potentially effective behavioral intervention agents (Anderson, Taras, & Cannon, 1996; Bondy & Frost, 1994; Freeman & Ritvo, 1976; Green, 1996a; Koegel, Egel, & Dunlap, 1980; Koegel & Rincover, 1974; Kozloff, 1975; Lovaas, 1977, 1996; McEachin et al., 1993; Rogers, 1996; Romanczyk, 1996; Schopler & Reichler, 1971; Wing, 1972). In fact, in a study of the maintenance effects of behavioral training with autistic children, Lovaas and Koegel (1973) concluded that clinic treatment without parent training failed to promote lasting gains.

Koegel, Schreibman, Britten, Burke, and O'Neill (1987) conducted a comprehensive study of the effects of behavioral training on children with autism. One group of children received treatment from clinicians without family involvement, while the second group was trained exclusively by their parents, who had previously been trained to use behavioral techniques. The authors measured treatment effects on the children as well as effects on the family. Results showed more initial improvement in the children and more durable treatment gains as a result of 25 to 50 hours of parent training than 225 hours of clinic training. In addition, the parent training group produced significant increases in the frequency of recreational and leisure activities. Finally, psychological and marital adjustment measures did not indicate abnormality in either group, implying that parent training did not adversely affect family dynamics.

A variety of natural environment training programs have been developed for professionals and parents interested in programming for children with autism. Table 15.2 lists several such programs and their major elements.

Even though some parents and family members of children with autism will not make use of them, *counseling, therapy, and support services* should be available. Specifically, these programs may offer (a) support groups for parents, siblings, and family members, including those sponsored by the Autism Society of America (ASA); (b) individual and group therapy resources; (c) crisis intervention services; and (d) counseling and support programs, including respite care. Parents of children with autism are no longer viewed as the cause of their children's disability; thus they do not necessarily require therapy. Such an exoneration, however, does not imply that many

Table 15.2

Parent Training Programs and Major Components

Program Title	Components	Reference
Responsive Parenting	Applied behavioral analysis. Eight 2-hour weekly meetings. Uses role playing. Requires certified group leaders.	Hall, 1981
Winning!	Parents of 3- to 12-year-olds. Basic behavioral techniques. Training modules include written material and videotapes. Movement based on mastery of previous skill. Uses role-plays and homework.	Dangel & Polster, 1984
CBTU Program	Goal setting, differential attention, positive reinforcement, precision request, problem solving. 6 to 8 weeks; 2-hour sessions. Written material, role-plays, modeling, home projects, problem-solving, booster sessions.	Jenson, 1985
RETEACH	10-week, data-based training. Behavior modification and language training. Specific lesson design format. Homework, pretest, posttest. Ongoing consultation.	Handleman & Harris, 1986
UCLA Young Autism Model	Applied behavioral analysis. Teaches language and socially appropriate behaviors. Initial 3-day parent training workshop, with 2-day follow-up twice per year.	Lovaas, 1996
Project TEACCH	Stresses self-care and language training. Emphasizes highly structured, sheltered environments rather than training sessions and consequences.	Smith, 1996

parents will not experience stress, depression, and other emotional responses directly associated with living day to day with a child with autism. Hence, appropriate support resources should be made available.

The various services for families of autistic children may be delivered in several formats. For instance, Auerbach (1968) delineated group formats appropriate for aiding parents and families in meeting their informational, support, advocacy, and counseling needs: (a) formal academic training (to increase understanding of child development, family relations, advocacy techniques, legislation, research, etc.); (b) group dynamics (to facilitate individual growth and self-validation); (c) group counseling (to assist in problem solving); and (d) group psychotherapy, to remove "pathological blocks that stand in the way of the continuing acquisition of knowledge and understanding needed to enable the growth process to continue" (p. 37). Auerbach noted that although teachers, psychologists, social workers, and psychiatrists could lead these groups, professional training should be matched with group objectives (e.g., use of psychologists or psychiatrists to conduct group psychotherapy sessions).

Additionally, Handleman and Harris (1986) described a consultation strategy for assisting parents and families to deal with issues associated with having a child with a disability. Their program (CONSULTED) does not focus on direct training, but on how to facilitate family problem solving. The nine basic elements of the strategy are identified below.

1. *Confer.* Assess what problems the family perceives and what kind of help they would like.

2. *Observe.* Look at the situation in the home or the community and document pertinent information about the perceived problem.

3. *Name problems.* Define the problem in specific terms.

4. *Set priorities.* Be sensitive to the needs of the parent; set priorities for solutions.

5. *Utilize resources.* Analyze what resources are available (e.g., space, respite care, materials, time).

6. *Label obstacles.* Analyze obstacles to success. For example, resistant family members, cognitive level of the child, lack of parental skills, or emotional needs of parents may promote failure. Refer for additional services if necessary.

7. *Try intervention.* Step aside so that the family can proceed with their own problem solution. Stay in touch for reinforcement and resources.

8. *Evaluate outcome.* Once a week, evaluate intervention progress with the parents.

9. *Determine next step.* Continue intervention, modify the plan, or proceed to another perceived problem.

Sibling Programs

An additional area of family support may involve siblings. Any brothers and sisters of the child with autism may require information, assurance, and other forms of emotional support (Berg, 1973; Grossman, 1972; Kaplan, 1969; Klein, 1972; Siegel, 1996). These needs are intensified by the fact that parents often focus inordinate attention on children with disabilities, sometimes ignoring the needs of other siblings. When informed and aware of their role, siblings can often facilitate growth and development of children with disabilities by serving as positive role models and behavior-change agents (Colletti & Harris, 1977; James & Egel, 1986; Luce & Dyer, 1996; Schreibman, O'Neill, & Koegel, 1983).

Siegel (1996) cautions that siblings of children with autism are at risk of becoming "parentified" (p. 150). This means that they might be forced to assume parental responsibilities on their own initiative or because they are required to do so by the actual parents. She delineates four typical patterns of coping with the special demands inherent in having a sibling with autism: (1) parentifying, (2) superachieving, (3) becoming a "family mascot" with a winning and humorous personality that attracts positive parental attention, or (4) withdrawing from family life. Withdrawal is the most maladaptive coping technique.

Knoblock (1982) described a sibling support group working toward the goal of (a) increasing children's awareness of disabilities, (b) providing a forum for children to share experiences, (c) encouraging group problem solving, (d) imparting information about educating children with disabilities, and (e) providing specific skill training. Several activities, including simulations, trust walks, communication through drawings, interviews, and information sharing over snacks, were used to facilitate involvement between children with autism and their siblings.

"Sibshops" (Meyer & Vadasy, 1994), peer support groups developed for 8- to 13-year-old siblings of children with developmental disabilities, have often been sponsored by agencies serving children with special needs, and are facilitated by a team of professional service providers (e.g., social workers, special education teachers and professors, psychologists, nurses). They typically meet once a week on Saturdays, from 10 a.m. until 2 p.m., for games, discussion and information activities, and making and eating lunch. The Sibshop model serves children from suburban and urban communities, and communities with unique cultural heritages (e.g., Alaska, New Mexico, and Hawaii). A dozen children and two facilitators is considered an optimum ratio, and the context is lively and recreational. Goals of the Sibshop model include providing opportunities for brothers and sisters of children with special needs to (a) meet other such siblings, (b) discuss common joys and concerns, (c) have an opportunity to learn how others handle situations commonly experienced by siblings of children with special needs, (d) learn more about the implications of their sibling's special needs, and (e) have their parents and professionals learn more about their concerns.

Respite Care and Other Support Services

Respite care may also be sought by many parents and families. These programs can take the form of in-home babysitting, center day care (after school and weekends), or placement of the child or adult with autism in a foster family, group home, or institution for 24 hours or longer. Respite care provides the family with time for social activities, vacations, or just a rest period away from their child with a disability (Siegel, 1996).

In response to a legislative recommendation that "families of autistic persons have significant need for support services, such as respite care, counseling, and training programs" (Joint Committee on Autism Report to the Texas Legislature, 1982, p. 4), the Texas Department of Mental Health and Mental Retardation provided funding for several pilot programs serving individuals with autism. One of these programs was developed by the Austin–Travis County Mental Health and Mental Retardation Center (ATCMHMR) to provide various forms of respite to families with children with autism in the area. The services included (a) after-school care, (b) Saturday programs, (c) in-home baby-sitting, (d) parent training, and (e) summer school. Participating mental health workers and teachers were trained in behavioral intervention techniques and consultation skills. Parents could participate in the services for any length of time they chose. A parent advisory board provided the project staff with feedback on family needs and program effectiveness. Community agencies such as the Austin Parks and Recreation Department and the Austin Community Schools provided additional recreational programming for the children.

To further support these efforts the local parent advocacy group (Capital Area Autism Society of America) organized informal and formal activities for the families in conjunction with the ATCMHMR project. These activities provided training and support for families. Siblings were often included in the respite and recreational activities. In addition, parents formed a volunteer group to disseminate information about services for adults with autism. Only 1 of the 20 children participating in the program was subsequently placed in an institution during their school-age years, suggesting that respite care services can provide the time necessary for families to develop resources and to feel empowered to deal with their child with autism.

Advocacy

Parents and families of children with autism should also have the opportunity to serve the general needs of persons with autism and related disabilities through participation in school and community programs. Such opportunities may take the form of serving on advocacy and advisory boards; disseminating information about autism; advocating for autism-related legislation, services, and resources; serving as volunteers in classrooms, agencies, or programs; or working as support and advocacy agents. Parents and family members with needs and interests in this area often work through and in conjunction with the Autism Society of America, a particularly effective and active organization. The ASA offers a "Fax on Demand" service that provides specific and thorough information quickly, at 800-FAX-0899.

Parents make very powerful advocates, and professionals might encourage parents who are willing to focus their energy on obtaining and maintaining appropriate services for all individuals with autism. Table 15.3 provides a list of state-administered organizations that are staffed by attorneys and advocates interested in the rights of individuals with disabilities. Each organization may have its own priorities in terms of specific issues.

Summary

Children with autism can be expected to present unique and significant challenges for parents and family members. The role of professionals who assist families in accommodating and adjusting to children with autism will be facilitated by (a) developing an individualized plan for various parent and family participation levels (awareness, open communication, advocacy and participation, problem solving and procedural application, and partnership) and (b) understanding potential parent and family needs. Assistance may be offered in the form of information sharing; partnership and consumer-advocacy training; natural environment training programs; counseling, therapy, and support services; and school and community participation programs.

Table 15.3

Parent Protection and Advocacy Organizations

Alabama
AL Disabilities Advocacy Program
Phone: 205-348-4928/800-826-1675

Alaska
Disability Law Center of Alaska
Phone: 907-344-1002/800-478-1234

Arizona
Arizona Center for Disability Law
Phone: 520-327-9547

Arkansas
Advocacy Services, Inc.
Phone: 501-296-1775/800-485-1775

California
Protection & Advocacy, Inc.
Phone: 916-488-9955/800-776-5746

Colorado
The Legal Center
Phone: 303-722-0300

Connecticut
Office of P & A for Persons with Disabilities
Phone: 860-297-4300/800-842-7303

Delaware
Disabilities Law Program
Phone: 307-575-0660

District of Columbia
University Legal Services
Phone: 202-547-0198

Florida
Advocacy Center for Persons with Disabilities
Phone: 850-488-9071/800-346-4127

Georgia
Georgia Advocacy Office, Inc.
Phone: 404-885-1234/800-537-2329

Hawaii
Protection & Advocacy Agency
Phone: 808-949-2922

Idaho
C0-Ad, Inc.
Phone: 208-336-5353/800-632-5125

Illinois
Equip for Equality, Inc.
Phone: 312-341-0022/800-537-2632

Indiana
Indiana Protection and Advocacy Services
Phone: 317-722-5555/800-622-4845

Iowa
Iowa P & A Service, Inc.
515-278-2502/800-779-2502

Kansas
Kansas Advocacy and Protection Services
Phone: 913-232-3469

Kentucky
Office for Public Advocacy and Division
for P & A
Phone: 502-564-2967

Louisiana
Advocacy Center for the Disabled
Phone: 504-522-2337/800-960-7705

Maine
Maine Advocacy Services
Phone: 207-626-2774

Maryland
Maryland Disability Law Center
410-234-2791/800-233-7201

Massachusetts
Disability Law Center, Inc.
Phone: 617-723-8455

Michigan
Michigan P & A Service
Phone: 517-487-1755/800-292-5896

Minnesota
Minnesota Disability Law Center
Phone: 612-332-1441/800-292-4150

Mississippi
Mississippi P & A System for DD, Inc.
Phone: 612-332-1441/800-292-4150

Missouri
Missouri P & A Services
Phone: 573-893-3333/800-392-8667

Montana
Montana Advocacy Program
Phone: 406-444-3889/800-245-4743

(continues)

Table 15.3 *Continued*

Native American
DNA-People's Legal Services, Inc.
Phone: 505-368-3216

Nebraska
Nebraska Advocacy Services, Inc.
Phone: 402-474-3183

Nevada
Nevada Advocacy & Law Center, Inc.
Phone: 702-383-8150/800-992-5715

New Hampshire
Disabilities Rights Center
Phone: 603-228-0432

New Jersey
Phone: 609-292-9742/800-922-7233

New Mexico
Protection & Advocacy, Inc.
Phone: 505-256-3100/800-432-4682

New York
New York Commission on Quality of Care
  for the Mentally Disabled
Phone: 518-473-7378/800-624-4143

North Carolina
Governor's Advocacy Council for Persons
  with Disabilities
Phone: 919-733-9250/800-821-6922

North Dakota
The North Dakota Protection & Advocacy
  Project
Phone: 701-328-2950/800-642-6694

Ohio
Ohio Legal Rights Service
Phone: 614-466-7264/800-282-9181

Oklahoma
Oklahoma Disability Law Center, Inc.
Phone: 405-525-7755/800-880-7755

Oregon
Oregon Advocacy Center
Phone: 503-243-2081/800-556-5351

Pennsylvania
Pennsylvania P & A, Inc.
Phone: 717-236-8110/800-692-7443

Rhode Island
Rhode Island Disability Law Center, Inc.
Phone: 401-831-3150/800-733-5332

South Carolina
P & A for People with Disabilities, Inc.
Phone: 800-782-0639/800-922-5225

South Dakota
South Dakota Advocacy Services
Phone: 605-224-8294/800-658-4782

Tennessee
Tennessee P & A, Inc.
Phone: 615-298-1080/800-342-1660

Texas
Advocacy, Inc.
Phone: 512-454-4816/800-252-9108

Utah
Disability Law Center
Phone: 801-363-1347/800-662-9080

Vermont
Vermont Protection & Advocacy
Phone: 802-229-1355

Virginia
Department for Rights of Virginians
  with Disabilities
Phone: 804-225-3962/800-552-3962

Washington
Washington P & A System
Phone: 206-324-1521/800-562-2702

West Virginia
West Virginia Advocates, Inc.
304-346-0847/800-950-5250

Wisconsin
Wisconsin Coalition for Advocacy
Phone: 608-0267-0214

Wyoming
Wyoming P & A System
Phone: 307-638-7668/800-624-7648

Note. Adapted from "State Training Parent Information Projects" (1998, January–February), *Advocate: The Newsletter of the Autism Society of America 30*, pp. 18–20.

References

American Psychiatric Association. (1994). *Diagnostic and statistical manual of mental disorders* (4th ed). Washington, DC: Author.

Anderson, S. R., Taras, M., & Cannon, B. O. (1996). Teaching new skills to young children with autism. In C. Maurice, G. Green, & S. C. Luce (Eds.), *Behavioral intervention for young children with autism: A manual for parents and professionals* (pp. 181–194). Austin, TX: PRO-ED.

Apolloni, T. (1984). Who'll help my disabled child when I'm gone? *Academic Therapy, 20,* 109–114.

Aekeson, B., & Forehand, R. (1978). Parents as behavior change agents with school-related problems. *Education and Urban Society, 10,* 521–540.

Auerbach, A. B. (1968). *Parents learn through discussion: Principles and practices of parent group education.* New York: Wiley.

Berg, K. (1973). Christina loves Katherine. *Exceptional Parent, 3*(1), 35–36.

Bettelheim, B. (1950). *Love is not enough.* Glencoe, NY: Free Press.

Biklen, D. (1990). Communication unbound: Autism and praxis. *Harvard Educational Review, 60,* 291–315.

Biklen, D. (1992, January). Typing to talk: Facilitated communication. *American Journal of Speech and Language Pathology,* pp. 15–17.

Birnbrauer, J. S., & Leach, D. J. (1993). The Murdoch early intervention program after 2 years. *Behaviour Change, 10,* 63–74.

Bondy, A. A., & Frost, L. A. (1994, August). The picture exchange communication system. *Focus on Autistic Behavior, 9*(3), 1–18.

Bourne, R. A. (1998). *CranioSacral therapy with dolphins* [On-line]. Description available: http//www.aquathought.com/idatra/symposium/96/upledger.html

Breslau, N., Staruch, K., & Mortimer, E. (1982). Psychological distress in mothers of disabled children. *American Journal of Disabled Children, 136,* 682–686.

Brown, J., & Prelock, P. A. (1995). Brief report: The impact of regression on language development in autism. *Journal of Autism and Developmental Disorders, 25,* 305–309.

Buscaglia, L. (1975). *The disabled and their parents: A counseling challenge.* Thorofare, NJ: Slack.

Colletti, G., & Harris, S. L. (1977). Behavior modification in the home: Siblings as behavior modifiers, parents as observers. *Journal of Abnormal Child Psychology, 1,* 21–30.

Connelly, B. (1998). Swimming with prisoners. *Dolphin Swim Programs* [On-line]. Available: www.dolphinproject-org/swim.htm

Creak, M. (1961). Schizophrenic syndrome in childhood: Progress of a working party. *Cerebral Palsy Bulletin, 3,* 501–504.

Dangel, R. F., & Polster, R. A. (1984). WINNING: A systematic, empirical approach to parent training. In R. F. Dangel & R. A. Polster (Eds.), *Parent training: Foundations of research and practice* (pp. 166–174). New York: Guilford Press.

Fewell, R. (1986). A handicapped child in the family. In R. R. Fewell & P. F. Vadasy (Eds.), *Families of handicapped children* (pp. 3–34). Austin, TX: PRO-ED.

Fiedler, C. R. (1986). Enhancing parent–school personnel partnerships. *Focus on Autistic Behavior, 1*(4), 108.

Freeman, B. J., & Ritvo, E. R. (1976). Parents as paraprofessionals. In E. R. Ritvo (Ed.), *Autism: Diagnosis, current research and management* (pp. 61–92). New York: Spectrum.

Frolik, L. A. (1983). Legal needs. In E. Schopler & G. B. Mesibov (Eds.), *Autism in adolescents and adults* (pp. 319–334). New York: Plenum Press.

Goldenberg, I., & Goldenberg, H. (1980). *Family therapy: An overview.* Monterey, CA: Brooks/ Cole.

Gorham, K. A. (1975). A lost generation of parents. *Exceptional Children, 41*(8), 521–525.

Green, G. (1994). The quality of the evidence. In H. C. Shane (Ed.), *Facilitated communication: The clinical and social phenomenon* (pp. 157–225). San Diego: Singular Press.

Green, G. (1996a). Early behavioral intervention for young children with autism: What does research tell us? In C. Maurice, G. Green, & S. C. Luce (Eds.), *Behavioral intervention for young children with autism: A manual for parents and professionals* (pp. 29–44). Austin, TX: PRO-ED.

Green, G. (1996b). Evaluating claims about treatment for autism. In C. Maurice, G. Green, & S. C. Luce (Eds.), *Behavioral intervention for young children with autism: A manual for parents and professionals* (pp. 15–27). Austin, TX: PRO-ED.

Grossman, F. K. (1972). *Brothers and sisters of retarded children: An exploratory study.* Syracuse, NY: Syracuse University Press.

Hall, M. C. (1981). *Responsive parenting.* Shawnee Mission, KS: Responsive Management.

Handleman, J. S., & Harris, S. L. (1986). *Educating the developmentally disabled: Meeting the needs of children and families.* San Diego: College-Hill Press.

Happé, F. (1994). *Autism: An introduction to psychological theory* (p. 109). Cambridge: Harvard University.

Hardman, M. L., Drew, C. J., Egan, M. W., & Wolf, B. (1993). *Human exceptionality: Society, school and family.* Needham Heights, MA: Allyn & Bacon.

Harvard Medical School. (1997). Autism. Part I. *The Harvard Mental Health Letter, 13*(9), 1–4.

Individuals with Disabilities Education Act of 1990, 20 U.S.C. § 1400 *et seq.*

Individuals with Disabilities Education Act Amendments of 1997, 20 U.S.C. § 1400 *et seq.*

James, S. D., & Egel, A. L. (1986). A direct prompting strategy for increasing reciprocal interactions between handicapped and nonhandicapped siblings. *Journal of Applied Behavior Analysis, 19,* 173–186.

Jenson, W. R. (1985). Skills preference in two different types of parenting groups. *Small Group Behavior, 16,* 549–555.

Joint Committee on Autism Report to the Texas Legislature. (1982). *Autism: An intricate dilemma.* Austin, TX: Author.

Kanner, L. (1985). Autistic disturbances of affective contact. In A. M. Donnellan (Ed.), *Classic readings in autism* (pp. 11–53). New York: Teachers College Press.

Kaplan, F. (1969). Siblings of retarded. In S. B. Sarason & D. J. Sarason (Eds.), *Psychological problems in mental deficiency* (4th ed., pp. 186–208). New York: Harper & Row.

Klein, S. (1972). Brother to sister, sister to brother. *Exceptional Parent, 2*(1–3), 10–28.

Knoblock, P. (1982). *Teaching and mainstreaming autistic children.* Denver: Love.

Koegel, R. L., Egel, A. L., & Dunlap, G. (1980). Learning characteristics of autistic children. In W. S. Sailor, B. Wilcox, & L. J. Brown (Eds.), *Methods of instruction with severely handicapped students* (pp. 101–134). Baltimore: Brookes.

Koegel, R. L., & Rincover, A. (1974). Treatment of psychotic children in a classroom environment. Learning in a large group. *Journal of Applied Behavior Analysis, 7,* 45–59.

Koegel, R. L., Rincover, A., & Egel, A. L. (1982). *Educating and understanding autistic children.* Boston: College-Hill.

Koegel, R. L., Schreibman, L., Britten, K. R., Burke, J. C., & O'Neill, R. E. (1987). A comparison of parent training to direct child treatment. In R. L. Koegel, A. Rincover, & A. L. Egel (Eds.), *Educating and understanding autistic children* (pp. 260–280). Boston: College Hill.

Kozloff, M. A. (1975). *Reaching an autistic child: A parent training program.* Champaign, IL: Research Press.

Kroth, R. L. (1985). *Communicating with parents of exceptional children.* Denver: Love.

Lovaas, O. I. (1977). *The autistic child.* New York: Lovington.

Lovaas, O. I. (1987). Behavioral treatment and normal educational and intellectural functioning in young autistic children. *Journal of Consulting and Clinical Psychology, 55,* 3–9.

Lovaas, O. I. (1996). The UCLA young autism model of service delivery. In C. Maurice, G. Green, & S. C. Luce (Eds.), *Behavioral intervention for young children with autism: A manual for parents and professionals* (pp. 241–248). Austin, TX: PRO-ED.

Lovaas, O. I., & Koegel, R. L. (1973). *Behavior modification in education, NSSE Yearbook.* Chicago: University of Chicago Press.

Lovaas, O. I., & Newsome, C. D. (1976). Behavior modification with psychotic children. In H. Keitenberg (Ed.), *Handbook of behavior modification and behavior therapy* (pp. 160–184). Englewood Cliffs, NJ: Prentice Hall.

Luce, S. C., & Dyer, K. (1996). Answers to commonly asked questions. In C. Maurice, G. Green, & S. C. Luce (Eds.), *Behavioral intervention for young children with autism: A manual for parents and professionals* (pp. 345–358). Austin, TX: PRO-ED.

Martin, J. (1997, September). *Overview of legal issues involved in educating students with autism and PDD under IDEA.* Paper presented at the Autism Conference, Region 20 Education Service Center, San Antonio, TX.

Maurice, C., Green, G., & Luce, S. C. (Eds.). (1996). *Behavioral intervention for young children with autism: A manual for parents and professionals.* Austin, TX: PRO-ED.

McEachin, J. J., Smith, T., & Lovaas, O. I. (1993). Long-term outcome for children with autism who received early intensive behavioral treatment. *American Journal on Mental Retardation, 4,* 359–372.

Meyer, D. J., & Vadasy, P. F. (1994). *Sibshops: Workshops for siblings of children with special needs.* Baltimore, MD: Brooks.

Miranda-Linné, F., & Melin, L. (1997). A comparison of speaking and mute individuals with autism and autistic-like conditions on the Autism Behavior Checklist. *Journal of Autism and Developmental Disorders, 27,* 245–263.

Mosley, M. (1998). *SWIMS/Dolphin assisted therapy* [Letter to Mr. Ray Clark, Council on Environmental Quality, on-line]. Available: www.dolphinproject-org/swim.htm

Olson, D. H., Russell, C. S., & Sprenkle, D. (1980). Marital and family therapy: A decade review. *Journal of Marriage and the Family, 42*(4), 973–993.

Rappaport, M. (1996). Strategies for promoting language acquisition in children with autism. In C. Maurice, G. Green, & S. C. Luce (Eds.), *Behavioral intervention for young children with autism: A manual for parents and professionals* (pp. 307–319). Austin, TX: PRO-ED.

Risley, T. R. (1968). The effects and side effects of punishing the autistic behaviors of a deviant child. *Journal of Applied Behavior Analysis, 1,* 21–34.

Ritvo, E. J., & Freeman, B. J. (1981). Definition of the syndrome of autism. In B. Wilcox & A. Thompson (Eds.), *Critical issues in educating autistic children and youth* (pp. 316–332). Washington, DC: National Society for Children and Adults with Autism.

Rogers, S. (1996). Brief report: Early intervention in autism. *Journal of Autism and Developmental Disorders, 26,* 243–246.

Romanczyk, R. G. (1996). Behavioral analysis and assessment: The cornerstone to effectiveness. In C. Maurice, G. Green, & S. C. Luce (Eds.), *Behavioral intervention for young children with autism: A manual for parents and professionals* (pp. 195–217). Austin, TX: PRO-ED.

Schopler, E., & Reichler, R. J. (1971). Parents as co-therapists in the treatment of psychotic children. *Journal of Autism and Childhood Schizophrenia, 1,* 87–102.

Schreibman, L., & Koegel, R. L. (1981). A guideline for planning behavior modification programs for autistic children. In S. M. Turner, K. S. Calhoun, & H. E. Adams (Eds.), *Handbook of clinical behavior therapy* (pp. 54–73). New York: Wiley.

Schreibman, L., O'Neill, R. E., & Koegel, R. L. (1983). Behavioral training for siblings of autistic children. *Journal of Applied Behavior Analysis, 16,* 129–138.

Siegel, B. (1996). *The world of the autistic child.* New York: Oxford University.

Simpson, R. L. (1996). *Working with parents and families of exceptional children and youth.* Austin, TX: PRO-ED.

Simpson, R. L., & Fiedler, C. R. (1989). Parental participation in Individualized Education Program (IEP) conferences: A case for individualization. In M. Fine (Ed.), *The second handbook on parent education: Contemporary perspectives* (pp. 145–171). New York: Academic Press.

Simpson, R., & Myles, B. (Eds.). (1998). *Educating children and youth with autism.* Austin, TX: PRO-ED.

Simpson, R., & Regan, M. (1986). *Management of autistic behavior.* Austin, TX: PRO-ED.

Simpson, R., & Swenson, R. (1980). The effects and side-effects of an overcorrection procedure applied by parents of severely emotionally disturbed children in a home environment. *Behavioral Disorders, 5*(2), 79–85.

Smith, T. (1996). Are other treatments effective? In C. Maurice, G. Green, & S. C. Luce (Eds.), *Behavioral intervention for young children with autism: A manual for parents and professionals* (pp. 46–47). Austin, TX: PRO-ED.

State training parent information projects. (1998, January–February). *Advocate: The Newsletter of the Autism Society of America, 30,* 18–20.

Turnbull, A., Summers, J., & Brotherson, M. J. (1984). *Working with families with disabled members: A family systems approach.* Lawrence: University of Kansas, University Affiliated Faculty.

Turnbull, A., & Turnbull, R. (1978). *The other side of the two-way mirror.* Columbus, OH: Merrill.

Webber, J. (1991). An interview with Daniel A. Torisky, President, Autism Society of America. *Focus on Autistic Behavior, 6*(2), 1–16.

Wing, L. (1972). *Autistic children: A guide for parents and professionals.* New York: Brunner/Mazel.

Wing, L. (1974). *Autistic children.* Secaucus, NJ: Citadel.

Wright, L. S., Matlock, K., & Matlock, D. (1985). Parents of handicapped children: Their self-ratings, life satisfaction and parental adequacy. *Exceptional Children, 32,* 37–40.

Yell, M. L., & Shriner, J. G. (1997). The IDEA amendments of 1997: Implications of special and general education teachers, administrators, and teacher trainers. *Focus on Exceptional Children, 30*(1), 1–19.

Zionts, P., & Simpson, R. (1988). *Understanding children and youth with emotional and behavioral problems.* Austin, TX: PRO-ED.

Families with Gifted Children

Reva C. Friedman

"O h, to have a gifted child!" begins an advertisement for a newsletter oriented toward parents of bright children, as if congratulating these couples upon a great achievement. On the other hand, "There is no greater burden than a great potential" is an often quoted line from a well-known Peanuts cartoon. Bright youngsters and their families are often caught in the paradox of these two statements. Resolving the dilemma so that talent is a blessing rather than a blight can be facilitated by an aware and supportive professional.

Families with highly intelligent offspring need to navigate particular and somewhat predictable challenges. To be effective at meeting these challenges, a collaborative partnership between professionals and families with gifted children must be grounded in an understanding of the phenomenon of exceptional ability within social and familial contexts. Although gifted individuals have been noted throughout recorded history, systematic programming, particularly in public school settings, is relatively recent.

The value of involving parents as partners with helping professionals is reflected in a broad spectrum of positive student outcomes (Alter, 1985; Barth, 1979; Emerick, 1992; Fine, 1990; Moon, Jurich, & Feldhusen, 1998). Likewise, enhancing parent involvement in the educational system produces positive effects for both the educational and family systems (Coleman, 1985; Haynes, Comer, & Hamilton-Lee, 1989; Walberg, 1984).

This chapter will explore how parent–professional partnerships that are centered in an understanding of the attributes of family systems can help youngsters with high potential to function successfully in the dynamic systems of family, school, and community. I will highlight issues particular to families with gifted children and connect these issues to the challenges of developing collaborative relationships. I will also suggest alternatives for working effectively with families.

Understanding Exceptional Ability

The past 4,000 years have witnessed tremendous changes in the ways in which giftedness is conceptualized, identified, and supported: once a mark of divinity, now contiguous with ordinary behavior; once neurotic, now normal; once inexplicable, now understandable and quantifiable. Every new development in understanding and measuring intelligence has had a salutary effect on the field of gifted child research and education (Grinder, 1985).

Modern professionals such as school psychologists working with families and their gifted children can explore the family's own conceptualization of giftedness, especially as it is reflected in their attitudes toward their child and the ways in which they describe their functioning as a family system. An outstanding researcher in the field, Dean Keith Simonton (in press), groups the vast array of theories about giftedness into three categories: biological (born to greatness); sociological (identified as great by the larger society); and psychological (achieving greatness). He uses this categorization as a framework for his psychometrically oriented biographical analyses and subsequent model-building research. However, the tripartite grouping also has meaning for school psychologists and other support professionals working with families. Simonton explores the underlying values that support each group of theories and builds hypotheses relative to the impact of each perspective. It is the combined effect of conceptualization and supporting values that shape a family's stance toward the child(ren) identified as having exceptional talent. A family aware of Simonton's framework can externalize and normalize the exceptionality and choose how to integrate giftedness into the family system and family members' collective and individual goals.

Biological Explanations

Pathological pedigrees and emergenetic inheritances characterize the biological perspective. Some researchers have tentatively concluded that about half of the variance in IQ scores in the general population as well as in the high end of the distribution is attributable to heredity (Plomin, 1997). Shared environmental factors also play a key role in similarities in the IQ patterns of children in the same family. However, these similarities can become subsumed by nonshared environmental factors that affect individuals across families. Once given this information a family can understand why one child and not others is identified as intellectually gifted and they can thus avoid blame or inappropriate self-congratulation. But because approximately half of the variance in IQ scores may be attributable to biological influences, the family can also frame itself in terms of a multigenerational transmission of talent and see the strengths and talents in all members of the identified child's family of origin.

Sociological Explanations

Theories of giftedness that focus on the social–cultural context are reflected in the notions of multiple contribution, cultural configuration, accumulative advantage, and symbolic interactionism. Multiple contribution refers to the phenomenon of the nearly simultaneous production of seemingly independent, yet strikingly similar, discoveries. The zeitgeist, as experienced in everchanging cultural configurations, clearly affects the fluctuations of values and circumstances that enhance or limit the opportunities for talent to emerge. Accumulative advantage, popularly referred to as the Matthew Effect (i.e., the rich get richer while the poor get poorer), offers a plausible explanation for a significant portion of individual variations in achievement.

The last sociological factor, symbolic interactionism, pertains to the powerful mutual influence between individual and referent group relative to defining a self and the subsequent impact on expectations and achievements. This perspective can help a family to understand that one member might be singled out as gifted simply due to the values of the larger culture. For example, Bill Gates, CEO of Microsoft and co-developer of the DOS computer operating system, possesses talents that would not necessarily have been recognized in another era. It is interesting to note that he dropped out of Harvard University.

Symbolic interactionism refers to the importance of the family system in enlarging its self-definition as it recognizes and accepts the talents of its identified gifted members. A bright child continues to develop a healthy self-concept and absorbs the values, expectations, and achievement motivations of the family referent group based in part on the extent to which the child and emerging constellation of abilities are woven into the fabric of the family's story.

Psychological Explanations

Simonton's (in press) third lens for studying extraordinary ability, the psychological, distinguishes giftedness that is achieved in the context of society from genius that results from the inheritance of superior genetic factors. He offers three clusters of psychological factors that predispose a child to giftedness: cognitive, motivational, and social.

Historically, cognitive preparation has referred to a precocious rate of mastery of knowledge; currently, it also refers to the speed at which information is encoded, retrieved, and applied (faster than one's average ability peers). Simonton asserts the importance of time in developing the cognitive underpinnings for expert performance, and the emergence of multifactored conceptions of intelligence as a critical precursor to extraordinary ability in one domain (as opposed to high but general abilities).

Motivation is the key nonintellective ingredient, acting as the psychological yeast that allows raw talent to rise and transform itself into extraordinary performance. Persistence, resiliency, optimism, perceiving oneself as the central agent in one's life, and attributional patterns that emphasize unstable, internal, controllable explanations such as effort characterize individuals who fulfill the early promise of their high abilities. There appears to be a biological predisposition to particular motivational patterns; however, environment plays an important role in the manifestation of persistence or helpless behaviors and beliefs. The home environments and early life experiences of individuals who attained eminence as adults were often characterized by hardship, poverty, or trauma (e.g., Goertzel, Goertzel, & Goertzel, 1978). Individuals who successfully navigate the destructive shoals of a hard early life may develop an emotional hardiness that helps them later to persevere with producing cutting-edge work. Walters and Gardner (1986) add another twist to this pattern from their biographical analyses of eminent individuals as children. They found a tendency of the highly able child's parents to be somewhat disengaged from the child's early talent, and speculated that a certain amount of benign neglect might allow extraordinarily talented young people to develop a strong motivational constitution and the courage to venture into cognitively uncharted waters.

The last psychological factor, social preparation, is operationalized as independence and iconoclasm. Through his biographical analyses of eminent individuals, Simonton (in press) notes the importance of traumatic events in disrupting the normal course of socialization; the individual is less invested in the status quo and more able to think and act transformationally. The last critical element of the social environment pertains to the individual's peers in the family system: Many authors have speculated as to the effects of birth order on the emergence of talent (e.g., Sulloway, 1990).

This view of giftedness through a psychological lens might be of practical use to families. For instance, a family could consciously provide time for a bright child to develop areas of expertise—while also reducing unreasonable expectations for adultlike performance that resulted from the child appearing to be precocious. This view also provides symbolic or exemplary models of resiliency for children with high potential, particularly relative to dealing with failure and learning to work patiently in stages to achieve goals. A third insight from this psychological viewpoint: Parents need to acknowledge their parenting contributions but nonetheless separate their identities and self-esteem from their bright children, and allow their children to own their successes and setbacks.

Clearly, the work of schools is relevant to the psychological–cognitive framework. Testing and classroom observations help to identify giftedness, which is usually defined as performance in the top 3% to 10% of the population in intelligence or creativity. New cognitively based theories of intelligence such as Robert Sternberg's work in information processing, Howard

Gardner's (1983) in multiple intelligences, and Mihalyi Csikszentmihalyi's (Csikszentmihalyi, Rathunde, & Whalen, 1993) in creativity and the ethnography of talent continue to broaden our definitions of talent and expand the educational options designed to nurture high ability. However, families might want to acknowledge all three perspectives to support their full understanding of the terms "giftedness," "talent," "bright," or "high potential/high achieving" relative to their child(ren) and to join with the school in its goals.

For the balance of this chapter, I will continue to use the above terms interchangeably. The psychological–cognitive framework will be my primary topic; however, I will try to remain sensitive to the importance of the sociological and biological frameworks in partnering successfully with families.

Describing "Gifted" Families from a Systems Perspective

Obviously families play a key role in the positive educational and social growth of gifted children. Family qualities that may help gifted children to achieve their potential include healthy parent–child interactions (Morrow & Wilson, 1964), positive shaping of values and attitudes (Moon et al., 1998), freedom to make decisions related to educational opportunities (Bloom, 1985), and support for establishing a peer group (Csikszentmihaly, Rathunde, & Whalen, 1993).

Of the many theoretical lenses that can be applied to looking closely at families with gifted children, gifted child education is the most predominant. As Moon et al. (1998) point out, that field is devoted to understanding the nature and promoting the nurture of children and youth with high intellectual potential. It focuses on cognitive development rather than affective development and highlights individual qualities or individual-in-school variables rather than the family context. Reviews of research on parents and families of bright youngsters have addressed the limited applications of univariate studies and anecdotal reports emanating from gifted child education (Dettmann & Colangelo, 1980; Frey & Wendorf, 1985; Hackney, 1981; Keirouz, 1990; Moon et al., 1998).

The systems approach to understanding families with gifted children underscores the developmental dynamics of talent; it delineates the critical ways in which family life affects the developmental trajectory of talent and provides insight into effective collaboration with children and families to enhance strengths and alleviate problems concomitant with high potential. Family systems as a conceptual framework has much to add to gifted studies. Its basic premises include the family as a multigenerational, emotionally dynamic system whose primary organizing themes shape and are shaped by its members (Bowen, 1978; Kerr & Bowen, 1988). In this section I will develop a systemically oriented profile of families with high-potential youngsters and highlight issues related to the emergence of exceptional talent in the family system.

Qualities of a Healthy "Gifted" Family System

Study after study has shown that families of gifted children epitomize self-actualizing family systems (Frey & Wendorf, 1985). Stable marriages and well-adjusted families appear to be the most effective talent incubators (Barbe, 1981; Beach, 1988; Bloom, 1985; Mathews, West, & Hosie, 1986; Moon et al., 1998; VanTassel-Baska, 1989). The various family subsystems, rules, and complementarity of roles create an open flexible environment that acknowledges the unique qualities of all family members and nurtures their cognitive and emotional growth.

Family Subsystem. Mutually supportive relationships, appropriate degrees of closeness, flexibility, and open expression of thought and feelings characterize the families with at least one child participating in a gifted education program (Cornell, 1983a, 1983b; Csikszentmihalyi et al., 1993; Frey & Wendorf, 1985). This pattern is strongly associated with positive outcomes such as higher overall child adjustment, self-esteem, and academic self-concept. These children have fewer discipline, self-control, and anxiety issues, as indicated by data gathered from child self-reports and teacher observations. When compared to families with no identified children, "gifted" families express higher values for recreational, intellectual, and cultural pursuits, although not in the context of an achievement or competitive framework (Cornell & Grossberg, 1987).

The well-functioning families of gifted children tend to be successful—reporting a high degree of achievement in both the previous and present generations. These families expect their children to be bright and are not surprised when a family member qualifies for placement in a gifted education program (Frey & Wendorf, 1985).

Parental Subsystem. "Participatory exploration" describes the way in which these parents structure family interactions, whether resolving conflict (Frey & Wendorf, 1985) or managing planning tasks (Cornell, 1983b). The contributions of each family member are solicited, valued, and incorporated by other family members into the family dialogue. Parents are democratic yet clear leaders in family discussions. They are flexible, adapting their approaches in accordance with their children's ages. In one study the researchers commented that even experimental tasks employed to assess family functioning were used as teaching opportunities and were linked by the parents to current family issues (Frey & Wendorf, 1985).

Couples handle differences easily and do not appear to feel threatened by conflicting opinions. However, this finding needs to be somewhat qualified, since marital adjustment was used in several studies as a selection criterion for further data gathering (e.g., Karnes & Shwedel, 1987). Cornell (1983a, 1983b) found that parents were likely to differ in perceptions of their children as gifted. Mothers tended to be more liberal in their definitions of giftedness (i.e., as special learning abilities) than fathers, who limited their definitions to prodigy- or genius-like performance. Thus, whereas mothers were more likely to perceive their children as gifted, fathers were less likely to apply the gifted label and also less likely to verbalize positive aspects of attributes associated with giftedness.

Looking more closely at the father–child relationship, Karnes and Shwedel (1987) discovered that fathers whose preschool children were identified as gifted reported substantially more involvement with the children in activities such as reading and hobbies and placed a high value on oral language. These fathers also displayed significantly more unconditional positive regard for their children. Fathers of nonidentified youngsters spent an average of two-thirds less time in reading activities with their children, valued psychomotor activities over language development, and emphasized dependence on the father rather than encouraging independence.

These findings become important when comparing parental perceptions of their children as gifted to the children's personality adjustment. Positive labeling of a child by parents is associated with parental pride in the child's accomplishments, healthier child personality qualities, and more intimacy in parent–child relationships, whether or not the child is formally identified (Cornell, 1983a; VanTassel-Baska & Olszewski-Kubilius, 1989). This influence of parental perceptions on the actualization of potential is further supported by research linking ability and birth order. In his analysis of archival and biographical data of eminent persons (e.g., presidents, prime ministers, and Nobel laureates), Albert (1980) concluded that parental interests and values combined with family position to accentuate the child's abilities: "He becomes the child who gets an intense socialization in those family interests and traditions" (p. 88).

The key role played by the parental subsystem is further supported by case studies of 120 eminent young persons (Bloom, 1985) and case studies of six prodigies (Feldman & Goldsmith, 1986). According to this research, the talent area is almost like a language spoken in the home. Parents routinely provide materials (e.g., musical instruments, typewriters) and lessons in the talent area they value (and often in which they share a proficiency). They are adept "talent scouts," and can recognize a "gifted" response from their child. Often they alert the school that their child has exceptional abilities.

Sibling Subsystem. Among nonproblem "gifted" families, sibling interactions are congruent with the parental subsystem interactions. There is little or no competition for parental approval, and no jealousy or resentment of the gifted label among siblings. Any teasing or antagonism appears to be contained by the parents. When the siblings under study are adolescents, they show a high degree of camaraderie, even when only one is identified as gifted (Frey & Wendorf, 1985).

However, this picture changes somewhat when we look more closely at the relationship between identified and nonidentified siblings. Cornell and Grossberg (1987) discovered that, among nonproblem families, when the parents report not thinking of the (nonidentified) sibling as having special talents, there are repercussions for that child. Nonidentified children appeared to be less well adjusted and more anxious and neurotic than their gifted siblings. They evidenced lower self-esteem, more defensiveness, and less drive to pursue and to develop their abilities than their identified siblings. The researchers hypothesized that these nonidentified children might have received negative messages about self-worth from the family system.

In its early stages, labeling appears to be most beneficial to the self-image of the gifted sibling, encouraging cooperation and communication, perhaps as a result of self-enhancing comparisons. In a study of 27 pairs of labeled and unlabeled siblings, Grenier (1985) discovered increased competition and diminished cooperation on the part of unlabeled siblings; in short, labeling damaged the sibling relationship. She noted, however, that these results were mitigated by the perceptions of positive treatment by the parents and by the increase in the age difference between the siblings.

Over time, the negative effects of labeling seem to reverse, at least from the perspective of the unlabeled sibling. Five years after identification of their sibling, unlabeled youngsters reported greater happiness regarding the gifted child's participation in special education programs and more openness in family communication about the gifted label and program participation. In fact, they perceived fathers as being happier about the label than the fathers actually reported (Colangelo & Brower, 1987). In contrast the identified sibling appeared to be more uneasy regarding family valuing and perceptions of him. The authors speculated that the gifted child might be the victim of self-generated unrealistic views as one manifestation of the effects of the label on the family. However, they failed to take into consideration that the gifted sample was in late adolescence (mean age = 19); thus, some of the perceptions could be an expression of developmental issues independent of the gifted label.

Rules and Complementarity. Well-functioning families of gifted children interact cooperatively with minimal conflict and maximum freedom for personal expression (Cornell & Grossberg, 1987). Kulieke and Olszewski-Kubilius (1989) and Moon et al. (1998) observed that families whose gifted children exhibited differing talents were characterized by particular value systems. For example, child-centeredness and supportive, close family relationships distinguished families with high-achieving and high IQ children. These families acted as educators in the home; they monitored homework, set high standards for educational outcomes, and modeled the pursuit of intellectual and cultural activities (Prom-Jackson, Johnson, & Wallace, 1987). The parents expressed support for more conventional values and were more likely to "push" their children for scholastic achievement (Getzels & Jackson, 1962). However, they saw themselves as successful parents, and their children also saw them that way (Strom, Strom, Strom, & Collinsworth, 1994).

In contrast, the family environment for creatively gifted children differs significantly from that of their nonidentified peers in the degree of overt control orientation. The family places relatively little value on set rules and procedures and more emphasis on independence (Robinson & Noble, 1991). This pattern is reflected, for example, in a study of creatively gifted women: Parental behavior tended to support questioning as legitimate rather than treating it as rebellious. Parents even actively supported values that were at odds with those expressed by the school (List & Renzulli, 1991).

Exceptional Talent in the Family System: Predictable Challenges

The presence of a gifted child can have negative as well as positive effects on the family. Particularly in the early years following the identification or labeling process, parents report an overpowering sense of responsibility. Their feelings might include fears regarding their ability to raise a gifted child or guilt about possibly neglecting their gifted child's growth. To the degree that parents fail to resolve these feelings, family interactions can be adversely affected. For instance, making the gifted child the focal point of the family leads to inappropriate comparisons among siblings and fosters competition. Sibling jealousy can be fueled by highlighting the limited access activities that are part of the gifted child's school program. In such a family environment, nonidentified children are less likely to view themselves as successful (Peterson, 1977). Conflict resolution is hampered, and one parent often becomes more peripheral with respect to discipline or school relations (Frey & Wendorf, 1985). Parents sometimes compensate for their feelings by placing excessive performance pressure on themselves and their children, which can stimulate chronic underperformance, stress reactions, and other psychological problems.

Some researchers speculate that the degree to which the gifted child has an adverse impact on the family is directly related to the perceived discrepancy between the gifted child's intellectual capacity and that of other family members (Ross, 1979). However, giftedness can be a positive family organizer. Albert (1980) concluded that, combined with values and goals, it can "pull together diverse personal and interpersonal factors to make a more coherent organization of a child's and a family's transactions" (p. 93).

Over time, labeling seems to affect the quality of family interactions. Behaving in adult ways at a young age—making decisions, juggling complex time demands, acting independently—distinguishes the bright child in her transactions within the family. Case studies and histories offer many instances of bright young people making key decisions about education in their talent area: setting performance standards, moving away from home at young ages to pursue advanced training, evaluating the quality of their instruction—even choosing their teachers (Bloom, 1985; Feldman & Goldsmith, 1986; Goldsmith, in press). Remembering that the precious child is not an adult and maintaining parental role boundaries compound the challenges parents face. If parents do not resolve their challenges successfully, an imbalance of power in the family can develop, particularly when only one child is labeled gifted. Cornell (1983b) found a tendency in these families for the parents to focus on the gifted child and to proceed according to the child's direction, ideas, and decisions.

Independent of the public act of identifying a child as gifted is the intrapersonal challenge of exceptional ability. The most common manifestation of this stressor is in asynchronous development. Simply put, a child with extraordinary conceptual ability may feel frustrated at being able to conceptualize a product while lacking the tools or skills to bring it to fruition. As youngsters develop more cognitive skills and emotional–motivational stamina, they may resolve this issue; however, giftedness appears to create certain "psychological vulnerabilities" (Moon et al., 1998, p. 65). Struggling with feeling different (Robinson & Noble, 1991), balancing achievement and affiliation needs (Clasen & Clasen, 1995), resolving the gaps among widely varying sub–self-concepts (Brounstein, Holahan, & Dreyden, 1991), and setting reasonable learning goals (Jenkins-Friedman & Murphy, 1988) can enhance a child's commitment to living a fully potentiated life.

Issues in Describing "Gifted" Families

As mentioned earlier families of gifted students tend to follow the typical profile of a well-functioning family system. With the parents at the helm, democratic yet clear captains of the family ship, the family successfully navigates past the shoals in the Sea of Life. However, a closer examination of these studies creates some skepticism. For example, many of the studies narrowly define their samples as two-parent intact families, or draw samples from university-based schools, in which the per capita income is at least at the middle to upper middle level (Frey & Wendorf, 1985; Moon et al., 1998) *Giftedness* is narrowly defined in these studies as a high score on intelligence or achievement tests. This delineation further limits the economic diversity of samples, because researchers have shown that low income tends to be associated with depressed scores on standardized ability and achievement measures (Hunsacker, 1994).

Moon et al. (1998) and other researchers assert that cognitive characteristics of highly intelligent children are relatively stable across ethnic groups and cultures, but the affective and social characteristics vary considerably within the cultural context of the student (Ford, 1996; Plucker, 1996; Steinberg, 1996). Some identifiable characteristics of gifted children appear to put them at a greater risk for underperformance in school and for psychological problems: lower socioeconomic backgrounds (Friedman, 1994; VanTassel-Baska, Patton, & Prillaman, 1991), single-parent families (Gelbrich & Kare, 1989), exceptionally high measured intelligence (Janos & Robinson, 1985), and giftedness in connection with a disability such as learning disability (Baum, 1994; Nielsen, Higgins, Wilkinson, & Webb, 1994). Nonmajority ethnicity is also associated with disproportionately low identification rates, greater vulnerability for underperformance, and a higher likelihood for refusing or exiting services.

Working with Families of Gifted Youngsters: A Systems Perspective

There is an abundance of literature on methods for educating parents of gifted children; however, the bulk of these approaches is school-centered. They assume that the school is responsible for the intellectual and affective development of the gifted child. In this framework parents are passive recipients of information, not teachers or facilitators of their child's growth. School counselors and psychologists are responsible for educating parents relative to the available services and reassuring them that their child's needs can best be met through expertly trained school personnel (Dettmann & Colangelo, 1980). The most popular format for parent education programs is a "one-shot" evening presentation by the gifted program staff (e.g., Wolf & Stephens, 1984), rather than sustained efforts that blend parents' expertise with the gifted program, or educational programs based on an assessment of parents' issues and needs.

Aside from the incompleteness of one-shot approaches, the content is often overly simplistic. Mathews (1981) questions the validity and objectivity of presentations such as the "I Know What You Are Going Through Because I Have a Gifted Child, Too" or "I Understand Your Child Because I Was/Am Gifted, Too" approaches. He asserts that these approaches are limited by their subjective examination of the issues. I would add that the very nature of parent education groups puts parents in a forced help-seeker role, which upsets the power balance between professional and parent, undermines the process of joining and partnering with families, and distances parents from the education process.

A far more useful framework for working with parents is a partnership approach (Dettmann & Colangelo, 1980; Fine, 1977; Fine & Pitts, 1980; Petr, 1998). This paradigm recognizes that all parties have knowledge and expertise that can be beneficial to the child's growth at home and school. Fine (personal communication, March 1988) identifies four objectives for a collaborative model of parent involvement: (1) educating; then (2) including parents in decision making; (3) assisting parents therapeutically so they will be able to cope more effectively with the issues surrounding their exceptional child; and (4) empowering parents to work actively on behalf of their child.

In my work with school personnel and parents of gifted children, I have found that the most enduring school–parent partnerships combine two elements: (1) a flexible role definition for the professional and (2) an empowerment-oriented systemic framework for assessment and intervention.

The School Psychologist's Role

In a recent article, William J. Doherty (1998) proposed that mental health professionals challenge themselves to be open minded and flexible, yet self-critical and accountable. Because human behavior is the product of many weak forces, he suggested that human problems can be treated by many partly successful approaches, and by individuals with different roles in the family's life. I likewise support a contingency model for developing an effective partnership with parents of gifted children. A contingency approach assumes that there is no single best way to work with parents; rather, the school psychologist must be able to function in many different roles to help families become more competent in mobilizing resources, having needs met, and achieving desired objectives. The notion of tailoring an approach to meet the needs of the learner and to capitalize on her strengths is foundational to the field of gifted child studies (Friedman & Gallagher, 1991); it is a logical basis for working effectively with parents (Dunst, Trivette, & Deal, 1988; Nielsen & Higgins, 1989).

Researchers outline a nearly inexhaustible array of functions applicable to the school psychologist working with parents of gifted children; however, several common themes emerge and can be grouped into a rough hierarchy of increasing involvement (e.g., Callahan, 1982; Colangelo, 1988; Dettmann & Colangelo, 1980; Fine, 1984; Hackney, 1981; Loven, 1978; Schatz & Sandborn, 1980). The first role, *collaborative diagnostician,* emphasizes an information exchange between school and family for the purposes of joint program planning. It assumes that all individuals have unique insights and information regarding the bright child, and that the most effective programming results from an open sharing of these data. The second role, *communication facilitator,* emphasizes promoting school–family interaction, for example, to avoid catching the child in competing system loyalties. The school psychologist, being a member of one system and having insights into the other, can thus serve as a mediator between the two and stimulate collaborative problem solving. Building on these functions, the *consultant* works with the family and school personnel on specific child-related issues. This role assumes that parents, child, and school share responsibility for solving problems. The school psychologist supports the involved parties in understanding the dynamics of an issue and in generating and implementing solutions. Both the school and family system have ownership of the problem as well as the solution; each is committed to working together for durable solutions in their common interest: the well-being of the gifted child. The most intensive involvement occurs in the *counselor* role, combining educator and therapist. In this instance the school psychologist works directly with gifted children, their parents, and teachers to address issues of concern.

An empowerment orientation to working with parents also incorporates a stance of least invasiveness. That is, as the family system appears more empowered, the school psychologist focuses on less intensive involvement and professional support.

A Systemic, Strengths-Oriented Framework for Assessment and Intervention

The key qualities of an empowerment model are its emphases on strengths, health, growth, and solutions (Saleebey, 1996; Weick, 1986). Such a model is systemically focused and far more holistic and dynamic than the linear biomedical model of diagnosis, prescription, and treatment (Fine & Holt, 1983). The child's issues and challenges are regarded as ongoing, interactional, and contextually defined in terms of the relationship between the self and the system (Walter & Peller, 1992; Wendt & Zake, 1984).

Fine and Holt (1983) asserted that viewing children's behavior from a systems perspective could expand the school-based professional's view of the contextual function of a particular behavior. This approach is especially well suited to working with gifted children, whose complex cognitive and affective functioning and often insightful systemic metacognitive processing can undermine needed interventions (Wendorf & Frey, 1985). A systems framework provides a perspective on the person-in-environment, which allows for greater family involvement and collaborative problem solving (Dunst & Trivette, 1987; Treffinger & Fine, 1979).

The Upstream Helping Model

A two-part recommendation for promoting effective partnerships between school professionals and families of gifted students is to (a) assess family strengths and needs and (b) use family strengths to respond to needs. The perspective from which the model operates is illustrated by the well-known story of the drowning man and the Good Samaritan:

> A person walking beside a river sees someone drowning. This person jumps in, pulls the victim out, and begins artificial respiration. Then another drowning person calls for help. The rescuer jumps into the water again and pulls the second victim out. This process repeats itself several times until finally the rescuer ignores the cries of the next victim and

begins to walk upstream. A bystander accosts him: "Where are you going? Can't you see that these people need you?" The rescuer replies: "You take care of them. I'm going upstream to find out who's pushing all these people in and see if I can stop it." (Egan, 1984, p. 23)

Egan's point is that helping professionals typically work downstream, treating the casualties of ill-functioning human systems. He suggests that they need to begin intervening "upstream," that is, to reframe the context and goals of their work as early and preventive. These ideas applied to working with families of gifted children and youth result in a foundation of empowerment rather than therapy, wellness rather than pathology, and upstream rather than downstream helping (see Culross & Jenkins-Friedman, 1988, for a more detailed application of this approach to addressing gifted students' affective needs).

Assessing Family Strengths and Needs

The first step in determining how to work with a particular family is to develop a complete family profile. Helping professionals may even want to analyze their own family backgrounds for practice identifying the rich variety of functional family patterns, as well as personal biases (Fine, 1991). A resource such as *Ethnicity and Family Therapy* (McGoldrick, Giordano, & Pearce, 1996) is especially useful for uncovering ethnically derived family themes and organizers.

The "Mirror Model" (Nielsen & Higgins, 1989) provides a structure for identifying family strengths and needs and tying separate actions to them. Two features make it especially germane: first, its inclusion of strengths as well as needs encourages helping professionals to analyze families from a perspective of functionality. Using strengths to help the family meet needs promotes family empowerment.

A second feature of the model is its delineation of strengths and needs in terms of the frequency with which the professional would be likely to encounter them in families. For example, all families probably have special knowledge of their child's strengths and need educators to demonstrate genuine concern for the child and family. However, low-income families probably have less clear educational goals and expectations for their children, given their organization around successful coping with the stress of daily living. Nielsen and Higgins (1989) suggest using group models and regular school system channels to meet common needs, and individual approaches for the more infrequently identified strengths and needs.

Identifying family behaviors relative to key systemic attributes provides insights into family strengths and options for applying strengths to address needs. Dunst et al. (1988) identify 12 attributes: commitment, appreciation of family members, use of time, sense of purpose, congruence, communication, role expectations, coping strengths, problem solving, positivism, flexibility, and balance. A helping professional can use a recording form to note specific behaviors relative to each quality and to identify intra- and extrafamily resources.

Incorporating a systemic perspective in assessing family functioning means exploring the family subsystems and their interrelationships. In particular the professional would seek to determine (im)balances among family subsystems, alliances among family members, and the degree to which the child's giftedness is a family "organizer" (Jenkins-Friedman, 1992).

Using Family Strengths To Respond to Needs

According to research on families with exceptional children, the way in which support and assistance are offered can either usurp or promote self-sustaining and adaptive behavior (Dunst & Paget, 1991; Fine, 1991). As mentioned earlier, in helping relationships an empowerment approach is proactive: It first assumes that help seekers are already competent or that they have the capacity to become competent. Second, the approach assumes that the social system plays a major role in an individual's success or failure. Thus, an individual's failure to demonstrate competence comes from the failure of social systems to provide relevant opportunities rather than from deficits within the person. Third, it assumes that the criterion for empowerment is met when the help seeker attributes change to his own actions; that is, he demonstrates a sense of control.

In addition to identifying 12 family attributes as mentioned earlier, Dunst and Trivette (1987) also propose 12 principles for empowering and enabling families. Four are presented below as having particular relevance to working with "gifted" families.

1. *Offer assistance that is reciprocal.* Accepting aid necessarily places the help seeker in a "one-down" position: "Reciprocity is likely to be the preferred mode of reducing indebtedness to the extent that recipients are made aware of this option and they perceive that the opportunity to reciprocate exists" (Greenberg & Westcott, 1983, p. 95). This principle especially fits parents of gifted children, whose overall competence would tend to make them uncomfortable with a help-seeker role. Identifying family strengths can reveal ways for equalizing assistance, as can using strengths to address needs. This principle also respects an organizing principle of solution-focused brief therapy: that the individual is the expert on herself. The therapist is there to support the individual, to articulate and organize her insights and information, and to develop strategies for identifying and achieving goals (Walter & Peller, 1992).

2. *Promote parents' natural resources and support networks.* Enhancing a sense of community and promoting the competence and well-being of the family's social network are empowering rather than dependency-producing

approaches (Hobbs, 1975). The importance of support networks has been noted in research on families with a child with disabilities: noncritical support networks were linked to lower levels of maternal psychological distress (Frey, Greenberg, & Fewell, 1989). Professionals should avoid replacing natural resources and support networks with professional services (Dunst & Trivette, 1987; Petr, 1998). This principle is important to consider when working with parents of newly identified gifted children, given their predictable tendency to reexamine parenting practices and even to question their competence to raise bright children. It is a useful principle to revisit as the child and family system pass developmental milestones, meet challenges, and make decisions related to the child's talent.

For instance, a defining characteristic of resilient, low-income families is their access to formal and informal support networks. A key aspect of upstream helping is to assist the family to map these resources and networks. Dunst et al. (1988, p. 78) identify five such nested networks. Families might think to draw support from two of these: (1) the immediate family (mother, wife, stepparent, sibling) and (2) the kinship network (ex-spouse, cousin, grandparent). However, the family might overlook or discount the utility of (3) its informal network (minister, bowling league, employer, neighbors), (4) professionals and organizations (child's teacher, public health department), and (5) influences of larger society (advertising, inflation). Dunst et al. (1988) propose identifying these potential sources of support and the particular ways in which they function, then using the information in problem solving.

3. *Solve problems as a team.* This principle is characterized by participative decision making. Involving parents as partners with an equal stake in developing, evaluating, and selecting choices for their child will help them feel valued and a key part of their child's education (Dettmann & Colangelo, 1980). For helping professionals to maximize effectiveness in enacting this principle, their goals for parents should be consonant with family values (e.g., providing a nurturing environment rather than acting as educators). Helping professionals need to recognize that the gifted child is an active participant in both family and educational systems and avoid creating a complex of conflicting loyalties.

For instance, Fine (1990) points out that school systems tend to value diversity on a conceptual level rather than operationally: "There is a persistence on the part of schools in establishing home–school policies as if every family were a two-parent family with one of the parents at home and with time available to engage in school visits" (p. 173). Professionals should recognize patterns such as single-parent or reconstituted families that may leave less time available to introduce school policies and values into the home. He asserts that the administration creates a zeitgeist that affects the way families are perceived: valued or discounted.

For example, avoiding the use of jargon is critical to working successfully with parents whose educational level is radically dissimilar from that of helping professionals. Formalization of interactions and use of specialized educational terminology can further alienate parents whose images of their own school experiences might already be negative. Thus, it is important to demystify the collaboration process and to identify common interests and values of the family and educational systems and to use those interests and values as a foundation for problem solving.

4. *Ensure family ownership of desired changes.* This principle is the prime determinant of the upstream helping model's success. As help seekers become more capable and competent, they also display greater independence and better problem-solving abilities (Dunst & Paget, 1991; Fish, 1991; Skinner, 1978). Encouraging parents' self-directedness helps them become more self-sustaining, and thus less likely to need help in the future (Colangelo, 1988).

In my opinion, this principle is the defining attribute of the empowerment model. In sum, if help-seeking and help-giving exchanges are to be effective, two conditions must be met: First, recipients of assistance must come to see themselves as no longer in need of support. Second, these individuals need to see themselves as responsible for both producing and maintaining the observed changes (Bandura, 1977). Again, this principle is relevant for successful "gifted" families, who tend to value inner control and independence (Moon et al., 1998).

Summary and Conclusions

This chapter offered frameworks for helping families understand the phenomenon of exceptional ability: biological, sociological, and cognitive–psychological. These emphasize that giftedness is a complex phenomenon with concomitant adjustment issues for bright children and their families. I discussed challenges to a collaborative relationship and presented principles for enhancing a school–home partnership. I suggested a flexible accountable role definition for professionals, along with a family systems perspective for working effectively with families of gifted children. Last, I proposed a strengths-oriented empowerment model for collaborating with families of gifted children and youth.

I believe that an empowerment orientation meshes well with the ways in which families with gifted children construct their "family story." They see themselves as successful in fulfilling the goals for being a family, and acting in accordance with the family values embedded in their ethnic heritage and identification with a particular socioeconomic status. Unfortunately, many parents of gifted children find the contacts with school dependency forming rather than empowering. It is dissonant for parents, who might at least partly explain the recognition of their child's abilities as a manifestation of their genetic contributions, to repeatedly hear the message that their gifted child's needs can best be met by expertly trained school personnel. Subsequent contacts with school counselors, psychologists, and gifted program teachers can leave these parents feeling excluded from responsibility for educational planning for their child, defensive about their parenting abilities, and distanced from the school program.

In contrast, a partnership paradigm recognizes that all parties have knowledge and expertise that can be beneficial to the child's continued growth at home and at school. An accompanying strengths-based, solution-focused orientation leads to mutual respect, teaming, optimism, and emphasis on successful functioning. It is a solid foundation on which to build collaborative relationships.

Acknowledgment

I would like to thank T. J. Gallagher for his contributions to an earlier version of this chapter.

References

Albert, R. A. (1980). Family positions and the attainment of eminence: A study of special family positions and special family experiences. *Gifted Child Quarterly, 24,* 87–95.

Alter, R. C. (1985). *Parent–school communication: A selective review and commentary.* Unpublished manuscript, Dellcrest Children's Center, Toronto.

Bandura, A. (1977). Self-efficacy: Toward a unifying theory of behavioral change. *Psychological Review, 84,* 191–215.

Barbe, M. (1981). A study of the family background of the gifted. In W. Barbe & J. S. Renzulli (Eds.), *Psychology and education of the gifted* (3rd ed., pp. 302–309). New York: Irvington.

Barth, R. (1979). Home-based reinforcement of school behavior: A review and analysis. *Review of Educational Research, 49,* 436–458.

Baum, S. (1994). Meeting the needs of gifted/learning disabled students. *Journal of Secondary Gifted Education, 5*(3), 6–22.

Beach, M. (1988). Family relationships of gifted adolescents: Strong or stressed? *Roeper Review, 10,* 169–172.

Bloom, B. S. (Ed.). (1985). *Developing talent in young people.* New York: Ballantine.

Bowen, M. (1978). *Family therapy in clinical practice.* New York: Aronson.

Brounstein, P. J., Holahan, W., & Dreyden J. (1991). Change in self-concept and attributional styles among academically-gifted adolescents. *Journal of Applied Social Psychology, 21*(3), 198–218.

Callahan, C. M. (1982). Parents of the gifted and talented child. *Journal for the Education of the Gifted, 4,* 247–258.

Clasen, D. R., & Clasen, R. E. (1995). Underachievement of highly able students and the peer society. *Gifted and Talented International, 10,* 67–76.

Colangelo, N. (1988). Families of gifted children: The next ten years. *Roeper Review, 11,* 16–18.

Colangelo, N., & Brower, P. (1987). Labeling gifted youngsters: Long term impact on families. *Gifted Child Quarterly, 31,* 75–78.

Coleman, L. (1985). *Schooling the gifted.* Menlo Park, CA: Addison Wesley.

Cornell, D. G. (1983a). The family's view of the gifted child. In B. M. Shore, F. Gagné, S. Larivee, R. H. Tali, & R. E. Tremblay (Eds.), *Proceedings of the Fourth World Conference on Gifted Education: Face to face with giftedness* (pp. 39–50). New York: Trillium Press.

Cornell, D. G. (1983b). Gifted children: The impact of positive labeling on the family system. *American Journal of Orthopsychiatry, 53,* 322–334.

Cornell, D. G., & Grossberg, I. N. (1987). Family environment and personality adjustment in gifted program children. *Gifted Child Quarterly, 31,* 59–64.

Csikszentmihalyi, M., Rathunde, K., & Whalen, S. (1993). *Talented teenagers: The roots of success and failure.* New York: Cambridge University Press.

Culross, R. R., & Jenkins-Friedman, R. (1988). On coping and defending: Applying Burner's personal growth principles to working with gifted/talented students. *Gifted Child Quarterly, 32,* 261–266.

Dettmann, D. F., & Colangelo, N. (1980). A functional model for counseling parents of gifted students. *Gifted Child Quarterly, 24*(4), 158–161.

Doherty, W. J. (1998, March/April). From hedgehog to fox: Retooling for an age of complexity. *Family Therapy Networker, 22*(2), 50–57.

Dunst, C. J., & Paget, K. D. (1991). Parent–professional partnerships and family empowerment. In M. J. Fine (Ed.), *Collaboration with parents of exceptional children* (pp. 25–44). Brandon, VT: Clinical Psychology.

Dunst, C. J., & Trivette, C. M. (1987). Enabling and empowering families: Conceptual and intervention issues. *School Psychology Review, 16,* 443–456.

Dunst, C. J., Trivette, C. M., & Deal, A. (1988). *Enabling and empowering families: Principles and guidelines for practice.* Cambridge, MA: Brookline Books.

Egan, G. (1984). People in systems: A comprehensive model for psychosocial education and training. In D. Larson (Ed.), *Teaching psychological skills: Models for giving psychology away* (pp. 21–43). Monterey, CA: Brooks/Cole.

Emerick, L. (1992). Academic underachievement among the gifted: Students' perceptions of factors that reverse the pattern. *Gifted Child Quarterly, 36*(3), 140–146.

Feldman, D. H., & Goldsmith, L. T. (1986). *Nature's gambit.* New York: Basic Books.

Fine, M. J. (1977). Facilitating parent–child relationships. *Gifted Child Quarterly, 21,* 487–500.

Fine, M. J. (1984). Integrating structural and strategic components in school-based intervention: Some cautions for consultants. *Techniques: A Journal for Remedial Education and Counseling, 1,* 44–51.

Fine, M. J. (1990). Facilitating home–school relationships: A family-oriented approach to collaborative consultation. *Journal of Educational and Psychological Consultation, 1*(2), 169–187.

Fine, M. J. (1991). The handicapped child and the family: Implications for professionals. In M. J. Fine (Ed.), *Collaboration with parents of exceptional children* (pp. 3–24). Brandon, VT: Clinical Psychology.

Fine, M. J., & Holt, P. (1983). Intervening with school problems: A family systems perspective. *Psychology in the Schools, 20,* 59–66.

Fine, M. J., & Pitts, R. (1980). Intervening with underachieving gifted children: Rationales and strategies. *Gifted Child Quarterly, 24,* 51–55.

Fish, M. (1991). Exceptional children in nontraditional families. In M. J. Fine (Ed.), *Collaboration with parents of exceptional children* (pp. 45–60). Brandon, VT: Clinical Psychology.

Ford, D. Y. (1996). *Reversing underachievement among gifted black students: Promising practices and programs.* New York: Teachers College Press.

Frey, J., & Wendorf, D. J. (1985). Families of gifted children. In L. L'Abate (Ed.), *The handbook of family psychology and therapy* (pp. 781–809). Homewood, IL: Dorsey Press.

Frey, K. S., Greenberg, M. T., & Fewell, R. R. (1989). Stress and coping among parents of handicapped children: A multidimensional approach. *American Journal on Mental Retardation, 94*(3), 240–249.

Friedman, R. C. (1994). Upstream helping for low-income families of gifted students: Challenges and opportunities. *Journal of Educational and Psychological Consultation, 5*(4), 321–338.

Friedman, R. C., & Gallagher, T. J. (1991). The family with a gifted child. In M. J. Fine (Ed.), *Collaboration with parents of exceptional children* (pp. 257–273). Brandon, VT: Clinical Psychology.

Gardner, H. (1983). *Frames of mind: The theory of multiple intelligences.* New York: Basic Books.

Gelbrich, J. A., & Kare, E. K. (1989). The effects of single parenthood on school achievement in a gifted school population. *Gifted Child Quarterly, 33*(3), 115–117.

Getzels, J., & Jackson, P. (1962). *Creativity and intelligence.* New York: Wiley.

Goertzel, M. G., Goertzel, V., & Goertzel, T. G. (1978). *Three hundred eminent personalities.* Boston: Little, Brown.

Goldsmith, L. T. (in press). Tracking trajectories of talent. In R. C. Friedman & B. M. Shone (Eds.) *Talents within: Cognitive and affective development.* Washington, DC: American Psychological Association.

Greenberg, M. S., & Westcott, D. R. (1983). Indebtedness as a mediator of reactions to aid. In J. D. Fisher, A. Nadler, & B. M. DePaulo (Eds.), *New directions in helping* (Vol. 1, pp. 45–70). New York: Academic Press.

Grenier, M. E. (1985). Gifted children and other siblings. *Gifted Child Quarterly, 29,* 164–167.

Grinder, R. E. (1985). The gifted in our midst: By their divine deeds, neuroses and test scores we have known them. In F. D. Horowitz & M. O'Brien (Eds.), *The gifted and talented: Developmental perspectives* (pp. 5–35). Washington, DC: American Psychological Association.

Hackney, H. (1981). The gifted child, the family, and the school. *Gifted Child Quarterly, 25*(2), 51–62.

Haynes, N. M., Comer, J. P., & Hamilton-Lee, M. (1989). School climate enhancement through parental involvement. *Journal of School Psychology, 27,* 87–90.

Hobbs, N. (1975). *The futures of children: Categories, labels and their consequences.* San Francisco: Jossey-Bass.

Hunsaker, S. L. (1994). Adjustments to traditional procedures for identifying underserved students: Successes and failures. *Exceptional Children, 61,* 72–76.

Janos, P. M., & Robinson, N. M. (1985). Psychosocial development in intellectually gifted children. In F. D. Horowitz & M. O'Brien (Eds.), *The gifted and talented: Developmental perspectives* (pp. 149–195). Washington, DC: American Psychological Association.

Jenkins-Friedman, R. (1992). Families of gifted children and youth. In M. J. Fine & C. Carlsen (Eds.), *The handbook of family–school intervention: A systems perspective* (pp. 175–187). Boston: Allyn & Bacon.

Jenkins-Friedman, R., & Murphy, D. L. (1988). The Mary Poppins effect: Relationships between gifted students' self concept and adjustment. *Roeper Review, 11*(1), 26–30.

Karnes, M. B., & Shwedel, A. (1987). Differences in attitudes and practices between fathers of young gifted and fathers of young non-gifted children: A pilot study. *Gifted Child Quarterly, 31*(2), 79–82.

Keirouz, K. S. (1990). Concerns of parents of gifted children: A research review. *Gifted Child Quarterly, 34*(2), 56–63.

Kerr, M. E., & Bowen, M. (1988). *Family evaluation.* New York: Norton.

Kulieke, M. J., & Olszewski-Kubilius, P. (1989). The influence of family values and climate on the development of talent. In J. L. VanTassel-Baska & P. Olszewski-Kubiliuss (Eds.), *Patterns of influence on gifted learners: The home, the self, and the school* (pp. 140–159). New York: Teachers College Press.

List, K., & Renzulli, J. S. (1991). Creative women's developmental patterns through age thirty-five. *Gifted Education International, 7,* 114–122.

Loven, M. D. (1978). Four alternative approaches to the family/school liaison role. *Psychology in the Schools, 15,* 553–559.

Mathews, F. N. (1981). Effective communication with parents of the gifted and talented: Some suggestions for improvement. *Journal for the Education of the Gifted, 4*(3), 207–210.

Mathews, F. N., West, J. D., & Hosie, T. W. (1986). Understanding families of academically gifted children. *Roeper Review, 9*(1), 40–42.

McGoldrick, M., Giordano, J., & Pearce, J. K. (Eds.). (1996). *Ethnicity and family therapy* (2nd ed.). New York: Guilford Press.

Moon, S. M., Jurich, J. A., & Feldhusen, J. F. (1998). Families of gifted children: Cradles of development. In R. C. Friedman & K. B. Rogers (Eds.), *Talent in context: Historical and social perspectives on giftedness.* Washington, DC: American Psychological Association.

Morrow, W. R., & Wilson, R. C. (1964). Family relations of bright high-achieving and under-achieving high school boys. *Child Development, 35,* 1041–1049.

Nielsen, M. E., & Higgins, D. (1989, November). *The Mirror Model for involving parents of gifted children.* Paper presented at the annual meeting of the National Association for Gifted Children, Cincinnati, OH.

Nielsen, M. E., Higgins, D., Wilkinson, S. C., & Webb, K. W. (1994). Helping twice-exceptional students to succeed in high school. *Journal of Secondary Gifted Education, 5*(3), 35–39.

Peterson, D. C. (1977). The heterogeneously gifted family. *Gifted Child Quarterly, 21*(3), 396–411.

Petr, C. G. (1998). *Social work with children and their families: Pragmatic foundations.* New York: Oxford University Press.

Plomin, R. (1997). Genetics and intelligence. In N. Colangelo & G. A. Davis (Eds.), *Handbook of gifted education* (pp. 67–74). Needham Heights, MA: Allyn & Bacon.

Plucker, J. A. (1996). Gifted Asian-American students: Identification, curricular, and counseling concerns. *Journal for the Education of the Gifted, 19*(3), 314–343.

Prom-Jackson, S., Johnson, S. T., & Wallace, M. B. (1987). Home environment, talented minority students, and school achievement. *Journal of Negro Education, 56*(1), 111–121.

Robinson, N. M., & Noble, K. D. (1991). Social–emotional development and adjustment of gifted children. In M. C. Wang, M. C. Reynolds, & H. J. Walberg (Eds.), *Handbook of special education* (Vol. 4, pp. 57–76). Oxford: Pergamon Press.

Ross, R. (1979). A program model for altering children's consciousness. *Gifted Child Quarterly, 23*(11), 109–117.

Saleebey, D. (1996, May). The strengths perspective in social work practice: Extensions and cautions. *Social Work, 41*(3), 296–305.

Schatz, E. M., & Sandborn, M. P. (1980). Some pragmatics of parent consultation. *Roeper Review, 3*(1), 40–43.

Skinner, B. F. (1978). The ethics of helping people. In L. Wispe (Ed.), *Sympathy, altruism and helping behavior* (pp. 249–262). New York: Academic Press.

Simonton, D. K. (in press). Gifted child, genius adult: Three life span developmental perspectives. In R. C. Friedman & K. B. Rogers (Eds.), *Talent in context: Historical and social perspectives on giftedness.* Washington, DC: American Psychological Association.

Steinberg, L. (1996). *Beyond the classroom.* New York: Simon & Schuster.

Strom, R., Strom, S., Strom, P., & Collinsworth, P. (1994). Parent competence in families with gifted children. *Journal for the Education of the Gifted, 18*(1), 29–54.

Sulloway, F. J. (1990). *Orthodoxy and innovation in science: The role of the family.* Unpublished manuscript, Harvard University, Cambridge, MA.

Treffinger, D. J., & Fine, M. J. (1979). When there's a problem in school. *G/C/T, 10,* 3–6.

VanTassel-Baska, J. L. (1989). The role of the family in the success of disadvantaged gifted learners. *Journal for the Education of the Gifted, 13*(1), 22–36.

VanTassel-Baska, J. L., & Olszewski-Kubilius, P. (Eds.). (1989). *Patterns of influence on gifted learners: The home, the self, and the school.* New York: Teachers College Press.

VanTassel-Baska, J. L., Patton, J. M., & Prillaman, D. (1991). *Gifted youth at risk: A report of a national study.* Reston, VA: Council for Exceptional Children.

Walberg, H. J. (1984). Families as partners in educational productivity. *Phi Delta Kappan, 65,* 397–400.

Walter, J. L., & Peller, J. E. (1992). *Becoming solution-focused in brief therapy.* New York: Brunner Mazel.

Walters, J., & Gardner, H. (1986). The crystallizing experience: Discovering an intellectual gift. In R. J. Sternberg & J. E. Davidson (Eds.), *Conceptions of giftedness* (pp. 306–311). New York: Cambridge University Press.

Weick, A. (1986, November). The philosophical context of a health model of social work. *Social Casework: The Journal of Contemporary Social Work,* pp. 551–559.

Wendorf, D. J., & Frey, J. (1985). Family therapy with the intellectually gifted. *The American Journal of Family Therapy, 13*(1), 31–38.

Wendt , R. N., & Zake, J. (1984). Family systems theory and school psychology: Implications for training and practice. *Psychology in the Schools, 21,* 204–210.

Wolf, J. S., & Stephens, T. M. (1984). Training models for parents of the gifted. *Journal for the Education of the Gifted, 5*(4), 247–258.

Working with Families of Children with Attention-Deficit/Hyperactivity Disorder

17

Steven E. Colson and Mary Dwyer Brandt

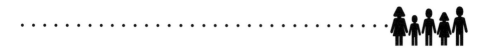

E xcept for the ubiquitous term *inclusion,* there currently is no bigger buzzword in the field of special education than *attention-deficit/hyperactivity disorder* (ADHD). From the covers of newstand magazines to entire issues of professional journals, from cartoons to graduate training courses, from tabloid television shows to federally funded research projects, ADHD is everywhere. If learning disabilities was the trendy topic of the 1970s and 1980s, certainly ADHD has become its successor in the 1990s and into the next century.

It has been difficult for educators, psychologists, and other professionals to keep current about ADHD—as well as for parents attempting to sort out competing information. Professionals spend considerable time explaining to parents the specifics of a student's learning and behavior differences along with setting goals and objectives aimed at improving performance. But professionals cannot stay on top of the explosion of new information on this topic, and parents of children with ADHD are sometimes put in the awkward position of educating the educators, with updates of information. Educators, in turn, are having to sort out research-based assessment techniques and intervention strategies from more controversial therapies.

Physicians are sworn to "first, do no harm." Educators would do well to adopt this professional standard and the best way to start is by becoming knowledgeable about the various types of disabilities. Increasingly, many children with special needs are being served in both the general education and the special education classroom. Major progress has been made in the ability to determine the etiology of many disorders, and associated research has provided insights into multidisciplinary treatments and interventions (Tyler & Colson, 1994). Educators and related service professionals need current data-supported information to assist them in the clinical judgments they make every day assessing, planning, and delivering instruction to students with ADHD.

This chapter will provide a brief update of ADHD along with suggestions for working collaboratively with parents during the assessment and intervention stages.

A Brief History of ADHD

Many professionals think ADHD was only recently "discovered." In fact, British neurologist George Still has been credited with authoring the first scientific paper at the turn of the century. He described a group of children who were defiant, resistive to discipline, overly emotional, inattentive, and showing little inhibitory volition (Still, 1902). Adhering to popular philosophic views of the times, he pronounced these children as suffering from a "defect in moral control" (p. 1009). Although this conception of those characteristics would hardly be respected today, Still and subsequent researchers did begin to take data on what constituted abnormal behaviors in children. Still presumed the cause was some underlying neurological deficit, a view strongly supported today by modern imaging devices that chart differences in brain activity.

After an encephalitis epidemic in North America in 1917–18, many researchers (Ebaugh, 1923; Hohman, 1922; Styker, 1925) began seeing a group of surviving children who had impairments in attention, regulation of activity, and impulse control. This additional information was helpful in building neurological theories of differences after acquired brain injury. At that time researchers made little attempt to differentiate between types of disabilities, such as learning disabilities or mental retardation. Most professionals were pessimistic in their prognosis for these children, although they did have some success with early attempts at behavior modification and increased supervision (Bender, 1942).

Soon, the term *Brain Damage Syndrome* began appearing, which had its origin in circular logic. If children with evidence of acquired brain trauma experienced subsequent problems with attention, impulsivity, and hyperactivity, then students with those same characteristics without formal documentation of etiology were presumed to have had some type of brain insult. Minimal brain damage soon metamorphosed into *minimal brain dysfunction,* an early term for learning disabilities. Early pioneers in the field of learning disabilities took successful strategies used in treating children with mental retardation and championed them for use with students with the same learning and behavioral differences who did not share that diagnosis.

During the 1950s these terms indicating brain differences aroused considerable criticism within the profession. Chess (1960) was instrumental in calling for an emphasis on hyperactivity and in developing objective diagnostic criteria. She was also credited with helping to shift the blame away from parents for this overactivity in their children. In the second edition of the *Diagnostic and Statistical Manual* (DSM) of the American Psychiatric Association (APA) (1968), professionals began using the term "Hyperkinetic Reaction to Childhood" to describe children with unusual levels of activity.

In the 1970s the emphasis switched from hyperactivity to attention deficits. Over 2,000 studies were published during the 1970s including the first scholarly review of the literature (Ross & Ross, 1976). Other significant advances included new models of attention deficit (Douglas, 1972), the rise of medication therapy, and the passage of the Education for All Handicapped Children Act (1975) which mandated special education services for children with a variety of disabilities. The 1970s ended with the publication of the third edition of the DSM (APA, 1980) in which researchers began differentiating *Attention Deficit Disorder with Hyperactivity* from inattention without the activity component, called *Attention Deficit Disorder without Hyperactivity*.

In 1987 the DSM was again revised and Attention Deficit Disorder without Hyperactivity was removed for it vagueness. At the same time an attempt was made to quantify the characteristics of attention-deficit disorder by using behavior rating scales in large clinical trials. The term *Attention-Deficit/ Hyperactivity Disorder* was used for the first time. Another term *Undifferentiated Attention-Deficit Disorder* was added, but with no formal criteria for diagnosis.

As parents of children with ADHD became more aware of the Education for All Handicapped Children Act (1975), now called the Individuals with Disabilities Education Act (IDEA, 1990; reauthorized in 1997), they asked for special services under this legislation. Often parents were told that ADHD in and of itself was not a disability unless a child also qualified under one of the existing educational categories. For example, parents were told if a child had ADHD *and* a learning disability, he could receive services under IDEA. But, if the child had *only* ADHD, he could not receive special services.

In 1991 the Department of Education released a "Clarification Policy To Address the Needs of Children with Attention Deficit Disorders within General and Special Education." The memo affirmed that students with ADHD are protected under IDEA. It also stated that if a child with ADHD is found ineligible for special education and related services under IDEA, he may still be protected under Section 504 of the Rehabilitation Act (1973). It concluded that special and general educators needed to work together in the provision of services and accommodations for children with ADHD.

The DSM had its most recent revision in 1994. The current set of diagnostic criteria is the most thorough to date, separating for the first time issues with attention from those of impulsivity and hyperactivity. Table 17.1 lists the diagnostic criteria for the three types of ADHD: ADHD–Predominantly Inattentive Type, ADHD–Predominantly Hyperactive/Impulsive Type, and ADHD– Combined Type. Although this set of diagnostic criteria is not embedded in IDEA, it is the most commonly used set of data-based criteria. School

Table 17.1

Criteria for ADHD

A. Either (1) or (2)

(1) six (or more) of the following symptoms of inattention have persisted for at least 6 months to a degree that is maladaptive and inconsistent with developmental level:

   (a) often fails to give close attention to details or makes careless mistakes in schoolwork, work, or other activities

   (b) often has difficulty sustaining attention in tasks or play activities

   (c) often does not seem to listen when spoken to directly

   (d) often does not follow through on instructions and fails to finish schoolwork, chores, or duties in the workplace (not due to oppositional behavior or failure to understand instructions)

   (e) often has difficulty organizing tasks and activities

   (f) often avoids, dislikes, or is reluctant to engage in tasks that require sustained mental effort (such as schoolwork or homework)

   (g) often loses things necessary for tasks or activities (e.g., toys, school assignments, pencils, books, or tools)

   (h) is often easily distracted by extraneous stimuli

   (i) is often forgetful in daily activities

(2) six (or more) of the following symptoms of hyperactivity–impulsivity have persisted for at least 6 months to a degree that is maladaptive and inconsistent with developmental level:

Hyperactivity

   (a) often fidgets with hands or feet or squirms in seat

   (b) often leaves seat in classroom or in other situations in which remaining seated is expected

   (c) often runs about or climbs excessively in situations in which it is inappropriate (in adolescents or adults, may be limited to subjective feelings of restlessness)

   (d) often has difficulty playing or engaging in leisure activities quietly

   (e) is often "on the go" or often acts as if "driven by a motor"

Impulsivity

   (f) often talks excessively

   (g) often blurts out answers before the questions have been completed

   (h) often has difficulty awaiting turns

   (i) often interrupts or intrudes on others (e.g., butts into conversations or games)

Table 17.1 *Continued*

B. Some hyperactive–impulsive or inattentive symptoms that caused impairment were present before age 7 years.

C. Some impairment from the symptoms is present in two or more settings (e.g., at school [or work] and at home).

D. There must be clear evidence of clinically significant impairment in social, academic, or occupational functional settings.

E. The symptoms do not occur exclusively during the course of a Pervasive Developmental Disorder, Schizophrenia, or other Psychotic Disorder and are not better accounted for by another mental disorder (e.g., Mood Disorder, Anxiety Disorder, Dissociative Disorder, or a Personality Disorder).

Code based on type:

314.01 Attention-Deficit/Hyperactivity Disorder, Combined Type: if both Criteria A1 and A2 are met for the past 6 months.

314.00 Attention-Deficit/Hyperactivity Disorder, Predominantly Inattentive Type: if Criterion A1 is met but Criterion A2 is not met for the past 6 months.

314.01 Attention-Deficit/Hyperactivity Disorder, Predominantly Hyperactive-Impulsive Type: if Criterion A2 is met but A1 is not met for the past 6 months.

Coding note: For individuals (especially adolescents and adults) who currently have symptoms that no longer meet full criteria, "In Partial Remission" should be specified.

From *Diagnostic and Statistical Manual of Mental Disorders* (4th ed.), by American Psychiatric Association, 1994, Washington, DC: Author. Copyright 1994 by American Psychiatric Association.

diagnostic team members would be wise to consult the information from this respected professional set of criteria for their decision making (see Table 17.1).

Helping Parents Understand the Assessment of ADHD

Parents have received conflicting messages about who should conduct an evaluation for ADHD. There are several options available but most parents will feel assured of a comprehensive evaluation when a multidisciplinary team is helping reach that decision. This team could be comprised of a developmental pediatrician, a behavioral psychologist, a special educator, and a social worker. Some parents, especially in rural areas, may not have that constellation of professionals available. Even in larger population centers it is rare to find a practice where all of these professionals meet collaboratively to share information before determining a diagnosis.

A single professional making the diagnosis may not take into account all of the important information. For example, a physician may make a diagnosis of ADHD after only a brief parent interview, never asking school personnel for behavior rating scales and a detailed description of the child during learning activities. Likewise, a brief parent interview in the physician's office may not elicit significant family stressors, which may be contributing factors. This, of course, sets up dissonance between sets of professionals and often leads parents to the erroneous conclusion that a diagnosis from a physician will automatically result in special education services under IDEA or general education modifications under a 504 Plan.

Regardless of the parents' access to, or willingness to pursue, medical evaluations, public schools have the obligation under IDEA and Section 504 of the Rehabilitation Act to perform a multidisciplinary evaluation for any student suspected of having a disability. Since ADHD is considered a disability, at least one member of the school diagnostic team must be knowledgeable about ADHD. This requirement, too, has been clarified by written remarks from the Department of Education. Of course, a parent may contest the determination made by the school team.

Parents and educators need to understand the difference between the terms *diagnosis* and *educational classification*. Physicians, clinical psychologists, and other mental health professionals use the DSM and other sources of information to determine diagnoses of mental conditions such as anxiety, depression, Tourette syndrome, and bipolar disorder. Diagnosis is a medical term and does not, in itself, determine whether a student is eligible for special education services. A medical diagnosis can lead the school assessment team to look more closely at the student's performance at school and, likewise, information from the school team can facilitate a more accurate diagnosis by the physician or psychologist.

Regardless of whether a student has a medical or psychological diagnosis, the school team must still assess the educational impact of the student's differences in behavior and learning. As mentioned earlier, diagnosis does not prove the need for special services. First, school assessment teams must look for the presence of the salient characteristics of the disability. This is where the DSM becomes particularly helpful in the question of ADHD. If the student exhibits the salient characteristics, as well as meeting all the other guidelines in the DSM (i.e., early onset, consideration of the student's developmental status), then the team must decide if these characteristics are having an adverse impact on the student's educational performance. If the team finds a significant adverse impact, then the student could qualify for special services under IDEA or Section 504. This determination of the student's eligibility must precede development of the individual education plan under IDEA or a plan under Section 504. The individual plan then leads to a discussion of what educational environment(s) will best suit the student. Parents may need help in understanding the complex and sometimes confusing nature of the evaluation components of both IDEA and Section 504.

Helping Families in the Collaborative Intervention Process Between Home and School

Many times the classroom teacher is the first professional that parents seek out for information about ADHD. Teachers, often collaborating with other professionals such as outside psychologists and pediatricians, provide information about the child's ongoing progress in both academics and social or emotional interactions. Effective teachers primarily need current information regarding intervention during the school day. To facilitate a home-based behavioral plan, they need reliable information about the impact of a child with ADHD on the entire family. The remainder of this chapter will describe typical family dilemmas in relating to these children as well as suggestions for creating a more functional family unit. The text will also delineate collaborative roles of parents, educators, and other professionals in the ADHD school-based and home-based intervention process.

Adjustment to ADHD, as with other disabilities, is a family affair. Certainly parents, but also the extended family including grandparents and siblings, share the experiences of denial, anger, bargaining, and acceptance originally researched and identified by Kubler-Ross (1969) in her work on loss, grief, and adjustment. In interactions with family, the child with ADHD characteristically shows inconsistent behaviors, failure to adopt and follow routines, frequent disagreement with siblings, and unpredictable behavior during transition times. Visits from grandparents or trips to friends and relatives can be stressful for the whole family, painfully exacerbating the child's inability to follow rules, repeat expected protocol, or calm down and listen.

What should families do when the needs of the child begin to supersede all other family interactions and serve as the driving force in family communication, recreational activities, home responsibilities, and even employment decisions? Frequently families attempting to reign in their out-of-control child superimpose such highly structured routines that family dynamics become rigid. The child with ADHD is rendered helpless, while the rest of the family becomes resentful, isolated, or both (Bender, 1997).

The genetic component of ADHD often adds to the parenting dilemma (Barkley, 1990). When one or both parents are also affected, the task of keeping the home balanced becomes even more tedious. Roles taken by the unaffected parent may expand to encompass management of not only the child but also the spouse. Since patience, consistency, and planning are not traits usually found in adults with ADHD, parenting can easily become a psychodrama with parents playing interchanging roles of persecutor or rescuer and the child chronically maintaining the stance of "victim."

Helping the Child Develop a Positive Sense of Self

Due to the hereditary nature of ADHD, many adults can trace generational connections to relatives who had problems in school, on the job, or in relationships. Many times contemporary parents working with their own children with ADHD are reliving the experiences they themselves had in childhood. Years of contending with their own seemingly endless series of failures and sense of incompetence resulted in internalization of a low self-concept and continued predisposition toward failure.

Children with ADHD, who are most in need of consistency, positive behavior management, and patience may experience a continuous cycle of negative disequilibrium because parents are struggling with the same issues as their affected offspring.

Hallowell (1993) as well as Nadeau (1995) supported reframing the issue of ADHD as familial rather than individual. In a solution-focused approach, ownership is shared by all family members and blame is not assigned. The family can apply constructive problem-solving techniques and learn to recognize and celebrate the positive attributes of the child with ADHD. Parents as well as children need opportunities to feel a sense of ownership and responsibility. When the family can work as a unit to identify and prioritize problem areas, decide on a plan with several options, and carry out the plan through a series of steps that can be revised and retried, their sense of competence is promoted.

Brooks (1997) refers to this building of self-concept in his work on fostering self-esteem using Attribution Theory. He stated,

> Children with positive self-esteem also believe that it is within their power to change an unsuccessful situation if they try harder. These children feel that failures are experiences from which they can learn. On the other hand children with low self-esteem are likely to attribute failure to an unchangeable inner lack of ability. (p. 3)

Professionals give special attention to self-esteem due to its residual nature and detrimental effects into adulthood. The literature abounds with suggestions for empowerment, ways to support a sense of belonging and value, and methods to demonstrate appreciation and encouragement (Nelsen, 1996). Studies of resilience have found that successful adults with ADHD have all had a significant charismatic role model in their lives from whom they gathered strength and support (Cordoni, 1996).

Though the professional can find a plethora of suggestions for building self-esteem, putting words into action is far more difficult. Parents can empathize easily with a child trying to do the right thing but not with a child who chronically acts in ways which elicit disappointment, frustration, and noncompliance.

Children with ADHD are almost continuously bombarded with messages such as "Why can't you try harder?" "You could do better if you wanted to," "What has gotten into you?" "You are so irresponsible," and "Why can't you be like your sister?" Messages like this are internalized by the child and frequently result in a poor self-image since these children with ADHD are masters at identifying their deficits. These children continuously encounter a hostile environment of insurmountable tasks and perceive the significant people in their lives as nonsupportive and uncaring. Children with ADHD desperately need someone to believe in them and generate hope that their lives will get better.

Feelings of competence result from a systematic process of helping the child recognize and develop her personal strengths. Parents should be encouraged to become advocates for their child by learning how ADHD manifests itself at home, at school, with peers, and within the family system. Learning to stop, look, listen, and then respond instead of reacting with immediate blame or anger can eliminate potential threats to a child's self-concept. Children need to be seen as in trouble, not the cause of trouble (Barkley, 1990).

In order for a child to believe in himself, he must first experience his parents' belief in him. An initial step in this process is for the parents to see him as a child first, separate from his behavior and disability. Catching a child being good instead of only responding to negative behaviors increases the probability of appropriate behaviors in the future. Giving children encouragement and recognition when they meet expectations provides them with the impetus for repeating appropriate actions. Ridicule and sarcasm should never be used since this type of metalinguistic communication is often misunderstood or misinterpreted by the child with ADHD.

Creating a Healthy Family System

What can be done to generate realistic hope? Because the entire family is affected, it is imperative for parents to work together to cope with ADHD issues. Techniques that work to promote harmony between both parents is a crucial first step. Consistency, commitment, creativity, and communication are necessary concepts for parents to understand and use in strengthening family relationships.

Everyone needs to feel acceptance at some level and communication provides it. If a concern or problem does not get resolved during initial attempts, then parents should keep working until a mutually satisfying solution is reached. Family members should attempt to keep conversations on a feeling level and personalized. Words that imply blame will only be talk stoppers; those that express feelings will generate empathy. Parents should tell each other about their individual needs. For example, complaining to your spouse about being tired will not effectively relay the message that you need to have a change of pace or a couple of hours by yourself. Directly identifying needs will help them to be met.

Parents need to take time to build a strong spousal relationship. Not respecting boundaries can cause confusion for children who then may play husband or wife roles. Spouses need time alone without the children. This may not happen with the spontaneity of prior dating days but the creativity does not have to be wasted. For example, taking turns planning a day trip, or scheduling a Sunday brunch instead of a Saturday night movie, as well as remembering and exploring what was attractive to one another before the children are ways to solidify healthy marital relationships.

A way to get over feeling guilty about leaving the children is to reframe the absence in the context of children needing a break from parents as well. Holding family meetings so everyone can feel a sense of sharing can be an effective tool. Parents need to take turns performing different parts of the daily routine. If dad always drives to karate while mom stays at home and cooks, then switching jobs could give each parent a perspective on the other's traditional role. Joining outside support groups comprised of other parents of children with ADHD can give each parent a resource for ideas in addition to the spouse. Support groups and resources for families who have a child with ADHD are listed in Table 17.2.

Managing behavior is a key intervention strategy in which parents need direct training. Often the child with ADHD is unsuccessful in pursuits that are easy for most individuals. By teaching the child these seemingly simple routines, parents can begin to change behavior patterns that have been chronically annoying and at times extremely disruptive. Parents may have already experienced their non-ADHD children learning simple routines either by observation or with only minimal instruction. They should realize that children with ADHD have difficulty learning in this way. Direct instruction is frequently not just desirable, but absolutely necessary.

A child with ADHD is better able to comply with a request such as "clean your room" if the parent breaks the larger task into a sequence of smaller ones, such as the following:

▶ **Step 1:** Pick up clothing and trash off the floor.

▶ **Step 2:** Put dirty clothes in hamper. Hang up clean clothes in closet or put them in a drawer.

▶ **Step 3:** Put trash in a large garbage bag. Empty wastebasket into trash bag.

▶ **Step 4:** Put anything remaining on the floor in the proper place or container (e.g., toys in toybox, books on shelves, games and crafts in bins or on shelves).

A caveat is attached to any technique that is used to enhance the child's attention to household tasks and rules. This process is educational in nature

Table 17.2
Parent Support and Resources Related to ADHD

Attention Deficit Disorder Association (ADDA)
80913 Ireland Way
Aurora, CO 80016
313-690-7548

Attention Deficit Information Network (AD-IN)
P.O. Box 790
Plymouth, MA 02360
508-747-5180

A.D.D. Warehouse (a clearinghouse for books and videos)
300 NW 70th Avenue
Plantation, FL 33317
800-233-9273

Center for Hyperactive Children Information, Inc. (CHCI)
P.O. Box 66272
Washington, DC 20035
703-415-1090

Children and Adults with Attention Deficit Disorder (CH.A.D.D.)
499 NW 70th Avenue
Suite 308
Plantation, FL 33317
305-587-3700
http://www.chadd.org

LD On-line
http://www.ldonline.org

Special Education Resources on the Internet (SERI)
http://www.hood.edu/seri/serihome.htm

Council for Exceptional Children
1920 Association Drive
Reston, VA 20191-1589
703-620-3660
http://www.cec.sped.org

and should be looked at as such. In an organizational process (such as room cleaning) the child must start with a finished product (clean room). Whether the finished product is initially achieved with the help of the parent or whether the parent chooses to prepare it in advance to avoid an adversarial encounter is not so important as the child's retaining the experience of it as a visualized positive image. Some children need to "see" the big picture in order to understand how the details fit. This kind of top–down processing is often overlooked in the traditional learning environment. Visualization is a powerful tool. The long-term goal of this approach is to enable a child with ADHD to be internally empowered rather than externally controlled.

Helping children increase their internal control and become their own agents of change addresses many of the core deficits identified as being present in children with ADHD. The meta-skills of organization, reflection, sequencing, and social intuition often are frequently missing in the child's repertoire and must be directly taught. Teaching children to observe their own behavior, reward themselves appropriately, solve problems, and guide themselves along a sequence of steps builds their sense of accomplishment and aids in developing a positive image. Additionally, these skills, once acquired, fill the universal need for self-determination while providing opportunities for children to be active participants in their own learning. All children have a desire to feel competent and should be afforded opportunities to demonstrate expertise. Children with ADHD often see themselves as drowning in an ocean of inadequacy. Parents can help these children make a difference within their own home and neighborhood environment in several ways, including the following:

• Parents can be good role models in the ways they solve problems. For instance, they can set a relaxed tone for this process by using humor in large doses and laughing at their own mistakes. Families can set aside time to talk not only about mistakes but also about how they felt while they were making them. They can also talk about what worked best in resolving situations (Nelsen, 1996).

• Parents can create a structure for making rules, setting consequences, and providing reminders. If a child with ADHD helps to make the rules, she will more likely remember them or accept help in being reminded. Family meetings can be used to make sure that a problem is viewed as a shared project, not a personal flaw.

• Parents can initiate a quality assurance committee. This type of buddy system encourages each person in the household to assume a nonjudgmental helping posture. It can promote family members' sense of individual ownership of their actions.

• Parents should take time to identify reinforcers that are truly motivating and are available contingently. These reinforcers also need to be rotated on a regular basis to keep motivation high. All consequences and response costs that occur because of unsatisfactory actions should be reasonable, related, and respectful.

• Parents should develop a realistic understanding of their child's strengths as well as weaknesses and should support the strengths by carefully structuring situations to make success achievable. Some specific suggestions include assigning special jobs, cultivating special interests, finding an extracurricular activity that builds confidence, playing with the child and watching for opportunities to teach her how to "socially engineer" a variety of situations that require peer interaction.

• Parents should remember that communication is a two-way street. They should take time to talk to the child at his level. This may mean sitting or kneeling to get to his eye level and using words that are age appropriate. Lecturing to a 6-, 7-, or 8-year-old will only produce poor compliance on the part of the child and frustration for the parent. Above all parents should keep expectations appropriate to the child's abilities and developmental stage. They should show the child they are really listening and model active listening principles like eye contact, reflective statements, and approachable body language.

• Parents should keep a sense of humor and playfulness. Often comic relief provides the atmosphere for approval in the face of mistakes. Parents should let the child know she is loved and accepted and that no one is perfect. They should compliment the child on her strengths. As one mother stated "My child is very courageous. She goes to school every day even though most of the time she is overwhelmed by the work and is lonely because she lacks friends." A child probably will not remember the math problems she got wrong but will remember the times she experienced an open, friendly, and sincerely encouraging adult.

Sibling Issues

Parents struggle with feelings of guilt about investing an inordinate amount of time and energy dealing with the child with ADHD including the daily struggle of meeting the child's special needs. These feelings of guilt often affect the other nondisabled children in the home. Though sibling harmony in families with both affected and nonaffected children has not received much study, the general trend of the existing research seems to indicate tolerance on the part of the brother or sister without ADHD (Johnson, 1996). This tolerance does not negate the fact that families with children with ADHD exhibit a higher degree of stress compared to those families that do not include children with ADHD. This stress appears to be primarily due to the magnification of common issues of rivalry between siblings.

Parents must make every effort to be firm but fair when handling routine disagreements.

Lack of privacy is frequently mentioned as problematic by siblings of children with ADHD. The sibling with ADHD may borrow things without asking, a behavior made worse by the item being lost, destroyed, or misused. Parents can help in this area by establishing boundaries both explicit and implicit. They can frequently bring up the topic of privacy using concrete examples modeled in the course of normal familial interchanges. They can also review, and even post, rules for borrowing and returning, knocking when doors are closed, and waiting to be asked to join an activity as opposed to barging in on a sibling's friends. In extreme cases parents have installed locks on bedroom doors or maximized the physical separation between bedrooms to maintain privacy.

Fighting and vying for attention are areas equally distressing for parents to handle. Many times parents rush in to settle disputes that were instigated by the sibling without ADHD assuming the child with ADHD was at fault. Parents can often significantly reduce the number of disagreements by initiating an "equal but not the same policy." Using this approach, parents communicate to each child that his needs will be met equally but possibly not in the same ways. Instead of allowing the same privilege or favor to all children in the family, they can provide different favors or privileges that are equally special to each child and that reflect individual preferences.

All children want to be loved, valued, and protected, and all parents have a genuine desire for harmony among family members. These goals are often derailed if a family member has attentional and impulse control issues. Parents must set firm but loving boundaries for all family members while taking into consideration each family member's individuality. Sibling issues will be ongoing and must be handled with consistent and proactive parental involvement.

Social Engineering

Children with inadequate attending skills typically have problems in multiple areas. They may not be able to perceive situations accurately, select appropriate responses, or execute the response even if they know what to do. Barkley (1990) stated, "It is not that ADHD children do not know what to do. They don't do what they know." Some children with ADHD can perceive, select, and execute appropriate responses but not frequently or consistently enough to be considered socially skillful.

Deficits in the area of social information processing often translate into problems at home and school with regard to completing work and relating appropriately with family members and friends. Some children with ADHD experience problems with shyness, and this internalized response can be just as socially isolating as an externalized behavior such as aggression. Either behavior carried to the extreme can result in some degree of peer rejection. As Bryan (1997) stated, "Bullies and victims both tend to be rejected by their peers."

Professionals make similar recommendations concerning the building of social competencies. One program (Sugai & Lewis, 1996) encourages the following sequence for parents:

• Name the skill or problem, for example: How would you greet another student? How would you initiate a conversation with a teacher if you have had a problem with homework?

• Identify the critical rules of the skill. Give the child a set of conditions that signal a routine to be used, for example: When you start to feel angry, stop what you are doing, take a deep breath, or walk away. A feeling becomes a signal to stop engaging in the problematic behavior and initiate new, more successful, behaviors.

• Set up simulated situations in which the child can try out the skill rules. The child can practice the acceptable behaviors and review the protocol. During this time parents can observe when the child needs to be prompted.

• Bridge the gap between contrived activities and the real world, where people are ultimately judged on their social abilities, by allowing for independent practice. Encourage the implementation of the skill outside of the formal instructional context by rewarding the child for observing the skill or practicing it within his natural environment.

It is important for parents to be aware of the normal development of a child's attentional skill level and therefore his capacity to meet the demands of a variety of situational circumstances. In general, management suggestions fall into the broad categories of initiating attention for an activity, sustaining activity for a task, listening, and remembering. Parents should take the time to plan ahead for situations in which their child has had problems in the past. A routine that provides consistency, structure, and predictability offers the best chance for success. One such plan is listed below and should happen well before the child and parents find themselves in the potentially problematic situation:

• Review the rules. Say or read them. Have the child repeat or read them.

• Contract with your child on a reward for appropriate behavior. Be sure the reward will be reinforcing and is available immediately or within a very short time.

• Have a consequence for noncompliance to the agreed upon rules. Be sure the child can restate the consequence in a way that shows she understands the boundaries of her behavior.

Other management suggestions that have proven to be helpful in parenting a child with ADHD include the list below. These can be useful tips for other caretakers such as grandparents and babysitters:

- Try to provide frequent and directive feedback as well as encouragement.
- Build success into tasks and give reinforcement frequently.
- Anticipate monotonous situations and alternate high- and low-interest activities.
- Make sure your child understands the expectations of the circumstance.
- Give short concrete directions of not over 10 words.
- Be willing to provide examples and repeat directions.
- Be sure the end of a task is discussed before the task begins. Room cleaning may seem like an endless endeavor, but breaking it into small steps—making the bed and picking clothes up off the floor—may encourage a child to move forward instead of procrastinating.
- Intersperse short independent activities with those requiring longer concentration and more guidance.
- Reward your child for listening.
- Give your child opportunities for leadership. Frequently praise the child during the process (e.g., "I liked the way you stayed right next to me while we shopped. I know you will continue to stay next to me while we are paying for our purchases").

The Continuum of Adjustment

Professionals in related disciplines can be helpful in guiding parents through the phases of adjusting to a child with ADHD in the family. Parents have to cope with the disparity of wanting an idealized "normal child" and the reality of parenting a child with special needs. These families often go through predictable but uneven stages of adjustment (Conoley & Sheridan, 1996).

A child with ADHD is often referred to as having no physical sequelae, unlike children with cerebral palsy, muscular dystrophy, and so forth. The parents suffer not only the pressure of having a child who is not quite able to keep up with peers but also one who very often misses the usual developmental or social milestones for no apparent reasons. Parents respond differently to the diagnosis. Some spend time denying that the problem is anything more than a "phase," while others begin shopping for cures or propose various actions in an attempt to change the reality of the diagnosis. Anger is not uncommon. It may however be demonstrated in different ways. Some parents may verbally lash out, blaming anyone and everyone for their unfortunate circumstance while others may withdraw and express intense feelings of guilt. In some instances feelings of shame, anxiety, and hopelessness can result in abnormal isolation during organized or routine social encounters. This type of behavior, though expected, should be addressed professionally if it persists. The final stages of acceptance and return to normalcy are often complicated by repeated negative experiences such as thoughtless actions by people who show little caring or understanding toward the child with ADHD or her caretakers.

Many, if not most, parents of children with ADHD require help to reach an acceptable level of closure and reconstruction. Mental health and education professionals can aid members of the child's immediate as well as extended family system to understand the child's progress with regard to customary developmental benchmarks. Counselors, social workers, and child development specialists can help family members maintain a balance between their hopes and reality. Healey (1996) illustrates this principle:

> No need exists to engage in speculation about what a 4 year old child will be able to do when she/he has reached the age of 21. While most parents want and have a need for professionals to be truthful as a prerequisite to be recognized as trustworthy persons with credibility, they do not need information that is bleak and replete with dismal prognosis. (p. 13)

Professionals need to be familiar with the grieving process and be ready to guide parents along the continuum of adjustment. A large part of the professionals' role is targeting those family members who are having difficulty coping with their own pain and frustration in relation to accepting their child's disability. This process is even more complicated for those families having children with less definitive disabilities such as attentional and impulse control disorders. But until parents of these children can cope effectively with their child's condition, they cannot fully direct their energies toward becoming active participants in the intervention process. The following suggestions are ways for professionals to encourage parents in their understanding of their child's disability, promote reasonable developmental expectations, and aid their assessment of their child's readiness for learning.

- Make sure any diagnosis or the results of any evaluation are relayed with compassion and hope.

- Take time to build rapport and ascertain what types of materials or means of communication would be most effective in disseminating information. Treat each family individually.

- Create an atmosphere of openness and encourage parents to express their true feelings.

- Anticipate questions and promote an atmosphere that encourages questioning.

- Have a list of ready resources within the community that parents can enlist.

- Spend considerable time repeating and responding to areas that are known to be problematic.

- Provide many types of encouragement and reinforcement to parents as they encounter possible roadblocks in their attempt to help their child obtain appropriate services.

- Do not be afraid to say you do not know and that you will try to find out. Showing some human frailty often goes far in establishing trust.

- Above all honor and normalize the parental adjustment process. Acceptance and adjustment happen concomitantly. Families going through these processes can provide professionals with knowledge and support from the home arena, and in turn professionals can offer assistance in meeting the diverse needs of families.

Andregg, Vergason, and Smith (1992), in their research on families, found that a frequent barrier to improving communication between parents and professionals is the lack of understanding professionals have of what it means to have a child with a disability. Their research indicated that parents of children with disabilities suffer a grief response similar to the response parents have when a child dies. In many ways parents of a child with a disability have lost a child they believed they had or the child they dreamed of having. Armstrong (1996) suggested that these feelings intensify each time they deal with an intervention system that is fragmented such as education and health care.

Families having children with mild or physically unobservable disabilities seem to have the opportunity for even more digressions in the grieving process than those having children with more severe disabilities. Following the initial diagnosis parents may become overly optimistic about the future, and they may begin to speculate in an unrealistic direction. Many families in fact deny the extent or permanence of the disability and tend to grieve repeatedly as their child fails to meet expected developmental and social milestones (Conoley & Sheridan, 1996). The relief associated with improvement is frequently marred when the family has to adjust and readjust to the child's unpredictable and uneven performance profile. Previous studies have measured the actual progress of families in terms of adjustment by evaluating the disabled child's role in the family. Other factors in family adjustment include religious beliefs, number of siblings, and whether or not the siblings are affected with ADHD (Thompson, 1996).

Other factors affect the degree to which the family is coping effectively with the inclusion of a child with special needs. These include the enmeshment or disengagement of the extended family system, the coping style of individual family members, and the occurrence of negative or positive events (e.g., school transitions, moves, job changes, birth of a sibling, and death of a family member or close friend). Well-functioning families are much quicker and better at adjusting to the child with ADHD and promoting that degree of mental health to the extended family members.

All families experience emotional swings and will go through periods of acceptance and celebration as well as times when they are angry with the child because she is not trying hard enough or is being irresponsible. Families may also experience anger toward their child's providers. They blame therapists, medical personnel, and educators when the child does not progress quickly or regresses. Reaching total acceptance of the child is difficult because the whole family must shift their expectations, hopes, and dreams. Parents have the responsibility of setting meaningful goals and advocating for their children to ensure adequate counseling, medical, and educational support. To do this well parents must actively seek collaboration with ancillary service providers.

Conclusion

Parenting any child with a disability can seem like an overwhelming task to many, if not most, parents. When a family has the benefit of current and reliable scientific information to help them decide appropriate treatment options, they more easily negotiate the special education maze. Throw into this scenario the plight of parents with children having ADHD. They are searching for assistance to sort out treatment approaches from the medical, psychological, and educational communities while trying not to put too much faith in unproven controversial therapies.

General and special educators, along with related service professionals, can significantly affect the lives of these parents and their children by providing them with accurate information. These professionals can also collaborate with their colleagues in other child-centered professions to plan and evaluate treatments. In many cases a classroom teacher will be the first professional to help guide parents through this process. It is imperative that all professionals working with children first educate themselves in order to empower parents to act as advocates for their children.

References

American Psychiatric Association. (1968). *Diagnostic and statistical manual of mental disorders* (2nd ed.). Washington, DC: Author.

American Psychiatric Association. (1980). *Diagnostic and statistical manual of mental disorders* (3rd ed.). Washington, DC: Author.

American Psychiatric Association. (1987). *Diagnostic and statistical manual of mental disorders* (3rd ed., rev.). Washington, DC: Author.

American Psychiatric Association. (1995). *Diagnostic and statistical manual of mental disorders* (4th ed.). Washington, DC: Author.

Andregg, M. L., Vergason, G. A., & Smith, M. C. (1992). A visual representation of the grief cycle for use by teachers with families of children with disabilities. *Remedial and Special Education, 13*(2), 17–23.

Armstrong, R. (1996). A holistic approach to attention deficit disorder. *Educational Leadership, 53*(5), 34–36.

Barkley, R. (1990). *Attention deficit hyperactivity disorder, a handbook for diagnosis and treatment.* New York: Guilford Press.

Bender, L. (1942). Postencephalitic behavior disorders in children. In J. B. Neal (Ed.), *Encephalitis: A clinical study.* New York: Grune & Stratton.

Bender, W. N. (1997). *Understanding ADHD: A practical guide for teachers and parents.* Englewood Cliffs, NJ: Prentice Hall.

Brooks, L. (1997). Fostering self-esteem in the child with learning disabilities: The search for islands of competence. *LDA Newsbriefs, 32*(1), 3–4.

Bryan, T. (1997). Assessing the personal and social status of students with learning disabilities. *Learning Disabilities Research and Practice, 12*(1), 63–76.

Chess, S. (1960). Diagnosis and treatment of the hyperactive child. *New York State Journal of Medicine, 60,* 2379–2385.

Conoley, J. C., & Sheridan, S. M. (1996). Pediatric traumatic brain injury: Challenges and intervention for families. *Journal of Learning Disabilities, 29*(6), 662–669.

Cordoni, B. (1996, November/December). A learning disability is only one part of a child. *LDA Newsbriefs,* pp. 3–6.

Douglas, V. I. (1972). Stop, look, and listen: The problem of sustained attention and impulse control in hyperactive and normal children. *Canadian Journal of Behavioral Science, 4,* 259–282.

Ebaugh, F. G. (1923). Neuropsychiatric sequelae of acute epidemic encephalitis in children. *American Journal of Diseases in Children, 25,* 89–97.

Education for All Handicapped Children Act of 1975, 20 U.S.C. § 1400 *et seq.*

Fowler, M. (1990). *Maybe you know my kid: A parent's guide to identifying, understanding, and helping your child with ADHD.* New York: Birch Lane Press.

Fulk, C. L. (1997, January/February). How to pinpoint and solve day-to-day problems. *Teaching Exceptional Children,* pp. 55–59.

Hallowell, E. M. (1993). Living and loving with attention deficit disorder: Couples where one partner has ADD. *C.H.A.D.D.E.R., 7,* 13–15.

Hartman, A., & Larid, J. (1983). *Family-centered social work practices.* New York: The Free Press.

Healey, B. (1996, November). Helping parents deal with the fact that their child has a disability. *CEC Today,* pp. 12–13.

Hohman, L. B. (1922). Post-encephalitic behavior disorders in children. *Johns Hopkins Hospital Bulletin, 33,* 372–375.

Individuals with Disabilities Education Act of 1990, 20 U.S.C. § 1400 *et seq.*

Individuals with Disabilities Education Act Amendments of 1997, 20 U.S.C. § 1400 *et seq.*

Johnson, C. (1996). Parent characteristics and parent–child interactions in families of non-problem children and ADHD children with higher and lower levels of oppositional–defiant behavior. *Journal of Abnormal Child Psychology, 24*(1), 85–104.

Kubler-Ross, E. (1969). *On death and dying.* New York: Macmillan.

Nadeau, K. G. (1995). *A comprehensive guide to attention deficit disorder: Research, diagnosis, and treatment.* New York: Brunner/Mazel.

Nelson, J. (1996). *Positive discipline.* New York: Ballantine Books.

Purvis, P., & Whelan, R. J. (1992). Collaborative planning between pediatricians and special educators. *Pediatric Clinics of North America, 39,* 451–469.

Rehabilitation Act of 1973, 20 U.S.C. § 701 *et seq.*

Ross, D. M., & Ross, S. A. (1976). *Hyperactivity: Research, theory, and action.* New York: Wiley.

Styker, S. (1925). Encephalitis lethargica–the behavior residuals. *Training School Bulletin, 22,* 152–157.

Still, G. F. (1902). Some abnormal psychical conditions in children. *Lancet, 1,* 1008–1012.

Sugai, G., & Lewis, T. J. (1996). Preferred and promising practices for social skills instruction. *Focus on Exceptional Children, 29*(4), 1–24.

Thompson, A. M. (1996). Attention deficit hyperactivity: A parent's perspective. *Phi Delta Kappan, 77*(6), 433–436.

Tyler, J. S., & Colson, S. (1994). Common pediatric disabilities: Implications for educators. *Focus on Exceptional Children, 27,* 1–16.

Ward, R., & Purvis, P. (1997). Twelve management tips for children with ADHD. *The ADHD Report, 5*(1), 16.

Building Blocks to Effective Partnerships: Meeting the Needs of Students with Emotional or Behavioral Disorders and Their Families

18

Nancy A. Mundschenk
and Regina M. Foley

S tudents with emotional or behavioral disorders are more likely than students in the general population to come from low-income families headed by a single parent whose formal educational level is less than that of age peers in the larger society (Rylance, 1997; U.S. Department of Education, 1997). Economics and social trends have an impact on the ways in which families can be involved in their child's education. Family involvement may be affected by difficulties with transportation, work schedules, child care needs, and economic pressures. Most school-based strategies for family involvement have been developed with the nuclear family in mind. In contrast, students with emotional or behavioral disorders may rely on the support of their extended families. Professionals should recognize that family structure is no guarantee of family functioning, and there are no simple formulas for family involvement. In their efforts to facilitate collaborative partnerships with families, professionals should be sensitive to the fact that activities designed for one family structure may not be appropriate for another (Cullinan, Epstein, & Sabornie, 1992) and different types of involvement may lead to different outcomes.

Collaborative partnerships between parents, teachers, and other service providers are an important component of educational service delivery systems for all students with disabilities but may be particularly critical for students with emotional or behavioral disorders. These students present patterns of behavior that may challenge even experienced teachers who struggle to find effective interventions that will result in meaningful gains. Parents, teachers, and community service providers who work in collaboration can establish a strong base of support that extends beyond the school day for a more comprehensive educational program.

Teachers still report varying perceptions of the levels of parental interest, support, and involvement in the educational lives of their children (Martin, Lloyd, Kauffman, & Coyne, 1995). Though most school personnel would agree that parental involvement is an important facet of effective educational programs, the amount of involvement tends to decline with increasing grade levels unless schools implement appropriate partnership experiences at each grade level (Epstein, 1995).

Most school personnel embrace the idea of increased family involvement and aim for improved positive interactions between home and school. But the vehicles for establishing those interactions are often overlooked or given cursory attention. The schools have a history of blaming parents and neglecting families in general. Professionals recognize that families are often trapped in a spiral where the child's behavior problems drive interactions and parents unintentionally reinforce their child's noncompliant and aggressive behavior (Kaiser & Hester, 1997; Patterson, 1986), which is often carried over into school. Professionals at the school may look to parents to modify their child's behavior when attempts at school are unsuccessful, or they may want a coordinated home–school effort. Unfortunately, the latter may simply mean that they want parents to mete out the punishment that was determined by the school. Although families may vary enormously in how active a part they can play in their child's education, most care deeply about the progress of their child and appreciate meaningful participation. Perhaps in better understanding families of students with emotional or behavioral disorders, professionals will better understand the students they are committed to serving. They must recognize the overlapping spheres of influence (Epstein, 1995) of home and school in order to establish meaningful partnerships that are more family focused, without losing sight of the outcomes they want for students with emotional or behavioral disorders.

The shift from a child-focused to a family-focused comprehensive service delivery system to meet youngsters' individualized needs evolved from the recognition of the importance of the family to the student's functioning (Knitzer, 1993). A child's development does not depend upon any one aspect of life experience (such as personal characteristics, family background, or educational services) but rather a compilation of life experiences (Fine & Gardner, 1994; Lambert, 1991). Furthermore, the unique strengths of the family unit are potential contributors to the service planning and delivery process (Fine & Gardner, 1994; Friesen & Koroloff, 1990). For example, families may have developed an elaborate set of coping resources such as informal (e.g., family, neighbors, friends) and community support networks (e.g., church, clubs) (Friesen & Koroloff, 1990), which assist the family in meeting the demands of a child with social–emotional difficulties. Families may also provide valuable information regarding the roles of individual family members, familial communication and decision-making patterns, and cultural values and patterns (Fine & Gardner, 1994).

Family–Centered Programs

Family-centered programs have been defined as a broad array of services that respond to individualized needs of the entire family (Friesen & Koroloff, 1990; Hanson & Carta, 1996; Kutash & Rivera, 1995). The goal of family-focused programs is to protect and strengthen the integrity of the family through the organization and provision of supports and resources (Agosta & Melda, 1996; Dunst, Trivette, & Thompson, 1990). This family-centered orientation involves the family members as collaborative partners in the identification, organization, and provision of necessary support services (e.g., physical needs, psychological services) (Dunst et al., 1990).

Family-centered services have a number of distinguishing features. First, family-centered services seek input from families on policy, design of service delivery systems, and evaluation of services (Agosta & Melda, 1996; Cheney & Osher, 1997). Families may be included as members of advisory committees that are charged with a variety of tasks such as program reviews and identification of potential policy revisions. Second, family-centered approaches actively involve the family in the decision-making process and reduce the emphasis on caregiver control (Hanson & Carta, 1996). Third, help givers in family-centered programs have more frequent contact and spend greater amounts of time with their clients (Trivette, Dunst, Boyd, & Hamby, 1996). Research shows that clients who receive high levels of contact from their service providers are more open to these services and, in turn, indicate they have greater personal control of their situation (Trivette et al., 1996). Fourth, culturally appropriate services appear to be a critical element of family-centered services (Hanson & Carta, 1996). Family-oriented service providers recognize that families vary in their linguistic, ethnic, cultural, or socioeconomic characteristics, and that such factors have an impact on the type and level of participation of family members in programming activities (Singh, 1995).

The breadth and depth of available family-centered services are sufficient to cover a broad range of needs for all family members. Family-focused services may address basic physical needs (e.g., food, clothing, shelter); informational needs such as availability and accessibility of community-based services (e.g., counseling, medical care, respite care); educational and vocational opportunities; case management services; advocacy services; and skill-building programs (e.g., behavior management training programs, parenting skill programs) (Kutash & Rivera, 1995). Similar to the breadth of services, the intensity of services is also based upon family needs (Hanson & Carta, 1996) and ranges from minimal services such as parents participating in a weekly parent support group to intensive complex service delivery plans that involve multiple agencies for each member of the family.

Support Groups

Support groups are small groups of individuals (e.g., parents, siblings) who meet regularly to discuss and share problems and information, engage in advocacy efforts, and offer support (Koroloff & Friesen, 1991). Support groups for parents and other family members provide one avenue for easing the burden of caring for children with emotional or behavioral disabilities (Koroloff & Friesen, 1991).

As an intervention, support groups function in several different capacities for their members. First, support groups serve as sources of information for participants (Koroloff & Friesen, 1991; Modrcin & Robinson, 1991). For example, parents may develop an increased awareness of their own needs and identify a broad range of available services. Second, regular group meetings provide opportunities for families to interact with others sharing similar experiences and to derive support from one another (Modrcin & Robinson, 1991; Telleen, Herzog, & Kilbane, 1989). Third, group members may work to advocate for legal and legislative actions to support effective services (Modrcin & Robinson, 1991). Finally, members of support groups may assist family members to identify their own strengths as a family, a process which can be useful in preserving the functioning of that family (Modrcin & Robinson, 1991).

Generally support group members appear to receive a number of benefits from participating in group activities. Previous reviews of the literature on the outcomes of support groups suggest that parents of children with emotional or behavioral disorders (a) develop a greater awareness of their child's developmental stages (Allen, Brown, & Finlay, 1992; Kutash & Rivera, 1995); (b) improve their attitude and parenting skills (Allen et al., 1992; Kutash & Rivera, 1995); and (c) improve family communication, particularly when interacting with their child with emotional or behavioral disorders (Kutash & Rivera, 1995).

Skill-Building Activities

Parent or family education may be a support service offered to parents as part of a family-centered program. Activities typically include one-to-one or group interactions that are designed to increase the competence of parents, couples, and other family members in parenting roles (Doherty, 1995). Parent education services may be directed toward improving any number of parenting skills such as behavior management or child–parent communication (Telleen et al., 1989).

Parent education programs appear to meet a number of parenting needs. First, parents who have participated in these programs have reported a greater understanding of their child's disability and increased their involvement in the child's treatment and educational planning process (Volenski, 1995). Second, participation in parent education activities appears to reduce parenting stress (Telleen et al., 1989; Volenski, 1995). Researchers have reported that parents feel less socially isolated (Telleen et al., 1989) and receive support from other parents participating in the program (Volenski, 1995). A final outcome of parent education programs is an increase in parental knowledge (Owen & Mulvihill, 1994). However, mothers appear to gain more information than fathers (Owen & Mulvihill, 1994). Some researchers have suggested that fathers may need a parent education program that is tailored to their knowledge level, socialization experiences, and availability of support (McBride, 1991; McBride & McBride, 1993; Meyers, 1993).

Family Empowerment and Advocacy

Some categories of disability have been represented by broad-based advocacy groups spearheaded largely by parents. But the parents of students with emotional or behavioral disorders, in contrast, have often been held responsible for the behavioral problems of their children; the resulting stigma has certainly impaired their ability to advocate on behalf of their children. Those parents who have adopted an advocacy stance and are vocal about what they want for their children are often seen as adversaries rather than advocates. Recently professionals have come to realize and appreciate the perspective that parents bring to any discussion regarding their child. The Federation of Families for Children's Mental Health, a national parent-run organization, is doing a great deal toward effective advocacy efforts on behalf of students with emotional or behavioral disorders and their families. Working to help empower families, the Federation aims at promoting collaboration between family members and professionals to improve services for students. It focuses on family participation in a system of care that recognizes the child as a person rather than a disability, and the family as a unit (The Federation of Families for Children's Mental Health, 1998).

By empowering families, professionals ensure that they become active participants in the treatment process. Professionals should encourage empowerment through shared responsibility and control, rather than foster dependency through "noncontingent helping" where they provide services and support for families without expecting proactive behavior from families in return (Howard, Williams, Port, & Lepper, 1997). Dunst, Trivette, and Deal (1988) identified three criteria for empowerment: (1) professionals assume that families are, or are capable of becoming, competent; (2) professionals create opportunities to enable families to display their strengths; and (3) professionals enable families to acquire a sense of control over family affairs so that the way in which the identified need is met is as important as having that need met. To facilitate this empowerment, professionals should encourage use of the family's existing supports and structures in dealing with challenges such as transportation, child care, and scheduling difficulties, rather than creating or identifying new structures and supports and asking families to integrate them.

The empowerment of parents and families through education is often identified as an aspect of a collaborative service delivery model (Cochran & Henderson, 1986; Fine, 1991; Friesen & Koroloff, 1990; Tarico et al., 1989). Practices that may serve as educational tools for parents and families include the use of advocates to guide parents through the agency's process and system (Evans et al., 1994; Koroloff, Elliott, Koren, & Friesen, 1994), parent mentors (Searcy, Lee-Lawson, & Trombino, 1995), effective case management (Illback & Neill, 1995), and skill-building programs such as those that help parents develop behavior management skills (Kutash & Rivera, 1995). In addition, knowledge-building practices may culminate in greater involvement of the parents in the service planning and delivery process. Researchers have reported that the knowledge level of parents of children with severe emotional or behavioral disorders was moderately correlated with families' level of collaborative involvement (Curtis & Singh, 1996).

Collaboration at the Organizational Level

In order to establish more effective working relationships with families of students with emotional or behavioral disorders, school and community agency personnel should evaluate their programs to determine the efficacy of existing policies and procedures relative to working with these families and incorporate practices that encourage collaborative efforts. The integration of parents and other family members as collaborators into the service planning and delivery process has a number of implications for the service delivery practices of community-based services and schools. First, the organization and administration of community-based services may need to be reviewed relative to the dimensions of a family-focused approach (Friesen & Koroloff, 1990). Important issues include the current level of service coordination with other agencies (e.g., eligibility and procedural requirements), availability of a range of services for clients, and fiscal funding flexibility that will allow for a comprehensive set of services to be provided to a child and family (Friesen & Koroloff, 1990; Nelson & Pearson, 1991). A lack of interagency coordination has been an obstacle to achieving the comprehensive programming developed for students with emotional or behavioral disorders. Although efforts to improve these linkages have been successful, obstacles to effective partnerships still exist and must be considered.

Collaboration among agencies may present a challenge when these agencies differ on critical issues such as the etiology of the student's problem, appropriate location of service delivery, and their own agency goals and philosophies with regard to serving students with emotional or behavioral disorders and their families. For example, public school personnel may feel that an alternative school program would best meet the needs of a student with emotional or behavioral disorders, while the administration of the alternative school may exclude such students by policy. A review of the current philosophy or orientation of the program may be necessary to ensure that agencies operate under principles of joint ownership of clients, and parents and family are fully integrated into the services rather than being blamed for a child's problems (Friesen & Koroloff, 1990; Nelson & Pearson, 1991).

A second aspect of service provision to be examined by administrators and other supervisory personnel is the current day-to-day programs and practices (Friesen & Koroloff, 1990). Collaborative models of parent involvement have a number of observable characteristics that include recognizing and valuing the parents' or families' role in the process (Cochran & Henderson, 1986; Tarico et al., 1989), including parents and families in all decision-making activities, educating parents and families on how to participate in decision making in a meaningful way, and engaging in reciprocal communication among parents, family, and service providers (Cochran & Henderson, 1986; Fine, 1991; Tarico et al. 1989).

Community agencies and schools can also work to establish collaborative partnerships. This process would require moving away from the one-directional partnerships that so often exist between these two groups of service providers where the focus and activities inhibit ongoing involvement. For example, many community agency services are short term in nature and may rely on grant funding for support. When that support terminates, school districts are often unprepared to continue funding programs that may be of benefit to students. Schools may see community agency services as an "add on" to their program and may be inclined to transfer responsibility for implementation and outcomes to that agency. This response is reinforced when community agency services are offered off-site of public schools.

Two-directional partnerships between schools and community agencies reflect a concerted effort to streamline procedures to make services more accessible, and to articulate policy statements that illustrate the collaborative basis for operating procedures. This may include sharing personnel, such as a liaison person jointly employed by the school and community agency to coordinate services for students with emotional or behavioral disorders, or alternating responsibility for staff development training sessions identified through needs assessment of both school and agency programs (see Figure 18.1).

Attitudes and Perceptions of Personnel

Although school and agency personnel assert that parents play a critical role in the development of their child, by practice parents are often excluded from important activities because of an underlying attitude that makes them feel unwelcome or uncomfortable. An important step in the actualization of collaboration within a family-focused service delivery model is a review of the attitudes and perceptions of school and agency personnel toward family

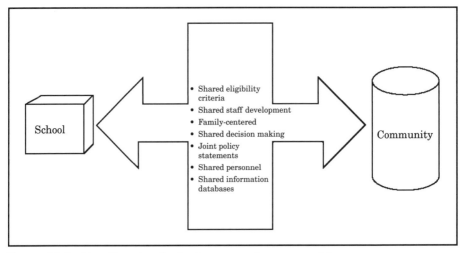

Figure 18.1. Two-directional school–community partnerships.

involvement activities. Parents of children with severe emotional or behavioral disorders have reported that one of the major barriers to services is the skepticism and minimization of their children's problems by pediatricians, teachers, and mental health professionals. Parents also indicated that they were often blamed for their children's problems (Tarico et al., 1989). Other findings have suggested similar perceptions of staff members serving children in a residential treatment center. In a survey of mental health practitioners, almost all (92% to 100%) of the participants identified a number of potentially favorable outcomes of family involvement for youth being treated in residential treatment centers (Baker, Heller, Blacher, & Pfeiffer, 1995). Among the reported possible positive outcomes of family involvement were the strengthening of the attachment between the parents and child, the improved adjustment of the parents, and more parental communication with staff members. However, the staff members also reported they were doubtful that the most frequent form of family involvement, regular visits, would have positive effects on their clients (Baker et al., 1995).

School and agency personnel may also be unaware of the reluctance of some parents to enter into collaborative relationships because of their own negative school experiences. This hesitancy may be reinforced by the reality that parents are most often contacted by schools or agencies when some problem needs to be resolved. Overcoming this reluctance requires a deliberate outreach that undermines past negative experiences. This outreach should include establishing environments where parents are viewed as important contributors to their child's program and are afforded regular opportunities for meaningful involvement. One high school, concerned about the lack of parent attendance at Open House, decided to replace the typical notice with a descriptive letter informing parents of proposed changes that would be discussed at the meeting and requesting their attendance and input. School personnel were surprised that over 50% of the parents participated, a significant increase in attendance from previous meetings (Foley & Mundschenk, 1997). When service providers celebrate family participation rather than assume a lack of family interest, collaborative relationships are more likely to develop.

Communication Skills of Agency and School Personnel

Previous research has suggested that both the communication skills and the level of interaction between service providers and family members are important aspects of service delivery (Modrcin & Robison, 1991; Tarico et al., 1989). Parents have reported they were appreciative of service providers who maintained open lines of communication with them and demonstrated regard and concern for the entire family's welfare (Tarico et al., 1989). A potential benefit of an open and concerned approach is that the service provider begins to establish a trustful relationship with the family (Modrcin & Robinson, 1991). For example, some researchers have suggested that practitioners acknowledge the familial stress of having a child with an emotional or behavioral disorder. The level of stress within the family may be determined through skillful questioning and paraphrasing of the responses of parents and siblings (Modrcin & Robison, 1991). Such techniques allow service providers to gain information about the resources and needs of the family, to adjust and respond to the stress of the situation, and to demonstrate concern and empathy for the family. Secondly, these techniques foster development of an awareness of the communication patterns occurring between help giver and family members. Previous research has tentatively indicated that the gender of the service providers may also influence the interaction between themselves and the family. Female family members appear to be more open to sharing information with female service providers than with male service providers (DeChillo, Koren, & Schultze, 1994).

In comparison to community-based service providers, school-based personnel are perceived as not as collaborative and less supportive of families by parents of a child with an emotional disorder (DeChillo et al., 1994). School personnel may need to be more cognizant of their interactions with parents in order to generate genuine collaboration (DeChillo et al., 1994). Examples of collaborative behaviors that convey a spirit of partnership include an attitude of respect, recognition of parents as coequal partners in planning activities, validation of parental perspective, use of their strengths in the service plan, and active collaboration-based generation of new ideas and strategies (Eber, Nelson, & Miles, 1997).

Service providers as a source of information appear also to be a valuable component of the service delivery process for families. Repeatedly, families have stressed the importance of information regarding the availability and access to services for their child and family (DeChillo et al., 1994; Modcrin & Robison, 1991; Soderlund, Epstein, Quinn, Cumblad, & Peterson, 1995; Tarico et al., 1989). For example, among the most frequently cited needs of parents is information about community services, transition programs, and alternative schools (Soderlund et al., 1995). Parents have indicated that agency staff who do not have the requested information about community services and resources are a mild barrier to obtaining services (Soderlund et al., 1995). Likewise, parents reported school-based professionals to be less knowledgeable of community resources and less helpful in connecting to services (DeChillo et al., 1994). Teachers themselves have reported frustration at the limited or delayed information coming from community agencies or classrooms in outside settings such as residential or day treatment schools, and the confusing and cumbersome procedures for obtaining that information (Foley & Mundschenk, 1997; Martin et al., 1995). School personnel should be aware that they may be required to initiate communication with agencies that do not have regular communication with their school such as Juvenile Justice personnel; they can also use a liaison person whose job is to coordinate agency responsibilities with public schools. It is imperative, then, that school personnel are assigned professional time to identify potential community agency services and to initiate and maintain collaborative activities.

The implementation of a family-focused model to the delivery of community-based services may require a reassessment of the time and intensity of service commitments of help-giving professionals (Illback & Neill, 1995). Generally parents appear to respond positively to services that afford ongoing contact with professionals (DeChillo et al., 1994; Tarico et al., 1989). A survey of parents of youngsters with severe emotional or behavioral disorders reported that greater frequencies of contact between parents and service providers were associated with sharing information, projecting a positive attitude of concern and care, taking into account parents' concerns and competing responsibilities, and integrating parents into the decision-making process (DeChillo et al., 1994). Also, greater amounts of time spent with families by professionals were correlated with activities that included finding, developing, coordinating, and funding services, and demonstrating flexibility by changing services based on parental feedback (DeChillo et al., 1994). Similarly, interviews conducted with parents of children with severe emotional or behavioral disorders indicated their perception of the helpfulness of services was related to the service provider's regard and concern for the child, maintenance of open communication with parents, and time spent explaining alternative treatments to parents (Tarico et al., 1989).

Communication Activities

By sharing information parents and teachers can operate with a more complete and accurate picture of the child. Teachers can gain insight into the child's background, skills, and behavior in nonschool settings. Parents can gain a better understanding of the child's performance in school. Both may develop a more accurate understanding of the expectations in these settings. Many schools employ one-directional communication strategies to convey information to parents. These strategies include newsletters, press releases, the school newspaper, student progress reports, and the school handbook. In our work, we have found some schools that simply rely on word of mouth. In one study parents reported that schools rarely solicited their input into critical school issues of interest to parents, such as disciplinary actions involving their child. The school typically communicated by letter; parents could only become involved if they took the initiative to do so (Mundschenk & Foley, 1994). Schools also rely on notes sent home with the students or through the mail—notes that parents may never see if the students have learned to expect and intercept negative communications from school. Unfortunately, parents of chronically disruptive students have a history of interactions with teachers and administrators that are most often the result of inappropriate student behavior. Communication with families regarding intervention plans and outcomes should occur at times of success as well as when a student is experiencing difficulty. To provide a more balanced pattern, one school implemented a policy where the building principal sent letters to parents of students who had achieved an educational goal or had demonstrated appropriate behavior. These letters came through the mail and were written on school stationary, just as with any other "official" school communication. Students were less likely to intercept school correspondence when the content could result in positive reinforcement from parents rather than punishment. Phone calls or home visits can also be used to inform parents of their child's progress. Although one-directional communication may be the appropriate vehicle for efficiently providing information, it may foster the perception that teachers are talking at parents rather than communicating with them. Collaborative activities require joint problem solving, which is best achieved through two-way communication.

Establishing two-way communication is one of the biggest challenges but one of the most important if professionals are to establish partnerships with families. Unlike one-directional communication it affords the opportunity for collaborative exchanges. School-initiated interactions often consist primarily of teachers providing a status report to parents on their child's academic or behavioral progress in school (Mundschenk & Foley, 1994). But teachers need to ask parents, "Do you have any questions or anything to add?" Asking parents for specific examples of skill generalization outside of school, such as positive interactions with siblings or homework completed independently, elicits important information and projects the attitude that teachers expect parents have something important to share.

School professionals often choose written forms of communication in order to document compliance with rules and regulations such as Individualized Education Plans (IEPs) or disciplinary reports. While this documentation is necessary to ensure the integrity of the program and procedural protections, it may not be the preferred method for parents. At formal meetings the focus can easily shift to filling out the paperwork rather than initiating a collaborative dialogue among parents and team members. By law and practice, service providers must ensure the development and maintenance of a participatory decision-making process. This means more than simply securing a parent signature on a school district form. Parents may be unfamiliar with the terminology used by professionals at the meeting, or they may be unclear about the goals that the school has identified for their child. These factors may help explain the observation that most parents participate passively in formal meetings with school personnel (Turnbull & Turnbull, 1990). Passive participation may be the parent's preferred method of involvement, or it may be the result of barriers that school personnel can identify and work to minimize. These barriers include logistical problems such as transportation, lack of understanding of procedural safeguards such as legal guidelines for disciplinary actions and behavior management strategies, and the feelings of inferiority that parents may have as the result of being outnumbered by professionals (Turnbull & Turnbull, 1990).

Ways to overcome these barriers are more easily identified when school personnel view families as a constituency group, actively encourage parent involvement, and value partnerships. Regular opportunities for family involvement may also help parents move from a passive stance to a more collaborative one with school personnel. There are a number of activities that schools can orchestrate that reflect different levels of involvement (see Figure 18.2). In one school, adult family members were encouraged to "hang out" in the school hallways during the changing of classes to greet and interact with students. The purpose in this case was not to act as hall monitors, but simply to be a presence in the building that illustrated the link between home and school. These family members were given school identification badges and invited into the faculty lounge for coffee and social conversation with school staff. Coordination of this program was the responsibility of a parent volunteer.

Technology is fast becoming a potential medium for communication as more schools go on-line and are connected to the Internet. Parents can call up the school's Web page to learn about school functions or obtain information of interest to families on the Internet (e.g., Federation of Families site at http://www.ffcmh.org/). Electronic mail can be used to foster communication between home and school while allowing participants to initiate and respond

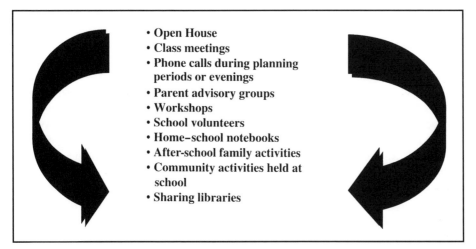

- Open House
- Class meetings
- Phone calls during planning periods or evenings
- Parent advisory groups
- Workshops
- School volunteers
- Home–school notebooks
- After-school family activities
- Community activities held at school
- Sharing libraries

Figure 18.2. Collaborative home–school activities.

to communication at a convenient time. Automated telephone systems enable schools to develop homework hotlines where parents can dial in to learn about current assignments. In addition, three-way conference calls may be an effective and efficient way to conduct collaborative activities particularly when parents have difficulty coming to school.

The use of videotaped vignettes from the classroom may help teachers provide parents with a realistic perspective on their child's behavior. Teachers can replay examples of improvement as well as instances of problematic behavior (Broome & White, 1995). Parents may see their child contributing appropriately to a class discussion or making disruptive remarks during the teacher's lecture. These vignettes can serve as a springboard for discussion. Videotapes can also be used to expand opportunities for family involvement; family members who are unable to attend a school event can view a videotaped recording of the event at a later time.

Given the variety of ways in which parents and school personnel can communicate, school professionals need to ascertain family preferences relative to the format, frequency, and location of communication. Many parents prefer more informal conversations with school personnel rather than the didactic sessions schools often provide (Turnbull & Turnbull, 1990). Some parents welcome home visits while others feel such visits pressure them to assume a level of involvement that makes them uncomfortable. It may also be helpful if the primary contact person is a staff member with whom parents feel at ease. Whatever the vehicle for communicating, school personnel should persevere in attempts to engage families in meaningful dialogue even when the desired outcomes are not immediately forthcoming.

Collaborative Processes

Another aspect of family-focused collaborative programming that may require examination is the current problem-solving and conflict management process. Collaboration-based services by nature provide more opportunity for the use of problem-solving processes and may require an increased need for conflict resolution (Friend & Cook, 1996). As the services become more family oriented and collaborative, the goals of the families and service providers may not always be in agreement (Friesen & Koroloff, 1990). For instance, families may begin making demands for services that are not readily available (Friesen & Koroloff, 1990), or they may question the accuracy of school reports of inappropriate behavior and disagree with the proposed intervention.

The interactive processes within a family-focused collaborative model may require an evaluation of the occurrence of meaningful parental participation during the decision-making process of planning and implementing services. Service providers may have to actively seek and integrate the participation of parents and other family members into the planning process. Parents have reported being invited and participating in the planning process to develop treatment plans for their children (Soderlund et al., 1995; Tarico et al., 1989). However, parents may perceive their input to be secondary, based on the actions of service providers (Tarico et al., 1989). Such off-putting actions include asking parents to review previously developed treatment plans (Tarico et al., 1989), failing to explain the purpose of the meeting, not asking parents for their perceptions of the effectiveness of various treatments used in the past or being considered for future use, and not having parents articulate their expectations for services or their child (Singh, Curtis, Wechsler, Ellis, & Cohen, 1997).

It can be difficult to talk collaboratively with parents about their child's behavior problems. Because parents have so often been blamed for these problems, they may become defensive and even lash out at school personnel. Professionals should approach these interactions with a deliberate effort to make the experience as positive and respectful as they can, and not to take personally the sometimes caustic statements that parents may make out of anger or frustration. The goal is not to lay blame at the feet of parents but rather to elicit their ideas and support for strategies to increase appropriate student behavior. Simpson (1996) offers some practical suggestions for working with angry parents that may help decrease the probability of these interactions.

Parental Expectations

Another facet of a collaborative service delivery model worthy of review is the flexibility of programs for meeting the variable expectations of parents. Reasons for varying parental expectations include readiness levels, resources, and competing responsibilities (Fine & Gardner, 1994; Singh et al., 1997). Some parents expect to receive services that meet the needs of the family as a whole (Tarico et al., 1989). They may prefer service providers who recognize the limits of the family's resources but at the same time acknowledge their ability to contribute meaningfully to the treatment process (Fine & Gardner, 1994). Table 18.1 summarizes what parents are looking for in a collaborative relationship with service providers.

Families also differ in behavioral and developmental expectations. When these expectations conflict with school or agency assumptions, personnel must work to develop culturally sensitive and relevant educational programs that respect the family functioning and reflect interventions, goals, and outcomes that are valid for that family.

Cultural Competence of Services

In a comprehensive system of care based on a collaborative approach, one of the core values and principles is cultural competence (Stroul & Friedman, 1986). Families from culturally and linguistically diverse backgrounds may exhibit expectations and perspectives at odds with what the school or agency proposes, or that simply affect the families' ability to collaborate with these service providers. Schools should examine the practices that respect cultural differences relative to cultural values, childbearing, and educational practices including behavior management strategies, family structure, communication patterns, cultural perceptions of mental illness, and acceptability of receiving assistance (Singh et al., 1997). Examples of culturally competent practices include determining the family structure (e.g., nuclear or extended, patriarchal or matriarchal), and working to understand how the client's behavior reflects communication patterns, perceptions of health, and religious influences (Cross, Bazron, Dennis, & Isaacs, 1989). This cultural sensitivity may be facilitated by home visits, informal as well as formal meetings with families, and the establishment of communication with neighborhood

Table 18.1

What Families Want in a Collaborative Relationship

- Accurate information on available community services and how to access them.
- Open and frequent communication which leads to a more trusting relationship.
- The expression of positive regard for the student and family.
- Flexibility in treatment plans based on parent feedback.
- Clear explanations of alternative treatments.
- Inclusion in decision-making process.
- Recognition of the needs and resources of the family.

churches as an outreach to the community. Because each family represents a unique blend of culture, experience, level of acculturation, and behavioral and developmental expectations, it is appropriate for professionals to identify cultural values and patterns directly from the families they serve.

Evaluation

The outcomes of services provided by agency personnel are another aspect of family-focused programs that may require evaluation. A common complaint of parents and teachers is that professionals design and implement treatment programs but fail to evaluate the outcomes or processes used. Some researchers have suggested that methods for documenting and reviewing the service delivery activities be included as part of the process. Examples of planning activities to be substantiated include the identification of a family's needs, strengths, and level of participation in the decision-making and service planning activities (Friesen & Koroloff, 1990). Agencies would also benefit from incorporating feedback from families to improve the delivery of services (Friesen & Koroloff, 1990). This feedback should include measures of the effectiveness of treatment programs and whether the effects reflect valued long-term outcomes for students with emotional or behavioral disorders. Summative and formative measures as well as combinations of ethnographic and social validity measures may be incorporated into the monitoring and evaluation procedures of programs (Eber et al., 1997). For example, an evaluation and monitoring system for a school-based wraparound program used surveys of parents and teachers, focus groups with school staff, and technical assistance meetings with school-based facilitators, parents, and staff as ways of identifying and addressing issues through the reallocation of resources, development of additional strategies, and provision of technical assistance (Eber et al., 1997).

Service Providers' Professional Development

A final issue to be reviewed in the refocusing of the service delivery process is the professional development and support of the service providers. Initially administrators and supervisors may need to determine the training and activities necessary for service providers to implement a family-focused approach (Friesen & Koroloff, 1990). In addition, it appears that most practitioners have had minimal preparation to engage in service coordination (Illback & Neill, 1995). Thus, administrators and supervisors may need to provide and support opportunities for professional development and supervision (Friesen & Koroloff, 1990; Illback & Neill, 1995). Examples include development of a repertoire of collaboration skills including communication skills (e.g., use of statements, questions, paraphrasing), recognition of one's own frame of reference, and using and evaluating interpersonal problem-solving and conflict resolution skills (Friend & Cook, 1996). Other service coordination skills to be developed may include case formulation, the use of complicated interventions, and enhanced sensitivity to a variety of issues (e.g., legal, cultural) (Illback & Neill, 1995). The support of field-based practitioners by administrative and supervisory staff has been strongly advocated as a critical component of the success of comprehensive systems of care that actively integrate families into the planning and treatment process (Eber et al., 1997; Friesen & Koroloff, 1990; Illback & Neill, 1995).

References

Agosta, J., & Melda, K. (1996). Supporting families who provide care at home for children with disabilities. *Exceptional Children, 62,* 271–282.

Allen, M., Brown, P., & Finlay, B. (1992). *Helping children by strengthening families: A look at family support programs.* Washington, DC: Children's Defense Fund.

Baker, B. L., Heller, T. L., Blacher, J., & Pfeiffer, S. I. (1995). Staff attitudes toward family involvement in residential treatment centers for children. *Psychiatric Services, 46,* 60–65.

Broome, S. A., & White, R. B. (1995). The many uses of videotape in classrooms serving youth with behavioral disorders. *Teaching Exceptional Children, 27,* 10–13.

Cheny, D., & Osher, T. (1997). Collaborate with families. *Journal of Emotional and Behavioral Disorders, 5,* 36–44, 54.

Cochran, M., & Henderson, C. R., Jr. (1986). *Family matters: Evaluation of the parental empowerment program.* New York: Cornell University Press.

Cross, T. L., Bazron, B. J., Dennis, K. W., & Isaacs, M. R. (1989). *Towards a culturally competent system of care* (Vol. 1). Washington, DC: CASSP Technical Assistance Center, Georgetown University Child Development Center.

Cullinan, D., Epstein, M. H., & Sabornie, E. J. (1992). Selected characteristics of a national sample of seriously emotionally disturbed adolescents. *Behavioral Disorders, 17,* 273–280.

Curtis, W. J., & Singh, N. N. (1996). Family involvement and empowerment in mental health service provision for children with emotional and behavioral disorders. *Journal of Child and Family Studies, 5,* 503–517.

DeChillo, N., Koren, P. E., & Schultze, K. H. (1994). From paternalism to partnership: Family and professional collaboration in children's mental health. *American Journal of Orthopsychiatry, 64,* 564–576.

Doherty, W. J. (1995). Boundaries between parent and family education and family therapy: The levels of the family involvement model. *Family Relations, 44,* 353–358.

Dunst, C. J., Trivette, C. M., & Deal, A. (1998). *Enabling and empowering families: Principles and guidelines for practice.* Cambridge, MA: Brookline.

Dunst, C. J., Trivette, C. M., & Thompson, R. L. (1990). Supporting and strengthening family functioning: Toward a congruence between principles and practice. *Prevention in Human Services, 9,* 19–43.

Eber, L., Nelson, E. M., & Miles, P. (1997). School-based wraparound for students with emotional and behavioral challenges. *Exceptional Children, 63,* 539–555.

Epstein, J. (1995). School/family/community partnerships: Caring for the children we share. *Kappan, 76,* 701–712.

Evans, M. E., Armstrong, M. I., Dollard, N., Kuppinger, A. D., Huz, S., & Wood, V. M. (1994). Development and evaluation of treatment foster care and family-centered intensive care management in New York. *Journal of Emotional and Behavioral Disorders, 2,* 228–239.

The Federation of Families for Children's Mental Health. (1998). Available: http://www.ffcmh.org/

Fine, M. J. (Ed.). (1991). *Collaboration with parents of exceptional children.* Brandon, VT: Clinical Psychology.

Fine, M. J., & Gardner, A. (1994). Collaborative consultation with families of children with special needs: Why bother? *Journal of Educational and Psychological Consultation, 5,* 283–308.

Foley, R. M., & Mundschenk, N. A. (1997). *Establishing collaborative partnerships: Appropriate service delivery for students with behavior disorders.* Paper presented at Seventh Annual Virginia Beach Conference, Virginia Beach, VA.

Friend, M., & Cook, L. (1996). *Interactions: Collaboration skills for school professionals* (2nd ed.). White Plains, NY: Longman.

Friesen, B. J., & Koroloff, N. M. (1990). Family-centered services: Implications for mental health administration and research. *The Journal of Mental Health Administration, 17,* 13–25.

Hanson, M. J., & Carta, J. J. (1996). Addressing the challenges of families with multiple risks. *Exceptional Children, 62,* 201–212.

Howard, V. F., Williams, B. F., Port, P. D., & Lepper, C. (1997). *Very young children with special needs: A formative approach for the 21st century.* Columbus, OH: Merrill.

Illback, R. J., & Neill, T. K. (1995). Service coordination in mental health system for children, youth, and families: Progress, problems, prospects. *The Journal of Mental Health Administration, 22,* 17–28.

Kaiser, A. P., & Hester, P. P. (1997). Prevention of conduct disorders through early intervention: A social-communicative perspective, *Behavioral Disorders, 22,* 117–130.

Knitzer, J. (1993). Children's mental health policy: Challenging the future. *Journal of Emotional and Behavioral Disorders, 1,* 8–16.

Koroloff, N. M., Elliott, D. J., Koren, P. E., & Friesen, B. J. (1994). Connecting low-income families to mental health services: The role of the family associate. *Journal of Emotional and Behavioral Disorders, 2,* 240–246.

Koroloff, N. M., & Friesen, B. J. (1991). Support groups for parents of children with emotional disorders: A comparison of members and non-members. *Community Mental Health Journal, 27,* 265–279.

Kutash, K., & Rivera, V. R. (1995). Effectiveness of children's mental health services: A review of the literature. *Education and Treatment of Children, 18,* 443–477.

Lambert, N. M. (1991). Partnerships of psychologists, educators, community-based agency personnel, and parents in school redesign. *Educational Psychology, 26,* 185–198.

Martin, K. F., Lloyd, J. W., Kauffman, J. M., & Coyne, M. (1995). Teachers' perceptions of educational placement decisions for pupils with emotional or behavioral disorders. *Behavioral Disorders, 20,* 106–117.

McBride, B. A. (1991). Parent education and support programs for fathers: Outcome effects on paternal involvement. *Early Child Development and Care, 67,* 73–85.

McBride, B. A., & McBride, R. J. (1993). Parent education and support programs for fathers. *Childhood Education, 70*(1), 4–9.

Meyers, S. A. (1993). Adapting parent education programs to meet the needs of fathers. *Family Relations, 42,* 447–452.

Modrcin, M. J., & Robison, J. (1991). Parents of children with emotional disorders: Issues for consideration and practice. *Community Mental Health Journal, 27,* 281–292.

Mundschenk, N. A., & Foley, R. M. (1994). Collaborative relationships between school and home: Implications for service delivery. *Preventing School Failure, 39,* 16–20.

Nelson, C. M., & Pearson, C. A. (1991). *Integrating services for children and youth with emotional and behavioral disorders.* Reston, VA: Council for Exceptional Children.

Owen, M. T., & Mulvihill, B. A. (1994). Benefits of a parent education and support program in the first three years. *Family Relations, 43,* 206–212.

Patterson, G. R. (1986). Performance models for antisocial boys. *American Psychologist, 41,* 432–444.

Rylance, B. J. (1997). Predictors of high school graduation or dropping out for youth with severe emotional disturbances. *Behavioral Disorders, 23,* 5–17.

Searcy, S., Lee-Lawson, C., & Trombino, B. (1995). Mentoring new leadership roles for parents of children with disabilities. *Remedial and Special Education, 16,* 307–314.

Simpson, R. L. (1996). *Working with parents and families of exceptional children and youth* (3rd ed.). Austin, TX: PRO-ED.

Singh, N. N. (1995). In search of unity: Some thoughts on family–professional relationships in service delivery systems. *Journal of Child and Family Studies, 4*(1), 3–18.

Singh, N. N., Curtis, J. W., Wechsler, H. A., Ellis, C. A., & Cohen, R. (1997). Family friendliness of community-based services for children and adolescents with emotional and behavioral disorders and their families: An observational study. *Journal of Emotional and Behavioral Disorders, 5,* 82–92.

Soderlund, J., Epstein, M. H., Quinn, K. P., Cumblad, C., & Peterson, S. (1995). Parental perspectives on comprehensive services for children and youth with emotional and behavioral disorders. *Behavioral Disorders, 20,* 157–170.

Stroul, B. A., & Friedman, R. M. (1986). *A system of care for children and youth with severe emotional disturbances* (Rev. ed.). Washington, DC: Georgetown University Child Development Center, CASSP Technical Assistance Center.

Tarico, V. S., Low, B. P., Trupin, E., & Forsyth-Stephens, A. (1989). Children's mental health perspectives: A parent perspective. *Community Mental Health Journal, 25,* 313–326.

Telleen, S., Herzog, A., & Kilbane, T. L. (1989). Impact of a family support program on mothers' social support and parenting stress. *American Journal of Orthopsychiatry, 59,* 410–419.

Trivette, C. M., Dunst, C. J., Boyd, K., & Hamby, D. W. (1996). Family-oriented program models, helpgiving practices, and parental control appraisals. *Exceptional Children, 62,* 237–248.

Turnbull, A. P., & Turnbull, H. R. (1990). *Families, professionals, and exceptionality: A special partnership* (2nd ed.). New York: Macmillian.

U.S. Department of Education National Center for Education Statistics. (1997). *Profiles of students with disabilities as identified in NELS:88.* Washington, DC: Author.

Volenski, L. T. (1995). Building school support systems for parents of handicapped children: The parent education and guidance program. *Psychology in the Schools, 32,* 124–129.

Sexuality, Transitions, and Advocacy

IV

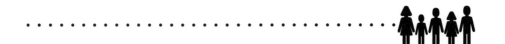

Issues in Social Sexuality for People with Disabilities, Their Families, and Professionals

19

Peggy Jo Wallis

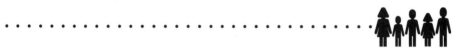

Everyone, regardless of abilities or disabilities, is a sexual being. Frequently those with disabilities have been denied this recognition by professionals, parents, and society. Despite recent medical advances in the treatment of sexual dysfunction and the advocacy of prominent spokespeople on the topic (e.g., actor Christopher Reeve discussing his ability to still father a child after his paralyzing injury), people with disabilities continue to be viewed as too asexual, hypersexual, eternally childlike, or severely handicapped to be concerned with issues of sexuality. Although recognition of historical errors in the treatment of people with disabilities has finally led to new priorities based upon normalization, the focus is most frequently on cognitive issues and daily living or vocational skills.

The issues that arise around social sexuality are difficult for parents and professionals alike, whether or not the person concerned has a disability. Few are trained in this topic, and it is one in which societal messages are conflicting. Society allows explicit sexual images in movies and printed material while simultaneously implying that sexuality is not something to be talked about openly. But social sexuality is inherent to our basic nature. People with disabilities have the right to have their sexuality recognized. Parents, professionals, and the people with disabilities themselves must find a way to be comfortable addressing educational and living considerations.

Professionals play a pivotal role as they work with and learn from both parents and their children with disabilities during the process of discussion and collaboration. They must recognize sensitive issues and concerns and deal with them in a straightforward yet empathetic manner. Frequently professionals must introduce the suggestion that education, intervention, or support might be warranted in the area of social sexuality. For parents and individuals with disabilities alike, this interaction with professionals might provide guidance in understanding and accepting the developmental process as well as assistance in making the decisions that are inherent in this process.

To provide objective assistance, professionals must become aware of the development and variation of values and emotionality connected with this subject, and acknowledge their own feelings and attitudes. They must also understand the concept of sexuality, the normal process of social-sexual development, the possible impact of disabilities on this process (for purposes of this chapter, disabilities will be considered generically unless otherwise noted), and the response of the parent to the maturation of the child. Only from this vantage point will professionals be prepared to begin considering appropriate guidance and intervention strategies.

Perceptions of Sexuality

Human sexuality encompasses the totality of who we are biologically, psychologically, and sociologically from birth until death. It is an ongoing lifetime process, not just a biological issue to be addressed at adolescence with discussions of "plumbing" and "disaster prevention." Although it encompasses significant physiological events and transitions, sexuality as a process also includes the basic elements of developing self-esteem, communication, and decision-making skills and the interaction of these three elements. How people feel about their bodies and the pleasures they can derive, the ways in which they express those feelings, and the determination of when and with whom they share these feelings are all key elements (Dixon & Mullinar, 1985).

The varying perceptions of exactly what sexuality means can cause significant difficulties. Some view sexuality in terms of a physical act, while others define it by the changes in visible physical characteristics that come with maturation. Most people think first of the physiological aspects (i.e., body changes, intercourse, and reproduction); they delay or omit altogether consideration of the other elements of sexuality, such as social and psychological aspects. But an understanding of sexuality in its entirety is especially important when addressing the needs of people with disabilities. They may have difficulties with self-esteem, problem solving, communication, decision making, acquiring information, and gathering experience. Professionals and parents need a broad perspective to encompass all the psychological–social–sexual issues.

General Attitudes and Values

Given the variety of views on sexuality, it is important for professionals to be sensitive to and aware of the particular values and attitudes of their clients—as well as their own views. Professionals convey their views both purposely through education and counseling and inadvertently through behavior, tone of voice, and body language. They and the parents who consult them may be "disabled" by views which, by being narrow in perspective or oppositional to certain behaviors, prove to be restrictive. Professionals and parents must therefore be particularly clear about their own attitudes and the messages they are conveying.

Sexuality can be a very emotional topic; each individual has particular feelings and biases. These beliefs are the product of a lifetime of discrete individual experiences. Various influences, including cultural beliefs and customs, the family, economics, peers, the law, the media, science, religion, and the school define each person's value system and perception (Dixon & Mullinar, 1985).

Each generation has its own experiences of each of these influences and thus a unique perspective on the way in which individuals should behave. Society's view of sexuality is constantly changing, from Victorian rigidness through the 1960s' openness to the present preoccupation with issues of AIDS and sexual abuse. But human attitudes, while influenced over time by prevailing trends, have had a constant thread: people are uncomfortable talking about sexuality. Therefore, when dealing with families, the professional should keep in mind the values of different generations and the almost universal discomfort with the topic of sexuality.

Parents, many lacking appropriate models themselves, have frequently avoided raising the topic with their children or approached it "red-faced." As reflections of society's values, educational institutions and professionals have also been reluctant to address the topic wholeheartedly, being fearful yet cognizant of the difficulty of melding all of the community and familial value systems into a whole. Students have received information, if at all, in a piecemeal fashion and usually after the time when the knowledge was necessary. This is particularly true for those with disabilities.

Attitudes Toward the Sexuality of People with Disabilities

Children and adolescents with physical or mental disabilities have very much the same concerns about sexuality as their nondisabled peers. They must learn to cope with generally the same biological changes as other children, as well as the new sexual feelings and desires that come in early adolescence. However, individual disabilities can complicate these tasks of growing up (Thornton, 1981).

It is society that frequently creates disabilities. Society tends to view someone first as "handicapped" and then as a person. Although many disabilities are products of birth, illness, or accident, the debilitating impact on a person's life often results from the misperceptions and devaluing behavior of others (Gordon, 1974). It is therefore not surprising that the sexual aspects of disability are unrecognized by some people, denied by others and, for still others, are a matter of distaste. Such attitudes will persist until the public at large becomes more aware of people with disabilities as fellow human beings of equal merit. At present, wholeness in form and function makes up part of the sexual ideal; the individual tends to become less acceptable as a sexual being, let alone as a sexual partner, to the extent that he falls short of that ideal (Stewart, 1979).

Historically, people with disabilities have been "desexualized" due to disbelief, fear, and the inability of others to recognize them as sexual beings. Active suppression resulting from fear of and for individuals with disabilities led to the control of their sexuality through mass institutionalization and passage of compulsory sterilization laws (Bregman & Castles, 1988). Inconsistent views of individuals with disabilities ranging from their having no sexual needs to the other extreme of males as sexually aggressive and females as sexually promiscuous have resulted in avoidance of the topic and the withholding of necessary information. Equally believed have been the misconceptions that "disability breeds disability" and that people with disabilities should stay with and marry their "own kind." All these views imply that people with disabilities are "defective" and that their most important characteristic is their disability (Cornelius, Chipouras, Makas, & Daniels, 1982).

People with disabilities, in not being recognized as sexually normal, are not encouraged or often permitted to express themselves sexually. That they are viewed as asexual, oversexed, or forever childlike encourages their suppression and dependency and perpetuates the view that if they are disabled in one way they are disabled in all ways, including their sexuality. These perspectives have led to segregation, punishment, the denial of their sexual expression, and a lack of social-sexual education and training. The result has been inappropriate behaviors, feelings of social inadequacy, and isolation.

Many of these attitudes have left people with disabilities susceptible to further misconceptions. The depiction of people with disabilities as innocent and vulnerable gives foundation to the myth that withholding knowledge about sexuality will deter them from engaging in certain inappropriate or unwanted behaviors. According to this view, if information is presented about sexuality, "putting things in their heads," individuals with disabilities will become overstimulated and involved in activities they otherwise would not have chosen or even given thought to. In truth, however, talking or not talking about social-sexual issues will not influence the reaching of puberty with the resultant physical and psychological changes.

The withholding of information can result in actions prompted by curiosity and ignorance, including inappropriate and frequently dangerous behaviors. Many people with disabilities have difficulty gaining information independently or developing healthy attitudes toward their own sexuality and sexual responsibility. Cognitive levels may limit reasoning, decision-making, and problem-solving capabilities, resulting in impulsive behaviors and lack of comprehension of the consequences of actions. Deficits in reading levels may restrict access to information. Verbal difficulties may preclude their asking questions, and so may a lack of knowledge of where, how, or whom to ask.

The inability to use and integrate observed social cues (either due to processing, visual impairment, or cognitive functioning) may deprive some people with disabilities of important social learning information. Some may have gotten the message that others do not view them as sexual, so they are uncomfortable asking about this topic. Lack of social concepts, access, or overprotection keeps them from partaking in social opportunities that would provide information. They are therefore on their own to gain information. Some will never seek it. Others may go about it by actions that are really questioning behaviors (touching, grabbing, etc.). By providing information, parents and professionals can decrease the occurrence of these inappropriate question-asking and exploratory behaviors.

It is sometimes assumed that there is an ideal time schedule for providing information concerning social sexuality and that providing information too soon is detrimental. In fact, there are no ill effects from providing information about sex at appropriate stages or ages. Harm can result, however, by withholding information until after the individual has a particular sexual experience. For the person with a disability who may not have garnered information through observation, reading, or questioning, natural occurrences of maturity (i.e., menstruation) can be upsetting and perhaps frightening. An understanding on the part of both parents and professionals of the expected physical and social development milestones, as well as the impact that disabilities may have upon this growth, is important in order to prepare and assist everyone involved through each transition.

Sexual Development

From the moment of birth, a person is affected by forces that influence sexual development. One of the strongest and earliest impacts is that of parent–infant bonding, which develops through touch, eye contact, and soothing talk. Once the relationship is established, it usually becomes reciprocal, with the parent (typically the mother) and the child drawing responses from each other (Grantham & Russell, 1985). The initial warmth and nurturing that take place give a sense to both the infant and parent of acceptance and create a foundation for the establishment of security and self-esteem.

This bonding, however, can be disrupted by a variety of factors. For babies born with a disability, parents may be confronted with the emotional loss of the "perfect" child, which may result in some difficulty accepting the infant. If parental grief or rejection is continuous, then socialization and affective development of the child is likely to be influenced (Schuster, 1987). Therefore the family members have to come to terms with the diagnosis. They must work through their own range of feelings and reactions as well as deal with the possibly altered behaviors of relatives and friends.

The child, due to medical or psychological difficulties, may not evoke a caring response from the parent or give a rewarding response in return (Grantham & Russell, 1985). The spasticity experienced by a child born with cerebral palsy may result in the infant's lack of "snuggling." Parents may have difficulty in evoking smiles from a blind baby because of lack of eye contact (Lewis, 1987). Additional factors, such as critical medical care leading to substantial separation and prolonged institutionalization may result in the infant not receiving initial nurturing or providing feedback to the parents. This may delay the development of trust and emotional security.

From the time a child is born, it is learning: learning in the first place to recognize its own body and the fact that the body has needs, learning, little by little, of the primary relationship between self and nonself (Stewart, 1979). As children continue through infancy (ages 0 to 1), this learning begins to take the form of exploration. At first they investigate the immediate environment: the crib, toys, their own fingers and toes. Infants will also explore their genitals, a behavior that may provoke dismay in those placing adult sexual connotations upon infants' actions. The response that this behavior elicits can have an impact on the children's future ability to view their bodies in a positive manner. Although exploration is a natural stage, some infants with disabilities may be delayed in reaching it. The parents may gradually feel concerned that their child is not developing in the same way as another child of the same age (Grantham & Russell, 1985). Further concern follows if the child, due to developmental delays, engages in certain exploratory behaviors later in the process when these are no longer age appropriate.

Self-image, independence, and gender identity begin to develop as children become aware (ages 1 to 2) of their own bodily functions and their ability to control them. Toilet training and the negative associations made between genitals and bodily wastes can have an impact on the child's sense of body image and sexuality. For many children with disabilities, the delay or difficulty in proceeding through this stage results in the postponing of skills of independence and socialization and the understanding of privacy. They may necessarily continue to rely on a parent or caretaker for dealing with bodily functions. Learned helplessness from infancy and toddler years can have a serious effect on the quality of interpersonal relationships, lasting into the adolescent and young adult years (Schuster, 1987).

In many children with disabilities of a congenital nature, eliminatory and "toilet" considerations need more attention than in the able-bodied child (Stewart, 1979). The necessity for a great deal of attention and assistance may result in a significant lack of privacy. These children may also experience gender confusion due to physical or developmental differences. Yet, children and adolescents need to have their bodily integrity respected (Miezio, 1983) in order to develop a healthy self-image.

Due to the nature of the disability or the overprotectiveness on the part of the parents or caregivers, some children are unable to have much privacy or independent free time. They therefore are not able to engage privately in natural developmental exploration and experimentation. If they attempt this exploration with other people around, they may be told their behavior is not socially acceptable (Fairbrother, 1983). They may practice these behaviors in inappropriate places where opportunity is possible (i.e., back of the school bus, coat room) or at a later age when the conduct is inappropriate. The result of these behaviors quite possibly is an inability to progress through the succeeding development stages of exploration, sex play, and social interactions. The children may be unable to develop independent adult characteristics, engage in appropriate behaviors, or fail to establish a sense of self-worth. If children cannot play easily with other children when the stage of interactional play arrives, the rehearsal for life that is implied by such play may be impeded (Stewart, 1979).

As children become less egocentric and more aware of others around them (ages 3 to 5), they become curious about their similarities and differences. They have many questions about sexual behavior and engage in sex rehearsal play (Calderone & Johnson, 1981). Children use this practice play to develop conscience and the beginnings of body image and to establish more firmly their gender identity. At this stage, as the child reaches school age, the next real teachers of the "facts of life" become peers, as they are all agents that modify the child's self-opinion (Symonds & Wickware, 1978).

Although people with disabilities may experience social isolation as adults, in terms of people in their network and the frequency of daily contact, as children they typically have larger networks than their nondisabled peers. The large network of children with disabilities is composed of relatives, adults, and, to a lesser extent, peers. But whereas children without disabilities, from ages 3 to 6, show a developmental shift in terms of an increase in proportion of peers to adults, children with disabilities do not show this change. Insufficient peer contact may restrict the child's opportunity to learn important social skills (Lewis, Feiring, & Brooks-Gunn, 1988) and independence and to develop an accurate body image.

Puberty is a biological process that cannot be halted. It is heralded by the physical changes the body undergoes resulting in visible differences in appearance. This is a time of heightened concern about body image, an awareness that began at an early stage when the child first became curious about the bodies of others. For the child with a disability, this concern about body image can result in a continuous difficulty in accepting obvious differences (Craft & Craft, 1983).

This period (ages 6 to 12) that concludes with puberty becomes especially difficult for many youngsters with disabilities as they are confronted by society's increased expectations and lower tolerance for frustration and failure. Limited access to social activities and lack of acceptance or minimal peer group interaction may delay or inhibit their social skill development. Overprotectiveness on the part of adults can directly impede the growth of children with disabilities. Physical maturity cannot be stopped (though some will deny its eventuality). However, adults with the best of intentions may curtail or even halt the social-sexual development of the child with disabilities. The result over time is people who are physically adults but who have the social status of children (Craft & Craft, 1983).

Adolescence is the state or process of growing up, the time of transition between childhood and adulthood. It is a "social" process in which the individual develops her understanding of her own social and sexual identity (Craft & Craft, 1983). During this time, the expectations of others, especially peers, become important. The adolescent must cope with the frustrations and failures of meeting those expectations. Some of the tasks of adolescence include developing identity and independence, assuming responsibilities, preparing for relationships, and developing values and ethical systems. Disabilities can complicate the completion of these tasks (Thorton, 1981).

Feedback from others helps the adolescent in developing his identity. But for many adolescents with disabilities, the feedback may be incomplete, unrealistic, or unavailable. Adolescence is a time when differences are negatively viewed by peers, and self-image and self-esteem can suffer (Thorton, 1981). Body image continues to be a central issue in this identity development as young adults come to terms with the ways in which their bodies are different from the popularized ideals (Miezio, 1983). For many adolescents with disabilities, obtaining information and feedback may be difficult. For instance, young people with vision or hearing impairments may have trouble acquiring information through the normal communication channels. These adolescents, with their growing awareness of sexuality often accompanied by various taboos, may become confused and anxious about their own and other people's bodies and about their feelings (Lewis, 1987).

For children with disabilities and parents alike, adolescence (ages 12 and above) can be a very difficult time. Young adults must struggle to adjust to bodily changes. Frequently, body growth occurs with greater speed than does emotional or conceptual ability to comprehend it. How well children adjust depends to a large extent on cognitive level, coping skills, how they are told about sexuality, and what support they receive from their families and from professional people (Fairbrother, 1983). As the sex drive intensifies and new emotions are felt, the young adult may examine and challenge attitudes and values established at an earlier age. This period is generally difficult for the entire family as the child's need to establish independence generates strains and stresses in family relationships. In particular, conflicts can arise concerning sexual matters (Calderone & Johnson, 1981). However, as noted earlier, this movement toward independence may be delayed or difficult for many adolescents with disabilities, and their parents may feel both frustration and concern. But some youngsters with disabilities may be satisfied with their limited freedom, a result of an inability to separate personal values from those of their parents. This suggests that autonomy should be understood as relative to the needs and abilities of each individual (Lewis et al., 1988).

For parents, the conflict between caretaking and letting go can be a particularly difficult one. Up until this period, their child has been a child, in both years and level of dependency. But parents with a child who will need ongoing care and some protection can easily go on and on treating the growing person as a child. For many parents, seeing their son or daughter as a perpetual child is the only way that they can accept or cope with the disability (Fairbrother, 1983).

Adult issues create tremendous stress for young people with disabilities and their families. Young people in need of both intimacy and private time must confront the attitudes of society, social isolation, parental overprotectiveness, and, in some cases, institutionalization (Bregman & Castles, 1988). The inability of some people with disabilities to conceptualize the abstract components of social sexuality and their lack of independence training and experience raise doubts about their decision-making abilities and their capacity to give informed consent to activities.

Parents must determine how involved they should become in making social arrangements for their young adult with a disability. In some cases the disability severely limits the young person's ability to move about or tend to his own body. In this case, sexual expression may require help (Miezio, 1983). Many parents of young adults who still need caretaking at a point when independence is the norm are discouraged and stressed by the lack of community opportunities, insufficient time to arrange for social activities, and the young adult's lack of social skills (Brotherson et al., 1988).

Planning for the transition into adulthood can be particularly difficult for the parents of young people with disabilities. They may be uncertain what the young person's adult roles and needs will be and unsure how to prepare them for the transition (Zetlin & Turner, 1985). Awareness of their child's imminent maturity may cause parents to wonder about their own future, as they cope with their own issues of aging and mortality.

Influences on Sexuality

Degree of Freedom To Make Decisions

Society expects adulthood to be accompanied by independence and separation from parents. According to this view, adults assume appropriate roles of responsibility, make their own decisions, and are responsible for the consequences of those choices.

Choices are one of the constants of adulthood. Decision making necessitates the recognition that there is a selection to be made, followed by a delineation of options and alternatives. Consequences for each of these options must be understood and willingly accepted with the decision.

For people with disabilities, independence may be impeded by physical and developmental disabilities or by the overprotectiveness of parents and professionals. Opportunity for self-determination may be limited by caretaking needs, mobility, and living situations. For some, self-esteem, which provides individuals with the notion that they have the right to make decisions, may have been sorely impaired, and cognitive levels may preclude the recognition and comprehension of the decisions to be made or even the perception that choices are available. The generation of alternatives may be restricted for some people with disabilities so only things that are presented to them or that are stimulated by impulse are seen as possibilities. Likewise, lack of experience and opportunity may limit their perceived and true choices. Some may be unable to formulate an understanding of the consequences that may follow the action they have chosen. As a result parents and professionals may have difficulty determining if informed consent has actually been provided.

An inverse relationship exists between an individual's ability to make a decision and the necessity for others to intervene in that process. The greater the ability of an individual with a disability to understand fully the decision to be made and to see the alternatives available as well as the resulting consequences, the less need for others to intervene in that decision. Conversely, in the case of an individual for whom recognition of decisions, available options, and outcomes is difficult, others will by necessity be involved in decision making for or with that person.

With regard to their child's sexuality, parents must determine when and how to make decisions and which decisions to make. They must confront their own feelings about sexuality and their attitudes about their adolescent engaging in such behaviors as masturbation, dating, intercourse, and entering marriage (Bregman & Castles, 1988). Decision making for parents may involve giving permission for the adult offspring to be sexual. Agency personnel and professionals must address legal, moral, and safety issues; deal with their own sexual attitudes; and reach a consensus on approaches with other staff members, while at the same time incorporating parental value systems.

One way in which professionals can further this decision-making process is by providing education to all parties involved. By providing information, discussing choices and consequences, and talking with parents, caregivers, and staff about decisions to be made, professionals can increase opportunities for independent or planned decision making for young adults with disabilities.

Education

The premise that all people have sexual needs leads to the conclusion that all people can cope better with those needs if they understand their physical and emotional manifestations. People need to know that they share these needs and feelings with everyone else. They need to know they are not alone in their strange new emotions, their happiness, and their misery (Fairbrother, 1983). However, because of myths, misconceptions, and fear, people with disabilities have typically received little or no formalized sex education (Craft & Craft, 1978). Yet they require accurate information and the opportunity to come to grips with their own sexuality in order to learn to express that sexuality in ways that are not harmful to themselves or others (Miezio, 1983).

People with disabilities need education in order to overcome the barriers (physical, social, emotional, and cognitive) that exist in the understanding of their own sexuality. Educational methods and strategies must provide access and understanding and be sensitive to what the young person's future may hold. For some young people, the best information would be behavioral and concrete in nature; for others, abstract concepts of relating might be explored.

Because sexuality is a lifelong process filled with a multitude of transitions, education must begin at an early age, not just at the onset of puberty, especially for those who learn slowly. The foundation of learning must be built early with some basic biological information and discussions of what "normal" behaviors are. Some children, such as those with visual impairments, may lack tools for learning the explicit and subtle behavior associated with gender expressions and social relationships. Professionals and parents should therefore start early to help these children feel at home with their bodies and emotions, and to express themselves in ways that will enhance personal development and social relationships (Schuster, 1987).

Parents and Family

Every child has an impact when it enters a family, but those with disabilities can have a particularly profound effect. Family members have expectations of children: how they will interact, the responsibilities they will assume, the development of independence (including bringing others into the family unit), and the eventual leaving for marriage, education, or employment. However, these social milestones may be reached or expressed in significantly different ways when a child has a disability.

Dealing with a child's sexuality is difficult for all parents. To think about it too early is to connect thoughts of "sex" with children, something that is viewed as socially and morally inappropriate for adults. Parents may also perceive the issue of sexuality as a problem to address in the distant future. If they do address the topic they may use a red-faced brusque manner that provides little information and a message that sexuality is not something to talk about or at the very best is an uncomfortable subject. More typical, however, is the natural tendency to ignore it for as long as possible, usually until secondary sex characteristics (e.g., facial hair) make the inevitable approach of adulthood impossible to ignore. For parents of some children with disabilities, this development may be delayed, thereby further deferring discussion of the issues associated with it.

By far, the most significant factor affecting an individual's sex life in the fullest meaning of the term is impressions from parents (Symonds & Wickware, 1978). Parents are their child's primary sex educators whether they talk about the topic or not, whether they present it comfortably or not. Everything that parents do contributes to being social-sexual educators of their child, from the way in which they interact physically to the way in which they talk to each other. Parents of children with disabilities can be the first and foremost providers of permission and limited information, if they can become comfortable with their child's sexuality. They can be the foundation for the young person's positive self-image, sexual independence, and comfort. Most important, as mentioned earlier, parents need to realize that ignoring sexuality does not cause it to go away. Parents have a responsibility to provide effective and relevant information about sexuality to all children, disabled or not (Cornelius et al., 1982).

How the parents handle the social sexuality of their child with disabilities derives initially from their own values and attitudes, not only toward their own sexuality but toward whether they connect it in any way to their child's disability. Those whose children were disabled at birth may have lingering feelings about the role that sex played in the results. Parents may feel responsible, guilty, or ashamed. Some may see the child's disability as a negative reflection of their sexuality.

Parents need to get beyond these feelings in order to nurture their child's own social sexuality. Certainly they should not choke down or deny their own feelings. They may, however, want to spend some time thinking about their values and attitudes (Miezio, 1983), to openly face their own sexuality, as well as acknowledge the sexuality of their child. This is difficult enough for parents of nondisabled children and even more so for parents of children with disabilities.

Disabilities bring into focus deep attitudes and values concerning physical attractiveness and sexual behavior. They may trigger parents' fear about their children's future when the time comes that parents can no longer care for them and protect them (Miezio, 1983). Other concerns include

1. How to talk about sexuality with their children, when to begin, what to say, and how to say it so that it can be understood.

2. How to help their children deal with and understand their sexual feelings, possibly including homosexual feelings.

3. Protecting their children from being abused and teaching them not to exploit others.

4. Determining whether their children should use birth control, what method should be used, when would sterilization be appropriate, and who should make these decisions.

5. Dealing with masturbation.

6. Determining their child's ability to make judgments and the ability to be independent and sexually responsible.

7. Determining if their children will marry or reproduce. Talking to their children about other options.

8. Understanding how a disability may affect a child's physical development and sexuality.

9. Helping their children to develop a feeling of positive self-esteem, confident body image, and comfort with their sexuality. Helping to give children a feeling that they have a right to be sexual but assisting them to make wise choices in the expression of sexuality.

10. Determining how to encourage and provide social opportunities for their children. Helping them decide who their friends will be. Do they know how to make friends? Can they discriminate between different types of relationships?

Professionals

Professionals can be as susceptible to the myths and misconceptions of social sexuality as anyone else. The same attitudes and values have had an impact on their lives, as mentioned earlier. Professionals should first explore their own feelings prior to beginning work with children and youth with disabilities or their families. By identifying their own views, they can avoid conflict with the family and engendering values that are not in keeping with those of the family. Professionals are expected to have all the information and be aware of all the resources. Many, however, may never have taken a course concerning social sexuality, and they may feel inadequate or overwhelmed when working with youngsters with disabilities and their families on this issue.

In a 1981 study conducted by the Sex and Disability Project, people with disabilities reported that they were not receiving as many sexuality-related services as they needed or wanted, chief among these being sex and disability courses (48.9%). Yet when rehabilitation counselors were polled, 72% said that they did not provide sexuality-related services to clients predominantly because "Clients don't ask for this service" (70%), followed by "lack of appropriate training" (51%) (Chipouras, 1981). The discomfort levels of both the person with disabilities and the provider act in collusion with strongly held societal myths to prevent provision of knowledge.

It is clear that many service providers need and want training about sexuality and disability. It is also obvious that disabled people are interested in receiving sex education and counseling services. To meet these needs, the provision of sexuality-related services must be considered a higher priority than it has been in the past. Policy makers and service providers need to view sexuality as an integral part of every person's well-being, and services addressing sexual issues should be included (if appropriate) in a client's overall plan (Chipouras, 1981).

Yet beyond the basics of information and knowledge provision are a number of value-laden issues that professionals need to approach when dealing with this topic:

1. How to provide appropriate professional recommendations, support, and feedback when the topic may be directly opposed to one's personal value system and therefore cause discomfort.

2. How to determine a client's level of knowledge prior to beginning an educational or counseling program.

3. How to determine a client's ability to understand his actions or someone else's and to make responsible decisions (informed consent).

4. How to facilitate the provision of information without overstepping boundaries or be in conflict with parental values.

5. How to work with parents so that they are more accepting and positive toward their child's sexuality.

6. How to determine when a client's behavior is a result of sexual abuse and not her disability. How to determine her ability to understand the consequences and therefore to counsel her appropriately.

7. How to deal with clients who exhibit aggressive behaviors perhaps as a result of sexual frustration (i.e., inability to masturbate).

8. How to proceed with educating or counseling students and clients without clear policies in place.

Issues and Interventions

There are many issues that parents and professionals must confront and address in cooperation. They must acknowledge that people with disabilities are sexual and demonstrate this understanding by providing education and information. They also need to provide opportunities for young people with disabilities not only to practice socialization but also, to the extent appropriate, to engage in adult relationships. The present lack of social experience may leave youngsters emotionally unprepared for the intimacy and involvement of adult sexual relationships (Bregman & Castles, 1988). This issue must be addressed so that young people can experience the intimacy of touching and caring that all human beings require. At present, because of their social isolation, many individuals with disabilities suffer from a deprivation of touching (Bregman & Castles, 1988).

Clearly the most critical intervention is the recognition and acknowledgment of the existence of and right to the expression of sexuality for all people. This simple acknowledgment is as meaningful for the professional as it is for the parent and the person with the disability. Without this basic acceptance, people with disabilities will forever be denied this most basic of human rights.

If this topic is to be dealt with effectively (and affectively), the professional will need greater information and training to feel comfortable with an increasingly active role. As a climate develops that encourages openness, parents and people with disabilities will have questions not only about their own sexuality but how to deal with others'. Educational programs for everyone should be encouraged and incorporated into any plan. These programs, of course, should be provided at the appropriate level and use accessible information. Comfort level is an extremely important element in addressing this topic, and having a good knowledge base is the chief factor in feeling more competent.

It is important that the professional work with the family progressively, rather than focus solely on the content of sexuality at any one period of time. Sexuality needs to be seen as a natural progression and life itself as a series of transitions. In viewing development in such a way, parents and their children with disabilities can not only pass through these stages successfully, but they can also predict and prepare for transitions, lessening the emotional trauma when the inevitable occurs. Assisting families to plan for the future in this way is a promising intervention that may improve the quality of life for the young adult and other family members (Zetlin & Turner, 1985).

Some segregationists would deny people with disabilities the opportunity to express their sexuality through lack of access. These segregationists range in views from extremists, who want to keep males and females completely apart, to the more frequently encountered people who panic when they see a loving relationship developing between two people with disabilities. They assume that it must lead either to sexual intercourse or to frustration if the pair are unable to consummate their desires. Very often, the segregationists' views are based on the false assumption, common in our modern world, that only sexual intercourse can satisfy sexual need (Fairbrother, 1983). Parents and professionals in partnership must find ways to ensure that a social-sexual continuum is available and to help people with disabilities to be sexually responsible together, rather than being kept apart.

Professionals must use their knowledge and assessment criteria to assist young people with disabilities and their parents in determining their future capabilities and goals and making appropriate decisions. Parents need support through this stage, as with all others. At this important and often stressful point of transition into adulthood for young people with disabilities, they and their parents need contacts with professionals that are particularly supportive and positive (Zetlin & Turner, 1985). Professionals can help families address some of the following questions about their child:

What are the parents frightened of?

What do they believe sex means to the people with disabilities that they know?

What signs of sexual awareness and need have they noticed?

What sort of relationships has the young person formed and have the parents or caregivers allowed them to develop freely?

Do they offer the young person alternatives, places where a relationship is socially acceptable?

If the decision is to have intercourse and the individual with a disability does not know how, should she be guided?

Should people with disabilities be encouraged to marry?

What criteria should parents expect before they encourage marriage?

Have people with disabilities the right to bear children?

What if the couple is not capable of independent living? Does that exclude them from marriage? (Fairbrother, 1983)

People with disabilities should have opportunities to practice their social skills and the chance to have a full realm of choice in their lives. Introducing social skills and appropriate information on sexuality early in a child's life makes each developmental transition easier. There is therefore a positive relationship between planning for adult needs and family functioning (Zetlin & Turner, 1985).

Conclusion

Because sexual expression is one of the most basic aspects of adult functioning, normalization theory holds that people with disabilities have a fundamental right to responsible and appropriate sexual gratification (Bregman & Castles, 1988). Yet, this view is still not widely advocated among the public, professionals, parents, and people with disabilities themselves. Guaranteeing this right should be a priority regardless of what moral or physical discomfort it creates. To do less—to deny someone the basic right to simple closeness and touch—will cause a great deal more damage and pain. Many barriers are slowly being eliminated. A primary one is limited access to information about sexuality. Another, the most desperate problem, is the lack of opportunities to form partnerships and loving relationships (Daniels, 1981).

People with disabilities, assisted by those who care about them, must labor to develop a world in which their need for social–sexual relationships is respected and their pleasure as sexual beings is encouraged. Often the sexual problems of people with disabilities are really the problems of parents, professionals, and others who come in contact with them. Because nondisabled people have more power, they may at times intrude upon the lives of people with disabilities, infringe on their adult rights, and try to shape their destinies. They may impose their own problems, attitudes, beliefs, prejudices, or lack of fulfillment. As a result, people with disabilities may be directed and constantly observed in their every move. They may rarely be allowed to be alone. They may not be given opportunities to explore relationships independently, to make mistakes, and to find fulfillment. People with disabilities may not need to change; what they need is loving guidance and the opportunity to fulfill themselves (Fairbrother, 1983).

References

Bregman, S., & Castles, E. (1988). Insights and interventions into sexual needs of the disabled adolescent. In A. Dell Orto & M. Blechar Gibbons (Eds.), *Family interventions throughout chronic illness and disability* (pp. 184–191). New York: Springer.

Brotherson, M. J., Houghton, J., Turnbull, A., Bronicki, G. J., Roeder-Gordon, C., Summers, J. A., & Turnbull, H. R., III. (1988). Parental planning for sons and daughters with disabilities. *Transitions Into Adulthood, 23,* 165–172.

Calderone, M., & Johnson, E. (1981). *The family book about sexuality.* New York: Bantam.

Chipouras, S. (1981). Sexuality-related services for disabled people. In D. Bullard & S. Knight (Eds.), *Sexuality and physical disability perspectives.* St. Louis: Mosby.

Cornelius, D., Chipouras, S., Makas, E., & Daniels, S. (1982). *Who cares? A handbook in sex education and counseling services for disabled people* (2nd ed.). Baltimore: University Park Press.

Craft, A., & Craft, M. (1978). *Sex and the mentally handicapped.* London: Routledge and Kegan Paul.

Craft, A., & Craft, M. (1982). Implications for the future. In A. Craft & M. Craft (Eds.), *Sex education and counseling for mentally handicapped people* (pp. 299–300). London: Costello.

Daniels, S. (1981). Critical issues in sexuality and disability. In D. Bullard & S. Knight (Eds.), *Sexuality and physical disability personal perspectives.* St. Louis: Mosby.

Dixon, H., & Mullinar, G. (Eds.). (1985). *Taught not caught: Strategies for sex education.* London: Learning Development Aids.

Fairbrother, P. (1983). The parents' viewpoint. In A. Craft & M. Craft (Eds.), *Sex education and counseling for mentally handicapped people* (pp. 95–108). London: Costello.

Gordon, S. (1974). *Sexual rights for the people who happen to be handicapped.* Syracuse: Center on Human Policy.

Grantham, E., & Russell, P. (1985). Parents as partners. In M. Griffiths & P. Russell (Eds.), *Working together with handicapped children: Guidelines for parents and professionals* (pp. 38–45). London: Souvenir Press and National Children's Bureau.

Lewis, M., Feiring, C., & Brooks-Gunn, J. (1988). Young children's social network as a function of age and dysfunction. *Infant Mental Health Journal, 9,* 142–157.

Lewis, V. (1987). *Development and handicaps.* Oxford: Basil Blackwell.

Miezio, P. M. (1983). *Parenting children with disabilities: A professional source for physicians and guide for parents.* New York: Marcel Dekker.

Schuster, C. S. (1987). Sex education of the visually impaired child: The role of parents. *Journal of Visual Impairment and Blindness, 81,* 98–99.

Stewart, W. F. R. (1979). *The sexual side of handicap: A guide for the caring professions.* Cambridge: Woodhead-Faulkner.

Symonds, M. E., & Wickware, L. (1978). Sex education of children with disabilities. In A. Comfort (Ed.), *Sexual consequences of disability* (pp. 243–245). Philadelphia: Stickly.

Thorton, C. (1981). Sex education for disabled children and adolescents. In D. Bullard & S. Knight (Eds.), *Sexuality and physical disability personal perspectives* (pp. 229–234). St. Louis: Mosby.

Zetlin, A. G., & Turner, J. L. (1985). Transition from adolescence to adulthood: Perspectives of mentally retarded individuals and their families. *Journal of Mental Deficiency, 89,* 570–579.

The Exceptional Child Grows Up: Transition from School to Adult Life

20

Edward M. Levinson, Lynne McKee, and Francis J. DeMatteo

P arents of adolescents frequently face emotional turmoil when the time comes for their children to make decisions regarding living arrangements, higher education, vocational pursuits, and marriage. Parents often wonder if they have taught their children the skills they need to make the realistic and informed decisions that would allow them to develop into content, responsible, and self-sufficient adults. If the children have disabilities, parents face even greater challenges at the time of this decision making. They may feel guilt and personal responsibility for their child's disability and have difficulty "letting go" when the time comes. Often, parents find that the vocational and lifestyle options for individuals with disabilities are still quite limited compared to those available for the nondisabled population.

Fortunately, society's views toward individuals with disabilities are changing. Although the right to work is not viewed as an entitlement, efforts are being made to extend the opportunity for meaningful employment and independent community living to a greater number of people with disabilities. The purpose of this chapter is to explore the issues involved in the transition of individuals with disabilities from school to adult society. The chapter will review the relevant literature on transition, the legislation that facilitated transition efforts, and transition models. Finally, it will discuss the critically important role of parent–professional collaboration in the transition process.

Overview

The life adjustment concerns expressed by parents are well founded. A number of researchers have explored the adjustment of people with disabilities into the community from the standpoints of employment, living arrangements, and general satisfaction with life. The President's Committee on the

Employment of the Handicapped reports that only 21% of people with disabilities will become fully employed, 40% will be underemployed and at the poverty level, and 26% will be on welfare (Pennsylvania Transition from School to the Workplace, 1986). Similarly, Rusch and Phelps (1987) have reported that 67% of Americans with disabilities between the ages of 16 and 64 are not working. Of those who are working, 75% are employed on a part-time basis, and of those not employed, 67% indicated that they would like to be employed.

Within the past 10 to 15 years, numerous statewide surveys have focused on the status of young people with disabilities who are no longer in school. Studies in Florida (Fardig, Algozzine, Schwartz, Hensel, & Westling, 1985), Washington (Edgar, 1987), Colorado (Mithaug, Horiuchi, & Fanning, 1985), Vermont (Hasazi, Gordon, & Roe, 1985; Hasazi et al., 1985), and Nebraska (Schalock & Lilley, 1986; Schalock et al., 1986) have indicated that the employment rate for individuals with disabilities is generally higher for females than for males and ranges between 45% and 70% depending upon the severity of disability and geographical location (rural, urban, metropolitan). A large number of those who are employed report to work on a part-time basis; many earn minimum wage or less. As a consequence, between 64% and 82% of those contacted did not live independently in the community but were at home with their parent or guardian.

The high school attrition rate appears to be higher among students with disabilities. Rusch and Phelps (1987) cite a survey done by Owing and Stocking in 1985 in which 30,000 sophomores and 28,000 seniors including those self-identified as having a disability were studied on a longitudinal basis. The findings indicated that those students with mild disabilities fared poorly regardless of whether they were receiving regular or special education. Twenty-two percent of the 1980 sophomores with disabilities dropped out of school between their sophomore and senior years as compared with 12% of students without disabilities. Furthermore, The Twelfth Annual Report to Congress on the Implementation of the Education of the Handicapped Act (U.S. Department of Education, Office of Special Education and Rehabilitative Services, 1990) specified that 47% of students with disabilities do not graduate from high school with a certificate of completion or a diploma. This finding is in line with Wagner and Shaver's 1989 study which determined that 44% of students with disabilities failed to graduate from high school while 36% dropped out of school. Students with learning disabilities and emotional disabilities appear to be particularly at risk of dropping out of school. Dropout rates for these students can exceed 40% and 50% respectively (Gajar, Goodman, & McAfee, 1993). Studies that have compared special education dropout rates with control group dropout rates or normative data have consistently demonstrated that students with disabilities leave school more often than students without disabilities (Ysseldyke, Algozzine, & Thurlow, 1992).

Recent research is consistent with previous studies but suggestive of some encouraging trends as well. D'Amico and Marder (1991) found that 57% and 67% of youth with disabilities who had been out of school at least 1 month and no more than 2 years were employed in 1987 and 1989, respectively. But even though the general employment rate increased, the rates for individuals with different types of disabilities continued to vary greatly. In 1989, the employment rate for individuals with learning disabilities was 67%; mental retardation, 56%; emotional disturbance, 48%; and multiple disabilities, 10% (Marder & D'Amico, 1992).

The large unemployment and high school dropout rates for individuals with disabilities indicate that special education has not successfully integrated these individuals into society. As a consequence, the economic cost to society of supporting the needs of people with disabilities may exceed $114 billion per year (Poplin, 1981). Historically, much of this money has been channeled into programs that support dependence rather than ones that facilitate independence (Pennsylvania Departments of Education & Labor and Industry, 1986).

The social, physical, and emotional benefits to be derived by individuals with disabilities from successful work and community adjustment are not to be slighted by the economic benefits to be derived by society. Historically, research has indicated that an individual's self-worth is intimately related to work performance and satisfaction (Dore & Meachum, 1973; Greenhaus, 1971; Kalanidi & Deivasenapathy, 1980; Snyder & Ferguson, 1976; Super, 1957) and that overall adjustment to work is associated with both physical and mental health (Kornhauser, 1965; O'Toole, 1973; Portigal, 1976) and overall life satisfaction (Bedeian & Marbert, 1979; Haavio-Mannila, 1971; Iris & Barrett, 1972; Orphen, 1978; Schmitt & Mellon, 1980). Obviously, the overall quality of life experienced by an individual with a disability will be influenced by the degree to which that individual successfully adjusts to work and community living.

Despite what many believe, the unemployment and underemployment rates among individuals with disabilities do not appear to be a function of a lack of available job opportunities. A review of occupational trends and predictions for the next few years indicates that jobs will be available for individuals who do not possess high skill levels. Projections indicate a significant increase in the number of jobs in health services, cleaning and building services, food preparation, other food services, and personal services (Silvestri & Lukasiewicz, 1987). With appropriate special education and transition services, many individuals with disabilities could successfully enter and maintain employment in these and other fields.

In an effort to ensure postschool opportunities, federal and state governments have made transition a priority for all individuals with disabilities. Efforts to integrate and coordinate special education, vocational education, vocational rehabilitation, and other adult services and to provide a more functionally oriented curriculum are aimed at preparing individuals with disabilities for an adulthood that includes a meaningful role in the community. Many of these efforts have been spurred by federal legislation.

Legislative Background

Legislation designed to assist individuals with disabilities in acquiring and maintaining employment and adjusting to community living has had an impact on the fields of vocational rehabilitation, vocational education, and special education. In the area of vocational rehabilitation, the Rehabilitation Act of 1973 (P.L. 93-112) provided federal support for the training of individuals with physical and cognitive disabilities. The law authorized grants to vocational rehabilitation agencies for counseling, training, referral, and other services and mandated that priority be given to those individuals with severe disabilities. This legislation required that the counselor, individual with disabilities, and parent or guardian participate in developing an Individualized Written Rehabilitation Plan describing the services to be provided to the individual and indicating what agency would be responsible for providing the identified services. An amendment to the act in 1978 (Developmental Disabilities Assistance and Bill of Rights Act) emphasized the provision of services to individuals with disabilities, including services related to independent living arrangements. This amendment also called for cooperative relationships between special education, vocational education, and vocational rehabilitation.

Section 504 of the Rehabilitation Act is sometimes referred to as the "bill of rights" for individuals with disabilities. It prohibits discrimination on the basis of disability in any program that receives federal monies. The act also calls for the mainstreaming of children with disabilities and for the provision of vocational counseling, guidance, and placement on a nondiscriminatory basis.

The Vocational Education Act of 1963 (P.L. 88-210) authorized federal grants to assist states in maintaining and improving vocational education, in developing new vocational education programs, and in providing part-time employment that would allow individuals to continue vocational training. The aim was to provide all individuals the opportunity to participate in quality realistic vocational training. This act also allowed federal funds to be used for occupational training for individuals with disabilities, but it did not mandate that any portion of the funds be used in this manner.

The Vocational Education Act of 1963 was amended in 1968 (Vocational Education Act Amendments) and again in 1976 to provide federal support for individuals with disabilities who had not been given equal access to publicly supported vocational education programs. This legislation called for state plans to link special education and vocational education, the use of procedural safeguards from the Education for All Handicapped Children Act (discussed below) to ensure that secondary school participants got necessary services, and the mainstreaming of individuals with disabilities.

In 1984 the Carl D. Perkins Vocational Education Act (P.L. 98-524) amended the Vocational Education Act of 1963. This far-reaching piece of legislation mandated increased services for both individuals with disabilities and disadvantaged citizens. The legislation required that parents and students had to receive information concerning vocational education opportunities no later than the beginning of the 9th grade and at least 1 year before the student was to enter the grade level at which vocational education was offered. Students and parents also had to be told the eligibility requirements for enrolling in these vocational programs. Once enrolled, students had to receive an assessment of interests, abilities, and special needs; special services including adaptation of curriculum, instruction, equipment, and facilities; guidance, counseling, and career development activities conducted by a professionally trained counselor; and special counseling services designed to facilitate transition from school to postschool employment or training.

A landmark piece of legislation that was an integral component of vocational education and rehabilitation was the Education for All Handicapped Children Act of 1975 (P.L. 94-142) and its corresponding amendments. The act mandated free appropriate public education for all children with disabilities between the ages of 3 and 22. The bill specifically called for "organized educational programs which are directly related to the preparation of individuals for paid or unpaid employment, or for additional preparation for a career requiring other than a baccalaureate or advanced degree." An amendment to the act in 1983 (P.L. 98-199) gave even greater emphasis to vocational education for students with disabilities by calling for state demonstration grants that would improve secondary special education programs, create incentives for employers to hire individuals with disabilities, increase educational opportunities at the postsecondary level, increase supported work opportunities, and make better use of job-training placement services for individuals with disabilities.

In October 1990 the Education for All Handicapped Children Act was amended and renamed the Individuals with Disabilities Education Act (IDEA, P.L. 101-476). In addition to reauthorizing and expanding many of the earlier provisions, IDEA added several new discretionary programs covering transition, services for children and youth with severe emotional disturbance, and research and dissemination related to attention-deficit/hyperactivity disorder (ADHD). Additionally, the law included transition services and assistive technology services as new definitions of special education services that must be addressed in a student's Individualized Education Plan (IEP). Rehabilitation counseling and social work services were also included as related services under this law. Last, the services and rights under this law were more fully expanded to include children with autism and traumatic brain injury.

Amendments to IDEA in June of 1997 (P.L. 105-17) placed a new emphasis upon using transition services as a vehicle to obtain improved outcomes for individuals with disabilities. Section 601(c) of the amendments implied that the implementation of IDEA had been stunted by both an overall lack of expectations and by an absence of attention toward reliable research into established teaching and learning methods for children and youth with disabilities (deFur & Patton, in press). In light of these findings, the amendments stated that the primary purpose of IDEA was to "ensure that all children with disabilities have available to them a free appropriate education that emphasizes special education and related services designed to meet their unique needs and prepare them for employment and independent living" (Section 601[d] Purposes [1] [A]). Furthermore, this legislation insisted that the ultimate goal of a free appropriate education under the amended IDEA was to "prepare students with disabilities for employment and independent living" (deFur & Patton, in press). The 1997 IDEA amendments introduced specific changes that affected services offered to students with disabilities. These changes included the definition and age requirement for the initiation of services, participation in statewide testing, and discipline evaluation and service requirements.

Definition and Age Requirement

Section 602(30) defines transition services as a coordinated set of activities for a student with a disability that

(A) is designed within an outcome-oriented process, which promotes movement from school to post-school activities, including post-secondary education, vocational training, integrated employment (including supported employment), continuing and adult education, adult services, independent living, or community participation;
(B) is based upon the individual student's needs, taking into account the student's preferences and interests; and
(C) includes instruction, related services, community experiences, the development of employment and other postschool adult living objectives, and, when appropriate, acquisition of daily living skills and functional vocational evaluation.

Because of evidence showing the benefits of early transition planning and the increasing dropout rate among individuals with disabilities, IDEA mandates that transition planning begin by age 14. More specifically, Section 614(d)(1)(A)(vii) of the legislation requires the following:

(I) beginning at age 14, and updated annually, a statement of the transition service needs of the child under the applicable components of the child's IEP that focuses on the child's courses of study (such as participation in advanced placement courses or a vocational education program).

Furthermore, the next provision states that specific transition planning and services that include other agencies are still required before the time the child reaches age 16. This section specifically requires the following:

> (II) beginning at age 16 (or younger, if determined appropriate by the IEP team) a statement of needed transition services for the child, including, when appropriate, a statement of the interagency responsibilities or any needed linkages.

Participation in Statewide Testing

Standardized testing is one means by which a school demonstrates its effectiveness. Because many standardized tests do not allow for the accommodations needed by a student with a disability, and because administrators are often concerned with having the highest possible test scores, students with disabilities have often been excluded from participating in statewide testing (deFur & Patton, in press). If a school's educational program is effective according to statewide testing, then the state government will direct more financial resources to the school. Thus, standardized testing serves as an accountability measure. When administrators exclude a group of students from standardized testing, the level of accountability the school feels toward that group decreases. Because legislators wanted to ensure that school systems were accountable for student progress, students with disabilities will now participate (with the necessary accommodations) in general state and districtwide assessments (deFur & Patton, in press). If participation in general state assessments is not appropriate, then the states are directed to implement alternate assessments for students with disabilities. All performance outcomes and participation rates must be reported to the federal government.

Discipline Evaluation

Students with disabilities may manifest behavior problems because their disabilities sometimes affect their social development. As a direct result, many students face suspension or expulsion, which can interrupt learning while causing a vicious cycle of poor academics and inappropriate behavior (deFur & Patton, in press). Students who experience these problems view dropping out of school as an alternative. Thus, "behavior issues become transition issues" (deFur & Patton, in press).

The 1997 amendments to IDEA state in Section 614(d)(3)(B)(i)

> that the IEP Team shall consider for a child whose behavior impedes learning, interventions, strategies, and supports, including positive behavioral interventions, strategies, and supports to address that behavior. In

addition, the legislation requires that a functional behavioral assessment be conducted for students who engage in behavior that constitutes a possible long term suspension or expulsion, if none currently exists as part of the IEP evaluation. (deFur & Patton, in press)

The 1997 IDEA amendments breathed new life into legislation for individuals with disabilities and suggest that all special education services should be built upon transition goals.

A Brief Review of Transition Models

Office of Special Education and Rehabilitation Services (OSERS) Model

OSERS Programming for the Transition of Youth with Disabilities: Bridges from School to Working Life was published in 1984 and became the generic roots from which many other transition models developed. In this document, transition is defined in the following manner:

> The transition from school to working life is an outcome oriented process encompassing a broad array of services and experiences that lead to employment. Transition is a period that includes high school, the point of graduation, additional postsecondary education or adult services, and the initial years in employment. Transition is a bridge between the security and structure offered by the school and the opportunities and risks of adult life. Any bridge requires both a solid span and a secure foundation at either end. The transition from school to work and adult life requires sound preparation in the secondary school, adequate support at the point of school leaving, and secure opportunities and services, if needed, in adult situations. (Will, 1984, pp. 9–24)

There are three underlying assumptions inherent in the OSERS model: (1) the individual who is leaving school is moving from a somewhat organized system into a more complex and confusing one that is not well understood by professionals, let alone by parents and consumers; (2) transition plans should address all persons with disabilities, and it is the professional's responsibility to identify the services needed to assist in the transition of each individual; and (3) paid employment is the goal of the transition plan. This model calls for a firm high school foundation in which the curricula in both special and vocational education provide students with job skills appropriate for the local community. Whenever possible, potential employers should have an opportunity to observe students' performance within community jobs.

The OSERS model provides for three "bridges" from high school to employment:

1. *Transition without special services.* Individuals using their own resources or those used by all citizens to find gainful employment or to continue their education at the postsecondary level

2. *Transition with time limited services.* Individuals using such services as vocational rehabilitation and job-training programs to assist in gaining employment; once employment is secured, the individual is able to function independently

3. *Transition with ongoing services.* Individuals using continuing adult services to obtain and maintain employment as an alternative to custodial or sheltered employment

In this model the final outcome of the transition plan is employment. This sole outcome was subsequently viewed by many as rather narrow; more recent models view the goal of transition to be independent living in the community, a component of which includes employment.

The Virginia Commonwealth University Model

Paul Wehman (1986) of Virginia Commonwealth University (VCU) has developed a plan that expands and enhances many of the concepts outlined in the OSERS model. His model suggests that the transition from school to the workplace is a three-stage process that includes the following:

1. input and foundation school instruction
2. planning for the transition process
3. placement into meaningful employment

The school instruction portion of this plan emphasizes the importance of a functional curriculum within which activities are specifically designed to prepare students for vocational placement. It calls for integrated school services, including exposure to natural work settings with training taking place within the community whenever possible. Finally, it calls for community-based instruction in which students over the age of 12 spend decreasing amounts of time in the classroom and increasing amounts of time at job sites learning job skills, interpersonal skills, and other skills that will directly benefit them when they leave the school environment.

The process of planning for transition includes the development of an individualized transition plan that lists the competencies to be achieved by the student and the transition services to be provided both during and following the school years. The plan is designed to emphasize functional skills required on the job, at home, and in the community. Participation of the parent or guardian is viewed as critical, and this model calls for parent education activities to improve the background information and skill effectiveness of parents as they participate in transition planning. Cooperation among the various agencies that will be involved with the student during the period of transition is another aspect of the planning phase. Finally, this model presents several alternative employment outcomes to persons with disabilities, including competitive employment, supported competitive employment, enclaves, and specialized industrial training.

Transdisciplinary Transition Model

The Transdisciplinary Transition Model (TTM) advocated by Levinson (1998) encompasses services from a variety of community agencies in addition to the schools, and consists of five phases: Assessment, Planning, Training, Placement, and Followup.

Assessment. An initial first step in transition planning is an assessment of a student's skills and individual needs. A variety of domains need to be assessed including intellectual–cognitive, educational–academic, social–interpersonal, occupational–vocational, independent living, and physical–sensory. Different assessment approaches and techniques can be used to gather information about a student. Assessment should not be the responsibility of one professional but instead should be conducted by a team of professionals, each of whom is responsible for gathering specific information about the student. Professionals involved in this process may be employed by the schools or by community agencies.

Planning. Following a thorough assessment of the student's individual needs and skills, the transdisciplinary transition team can use the information gathered to develop a transition plan for the student to be included in the student's IEP. This plan should specify goals and objectives and the professionals and agencies responsible for providing needed services. Additionally, the plan can include a time frame for service provision.

Training. Following the development of a transition plan as part of the student's IEP, instruction and training is initiated. In addition to school personnel, professionals from a variety of agencies may be involved in training the student. Training should focus on assisting the student in acquiring those skills that will allow for successful functioning in the community.

Placement. Once instruction and training have been completed, the student is ready to be placed in a job, in a residence, or in a postsecondary educational setting. A variety of options exist, and the appropriateness of any one option for a student depends upon his level of functioning.

Followup. In the final phase of the transdisciplinary transition model, the success of the placement is evaluated. This assessment may lead to termination of some support services, initiation of other services, or a change of placement.

Levinson (1998) recommended that transition should be conceptualized as a component of a K–12 career education program, and that career development theory should form the basis for program development. Additionally, he suggested that assessment might be the most critical component of transition planning, in that individual transition plans are developed based upon the needs identified from the assessment.

Other Transition Models

Several other transition models have been developed in various states including Missouri, Minnesota, Pennsylvania, Washington, and Oregon. Some, like the OSERS and VCU models described above, emphasize employment as the primary goal of the transition process. Others view transition from a broader perspective and see employment as being but one component of the overall transition effort.

Halpern (1985) developed a model that emphasizes the nonvocational aspects of transition. This model was directly related to his definition of transition:

> Transition refers to a change in status from behaving primarily as a student to assuming emergent adult roles in the community. These roles include employment, participation in post secondary education, maintaining a home, becoming appropriately involved in the community, and experiencing satisfactory personal and social relationships. The process of enhancing transition involves the participation and coordination of services, and natural supports within the community. The foundations for transition should be laid during the elementary and middle school years, guided by the broad concept of career development. Transition planning should begin no later than age 14, and students should be encouraged to the full extent of their capabilities, to assure a maximum amount of responsibility for such planning. (Halpern, 1994)

Halpern viewed successful community adjustment as the goal of transition and he believed that quality of life and social and interpersonal issues were just as important as employment. Through research conducted in Washington, Oregon, California, and Colorado, Halpern concluded that success in employment did not necessarily correlate with success in other areas of life. Consequently, he advocated programs that consider all life dimensions when determining need for services.

The use of a functional curriculum, with emphasis placed on vocational and career as well as life-skills issues, is inherent in most transition models.

Brolin (1986) developed a "Life-Centered Career Education (LCCE) Model for the Transition from School to Work," which emphasized the inclusion of career-oriented education even at the preschool level. Brolin presented 12 propositions, generated from research in a variety of areas, that he believed would facilitate the training of individuals with disabilities and assist in their acquiring the skills necessary to become self-sufficient adults. Included in these propositions were the integration of career education in all areas of instruction; "hands-on" learning experiences wherever possible; active partnership among schools, parents or guardians, business, and industry and community agencies; and the creation of a position for a Training Resource Coordinator who would assume responsibility for transition services. Brolin described these guidelines as a total-person approach that emphasized all aspects of the individual's development, not just vocational development.

Finally, some transition advocates are concerned that the current Excellence in Education Movement may hamper efforts to get functional curricula into classrooms where needed. This education movement calls for a set number of credits in English, mathematics, science, social studies, and other areas. Not only are many of the courses in these areas not necessarily "functional" for all students, but the requirement that all students be subjected to such an academically oriented curriculum could take time away from functional, life skill, and vocational instruction. Relatedly, many professionals are currently recognizing the need for alternative diplomas that would indicate the specialized instruction the student received and would reflect the student's accomplishments more adequately than a certificate of attendance, which is the current alternative to a regular diploma. Although these issues are as yet unresolved, they will most certainly influence transitioning efforts in the coming years.

Characteristics of Effective Transition Programs

Though transition programs vary from one locality to the next, the professional literature in the field suggests that certain characteristics are associated with successful programs. Readers will recognize many of these as elements from the models just discussed. According to the literature, successful transition programs are characterized by a comprehensive transdisciplinary assessment of a student's skills and needs; the development of an individual transition plan based upon the results of the assessment; involvement of parents in the transition planning process; involvement of the private sector and local business people in the transition process; involvement of community agencies and the development of interagency agreements; integration of academic, vocational, interpersonal, and career development skills into the curriculum; on-the-job training of students; follow-up services to students placed in jobs; and an evaluation of the effectiveness of the program. Though not all transition programs will incorporate all of the aforementioned characteristics, a majority of these characteristics are present in effective programs. The following section addresses one of these characteristics: involvement of parents.

Working with Parents

Any effort at improving the school to work transition for disabled youth that fails to incorporate parental involvement as a major component of the process will have limited success. . . . A mutual trust relationship between parents and professionals needs to be nourished. . . . The parent/ student will have to choose the type of activity or service outcome that is important to them. Preferably, this sort of decision making should not be done in isolation, but more appropriately through the participation of the parent, client, professional team. (Pennsylvania Departments of Education & Labor and Industry, 1986, p. 83)

For school professionals, the successful transition of a student with disabilities from high school to work and community living is extremely rewarding. It serves to validate the meaning of education and confirms that the IEPs that have been developed for students over the years have been meaningful and appropriate. Fortunately, transition is often a smooth and relatively easy process. Students, parents, school professionals, and community representatives agree regarding the academic, vocational, and independent living skills necessary to achieve transition objectives, and the resources available to assist the student in meeting these objectives are already available in the community.

Sometimes, however, transition planning is a difficult and frustrating activity. Parents and school professionals can disagree regarding what would be most appropriate for a student following graduation. In some cases students but not parents are ready for the transition to occur. In the case of students with more severe disabilities, school personnel often advocate for group home or semi-independent living arrangements with sheltered employment. Parents frequently refuse these options, choosing instead to have the student remain in the home; suggestions regarding therapeutic day activities or sheltered employment are disregarded. This leads school professionals to worry about what will happen to students as parents grow older and become unable to care for them. School personnel are often concerned that the student, who has had stimulating activities and developed meaningful relationships with peers while in school, will become bored and unhappy while living at home. When school professionals and parents differ regarding a child's post–high school plans, it is extremely important that school staff avoid negative judgments about parents and make every effort to view the situation from the parents' perspective. As frustrating as it may be, the only thing school personnel can do in some cases is to provide parents with information and resources which they might use in the future when they are ready to deal with transition issues.

In the case of students with mild disabilities, other obstacles confront school personnel. The student sometimes expresses little interest in post–high school life. She may not have acquired the skills needed for independent living and meaningful work, and show no interest or motivation to do so. In other cases the student does have the interest or necessary skills to perform various jobs; however, opportunities for employment in these areas is not available in the local community. These situations, and others like them, will test the creativity and resourcefulness of the transition team.

Additionally, school personnel themselves often serve as barriers to the development of a successful transition plan. Too often transition planning is not given the attention it deserves. School personnel often view high school graduation as the only important goal; they believe that the student's life after leaving high school is not their responsibility and therefore is of little significance. This attitude leads one to question the meaning of education. If students graduate but cannot successfully take on adult roles, has the educational system failed? As discussed previously, legislation mandates that transition planning be initiated by age 14. It is important that transition planning be taken seriously by all involved in the process; merely giving lip service to the process does a disservice to all students.

With this in mind, we now explore the role of parents and professionals in transition planning.

Involving Parents in Transition Assessment and Programming

The involvement of the parent in the educational process must begin early in the child's life. A parent who has not been involved in the child's educational planning prior to adolescence is not likely to become involved suddenly at the time of transition. It is important that "transition awareness" on the part of the parent begins early in the child's academic career and be ongoing throughout the child's life. To be most effective, students and their parents should be involved in career development activities from early elementary school onward. In addition, parents of students with disabilities should be actively involved in IEP development from the time their child is placed in special education until the child graduates from high school.

Izzo and Shumate (1991) suggest the following reasons why parents should be involved in the transition process:

- Parents can serve as critical resources in program planning because they know their children better than anyone else.

- Parents can play an important role in maintaining continuity of training and purpose.

- Parents can become system advocates who act as catalysts for changes professionals desire but are hindered from accomplishing.
- Parents can act as role models and teachers who communicate the connection between positive learning and job success to their children.
- Parents can complement professional efforts by providing support and encouragement to their children.
- Parents can report the positive results to the community.

The specific role that parents play in transdisciplinary transition assessment and planning will vary. There are numerous ways to involve parents in this process, some of which are not feasible in every locality. Parents can be involved in the assessment process by

- Becoming the cornerstone of the transdisciplinary transition assessment team. Parents can provide the team with data concerning the child's interests, work habits, skills, and personality characteristics and can complete interviews, rating scales, and checklists.
- Participating in the development of their child's IEP. Parents can suggest applicable educational and vocational objectives and, more specifically, assist in the development of objectives in the areas of employment, residential living, and community functioning.
- Becoming a member of local, state, and federal advisory councils.
- Joining advocacy groups for individuals with disabilities.

Research has demonstrated that the role of the family in the transition process is critical. As Johnson and Rush (1993) stated, "Lack of parent participation and involvement may be detrimental to the achievement of successful transition outcomes" (p. 6). Additionally, Everson, Rachal, and Michael (1992) discovered that interagency teams that adopted parents as co-members and decision makers were "more effective in stimulating service delivery change at the individual, local, regional, and state levels" (p. 48).

However, as Ott (1991) suggested, family involvement in the school in any form has only rarely matched the enthusiastic rhetoric advocating it or the considerable body of research supporting it. After surveying 200 families of students with disabilities, McNair and Rusch (1990) concluded that parents were not as involved in the transition process as they desired to be. Furthermore, McNair and Rusch discovered that

- Approximately 70% of parents desired involvement; however, a little more than 30% were actually involved.
- Significantly more parents desired an equal role in decision making than were given the opportunity.
- Although 12% of parents reported no involvement with the transition team, fewer than 2% reported that they desired no involvement.

- Parents wanted to be more involved than they were in finding jobs and arranging community living for their children.

In studying individuals with moderate and severe disabilities, Schalock et al. (1986) found that students whose families were moderately to highly involved in their programming were more successful on employment outcome measures than were students whose families had low involvement. Further findings indicated that those who had high family involvement received higher wages and worked more hours per week than did those with low family involvement. Schalock and Lilley (1986) reported that family involvement has been shown repeatedly to be related to successful living and employment. In a similar study Hasazi, Gordon, and Roe (1985) found that among all postschool individuals with disabilities, 84% had found work through the self–family–friend network. The value of active family involvement in achieving successful transition appears to be well documented. Unfortunately, research suggests that as a child grows older, the family typically becomes less involved in the educational planning process. Johnson, Bruininks, and Thurlow (1987) cited a 1982 study by Lynch and Stein which found that parents of older students participated in IEP conferences significantly less often than did parents of younger children.

Teachers are apparently dissatisfied with such decreased parental involvement and desire more collaboration with parents. After sending questionnaires to administrators, teachers, and parents in the state of Oregon, Benz and Halpern (1987) reported that 36% of the responding school personnel were dissatisfied with parental support while 44% indicated that they would like more communication and parent involvement in classroom activities. Over half of the parents indicated they had contact with their child's teacher once per term or less. Relatedly, one third of the parents indicated that they had no idea what their children would be doing in terms of employment either 1 or 10 years following high school, and one quarter of them had no idea where their children would be living 1 or 10 years after school. Similarly, in a survey of special education administrators in New Hampshire, only 11% of the reporting districts indicated that parents were routinely invited to attend team meetings, whereas 52% reported that parents were either seldom or never invited to attend these team meetings (Ott, 1991).

Barriers to Active Parent Involvement

Several obstacles impede the establishment of an effective collaborative relationship between parents and professionals (Brynelsen, 1984; Murray, 1990). The following are examples of the numerous hurdles faced by parents when working with professionals (Murray, 1990): lack of confidence in themselves as parents, problems in balancing the demands of their children with other family needs, under- or overestimation of their child's potential and the contributions that professionals can make, and negative past experiences with professionals. The following are among the obstacles faced by professionals when working with parents: no preparation in working with parents, anxiety or resistance toward the idea of parent involvement, a tendency to adopt an authoritarian approach with parents, uncertainty about admitting limitations in skill or knowledge, having high or low expectations for parents, using professional jargon, withholding or refusing access to information, and emphasizing weaknesses rather than strengths in the child.

In a survey of the literature, Ott (1991) identified three common barriers to effective school–family collaborative planning: a reliance on an "expert" model of consultation and problem solving, competition between parents and school personnel, and economic considerations.

The "Expert" Model. Educators sometimes communicate the message that decision making is solely their responsibility and that parents have little say. When parents are treated as being less knowledgeable, powerful, and important than school personnel, they may assume a more passive and withdrawn position. Unfortunately, school personnel are often more comfortable with passive uninvolved parents than they are with assertive involved parents. Hence, school personnel sometimes behave in subtle (and not so subtle) ways to encourage such passivity.

Competition Between Home and School. The expert stance adopted by educators frequently elicits a defensive posture on the part of parents. Parents sometimes react in this way because they feel responsible for the difficulties their children may be experiencing in school. In many cases, parents feel that expert educators are usurping their role as parents by taking responsibility for making important decisions. These feelings can provoke resentment, hostility, anger, and frustration. When educators adopt an expert stance that constricts the parent's freedom of choice, a natural competition between parent and professional may result.

Economic Considerations. Parent involvement in transition planning may be inconvenient and costly for both parents and professionals. Because parents live according to their daily work schedule and depend upon the weekly paycheck, they are often unable to meet with school personnel during the work day. Consequently, school personnel may have the frustrating job of contacting and scheduling parents for daytime meetings. These factors permit both parents and professionals to be comfortable with parental noninvolvement.

Overcoming Barriers to Parental Involvement: The Professional's Responsibility

Professionals should be trained to work with parents during the initial planning stages of a transition program (Ott, 1991). At a minimum, professionals should be trained to

1. Communicate with parents in a language they can easily understand (for example, avoiding acronyms).

2. Reinforce parents for their strengths, their successes, and their involvement in the transition planning process.

3. Encourage parents to believe that they are experts who possess knowledge about their children that school personnel do not have. Parents should be made aware that this knowledge is critical to effective transition planning.

4. Refrain from patronizing parents. Professionals should be trained to show respect, encouragement, and understanding while incorporating parental ideas into transition plans.

5. Recognize that parents may be perceiving the situation from a very different perspective. Explore that and let the parents know they are entitled to a different viewpoint.

The professional must also assist the parent in viewing education from a multidimensional perspective. As noted elsewhere in this volume, the professional must assume multiple roles when assisting parents. These roles include therapist, expert, and advocate.

Therapist. Professionals must be aware that even at the level of transition, many parents continue to experience guilt regarding their child's disability. Likewise, parents are frequently apprehensive about their child's future. In fact, many parents who have successfully dealt with these feelings while the child was in school experience renewed guilt and anxiety when they realize that their child is ready to begin life as an adult. Some parents never fully accept the idea that their child has a disability; these parents keep expecting that at some point in time their child will be "normal." These feelings and issues can frequently present obstacles to objective and realistic decision making on the part of parents while jeopardizing collaborative transition programming. As such, they must be identified and resolved by the professional before additional programming is initiated. In some cases, short-term counseling may be necessary to resolve these issues.

Expert. The role of expert requires that the professional assume both an educational and problem-solving perspective when working with parents in transition. As an expert, the professional must educate parents about the kinds of decisions they and their children must make, and the type of information that must be considered if they are to make realistic and informed decisions about postschool life. The types of decisions that must be made vary but include the vocational, residential, independent living, and recreational options that may be appropriate for their child. The type of information the professional must provide to parents in order to facilitate such decision making is twofold: (1) information about their child (i.e., his abilities, interests, values, and personality characteristics) and (2) information about the vocational, residential, independent living, and recreational options that are available. Although it is the professional's responsibility to ensure that this information is available to the parent, the professional should also encourage the parents to gather as much of this information as they can on their own. Once they have pooled this information, the parents and professional can jointly assume a problem-solving perspective in making necessary transition decisions.

Advocate. As mentioned throughout this chapter, the transition process is complex and often confusing to parents. Many different professionals and agencies are involved and assume different roles in the process. To complicate matters, agencies frequently use different criteria to determine eligibility for services, and professionals often disagree. As an advocate for the parents and their child, the professional is responsible for sorting through this confusion, identifying services to which the child is entitled, and clarifying and resolving all disagreements among the various professionals. As an advocate, the professional should attempt to organize and present all information to the parent in an orderly and coherent fashion. In addition to preserving the rights and privileges of the parents and child, the advocate also acts as a liaison between the parent and other involved agencies and professionals. The importance of this role will become clearer when team planning is discussed next.

Team Planning

In an effort to provide better organized transition services to individuals with disabilities, many states have developed interagency agreements. These agreements involve educational and vocational rehabilitation personnel and other adult service providers who function as a team in facilitating transition. Typically, such teams consist of any combination of teachers (regular education, vocational education, and special education), psychologists (school and clinical), counselors (school and vocational rehabilitation), vocational evaluators, social workers, and administrators. The professional should be familiar with three primary types of teams: (1) the multidisciplinary team in which each professional independently makes recommendations, which are compiled by one team member into a final report; (2) the interdisciplinary team in which the client is evaluated by a variety of professionals who then make decisions by group consensus; and (3) the transdisciplinary team in which professionals continue to be involved after the initial assessment in terms of interaction, evaluation, and assessment, but one professional assumes the responsibility of carrying out the recommendations and working directly with the client and family (Levinson, 1998; Pennsylvania Departments of Education & Labor and Industry, 1987).

In terms of working with clients and their families, and in view of the ongoing nature of the transition process, the transdisciplinary team approach offers numerous advantages over other team planning models. Although most Individualized Education Plans are completed by interdisciplinary teams, the transdisciplinary team may be more effective in some cases for the following reasons:

• It is easy for a client and her family to be intimidated in an interdisciplinary team meeting. When many "experts" are discussing what is "best," the feelings of the client or client's parents can be overlooked. To avoid this problem, the transdisciplinary approach has one professional function as the main contact person between the family and the team.

• The transition process is an ongoing one. Given that both educators and adult service providers have large caseloads, the transdisciplinary model is more economical.

• The transdisciplinary model is less confusing for the client and his family. They know exactly whom to contact with their questions or concerns.

• The responsibility for the transition plan rests primarily in the hands of one individual. There is less likelihood of "buck passing" if one person bears the primary responsibility for overseeing the plan.

• Unfortunately, issues of "turf" and "territory" frequently arise during team approaches. When a client and family become involved in these issues, the outcome is never positive. The transdisciplinary model is less likely to involve clients in these issues.

Individual Planning

Philosophically, professionals should view themselves as advocates for the client and the client's family, and should attempt to facilitate realistic and informed decision making. To the maximum extent possible, responsibility for decision making should rest with the client and the client's family. The professional's role is to provide the client with the information necessary for realistic and informed decision making and to attempt to remove obstacles (such as guilt or anxiety) that may impede such decision making.

The professional working with a client and family to facilitate successful transition from school to adult life must be knowledgeable about a number of topics that cross several major disciplines including psychology, vocational education, vocational rehabilitation, and special education. Although these topics cannot be described in detail within this chapter, the professional working as a member of a transdisciplinary transition team should have a general understanding of three important topics: (a) transition assessment, (b) vocational or life skills instruction and functional academics, and (c) vocational and residential placement options and considerations.

Transition Assessment

Professionals should try to follow certain strategies when planning assessments with regard to transition. First, they should structure assessments with career development theory in mind and interpret all assessment data in light of this theory. They cannot design or implement a valid assessment program without knowing what developmentally appropriate behavior to expect of an individual at any given point in time. Through an understanding of career development theory, they can decide what traits to assess in a particular individual at any given grade or age level. Career development theory will also lend perspective to the assessment results, allowing users of the assessment data to generate developmentally appropriate recommendations for the student. Second, a transdisciplinary team should conduct the assessments, which should embody a multitrait, multimethod theoretical perspective (Levinson, 1993). Third, the team should only use instruments with acceptable psychometric properties that have been adequately standardized. Last, assessment should be an ongoing process rather than a one-time occurrence. In that assessment is linked to career development which is a continuous process, it should naturally be a somewhat continuous process as well.

Consistent with these recommendations, many vocational assessment programs based in the schools are multilevel programs. At each level, the assessment process has different purposes (based upon what is developmentally appropriate), uses a variety of assessment techniques and strategies, and is designed to gather different types of information. Different professionals are responsible for several aspects of the assessment, and assessment responsibilities are assigned based upon a professional's knowledge and expertise. Programs usually consist of either two or three levels of assessment. As summarized by Anderson, Hohenshil, Buckland-Heer, and Levinson (1990), *Level 1* assessments begin during the elementary school years; focus upon an individual's needs, values, interests, abilities, interpersonal skills, and decision-making skills; use vocational and career exploration activities; and have the goal of building self awareness. *Level 2* assessments generally occur during the middle school or junior high school years; focus more specifically on vocational interests, vocational aptitudes, work habits, and career maturity; use interviews, observations, and standardized norm-referenced assessment instruments; and have the goal of continuing to encourage career exploration and assisting individuals in making tentative choices regarding educational and career goals. A *Level 3* assessment generally occurs during the high school years, often employs more experientially based assessment devices like work samples and situational assessments, and focuses upon the specific training needed to obtain postschool education or employment.

Generally, such assessments should be completed as part of a student's triennial reevaluation (which is required by law) and be initiated early in a student's educational career (as early as the 6th grade) (Levinson & Capps, 1985). Along with sharing the assessment results with the client and his family as part of the vocational decision-making process, the professional should use the results of the assessment as the foundation for planning and initiating vocational education and instruction. For a comprehensive treatment of issues associated with the establishment and implementation of school-based vocational assessment programs, readers are referred to Levinson (1993).

Vocational and Life Skills Instruction and Functional Academics

As mentioned earlier, professionals involved in transition efforts with clients with disabilities should advocate a functional skills approach to instruction. They should use transition assessment results to determine what functional life skills (including academic skills in reading, writing, and computation) need to be taught because they are necessary for independent functioning in the community and on the job. Similarly, transition assessment results should provide the professional with some preliminary information relative to the appropriateness of training in various occupational areas. The assessment should identify realistic vocational training options for a client; then the training itself should develop the skills necessary for entry-level employment in the occupational area. It should gradually introduce advanced skills for higher level jobs. For clients with more severe disabilities, instruction should be a continual process of teaching a skill, testing to assess acquisition, and teaching until mastery. Once mastery is reached, the next sequential skill leading to entry-level employment can be taught. Ideally, in order to facilitate generalization of skills from training to the job, some training should be conducted on the job. A similar approach to the instruction of life skills and functional academics can be used as well.

Vocational and Residential Placement Options and Considerations

The vocational and residential placement options for individuals with disabilities are numerous, varied, and expanding. Vocational options can be categorized as competitive employment, in which individuals are placed in competitively salaried community jobs without ongoing support services; supported employment, in which individuals are placed in jobs with special assistance from job coaches who provide ongoing support (including training, retraining, and problem resolution); and sheltered employment, in which individuals are placed in businesses operated by human service agencies, typically termed "sheltered workshops" or "work activity centers."

Professionals can choose from a variety of approaches to facilitate the job placement of individuals with disabilities, including job-seeking skills training, job matching and referral services, job adaptation, and community-based training and supported employment. Job-seeking skills training teaches individuals (usually via classes) the skills necessary to obtain and keep a job (skills such as resume preparation and interviewing), after which individuals assume responsibility for seeking out their own jobs. Job matching and referral services are placement resources in which job openings are collected and matched to the interests and capabilities of job applicants. This service is frequently used in combination with other services. Job modification is a type of selective placement approach that focuses on adaptation of job tasks and the working environment in order to accommodate the needs and limitations of the individual. Community-based training and supported employment, including on-the-job training and work-study programs, is a placement process in which training is provided by an employer, and vocational counselors or job coaches monitor client progress and assist in remediating job-related difficulties. Selection of an appropriate job-placement strategy should be made in consultation with the client and client's family and depends on the individual needs and characteristics of the client.

There are several residential living options that may be considered for an individual with a disability. These include living independently, living with the family, supervised living, residential care living, family life home, and intermediate care facilities. The appropriateness of a particular option for an individual depends upon her independent living skills. The least restrictive option appropriate for the individual given her needs should be considered—and those that allow maximum interaction with individuals without disabilities. Prior to placement, the professional should assess and develop community support for the placement. For a thorough discussion of residential living options for individuals with disabilities, readers are referred to Levinson (1998).

In addition to being knowledgeable in the previously identified areas, the professional involved in transition must

1. Be knowledgeable about the roles, responsibilities, and expertise of the other transition team professionals and be able to refer the client and his parents to these other professionals when appropriate.

2. Be knowledgeable about the support service agencies available in the local community and establish liaison relationships with these agencies.

3. Be knowledgeable about the employment options, occupational training alternatives, and residential living options that exist in the local

community so that this information can be used by the professional in collaboration with the client and parents during decision making.

4. Be knowledgeable about local job market trends and consider how such trends may eventually alter the occupational training and placement options currently available.

Summary

Given the recent federal and state initiatives aimed at facilitating transition of individuals with disabilities, it is likely that an increased number of mental health and social service workers will become involved in transition efforts. The success of these efforts may ultimately influence the overall quality of life experienced by individuals with disabilities. For this reason, transition presents a new and critically important challenge to the professional working with those individuals and their parents. This chapter has reviewed transition models and the federal legislation that spurred development of these models. The roles of professionals in facilitating transition efforts have been reviewed, particularly in regard to the responsibilities these professionals have to parents. Professionals will assume numerous roles when working with parents and will need to function as part of a team when facilitating transition efforts. They will need to understand the role of other team members and structure their role accordingly and will need to have some working knowledge of transition assessment, vocational and life skills instruction and functional academics, and vocational and residential living options.

References

Anderson, W. T., Hohenshil, T. H., Buckland-Heer, K., & Levinson, E. M. (1990). Best practices in vocational asessment. In A. Thomas & J. Grimes (Eds.), *Best practices in school psychology–II* (pp. 114–138). Washington, DC: National Association of School Psychologists.

Bedeian, A. G., & Marbert, L. D. (1979). Individual differences in self-perception and the job–life satisfaction relationship. *Journal of Social Psychology, 109,* 111–118.

Benz, M. R., & Halpern, A. S. (1987). Transition services for secondary students with mild disabilities: A statewide perspective. *Exceptional Children, 53*(6), 507–514.

Brolin, D. E. (1986) A model for providing comprehensive transitional services: The role of special education. In J. Chadsey-Rusch & C. Hanley-Maxwell (Eds.), *Enhancing transition from school to the workplace for handicapped youth: Personnel preparation implications* (pp. 116–128). Champaign, IL: National Network for Professional Development in Vocational Special Education.

Brynelson, D. (1984). *Working together: A handbook for parents and professionals.* (British Columbians for Mentally Handicapped People, Vancouver). Toronto: National Institute on Mental Retardation.

Carl D. Perkins Vocational Education Act. (1984). Public Law 98-524.

D' Amico, R., & Marder, C. (1991). *The early work experiences of youth with disabilities: Trends in employment rates and job characteristics.* Menlo Park, CA: SRI International.

deFur, S., & Patton, J. (in press). *Transition and school-based services.* Austin, TX: PRO-ED.

Developmental Disabilities Assistance and Bill of Rights Act. (1978). Public Law 95-602.

Dore, R., & Meachum, M. (1973). Self-concept and interests related to job satisfaction of managers. *Personnel Psychology, 26,* 49–59.

Edgar, E. (1987). Secondary programs in special education: Are many of them justifiable? *Exceptional Children, 53*(6), 555–561.

Education for All Handicapped Children Act of 1975, 20 U.S.C. § 1400 *et seq.*

Education of the Handicapped Act Amendments of 1983, 20 U.S.C. § 1400 *et seq.*

Everson, J. M., Rachal, P., & Michael, M. G. (1992). *Interagency collaboration for young adults with deaf-blindness: Towards a common transition goal.* Sands Point, NY: Technical Assistance Center, Helen Keller National Center (ED 345 456).

Fardig, D. B., Algozzine, R. F., Schwartz, S. E., Hensel, J. E., & Westling, D. L. (1985). Postsecondary vocational adjustment of rural, mildly handicapped students. *Exceptional Children, 52*(2), 115–121.

Gajar, A., Goodman, L., & McAfee, J. (1993). *Secondary schools and beyond: Transition of individuals with mild disabilities.* New York: Merrill.

Greenhaus, J. H. (1971). Self-esteem as an influence on occupational choice and occupational satisfaction. *Journal of Vocational Behavior, 1,* 75–83.

Haavio-Mannila, E. (1971). Satisfaction with family, work, leisure, and life among men and women. *Human Relations, 24*(6), 585–601.

Halpern, A. (1994). The transition from youth to adult life: A position statement of the Division on Career Development and Transition. *Career Development for Exceptional Individuals, 17,* 115–124.

Halpern, A. S. (1985). Transition: A look at the foundations. *Exceptional Children, 51*(6), 479–486.

Hasazi, S. B., Gordon, L. R., & Roe, C. A. (1985). Factors associated with the employment status of handicapped youth exiting high school from 1979 to 1983. *Exceptional Children, 51*(6), 455–469.

Hasazi, S. B., Gordon, L. R., Roe, C. A., Hull, M., Finck, K., & Salembier, G. (1985). A statewide follow-up on post high school employment and residential status of students labeled "mentally retarded." *Education and Training of the Mentally Retarded, 20*(4), 222–235.

Individuals with Disabilities Education Act Amendments of 1997, 20 U.S.C. § 1400 *et seq.*

Iris, B., & Barrett, G. V. (1972). Some relations between job and life satisfaction and job importance. *Journal of Applied Psychology, 56*(4), 301–307.

Izzo, M. V., & Shumate, K. (1991). *NetWORK for effective transitions to work: A transition coordinator's manual.* Columbus: Center on Education and Training for Employment, Ohio State University.

Johnson, J. R., Bruininks, R. H., & Thurlow, M. L. (1987). Meeting the challenge of transition service planning through improved interagency cooperation. *Exceptional Children, 53*(6), 522–530.

Johnson, J. R., & Rush, F. R. (1993). Secondary special education transition services. *Career Development for Exceptional Individuals, 16*(1), 1–18.

Kalanidi, M. S., & Deivasenapathy, P. (1980). Self-concept and job satisfaction among the self-employed. *Psychological Studies, 25,* 39–41.

Kornhauser, A. W. (1965). *Mental health of the industrial worker.* New York: Wiley.

Levinson, E. M. (1993). *Transdisciplinary vocational assessment: Issues in school-based programs.* Brandon, VT: Clinical Psychology.

Levinson, E. M. (1998). *Transition: Facilitating the post school adjustment of students with disabilities.* Boulder, CO: Westview Press.

Levinson, E. M., & Capps, C. F. (1985). Vocational assessment and special education triennial reevaluations at the secondary school level. *Psychology in the Schools, 22*(3), 283–292.

Marder, C., & D'Amico, R. (1992). *How well are youth with disabilities really doing? A comparison of youth with disabilities and youth in general.* Menlo Park, CA: SRI International.

McNair, J., & Rusch, F. R. (1990). Parent involvement in transition programs. In F. R. Rusch (Ed.), *Research in secondary special education and transitional employment.* Champion: University of Illinois.

Mithaug, D. E., Horiuchi, C. N., & Fanning, P. N. (1985). A report on the Colorado statewide follow-up survey of special education students. *Exceptional Children, 51*(5), 397–404.

Murray, J. (1990). Best practices in counseling parents of handicapped children. In A. Thomas & J. Grimes (Eds.), *Best practices in school psychology II.* Washington, DC: National Association of School Psychologists.

Orphen, C. (1978). Work and non-work satisfaction: A causal correlational analysis. *Journal of Applied Psychology, 63*(4), 530–532.

O'Toole, J. (Ed.). (1973). *Work in America: Report of a special task force to the Secretary of Health, Education, and Welfare.* Cambridge, MA: MIT Press.

Ott, C. (1991). *Family involvement on the intervention assistance team: An untapped resource for building home–school partnerships.* Paper presented at the annual conference of the National Association of School Psychologists, Dallas, TX.

Pennsylvania Departments of Education & Labor and Industry. (1986). *Pennsylvania Transition from School to the Workplace* (pp. 3, 7, 83). Harrisburg, PA: Author.

Poplin, P. (1981). The development and execution of the IEP: Who does what, when, to whom? In T. H. Hohenshil & W. T. Anderson (Eds.), *School psychological services in secondary vocational education: Roles in programs for handicapped students* (pp. 26–39). Blacksburg, VA: Virginia Tech. (ERIC Reproduction No. 215245)

Portigal, A. H. (1976). *Towards the measurement of work satisfaction.* Paris: Organization for Economic Cooperation and Development.

Rehabilitation Act of 1973, 29 U.S.C. § 701 *et seq.*

Rusch, F. R., & Phelps, L. A. (1987). Secondary special education and transition from school to work: A national priority. *Exceptional Children, 53*(6), 487–492.

Schalock, R. L., & Lilley, M. A. (1986). Placement from community-based mental retardation programs: How well do clients do after 8 to 10 years? *American Journal of Mental Deficiency, 90*(6), 669–676.

Schalock, R. L., Wolzen, B., Ross, I., Elliot, B., Werbel, G., & Peterson, K. (1986). Post-secondary community placement of handicapped students: A five-year follow up. *Learning Disability Quarterly, 9,* 295–303.

Schmitt, N., & Mellon, P. M. (1980). Life and job satisfaction: Is the job central? *Journal of Vocational Behavior, 16*(1), 51–58.

Silvestri, G. T., & Lukasiewicz, J. M. (1987). A look at occupational employment trends to the year 2000. *Monthly Labor Review, 110*(9), 46–63.

Snyder, C. D., & Ferguson, L. W. (1976). Self-concept and job satisfaction. *Psychological Reports, 38,* 603–610.

Super, D. (1957). *The psychology of careers.* New York: Harper.

Vocational Education Act. (1963). Public Law 88-210.

Vocational Education Amendments. (1968). Public Law 90-576.

Wagner, M., & Shaver, D. M. (1989). *The transition experiences of youth with disabilities: A report from the National Longitudinal Transitional Study.* Menlo Park, CA: SRI International.

Wehman, P. (1986). Transition for handicapped youth from school to work. In J. Chadsey-Rusch & C. Hanley-Maxwell (Eds.), *Enhancing transition from school to the workplace for handicapped youth: Personnel preparation implications* (pp. 26–43). Champaign, IL: National Network for Professional Development in Vocational Special Education.

Will, M. (1984). OSERS programming for the transition of youth with disabilities: Bridges from school to working life. In J. Chadsey-Rusch & C. Hanley-Maxwell (Eds.), *Enhancing transition from school to the workplace for handicapped youth: Personnel preparation implications* (pp. 9–24). Champaign, IL: National Network for Professional Development in Vocational Special Education.

Ysseldyke, J. E., Algozzine, B., & Thurlow, M. L. (1992). *Critical issues in special education* (2nd ed.). Princeton, NJ: Houghton Mifflin.

Empowering Parents To Participate: Advocacy and Education

21

Craig R. Fiedler and Wayne H. Swanger

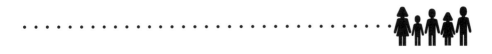

T he Individuals with Disabilities Education Act (IDEA) Amendments of 1997 (Public Law 105-17) continued a legislative history begun in 1975 of placing a high value on parent participation in educational planning and decision making. In fact, the 1997 amendments granted parents new rights to participate in all educational decisions and decision-making processes. Some of the most important special education procedural rights of parents now include

- Guarantee of a free appropriate public education for children with disabilities.

- Notification whenever the school proposes to evaluate a child, wants to change a child's educational program, or refuses a parent's request for an evaluation or a change in placement.

- The ability to initiate a special education evaluation if the parents think their child is in need of special education or related services.

- Requirement of informed parental consent prior to the initial evaluation and placement of a student in special education.

- Power to obtain an independent education evaluation if parents disagree with the outcome of the school's evaluation.

- Right to review all educational records.

- Requirement that the school must fully inform parents of all rights that they have under the law.

- Participation in the development of an Individualized Education Plan (IEP) for a child in special education.

- Requirement that children with disabilities be educated in the least restrictive environment.

- Ability to request a due process hearing to resolve differences with the school that could not be resolved informally (Simpson, 1996; Yell, 1998).

The 1997 IDEA amendments emphasized the responsibility of parents and school personnel to work together to develop effective IEPs. One of the new requirements specified parents' rights to participate in group decision making to determine eligibility and placement of their children with disabilities. Prior to the 1997 amendments in some states parents only had a right to be included in IEP meetings (Heumann & Hehir, 1997). Also required is inclusion of a general education teacher as a participant at IEP meetings (Yell, 1998). In an effort to enhance accountability, the amended IDEA required a statement of measurable annual goals, as well as short-term objectives to assess if a student is making progress toward the annual goals (Yell, 1998). School personnel are required to keep parents regularly informed on their child's progress. Another change strengthened accountability by explicitly requiring that an IEP detail the aids, supports, and accommodations a student would receive within general education classrooms (Heumann & Hehir, 1997). A final 1997 change that affected parents' educational participation and advocacy efforts was the requirement that all states establish a mediation system that would encourage parents and school officials to resolve their differences in a nonadversarial manner.

The IDEA amendments of 1997 made clearer the Congressional intent to empower parents as active advocates and educational decision makers. However, merely passing a law that established an opportunity for parents to participate in educational planning and decision making could not ensure that such participation would automatically occur, especially if parents and professionals alike did not actively embrace the spirit of this new partnership (Simpson, 1996; Turnbull & Turnbull, 1997). This new role perception of parents created an expectation and need for parent and family support and empowerment to enhance their advocacy efforts and participation in the educational decision-making process. Indeed, parents who did participate and exert their rights through effective advocacy had a far better chance of securing an appropriate education for their child than did those parents who remained uninvolved, unprepared, and uninformed (Herr, 1983).

This chapter will address the critically important issue of parent participation in educational decision making and parental advocacy, which is sometimes necessary to ensure appropriate services. Educational professionals must be able to enhance parental participation and advocacy through collaboration and empowerment attitudes and approaches. Instead of a professional attitude that considers parental participation as troublesome and irrelevant, a new vision is required, one recognizing parents as potential partners and collaborators. This collaborative concept of parent participation in educational matters essentially attempts to empower and enable parents to work actively on behalf of their exceptional child. This new partnership requires advocacy efforts by parents and professionals alike. Specifically, this chapter will identify basic parent and family collaboration and empowerment concepts; discuss barriers to more active parent participation; describe what is meant by educational advocacy; present specific strategies and considerations for enhancing parental participation and advocacy, especially at IEP conferences (while adhering to the belief that parents should be allowed to participate in their children's education according to their preferences); outline the basic characteristics and skills required of both parents and professionals in their advocacy efforts; and discuss pertinent considerations in resolving, in a nonadversarial fashion, parent–professional conflict, which at times arises from assertive advocacy.

Parent–Professional Collaboration and Empowerment

The traditional model of parent–professional interaction, which expected parents to comply passively and gratefully with professional decisions about their exceptional children, perpetuated the "mere parents" myth and fostered excessive dependence on professionals and the educational system (Turnbull & Turnbull, 1997). In the past few years, this traditional model has largely given way to a new paradigm of special education decision making. This new paradigm has been variously labeled as "family-centered," "family empowerment," and "self-determination" (Summers, 1992). It acknowledges the expertise of parents and their rightful decision-making authority by advocating a collaborative parent–professional partnership that seeks to empower parents. Empowerment means the enhanced ability to take action to get what one wants and needs (Cochran, 1992; Dunst, Trivette, & LaPoint, 1992).

This new collaboration and empowerment paradigm has been articulated and operationalized by Turnbull and Turnbull (1997). Essentially, they maintain that professionals, through collaborative partnerships with parents, can empower families of exceptional children by increasing parent motivation and knowledge or skills. Parent motivation is bolstered by five factors: self-efficacy (believing in one's capabilities); perceived control (believing that one's capabilities can be applied so as to control what happens to oneself); hope (believing that one will get what one needs); energy (lighting the fire and keeping it burning); and persistence (putting forth a sustained effort). Parent knowledge and skills consist of information (on special education legal rights, on appropriate educational services, on community resources); problem solving (knowing how to bust barriers); coping skills (knowing how to handle what happens to oneself); and communication skills (successfully expressing needs and wants in interpersonal interactions with professionals). As parents become more empowered, true parent–professional partnerships are realized. Empowered parents are more effective in their advocacy efforts, thus ensuring that their exceptional children receive appropriate educational services. This parent–professional collaboration and empowerment paradigm represents an ideal for educational decision-making partnerships. The next section will discuss the all too frequent reality: the existence of numerous barriers to parent participation in educational decision making.

Barriers to Parent Participation

Before reviewing several identified barriers to parent participation in educational decision making, we will consider the extent to which parents of exceptional children participate in the decision-making process of IEP conferences. Most of the research on parent participation has focused on levels of participation at IEP conferences because those meetings represent the most typical and crucial interactions between parents and educators as envisioned by the IDEA.

Research on Parent Participation in IEP Conferences

Although parents are supposed to be active equal partners in educational processes, research data indicate this is often not the case. Many parents do not attend educational meetings or participate fully in meetings when they do attend. Bailey and associates reported that approximately 20% of parents did not attend IEP meetings (Bailey, Buyose, Edmondson, & Smith, 1992). Other researchers found that 39% of parents did not attend IEP meetings the third year following their child's placement in special education (Harry, Allen, & McLaughlin, 1995).

When in attendance at IEP meetings, parents frequently do not participate as equal partners. In a review of IEP participation research, Smith (1990) reported parents were more likely to be the recipients of educational decisions rather than collaborative decision makers. Lack of parent participation in IEP meetings has been a persistent problem. In 1980 parents provided fewer than 25% of total IEP contributions (Goldstein, Strickland, Turnbull, & Curry, 1980). Goldstein et al. observed the IEP conferences of 14 elementary students with mild disabilities and analyzed the topics of discussion, frequency of contributions by each conference participant, and overall satisfaction with conference participation and decisions made. The researchers concluded that parents were by no means equal participants or actively involved in the decision-making process even though the parents themselves reported a high degree of satisfaction with those conferences and their role. A more recent study revealed that approximately 15% of IEP meeting time consisted of parent interactions (Vaughn, Bos, Harrell, & Lasky, 1988). It is not surprising that more than one third of special education teachers surveyed indicated they were dissatisfied or very dissatisfied with parent involvement in their children's education (Berg & Halpern, 1987).

The research on parent–professional partnerships in developing IEPs is not encouraging. There is a discrepancy between the ideal quantity and quality of parent participation and the reality. Most studies have concluded that IEP meetings tend to function as legal formalities where a previously developed IEP is merely presented to the parents for their information and approval (Goldstein et al., 1980; Harry et al., 1995; Vaughn et al., 1988). These findings reinforce the conclusion of Turnbull and Turnbull (1997): "The dominant theme of all the research and testimony is that schools try to comply with legal mandates and procedures but do not make an effort to foster empowerment through collaboration" (p. 231). Fiedler (1986) offered two explanations for these research findings. First, minimal or passive parent participation in their child's education may reflect the parents' genuine preferences. The implications of this reality on parent–professional interactions will be discussed later in this chapter. Second, the passive participation of parents in IEP conferences may result from numerous barriers that preclude them from more active participation.

Barriers to Active Parent Participation

For parents to become productive participants and advocates in their children's education, professionals must recognize the barriers that prevent active parent participation. These barriers either operate indirectly by damaging parent–professional interactions and, ultimately, their relationship, or have a direct adverse impact on parents' participation by limiting their time, energy, knowledge, and psychological support, which are necessary for their active participation and advocacy.

The barriers briefly reviewed in this section include cultural and language differences, poverty, parental lack of knowledge about special education procedures, parental lack of adequate information to assist them in their educational decision making, negative professional attitudes toward parents, parental burnout and parental alienation and isolation.

First, cultural factors may negatively affect parent participation. In particular, differences in language limit input from parents and parents' understanding of discussions at educational meetings and formal or informal communications from school personnel. Although the use of interpreters is mandated by law to address language barriers in parent–school communications, many serious problems arise in the use of interpreters at educational meetings. For example, Plata (1993) listed the following concerns when using interpreters:

- Immediate oral translations can be stressful for interpreters.
- Some loss of meaning typically occurs in translation.
- Provincial meaning of words and concepts can result in miscommunication.
- Negative feelings may be generated between interpreter and discussants.

Poverty is another factor that may negatively affect parents' participation in IEP meetings. A disproportionate number of students with disabilities are from families of lower socioeconomic status. There are many concomitant problems such as long work hours, limited transportation availability, and lack of childcare (Salend & Taylor, 1993). These logistical barriers frequently are cited as reasons for parents not attending IEP meetings (Kitsiyanni & Ward, 1992; Leyser, 1985).

Parents' limited knowledge of special education processes, rights, and procedures may negatively affect their participation in educational decision making. Many parents have a general lack of understanding of educational rights, concepts, programs, assessment, and services. For example, in one survey intended to examine the needs of parents of young children with disabilities, 50% of the parents wanted to know more about what services were available for their children, and 51% of the parents wanted to know how the system worked (Sontag & Schacht, 1994). Parents often are aware of their lack of knowledge regarding educational services and program options and, as a consequence, may find it difficult to participate in educational meetings with professionals due to their sense of their own limited understanding. Vaughn et al. (1988) indicated that a number of parents reported they felt nervous and confused at IEP meetings. Other researchers reported parents did not attend IEP meetings because they were uncomfortable with the use of jargon frequently employed at such meetings (Harry et al., 1995).

There is evidence to suggest educators do not provide sufficient information to many parents that might otherwise encourage increased participation. For example, a survey by Katsiyanni and Ward (1992) revealed that over 10% of parents reported they did not receive a written statement of their educational rights and over 13% did not get an explanation of those rights. In addition, League and Ford (1996) reported fathers of children with disabilities indicated they often did not receive the type of communication they needed from the school or the child's teacher that would enable them to participate in their children's education in terms of managing misbehavior, advocating for appropriate services, and motivating and encouraging academic performance.

Another barrier to parent participation in educational meetings is related to the traditional professional attitude and perspective toward parents. Professionals often view parents as mere recipients of educational deci-

sions. Data suggest professionals often communicate this attitude in interactions with parents. For example, Sontag and Schacht (1994) reported parents of young children were told by professionals what their child's problem
was and what could be done about it without any attempt to solicit parental
input into the decision-making process. Surprisingly, over half of the parents
reported they helped make decisions about their child's program anyway.
These data suggest parents were not viewed by school personnel as full and
equal partners in evaluation and educational programming decision making.
When parents perceive themselves as mere recipients of educational decisions made by professionals, they are less likely to attend IEP meetings; they
feel their input is discounted and they are unable to influence outcomes
(Harry et al., 1995). Harry et al. stated that in such situations the main activity of an IEP meeting is to secure a signature rather than to promote collaboration. It is not surprising that IEP meetings often last an average of only
20 to 30 minutes under these conditions.

Evidence suggests parents may become less involved over time in educational processes such as IEP meetings. They may become weary following
years of struggle at home, with school personnel, and with various other professionals. In effect, parents may suffer "burnout" and as a consequence might
not attend IEP meetings or other parent–teacher conferences. Moreover, parents often experience less community acceptance and greater isolation as
their children progress through the school years (Brotherson, Berdine, & Sartini, 1993). It is not surprising therefore that parents of secondary students
with disabilities often are perceived as being less involved in educational processes than parents of younger students (Lynch & Stein, 1982).

Over time parents also may reduce their participation in educational
decision making as a result of increased alienation or disenfranchisement.
For example, Harry et al. (1995) reported low- to low-middle–income African
American parents of students with disabilities and parents of nondisabled
peers who were entering urban public schools voiced high expectations for
their children and positive views regarding participation in educational processes. Over time participation became perfunctory for parents of students
with disabilities in comparison to parents of nondisabled students. In addition, parents of students with disabilities experienced increasing difficulties
in understanding and effectively interacting with the special education system (Lynch & Stein, 1987).

In summary, there are numerous barriers to full and equal parent participation in educational decision-making processes. Cultural differences
between parents and professionals may be barriers to participation. Parents
may lack the prerequisite knowledge to be effective collaborators or to be confident in their ability to contribute to the decision-making process. Educators
may view parents as recipients of professional decisions rather than as collaborators. And, over time, parents may become less active in educational
processes due to a sense of burnout or disenfranchisement.

Increasing Parent Participation

Many barriers that prevent active parent participation relate directly to professionals' attitudes and interpersonal skills. Regarding professional attitudes Fiedler (1986) noted,

> More positive attitudes and assumptions toward parents are promoted by emphasizing the role of parents as family members. This role is based on the premise that successful family life requires that the needs of all family members, including parents, must be identified and addressed. This premise adheres to basic principles incorporated in family systems theory, which views the family as a social system with unique characteristics and needs. Accordingly, underlying family systems theory is the basic belief that the individual members of a family are so interrelated that events affecting one member will inevitably affect all family members. (pp. 1–2)

Undoubtedly, parent–professional interactions that address the needs of the entire family unit will provide the foundation for more positive relations between the two and the establishment of a true partnership as envisioned by the IDEA. In addition to developing more appropriate and positive professional attitudes toward parents, parent–professional collaborations and partnerships are largely dependent upon interpersonal factors. Four interpersonal factors are fundamental to establishing these relationships: (a) willingness to listen; (b) recognition of trust as a basic element of cooperation; (c) knowledge and acceptance of individual values; and (d) willingness to accommodate a partnership relationship (Simpson & Fiedler, 1989).

Willingness To Listen. Listening to parents is the most fundamental way in which professionals can communicate interest and willingness to accept parents as educational partners. Active listening enables professionals to develop greater understanding of and empathy for parental issues and stressors and to be better equipped to offer appropriate support, whether it be informational, educational, psychological, or simply a referral to another agency or resource. Also, listening communicates respect and encourages parents to become more actively involved in educational planning and decision-making discussions.

Recognition of Trust. Trust is an essential ingredient in parent–professional relationships. Indeed, parents who do not trust professionals will be disinclined to form a productive partnership and will not be as actively involved in their children's education. Simpson (1996) identified some requirements for developing parent–professional trust: (a) willingness to be involved in the educational process, (b) acceptance that both parents and educators have a commitment to children, (c) willingness to serve as a child advocate, (d) positive outlook, (e) willingness on the part of parents and professionals to reinforce and confront one another, (f) sensitivity to individual needs and emotions, and (g) desire to trust.

Acceptance of Individual Values. Personal values determine many of our decisions and much of our behavior. Professionals must not presume that their values are more acceptable than those of parents. Simpson and Fiedler (1989) cautioned that

> when attempting to make value-based decisions, professionals should anticipate differences of opinion. Such differences should not be perceived as problematic; however, they do require that parents as well as educators recognize their own values and accept that others will often have different goals and beliefs. (p. 163)

Accommodation of Partnership Relationship. Finally, professionals must actively promote and accept parents as participants in the educational process. This requirement cannot be legislated; it must be demonstrated by words and actions. Professionals who actively seek to eliminate or minimize barriers to parent participation, who are willing to listen to parents, who develop mutual trust, and who acknowledge and accept individual values will be promoting and supporting parents as active participants in the educational process.

Active parent participation in educational decision making is further enhanced by (a) maintaining positive professional attitudes that avoid judgmental stereotypes of culturally diverse families; (b) providing effective interpreter services to minimize language barriers; (c) providing parents with relevant information and skill training to enhance their advocacy efforts; and (d) initiating preservice teacher education preparation programs that inculcate a collaborative perspective in working with parents. Educators must recognize that cultural differences exist between families and themselves. These differences can affect the collaborative interactions between parents and professionals (Allen, 1993; Harry, 1992). But although cultural factors may affect the extent and quality of parent participation in educational processes, the manifestations of these cultural differences are not entirely predictable. Families from the same culture may interact with educational professionals in significantly different ways. Such differences may be due to variations in the level of acculturation, experience with discrimination, and structure of the family (Salend & Taylor, 1993). Therefore, professionals must avoid the use of stereotypes when interacting with culturally diverse families.

Language differences can be a serious obstacle to parent participation. An interpreter may be necessary to provide parents whose primary language is not English an opportunity to fully participate in educational decision making. Guidelines should be developed for selecting an interpreter. Plata (1993) recommended that an interpreter demonstrate the following characteristics:

- Proficiency in the desired language

- Familiarity with the culture

- Knowledge of special education concepts, terminology, rights, and procedures

- Willingness to assume a secondary role in the educational decision-making process

- Ability to read and write in English

- Ability to interact with individuals from diverse educational, cultural, and training backgrounds

- Trustworthiness

Plata further recommended that if non–English-speaking parents are to be full participants in the educational process, programs must be developed to train, monitor, evaluate, and compensate quality interpreters.

Other researchers have suggested numerous other ways to facilitate participation of non–English-speaking parents. For example Salend and Taylor (1993) offered the following: (a) determine language ability and parents' needs, (b) provide training sessions and materials in native language, and (c) hire bilingual personnel.

Parents may often lack knowledge and skills that would empower them to be more effective participants in educational decision making. Advocacy training and support for parents may need to focus on topics such as the legal rights of parents in the special education system, basic advocacy skills, assertive communication skills, strategies for parent participation in educational evaluation procedures, strategies for parent participation in IEP decision making, and techniques for parent monitoring of educational programming and progress. Several approaches can be taken to provide parents with information and skills to enhance their participation in educational processes. First, professionals can assess parents' need for information and skills through informal contacts and meetings with parents. These contacts and meetings might occur in the form of community outreach activities or preconference meetings with parents, for example (Salend & Taylor, 1993). Second, formal training opportunities could be provided to parents (Miller, 1995; Miner & Bates, 1997). Training could take place in or out of school settings. Recent research indicates that training parents to use a person-centered planning activity may result in greater parent participation at IEP meetings and high levels of parent satisfaction (Miner & Bates, 1997).

Professionals can be assisted in working more effectively with parents (Lowenthal, 1996). Preservice and inservice preparation programs may encourage teachers to view parents as partners in educational decision making rather than as recipients of professional decisions. Course work for collaborating with parents is available in many teacher preparation programs.

Following a survey of special education teacher preparation programs and inservice teachers, Hughes, Ruhl, and Gorman (1987) reported that a majority of programs offered a course on working with families, but a small proportion of inservice teachers actually took such a course. Evidence suggests that these teacher preparation programs are effective in modifying teachers' perceptions of parent participation in educational processes. Hughes et al. reported that preservice preparation in working with families was significantly correlated with teachers' confidence in their ability to communicate effectively with parents. Teacher preparation programs may be increasing their emphasis on promoting parent–teacher collaboration: Researchers reported that younger teachers had more positive views regarding parent involvement in educational processes than older teachers (Bennett, Deluca, & Bruns, 1997).

In summary, effective collaboration between educators and parents frequently does not occur in educational decision-making processes. Among the numerous barriers to parent participation are cultural and language differences, lack of parent knowledge, and parent and professional attitudes. By avoiding stereotyping, using recommended practices for translators, and providing collaborative training for parents and teachers, school professionals can realize the benefits of full parent participation in educational decision making.

Educational Advocacy

Advocacy is the representation of rights and interests of oneself (or others) in an effort to bring about change and to eliminate barriers to meeting identified needs (Alper, Schloss, & Schloss, 1994). When the educational system is working well, there is little need for advocacy. In such situations, the advocate's role is to serve as a "guardian of the process" to ensure that the educational system continues to function well by providing appropriate services to exceptional children (Bonney & Moore, 1992). In ensuring an appropriate education for exceptional children, advocacy takes two forms: (a) the responsibility of professionals to serve as advocates for exceptional children and (b) professionals' obligation to prepare parents adequately to fulfill their advocacy role.

The Need for Educational Advocacy

There will likely always be a need for professional educational advocacy on behalf of exceptional children. Reasons for educational advocacy include historical discrimination experienced by individuals with disabilities, current outcome findings of what happens to graduates of special education programs, and parental inability to serve as educational advocates. First, the legislative history of the original Education for All Handicapped Children Act (P.L. 94-142, 1975) is replete with testimony on the ills the new legislation was intended to correct in terms of inadequate educational services for exceptional children (U.S. Department of Education, 1996). The historical segregation and discrimination individuals with disabilities encountered in the first 200 years of this country have been well chronicled (Cutler, 1993; Stainback, Stainback, & Forest, 1989). Indeed, the passage of P.L. 94-142 in 1975 was largely hailed as a significant civil rights victory for exceptional children.

Unfortunately, inequalities, lack of access, and inadequate educational services are still the norm for many exceptional children (Brantlinger, 1991). Although professional and parent advocacy has secured broader public support for educational services for exceptional children, appropriate individualized services for many exceptional children are still unrealized today (Audette & Algozzine, 1997). The most recent *Annual Report to Congress on the Implementation of The Individuals with Disabilities Education Act* contains many disturbing statistics on inequitable and inadequate educational services received by inner city exceptional children (U.S. Department of Education, 1996). One prevailing problem that remains is the overrepresentation of African American children in special education programs. Further, it is estimated that 26% of all exceptional children will drop out of school prior to graduation or program completion (U.S. Department of Education, 1996). This dropout statistic is especially alarming because the special education outcome research has cited a strong correlation between high school graduation and postschool success for exceptional children (U.S. Department of Education, 1996). Special education outcome studies have generally yielded bleak results for postschool adjustment of exceptional students (Blackorby, Edgar, & Kortering, 1991; Chadsey-Rusch, Rusch, & O'Reilly, 1991; Edgar, 1995; Edgar & Polloway, 1994; Nelson, 1996; Wagner, 1989). Generally, studies report a higher unemployment rate, less postsecondary training experiences, greater residential dependence on parents, and poor social adjustment of special education students. Finally, Simpson (1996) cited a number of demographic statistics that clearly place more children at risk for school and community problems as a result of increasing poverty, more single-parent households, a growing number of infants born to cocaine-addicted mothers, an ever-growing teenage pregnancy rate, increasing violence among young people, and a child abuse rate that is approaching epidemic proportions.

Parents are the most natural individuals to serve as their children's advocates for a variety of reasons. First, parents have a legally recognized responsibility to be active educational decision makers and to ensure that the schools comply with legal mandates (Turnbull & Turnbull, 1997). Second, parents have an emotional investment in their child's welfare that goes well beyond the emotional investment of even the most caring professional. Third, parents are usually more of a constant in their child's life, because educators and other professionals frequently change from year to year. Thus, parents are in the best position to take a longitudinal perspective on their child's progress and deficits over time. Fourth, parents can also be persuasive advocates: they possess direct first-hand experiences with the educational system and their perspective can be compelling to legislators and policy makers. Finally, parents are freer than most professionals to speak out and challenge the educational system without fear of employment reprisals (Friesen & Huff, 1990).

However, many parents are unable to assume this advocacy role and responsibility on behalf of their exceptional children. Many families do not know what services should be available to their children and lack knowledge of basic legal rights (McBride, 1992). Due to various life circumstances, some parents are unable to devote enough time or emotional energy to advocate actively. For some families, cultural barriers including school insensitivity to diverse cultural norms and expectations may stand in the way of parental advocacy (Stoecklin, 1994). Some parents feel a stigma is associated with their child's disability and are reluctant or embarrassed to advocate against the educational system. Many parents are isolated and lack sufficient support for their advocacy efforts (Friesen & Huff, 1990). Professionals may contribute to parental inability or unwillingness to serve as educational advocates by displaying negative attitudes toward assertive parents and failing to build parents' confidence in taking advocacy initiatives (Friesen & Huff, 1990). And, finally, many parents are simply intimidated by professionals and special education procedures and become overly dependent on professional decision making instead of asserting their independent voice (Smith, 1992).

Professional Educational Advocacy

With respect to educational advocacy, Fiedler (1986) noted that "special education professionals have historically avoided advocacy responsibility because of insufficient training, legal ramifications, pressure from superiors, and competing time and energy demands" (p. 7). However, both the Council for Exceptional Children (1983) and the American Association on Mental Retardation (Antonak, Mallory, & Thede, 1986) have concluded that special education professionals have advocacy responsibilities to the children and families they serve, including the following:

1. Professionals should seek to improve government provisions for the education of exceptional children.

2. Professionals must work cooperatively and supportively with other providers to improve the provision of special education and related services to exceptional children.

3. Professionals should document and objectively report to their supervisors inadequacies in resources and promote appropriate corrective action.

4. Professionals should monitor for inappropriate placements in special education and intervene at the appropriate level to correct the situation when inappropriate placement exists.

5. Professionals must follow laws and regulations that mandate a free appropriate public education to exceptional students and the protection of the rights of exceptional persons to equal opportunities in society.

Like legal mandates, ethical mandates will not automatically change professional willingness to take on advocacy responsibilities. At the very least, professionals who aspire to be successful educational advocates must possess requisite *dispositions* (an advocacy disposition, an ethical disposition, and a family support or empowerment disposition), *knowledge* (knowledge of special education legal rights and procedures, knowledge of dispute resolution mechanisms, and knowledge of systems change theories and strategies), and *skills* (skills in interpersonal communication, collaboration, conflict resolution, advocacy methods and strategies, and ethical analysis). Professionals may use the above-referenced dispositions, knowledge, and skills either directly, in their advocacy for an exceptional child whose parents are unable to fulfill this role and responsibility, or indirectly, by supporting the advocacy efforts of parents.

Parental Educational Advocacy

Professional support of parent educational advocacy efforts should focus on two broad topics: providing information on legal rights and enhancing parent participation in the IEP process. Both will be discussed briefly.

Providing Information on Legal Rights. It is not sufficient that professionals merely provide parents with a written notice describing their child's educational rights. Indeed, Yoshida, Fenton, Kaufman, and Maxwell (1978) found that many parents do not receive adequate notice of their procedural safeguards as accorded by the IDEA. Perhaps part of the problem with regard to ensuring adequate notice is the rather high level of reading skills necessary to comprehend the disseminated material. A nationwide survey of state departments of education (McLoughlin, Edge, Petrosko, & Strenecky, 1981) revealed that materials disseminated to parents consistently had a 14th- to 15th-grade level readability rate. Such a high level restricts access to information by parents with limited educational backgrounds. Roit and Pfohl (1984) also expressed concern that parent information materials distributed by educational agencies may not be comprehensible to a large number of parents of exceptional children. In addition these authors suggested that school personnel assume greater responsibility for evaluating the knowledge acquired by parents through the disseminated materials. This admonition seems particularly pertinent when considering the Council for Exceptional Children's (1983) ethical mandate that professionals should inform parents of the educational rights of their children and of any proposed or actual practices that violate those rights.

On what legal rights and educational procedures should professionals ensure that parents have been sufficiently informed? Parent educational advocacy may be categorized according to the following areas: notice, consent, participation, access, verification, and oversight (South Dakota Statewide Systems Change Project, 1995). At a minimum, professionals should provide parents with information about their legal rights in each of these six areas.

Notice. Parents are entitled to notice of any proposed school actions or changes in programs or services for exceptional children. Therefore, parents should be provided with information about the required contents of school notices, the timing of notices, and the consequences if the school fails to provide parents with an adequate notice.

Consent. Parents must provide their informed written consent prior to an initial special education evaluation and placement of their exceptional children. To understand fully this legal safeguard, parents must know the following: the meaning of "informed and voluntary consent," their right to revoke consent, and the consequences of withholding their consent.

Participation. Parents are legally entitled to participate fully in the referral, evaluation, IEP development, and placement processes for their exceptional children. To participate fully in these decision-making processes, parents must know legal requirements for referring and evaluating children suspected of needing special education services. In addition, parents must be knowledgeable about the required components of an IEP and how parents can affect the writing of an appropriate IEP. Finally, parents must know about the legal requirement for educating all exceptional children in the least restrictive environment, what constitutes a "free and appropriate public education" and what are "related services" under the law.

Access. Parents have legal rights to inspect and review their exceptional children's educational records. To enforce this right effectively, parents must know about their right of confidentiality and their right to seek an amendment of inaccurate or misleading record information.

Verification. Parents are entitled to obtain an independent educational evaluation if they disagree with the school's evaluation report. To ensure that parents can invoke this legal safeguard, professionals must inform parents about the requirements for obtaining an independent educational evaluation and who pays for the costs of such evaluations.

Oversight. Parents are entitled to disagree with school decisions by initiating and participating in due process hearings. To enforce this right, parents must understand the procedures for requesting a due process hearing, the procedural aspects of the hearing, their appeal rights if they are dissatisfied with the outcome of the hearing, and alternative dispute resolution processes such as mediation.

The above-referenced information on parents' legal rights could be disseminated to parents via a workshop format or in an informational packet developed by the school district. In either format, ensuring parent understanding should be an affirmative professional obligation.

Enhancing Parent Participation in the IEP Process. Educational programs should involve parents to the maximum extent possible, while at the same time acknowledging the parents' rights to choose minimal participation. More participation is not necessarily better participation (Turnbull & Turnbull, 1982). Adhering to the family systems perspective, professionals should tolerate and encourage a range of parent participation options matched to the needs and interests of each family.

To show the range of parental participation options, we will briefly discuss seven potential parent participation levels. Professionals, in close collaboration with parents, should identify the needs, interests, and abilities of parents and then match family resources to a preferred level of parent participation. Parent participation options include the following (Fiedler, 1986):

1. *Attendance and approval of teacher priorities:* Parents attend IEP meetings, receive feedback about their child, and receive and approve proposed IEP goals.

2. *Sharing information:* Parents provide information to the educational staff regarding, for example, their child's current level of functioning within the family, effective and ineffective teaching strategies, preferred and nonpreferred activities, and so forth.

3. *Suggesting goals:* Parents suggest specific skills or goals that they would like to see incorporated into the educational program.

4. *Negotiating goals:* When differences of opinion arise, parents and educational staff negotiate to agreement on IEP goals and implementation strategies.

5. *Collaboratively analyzing and monitoring implementation:* After reaching agreement on the IEP, parents help monitor day-to-day performance to assure achievement of goals, help include new goals when performance criteria are met, and reexamine goals that are not being met for respecification of goals or procedures.

6. *Joint programming:* Parents select specific IEP goals that they will implement in the home and/or community settings, simultaneously and in cooperation with the school's implementation of the goals.

7. *Independent programming:* Parents undertake training of educational goals in the home or community. (p. 6)

After an acceptable level of parent participation has been chosen, parents should receive information and support on how to function at that level. This information and support may be provided via reading materials made available to parents, at formal workshop sessions, or through the establishment of parent support groups. Table 21.1 summarizes the skills to be trained within each of the seven parent participation levels (Simpson & Fiedler, 1989). Considerations for each level of participation are provided for three phases: prior to the IEP conference, during the conference, and after the IEP conference.

In addition to recognizing and supporting parents in efforts to determine a comfortable and realistic level of parent participation, professionals should consider the following guidelines for enhancing parent–professional partnerships.

1. *Inventory parent preferences for the IEP conference.* Turnbull and Turnbull (1986) devised a questionnaire to solicit parent preferences on the following questions pertaining to an IEP conference:

   - What people would you like to bring with you to the conference?

   - What professionals do you want to attend the conference?

   - What time would be convenient to hold the meeting?

   - Where should the meeting be held?

   - Do you need any childcare or transportation assistance?

   - What kind of information would you like to receive prior to the conference?

   - Do you want to share information with the school in advance of the conference?

2. *Allow enough time for meetings.* The single most important contribution to effective conferences is allowing enough time. Assess the agenda, allow time for discussion and reaching consensus, set realistic time estimates, and schedule accordingly.

3. *Make preliminary contacts informal and welcoming.* Parents will respond more favorably if they have had opportunities to chat informally with professionals prior to attending a formal meeting such as an IEP conference.

4. *Assign a conference liaison to the parents.* Parents need to know that there is one person who is principally knowledgeable about their child's educational experience and can answer their questions.

5. *Divide the evaluation and IEP components of the decision-making process into separate conferences.* Especially for parents new to the special education system, receiving both evaluation information and making educational placement and programming decisions in one meeting is intellectually and emotionally overwhelming.

Table 21.1
Considerations for Parent IEP Participation

Levels of Involvement	Phase of Participation		
	Pre-IEP Conference	During IEP Conference	Post-IEP Conference
I. Attendance and Approval	1) Plan for the meeting: a) Determine the site of the conference. b) Plan to arrive on time. c) Identify a babysitter to avoid having to bring young children to the meeting. d) Determine how much time has been allotted for the conference. e) Attempt to identify who will attend the meeting. 2) Consider bringing a friend or relative to the meeting if you are uncomfortable attending alone. 3) Develop a positive attitude regarding the meeting as opposed to assuming an adversarial position. 4) Familiarize yourself with legal and legislative special education mandates. In particular, review handbooks and pamphlets relating to the IDEA.	1) Maintain a positive attitude during the conference. 2) Maintain a businesslike demeanor: a) Dress in a businesslike manner. b) Bring writing materials. c) Avoid isolation via the seating arrangement. d) Listen carefully. e) Introduce yourself and request that others at the meeting do the same, including specifying their role. 3) Be willing to accept responsibility for problems that are outside school. Similarly, do not expect school personnel to solve your personal or family problems. However, you may seek referrals from school personnel for such services.	1) Be willing to attend meetings and to offer support and approval.

Table 6.1 *Continued*

	Phase of Participation		
Levels of Involvement	**Pre-IEP Conference**	**During IEP Conference**	**Post-IEP Conference**
II. Sharing Information	In addition to the above, 5) Maintain and organize developmental, school, and clinical records on your children and review these records (including previous IEPs) prior to conferences. 6) Develop a list of information and other data you wish to share at IEP conferences. Write this information down because you may not remember it at conference time.	In addition to the above, 4) Bring background information and other information that you may wish to share at the conference.	In addition to the above, 2) Obtain and file a copy of the IEP and any other information needed for future reference. 3) Family members, including the child about whom the meeting was held (if appropriate), should be provided conference information.
III. Suggesting Goals	In addition to the above, 7) Identify with family members (including the child about whom the conference will be held) prioritized goals for the child.	In addition to the above, 5) Assertively maintain a participatory status during the conference. Ask for clarification about items and concepts that you fail to understand and that are not explained; solicit input and feedback from individuals who might not otherwise share information; make suggestions you consider important; request a copy of the completed IEP; and request additional meeting time if the allotted schedule is insufficient for completing the IEP. 6) Present to IEP participants parent and family goals for the child.	In addition to the above, 4) Prepare notes about the meeting following the conference. These notes should reflect happenings during the conference and should be filed with the student's IEP. 5) Contact the appropriate personnel if clarification or additional information is required. 6) Reinforce educators for their work, for example, through letters and phone calls following the IEP conference.

(continues)

Table 6.1 *Continued*

		Phase of Participation	
Levels of Involvement	**Pre-IEP Conference**	**During IEP Conference**	**Post-IEP Conference**
IV. Negotiating Goals	In addition to the above, 8) Consider enrolling in assertiveness training and problem-solving workshops.	In addition to the above, 7) Positively and assertively work with educators during the IEP conference. Present and advocate for priority goals. However, avoid arguing over minor details or attempting to dominate the meeting.	Same as above.
V. Monitor Implementation	In addition to the above, 9) Consider enrolling in workshops on child and program assessment and evaluation.	In addition to the above, 8) Establish the manner in which goals and objectives will be monitored and how this information will be communicated to educators.	In addition to the above, 7) Maintain an ongoing record of IEP progress and skill development.
VI. Engage in Joint Programming	In addition to the above, 10) Familiarize yourself with teaching strategies and behavior management procedures.	In addition to the above, 9) Establish the manner in which goals and objectives will be monitored and how this information will be communicated to educators.	Same as above.
VII. Engage in Independent Programming	In addition to the above, 11) Develop proficiency in independently carrying out teaching strategies and behavior management procedures.	In addition to the above, 10) Establish the conditions under which goals and objectives will be independently pursued by parents and the manner in which this information will be communicated.	Same as above.

Note. Adapted from "Parent Participation in Individualized Education Program (IEP) Conferences: A Case for Individualization," by R. L. Simpson and C. R. Fiedler, in M. J. Fine (Ed.), *The Second Handbook on Parent Education: Contemporary Perspectives* (pp. 156–158), 1989, San Diego, CA: Academic Press. Copyright 1989 by Academic Press. Adapted with permission.

6. *Avoid premature solutions.* Professionals should remain flexible and not get narrowly locked into only one solution for a perceived problem.

7. *Don't wait.* If a child has a problem or the professional is aware of a particular parental concern, do not wait until the formal conference to raise the issue or problem initially.

8. *Avoid jargon.*

9. *Learn from the parents.* Acknowledge the parents' expertise about their child's interests, behaviors, and history.

10. *Encourage open honest communication.*

11. *Evaluate the IEP conference.* Ask parents to evaluate their conference experiences and use their feedback to make conferences more responsive to parents' needs.

In addition to adhering to the above guidelines for fostering more active parent participation in IEP conferences, professionals should consider employing either of the following two tools for educational planning: Bateman (1995) proposed a useful three-step process for developing educationally useful IEPs. This planning process encourages active parent participation in IEP development. The three steps are as follows: (1) Professionals and parents brainstorm and list the exceptional child's educational needs and characteristics. After completing this list, the needs and characteristics are clustered (e.g., reading needs, study skill needs, social interaction needs). (2) Professionals and parents identify what the school will do to meet each need or characteristic (e.g., special education programming, related services, general classroom modifications). (3) Professionals and parents determine what changes in the exceptional child's behavior will be regarded as indications that the service the school is providing is effective.

A second educational planning tool, the Making Action Plans (MAPS), provides an alternative to traditional IEP meeting practices (Falvey, Forest, Pearpoint, & Rosenberg, 1994; Vandercook, York, & Forest, 1989). In the MAPS planning process, a facilitator leads a group (including professionals, family members, the exceptional child, and peers of the exceptional child) in a discussion of the following seven questions:

- What is the exceptional child's history?
- What are your dreams for the exceptional child?
- What are your nightmares?
- How would you describe the exceptional child.
- What are the exceptional child's strengths, gifts, and talents?
- What are the exceptional child's needs?
- What is the educational plan of action for the exceptional child?

This MAPS process, as reflected in the above questions, takes a positive orientation by focusing on the exceptional child's strengths, instead of dwelling on deficiencies. Active parent participation is inherent in this process and technical jargon is largely avoided. Both of these educational planning tools, Bateman's three-step process and MAPS, offer professionals alternatives to traditional IEP conferences where parents tend to behave in a very passive manner.

Nonadversarial Approaches to Parent–Professional Conflict

Although research findings indicate many parents approach educational decision making passively, the convergence of a number of factors may result in increased likelihood of conflict between parents of exceptional children and professionals. Families of exceptional children contend with a unique constellation of variables that affect parents' perspectives on appropriate educational programming and placement for their children. On the other hand, demands for school reform, tax reduction, and academic excellence may affect the perspectives of school personnel. Consequently, educators and parents may approach program and placement decisions from different perspectives.

The amended IDEA (1997) guarantees schools, students with disabilities, and their parents the right to procedural due process. Conflicts between parents and school personnel can be formally resolved through participation in due process hearings. Goldberg (1989) identified the required elements of a due process hearing: (a) the hearing officer must be unbiased; (b) participants must receive adequate notice regarding the hearing; (c) participants must have ample opportunity to respond; (d) participants have the right to call witnesses on their behalf; (e) the decision must be based on evidence presented at the hearing; (f) participants must have the right to legal representation; (g) a record of the proceedings must be kept; (h) a statement of the reasons for the decision must be provided; and (i) public attendance must be permitted. If the school district or the parents are dissatisfied with the due process hearing decision, either party may appeal that decision to a federal or state court.

Failure to resolve conflicts prior to due process hearings or litigation has several disadvantages. First, the due process hearing is an overly adversarial legal proceeding that leads to antagonism, hostility, and alienation between school personnel and parents (Goldberg & Huefner, 1995; Zirkel, 1994). Second, parents often report their perceptions that the hearing process is unfair (Goldberg & Kuriloff, 1991). Third, due process hearings are time consuming and can take years to resolve (Zirkel, 1994). Fourth, the hearings are financially and emotionally costly to both parents and school personnel (Fiedler, 1993). For example, Zirkel (1994) cites one due process hearing where the cost of the transcript was $27,000 and the hearing officer's fees amounted to $20,000. Moreover, the emotional costs experienced by parents and school personnel participating in due process hearings may be even more significant than the financial costs. Fifth, participation in a due process hearing results in the removal of the decision-making authority from the parties in dispute. When the parties in dispute (parents and school personnel) lose their self-determination and must rely upon the decision of a hearing officer, they feel less inclined to abide by a decision imposed upon them by this outside authority (Fiedler, 1993). Sixth, research findings have consistently revealed that the due process hearing system is accessible primarily to parents in the middle- and upper-income levels who are well educated (Fiedler, 1993; Goldberg, 1989). Seventh, the hearing system has been criticized as representative of the special education profession's tendency to turn over questions of ethical judgment or educational decision making to legal procedures instead of resolving such dilemmas within the profession (Kauffman, 1984). Finally, parent participation in due process hearings may result in negative consequences for the exceptional child involved. For example, many parents reported that their children's attitude deteriorated during the hearing process (Budoff, 1976). Another consequence of due process participation may be negative treatment directed toward the exceptional child at school (Strickland, 1982).

One promising method for resolving educational disputes prior to a due process hearing is mediation. Morgan, Whorton, and Zink (1995) defined mediation as the following: "a tool used to aid disputing parties (i.e., complainant, respondent) in reaching an agreement. A third party listens to both arguments and assists the disputants in reaching a consensus" (p. 288). Mediation differs from due process hearings and litigation in numerous ways. The following differences were cited by the Center for Law and Education (1995):

1. Mediation is an informal process, whereas a hearing is a formal proceeding.

2. In mediation parents can voice their concerns, whereas in a hearing a counsel or advocates speak for them.

3. In mediation, agreement is voluntary, whereas in a due process hearing, a hearing officer imposes a decision.

4. Disputants actively shape the final agreement in mediation, whereas a hearing officer renders a decision in a due process hearing.

5. In mediation, cooperative problem solving is promoted, whereas in a due process hearing, hostility is generated.

6. Mediation may last from 2 to 4 hours, whereas due process proceedings may last 1 to 4 days or longer.

7. In mediation, discussion focuses on educational planning for the student, whereas in a due process hearing, testimony is presented to influence a decision concerning the educational program.

Resolution of conflicts through mediation has many advantages over due process hearings or litigation for parents and school personnel. Primm (1990) identified the following advantages: (a) discovery of mutual interests and benefits, (b) development of mutual respect, and (c) exploration of multiple options.

In addition to mediation procedures, Schrag (1996) identified the following alternative resolution strategies for special education disputes which have been used around the country.

Independent Ombudsperson. The ombudsperson works independently of the school district and serves as a neutral third party in assisting parents and school personnel in reaching mutually satisfactory solutions to their disputes. The ombudsperson gathers relevant factual information pertaining to the dispute and makes recommendations to both parties in an effort to resolve the dispute.

Impartial Reviews. As Schrag (1996) stated, "An impartial review team is two or three impartial/knowledgeable professionals who spend one full day or two half days on site to review the situation in conflict and render a written second opinion" (p. 13). The advantage of this impartial review process is that both the parents and school personnel are afforded an opportunity to review the merits of their positions prior to committing to an adversarial due process hearing.

Advisory Opinion Process. In this process the parents and school personnel are allowed one hour to present their case to a hearing officer. The hearing officer, after hearing from both parties, renders an oral nonbinding advisory opinion. The parties may still proceed to a due process hearing if the advisory opinion does not resolve the dispute.

Neutral Conferences. In this process, a third person serves as an arbitrator who reviews the facts of a special education dispute and issues a nonbinding decision.

Summary

The IDEA Amendments of 1997 have strengthened parental participation rights in the educational decision-making process. This chapter attempted to suggest how professionals could turn that legislative mandate into a practice reality by recognizing the barriers that have historically precluded active parent participation, by assuming the responsibilities of becoming educational advocates for exceptional children and their parents, by taking actions to enhance parental participation in IEP conferences, by actively practicing the skills of effective advocacy, and by working to resolve parent–professional conflict in a nonadversarial manner. Truly supportive and effective professionals recognize that their client responsibilities extend beyond the individual child they are serving and encompass that child's parents and entire family unit. This ecological perspective is essential in realizing one's potential as an effective professional in the 21st century.

References

Allen, N. N. (1993). *The parent professional partnership: African American parents' participation in the special education process.* Final report. Washington, DC: Maryland Institute for the Study of Exceptional Children and Youth, Department of Education.

Alper, S. K., Schloss, P. J., & Schloss, C. N. (Eds.) (1994). *Families of students with disabilities: Consultation and advocacy.* Needham Heights, MA: Allyn & Bacon.

Antonak, R. F., Mallory, B. L., & Thede, D. L. (1986). A proposed set of ethical principles for developmental disabilities professionals. *Mental Retardation Systems, 3*(1), 12–22.

Audette, B., & Algozzine, B. (1997). Re-inventing government? Let's re-invent special education. *Journal of Learning Disabilities, 30*(4), 378–383.

Bailey, D. B., Buyose, V., Edmondson, R., & Smith, T. M. (1992). Creating family-centered services in early intervention: Perceptions of professionals in four states. *Exceptional Children, 58*(4), 298–309.

Bateman, B. (1995). *Better IEPs: How to develop legally correct and educationally useful programs.* Longmont, CO: Sopris West.

Bennett, T., Deluca, D. A., & Bruns, D. (1997). Putting inclusion into practice: Perspectives of teachers and parents. *Exceptional Children, 64*(1), 115–131.

Berg, W. K., & Halpern, A. S. (1987). Transition services for secondary students with mild disabilities: A statewide perspective. *Exceptional Children, 53,* 507–514.

Blackorby, J., Edgar, E., & Kortering, L. J. (1991). A third of our youth? A look at the problem of high school dropout among students with mild handicaps. *Journal of Special Education, 25*(1), 102–114.

Bonney, L. G., & Moore, S. (1992). Advocacy: Noun, verb, adjective or profanity. *Impact, 5*(2), 7.

Brantlinger, E. (1991). Home–school partnerships that benefit children with special needs. *The Elementary School Journal, 91*(3), 249–259.

Brotherson, M. J., Berdine, W. H., & Sartini, V. (1993). Transition to adult services: Support for ongoing parent participation. *Remedial and Special Education, 14*(4), 44–51.

Budoff, M. (1976). *Procedural due process: Its application to special education and its implications for teacher training.* Paper presented at the meeting of the American Educational Research Association, San Francisco.

Center for Law and Education. (1995). *When parents and educators do not agree: Using mediation to resolve conflicts about special education.* Boston: Author.

Chadsey-Rusch, J., Rusch, F. R., & O'Reilly, M. F. (1991). Transition from school to integrated communities. *Remedial and Special Education, 12*(6), 23–33.

Cochran, M. (1992). Parent empowerment: Developing a conceptual framework. *Family Science Review, 51*(1 & 2), 3–21.

Council for Exceptional Children. (1983). Code of ethics and standards for professional practice. *Exceptional Children, 50*(3), 205–209.

Cutler, B. C. (1993). *You, your child, and special education: A guide to making the system work.* Baltimore: Brookes.

Dunst, C. J., Trivette, C. M., & LaPoint, N. (1992). Toward clarification of the meaning and key elements of empowerment. *Family Studies Review, 5*(1 & 2), 111–130.

Edgar, E. (1995). *First decade after graduation: Final report.* Seattle: University of Washington. (ERIC Document Reproduction Service No. ED 397 573)

Edgar, E., & Polloway, E. (1994). Education for adolescents with disabilities: Curriculum and placement issues. *Journal of Special Education, 27*(4), 438–453.

Education for All Handicapped Children Act of 1975, 20 U.S.C. § 1400 *et seq.*

Falvey, M. A., Forest, M., Pearpoint, J., & Rosenberg, R. (1994). Building connections. In J. S. Thousand, R. A. Villa, & A. I. Nevin (Eds.), *Creativity and collaborative learning: A practical guide to empowering students and teachers* (pp. 347–368). Baltimore: Brookes.

Fiedler, C. R. (1986). Enhancing parent–school personnel partnerships. *Focus on Autistic Behavior, 1*(4), 1–8.

Fiedler, C. R. (1993). Parents and the law: Conflict development and legal safeguards. In J. L. Paul & R. J. Simeonsson (Eds.), *Children with special needs: Family, culture, and society* (pp. 256–278). Fort Worth, TX: Harcourt Brace Jovanovich.

Friesen, B., & Huff, B. (1990). Parents and professionals as advocacy partners. *Preventing School Failure, 34*(3), 31–37.

Goldberg, S. S. (1989). The failure of legalization in education: Alternative dispute resolution and The Education for All Handicapped Children Act of 1975. *Journal of Law and Education, 18*(3), 441–454.

Goldberg, S. S., & Huefner, D. S. (1995). Dispute resolution in special education: An introduction to litigative alternatives. *Education Law Reporter, 99,* 703–803.

Goldberg, S. S., & Kuriloff, P. J. (1991). Evaluating the fairness of special education hearings. *Exceptional Children, 57*(6), 546–555.

Goldstein, S., Strickland, B., Turnbull, A. P., & Curry, L. (1980). An observational analysis of the IEP conference. *Exceptional Children, 48*(4), 360–371.

Harry, B. (1992). Restructuring the participation of African-American parents in special education. *Exceptional Children, 59*(2), 123–131.

Harry, B., Allen, N. N., & McLaughlin, M. (1995). Communication versus compliance: African-American parents' involvement in special education. *Exceptional Children, 61*(4), 364–377.

Herr, S. S. (1983). Rights and advocacy for retarded people. Lexington, MA: D.C. Heath.

Heumann, J. E., & Hehir, T. (1997). Believing in children: A great IDEA for the future. *Exceptional Parent, 27*(9), 2–4.

Hughes, C. A., Ruhl, K. L., & Gorman, J. (1987). Preparation of special educators to work with parents: A survey of teachers and teacher educators. *Teacher Education and Special Education, 10*(2), 81–87.

Individuals with Disabilities Education Act Amendments of 1997, 20 U.S.C. § 1400 *et seq.*

Kauffman, J. M. (1984). Saving children in the age of big brother: Moral and ethical issues in the identification of deviance. *Behavioral Disorders, 10*(1), 60–70.

Kitsiyanni, A., & Ward, T. J. (1992). Parent participation in special education: Compliance issues as reported by parent surveys and state compliance reports. *Remedial and Special Education, 13*(5), 50–55.

League, S., & Ford, L. (1996, March). *Fathers' involvement in their children's special education program.* Paper presented at the annual meeting of the National Association of School Psychologists, Atlanta, GA.

Leyser, Y. (1985). Parent involvement in the school: A survey of parents of handicapped students. *Contemporary Education, 57*(1), 38–43.

Lowenthal, B. (1996). Integrated school services for children at-risk: Rationale, models, barriers, and recommendations for implementation. *Intervention in School and Clinic, 31,* 154–157.

Lynch, E. W., & Stein, R. C. (1982). Perspectives on parent participation in special education. *Exceptional Education Quarterly, 3*(2), 56–63.

Lynch, E. W., & Stein, R. C. (1987). Parent participation by ethnicity: A comparison of Hispanic, Black, and Anglo families. *Exceptional Children, 54*(2), 105–111.

McBride, M. (1992). Self-determination and empowerment: The parent case management program. *Impact, 5*(2), 14.

McLoughlin, J. A., Edge, D., Petrosko, J., & Strenecky, B. (1981). P.L. 94-142 and information dissemination: A step forward. *Journal of Special Education Technology, 4*(4), 50–56.

Miller, J. E. (1995). *Improving parent participation in the educational process of 17 secondary students who are mildly disabled and exhibiting at-risk behaviors in a rural district setting.* Unpublished manuscript, Southeastern Nova University.

Miner, C., & Bates, P. (1997). The effect of person-centered planning activities on the IEP/transition planning process. *Education and Training in Mental Retardation and Developmental Disabilities, 32*(2), 105–112.

Morgan R. L., Whorton, J. E., & Zink, S. K. (1995). Use of mediation and negotiation in the resolution of special education disputes. *Education, 116*(2), 287–296.

Nelson, J. R. (1996). Designing schools to meet the needs of students who exhibit disruptive behavior. *Journal of Emotional and Behavioral Disorders, 4*(3), 147–161.

Plata, M. (1993). Using Spanish-speaking interpreters in special education. *Remedial and Special Education, 14*(5), 19–24.

Primm, E. B. (1990). Mediation: A comment under Part B; Common sense for Part H. *Early Childhood Reporter,* 4–6.

Roit, M. L., & Pfohl, W. (1984). The readability of P.L. 94-142 parent materials: Are parents truly informed? *Exceptional Children, 50*(6), 496–505.

Salend, J. S., & Taylor, L. (1993). Working with families: A cross-cultural perspective *Remedial and Special Education, 14*(25), 32–39.

Schrag, J. A. (1996). *Mediation and other alternative dispute resolution procedures in special education.* Alexandria, VA: Project FORUM, National Association of State Directors of Special Education. (ERIC Document Reproduction Services No. ED 399 736)

Simpson, R. L. (1996). *Working with parents and families of exceptional children and youth: Techniques for successful conferencing and collaboration.* Austin, TX: PRO-ED.

Simpson, R. L., & Fiedler, C. R. (1989). Parent participation in individualized educational program (IEP) conferences: A case for individualization. In M. J. Fine (Ed.), *The second handbook on parent education* (pp. 145–171). San Diego: Academic Press.

Smith, J. (1992). Making the system work: The multicultural family inclusion project. *Impact, 5*(2), 10.

Smith, S. W. (1990). Individualized education programs (IEP) in special education—From intent to acquiescence. *Exceptional Children, 57,* 6–15.

Sontag, J. C., & Schacht, R. (1994). An ethnic comparison of parent participation and information needs in early intervention. *Exceptional Children, 60*(5), 422–433.

South Dakota Statewide Systems Change Project. (1995). *Welcoming parents as partners.* Pierre: South Dakota State Department of Education and Cultural Affairs. (ERIC Document Reproduction Service No. ED 391 324)

Stainback, S., Stainback, W., & Forest, M. (1989). *Educating students in the mainstream of regular education.* Baltimore: Brookes.

Stoecklin, V. L. (1994). Advocating for young children with disabilities. *Quarterly Resource, 8*(3), 1–35.

Strickland, B. (1982). Parental participation, school accountability, and due process. *Exceptional Education Quarterly, 3,* 41–49.

Summers, J. A. (1992). Decision making in the 90's: A new paradigm for family, professional, and consumer roles. *Impact, 5*(2), 2–3, 20.

Turnbull, A. P., & Turnbull, H. R. (1982). Parent involvement in the education of handicapped children: A critique. *Mental Retardation, 20,* 115–122.

Turnbull, A. P., & Turnbull, H. R. (1986). *Families, professionals, and exceptionality: A special partnership.* Columbus, OH: Merrill.

Turnbull. A. P., & Turnbull, H. R. (1997). *Families, professionals, and exceptionality: A special partnership.* Columbus, OH: Merrill.

U.S. Department of Education. (1996). *Eighteenth annual report to Congress on the implementation of the Individuals with Disabilities Education Act.* Washington, DC: Author.

Vandercook, T., York, J., & Forest, M. (1989). The McGill Action Planning System (MAPS): A strategy for building the vision. *The Journal of the Association for Persons with Severe Handicaps, 14*(3), 205–215.

Vaughn, S., Bos, C. S., Harrell, J. E., & Lasky, B. A. (1988). Parent participation in the initial placement/IEP conference: Ten years after mandated involvement. *Journal of Learning Disabilities, 21,* 82–89.

Wagner, M. (1989). *The transition experiences of youth with disabilities: A report from the National Longitudinal Transition Study.* Paper presented to the Division of Research, Counsil for Exceptional Children, San Francisco.

Yell, M. L. (1998). *The law and special education.* Upper Saddle River, NJ: Merrill/Prentice Hall.

Yoshida, R. K., Fenton, K., Kaufman, M. J., & Maxwell, J. P. (1978). Parental involvement in the special education pupil planning process: The school's perspective. *Exceptional Children, 44,* 531–534.

Zirkel, P. A. (1994). Over-due process revisions for the Individuals with Disabilities Education Act. *Montana Law Review, 55,* 403–414.

Author Index

Subject Index

Abuse, 195–213
 case study, 199–200
 intervention, 203–205
  attitudinal considerations, 205
  therapeutic options, 203–205
 multidimensional view, 206–210
  belief–insight level, 208–209
  education–information level, 207–208
  family emphasis, 210
  skill acquisition and problem-solving
   levels, 209–210
 overview, 195–196
Acceptance
 to diagnosis of a child with mental
  retardation, 221
Accidents
 toddlers and, 109–110
Active Parenting, 203–204
Adolescents, parenting of, 121–126
 acceptance, 13–14
 anticipating parent–adolescent conflict,
  124–125
 assessing parent and peer influence,
  123–124
 conflicts, 124–126
 developing a sense of identity, 122–123
 developmental impact of a child with mental retardation, 224–225, 232
 learning disabilities and, 279–280
 resolving parent–teen issues, 125–126
 sexual development, 397–399
 transition to adult life, 409–435
  legislative background, 412–416
   definition and age requirement,
    414–415
   discipline evaluation, 415–416
   participation in statewide testing, 415
  models, 416–419
   Office of Special Education and Reha-
    bilitation Services (OSERS),
    416–417
   transdisciplinary transition model,
    418–419

Virginia Commonwealth University,
   417–418
 overview, 409–412
 programs, characteristics of effective,
  420–432
  individual planning, 428–429
  team planning, 427–428
  transition assessment, 429–430
  vocational and life skills instruction,
   430
  vocational and residential placement
   options and considerations, 430–432
  working with parents, 421–427
Adoptive parents, 59–62
 characteristics and issues, 59–61
 guidelines for professionals, 61–62
Advocacy
 adolescent, 124
 of autistic child, 309, 317–318, 319–320
 consumer, autistic child and, 312
 educational, 447–458
  need for, 447–449
  parental, 450–458
  professional, 449–450
 parent, 92–93
 training and support, 446
 in transition from child to adult, 427
African Americans
 as single parents, 50
Age
 legislation and, 414
 siblings and, 71–72

Alienation, and child abuse, 204
America 2000: An Education Strategy, 95
Anxiety, 29
ASA. *See* Autism Society of America
Asian culture
 demographics, 134
 labels and stereotypes, 136
ATCMHMR. *See* Austin–Travis County Men-
  tal Health and Mental Retardation
  Center

About the Editors

Marvin J. Fine is a professor in the Department of Psychology and Research in Education at the University of Kansas where he is involved in training school psychologists. He has a major interest in family–school relationships and has published extensively on this topic. He is a strong advocate for collaborative parent–teacher planning and offers training to both teacher and parent groups.

Richard L. Simpson is a professor of Special Education and School Psychology at the University of Kansas. He has also worked as a teacher of students with behavior disorders, a school psychologist, a clinical psychologist, a director of a program for students with severe emotional disturbance and autism, and an administrator of a mental health organization's prevention and support program. Simpson is senior editor of *Focus on Autism and Other Developmental Disabilities*, as well as an author of numerous books, articles, and book chapters dealing with parents and families, children and youth with emotional or behavioral disorders, and children and youth diagnosed with autism and Asperger's syndrome.